Individual Diversity and Psychology in Organizations

Individual Diversity and **Psychology** in **Organizations**

Edited by

Marilyn J. Davidson and Sandra L. Fielden
University of Manchester Institute of Science and Technology, UK

WILEY

Other Wiley Editorial Offices

John Wiley & Sons Inc., 111 River Street, Hoboken, NJ 07030, USA

Jossey-Bass, 989 Market Street, San Francisco, CA 94103-1741, USA

Wiley-VCH Verlag GmbH, Boschstr. 12, D-69469 Weinheim, Germany

John Wiley & Sons Australia Ltd, 33 Park Road, Milton, Queensland 4064, Australia

John Wiley & Sons (Asia) Pte Ltd, 2 Clementi Loop #02-01, Jin Xing Distripark, Singapore 129809

John Wiley & Sons Canada Ltd, 22 Worcester Road, Etobicoke, Ontario, Canada M9W 1L1

Wiley also publishes its books in a variety of electronic formats. Some content that appears
in print may not be available in electronic books.

Library of Congress Cataloging-in-Publication Data

Individual diversity and psychology in organizations / edited by Marilyn J. Davidson
and Sandra L. Fielden.
     p. cm.—(Wiley handbook in work & organizational psychology)
     Includes bibliographical references and index.
     ISBN 0-471-49971-4
     1. Diversity in the workplace.   2. Organizational effectiveness.   3. Multiculturalism.
I. Davidson, Marilyn.   II. Fielden, Sandra L.   III. Series.

HF5549 .5 .M5I535   2003
658 .3′008—dc21   2003003581

British Library Cataloguing in Publication Data

A catalogue record for this book is available from the British Library

ISBN 0-471-49971-4

Typeset in 10/12pt Times by TechBooks, New Delhi, India
Printed and bound in Great Britain by TJ International Ltd, Padstow, Cornwall, UK
This book is printed on acid-free paper responsibly manufactured from sustainable forestry
in which at least two trees are planted for each one used for paper production.

Contents

About the Editors

Marilyn J. Davidson, *Manchester School of Management, University of Manchester Institute of Science and Technology, PO Box 88, Manchester M60 1QD, UK*

Marilyn J. Davidson is Professor of Managerial Psychology in the Manchester School of Management at the University of Manchester Institute of Science and Technology, UK. She is currently Head of the Psychology Group and Co-Director of the Centre for Diversity and Work Psychology. Her research and teaching interests are in the fields of occupational stress, the management of diversity, equal opportunities, women in management and female entrepreneurs. She has published over 150 academic articles and 15 books, e.g. *Shattering the Glass Ceiling—the Woman Manager* (with C.L. Cooper); *Women in Management: Current Research Issues, Volume II* (edited with R. Burke); and *The Black and Ethnic Minority Woman Manager—Cracking the Concrete Ceiling* (shortlisted for the Best Management Book of the Year). Marilyn is former Editor of the MCB University Press journal *Women in Management Review*; Associate Editorial Board Member of the *Journal of Occupational and Organizational Psychology*, the *Journal of Gender Work and Organization*, and the *International Review of Women and Leadership*. She is a Fellow of the Royal Society of Arts; a Fellow of the British Psychological Society; a Chartered Psychologist; a member of the Division of Occupational Psychology (BPS); and a member of the Division of Psychology of Women Section (BPS).

Sandra L. Fielden, *Manchester School of Management, University of Manchester Institute of Science and Technology, PO Box 88, Manchester M60 1QD, UK*

Dr Sandra L. Fielden is a lecturer in organizational psychology at Manchester School of Management, University of Manchester Institute of Science and Technology, UK. She is also Director of the Centre for Diversity and Work Psychology and has been involved in applied research within the public and private sector, including European-funded research into small business start-up and economic growth. Her research and teaching interests are in gender, diversity, women's entrepreneurship, equal opportunities, health, occupational stress, psychological contract and organizational change. Sandra lectures on a number of postgraduate degrees, including the NHS Effective Leadership MSc and MSc in Organizational Psychology, at Manchester School of Management, plus courses on change and entrepreneurship on the MBA programme at Manchester Business School. She is widely published and is editor of the MCB University Press journal *Women in Management Review*, for which she has received the 2002 Leading Editor award for her work in developing the journal. Sandra is a Chartered Psychologist and an Associate Fellow of the British Psychological Society.

About the Contributors

Carolann Ashton, *Fernhill, Uplands, Gowerton, Swansea SA4 3ET, UK*
   Carolann Ashton has been an innovator in the field of diversity and training for 14 years. In 1985, at the age of 23, she worked on a range of projects within central government, eventually taking up a peripatetic role travelling across the UK and Northern Ireland. In 1991 she accepted a job with BBC Television as their Equalities Training Manager, where she developed and implemented their award-winning Equalities Training Strategy. In 1996 she took time out to develop her own very successful training business specializing in working with senior teams to develop equality strategies linked to key business objectives. Carolann has also recently worked for both Littlewoods and Ford as a consultant to their Diversity/European Diversity Teams. She is currently focusing on expanding her consultancy work and will shortly begin her PhD.

Mary Barrett, *Deputy Director and Director of Masters' Course, Graduate School of Management, Griffith University—Gold Coast, PMB 50, Gold Coast Mail Centre, Queensland 9127, Australia*
   Mary Barrett gained a PhD in French and literary theory in the mid 1980s and taught in that field at the University of Queensland. She gained an MBA in 1993 and worked in human resource management and policy development in university administration and government for several years before becoming a management academic in 1992. Her professional experience includes Australia and the United States where she held a Fulbright Postdoctoral Research Fellowship at the University of California at Berkeley and the University of California Office of the President. Mary has taught in general management and human resource management at four Australian universities and is currently Associate Professor in Management at Griffith University. She researches and publishes in the areas of women in management (including as owners of their own businesses), family business, leadership and management theory.

Chris Brotherton, *Head of Department and Professor of Applied Psychology, Heriot-Watt University, Department of Applied Psychology, Edinburgh EH14 4AS, UK*
   Chris Brotherton is Professor of Applied Psychology at Heriot-Watt University in Edinburgh, Scotland. He formerly held senior posts in Nottingham University and University of Ulster. Chris began his working life as a Printer's Compositor before winning scholarships to Ruskin College, Oxford and to the University of Hull. He is an active member of the British Psychological Society and has extensive research and consulting experience with industry. He chairs the Faculty of Psychology and Management of the Chartered Institute of Personnel and Development. Among his most recent publications is *Social Psychology and Management—Issues for a Changing Society* published by Open University Press.

Catherine Cassell, *Senior Lecturer in Organization Behaviour, Sheffield University Management School, 9 Mappin Street, Sheffield S1 4DT, UK*
   Catherine Cassell is a Professor of Organizational Psychology and Director of Research at Sheffield University Management School. Her main research focus has been on the use of qualitative methods in organizational research and she has co-edited (with Gillian Symon) three books in this area for Sage. She also has a keen interest in organizational change and development and has published in the areas of manufacturing change, managing diversity and business ethics.

David Clutterbuck, *Clutterbuck Associates, Burnham House, High Street, Burnham, Buckinghamshire SL1 7JZ, UK*

Dr David Clutterbuck introduced the concept of structured mentoring programmes to the UK in the early 1970s. His book *Everyone Needs a Mentor* (1985, now in its third edition) is the classic European text on the topic. Since then he has written or co-authored *Mentoring in Action, Learning Alliances, Mentoring Executives and Directors* and *Mentoring and Diversity*, as well as numerous other shorter publications. David co-founded EMC and is a member of the Mentoring and Coaching Research Group at Sheffield Hallam University, where he is a visiting professor. He lectures and consults globally on mentoring themes and his company, Clutterbuck Associates, has franchisees or licensees in 35 countries. An active mentor (8 mentees) himself, he maintains a continuous stream of research programmes into aspects of mentoring and one long-term project—a longitudinal study of mentor/mentee behaviours, for which he welcomes additional participants. David can be reached at dclutterbuck@item.co.uk.

Ardha Danieli, *Lecturer in Qualitative Research Methods and Organizational Analysis, Industrial Relations and Organizational Behaviour Group, Warwick Business School, University of Warwick, Coventry CV4 7AL, UK*

Dr Ardha Danieli is a Lecturer in Qualitative Research Methods and Organizational Analysis in the Industrial Relations and Organizational Behaviour group at the University of Warwick Business School. Her research interests include: discrimination and inequality in employment particularly as it affects disabled people and women; gender in industrial relations and organizations, and researching inequality. Other research interests include the exercise of power in managing change and the construction of identity. She has published on these subjects in the *Journal of Management Studies*, *Sociological Review*, *Management Learning* and *Personnel Review*. She is an Associate Editor of *Gender, Work and Organization*.

Penny Dick, *Lecturer in Organizational Behaviour, Sheffield University Management School, 9 Mappin Street, Sheffield S1 4DT, UK*

Dr Penny Dick is a Lecturer in Organizational Behaviour at Sheffield University Management School. She is a Chartered Occupational Psychologist with a wide array of industrial experience. Her research interests and publications are in the management of diversity and organizational stress, particularly in emergency service settings.

Jill Earnshaw, *Dean of Management Studies, Manchester School of Management, UMIST, PO Box 88, Manchester M60 1QD, UK*

Jill Earnshaw BSc, PGCE, LLB Barrister, MSc graduated in Chemistry from Manchester University and later retrained as a lawyer. From 1979 to 1989 she held lecturing posts in the Manchester School of Management, UMIST and Manchester Metropolitan University, at which time she took up full-time employment at UMIST. She is now a Senior Lecturer in Employment Law and Dean of Management Studies. In 1990 Jill was also asked to sit as a part-time Chairman of Employment Tribunals and from 1995 to 2000 she was a member of the Training Panel, devising and delivering training to Employment Tribunal Chairmen. Jill's research interests lie in the legal issues surrounding sexual harassment and workplace stress, and she is co-author (with Professor Cooper) of *Stress and Employer Liability* published by CIPD. In 1997 she carried out a research project funded by the DTI on the subject of workplace disciplinary and grievance procedures in small firms and she has recently completed a study for the DfES focusing on teacher capability procedures. She is currently involved in the 'Future of Work' research project.

Andrew W. Gale, *Dept of Civil and Construction Engineering, UMIST, PO Box 88, Manchester M60 1QD, UK*

Dr Andrew Gale is a Senior Lecturer in Project Management at the Manchester Centre for Civil and Construction Engineering, UMIST, Manchester. Andrew is the programme director for the MSc in Project Management (for Rolls-Royce, AMEC and TRW). He is a Chartered Civil Engineer and Specialist in construction project management, with 13 years' industrial experience, including 5 years in Saudi Arabia and Egypt. Since 1985 he has developed an academic career. Andrew has obtained, competitively, over £1.5 million worth of research and consultancy grants since 1990 and published over 90 papers, technical articles and books. He has over 12 years' experience in working with Russian construction firms and academic institutions in St Petersburg and north-west Russia, funded by the European Union, Know-How Fund and DFID; over 17 years' experience in research on construction organization and project culture, with specific interest in diversity, equality and inclusion; and consultancy experience with Ove Arup & Partners and Glaxo Wellcome.

Jean Hartley, *Reader in Organizational Change, Local Government Centre, Warwick Business School, University of Warwick, Coventry CV4 7AL, UK*

Jean Hartley is Professor of Organizational Analysis, The Local Government Centre, Warwick Business School, University of Warwick, UK. Jean is responsible for the Centre's research programmes on organizational change, leadership and learning in public service organizations. She is the Research Director of the team monitoring and evaluating the Beacon Council Scheme (concerned with interorganizational learning and corporate and service improvement) and for the research on the implementation of Best Value through the Better Value Development Programme. She was also a member of the Best Value national evaluation team. Her work on leadership and the management of influence includes developing a self-assessment instrument for political leadership. She is also the Academic Director of the Warwick MPA, the "MBA for the public sector". She has published three books and many articles.

Andrew Hede, *University of the Sunshine Coast, Maroochydore DC, Queensland 4558, Australia*

Andrew Hede is Professor of Management and was formerly Foundation Dean of Business at the University of the Sunshine Coast. He graduated in the mid-1970s from Sydney University with a doctorate in Psychology. He is also a registered psychologist. He has had extensive experience as a senior manager in the Australian Commonwealth and State public services as well as private sector experience as the inaugural director of the Public Policy Research Centre in Sydney. He has more than 100 publications on a range of issues including community noise, leadership, organizational conflict, senior Civil Service, public policy, women in management and employment equity.

Deborah Hicks-Clarke, *Manchester Metropolitan University Business School, Aytoun Street, Manchester M3 8GH, UK*

Deborah Hicks-Clarke, PhD, is a Lecturer at Manchester Metropolitan University and a member of the CIPD. Her areas of research interest include HRD, diversity and OB and she has published in these areas. She is currently engaged in research examining male and female stress coping strategies and work–life balance issues.

Charlotte Holgersson, *Stockholm School of Economics, Box 6501, SE-113 83 Stockholm, Sweden*

Charlotte Holgersson, MSc in Economics and Business Administration, is a researcher at the Center for Management and Organization at the Stockholm School of Economics. She is also a lecturer at the same school. She is active in the research programme Fosfor (Feminist Organization Studies) where she is conducting a project on the recruitment of managing directors. She is co-author of books (in Swedish) *Ironi och sexualitet—om ledarskap och kön* (Irony and Sexuality—on Management and Gender) (1998) and *Det ordnar sig* (It will be in order. Theories on Organization and Gender) (2001) and has published a chapter in English in the book *Invisible Management* (2001).

Paul Iles, *University of Teesside Business School, University of Teesside, Borough Road, Middlesbrough TS1 3BH, UK*

Paul Iles is a Professor of Strategic HRM at Teesside Business School, University of Teesside. Previously he was Professor of HRD at Liverpool Business School, Liverpool John Moores University. A chartered psychologist, associate Fellow of the BPS and Fellow of the CIPD, his interests are in managerial assessment and development, careers, HRD, diversity, learning/knowledge management and international HRM/HRD. He has published in these areas in a variety of international journals, as well as being the author or co-author of four books on assessment, development and learning. He is a visiting professor at the University of Mauritius and University of Paris, and has been a trainer and consultant to various private, public and voluntary sector organizations.

Phil Johnson, *Principal Lecturer in Organization Behaviour, Sheffield Business School, Sheffield Hallam University, Stoddart Building, Pond Street, Sheffield S1, UK*
Dr Phil Johnson is a Principal Lecturer and Research Leader in the School of Business and Finance at Sheffield Hallam University. He has published in the areas of research methodology, epistemology, business ethics and organization behaviour. His current empirical research is into aspects of supply chain management.

Roberta Youtan Kay, *812 Jessica Place, Nipomo, California 93444-5600, USA*
Roberta Youtan Kay is an international corporate trainer and consultant who has led workshops and seminars for both public and private organizations for almost two decades. Roberta holds Master's Degrees in Organizational Psychology and Marriage and Family Counselling. She is a member of the American Society for Training and Development, the Organizational Development Network, and the California Association for Marriage and Family Therapists. Her main areas of expertise include cultural diversity, conflict resolution, team building, interpersonal communications and stress management. Her publications have appeared in *Cultural Diversity at Work* and *Employment Relations Today*.

Gill Kirton, *Lecturer in Business Management, Centre for Business Management, Queen Mary, University of London, Mile End Road, London E1 4NS, UK*
Gill Kirton is Lecturer in Business Management at the University of London. She has a long-standing interest in equality issues and is the co-author of *The Dynamics of Managing Diversity* (2000, Butterworth Heinemann). She has also published several articles on women's roles in trade unions.

Alison M. Konrad, *School of Business and Management, Temple University, 1810 North 13th Street, Philadelphia, PA 19122-6083, USA*
Alison M. Konrad is a Professor of Human Resource Administration at Temple University's Fox School of Business and Management. She was Chair of the Academy of Management's Gender and Diversity in Organizations Division in 1996–97 and President of the Eastern Academy of Management in 1997–98. She is currently serving as Associate Editor for *Group and Organization Management* and *Gender, Work and Organization*, and is a member of the editorial board for the *Academy of Management Review*. She has published over 30 articles and chapters on topics relating to workplace diversity in outlets such as the *Academy of Management Journal*, *Administrative Science Quarterly*, *Gender, Work and Organization*, *Group and Organization Management*, *Human Relations*, *Psychological Bulletin*, *Sex Roles*, *Strategic Management Journal*, *Women in Management Review* and others. Her current work focuses on work values, work–life balance, the impact of race on perceptions of promotion fairness, evaluating the effectiveness of diversity management initiatives, and identifying human resource management practices to enhance job retention among former welfare clients.

Andrew Korac-Kakabadse, *Cranfield School of Management, Cranfield University, Cranfield, Bedfordshire MK43 0AL, UK*
Andrew Korac-Kakabadse is Professor of Management Development and Deputy Director of the Cranfield School of Management. He is also European Vice Chancellor for the International Academy of Management. He has worked in the health and social services field and then undertook various consultancy assignments concerned with local government reorganization and large capital projects in developing countries. He is currently a consultant to numerous organizations— ranging from banks; motor manufacturers; high-tech companies; oil companies, police and other public sector organizations and numerous multinational corporations. He has consulted and lectured in the UK, Europe, US, Russia, South-East Asia, Gulf States and Australia. His current areas of interest focus on improving the performance of top executives and top executive teams, excellence in consultancy practice and the politics of decision-making. He recently completed a major world study of chief executives and top executive teams. His data base covered 14 nations and over 7500 business organizations; including studying the strategic skills of top management in Japan, China, Hong Kong and the US. He is also the Director of the Cranfield Centre for International Management Development. He has published 21 books, 14 monographs and 132

articles; including the best-selling books *Politics of Management*; *Working in Organizations*; *The Wealth Creators*; *Essence of Leadership*; *Success in Sight: Visioning*; *Geo-Politics of Governance* and *Smart Sourcing: International Best Practice*. He is a co-editor of the *Journal of Management Development*, is the outgoing editor of the *Journal of Managerial Psychology* and is the associate editor of the *Leadership and Organization Development* journal. He has a BSc (Environmental Sciences) (Salford University); MA (Public Administration) (Brunel University); PhD (Management) (Manchester University); Diploma in Psychiatric Social Work (Manchester University), as well as being Fellow of the British Academy of Management, Fellow of the British Psychological Society and Fellow of the International Academy of Management.

Nada Korac-Kakabadse, *Professor of Management and Business Research, University College, Northampton, UK*

Nada Korac-Kakabadse is currently Professor of Management and Business Research at University College, Northampton. Previously she was a Senior Research Fellow at the Cranfield School of Management. She was employed as a Senior Information Technology Officer with the Australian Public Service Department of Employment, Education and Training. She has worked for international organizations in Scandinavia, the Middle East and North Africa, as well as for the Canadian Federal Government. Her research interest focuses on information technology and organizational dynamics; diversity management; performance improvement in private and public sector organizations and excellence in politics of decision-making. She has a BSc in Mathematics and Computing; a Graduate Diploma in Management Sciences; a Master's Degree in Public Administration and a PhD in Management. She has co-authored (with A. Korac-Kakabadse) five books—*Smart Sourcing: International Best Practice* (2002); *Geo-Politics of Governance* (2001); *Creating Futures* (2000); *The Essence of Leadership* (1999); and *A Study of the Australian Public Service* (1998). She has contributed 35 chapters to international volumes and has published 45 scholarly and reviewed articles. She is co-editor of the *Journal of Management Development and Corporate Governance*.

Alexander Kouzmin, *Graduate College of Management, Southern Cross University, P.O. Box 42, Tweeds Heads, NSW 2485, Australia*

Alexander Kouzmin currently holds a chair in Management at Southern Cross University. Previously he held the Chair in Organizational Behaviour at the Cranfield School of Management (2000–2003) and prior to that the Foundation Chair in Management in the Graduate School of Management at the University of Western Sydney, Australia (1991–2000). His research interests include organizational design, technological change, project management, comparative management, administrative reform and crisis management. He has published eight volumes of commissioned work. Among these are his edited *Public Sector Administration: New Perspectives* (Longman Cheshire, 1983); his co-edited (with N. Scott) *Dynamics in Australian Public Management: Selected Essays* (Macmillan, 1990); (with L. Still and P. Clarke) *New Directions in Management* (McGraw-Hill, 1994); (with J. Garnett) *Handbook of Administrative Communication* (Marcel Dekker, 1997); and (with A. Hayne) *Essays in Economic Globalization, Trans-national Policies and Vulnerability* (IOP Press, 1999). He has contributed 60 chapters to many national and international books and has published some 200 papers and review articles in more than 65 leading international refereed journals. He is on 11 international editorial boards and is a founding co-editor of the international *Journal of Contingencies and Crisis Management*, published quarterly since 1993.

Frank Linnehan, *Lebow College of Business, Drexel University, 101 N.33rd Street-Academic Building, Philadelphia, PA 19104, USA*

Frank Linnehan is an Assistant Professor of Human Resources at Drexel University's LeBow College of Business. After working for 17 years in the financial services industry, Dr Linnehan earned his PhD in Human Resources Administration at Temple University. Frank joined Drexel in 1997 and teaches graduate and undergraduate course in HR and Organization Behaviour. Dr Linnehan's research interests include equal employment opportunity, affirmative action and diversity initiatives in the workplace, as well as school-to-work transitions for younger workers. He has published articles in such journals as the *Academy of Management Journal*, *Applied Psychology: An International Review*, *Educational Evaluation and Policy Analysis*, *Journal of*

Vocational Behavior and *Social Psychology of Education*. His current interests focus on intergenerational mentoring in the workplace, work-based learning programmes and the impact of race on promotional fairness.

Tony Montes, *Ashridge Management College, Berkhamsted, Hertfordshire HP4 1NS, UK*

Tony Montes is a faculty member of Ashridge Management College in Hertfordshire. He focuses on leadership, organization behaviour and diversity issues for both open and tailored programmes. Prior to Ashridge, he performed various roles with Shell, the most recent of which was as Global Diversity Consultant. His career includes leadership roles in logistics and supply distribution, HR development and training, and transformation management. He was posted in Malaysia as a Senior Learning Consultant and was a lead resource in the consortium of management development programmes for Shell companies in the Asia Pacific region. Tony's expertise and interests are in developing business transformation strategies and processes, helping people and organizations through change and transition, addressing global leadership and culture issues, valuing and leveraging differences, and developing networks and change agents. He draws from several years of organization effectiveness practice supported by a broad range of capabilities developed through consulting and engaging small and large groups in diverse work environments. He is the subject leader and curriculum director for HR in the Ashridge Diploma for General Management. His work in the UK also involves leadership development of ethnic minority senior civil servants, under the Cabinet Office's Pathways scheme, consulting for the leadership team of Microsoft UK, Microsoft EMEA on Diversity transformation, the Improvement and Development Agency for Local Government, and the Commission for Racial Equality.

Lee A. Morris, *3400 E. Maxwell Dr, Oklahoma City, OK 73121, USA*

Lee A. Morris, Ed.D., is President of Research and Training Associates. Formerly, he was the Director of Education and Aerospace in the College of Continuing Education at the University of Oklahoma. Dr Morris occasionally teaches courses dealing with diversity issues for the Department of Human Relations at the University of Oklahoma.

Jane O'Sullivan, *School of English, Communication and Theatre, University of New England, Armidale, NSW 2351, Australia*

Jane O'Sullivan, PhD, is a Lecturer in the School of English, Communication and Theatre, University of New England, Australia. Her research interests focus on representations of gender in film and popular culture.

Lyndsay Rashman, *Senior Research Associate, Local Government Centre, Warwick Business School, University of Warwick, Coventry CV4 7AL, UK*

Lyndsay Rashman is Senior Research Associate, The Local Government Centre, Warwick Business School, University of Warwick, UK. Lyndsay's research interests are in organizational and cultural change in public services for the individual and the whole organization, knowledge transfer and interorganizational learning. Lyndsay has 20 years' experience in local government, most recently with Tameside Metropolitan Borough Council with responsibility for organizational development. Lyndsay was Research Manager for the research project concerned with monitoring and evaluating the Beacon Council Scheme in local government and has published reports and articles on interorganizational learning and organizational change from this research. She previously was a researcher on Warwick research on leadership and the management of influence.

Sandi Rhys Jones OBE, *Rhys Jones Consultants, 5th Floor, 9 Hatton Street, London NW8 8PL, UK*

Sandi Rhys Jones has more than 30 years' experience in marketing, communications and management services in construction, working for every sector of the industry. Her particular interest in diversity in construction developed more than 10 years ago, while studying for an MSc in Construction Law and Arbitration at King's College London. Her thesis, published in 1992, identified gender issues as an element of the adversarial nature of the construction industry. In 1994 she was invited to chair the government/industry working group on equal opportunities in construction, set up following the far-reaching review of the industry by Sir Michael Latham. The working group's report *Tomorrow's Team: Women and Men in Construction* was well received and a number of its recommendations implemented. She recently co-chaired a Housing Forum working group of the Rethinking Construction initiative led by Sir John Egan, producing a practical report, *Recruitment, Retention and Respect for People*. In 1998 Sandi was awarded the OBE for promoting women in construction.

Norma M. Riccucci, *Graduate Department of Public Administration, Rutgers University, Campus at Newark, 360 King Blvd, Hill Hall, Newark, NJ 07102, USA*

Norma M. Riccucci is Professor of Public Administration in the Graduate Department of Public Administration at Rutgers University, Newark, USA. She has published extensively in the areas of public management, employment discrimination law, affirmative action and public sector labour relations. *Managing Diversity in Public Sector Workforces* is forthcoming from Westview Press.

James Romero, *Director, Office of Continuing Medical Education, University of Oklahoma Health Sciences Center, 800 NE 15th, Rogers Building, Room 201, Oklahoma City, OK 73190, USA*

James Romero, PhD, is the Director of the Department of Continuing Medical Education at the University of Oklahoma Health Sciences Center. Dr Romero is in charge of coordinating all national, regional and local continuing education courses and programmes dealing with health and medical topics.

Graham Shaw, *Centre for Business and Diversity Ltd, 1 Dairy Cottages, Little Hawkwell Farm, Maidstone Road, Pembury, Kent TN2 4AH, UK*

Graham Shaw is the Director of the Centre for Diversity and Business. Graham founded the Centre in 2000 as a global network of associates working to develop the 'business case' for diversity. Through a series of international partnerships in Europe, South Africa, Australia and North America he has promoted the development of programmes, events, tools, materials, networks and human resources to assist individuals and organizations. He has recently worked on the establishment of an international Diversity Dialogue group and published research on public–private partnerships and ethnic minority employment. Graham is also a member of the editorial committee of *Profiles in Diversity*, a journal based in the US, and partners with colleagues in Canada on the development of measurement tools for those involved in diversity management.

Alison Sheridan, *School of Marketing and Management, University of New England, Armidale, NSW 2351, Australia*

Alison Sheridan, PhD, is a Senior Lecturer in the School of Marketing and Management, University of New England, Australia. She has an abiding interest in women's experiences of the paid workforce.

J. M. Smith, *Manchester School of Management, UMIST, PO Box 88, Manchester M60 1QD, UK*

Dr Mike Smith is Senior Lecturer in Work Psychology at Manchester School of Management, UMIST. He has wide experience of teaching and applying psychology at the highest levels. From a sound academic base in one of Europe's most prestigious University Schools of Management he has established an international reputation in the fields of selection and testing, career guidance, repertory grids, competency determination and organizational surveys. He has also served on a number of national bodies including the Council of the British Psychological Society and committees of the Manpower Services Commission. Publications include over 100 papers and articles and 12 books on selection, motivation to work and organizational psychology. He has been a member of the Board of Europe's largest and most prestigious career counselling company. His teaching and research are enriched by the practical experience provided by consultancy assignments in many prestigious organizations both in the UK and overseas.

Dianne Sodhi, *Research Fellow, Salford Housing and Urban Studies Unit, School of Environment and Life Sciences, Allerton Building, Frederick Road, University of Salford, Greater Manchester M6 6PU, UK*

Dianne Sodhi is Research Fellow within the Salford Housing and Urban Studies Unit at the University of Salford with a particular interest in 'race' and housing and has been responsible for a number of research projects in this field. She is a member of Career Opportunities for Ethnic Minorities North West (a human resource group set up to promote equality for black and ethnic minority staff within the social housing movement) and is involved in the development of a Race and Housing Database at the Ahmed Iqbal Ullah Race Relations Archive in Manchester.

Peter Somerville, *Director, Policy Studies Research Centre, University of Lincolnshire and Humberside, Brayford Pool, Lincoln LN6 7TS, UK*

Peter Somerville, BA, MA, DPhil, MIH, is Professor of Social Policy and Head of the Policy Studies Research Centre at the University of Lincoln. He has been responsible for major research projects in the field of 'race' and housing, including on Career Opportunities for Ethnic Minorities in the North West (1998) for the National Housing Federation and Housing Corporation and on Building Equality in Black and Minority Ethnic Employment (1999) for the Housing Corporation, published as *A Question of Diversity: Black and Minority Ethnic Staff in the RSL Sector* (2000). He has also been responsible for numerous research projects in the field of resident involvement and empowerment, including research into estate agreements, the right to manage, and community control. His most recent publications include *Social Relations and Social Exclusion*, published by Routledge (2000), and *Race, Housing and Social Exclusion*, published by Jessica Kingsley (2002).

Andy Steele, *Director, Salford Housing and Urban Studies Unit, School of Environment and Life Sciences, Allerton Building, Frederick Road, University of Salford, Greater Manchester M6 6PU, UK*

Andy Steele is Professor of Housing and Urban Studies and Director of the Salford Housing and Urban Studies Unit at the University of Salford. He specializes in research in 'race' and housing and has been responsible for over 40 externally funded research projects in this field. He has published widely, including the recently co-edited book *Race, Housing and Social Exclusion* (2002).

Donna M. Stringer, *Executive Diversity Services, Inc, 675 South Lane Street, Suite 305, Seattle, WA 98104, USA*

Donna M. Stringer, PhD, President of EDS, is a social psychologist with more than 25 years' experience as a manager, teacher and trainer of multicultural issues. Donna is a dynamic trainer and speaker who has trained thousands of people. She serves as a faculty member of the Intercultural Communication Institute in Forest Grove, Oregon, and is an adjunct faculty member on three higher education campuses. Donna has been teaching instructional design and providing training for diversity trainers for almost two decades. She is an active researcher who has published extensively in the areas of diversity, management and sex roles. Her newest book is *52 Activities for Exploring Values Differences* published by Intercultural Press, 2003.

David L. Tan, *Associate Professor and Director, Adult and Higher Education Program, Department of Educational Leadership and Policy Studies, University of Oklahoma, Norman OK 73701, USA*

David L. Tan, PhD, is Associate Professor and Director of the Adult and Higher Education Program at the University of Oklahoma. He teaches research methodology, higher education finance, assessment, research on the college student, and leadership development.

Anna Wahl, *Stockholm School of Economics, Box 6501, SE-113 83, Stockholm, Sweden*

Anna Wahl, PhD and Associate Professor at the Center for Management and Organization at the Stockholm School of Economics, is leader of the research programme Fosfor (Feminist Organization Studies). Fosfor comprises a series of projects and has on the theoretical level dealt with development of organization and management theory from a gender perspective. On an empirical level studies have been carried out on women in male-dominated professions and environments, top management and other executives within the private sector, both men and women, and change agents in working life. Her own research has focused on gender structures in organizations, constructions of gender and management, sexuality in organizations and strategies for change at organizational and individual level. She has published several books and articles in Swedish and English, e.g. a chapter in the book *Invisible Management* (2001). Her most recent (co-authored) book in Swedish is *Det ordnar sig* (It Will Be in Order. Theories on Organization and Gender) (2001).

Michael L. Wheeler, *OEStrategies, Inc., PO Box 190721, Miami Beach, Florida 33119, USA*

Michael L. Wheeler is a strategic management consultant and business writer specializing in the area of workforce diversity. For over a decade he has worked closely with Fortune 500 companies on a variety of projects and research. Recent publications include four annual special sections in *Business Week* dedicated to diversity as well as numerous research reports and publications for the Conference Board. Mr Wheeler was invited to the White House by First Lady Hillary Clinton in recognition of his work; and his advice was sought for President Clinton's White House Initiative for One America. He was recently invited to a Roundtable discussion with the Honorable Cari M. Dominguez, Chair of the US Equal Employment Opportunity Commission. His work has been cited in major newspapers and professional journals including the *Wall Street Journal*, the *New York Times, Washington Post, Personnel Journal* and *Training Magazine*. He has appeared as a special guest on Larry King Live Radio, CNBC and Money Radio. Mr Wheeler holds a BA in Organizational Communication from the California State University and an MS in Human Resources Management from the Milano Graduate School of Management at the New School for Social Research where he is an adjunct professor.

Elisabeth M. Wilson, *Institute for Development Policy and Management, University of Manchester, Crawford House, Precinct Centre, Oxford Road, Manchester M13 9GH, UK*

Dr Elisabeth Wilson's first career was in social work, and after taking an MBA she lectured at Liverpool John Moores University, where she gained her PhD, before moving to the Institute for Development Policy and Management at Manchester University. Her principal research interest has been in gender and organization. She has published articles and book chapters in this field as well as editing a recent volume, *Organizational Behaviour Re-assessed: The Impact of Gender* (Sage, 2001). Other research interests have been in the field of managing diversity, yoga and management, and public sector structure and culture. She is currently researching gender and diversity issues in organizations in India, as well as exploring postcolonialism and critical approaches to management.

Carol Woodhams, *Lecturer, Department of Business Studies, Manchester Metropolitan University, Aytoun Building, Aytoun Street, Manchester M1 3GH, UK*

Dr Carol Woodhams is a Lecturer in Human Resource Management in the Human Resource Management and Organizational Behaviour Group at the Manchester Metropolitan University Business School. She has recently completed a doctorate and continues to research in the area of disability and equality management. Other research interests include the management of diversity and equality legislation.

Series Preface

Peter Herriot
University of Surrey

The dictionary definition (Random House, 1987) of 'handbook' runs as follows:

- A book of instruction or guidance, as for an occupation; a manual
- A guidebook for travellers
- A reference book in a particular field
- A scholarly book on a particular subject, often consisting of separate essays or articles

These definitions are placed in the historical order of their appearance in the language. So the earliest use of a handbook was as a set of instructions which members of particular occupations kept to hand, in order to be able to refer to them when they were at a loss as to how to tackle a problem at work. The most recent definition, by way of contrast, refers to a scholarly book consisting of separate essays or articles.

It is the modest ambition of the Wiley Handbooks in the Psychology of Management in Organizations to reverse the course of (linguistic) history! We want to get back to the idea of handbooks as resources to which members of occupations can refer in order to get help in addressing the problems which they face. The occupational members primarily involved here are work and organizational psychologists, human resource managers and professionals, and organizational managers in general. And the problems which they face are those which force themselves with ever greater urgency upon public and private sector organizations alike: issues such as how to manage employees' performance effectively; how to facilitate learning in organizations; how to benefit from a diversity of employees; and how to manage organizational change so that staff are engaged and supported.

Now the claim to provide something useful for professionals, rather than a set of scholarly articles, is a bold one. What is required if such a claim is to be justified? First, practising professionals need a clear theoretical basis from which to analyse the issues they face, and upon which to base their solutions. Practice without underpinning theory is merely applying what has worked in some situations to other ones without knowing why, and hoping that they will work there too. This is blind empiricism.

Theory without practice, on the other hand, is mere indulgence. It is indulgent because theories in applied science can never be properly tested except by application, that is, their attempted use in solving problems in the real world. A handbook in the original sense of the word will therefore contain elements of practice as well as statements of theory. The Wiley Handbooks of the Psychology of Management in Organizations seek to demonstrate by descriptions of case studies, methods of intervention, and instruments of assessment, how theory may be applied in practice to address real organizational issues.

It is clear that Work and Organizational Psychology is a core discipline for addressing such issues as those listed above. For they are all issues which depend for their solution upon an understanding of individuals' behaviour at work, and of the likely effects of various organizational interventions upon the stakeholders involved. These latter include employees, customers, shareholders, suppliers and the wider community (Hodgkinson & Herriot, 2001).

The success criterion for these handbooks, then, is a simple one: will professionals find them useful in their practice? If they also help in the development of apprentice professionals, for example by being used on training courses, then so much the better. The field of Work and Organizational Psychology is currently at risk from a failure to integrate theory and practice (Anderson et al., 2001). Theory and research often seem to practitioners to address issues of interest only to academics; practice appears to academics to lack careful empirical, let alone theoretical, underpinning. These handbooks will help to bridge this divide, and thereby justify the title of 'Handbook'.

What is clear is that if we psychologists fail to impact upon the urgent issues which currently crowd in upon organizations, then those who claim to address them better or faster than us will gain power and influence. This will happen even if the solutions which they provide offer little longer-term benefit to clients. The Wiley Handbooks in the Psychology of Management in Organizations provide a resource to help professionals serve their clients more effectively.

This third handbook in the series is edited by Marilyn Davidson and Sandra Fielden. Our globalized world is characterized by major increases in the mobility both of labour and also of work. Each nation's workforce contains a greater variety of people, and so, by definition, does its domestic market. At the same time, its market is becoming more global and therefore more varied. Work migrates by means of information technology, so that employees in India, for example, are serving customers in the United Kingdom. How may organizations best manage this increased diversity?

For, as Marilyn and Sandra argue, manage it they must. If they fail to do so, they will miss out on a wide range of talented potential employees; and they will fail to satisfy clients and customers from a similar wide range of backgrounds. What is more, they will fail to tap those individual differences which foster creativity and innovation. The distinguished contributors to this handbook provide an invaluable summary of the state of knowledge in a field which is only around 10 years old. They also give some illuminating case studies and methods for intervention which will help anyone seeking to derive benefit from diversity.

REFERENCES

Anderson, N., Herriot, P. & Hodgkinson, G.P. (2001). The practitioner–researcher divide in Industrial, Work, and Organisational (IWO) Psychology: where are we now, and where do we go from here? *Journal of Occupational and Organisational Psychology*, 74, 391–411.
Hodgkinson, G.P. & Herriot, P. (2002). The role of psychologists in enhancing organisational effectiveness. In I. Robertson, M. Callinan & D. Bartram (eds) *Organisational Effectiveness: The Role of Psychology*. Chichester: Wiley.
The Random House Dictionary of the English Language, 2nd edn (1987). New York: Random House.

Preface

The phenomenon of managing diversity in the workplace is relatively new and has only appeared in the published literature over the past decade or so. Not surprisingly, as is evidenced throughout this book, there is still some controversy over what we actually mean by diversity. Nevertheless, a proposed definition by Kandola and Fullerton (1994: 8) provides an acceptable starting point:

> The basic concept of managing diversity accepts that the workforce consists of a diverse population of people. The diversity consists of visible and non-visible differences, which will include factors such as sex, age, background, race, disability, and personality and work style. It is founded on the premise that harnessing these differences will create a productive environment in which everybody feels valued, where their talents are being fully utilized and in which organizational goals are met.

During the 1970s, in most Western countries, much emphasis was placed on achieving equal employment opportunities and reducing discrimination in organizations by way of introducing equal opportunity (EO) legislation, particularly aimed at sex and race. However, the lack of success of imposed EO legislation has not only sometimes led to degrees of resistance or 'backlash' (particularly in countries with affirmative action legislation), but also often failed to successfully create EO by expecting employees of different gender and backgrounds to *assimilate*, once in the organization (Davidson & Burke, 2000).

Therefore, the assumptions underlying EO were consequently similar to those behind the *melting pot* of a country. Assumptions such as these are problematic, as the specific culture and uniqueness of individuals are undermined. Moreover, Burn (1996) proposed that the metaphor of the *melting pot* should be exchanged for that of the *salad bowl*, as it reflects how different cultures can combine and still preserve their own 'flavour'. The underlying assumptions of managing diversity are in line with the philosophy behind the salad bowl, as both concepts emphasize the *value of individual differences* (Liff & Wajcman, 1996).

Thus, the concept of managing diversity has gained popularity since the early 1990s, and has also been fuelled by changing demographic trends (e.g. the increasing proportion of minority groups in the US workforce and by the increasingly multicultural and international business environment (Cassell, 1997)). Consequently, the focus has also switched towards making EO attractive to employers via the business case of diversity management. Organizations can no longer afford to discriminate against applicants and employees on the basis of gender, age, race, disability, etc., because firstly, many skilled employees would be forgone, and secondly, competitiveness will increasingly depend on the ability to satisfy and understand customers from different cultures and backgrounds.

This handbook addresses issues relevant to successfully managing diversity initiatives in organizations. While it attempts to take a cross-cultural approach, unfortunately to date the majority of work in this area has been predominantly from the USA, the UK and Australasia, with limited literature pertaining to mainland Europe and other industrialized countries. Keeping this in mind we hope that all countries will be able to gain valuable experiential lessons from contributors, that could be adapted and incorporated into diversity practice and legislation globally. This book provides an up-to-date overview of both current research findings and practical applications within organizations, with a special emphasis on the psychological issues related to attitudes and perceptions at the individual and organizational level. Managing diversity initiatives seek to fully develop the potential of each employee and turn the different sets of skills that each employee brings into a business advantage. Through the fostering of difference, team creativity, innovation and problem-solving can often be enhanced. The focus is, therefore, much more on the individual rather than the group. Having a diverse workforce not only enables organizations to understand and meet customer demand better, but also helps attract investors and clients, as well as reduce the costs associated with discrimination.

This volume is divided into six parts and consists of chapters covering both academic and practical issues. **Part I** covers topics associated with the strategic approaches taken to diversity, why organizations should be interested in diversity (including the history and definition) and the business case or lack of it. This section also explores the importance of diversity from both the individual psychological and behavioural perspectives, as well as organizational benefits and advantages. In the first chapter, Gill Kirton examines the developing strategic approaches to diversity policy emphasizing the role of two key policy levers—training and development and mentoring and auditing—to illustrate the challenges of translating policy into practice. In the next chapter, Carolann Ashton examines the business case for diversity in innovation. She explores the relationship between successful innovation, giving case study examples and matching cost profiles. In the following chapter, Catherine Cassell and Phil Johnson examine the implications of debates deriving from business ethics, relating to how we understand diversity and how it is managed. In particular, they argue that the business ethics literature provides another set of concepts, which can be used as tools to clarify the underlying principles behind managing diversity initiatives. Michael Wheeler's chapter is both conceptual and practical and explores a framework for understanding diversity as a critical factor influencing organizational effectiveness. His strategic diversity model provides an action plan and overall strategic measurement process relating to creating, managing, valuing and leveraging diversity in organizations.

Part II concentrates on the legal and cultural issues surrounding diversity in varying countries and explains how these differences present alternative contexts for practice, and how much/little they affect the working lives of individuals. Jill Earnshaw explores the extent to which legislative provisions and their associated case law can aid in organizational moves towards greater diversity. In addition, she also describes the various avenues for individual redress against such treatment as bullying and harassment, while also questioning the appropriateness of legal remedies. Following on with a legal theme, Alison Konrad and Frank Linnehan's chapter focuses on the nature of affirmative action (AA) programmes and summarizes evidence regarding their effects (particularly in the US). Their empirical evidence suggests that while AA has been generally effective in improving educational and employment opportunities for disadvantaged groups, it also questions the claims that individuals have negative attitudes towards AA programmes, or that AA programmes stigmatize beneficiaries. Australia is another country that introduced AA programmes, and principles and practice of gender diversity are then examined in the Australian context by Mary Barrett and Andrew Hede. They present a perspective on the most advanced current thinking and practice in Australia in gender-based diversity and, through specific case-study examples, also illustrate some of the dilemmas arising from changing paradigms in diversity management generally. In the next chapter, Penny Dick argues that the empirical evidence linking the management of diversity to different levels of achievement and affective outcomes is limited and that the majority of studies have focused on diversity per se, not its management. She concludes by arguing that the diversity literature needs to adopt a more theoretical and critical emphasis to achieve understanding in this field. Finally, unlike the UK, US and Australia, the concept of managing diversity has gained little headway in India and Elisabeth Wilson examines sources of difference within the Indian workforce, concentrating on caste and gender. In her academic review, she highlights the application of reservation, a form of affirmative action, as a means of enabling disadvantaged groups to gain public sector employment.

Part III centres around the specific forms of diversity, i.e. gender, disability, race and age, and illustrates the major differences between them. In Chapter 10, Deborah Hicks-Clarke and Paul Iles explore the relationship between diversity climate, gender and performance and the impact of diversity climates on work and organizational attitudes. The managing diversity paradigm is also explored through an analysis of the business case, the costs and benefits of managing diversity, and research on diversity climates. Carol Woodhams and Ardha Danieli present an analysis of the operation of diversity on the basis of disability. Moreover, they conclude that as a tool to effect organizational progress, the managing diversity approach of 'dissolving difference' has weaknesses for both organizations and disabled employees. In the following chapter, Andrew Gale, Marilyn Davidson, Peter Somerville, Diane Sodhi, Andy Steele and Sandi Rhys Jones adopt a practical approach to managing racial equality and diversity in the UK construction industry (the UK's largest industrial sector). This chapter reviews the literature pertaining to the under-representation of black and minority ethnic groups in the construction industry, and includes good practice guidelines and examples for improving the situation with respect to racial equality. The last chapter in this section addresses the subject of age and ageism in the future of employment and calls for a positive celebration of difference and diversity. Chris Brotherton's review reveals that age discrimination is a major problem despite the psychological evidence on age and ability, which demonstrates that there is no empirical basis for detrimental treatment being given to people on the basis of age.

Part IV turns our attention to diversity training and its effectiveness, with a heavy emphasis on practical applications. Roberta Kay and Donna Stringer provide practical guidance on how organizations can best design effective diversity programmes, including content, process and selection of a training team. They also offer a number of case studies to demonstrate the types of issues that might arise in such training and some of the approaches trainers might use in handling those issues. Mentoring is also increasingly used to help organizations achieve diversity management objectives. David Clutterbuck's chapter explores some of the issues surrounding mentoring across the spectrum of diversity. In particular, he points out that the more different the backgrounds of mentor and mentee, the greater the skill required by both parties to make the most of the relationship. Jean Hartley and Lyndsay Rashman's chapter examines UK public service organizations and specifically local government, and argues that diversity has been undertheorized in the current major period of organizational and cultural change. Furthermore, they also emphasize the importance of networking within and between organizations, as a crucial element of change. Carrying on with the theme of change, the last chapter in this section is practical in its orientation and discusses the changing demographics in the US workforce and the role that diversity training can play in dealing with these changes. David Tan, Lee Morris and James Romero present a workable diversity training model, an evaluation of its effectiveness and practical suggestions for developing and implementing a successful diversity training programme.

Part V of this book focuses on academic and theoretical analyses of stereotypes, attitudes and bias in relation to diversity within organizations. Alison Sheridan and Jane O'Sullivan argue that representations of gender and work in popular cultural texts (such as mainstream Hollywood cinema), contribute to the disparity between the spirit of diversity management and its manifestations in organizations. They propose that in order to enter and survive in many organizations, people who are seen to be too different from the privileged and notionally mainstream identity group must somehow camouflage their difference in order to 'pass' as being the dominant group.

The attitudes and reactions of male managers to gender diversity activities in organizations are discussed by Anna Wahl and Charlotte Holgersson. Their chapter reviews two empirical studies conducted in the Swedish private sector and the results indicate that the gender structure of the organization had a decisive impact on men's reactions to gender diversity. In the next chapter, Mike Smith examines the academic literature in relation to bias in job selection and assessment techniques. Concepts of fairness and bias are distinguished and defined, and methods of establishing whether bias exists in selection are critically reviewed.

Finally, **Part VI** addresses the future in relation to the management of individual diversity and psychology in organizations beyond the millennium. Norma Riccucci investigates some of the programmes that US organizations have introduced to prepare for increased social and cultural diversity in their workforces. She concludes that in the past, there have been a host of problems with the way in which diversity programmes have been conceptualized and implemented, and that in future, organizations will need to develop viable programmes and policies or reconceptualize existing ones.

Nada Korac-Kakabadse, Alexander Kouzmin and Andrew Korac-Kakabadse critically review the research relating to the effects of information technology (IT) at the beginning of the third millennium, and its present and future ramifications for labour organization, business and culture. A need for self-reflection and a critical examination of adopted management models, especially those within embedded ethnocentric contexts of shared beliefs, values and cognitive structures, are also explored. Finally, Tony Montes and Graham Shaw's chapter provides practical issues and challenges that the future of workforce diversity brings in the new millennium. They also provide a framework that can be used to progress diversity aspirations in the form of a Diversity Assessment tool which has been used successfully by a number of UK companies.

Undoubtedly, managing diversity is a complex issue for both individuals and organizations. This is reflected in common major themes discussed by the chapter contributors, related to the problems associated with the application of the theoretical components of managing diversity into practice (which also involves the complexities of differences in organizational cultures both within and between countries); and to date, the limited number of sound, methodological studies investigating the effectiveness of diversity initiatives.

We conclude from the evidence presented in this book that the future success of the management of diversity in organizations lies not solely in legislation or corporate policy. We strongly propose that the effectiveness of diversity programmes is reliant also on the attitudes, perceptions and behaviour of individuals at all levels (from the top down) of the workforce, combined with an appropriate organizational and social cultural climate.

Hopefully, this handbook will help the reader to gain a much clearer insight into the issues and practicalities of successful and effective diversity management. In the words of Lawthorn (1999: 405):

> If occupational/organizational psychology is to make a difference, practitioners and theorists need to see the wood and the trees, the shadows and the showcase of the managing diversity debate.

Marilyn J. Davidson and Sandra L. Fielden

REFERENCES

Burn, S. (1996). *The Social Psychology of Gender*. New York: McGraw-Hill.

Cassell, C. (1997). The business case for equal opportunities: implications for women in management. *Women in Management Review*, **12**(1), 11–16.

Davidson, M. J. & Burke, R. (eds) (2000). *Women in Management: Current Research Issues*, Volume II. London: Sage.

Kandola, R. & Fullerton, J. (1994). *Managing the Mosaic: Diversity in Action*. London: Institute of Personnel and Development.

Lawthorn, R. (1999). Against all odds: managing diversity. In N. Chmiel (ed.) *Introduction to Work and Organizational Psychology—a European Perspective*, pp. 388–406. London: Blackwell.

Liff, S. & Wajcman, J. (1996). 'Sameness' and 'difference' revisited: which way forward for equal opportunity initiatives? *Journal of Management Studies*, **33**(1), 79–94.

Acknowledgements

We would like to thank and acknowledge the valuable assistance of Cath Hearne for her expertise in the coordination of the manuscripts and the managing of correspondence. Her enthusiasm and initiative have proved invaluable. Finally, we are also grateful to Stuart Fielden for his time given to proof-reading.

PART I

Strategic Approaches to Diversity

CHAPTER 1

Developing Strategic Approaches to Diversity Policy

Gill Kirton
Queen Mary, University of London, UK

SUMMARY

This chapter considers how organizations might develop diversity policy in the context of the social, economic and legal environments of the UK. It is suggested that the dominant 'equal opportunities' paradigm has not yet been supplanted by a 'diversity' paradigm and the chapter therefore explores possible types of diversity policy, which are broadly characterized as reactive and proactive. The chapter discusses the role of two key policy levers—training and development and monitoring and auditing—to illustrate the challenges of translating policy into practice. In conclusion, the chapter argues that abandoning altogether traditional 'equal opportunity' policy would be a retrograde step, while asserting that if approached with caution, the diversity discourse does have potential to push forward the equality project.

INTRODUCTION

Diversity is infinite: everyone is different from everyone else. If we take diversity to mean the multiplicity of characteristics that combine to make us individuals, we risk producing a definition so broad as to become meaningless (Heneman et al., 1996). On the one hand if we are to search for a definition that can be operationalized in the form of organizational policy, then it is necessary to narrow the definition in order to focus policy efforts. On the other hand, a broad conceptualization of diversity has the capacity to recognize not simply individual diversity, but also the heterogeneous nature of diverse social groups within the workforce (Liff, 1999), for example women, minority ethnic groups, disabled

Individual Diversity and Psychology in Organizations. Edited by Marilyn J. Davidson and Sandra L. Fielden.
© 2003 John Wiley & Sons, Ltd.

people and so on. The definition adopted for the purposes of a discussion in this chapter of developing diversity policy within organizations is one which locates the diversity debate in the categories of gender, ethnicity, age and disability because, as we shall see later, these demographic characteristics strongly influence employment outcomes. That said, the overlapping and sometimes fluid nature of these categories is recognized. For example, motherhood impacts upon women's relationship with employment, but not all women are or will become mothers. Thus different women will have different needs and aspirations over the life course.

It is also relevant in defining diversity that in the UK, in practice, when organizations talk about diversity policy they are usually referring to a set of procedures and practices, which were once labelled 'equal opportunities'. Equal opportunities policies (EOPs) have traditionally been concerned with the employment disadvantage and discrimination experienced by certain groups of workers, especially women, minority ethnic people, disabled people, older workers and lesbians and gay men. The general thrust of EOPs has been for organizations to develop procedures and practices to eliminate discriminatory behaviour by line managers and other gatekeepers and in so doing reduce the disadvantage experienced by individual members of the groups covered by the policy. One of the criticisms of this approach has been that it is negative, in the sense that failure to comply is associated with penalties (imposed by legislation) and punitive actions (for example, the disciplining of anyone found contravening policy). In other words, the positive benefits of compliance and commitment to the ideals or goals of the policy are not effectively sold to organizational members. In contrast, diversity policy seeks not only to recognize workforce diversity, but to value it rather than see it as a problem requiring a remedy. While there can be no argument with the valuing of diversity as a goal, the question which diversity policies need to address is how organizations can achieve that objective, particularly in view of the fact that to have a diverse workforce is no guarantee of that diversity being valued. Therefore, the project should begin but not end with achieving workforce diversity.

This is the background for this chapter's discussion of how organizations might develop strategic approaches to diversity policy. First, the social, economic and legal contexts of diversity policy development in the UK are discussed. The segmented nature of the labour market is highlighted, which gives rise to different patterns of employment among diverse employee groups. Second, the internal contexts of organizations are explored. Here, the emphasis is on dominant, hegemonic organizational cultures, which reproduce and reinforce normative values and behaviours, which run counter to a valuing diversity paradigm. Finally, the chapter turns its attention to consider how organizations might learn to value diversity. In other words, what kinds of policy levers might be contained within a diversity policy to push forward the terrain from an approach based on redressing discrimination towards one based on positive conceptions of difference?

THE EXTERNAL CONTEXTS OF DIVERSITY POLICY DEVELOPMENT

THE SOCIAL AND ECONOMIC CONTEXTS

Gender, race and ethnicity, age, whether or not one is disabled, are all factors which influence employment outcomes. The external labour market in which organizations are situated is sharply segmented (Kirton & Greene, 2000). However, it is not the intention of this chapter to enter into a detailed discussion of the employment inequalities which result from this segmentation. That said, the labour market patterns of various groups of employees is a relevant area for consideration here because it shapes the context in which diversity policy is developed, adding weight to the argument (made below) that diversity policy should build upon equality policy.

Female employment in the UK is now at the highest rate ever, with women comprising 45 per cent of the workforce and just below 70 per cent of women in employment. The largest employment rate increase in the last decade has been among women with children aged below five. The vast majority of women (88 per cent) work in the service industries and the main occupations for women are clerical (where 24 per cent of women have jobs), professional/technical (22 per cent), personal/protective (16 per cent), managerial (12 per cent) and sales (12 per cent) (EOR, 2001). These factors point to greater gender diversity in the labour market than previous generations have witnessed and indicates that organizations might need to adjust their employment strategies to recruit and retain this increasingly important labour source.

Non-white ethnic minority people comprise about 6 per cent of the British workforce. Recent analysis of Labour Force Survey data shows that ethnic minorities are disproportionately found in lower-skilled and lower-grade jobs. In particular, they are underrepresented in senior management grades in large organizations (Hoque & Noon, 1999). This is despite progress having been made by most ethnic minority groups in qualification levels. It is notable that in terms of occupational and educational attainment there are considerable differences between different ethnic minority groups (Kirton & Greene, 2000).

Disabled people make up 13 per cent of the working-age population. They are over-represented in low-skilled, low-status jobs and are three times more likely than non-disabled to be unemployed (DfEE, 1997). The likelihood of an organization employing disabled people is linked to size (with larger organizations more likely) and sector (manufacturing most likely) (Honey et al., 1993).

Ageism is sometimes described as the fourth main form of discrimination in employment. Age intersects with other diversity issues: gender, race and disability, with women, ethnic minorities and disabled people experiencing age disadvantage to the greatest extent. People over the age of 50 are disproportionately represented among the long-term unemployed and older employees are less likely to receive training from their employers (DfEE, 1997).

The segmented nature of the labour market briefly sketched above produces inequalities of pay and opportunities among diverse social groups. Thus, the labour market tends to produce discrimination and inequality (Dickens, 1999) rather than to value diversity. This is the external social and economic context in which organizations develop diversity policy.

THE LEGAL CONTEXT

The British legal and regulative framework for diversity and equality is set out in Table 1.1 and discussed more fully in Chapter 5. It can be seen that at present UK organizations can be held legally liable for cases of discrimination on grounds of gender, race and disability. There also exists a code of practice designed to promote age equality. British anti-discrimination legislation adopts a complaints-based approach, which concentrates

TABLE 1.1   UK legal/regulative framework for diversity and equality

---

Sex Discrimination Act (SDA) (1975)

Covers discrimination on grounds of gender, marital status and gender reassignment

Recognizes direct and indirect discrimination. *Direct* discrimination is where a person from one group is treated less favourably than are people not in that group. *Indirect* discrimination occurs where an apparently neutral employment practice has a disproportionately disadvantageous effect upon a particular group

Race Relations Act (RRA) (1976)

Covers discrimination on grounds of colour, race, nationality, or ethnic or national origins

The wording of the SDA and RRA are almost identical, therefore decisions of the tribunals and courts made under one Act are used to interpret the other

Disability Discrimination Act (DDA) (1995)

Covers discrimination against people with disabilities. Disability is defined as a physical or mental impairment, which has a long-term adverse effect on the person's ability to carry out normal day-to-day activities

Prohibits less favourable treatment, but allows the employer the defence of justification in some material and substantial circumstances

Code of Practice for Age Diversity in Employment (1998)

Does not have the force of the law, but urges employers to ensure that age is not a barrier to jobs and opportunities

---

on providing redress for individual victims of discrimination through the Employment Tribunal system, rather than seeking to promote equality (Johnson & Johnstone, 2000). For this reason, British legislation in this area has been criticized as being weak and minimalist in its nature. In order to avoid legal liability, employers are advised to adopt formal procedures to ensure that discrimination does not take place. Advice on how to do this is found in various codes of practice available from the Equal Opportunities Commission, Commission for Racial Equality and the Disability Rights Commission which, although not legally binding, provide guidance as to good practice.

The legislation outlined has underpinned traditional EOPs in the UK context and a shift to diversity policy does not render this requirement any less important. Therefore, it remains essential that organizations have policy mechanisms for ensuring that discrimination does not take place and that organizational members do not adopt discriminatory behaviours. Indeed, the need to comply with legislation represents a sound business case argument for developing policy. It is argued that it is not in the organization's interest in financial, productivity and public relations terms to be placed in the position of defending complaints of discrimination (Cameron, 1993). Yet, contrary to this, complaints to Employment Tribunals are increasing (EOR, 1999c), indicating that overall compliance with the law is partial. To risk stating the obvious, the rising number of complaints suggests that many organizations do not value diversity. Therefore, the law, albeit minimalist, provides a valuable safety net for many employees and has been an important trigger to EOP development. However, the UK legislation's partial nature (covering only two groups of employees until fairly recently) has typically constrained the breadth of coverage of EOPs and led most organizations to concentrate on gender and race equality. In terms of diversity policy development, the concern remains that some employers, who have been unconvinced by the economic arguments for complying with the law, will be similarly unconvinced by business arguments for valuing diversity. Generally speaking then, it is employers who have hitherto adopted strong EOPs (with the law as their foundation), who are likely to build on these to develop proactive diversity policy. The chapter now turns to explore the internal context of diversity policy.

THE INTERNAL CONTEXT OF DIVERSITY POLICY DEVELOPMENT—ORGANIZATION CULTURE

Organizational culture is usually defined in terms of shared symbols, languages, practices and deeply embedded beliefs and values (Newman, 1995). This implies a high degree of homogeneity within the organization, which may not constitute an accurate picture, or alternatively, the organization may be seeking to become more diverse and for this reason cultural homogeneity may be perceived as undesirable. In any case, it would be naive to suggest that diversity and cultural homogeneity could coexist without coming into conflict. To look at this another way, diversity might create problems for some organizations whose cultures are not inclusive. In terms of defining organizational culture, it would be more accurate to say that the cultural values of the dominant group come to be seen as residing in the organization, but that subcultures also exist. Nevertheless, the dominant group—the power holders—is the group able to use their structural position to impose their own cultural values on other organizational members. Thus, organizational cultures are infused with power inequalities. Since white males dominate management, it is this group whose cultural values come to be seen as the norm. Other groups are required to conform to and assimilate within this norm. Alvesson and Billing (1997: 107) talk about the 'pressure for homogeneity and culturally competent behaviour'. This involves individuals, consciously or unconsciously, conforming and adapting to organization norms in order to fit in or progress their careers, for example by adopting the expected and desired language, work style, appearance and so on. The demand for 'cultural competence' reinforces and reproduces the dominant monoculture, from which those who do not comply, or conform, remain excluded.

It is worth providing a few detailed examples of cultural processes at work in organizations. Performance appraisal is a widespread organizational practice, which is supposed to evaluate objectively and fairly employee performance. However, the objectivity and fairness of appraisal have been questioned. It is argued that performance appraisal systems are framed by the cultural beliefs, values and assumptions of the people who design them. Cultural values then determine who is judged a good employee and who is deemed suitable for training or promotion opportunities. The problem is that in a diverse workforce cultural values and assumptions will not be homogeneous; what is felt to be a fair judgement of ability and potential by one subgroup might not be shared by another (Chen & DiTomaso, 1996), possibly resulting in some people not feeling valued. Another important area of human resource practice is recruitment and selection (see also Chapter 20). Case studies conducted in the UK context by Collinson et al. (1990) examine this sphere. Their study of the insurance industry uncovers the cultural assumptions underlying male managers' stereotypes of male and female attributes. When evaluating male candidates, involvement in sport was a definite advantage, whereas a female's sporting achievements were read as indicative of a 'very narrow existence' (1990: 147). Another example was behaviour described as 'pushy' when exhibited by a female candidate and as 'showing initiative' when a male candidate was involved (1990: 101). Thus women were less likely to be recruited to what were viewed as gender-incongruent jobs.

These examples illustrate the difficulties involved in valuing diversity in an organiza-tional context where power holders constitute a largely homogeneous group. Further, in some cultural contexts a diversity discourse could be used to exclude as much as to include. Rutherford's (1999) case study of banking illustrates how the discourses of gendered biological and psychological difference might be used to justify the scarcity of women in management grades and in so doing reproduce the status quo of male domination. After all, if women were not suited to management in banking what would be the point of creating policies to attempt to improve their representation there? Thus, jobs become infused with stereotyped characteristics, which are believed to be linked to gender, race (Liff & Dickens, 2000) and to some extent, age.

Miller (1996: 207) describes organizational culture as an 'abstraction' and 'therefore a most difficult thing to manage'. He suggests that while the organization may be able to address the more tangible manifestations of the dominant culture, which may create an adverse environment for certain groups of workers, it is much harder to address the more fundamental values and assumptions held by organizational members. Thus, policy intervention at a superficial level—for example, tinkering with cultural symbols such as uniforms, dress codes or the layout of buildings—will not create new shared values at a fundamental level. In addition, some organizational members might eschew culture change efforts and adhere to the traditional core values of the dominant culture (Miller & Rowney, 1999), rendering the construction of a valuing diversity culture less plausible. Following from this, in their research Collinson et al. (1990) emphasize human agency, arguing that human beings retain a relative autonomy and a capacity to act in a manner of their own choosing irrespective of organizational policy. In this vein, line managers, and other gatekeepers, are able either to act in accordance with diversity policy or in opposition to it. Hoque and Noon's (1999) study of race discrimination in the recruitment process, for example, shows that managers' actions are often responsible for unfairness (rather than the policy or procedures per se). Also, other (lower level) employees will not abandon their own stereotypes and prejudices simply because the organization states that it values diversity. To summarize, organizational culture is important for diversity policy because employees who are perceived as different can feel undervalued and excluded by informal cultural practices.

DEVELOPING DIVERSITY POLICY

The above discussions of the outer and inner contexts of organizations suggest that the valuing of diversity will not occur naturally. Organizations, including individual organizational members, will need to be persuaded of the (ethical or economic) merits of valuing diversity. Following from that, specific and measurable policy initiatives will need to be developed if change is to occur. This section of the chapter considers the ideology, triggers and characteristics of diversity policy. It is not the intention here to offer a precise set of policy prescriptions, rather to delineate broad approaches.

APPROACHES TO DIVERSITY

At present in the UK 'equal opportunities' is the dominant term used by organizations to frame their approach to managing difference, discrimination and disadvantage. That said, it has never been entirely clear whether the aim of equal opportunities should be equal access, equal treatment or equal outcomes (or of course all three). (For a fuller discussion see Miller, 1996; Webb, 1997; Kirton & Greene, 2000.) However, EOPs tend to be associated with treating everybody the same (Skinner, 1999). In contrast, within diversity policy, in order to value diversity it might be necessary to recognize difference with different treatment (for example, disabled people might have particular requirements related to their disability). The situation becomes complex because sometimes, in the interests of fairness (and it is clearly necessary to treat people fairly if they are to feel valued), it will be essential to treat people the same (for example, by having standardized recruitment and selection procedures). This conceptual muddle notwithstanding, recent evidence indicates that around two-thirds of workplaces are covered by formal written EOPs (Cully et al., 1999). In contrast, there is little information available about the spread and coverage of diversity policy. Although the aim of diversity policy—to value diversity—is seemingly more transparent and straightforward than the aim of EOPs, there remains a lack of precision about what this involves. What is clear is that a diversity policy will sit uncomfortably with a drive for lower costs, because resources will be necessary to make the policy meaningful and real (Skinner, 1999). The UK Chartered Institute of Personnel and Development (CIPD) suggests that 'diversity takes equality forward' (IPD, 1996). It 'develops and complements established approaches to equal opportunities' and 'builds on an understanding of the need for equal opportunity policies' (IPD, 1996: 1). Further, it is argued that EOPs provide a solid platform on which diversity policy can be built, and for this reason diversity policy will be most successful where this approach is taken (Cornelius et al., 2001). The term 'diversity model of equal opportunity' has also been coined (Webb, 1997: 163–4) to 'signify a commitment by the employer to create a workplace which facilitates the inclusion of all social categories and enables everyone to contribute to the business'. Thus, in the UK context discussions about diversity policy cannot be entirely divorced from traditional equal opportunity approaches. It remains unclear how UK organizations will operationalize diversity and how this might diverge from or transform traditional EOPs.

The proponents of diversity approaches usually emphasize the advantages to business in valuing diversity. This discussion typically centres on four main areas: taking advantage of diversity in the labour market; maximizing employee potential; managing across borders and cultures; creating business opportunities and enhancing creativity (Cornelius et al., 2001). The first area concerns the changing demography of the British labour market, examined earlier. To reiterate, the most salient changes for employers are the decline of young workers entering the full-time, permanent workforce and the increase of women available for employment. Together, these factors indicate that many employers will seek to recruit women and older workers (although young people in full-time education continue to be available for part-time work). The second area emphasizes the harnessing of the human capital possessed by diverse groups. This argument holds that prejudice, discrimination and within-organization disadvantage create low morale and disaffection, which in turn lead to poor individual and organizational performance. Here, employers need to confront prejudice and discrimination and seek to eliminate them, so that human capital can be fully utilized. The third area is particularly concerned with the globalization of world markets and the international labour and product markets that many organizations operate within. It is believed that a diverse workforce can make a positive contribution to such organizations. From this perspective, it is worthwhile organizations proactively seeking to recruit and retain diverse employees. The fourth area concerns customer markets. The assumption is that organizations could gain access to new markets by tapping the culturally specific experiences and insights that a diverse workforce possesses. Again, diversity adds value to the organization. To be effective in economic business terms, diversity policy would need to tackle the area(s) appropriate to the particular organizational context and circumstances. Placing the emphasis on a narrow conception of the organizational benefits to be derived from diversity might result in a partial rather than comprehensive policy. For example, a narrow approach might render organizations more amenable to valuing certain types of diversity over others. There is no evidence to suggest that an organization that values gender diversity will necessarily place an equivalent value upon ethnic diversity, especially as women comprise overall a larger customer market than do ethnic minorities.

Furthermore, there is no assumption made here that all organizations stand to benefit (in a narrow sense) either from equality or from diversity—this assumption rests on shaky foundations and its veracity needs to be challenged. Dickens (1994), for example, points to the partial and contingent nature of economic rationales for diversity, which often pay insufficient attention to the wider context in which organizations operate. For example, policy initiatives developed to attract and retain women often arise from a shortage of young labour and when employers need to fill part-time jobs, rather than stemming from a belief that women add value to the organization. Other employers in certain geographical locations can attract minority ethnic labour into lower-level jobs without pursuing either equality or proactive diversity policy, simply because this group is over-represented in low-skill, low-pay work (Edwards, 1995). In other words, some organizations are able to flourish with un(der)valued diverse workforces, while others need pursue neither equality nor diversity in order to deliver profits or other organizational objectives.

TYPES OF DIVERSITY POLICY

With these caveats in mind, an attempt is now made to map out possible approaches to diversity in order to frame a discussion of the types of policy initiatives that might be followed by organizations seeking to learn to value diversity. This has been developed from a review of the literature in the area. Table 1.2 proposes two different types of diversity policy—the reactive and proactive. As can be seen, the reactive approach rests on a narrow conception of business interests. In contrast, the proactive approach looks at the longer-term, broader picture and sees the organization as having social and ethical responsibilities, which underpin the organization's long-term health and viability. Thus, the definition of 'business case' interests can be narrowly or broadly conceived. Dickens (1994) makes an argument for broadening these to include social, ethical and environmental issues, so that even where short-term gains are not apparent organizations might become convinced to attach a greater importance to valuing workforce diversity.

As with any typology, it is intended as a classificatory tool to aid discussion and analysis. In reality organizations may not fit neatly into either category. There are a number of possible reasons for this. First, an organization may have adopted the language and rhetoric of diversity to describe its former EOP in order to downplay equality issues and to suggest neutrality towards diverse social groups, thereby signalling that inequality is not an issue within the organization (Kirton & Greene, 2000). This organization is unlikely to have a clearly articulated approach to diversity policy and practice; instead it may simply declare that it values all individuals, whatever their backgrounds. Second, an organization may straddle both the reactive and the proactive approaches by developing different policy initiatives in relation to different groups of employees. For example, an organization seeking to attract more female customers might be proactive in relation to recruiting, retaining and developing women employees, but less so in relation to other groups.

The discussion now moves to elucidate further the features of proactive diversity policy, because it is this approach that offers the greatest potential for the depth of transformation required for organizations to value diversity. In contrast, with reactive diversity policy any change is likely to be either short term, superficial, or both. Clearly, this is not to say that the proactive organization is not interested in some aspects of the shorter agenda of the reactive approach. It is merely a question of emphasis and the investment in the development of a longer agenda.

PROACTIVE DIVERSITY POLICY

Table 1.2 suggests that proactive diversity policy would be underpinned by ethical beliefs and values. This is in contrast to reactive diversity policy, which would seek simply to utilize workforce diversity to further measurable and short-term business interests. The problem with the reactive approach is that employees might feel exploited by the policy (Thomas & Ely, 1996 in Cornelius et al., 2001), in which case the organization could not expect to co-opt employees to its aspirations. Further support for the proactive approach arises from the increasing interest in ethical issues in business and organizations. This is captured by GrandMet's statement cited in CIPD's position paper on 'managing diversity': 'Customers are increasingly looking through the front door of the companies

TABLE 1.2   Types of diversity policy

	Reactive diversity policy	Proactive diversity policy
Ideology	Utilitarian instrumentalism Business case Diversity viewed as cost	Ethical rationality Social justice Diversity viewed as asset
Triggers	Labour and skills shortages Declining profits Shareholders' needs	Corporate reputation Attract investors Multiple stakeholders' needs
Characteristics	Abandons EOP Legal compliance Focus on recruitment Add-on initiatives Managerial autonomy Mission statement Dependent on statements of intent Management-led Narrow agenda Short term	Builds on EOP Goes beyond the law Focus also on promotion blocks Mainstreaming Managerial accountability Ongoing publicity Dependent on monitoring and auditing Consultation with stakeholders Broad agenda Long term

they buy from. If they do not like what they see in terms of social responsibility, they will not go in' (IPD, 1996).

The triggers to a policy built on the foundation of social and ethical responsibility would be centred on corporate reputation, the wish to attract new investors or the perceived need to consider the interests of organizational stakeholders. Here, corporate reputation would be seen to be contingent on being a 'good employer' and linked to this the perceived need to fulfil social obligations by embracing equality, justice and diversity. Within proactive diversity policy consultation with stakeholders—consumers, community groups, employee groups and trade unions for example—would be worthwhile because it is essential that future policy developments will be informed by feedback from those involved with the organization. Thus, lack of diversity or failing to value diversity cannot be justified on the basis that there is no short-term gain. This means that the organization needs to develop policy, which is less concerned with measuring and quantifying specific gains and outcomes for the business, and instead looks for qualitative improvements in the experiences of the workforce. A good example of a UK company practising this approach is the Littlewoods Organization. Each of the businesses within the company has its own diversity action plan, which is linked to every business function. The plan identifies how diversity and equality can add value to the business, customers and the community (EOR, 1998).

Proactive policy would encompass several characteristics as shown in Table 1.2. There are several points which are worthy of further explication, but it goes without saying that the proactive organization would see diversity policy as extending and complementing the policy provisions of the existing EOP, rather than supplanting it. It is also self-evident that this approach would be compliant with equality legislation.

Where this approach has something more distinctive to offer is in its commitment to work towards valuing diversity, rather than seeing it as a problem to be managed or resolved. This would involve a 'mainstreaming' approach, which integrates diversity and equality considerations into all business and employment policies (Rees, 1998), rather than being dependent on 'add-on' initiatives geared towards tackling a particular issue such as women's under-representation in senior management. It is also necessary to ensure that diversity policy does not just benefit higher-level employees (Richards, 2000). There needs to be consideration given to how diversity at the lower levels of the organizational pyramid can also be valued. Again, Littlewoods is a good example. There, it is planned that managers' performance will be assessed on diversity outcomes, for example the ethnic minority profile of their departments, how they respond to jobshare requests and on community involvement initiatives (EOR, 1998). Also, diversity policy should be integral to the management of change so that any achievements are built upon rather than lost, if the organization undergoes restructuring, 'downsizing' or some other such change.

LINKING POLICY TO PRACTICE

It has been suggested that statements of policy are poor indicators of good practice in this area (Noon, 1993). Indeed, it might be that such statements are being used simply as 'window dressing' (Hoque & Noon, 1999). This section discusses the role of two key policy levers—training and development and monitoring and auditing—in translating diversity policy into practice (see also Chapters 14 and 17). Training and development can be used for two diversity-related purposes. First, to communicate the aims of the policy (at employee induction, for example), to raise employee awareness of diversity issues and to instruct managers and other employees of their roles and duties in relation to diversity policy (for example, managers' performance objectives might be tied to diversity outcomes). Second, training programmes might be utilized as a way of achieving greater diversity in certain occupations or at certain levels of the organization.

The first type of diversity training seeks to alter employee behaviour so that a culture of valuing difference can emerge. However, there is some evidence, in the US context at least, of employee resentment of training that attempts to manipulate the beliefs and attitudes of employees: 'Diversity training seemed to fuel the fires of a national backlash. Many people came to believe that the point of diversity training was to change white men' (Zhu & Kleiner, 2000: 6). These authors argue that diversity education needs to be a 'cultural issue' rather than a 'training issue' if it is to be effective. In other words, the contention is that people will not learn how to value diversity simply by being exposed to a one-off training course, especially if forced to attend. In the UK context, despite the existence of training, it has been found that assessments of employees were based on stereotypes of the 'traditional' worker, instead of accommodating diversity (in this case the needs of part-time workers) (Skinner, 1999). In contrast, in the Australian context positive benefits of diversity training have been identified from a study of a major corporation (Sinclair, 2000), where participants reportedly developed awareness of their own stereotypes and a new respect for others. Based on these studies, the utility and efficacy of diversity training are debatable, but effectiveness is likely to be contingent upon the specific organizational context, as well as upon how the training process is managed. In order to pre-empt some of the possible pitfalls, organizations need to take some precautions. In addition to providing training geared towards developing greater understanding of diverse employees (which may or may not result in the desired outcome), organizations need to find ways of rewarding positive contributions to diversity, through the performance appraisal system, for example (EOR, 2001). They also still need to be prepared to confront the existence of behaviours in opposition to a diversity paradigm, such as discrimination and harassment. The latter involves providing specific examples of inappropriate and unacceptable behaviours, together with the methods of discipline to be applied. A degree of 'backlash' or resentment is inevitable, given that valuing diversity in organizations will involve some loss of privilege for some groups (Sinclair, 2000). The possible resulting behaviours of angry individuals and groups cannot simply be ignored.

The second type of diversity training essentially seeks to break down various forms of vertical occupational segregation. In particular, it seeks to tackle the problem of the 'glass ceiling' encountered by certain groups of employees. The aim is to achieve diversity at the higher levels of the organization. There are a number of organizations which have adopted this approach in relation to women. The Royal Mail, for example, has developed an in-house training course for women in non-managerial positions who wish to explore personal development opportunities (EOR, 1996). British Telecom has developed a course for women middle managers to assist them in progressing their careers within the male-dominated context of the telecommunications industry (EOR, 1999a). Lloyds TSB, in the banking and finance industry, has a similar programme for ethnic minority employees (EOR, 1999b).

TABLE 1.3   A diversity audit

1 *Where are employees located?*
Produce a breakdown by grade, job and site on the basis of gender, ethnicity, age and disability. This will help identify patterns of segmentation and possible blocks to internal horizontal or vertical mobility

2 *What educational, vocational and professional qualifications do employees hold?*
Combined with the information gained from the exercise (1) above, this will help identify employees who are underemployed and who might be suitable for development and promotion. It will also help to identify any patterns of career underachievement among diverse employees

3 *What skills and experience do employees have?*
This is a complementary exercise to (2) above, which trawls for a wider profile of experience and expertise, which may not be reflected in formal qualifications

4 *Auditing and monitoring access to training and development opportunities*
Review the routes to promotion and horizontal mobility. Identify patterns of access and take-up among diverse employees

5 *Auditing and monitoring recruitment and appraisal procedures, processes and outcomes*
This will identify any biases in procedures and processes and whether stereotypes inform decisions

6 *Cohort analysis*
This involves tracking the career progress of a diverse group of employees over a period of time and helps identify obstacles

7 *Employee attitude survey*
This will complement the data gathered from the exercises above. Its aim is to explore diverse employees' perceptions of the organization

Source: adapted Kirton and Greene (2000) *The Dynamics of Managing Diversity*. Reprinted by permission of Butterworth-Heinemann.

Although these initiatives appear to meet diversity objectives by seeking to recast workforce composition and value difference, they also meet controversy on grounds that employees are selected for their demographic characteristics rather than on the basis of merit. From the point of view of the beneficiaries of targeted training, being positioned as in need of assistance can be a stigmatizing experience. This presents a dilemma, which is not easily resolved.

Another important principle of good diversity practice for organizations is to develop ways of monitoring and evaluating the outcomes of policy initiatives. Various bodies such as the Equal Opportunities Commission (EOC), Commission for Racial Equality (CRE) and CIPD recommend this approach. Noon (1993: 45) goes so far as to argue that

> in an increasingly competitive environment, where according to a plethora of HRM literature, people are deemed to be an organisation's 'most valued asset', can companies afford not to be making high quality decisions with regard to their personnel? Arguably, a thorough monitoring policy, covering gender, ethnic grouping, disability and age, may become a competitive advantage in the future.

Table 1.3 sets out the elements of a diversity audit.

The objective of the audit is to gather information about the workforce, with the aim of utilizing the findings to inform diversity policy development and implementation. The findings should indicate the extent to which diversity exists in the organization and the extent to which diversity is valued. This might subsequently lead to the implementation of remedial policies, for example recruitment initiatives designed to draw in more diversity such as advertising in the ethnic minority press. Or better-quality part-time work might be considered in order to offer alternative work arrangements and career paths to working parents. An audit might also identify the ways in which an organization is underutilizing the skills and abilities of diverse employees (Liff & Dickens, 2000). Policy can then be oriented towards areas where there appear to be blockages to the valuing of diversity, perhaps by introducing targeted training programmes. These are all simply examples to illustrate the ways in which it is possible for organizations to respond in practical terms to diversity issues and also to demonstrate the dynamic nature of policy in this area. A further benefit of a diversity audit lies in the importance of understanding *practice* as it relates to policy. Put another way, organizational practice does not always accurately reflect policy, but if diversity policy is to be more than vacuous rhetoric, there have to be mechanisms for ensuring it is being followed by organizational members, especially gatekeepers and decision-makers.

CONCLUSIONS

Critics of equal opportunity argue that this policy approach has failed to deliver equality (Kandola & Fullerton, 1994). While it is true to say that employment inequalities do still exist, overt discrimination on grounds of gender and race is less commonplace than it was prior to the development of the sex and race discrimination acts and of organizational EOPs. Therefore, the traditional equality approach has had some, albeit limited, impact. The limitations mainly arise from the wider context in which the organization is situated. In other words, even relatively strenuous efforts to tackle discrimination and disadvantage within the organization are hampered by structural inequalities at a societal level, in particular the interrelationship between education, training and employment (Rees, 1998). The continued existence of social inequalities could be said to indicate that as a society we are not yet ready to value diversity—adopting the language will not make it happen. However, this should not be used as an excuse for organizational inertia or fatalism. Businesses have social responsibilities (one of these is to treat employees fairly) and they also have a need for social legitimacy in order to survive in the longer term (Miller & Rowney, 1999). This would point to a need for organizations to value workforce diversity, irrespective of the purchase of short-term business case arguments discussed earlier.

The concept of diversity has been subjected to a substantial critique because of its focus on the needs of businesses and organizations, but it can also be useful for organizational policy-makers and practitioners as a way of gaining access to some of the resources necessary to achieve gains for employees. In particular, the new discourse of diversity provides the opportunity for the message about difference to be heard. However, recognition of difference and the adoption of diversity policy should not be used as an excuse for the ad hoc or inconsistent treatment of individual employees, which might reproduce historic inequalities and take the organization further from, not closer to, valuing diversity. Organizations can develop proactive diversity policy, starting the journey towards learning to value diversity, but it must be recognized that the project will be a long-term one. Diversity goals cannot be realized without first dismantling the many obstacles to organizational equality. The problem in the UK context is that most organizations are predominantly concerned with the bottom line—short-term profitability—(Sisson, 1995) and this orientation militates against long agendas. This renders it all the more important that the retrograde step of abandoning or neglecting equal opportunity policy should be avoided. Nevertheless, it must be recognized that policy approaches which focus on certain groups of employees—most typically women and ethnic minorities—have engendered some employee resentment (Cockburn, 1991; Miller & Rowney, 1999). All in all, perhaps it is now an appropriate juncture in the history of equality initiatives to develop more inclusive definitions. One of the strengths of the diversity discourse is its capacity to stretch beyond the narrow confines of the law associated with traditional equality approaches and to recognize individual as well as group-based difference.

In conclusion, diversity policy development needs to be approached with caution. First, it needs to build on existing and traditional equal opportunities, in order that the safety net is not dislodged, particularly for groups of employees whose diversity might not add obvious value to the organization, but who from an ethical perspective still have a right to expect fair treatment. Second, it needs to articulate a strong case for diversity and show how in practical terms the goal of valuing diversity is to be achieved by making clear linkages to specific policy levers. Third, the policy should not be viewed as static: there are no once-and-for-all solutions. Rather, it must be regularly reviewed following comprehensive evaluation of policy initiatives through an ongoing monitoring and auditing process. Finally, organizations must be prepared to confront policy failures as well as to celebrate successes, in order to rise to the challenge of learning to value diversity.

REFERENCES

Alvesson, M. & Billing, Y. (1997). *Understanding Gender and Organisations*. London: Sage.

Cameron, I. (1993). Formulating an equal opportunities policy. *Equal Opportunities Review*, No. 47, 16–20.

Chen, C. & DiTomaso, N. (1996). Performance appraisal and demographic diversity: issues regarding appraisals, appraisers and appraising. In E. Kossek & S. Lobel (eds) *Managing Diversity: Human Resource Strategies for Transforming the Workplace*. Oxford: Blackwell.

Cockburn, C. (1991). *In the Way of Women*. Basingstoke: Macmillan.

Collinson, D., Knights, D. & Collinson, M. (1990). *Managing to Discriminate*. London: Routledge.

Cornelius, N., Gooch, L. & Todd, S. (2001). Managing difference fairly: an integrated partnership approach. In M. Noon & E. Ogbonna (eds) *Equality, Diversity and Disadvantage in Employment*, Basingstoke: Palgrave.

Cully, M., Woodland, S., O'Reilly, A. & Dix, G. (1999). *Britain at Work*, London: Routledge.

DfEE (Department for Education and Employment) (1997). *Labour Market and Skill Trends 1997/8*.

Dickens, L. (1994). The business case for women's equality. Is the carrot better than the stick? *Employee Relations*, **16**(8), 9–19.

Dickens, L. (1999). Beyond the business case: a three-pronged approach to equality action. *Human Resource Management Journal*, **9**(1), 9–19.

Edwards, J. (1995). *When Race Counts: The Morality of Racial Preference in Britain and America*. London: Routledge.

EOR (1996). Women in the Post Office. *Equal Opportunities Review*, No. 66, 13–19.

EOR (1998). Littlewoods: increasing diversity, increasing profits. *Equal Opportunities Review*, No. 81, 20–28.

EOR (1999a). BT: championing women in a man's world. *Equal Opportunities Review*, No. 84, 14–20.

EOR (1999b). Improving recruitment and promotion opportunities for ethnic minorities. *Equal Opportunities Review*, No. 85, 15–20.

EOR (1999c). Compensation awards 1998: a record year. *Equal Opportunities Review*, No. 86, 14–18.

EOR (2001). Diversity now the ultimate test of management capacity. *Equal Opportunities Review*, No. 96, 11–17.

Heneman, R., Waldeck, N. & Cushnie, M. (1996). Diversity considerations in staffing decision-making. In E. Kossek & S. Lobel (eds) *Managing Diversity: Human Resource Strategies for Transforming the Workplace*. Oxford: Blackwell.

Honey, S., Meager, N. & Williams, M. (1993). *Employers' Attitudes towards People with Disabilities*. Brighton: Institute of Manpower Studies.

Hoque, K. & Noon, M. (1999). Racial discrimination in speculative applications: new optimism six years on? *Human Resource Management Journal*, 9(2), 71–82.

IPD (1996). Managing diversity: an IPD position paper. London: Institute of Personnel and Development.

Johnson, L. & Johnstone, S. (2000). The legislative framework. In G. Kirton & A. Greene (eds) *The Dynamics of Managing Diversity*. Oxford: Butterworth Heinemann.

Kandola, R. & Fullerton, J. (1994). *Managing the Mosaic: Diversity in Action*. London: IPD.

Kirton, G. & Greene, A. (2000). *The Dynamics of Managing Diversity*. Oxford: Butterworth Heinemann.

Liff, S. (1999). Diversity and equal opportunities: room for a constructive compromise? *Human Resource Management Journal*, 9(1), 65–75.

Liff, S. & Dickens, L. (2000). Ethics and equality: reconciling false dilemmas. In D. Winstanley & J. Woodall (eds) *Ethical Issues in Contemporary Human Resource Management*. London: Macmillan.

Miller, D. (1996). Equality management: towards a materialist approach. *Gender, Work and Organisation*, 3(4), 202–214.

Miller, G. & Rowney, J. (1999). Workplace diversity management in a multicultural society. *Women in Management Review*, 14(8), 307–315.

Newman, J. (1995). Gender and cultural change. In C. Itzin & J. Newman (eds) *Gender, Culture and Organisational Change*. London: Routledge.

Noon, M. (1993). Racial discrimination in speculative application: evidence from the UK's top 100 firms. *Human Resource Management Journal*, 3(4), 35–47.

Rees, T. (1998). *Mainstreaming Equality in the European Union*. London: Routledge.

Richards, W. (2000). Evaluating equal opportunities initiatives: the case for a 'transformative' agenda. In M. Noon & E. Ogbonna (eds) *Equality, Diversity and Disadvantage in Employment*. Basingstoke: Palgrave.

Rutherford, S. (1999). Equal opportunities policies—making a difference. *Women in Management Review*, 14(6), 212–219.

Sinclair, A. (2000). Women within diversity: risks and possibilities. *Women in Management Review*, 15(5/6), 237–245.

Sisson, K. (1995). Human resource management and the personnel function. In J. Storey (ed.) *Human Resource Management: A Critical Text*. London: Routledge.

Skinner, D. (1999). The reality of equal opportunities: the expectations and experiences of part-time staff and their managers. *Personnel Review*, 28(5/6), 425–438.

Thomas, D. & Ely, R. (1996). Making differences matter: a new paradigm for managing diversity. *Harvard Business Review*, September–October, 79–90, in Cornelius et al. (2001).

Webb, J. (1997). The politics of equal opportunity. *Gender, Work and Organisation*, 4(3), 159–169.

Zhu, J. & Kleiner, B. (2000). The value of training in changing discrimination behaviour at work. *Equal Opportunities International*, 19(6/7), 5–9.

CHAPTER 2

The Importance of Diversity in Innovation

Carolann Ashton

Diversity Consultant, Swansea, Wales, UK

SUMMARY

Diversity has made several transitions during the last five decades. The current paradigm and the one that private sector companies have become interested in is the business case for diversity. This is a process of looking at diversity through the eyes of the multiple identities of the consumer, and distinguishing the demographics and statistics that will help to identify growth markets and consumer changes. It engages companies in the benefits of understanding all of their customers, in order to sustain their competitive advantage.

However, can this or any of diversity's previous incarnations be considered innovative? Certainly some of the companies that have embraced the business case have adopted innovative ideas, but only in selected areas of the company where the appropriate environment and leadership exist for such innovation. So, the big question remains, 'Do companies really want to change in ways that allow diversity to be successful?' For this would mean massive cultural change and a process of internalizing different perspectives and incorporating them into the main work of the organization.

Innovation needs a concentrated energy of effort behind it and despite their engagement in the issue, few companies could boast this energy. Of course, one of the fundamental flaws to this 'business case' approach is that no one has yet developed an innovative way of measuring its success, for true innovation cannot be measured through the company balance sheet alone.

Individual Diversity and Psychology in Organizations. Edited by Marilyn J. Davidson and Sandra L. Fielden.
© 2003 John Wiley & Sons, Ltd.

INTRODUCTION

Diversity has been predicated on a range of social, moral and business imperatives during the last 50 years, but have any of its manifestations been truly innovative? The business case for diversity, which is currently in the ascendancy, has certainly attracted the attention of the business community, but will its influence lead to any fundamental and lasting change? In a world driven by the bottom line do we have in place the kind of measures to convince business that fully embracing diversity will bring about positive change?

HISTORICAL CONTEXT

In the 1960s, 1970s and 1980s most of the work on equal opportunities in the UK was done by public sector organizations in local or central government, and they did a good job of identifying the moral 'in a stable society all segments of the population have a stake in the society's prosperity and equal access to its benefits' (Price Mueller, 1998: 3) and social arguments for change in this area; however, private sector businesses rarely identified anything in it for them, unless it was to avoid the embarrassment of an Employment Tribunal.

Meanwhile, in the late 1990s Employment Tribunals were given the power to award unlimited awards for sex, race and disability discrimination (Sex Discrimination Act 1975; Race Discrimination Act 1976; Disability Discrimination Act 1995) cases in an attempt to bring more companies into line, but this punitive approach did not work either. New European directives, such as 'the employment, directive', which is designed to establish a general framework for equal treatment in employment, will mean that employees will also be protected on grounds of religion or belief, sexual orientation and age. But as with its predecessors, legislation alone will not change company, or societal, behaviour.

For many years a new paradigm was sought; in 1987 in America, a highly influential book entitled *Workforce 2000* (Johnstone & Packer, 1987) was produced by the Hudson Institute showing startling workforce demographic trends, and here the term 'managing diversity' was initiated. In the 1990s and up to the present date, the focus has been on diversity as an entire concept; R.R. Thomas's 1990 *Harvard Review* article 'From affirmative action to affirming diversity' opened the floodgates for a range of literature on the topic.

The 'business case for diversity' has grown from the desire to fully include big business in issues of diversity, by concentrating on issues with which business people could connect. The UK and much of Europe have adopted the term 'business case for diversity' from the USA, where business and entrepreneurship are a fundamental part of the culture.

The current environment in which we live, driven by the increasing impact of information and communication technologies, by economic globalization and the need for innovation, has meant that 'human capital' has become the primary source of productivity and competitiveness. This business and cultural dependence on people with the skills of problem-solving and communication to information and risk management and self-organization (Seltzer & Bentley, 1999) is the ideal business critical requirement for developing the individual and being totally diverse, yet one needs to question why this is still not happening.

IS DIVERSITY INNOVATIVE?

Kandola and Fullerton (1994) say, 'Diversity is a concept which recognizes the benefits to be gained by differences' (p. 12) and further explain it by stating that it

> consists of visible and non-visible differences which will include factors such as sex, age, background, race, disability, personality and work style. It is founded on the premise that harnessing these differences will create a productive environment in which everybody feels valued, where their talents are being fully utilized and in which organizational goals are met. (p. 19)

However, many organizations talk about diversity, they link it into their business objectives, they recruit from a wider pool of talent and yet they still appear outwardly to be the same. They maintain the same outlook, the same approach to work, and the same power base. If you challenged most organizations to demonstrate the ways their organization has changed since diversity became one of their objectives, the response would probably be uninspiring and the measurement limited.

Diversity is now seen as an essential part of most organizations; however, there is still very little understanding of what diversity actually means in terms of the day-to-day management of people and little knowledge of how to measure its success effectively.

Reena Bhavnani (2001) offers a more rounded and comprehensive definition of diversity:

> the ability to incorporate new perspectives, new ways of doing things, such that people feel valued for their group and individual difference. At the same time they are not stereotyped by expectations as always representing members of a group, or limited by expectations that they cannot do this, have no way to develop, or can only excel in one way.
>
> Diversity means questioning the ways we all speak with other people, the ways we treat each other, either defensively or in a hostile manner, patronizingly or with low expectations. It means the ability to shift from seeing all people as having one identity, which may be the most visible or most strongly ascribed, to seeing people with multiple identities, which defines them in all sorts of complex ways. These singular ascribed identities include the colour of someone's skin, whether they are women or men, old or young, gay or straight, disabled or able-bodied. We must all see others and ourselves as people with multiple identities. For example, one person may be a father, a worker, of Indian origin, Muslim, an engineer and a customer. These different identities may matter in different combinations or separately, in important ways, at different places, at different times. We must be able to move from one to several to a few to one, in order that respect and empathy is maintained, and not put people into one or two boxes from where they find it hard to emerge. (p. 5)

DO WE WANT CHANGE?

Do organizations really want to change in the ways that allow diversity to be successful? The American researchers, Thomas and Ely (1996), argue, on the basis of their six-year research project, that diversity is not meeting its true potential because managers still hold onto a flawed assumption about diversity which needs to be replaced with a broader understanding. They looked at 12 US organizations in relation to:

- How they had successfully achieved and sustained racial and gender diversity
- The impact of diversity on practices, processes and procedures

- How leaders had influenced whether diversity became an enhancing or detracting element in the organization

They worked particularly closely with three companies, a law firm, a bank and a consulting firm, who had attained a high level of demographic diversity. The following perspectives which they identify as having guided most diversity initiatives were the *discrimination and fairness paradigm* and the *access and legitimacy paradigm* and the emerging paradigm they identified at that time was *the connecting diversity to work perspectives paradigm*:

- *Discrimination and fairness paradigm*—'progress measured by how well the company achieves its recruitment and retention goals rather than by the degree to which conditions in the company allow employees to draw on their assets and perspectives to do their work more effectively. The staff one might say get diversified but the work does not'. The company operates as if everyone were the same, despite its efforts to recruit diversely.
- *Access and legitimacy paradigm*—this paradigm has a market-driven motivation, our customer base is diverse and therefore so must be our employees. Differences are celebrated as a way of accessing niche markets, however these differences are not analysed to see how they actually affect the work that is being done. 'Many organizations using this paradigm have diversified only in those areas in which they interact with particular niche-market segments' (Thomas & Ely, 1996). Often larger organizations perceive the experience of these 'diverse' individuals as limited or specialist and so their development and careers are restricted.
- *Connecting diversity to work perspectives*—a process of internalizing the differences among employees so that an organization can learn and grow because of them, incorporating different perspectives into the main work of the organization. A way of recognizing that employees frequently make choices and decisions at work that draw on their cultural background.

In fact diversity is not on a linear path, it is a process operating at different levels while also moving backwards and forwards. Some organizations have well-resourced diversity teams, linked to senior management structures and decision-making processes; they are perceived as influential and successful, however once the top management change, as they do on a regular basis in large commercial organizations, the process of convincing the successor to the throne begins again. This process requires a great deal of energy and can halt the progress of diversity, often sending it backwards. Nevertheless, these organizations are also extremely successful on an initiatives-led basis, reflecting the *work perspectives paradigm* in pockets within those organizations, where they are led by innovative managers and supported by an innovative diversity team. It is these managers who need to be groomed and supported; they are the ones who consistently influence change among their peers and seniors.

Even though we are now six years on from the original research and there is great scepticism about the existence of any organization, especially a large one, that can fully meet the criteria of the third paradigm, Thomas and Ely (1996) do outline some in their work. Organizations that have made the leap to the third paradigm have:

- Made the mental connection and are actively seeking opportunities to explore the issues

- Legitimated open discussion
- Actively worked against forms of dominance and subordination that inhibit all contribution
- Made sure that organizational trust stays intact

To their credit, Thomas and Ely (1996) also agree that this paradigm is in its emergent stage and fully reliant on the leadership's vision of the purpose of a diversified workforce. Could this third paradigm make the process of diversity more innovative? 'Innovation is the realization of value from a new solution to a problem, changing the rules of the game, so innovations must create value, new solutions that fail to produce value are ideas but not innovation' (Ruggles, 2001, CBI website).

To innovate means to 'break away from established patterns' (Mintzberg et al., 1999: 708). Of course diversity can be said to do that to a degree, but is it enough to be considered an innovation? Not all of Thomas and Ely's paradigms would meet the principles of innovation defined and explained fully by Peter Drucker in his book *Innovation and Entrepreneurship* which was first printed in 1985 and has been reprinted 12 times in the subsequent years, most recently 2001. Yet innovation is not as imaginative a process as one might imagine.

According to Drucker (1985), 90 per cent of all innovation is 'purposeful and systematic' and the other 10 per cent is a 'flash of genius'; however, the latter tend to remain brilliant ideas rather than become innovations. Focusing on the 90 per cent, purposeful, systematic innovation needs:

- An analysis of the opportunities—all opportunities should be analysed systematically and studied on a regular basis
- Innovators to go out and 'look and listen'—because innovation is both conceptual and perceptual we need to engage both the right and left side of our brains when we look at figures, people and processes working out what innovation needs in order to meet our customers' needs
- To be simple—focused on a specific need that is satisfied and on a specific end result that it produces, and it must be remembered that it will need to be implemented by ordinary people
- To start small—with pilots which can be developed and adjusted and which can have an immediate application
- Leadership commitment—if it does not achieve this from the beginning, it is unlikely to be innovative enough and may simply create an opportunity for the competition

However, King and Anderson (1995) are sceptical of the need to force the identification of a universal model of innovation, when the nature of innovation can be very different. Indeed there is a shortage of empirical studies on the innovation process, and King and Anderson (1995) examine Schroeder et al. (1989) who put forward a model based on longitudinal study of seven varied major innovations and described the following common factors:

1. Innovation is stimulated by shocks, either internal or external to the organization.
2. An initial idea tends to proliferate into several ideas during the innovation process.
3. Unpredictable setbacks and surprises are inevitable; learning occurs whenever the innovation continues to develop.

4. As innovation develops, the old and the new exist concurrently and over time they are linked together.
5. Restructuring of the organization often occurs during the innovation process.
6. Hands-on top management throughout the innovation period.

WHAT IS THE BUSINESS CASE?

The business case is the means by which diversity practitioners can connect with the powerful people who run big business. It is the means by which they can engage the chief executive, financial director and the board in the debate around diversity. To be honest it is the ticket into the boardroom. Until diversity practitioners realized this, they were relegated to the depths of Human Resources (HR) and seen to be interesting but certainly not integral. However, the struggle between an independent diversity function focused on change or its integration into a HR function focused on stability is still hard fought. Some enlightened companies have recognized the benefits of the former, and indeed some HR functions have successfully absorbed diversity in a way that is appropriate for their organization.

The power of demographics and a change in the expectations of customers have opened the door to the inner sanctum. Diversity professionals have learned to connect diversity firmly into the business drivers and it has certainly made our experiences with business easier. However, there is a price to be paid, and that is of having to pack diversity into already narrowly defined business processes, especially analysis of success. The current business case in Europe and the UK comprises data outlined below, which includes issues related to European trends, the working age population, the ageing population, the increasing female working population, migration, household changes, the underutilization of labour and changing consumer demands.

THE EUROPEAN TRENDS AFFECTING THE 'BUSINESS' OF DIVERSITY

> The combined total consumer spending of the 14 countries in Western Europe amounted to nearly $5,000 billion in 1995. This was 29% of the world's expenditure. Expenditure is forecast to rise by 2.6% a year on average between 1994 and 2005. The fastest growth is on leisure and education, transport and communications (3.2%). Rising incomes will stimulate desire on the part of consumers for greater choice in all their spending. (Bhavnani, 2001, p. 18)

In the UK:

- The ethnic minority population is growing by 2.5 per cent every year and has a disposable income of £12bn. They spend £24bn a year (*Guardian*, 2001a).
- The booming ethnic cosmetics and toiletries market—which is expected to grow in value from £77.2m. in 1999 to £177.8m. by 2004—is the most developed ethnic marketing sector (*Guardian*, 2001b).
- The annual income of the over 50s currently exceeds £160bn; they have an 80 per cent share of the UK's private wealth (Bhavnani, 2001).
- The value of the disability market is estimated to be £40bn per annum (Employers' Forum on Disability, 2002).

- One out of every four customers is disabled or has a disabled person in their immediate circle (Employers' Forum on Disability, 2002)
- Nearly one in three of the workforce is now over 40 (Employers' Forum on Age, 2002).
- The value of the pink economy in income terms is up to £95bn. The disposable income of the lesbian and gay community is estimated at £10bn (Gay Business Association, 2001).
- Seven million adults in England and Wales have yet to reach literacy and numeracy skills of an 11-year-old. It is estimated that basic skills deficiencies cost an average business with over 50 employees approximately £150k (Bhavnani, 2001).

The face of Europe is changing and many factors are influencing the development of the company of the future, most importantly the seven points below which are adapted from The Business Benefits of Diversity (Bhavnani, 2001).

1. THE WORKING AGE POPULATION

The global demographics tell us that the world population is growing at a rate of 1.2 per cent annually, implying a net addition of 77 million people per year. Six countries account for half of that annual increment; India 21 per cent; China 12 per cent; Pakistan 5 per cent; and Bangladesh, Nigeria and the USA for 4 per cent each. We also know that:

- Globally, life expectancy is expected to rise from 65 years to 74 years between 2045 and 2050.
- The number of older people (60+) is set to triple, increasing from 606 million in 2000 to nearly 1.9 billion by 2050.
- Currently 6 out of 10 of those older people live in less developed regions, by 2050, 8 out of every 10 will do so.
- In more developed regions, the population aged 60+ currently constitutes 19 per cent of the population, by 2050 it will account for 32 per cent of the population.
- Over the current decade, the number of excess deaths because of AIDS among the 53 most affected countries is estimated at 46 million and that figure is projected to ascend to 278 million by 2050.
Source: United Nations Populations Division, 2002.

Figure 2.1 shows the working age trends in the UK.

2. AGEING OF THE POPULATION

Also, European countries are experiencing low fertility levels combined with higher life expectancy, resulting in considerable ageing of the population. These trends have important influences on many spheres of social life, e.g. the increasing numbers of households without children, and households with single adults are increasing, particularly because of widows living longer and increasing divorce rates. The proportion of people in society who are over 45 is rapidly increasing and this is the age at which the incidence of disability begins to increase considerably. The ageing population of tomorrow will be more interested in consuming services rather than goods (see Chapter 20).

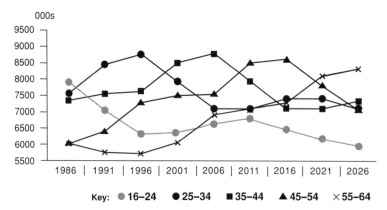

FIGURE 2.1 Working age projection for UK, 1986–2026.
Source: Employers' Forum on Age, Fact Sheet 1999

3. WOMEN IN EMPLOYMENT INCREASING MORE THAN MEN

However, women will play a greater role and have more economic power than ever before, because over the past 40 years we have seen an increase in the labour force participation rate from 60 per cent in 1950 to 70 per cent in 1990. The overall labour force increase of 7.1 million up to 2010 consists of an increase of 7.3 million women but a loss of 0.2 million men. Table 2.1 sets out the increasing female participation rates for women in part-time employment in a range of countries. As you can see, Iceland has the highest rate of women in employment and Turkey the least.

4. MIGRATION

As well as the growth of women's participation, there will be a growth in the numbers of people offering their labour across European borders. Skill and population shortages have meant that governments have increasingly turned to recruiting personnel from India, the Philippines, South Africa, etc. to fill shortages in areas like teaching, nursing and IT. Europe needs these workers! Research suggests that improvement in the labour market situation of Europe will result in a greater demand and supply of migrants from the South. As the EU's countries thrive and its populations age, they are increasingly turning to foreigners.

- International migration is projected to remain high during the first half of the century. Averaged over 2000 to 2050, the major net gainers of international migration are set to be: USA (1.1 million annually); Germany (211 000); Canada (173 000); UK (136 000); Australia (83 000).
- Major net senders of migrants will be: China (-303 000 annually); Mexico (-267 000); India (-222 000); Philippines (-184 000); Indonesia (-180 000).
- Around 3 per cent of the world's population currently reside in a country other than where they were born.
  Source: *International Migration Report 2002*, Department of Economic and Social Affairs, United Nations Populations Division.

Economies are surging and growth in the gross domestic product (GDP) in the EU is expected to reach 2.7 per cent in 2004, while the standardized rate for the OECD area

TABLE 2.1 Part-time employment

	Percentage of adult employment that is part-time				Women's share of part-time employment (%)	
	1990/1993		1998/2000			
Country or area	Women	Men	Women	Men	1990/1993	1998/2000
Asia						
Turkey	19	5	15	4	63	66
Republic of Korea	7	3	11	6	59	55
Eastern Europe						
Bulgaria	2	2	1	<1	48	67
Czech Republic	6	2	6	2	69	71
Estonia	...	...	11	6	...	63
Hungary	4	2	5	2	66	71
Latvia	12[c]	12[c]	13	11	48[c]	51
Lithuania	...	...	11	6	...	63
Poland	13	9	14	9	54	57
Romania	17[b]	10[b]	18	13	60[b]	54
Slovakia	5	2	3	1	73	72
Slovenia	4	3	8	5	53	55
Western Europe						
Austria	20	2	30	4	88	83
Belgium	30	5	37	7	80	79
Denmark	29	10	23	9	71	68
Finland	11	5	14	7	67	65
France	22	4	25	6	80	79
Germany	25	2	33	5	89	84
Greece	12	4	15	5	60	63
Iceland	40	8	35	9	82	77
Ireland	21	4	32	8	72	76
Italy	20	5	23	5	71	72
Luxembourg	22	2	28	2	86	92
Netherlands	53	13	55	12	70	77
Norway	40	7	35	8	83	79
Portugal	12	3	15	5	74	71
Spain	12	1	17	3	80	78
Sweden	25	7	22	7	78	74
Switzerland	43	7	47	8	82	83
United Kingdom	40	5	41	9	85	80
Other developed regions						
Australia	39	11	44	13	71	73
Canada	27	9	27	10	70	69
Japan	33	10	38	11	71	70
New Zealand	35	8	38	13	77	71
United States	20	8	19	8	68	68

Source: adapted from: Table 5b, Part-time employment, *The World's Women 2000: Trends and Statistics*, United Nations Statistics Division

Notes:

[a] Part-time employment refers to less than 40 hours per week while previous year refers to less than 25 hours per week.

[b] Data refer to 1994.

[c] Data refer to 1995.

Technical notes: Table 5b presents statistics on part-time workers—i.e. persons with jobs whose working hours total less than 'full time' (persons who work 30 hours or more per week are considered 'full-time workers' and those who work less than 30 hours per week are considered 'part-time workers'.)

The two types of data presented in this table are total part-time employment as a percentage of total employment, calculated separately for women and for men, and the proportion of women among all part-time workers. The statistics refer to two periods, 1990/1993 and 1998/2000, and have been compiled from the International Labour Office's (ILO) Key Indicators of the Labour Market (KILM) database.

THE IMPORTANCE OF DIVERSITY IN INNOVATION

TABLE 2.2   Indicators on households and childbearing

Country or area	Average household size (%) 1991/1994	women-headed households (%) 1991/1997	Contraceptive use, married women (%) 1991/2001	Total fertility rate (births per woman)		Births per 1000 women aged 15–19 (%) 2000–2005
				1990–1995	2000–2005	
Developed regions						
Australia	3.0[a]	..	76[a]	1.9	1.8	18
Austria	..	..	51	1.5	1.2	12
Belgium	..	..	78	1.6	1.5	8
Bosnia and Herzegovina	..	..	..	1.5	1.3	23
Canada	2.8	30	75	1.7	1.6	19
Croatia	3.1	..	..	1.5	1.7	19
Denmark	2.3[a]	42	78[a,l]	1.7	1.7	7
Finland	2.5[a]	42	77[a]	1.8	1.6	7
France	2.6[a]	..	75	1.7	1.8	9
Germany	2.3[a,m]	27[a,m]	75	1.4	1.3	11
Greece	3.0	20	..	1.4	1.2	10
Ireland	3.3	26	..	2.0	2.0	16
Italy	2.9	..	60	1.3	1.2	6
Japan	3.0[a]	17[a]	59	1.5	1.3	4
Malta	3.3[a]	..	..	2.0	1.8	12
Netherlands	..	..	79	1.6	1.5	4
New Zealand	2.8	37	75	2.1	2.0	31
Poland	3.1[a]	31[a]	49	1.9	1.3	16
Portugal	3.1	20	..	1.5	1.5	17
Russian Federation	2.8[a]	..	73	1.5	1.1	32
Serbia and Montenegro[r]	3.6	22	..	2.0	1.6	25
Spain	..	..	81	1.3	1.1	6
Sweden	2.2[a]	37[a]	..	2.0	1.3	5
Switzerland	2.4[a]	28[a]	82	1.5	1.4	5
United Kingdom	..	..	82[n]	1.8	1.6	24
United States	2.6[a]	36	76	2.1	1.9	49

Source: adapted from Table 2b, Indicators on households and childbearing, *The World's Women 2000: Trends and Statistics*, United Nations Statistics Division

Notes:

[a] Data refer to a year between 1985 and 1990.

[l] For all sexually active women of reproductive age.

[m] Data shown are for the former Federal Republic of Germany.

[n] Data exclude Northern Ireland.

Technical notes: Indicators of fertility presented in table 2b are estimates and projections prepared by the Population Division of the United Nations Secretariat in 2001 and are given as five-year averages. The total fertility rate is defined as the number of children that would be born to a woman if she were to live to the end of her childbearing years and bear children at each age in accordance with prevailing age-specific fertility rates. Births per 1 000 women aged 15–19 refers to the number of children born alive in one year per 1 000 women aged 15–19.

is projected at 7.5 per cent for the same year (source: *OECD Economic Outlook No. 72*, December 2002).

Some 11.7 million non-EU nationals live in the EU, making up 3.2 per cent of the population. By contrast, only 5.6 million EU nationals were living in another EU nation (in 1996 it was 1.5 per cent).

5. HOUSEHOLD CHANGES

Increased participation of women has also led (along with other factors) to another important change over the past decade: the postponement of family, marriage and children, reflected in higher ages of first marriage and first birth. Furthermore, the proportion of those who are single or childless is increasing. These trends may be reflective of increasing participation of women in the labour market and decreasing numbers of women having three or more births. The increasing numbers of cohabiting couples contribute to lower fertility, as cohabiting couples very often remain childless. A consensual union, it is argued, gives women more means to negotiate duties and to control power structures than within traditional marriage. The increasing economic independence of women gives more possibilities of negotiation over household powers and spending commitments.

6. UNDERUTILIZATION OF LABOUR

However, despite the high proportions of diverse labour on offer, much of it is underutilized by sex, age and ethnicity. Evidence for older people shows their productive capacity is grossly underutilized. Older workers are more flexible because of a decline in parental responsibilities. It could be argued that they are slower to change, but this may not be the case because the impact of change itself is so fast everyone has to keep updating him or herself. The economy will need to use this labour more.

7. CHANGING CONSUMER DEMANDS AND EXPENDITURE

Lastly, the rise in GDP from 1997, and a continued recovery in most of Europe, suggest that private consumption will gather pace in most European countries. The combined total consumer spending of the 14 countries in western Europe amounted to nearly $5000bn in 1995. This was 29 per cent of the world's expenditure. Expenditure is forecast to rise by 2.6 per cent a year on average between 1994 and 2005. The fastest growth is on leisure and education, transport and communications (3.2 per cent), miscellaneous goods and services and health.

High growth (above 45 per cent) or average growth (25–45 per cent) is forecast for most European countries in the transport and communications sector. Expenditure on car purchases represents a quarter or more of this total expenditure; high car ownership has not restrained demand much, since this has been offset by rising demand for a second car in Europe. Demand for special features, such as environmentally friendly options, is also expected to become important (Corporate Intelligence on Retailing, 1998). Rising incomes will stimulate desire on the part of consumers for greater choice in all their spending.

People who are older are more likely to have a disability and as this is a growth market, they will be searching for markets for particular adapted products and services. Women are gaining power in decisions about disposable income and may demand particular products and services that best serve their needs. The differences in household structures, the high disposable income across differing white and black ethnic groups, imply differing styles and sizes of products and services.

Increasing legislation on gender, sexuality, race and disability will add to consumer voices that will stress differing needs and lifestyles as well as adaptations of current products and services. Consumers will demand niche marketing and product design.

THE RIGHT ENVIRONMENT FOR DIVERSITY INNOVATION

> A giraffe and an elephant consider themselves friends, but when the giraffe invited the elephant into his home to join him in a business venture, problems ensued. The house was designed to meet the giraffe's needs with tall ceilings and narrow doorways, and when the elephant attempted to manoeuvre, doorways buckled, stairs cracked and walls began to crumble. Analysing the chaos, the giraffe saw that the problem with the door was that it was too narrow. He suggested that the elephant take aerobics classes to get him 'down to size'. The problem with the stairs, he said, were that they were too weak. He suggested that the elephant take ballet lessons to get him 'light on his feet'. But the elephant was unconvinced of this approach. To him, the house was the problem. (Adapted from *Building a House for Diversity* by R. Roosevelt Thomas Jr, 1999: 3–10)

It is natural to think of other people's needs in terms of our own. The giraffe was trying to be helpful, but saw the situation from his perspective, not through the eyes of his friend, and after all what was the other alternative—adapt his house? That would cost a fortune, take time and be uncomfortable for him. Can this be a failing of the business case approach? Even if we can get managers to see the need to 'adapt' in whatever way, not everything we do can be evaluated in monetary terms.

> Creating an innovative culture is not so much a matter of instituting new practices as it is of remembering to import and value in the workplace modes and states of mind which we all know and make use of in our leisure hours. (Claxton, 2001: 41)

This seems to imply that we need to be engaging our managers as whole people, not just the part of themselves they bring to work. While this seems a fine principle, the managers interviewed by Michael Maccoby in 1976 and highlighted in Daniel Goleman's book *Emotional Intelligence* (1996) serve as a stark reminder of reality, even 25 years on. Many 'feared that feeling empathy or compassion for those they worked with would put them in conflict with their organizational goals' (p. 149). One needs to ask whether organizational goals are so very different today.

So what about a more innovative environment to approach these issues? That according to Argyris (1991) 'requires . . . the continuous process of questioning the effectiveness of underlying operating norms, beliefs and assumptions'. These have been questioned by experts for years and yet cultures remain slow to change. Are our senior managers up to the job? Drucker (1985) identifies three conditions for innovation:

1. Hard work—innovation requires knowledge, ingenuity, talent and a predisposition, but at the end of the day it will only succeed through hard, focused, purposeful work making great demands on diligence, persistence and commitment—if these are lacking no amount of talent, ingenuity and predisposition will matter.
2. Building on the individual's strengths—the innovation must be important to them and make sense to them. Does it 'fit' the company and me?
3. An effect in economy and society—a change in people or in process, so it is important to stay close to the market by which it is being driven.

Thomas and Ely (1996) believe that there are eight preconditions for making a shift to the 'connecting diversity to work perspectives' paradigm mentioned earlier:

1. The leadership must understand that a diverse workforce will embody different perspectives and approaches to work, and must truly value variety of opinion and insight.
2. The leadership must recognize both the learning opportunities and the challenges that the expression of different perspectives presents for an organization.
3. The organizational culture must create an expectation of high standards of performance from everyone.
4. The organizational culture must stimulate personal development.
5. The organizational culture must encourage openness.
6. The culture must make workers feel valued.
7. The organization must have a well-articulated and widely understood mission.
8. The organization must have a relatively egalitarian, non-bureaucratic structure.

PEOPLE AND INNOVATION

Drucker (1985) says that innovative effort needs a core of unity otherwise it flies apart: 'innovation needs a concentrated energy of a unified effort behind it' (p. 125). He also requires that the people who put it into effect understand each other, and this too requires a unity and a common core.

Homogeneous and static is the fate of any company that refuses to see the writing on the wall. Of course, companies will not suddenly collapse because of the lack of diversity; no, they will gradually decline as they fail to fully understand the marketplace and generate new and innovative ideas.

The most successful diversity teams have drawn together very different people, but people who share the same goal—each of them having different ways of achieving their goals and some challenging and causing friction within the team. Nevertheless this dynamic worked because the teams were truly diverse—a wide range of ages, different ethnic origins, a balance of men and women, etc. However, the most difficult job was the one of managing these 'innovative' teams.

If we manage diversity effectively, according to Thomas (1990) we can get 'from employees first, everything we have a right to expect, and, second, if we do it well—everything they have to give'.

Ernst H. Drew, head of the chemical company Hoechst Celanese, became aware of the benefits of diverse teams by watching problem-solving groups at work (Elkington, 1997):

> They had ideas I hadn't even thought of. For the first time we realized diversity is a strength as it relates to problem solving. Before we just thought of diversity as the number of minorities and women in the company, like affirmative action. Now we knew we needed diversity at every level of the company where decisions are made. (p. 330)

Organizations should 'nurture jazz band cultures' said Nigel Nicholson at the CIPD National Conference (2001), a culture where all that mattered was 'Can you play?' and 'Do you like the music?' (p. 13). This viewpoint has great value, instead of looking for energy and innovation in our people we are busy measuring their ability to 'fit in' to what already exists, to follow Thomas and Ely's (1996) access and legitimacy paradigm. Companies talk about change, but are they scared of making it happen in any meaningful way? Risk as a management competency is seriously underrated and people who make us feel uncomfortable tend not to get through the selection process. It takes a very secure manager to proactively seek out and employ difference.

There is a chasm opening up between the perception that leaders of the future need integrity and vision and the ability of organizations and individuals to recognize those qualities and feel sure enough of their own abilities to manage them. Ways need to be found to make shifts in the abilities of individuals, especially at the top, to act in a different way. However, this is not easy as most board members, in my experience, feel themselves too busy to attend training and too senior to admit to any flaws. If only they could understand the power of such an approach in the path to culture change.

EMOTIONAL INTELLIGENCE

Emotional intelligence is one such approach. It is a concept that has been discussed by experts since the 1920s; Rueven Bar-On contributed the phrase 'emotional quotient' (EQ) in the 1980s and Mayer and Salovey formally defined the term 'emotional intelligence' in 1990. There are now several pieces of research linking EQ to success at senior management level. Indeed research suggests that the contribution of EQ to occupation performance is 27 per cent as opposed to the 6 per cent that is attributable to IQ.

The Bar-On EQ-i is the most extensively normed of all the emotional intelligence instruments; it has been assessed by BUROS[1], and has been scientifically demonstrated to be both reliable and valid. It has been administered to over 42 000 people in more than 36 countries and sets about capturing emotional intelligence by dividing it into five composites and further dividing it into 15 components. The five composites are:

- Intrapersonal
- Interpersonal
- Adaptability
- Stress management
- General mood

Interest in emotional intelligence has grown in the UK during the last three years, and the emotional intelligence community are now making direct links between emotional intelligence and ethics (Orme & Ashton, 2002). Diversity professionals would be well advised to explore its efficacy. Even the most successful and innovative diversity teams, which brought management buy-in, performance-based diversity objectives for senior managers, praise as 'employers of choice' and numerous awards, did not bring about the kind of organizational culture change which could sustain itself once those committed individuals left the organization.

Sustainable success relies on people making a personal change and investment to which they are committed and becoming fully aware of the personal issues that may get in the way of that success. Non-cognitive criteria have largely been sidestepped by diversity professionals in recent years in their desire to be perceived as business partners. This is a narrow vision; diversity must not lose sight of the benefits gained from the social and moral paradigms, and accept that in the rush to engage big business, we may disengage the individual. As innovators and role models of sustainability, diversity professionals must not allow the fear of again being sidelined to lead them to 'safer ground'. Safe environments do not bring about change!

Some diversity teams have participated in Bar-On EQ-i assessment to great personal and team effect, using it as a tool to identify issues that may block their personal success. However, it has yet to be used to identify the diversity 'star performers' and set a benchmark for the kind of individual who would be successful as a diversity professional or as a diversity champion. Making stronger connections between emotional intelligence and diversity is one way in which we can select the most appropriate diversity innovators who can introduce and sustain change.

Having established that the individual is an important part of the innovation and diversity process, one needs to ask what are the methods organizations use to measure and validate such originality. Are they up to the job?

MEASUREMENT

Despite the fact the business case approach has been in evidence for over a decade, the actual measurement of success remains elusive. The strongest measurement is usually a negative one, i.e. how much did our Employment Tribunals cost us? How much does it cost us to replace the diversity of people who have joined our company and then are unable to tolerate the culture or access flexible enough working patterns?

The National Worklife Forum (2000) suggests it costs £5 000 to replace a bank clerk, £10 000 to replace a supermarket deputy manager and £50 000 for an Inland Revenue inspector. Even this estimate, which is based on obvious costs like recruitment and training, fails to take into account the hidden costs such as the loss of intellectual capital, or the dip in morale for close work colleagues. However, one study in the US showed that the share values of companies indicted under equal opportunity legislation declined relative to others (Hersch, 1991).

The bottom line, when it is measured, contains mostly information on financial cost. This seems a very narrow and naive way of assessing something so linked to people, performance and innovation. The measurement of diversity is extremely broad and partly subjective, and it needs to be seen within the totality of the company's strategic intentions over a longish period of time. The measurement of results on business is one thing; however, performance is another. 'You cannot measure that which you have not defined', say Barrell et al. (1992: 166) and they are right. So how can diversity be defined in a way that will tap into the richness of its impact and make it acceptable to all of its stakeholders?

Patricia Digh (2000) offers a 'radical perspective on diversity measurement', one which encourages changing the idea of the 'bottom line' to include the reflection of 'hidden values that are not visible in traditional accounting'. For these, she explains, are more important as we move from the industrial paradigm to the knowledge paradigm where growing numbers of organizations, especially in the service sector, have few visible assets.

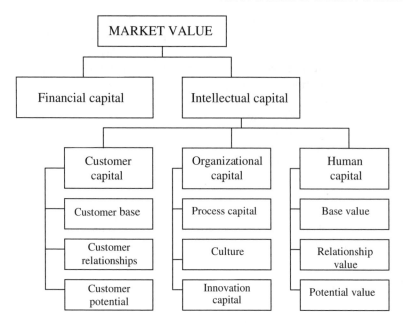

FIGURE 2.2   The Skandia Value Scheme
Source: Digh, P. (2000). Reproduced with permission from LexisNexis Butterworths Tolley

Digh (2000) and Funk (2001) highlight the example of Skandia, a Swedish insurance company who have developed a new perspective around the reporting of hidden values and have therefore transformed their bottom line and unwittingly created a new diversity metric. This approach, called 'the business navigator' or the 'Skandia Value Scheme', was developed when Skandia recognized that their true market was both their financial and their intellectual capital. Their view is that intellectual capital consists of human capital and structural capital and the areas of intellectual capital should be fully visible. Therefore they have published a supplement to their annual report addressing its intellectual capital in terms of innovation, customer loyalty and employee talent (see Figure 2.2).

The link between shareholder value and environmental and social performance is a phenomenon that has spawned a large body of research, literature and investment activity in recent years. However, diversity has not yet been singled out as a key component; nevertheless it is arguably one of the future keys to a sustainable business.

Certainly the question of social responsibility has become more of a core issue for businesses. About 80 per cent of FTSE-100 companies now provide information about their environmental performance, social impact or both.

The CBI's Value Creation Index is providing ongoing research in this area. It provides insights into the 'value drivers' that are strongly correlated with market value. Although the drivers can vary according to the industry, there is a consistency related to management credibility, innovativeness, ability to attract talented employees and research leadership.

Indeed in 1998 Sally Winter, in a British survey of FTSE-100 companies, found that over 25 per cent were assessed as very good regarding family-friendly policies. She also found that those companies had outperformed other companies in terms of higher share performance. On average their shares had risen by 141 per cent over a five-year period from 1993, in contrast to the FTSE-100 average of 78 per cent (Bhavnani, 2001).

However, facts and figures are only part of the story. Ricardo Semler, who owns a Brazilian company called SEMCO and was elected business leader of the year by a poll of 52 000 Brazilian executives in 1990 and 1992, said 'I don't think a company's success can be measured in numbers, since numbers ignore what the end user really thinks of the product and what people who produce it really think of the company' (Semler, 1994).

Consumers are certainly more driven now than ever before by ethics and social responsibility. In fact the Co-operative Bank have increased their market share by promoting their ethical policy through cinema and direct mail marketing (MORI, 2000). Furthermore, according to Bhavnani (2001):

- A recent poll suggested that 17 per cent of consumers are likely to be influenced by ethical considerations when making purchasing decisions, with another 5 per cent regularly taking account of a business's ethical performance when shopping.
- ASDA has launched its own Store of the Community standard and is expecting every one of its 241 stores to have made the grade by 2001.
- Travelsphere were the first travel company to offer a specialized service for blind and partially sighted people, creating a new market to the tune of more than £1m. in sales.

Littlewoods is well documented for its business-driven approach to diversity (Equal Opportunities Review, 1998). At that time, they were a family-owned company encompassing a range of different 'businesses' including *home shopping* via a catalogue and the internet, *Business Express* a delivery company, over 100 *high street Littlewoods stores*, *130 Littlewoods catalogue discount stores* and a printing company *J&C Moores*. Their process of measurement began at the top with managing directors and divisional directors having the responsibility of divisional action plans and programmes to implement diversity.

All managers set quantifiable, time-lined, finance-driven, objectives which linked diversity into their business plans, their budgets and their business management systems, making them fully accountable. These would be reviewed and challenged by the chief executive and chairman who took personal responsibility for driving the issue. Some of the individual initiatives were as detailed below.

1. COMMUNITY RECRUITMENT INITIATIVE—NEW OLDHAM STORE

The objective was to recruit a workforce representative of the local community:

- Local travel-to-work census data were examined
- Local community groups were identified and contacted
- Information translated into appropriate languages
- Leaflet drops in areas with high numbers of ethnic minorities
- Training and enterprise councils (TECs), local race equality councils (RECs), chambers of commerce, placement assessment counselling teams (PACT) and local authorities were contacted
- An open day and free helpline were provided

The results were:

- Free local media because of the innovative approach
- £14 000 worth of practical help from agencies mentioned above
- 950 applications compared to the usual 200 providing a wider pool of talent
- 34 per cent of applicants were from ethnic minorities compared with usual 5 per cent, resulting in 25 per cent of eventual workforce
- Employee turnover reduced in first year from 35 to only 5 per cent
- £123 499 higher initial sales performance over other comparable stores

2. LEICESTER STORE

The objective was to connect more effectively with its diverse customer base. It:

- Recognized that a wide proportion of its 28.5 per cent ethnic minority community celebrated Divali
- Ran a Divali poster competition in the Leicester Store for children in local schools to design a poster. The winning design was adapted for in-store and window posters, which were carried by 45 Littlewoods stores during 1997
- Stocked particular products that were likely to sell well in the lead-up time to the festival
- Released a publicity package to local newspapers
- Reported a 24 per cent rise in gift sales over the same period the previous year

However, the reasons for measuring success are wider than meeting stakeholders' expectations and should incorporate the concept of the learning organization. According to Barrell et al. (1992), measurement is a tool for learning and if organizations do not learn then there is much less chance of meeting stakeholder expectations. Measurement is useful to:

- *Control and improve*—monitoring progress during an ongoing project in order to highlight any corrective actions
- *At the end of a project*—to identify what was done well and what badly, leading to a better job next time

The process should include:

- Clear business plans
- A clear tracking system
- A financial plan broken down into manageable parts
- Activity schedules and timetables
- Bringing in people external to the team to challenge group assumptions

So the widest approach to measurement is most appropriate and one that links to the company's soul. These are the things that will be attracting the consumer and the investor of the future. Stakeholders are interested in more than simply how much money a company makes; they are now interested in the ethical approach of that company and in how people are treated. The importance of brand image in a marketplace, which is competitive, can offer identical goods and services, and infinite consumer choice is now more reliant on intangibles, such as the way people feel about a company or a product. How then can it be possible to assess companies on profit alone?

CONCLUSIONS

Diversity has great potential as an innovative tool. The diversity paradigm has developed and matured during the last 50 years, with the concept of the business case emerging as the key driver in recent years. The shift to the knowledge economy and the reliance on the power of the individual to provide competitive advantage have made the management of diversity an imperative. However, the power of the business case can only be fully utilized if companies not only attract diversity, but also allow that diversity the freedom to transform cultures. This is the challenge as seen by authors such as Ruggles (2001) who asks the question, can diversity really 'change the game'?

New solutions are not of themselves innovative. Many companies can break away from established patterns for a short period of time, but once the pressure is taken off, people move on and companies' politics shift. Then, diversity contracts and the knowledge which resides mainly with the diversity specialist also disappears and the company finds itself, a few years on, relearning what it allowed itself to lose.

Equating diversity with the amount of money it can attract to the business bottom line alone is naive, even though many companies now have objectives for managers and diversity linked to business objectives. The benefits are short-lived, unless the culture begins to shift, for those innovative, creative and diverse people who were recruited will leave and take their knowledge with them. Companies who do not meet their needs will end up training a workforce for their competitors.

Research tells us that consumer pressure to provide goods and services that meet ethical and social standards is growing. Stakeholders have instant access to information about companies and require them to be open about their environmental and social performance, and misfortune awaits the company that attempts to 'cook the books'. Diversity falls into this category and yet there is no accurate way of measuring its impact on the overall performance of a company.

However, individual initiatives can be measured according to their financial benefits and the specific impact they have on local communities. Nevertheless, rarely do these initiatives find their way into the fabric of the company to become best practice nor do they tend to be advertised by the company, unless like the Co-operative Bank they have taken the decision to use it proactively to increase their market share.

New measures like the CBI's Value Creation Index are providing ongoing research into 'value drivers' and yet companies still do not have any innovative ways of accurately measuring the impact of diversity against performance. An innovative approach would dictate the need to lead the field in this area and shape a new paradigm for diversity measurement. Which company will pick up the gauntlet?

NOTE

1. The Buros Institute, publishers of the *Mental Measurements Yearbook* and *Tests in Print*, provides critical analyses of tests and testing instruments.

REFERENCES

Argyris, C. (1991). Teaching smart people how to learn. *Harvard Business Review*, May–June, 99–109.

Barrell A., Herriot W. & Mitchel R. (1992). *How to Profit from Innovation*. Cambridge: Director Books.

Bhavnani, R. (2001). Ford Europe—The Business Benefits of Diversity (forthcoming, no publisher as yet).

Claxton, G. (2001). The innovative mind: becoming smarter thinking less. In J. Heary (ed.) *Creative Management*. London: SAGE.

Corporate Intelligence on Retailing (1998). *Consumer Spending Forecasts for Western Europe, 1998–2005*. London.

Digh, P. (2000). Create a new balance sheet: measuring intellectual capital as part of your diversity strategy. *Equal Opportunities Review*, No. 91, May/June, 30. London: Industrial Relations Services.

Drucker, P.F. (1985). *Innovation and Entrepreneurship*. Oxford: Butterworth-Heinemann.

Elkington, J. (1997). *Cannibals with Forks: The Triple Bottom Line of 21st Century Business (Conscientious Commerce)*. Oxford: Capstone Publishing.

Employers' Forum on Age website (2002). www.efa.org.uk

Employers' Forum on Disability website (2002). www.efd.org.uk

Equal Opportunities Review (1998). No. 81, September/October, 20–28. London: Industrial Relations Services.

Eurostat and Council of Europe 'Fertility and Family Indicators' 1999, adapted from 'Focus on European Lifestyles 1999' and *Eurostat Yearbook 2001*. www.europa.eu.int

Funk, K. (2001). *Sustainability and Performance: Uncovering Opportunities for Value Creation*. Centre for Business Innovation, July. London: Cap Gemini Ernst & Young.

Gay Business Association website (2001). www.gba.org.uk

Goleman, D. (1996). *Emotional Intelligence*. London: Bloomsbury Publishing.

Guardian (2001a). Marketing to a multicultural Britain. media.guardian.co.uk (26 June).

Guardian (2001b). Lloyds TSB advert, 27.06.01.

Hersch, J. (1991). Equal employment opportunity law and firm profitability. *Journal of Human Resources*, **26**.

Johnstone, W.B. & Packer, A.H. (1987). *Workforce 2000: Work and Workers for the 21st Century*. Indiana: The Hudson Institute.

Kandola, R. & Fullerton, J. (1994). *Managing the Mosaic*. London: Chartered Institute for Personnel and Development.

King, N. & Anderson, N. (1995). *Innovation and Change in Organisations* (series editor C. Fletcher). London: Routledge.

Mintzberg, H., Quinn, B. & Ghoshal, S. (1999). *The Strategy Process*. New Jersey: Prentice Hall.

MORI (2000). Winning with integrity (November 2000). www.dtisocietyandbusiness.gov.uk

National Worklife Forum (2000). *Worklife Strategies for the 21st Century*. London.

Nicholson, N. (2001). Chartered Institute of Personnel and Development (CIPD) National Conference—report by R. Johnson, *Diversity in Adversity, People Management* 8 November 2001, p. 13.

OECD (2002). *Economic Outlook No 72*, December 2002, OECD.

OECD Statistical Annex 2001, Table B, Labour Force Participation Rate. www.oecd.org

Orme, G. & Ashton, C (2002). Ethics: a foundation competency. *Competency Emotional Intelligence Journal* **10**(1), Autumn, 19–25. London: IRS.

Price Mueller, K. (1998). Diversity and the bottom line. *Harvard Management Update*, No. U9804C April, 3–4.

Punch, A. & Pearce, A. (2001). *Europe's Population and Labour Market beyond 2000*. Strasbourg: Council of Europe.

Ruggles, R. (2001). Centre for Business Innovation website. www.cbi.cgey.com

Schroeder, R.G., Van de Ven, A., Scudder, G.D. & Polley, D. (1989). The development of innovation and ideas. In A. Van de Ven et al. (eds) *Research on the Management of Innovation: The Minnesota Studies*. New York: Harper & Row.

Seltzer, K & Bentley, T. (1999). *The Creative Age*. London: DEMOS.

Semler, R. (1994). *Harvard Business Review*, January, 64–74.

Thomas, D.A. & Ely, R.J. (1996). Making differences matter: a new paradigm for managing diversity. *Harvard Business Review*, September–October, 79–90.

Thomas, R. Roosevelt (1990). From affirmative action to affirming diversity. *Harvard Business Review*, March–April, 107–117.

Thomas, R. Roosevelt (1999). *Building a House for Diversity*. New York: AMACOM.

United Nations Populations Division (2002). Highlights. *World Population Prospects: The 2002 Revision*, United Nations Populations Division.

United Nations Populations Division (2002). *International Migration Report 2002*. Department of Economic and Social Affairs, United Nations Populations Division.

United Nations Statistics Division (2002). Part-time employment. *The World's Women 2000: Trends and Statistics*, United Nations Statistics Division.

United Nations Statistics Division (2002). Indicators on households and childbearing. *The World's Women 2000: Trends and Statistics*, United Nations Statistics Division.

CHAPTER 3

Diversity in the Context of Business Ethics

Catherine Cassell
Sheffield University Management School, Sheffield, UK

Phil Johnson
Sheffield Hallam University, Sheffield, UK

SUMMARY

This chapter examines the implications of debates deriving from business ethics for how we understand diversity and how it is managed. The chapter firstly considers how business ethics is currently manifested in contemporary organizations. It then considers the different approaches within the ethical literature and their implications for diversity and its management. Finally the chapter considers some of the issues and tensions that arise from those links.

INTRODUCTION

Today, business ethics is generally recognized as an important dimension of organizational behaviour and is less likely to be cynically dismissed as an oxymoron. Of course this was not always the case. Indeed it is usually accepted that until the late 1980s there was a relative silence about the ethical dimension to business (Bird & Waters, 1989). When this 'moral muteness' was occasionally broken it was only too often to dismiss business ethics as sentimental and mischievously disruptive, since it gave rise to a utopian irrationality hostile towards business (e.g. Drucker, 1973). Indeed business was usually seen as the rightful preserve of an economic rationality which was, by that fact, ethically neutral.

Individual Diversity and Psychology in Organizations. Edited by Marilyn J. Davidson and Sandra L. Fielden.
© 2003 John Wiley & Sons, Ltd.

So why has the recent interest in business ethics emerged? It seems that there are a number of reasons. Firstly, it became apparent that moral issues were an integral aspect of everyday management practice (e.g. Jackall, 1988; T. Donaldson, 1989). There is little evidence that managers are behaving any more or less ethically than in the past, but a growing amount of media scrutiny of the behaviour of large companies and a variety of spectacular business 'scandals' which took place in the 1990s such as the Guinness and Robert Maxwell affairs, have led to a series of debates about the efficacy of the 'free market' and the impact of globalized businesses upon their employees and their host communities (e.g. De George, 1987; French, 1995). While the ethical debates arising from such 'scandals' have questioned the processes by which socially approved objectives are met, many of those objectives themselves have been challenged as commentators call for society as a whole to reconsider what its priorities are and how they might best be achieved (e.g. Handy, 1994).

Therefore a further reason partially behind the current surge in interest in business ethics appears to be a questioning of the exclusive dictates of neo-classical economics which located managerial responsibility in the pursuit of what were assumed to be shareholder interests (Etzioni, 1988). For Stark (1993) this has challenged and deval-ued 'traditional' business interests in favour of ostensibly more important, or equally important, interests that derive from other organizational stakeholders. As Kaler (2000) argues, perhaps a virtuous circle is at work as the activities of campaign groups (e.g. Friends of the Earth, Greenpeace) have begun to raise expectations regarding the ethical performance of business. The resultant pressures have impelled businesses to articulate ever-increasing moral commitments which in turn have caused the public's expectations to rise even further.

Additionally there is some evidence that firms can benefit from being perceived as ethical. Rosenblatt and Schaeffer (2000) extend this beyond perception and argue that there is a link between corporate success and adherence to ethics. They point to the work of Deshpande (1996) who notes that executives associate business success with a conducive ethical climate and argue that within the literature the assumed association is between organizational failure and ethical problems. Therefore ethical behaviour is seen to enhance the bottom line.

Whatever the reason for the interest in business ethics, it would seem that the old certainties about how to manage have been unsettled (Alvesson & Willmott, 1996: 1). The anxieties created by this situation have probably given impetus to moral dissensus and debate as previously accepted management norms are violated (Primeaux, 1992). This poses difficulties for organizational decision-makers as it in-creases the probability of personal moral dilemmas and public disputes. Hence the de-velopment of business ethics may be understood as a contemporary response to the perceived need for some form of guidance in an otherwise confusing and uncertain world.

With this scenario in mind, the aim of this chapter is to examine the implications of debates deriving from business ethics for how we understand diversity and how it is managed. Firstly, we will consider how business ethics is currently manifested in contemporary organizations. We will then consider the different approaches within the ethical literature and their implications for diversity and its management. Finally, we will turn to some of the issues and tensions that arise from those links.

BUSINESS ETHICS IN CONTEMPORARY ORGANIZATIONS

Although business ethics is itself a substantively diverse discipline, one persistent yet by no means exclusive theme has been to understand it as aiming to (re)establish some form of moral order to business. From this perspective, business ethics entails the rationalist application of normative ethical theory to business (e.g. Ozar, 1979; Davis, 1982; Velasquez, 1988; J. Donaldson, 1989; Hoffman & Moore, 1990). It is based upon the notion that ultimately there exist canonical moral principles which are accessible and universally applicable to the conduct of business regardless of sociohistorical context. Although there is some disagreement as to the extent to which it is possible to fully elucidate a coherent set of absolute ethical principles, there is a concern to formulate a framework of ethical standards that are taken to approximate those principles.

Into this framework are encoded prescriptions about what is right and wrong in the conduct of business which articulate conceptions of human welfare. Here guidelines are specified as to what should be avoided and done in order to achieve those prescribed standards and thereby improve the conduct of business—or at least make it more reasonable by challenging the economic pragmatism which is assumed to dominate business practice (Sorrell & Hendry, 1994). Indeed, an important aspect of this programme is to access, describe and evaluate current and past business practices, such as diversity, in the light of these rationally grounded philosophical criteria via an ethical audit 'devoted to systematic empirical inquiry about how corporations contribute to and detract from the ability of their stakeholders to live well' (MacKenzie, 1998: 1395). This is therefore based on the assumption that it is possible to judge business behaviour with reference to its conformity with some universally applicable framework of ethical standards.

Just how ethical issues are formally embodied within work practices and procedures can vary. A key issue for those concerned with diversity is how the recognition and valuing of diversity can be encompassed within an organization's ethical stance. For instance, research in the business ethics area indicates that the most common and important way in which ethics are institutionalized is through the design and implementation of a corporate code of ethics (e.g. Manley, 1992; Webley, 1992; Stevens, 1994). Their significance in current organizational practices is reinforced by the observation that other means of institutionalizing ethics, such as recruitment and selection or training, are dependent upon the prior codification of corporate ethics (Sims, 1991; Milton-Smith, 1995). Despite a degree of definitional ambiguity, most authorities agree that a corporate code entails two important aspects. The first is a visible and public statement of ostensible organizational values expressed as duties and obligations to a variety of stakeholders in the form of a set of ethical standards for behaviour which indicates what is and what is not acceptable (T. Donaldson, 1989). The second is concerned with *how* those principles are to be operationalized, monitored and reinforced by various formal sanctions so as to at least ensure members' compliance (Molander, 1987; Weller, 1988; Hyman et al., 1990). Here the establishment of the moral authority articulated by the code should be a top-down rational process where those with superior ethical knowledge legitimately impose their will upon others.

The use of such codes has traditionally been one of the ways in which organizations have addressed issues of equal opportunity, particularly with reference to prohibiting discriminatory behaviour. For instance, Cassell (1996) suggests that corporate codes that seek to institutionalize ethical principles and encourage ethical behaviours within organizational life usually have some reference to discriminatory issues. These codes focus on an individual's right to be treated and respected as an individual regardless of any characteristic along which they can be discriminated upon, for example age, race or sex.

However, the adoption and implementation of codes are not that straightforward. For instance, J. Donaldson (1989) suggests that the main function of a code is to provide a 'guide' to members, while Maitland (1988) observes that the presence of a code helps to relieve managers of the problem of having to make personal judgements concerning an organization's obligations to various stakeholder groups while legitimizing what the code defines as ethical behaviour (Trevino & Nelson, 1995; Adams et al., 2001). In contrast, Bowie (1979) emphasizes how ethical codes can be used as a means of avoiding the need for government regulation on the grounds that the ethical code indicates the willingness and ability of the organization to establish, and enforce, self-regulatory standards of behaviour which do not merely comply with existing legal requirements, but are usually in excess of them. In addition, a code might provide an important medium for influencing both the general climate of public opinion concerning the organization, and managing the relationship with particular stakeholder groups (Murphy, 1995): issues of particular significance in the public sector given the position of trust and power accorded to non-elected officials (Ashkanasy et al., 2000). This indicates how the processes of code creation and promulgation may embody not merely the ethical beliefs of its initiators as expressed through their perception and incorporation of particular stakeholder interests, but also their political–economic analysis of the strategic context within which their organization operates.

Within the diversity arena, it would seem that the adoption of a code may not necessarily lead to the success expected. Kandola and Fullerton (1994) examined the most frequently implemented diversity activities in their survey of diversity awareness and practice in the UK. 'Having a policy on equal opportunities' was implemented in 94 per cent of the firms they surveyed. This is where equal opportunities initiatives are codified into a policy document. However, this was not rated as one of the 10 most successful initiatives by HR managers. Rather the initiatives they rated as being the most successful were those which provided universal benefit, for example introducing equal rights and benefits for part-time workers and eliminating age criteria from selection criteria. Therefore practical initiatives were seen as more successful than the codification of principles.

A development within the area of codes can be seen in the recent proliferation of the adoption of values statements by organizations. Jick (2000) suggests that in the current climate of organizational change and disruption, some companies are identifying and implementing sets of organizational values as a way of dealing with the need to behave ethically in an increasingly complex environment. He suggests that: 'The biggest challenge for organizations is not to identify the values they want to live by, but rather to live by the values they've identified and to embed them in the organization's "genetic code"' (p. 251). Jick outlines how Seagram, a major player in the worldwide beverage and entertainment industry, implemented a values-based management programme in conjunction with a major re-engineering initiative. One of the key values in the values statement is respect: 'We treat everyone with dignity and we value different backgrounds, cultures and viewpoints' (p. 252). Jick argues that although no formal evaluation of the values statement has taken place, there are some quantitative factors of success of the overall initiative, for example increased customer satisfaction and overall growth in the company.

A values statement is clearly different from a corporate code of ethical conduct. Hall (1993) suggests that although in some companies the two may overlap, they also fill quite different roles. Rather than stating broad values, corporate codes are specific guidelines that serve the purpose of mandating behaviour standards and clarifying responsibilities. Hall also suggests that there should be clear statements of the requisite disciplinary action that should be taken if an individual breaches a code.

However, within a prescriptive approach, there are problems around the legitimacy of the moral authority which underpins any construal of the ethical, as expressed in relevant codes. Firstly, we all have different personal moral codes. In Jick's case study of Seagram mentioned earlier, the following interesting difference is highlighted, with regard to how members of the organization interpret the value of respect for diversity:

> To some of the old guard at Seagram, the value of 'respect' means keeping your mouth clean and your head down and treating those who rank above you with respect. To some of the newer, younger, and more innovative thinkers, they interpret respect differently and feel themselves to be disrespected by their elders. (2000: 265)

An additional complication arises in that it is difficult to find unambiguous criteria that enable the adjudication of ethicality. This is because there is a variety of different normative ethical theories each of which embraces different assumptions about, and prescriptions for, what is good or bad in the conduct of business affairs (Cooke, 1986). Instead of having available one set of rationally accessible moral precepts, any manager is confronted by an array of competing prescriptions derived from different moral philosophies (see Derry & Green, 1989; Duska, 1993; Michalos, 2001) and the dilemma of choosing *which* to draw upon for guidance. Alternatively, the manager could try to combine the differing approaches and thereby discern the optimum solution to the problem. But this raises the problem of whether different moral philosophies are commensurable (see MacDonald & Beck-Dudley, 1994). We are therefore left with the problem of which is the most appropriate ethical position to adopt in relation to diversity. We will now illustrate this problem by looking at how from within a prescriptive approach to business ethics managing diversity will be attributed a varying ethical status.

PRESCRIPTIVE ETHICAL VIEWS OF DIVERSITY AND DIVERSITY MANAGEMENT

Within a prescriptive approach it is possible to draw upon two quite different schools of ethical thought that vary in terms of the ethical precepts deployed. One is called a teleological or consequentialist approach. This claims that judgements as to whether or not human actions are right or wrong can only be accomplished with reference to the nature of the consequences of those actions for human beings. The most important version of this approach is known as utilitarianism which stresses the greatest good to the greatest number. An important alternative to utilitarianism is concerned with rights and duties. It derives from the deontological tradition and has a basis in Judaeo-Christian philosophical beliefs and the writings of Immanuel Kant. This deontological approach articulates the view that if a human action is to be judged as right, it has to have certain characteristics that are independent of its consequences. Therefore there is no appeal to the beneficial or harmful consequences of actions in determining their ethicality, rather it is in the virtue of being a particular action, according to particular principles, which bestows ethicality. We shall now turn to the particular understandings of 'diversity' created by these alternative ethical perspectives.

UTILITARIANISM

The underlying theme of utilitarianism is that any action or policy should be evaluated on the basis of the benefits or costs that that action has for society as a whole. Consequently in any situation where a practice is being assessed, the 'right' or most 'moral' line of action is the one that will produce the most 'utility' for the majority. When this approach is applied to issues of diversity, the analysis is initially straightforward. Given that different individuals have different skills and abilities, and that different jobs require different abilities, in cost–benefit terms, the approach that produces the most utility is for individuals to be in the jobs which most suit their skills and abilities, regardless of any other characteristic.

Framed in a different way, the utilitarian approach has provided the basis for a lot of the literature on the management of diversity (e.g. Thomas, 1990; McEnrue, 1993) where the emphasis is on how in *economic* terms (implicitly measured by shareholder value), it is crucial that organizations make the most of the skills and talents of the whole workforce regardless of the nature of the composition of that workforce. The 'business case' for including a variety of diverse groups at all organizational levels effectively operates on a similar cost–benefit analysis, where it is argued that it is better for the organization as a whole that everyone's skills and abilities are utilized. Therefore, this philosophical approach can be seen as the root of many diversity initiatives. Hence a particularly narrow operationalization of 'utility' frames the business case to provide a semblance of moral justification. Problems emerge when we consider that individuals and groups have very different interpretations of what is best for society and what creates the most utility. One could argue for example that as women are the child bearers of society, it makes the most sense in terms of society's productivity for women to spend their time working in the home child rearing: bringing up the families of the future, rather than attempting to have an active role in the labour market. This highlights how the operationalization of utility is problematic and always, implicitly value-laden. The key question is whose values are perceived as appropriate and why?

In itself the notion of 'society as a whole', or in this context 'the organization as a whole' causes problems. Essentially it is a unitary conception which naively assumes that interests are shared by all groups within the organization, rather than recognizing that different stakeholder groups may have irreconcilable differences of interest and varying amounts of power at their disposal in the pursuit of those interests. These concerns have been echoed by writers within the managing diversity field where the implications of the business case have been critiqued. Prasad and Mills (1997) suggest that the economic showcasing of diversity is both credible and persuasive to the public. However, the underlying economic assumptions of that case are drawn from human capital theories where people are treated explicitly as economic resources with their skills, qualifications and characteristics having potential value for the firms that employ them. This has a number of implications. If we take women as a group for example, it could be argued that opportunities for women employees in the labour force are enhanced when the perceived economic climate necessitates it. Where historians have conducted studies on the changes in women's participation in the labour force, interesting information has emerged about the conditions under which women have been encouraged to leave their homes and work (Alpern, 1994; Farley, 1994). A key theme in many such accounts is the role of war and the utilization of women in jobs traditionally associated with men when economic necessity demands it (e.g. Chafe, 1977; Campbell, 1984). In this utilitarian context then, regarding the business case for managing diversity, the key question must be what happens when demographic trends alter and skill shortages disappear? As Dickens (1994) suggests: 'Organizations can, and do, obtain cost benefits from the non-recognition (but utilization) of women's skills, the undervaluing of women's labour, and from the exploitation of women as a cheap, numerically flexible (easily disposed of) workforce' (p. 13).

It would seem that a utilitarian perspective highlights some of the problems encountered within a business case for managing diversity. These problems have been raised by researchers considering other characteristics on which people differ, for example disability (Woodhams & Danieli, 2000; see Chapter 9); ethnicity (Jones et al., 2000); and parents of disabled children (Lewis et al., 2000). Indeed there may be a need to have more comprehensive conceptualizations and operationalization of utility that reflect the interests of the broader spectrum of stakeholders—but in turn this raises the question of whether or not their interests are actually commensurable. Meanwhile the problem of incommensurability is raised in a different form when we turn to alternative ethical theories which express a very different vision of what is morally right or wrong.

RIGHTS

Rights focus on individuals and their life experiences rather than taking a societal focus as utilitarianism does. Kant's (1964) categorical imperative, for instance, suggests that everyone should be treated as a free person equal to everyone else. From the perspective of considering diversity, one could argue that individuals have the positive right to be valued regardless of their differences and not to be discriminated against in their organizational life, and that others have a duty to provide an individual with that right. Velasquez (1992) suggests that discriminatory behaviours on the basis of an individual's difference violate this principle in two ways. Firstly, discrimination is based on the view that one group is inferior to another, for example that older workers are less competent than younger workers, or that women are less ambitious than men. Such stereotypes can undermine the self-esteem of such groups and therefore violate their right to be treated as equals. Secondly, discrimination places members of diverse groups in lower economic and social positions where opportunities are considerably less than their counterparts. This again contravenes the right to be treated as a free and equal person. In asking the question whether it is morally right or wrong to discriminate against others, Kantian theory presents two criteria for determining a moral right: universability and reversibility. Universability suggests that an individual's reasons for acting in a particular way must be reasons that everyone could act on, whereas reversibility is the extent to which an individual would be happy to have others treat them in the same way. Clearly, individuals would not want their own discriminatory behaviour universalized, they would not want to be discriminated against themselves, consequently discrimination on the basis of difference from this perspective is morally wrong.

From this ethical stance doing the right thing for the wrong reason is also morally objectionable. To take an example, one could argue that the business objectives of a company tend to express management's perceived strategic interests. Hence managing diversity so as to meet business objectives is a way of taking actions that arise from self-interest, which are beneficial to others. This could be construed as morally objectionable as it is incompatible with the motivations required by Kant. Indeed from this point of view an ethical approach to diversity rests upon commitment to diversity out of a sense of duty and hence support for diversity regardless of its perceived impact upon competitive advantage. Indeed from a Kantian stance, the business case for diversity is de facto unethical—a point reinforced by the probability that doing the right thing may cease if the promised competitive advantage is not forthcoming. Of course from a utilitarian perspective, such a judgement may not necessarily be the case depending upon how one operationalizes and measures the greatest good for the greatest number.

However, one of the problems of the deontological approach is its relativistic nature, as ethicality is in the eye of the beholder and hence is a differential outcome of individuals' interpretive frameworks in terms of how they view their own organizational life. A woman manager could, for example, discriminate against a female subordinate as a result of the stereotypes she holds about women's commitment to work. She may also agree that it is right that she has been discriminated against herself. In this example, discriminatory behaviour would be seen to be morally right, a clear problem for this approach. It is difficult to see how these approaches tie in with managing diversity, indeed many exponents of managing diversity have sought to distance themselves from the notion of ethical underpinnings and the moral responsibility of organizations to take account of the rights of their staff, preferring to focus on arguments located within a 'business' discourse.

JUSTICE

Justice and fairness are concerned with the comparative treatment given to groups, therefore there is a direct analysis of diversity here. Distributive justice focuses on the fair distribution of society's benefits and burdens: in this case failing to manage diversity clearly contravenes that principle. Another approach is to see justice as equality, the argument being that as all people are equal, everyone should be treated equally. As Velasquez (1992) states, discrimination in employment is wrong because it violates the basic principle of justice by differentiating between people on characteristics (e.g. race, sex) that are not pertinent to the job they are to perform.

The notion of organizational justice is becoming an increasingly popular one within the literature on organization behaviour. A key distinction is made between procedural justice which focuses on the fairness of organizational practices and procedures, and distributive justice, which is the perceived fairness of any organizational outcome. The arguments underlying justice approaches tie in neatly with the traditional approaches to equal opportunities based on notions of justice and fairness. There is also evidence that it is a useful context for examining other aspects of diversity. As discussed in depth in Chapter 10, Hicks-Clarke and Iles (2000) argue that an individual's perceptions of organizational justice are an important element of the diversity climate of an organization. As part of their research into diversity climates, they discovered that the perception of organizational justice strongly predicted organizational commitment, job satisfaction, career planning, career commitment, satisfaction with manager, career satisfaction and career future satisfaction in a sample of 245 National Health Service workers.

Having reviewed the prescriptive approaches, it would seem that establishing, or even imposing, a moral order for business is difficult in that we could argue that trying to create a consensus about a moral or ethical code goes against the very notion of valuing the views of diverse groups with diverse sets of interests.

ALTERNATIVES TO PRESCRIPTION IN BUSINESS ETHICS

The problems encountered by the various prescriptive approaches to business ethics around dissensus and incommensurability have pushed some ethicists to forlornly shun any attempt at prescription and become sceptical of any claim to moral authority. This systematic doubt derives from the premise that all ethical judgements are intimately connected with the cultures to which people defer and refer, in making sense of their worlds and in constructing their moral behaviour. As Sumner puts it '... the notion of right is in the folkways. It is not outside them of independent origin, and brought in to test them. In the folkways whatever is, is right' (1988: 20).

Cross-cultural empirical evidence (e.g. T. Donaldson, 1989) is used to support this assertion of ethical plurality and to justify the view that the ethical is a product of the social and historical context and therefore is *relative* to the particular constellation of beliefs, values and recipes of knowledge that characterize a particular culture (MacIntyre, 1989). Since the ethicist's own culture cannot be pragmatically discarded so as to attain some position of clarified reason, any claim to a moral authority is inevitably ethnocentric. Even though there may be a degree of social agreement about morality within and between modern societies, and even though the people who make moral claims will often allude to their universality, there are no overarching rational grounds for moral authority. It follows that business ethics must suspend moral judgement.

Often the aims and focus of this approach to business ethics is the ethnographic description of organizational culture(s). Although they do not consider that ethics and culture are necessarily identical, some writers (e.g. Schein, 1985; Pastin, 1988) do suggest that ethics constitute 'the core' of organizational culture. In this way the 'ethical climate' that prevails influences the individual's interpretation of organizational experience and his/her own behaviour (Victor & Cullen, 1988). Others have approached this culture–ethics relationship either by exploring how some cultures might inhibit or prevent the discussion of ethical issues (e.g. Jackall, 1988; Bird & Waters, 1989) or by developing models that identify the sociopsychological and cultural factors which influence the nature of ethical and unethical decision-making (e.g. Trevino, 1986; Jones, 1991).

This consideration of culture is interesting given the emphasis on cultural change within the managing diversity literature. Valuing difference is seen as an important concept within that literature because it is specifically linked to an organization's culture and values. A key element is to move towards 'cultures of inclusion' (Thornberg, 1994), recognizing that various organizational practices often lead to certain groups feeling left out or unwelcome. One implication of the ethical scepticism evident here is that any top-down approach to managing ethics, and for that matter diversity, is thrown into disrepute (Rehg, 1994). For instance, Sinclair (1993) (re)constructs management's moral authority: instead of trying to institutionalize standards and practices that derive from their cultural particularism, the task of management becomes one of understanding the configurations of extant subcultures and their areas of potential consensus that could form the basis of a core of organization-wide cultural norms and practices. This perspective could provide us with new insights into the supposed ethicality or potential success of a range of managing diversity initiatives.

To take an example, Walker and Hanson (1992) describe some of the components of the 'valuing differences' philosophy that has been introduced and implemented at DEC (Digital Equipment Corporation), a company with 120 000 employees in 64 countries throughout the world. The philosophy emerged from a bottom-up movement and 'focuses employees on their differences. Employees are encouraged to pay attention to their differences as unique individuals and as members of groups, to raise their level of comfort with differences, and to capitalize on differences as a major asset to the company's productivity' (p. 120).

The 'valuing differences' work is done in a variety of ways including awareness and skills training, celebrating differences events (eg: Gay and Lesbian Pride week, Hispanic Heritage month) and leadership groups and support groups. A particularly radical intervention is that of the establishment of an informal network of small ongoing discussion groups, known as core groups, described as 'groups of 7–9 employees who commit to coming together on a monthly basis to examine their stereotypes, test the differences in their assumptions, and build significant relationships with people they regard as different' (p. 121). The authors conclude that 'capitalizing on diversity means helping employees become their very best by learning to accept, trust and invest in others' (p. 136). They propose that Digital have yet to learn how to quantify the impact of the valuing differences programme on profitability, but evidence would suggest that the company has some specific concrete advantages from the programme so far. The authors outline these as:

- A solid reputation as one of the best places to work—not just for women and minorities, but for everyone
- Empowered managers and leaders who empower others
- Greater innovation
- Higher employee productivity
- Effective global competition

Clearly the authors see the programme as being highly beneficial to the organization on a number of criteria.

Another example which is perhaps more typical is outlined by Ellis and Sonnenfeld (1994) in their review of corporate diversity programmes. They describe how National Transportation Systems (NTS) run a one-day 'Diversity' workshop which is mandatory for all full-time managers and supervisors. The aim of the workshop is: 'to increase managers' awareness of the growing diversity of the workforce, to teach them the necessity of learning how to manage that diversity, and to help them identify personal biases that may interfere with their ability to manage cultural diversity' (p. 85).

The workshop begins with an introductory video which features the CEO explaining the importance of diversity and its link with the bottom line. A discussion then takes place about each participant's race and gender biases. As Ellis and Sonnenfeld suggest, for the workshop to be successful, individuals have to feel safe enough to reveal sensitive information about themselves. They suggest that the two key criteria that impact upon this are the quality of the facilitator and the cultural mix of participants. The authors summarize the overall impact of this diversity initiative:

> NTS is making great strides in enhancing its ability to manage diversity and promul-
> gating the message that the firm values cultural differences, but its biggest hurdle
> in this area may be the cultural homogeneity of top level management, virtually all
> of the corporate leaders are white males. This homogeneity leaves subordinates to
> diverse backgrounds with few top level role models and inadvertently sends out the
> message that to make it to the top of the firm, one needs to be a white male. (p. 88)

The example from NTS is perhaps more typical in that it focuses on a top-down implementation of a diversity philosophy through the mechanism of training. However, the
top-down approach is problematic from this ethical approach. In contrast, Sinclair (1993)
shuns the imposition of an assumed management-derived ethics. Instead, by fostering
and sponsoring subcultural coexistence, the task of management is reconfigured to one
of encouraging members' reflexive and critical thought through self-scrutiny, debate and
the establishment of consensus prior to action. According to Sinclair (1993: 69–70), it is
through such processes that members weigh up personal and organizational obligations
and responsibilities before finally applying the resultant standards and making a decision. A potential implication of Sinclair's argument is that those individuals and groups
whose perspectives are ordinarily silenced in organizations must be given voice. The
demand is for members' conscious self-determination of social values. In a sense this
embraces a new construction of diversity in organizations: any approach can be ethical if
it is grounded in the democratic consensus of the diverse groups who constitute an organization. Therefore identification and involvement of all potential groups and individuals
presumably must start with the mobilization of every organizational stakeholder.

These alternative approaches to prescriptive business ethics encourage us to think and
question notions of diversity and its management in a different way. Rather than assuming
that ethical behaviour that is best for all can be defined and a diversity management
programme subsequently implemented, we are left with the issue of democratization in
relation to diversity, bearing in mind the political nature and implications of difference.
Therefore the demand is that the diverse approaches silenced by top-down approaches
must be given voice, as democracy is the only ethical basis for business ethics.

CONCLUSIONS

It would seem that there are a number of clear links between business ethics and the
management of diversity. Both have had a relatively short time as an area of legitimate
academic research, and both have initially been driven very clearly from a practitioner
perspective. Business ethics emerged as a focus for contemporary discussion. This was
partly as a response to business needs: companies that are perceived as 'unethical' tend to
be unpopular with customers. Similarly, the notion of managing diversity began to emerge
during the 1980s as a result of worldwide changing demographic trends and the perceived

need to recruit and retain people in the workforce from traditionally disadvantaged groups. In this case too, the underlying principles were driven by shareholder interest with a focus on the business benefits that could accrue from making the most of a more diverse workforce (Cassell, 2001). Theoretically and philosophically, however, there is little similarity between the two. Smith and Johnson (1996) suggest that the philosophical debates that underlie business ethics can be traced back to antiquity, though as Ackers (2001) suggests, the process of translating ethics from personal behaviour to business practice is not that straightforward. Compared to the ethics literature, the managing diversity literature is very new and has been criticized in places for being largely atheoretical (Cassell & Biswas, 2000). Indeed Prasad and Mills (1997) suggest that management academics have adopted an approach which they describe as 'distant cheerleading' (p. 5) where although they endorse the importance of managing diversity, it is not treated as a serious research area.

Although many managers may still remain alienated from and by business ethics (Stark, 1993; Sorrell, 1998) and despite its relatively marginal academic status outside North America, as we have outlined above, some of the debates that business ethicists have engaged in and the problems that they have encountered, are directly relevant to how we understand the case for 'diversity' in terms of either a *moral* or a *business* imperative. In particular the business ethics literature provides another set of concepts which can be used as tools to unpack and make sense of the underlying principles behind managing diversity initiatives. It remains to be seen the extent to which those concepts will be used and applied in this context.

REFERENCES

Ackers, P. (2001). Employment ethics. In T. Redman & A. Wilkinson (eds) *Contemporary Human Resource Management: Text and Cases*. Harlow: Financial Times/ Prentice-Hall.

Adams, J.S., Tashchian, A. & Shore, T.H. (2001). Codes of ethics as signals of ethical behaviour. *Journal of Business Ethics*, **29**, 199–211.

Alpern, S. (1994). In the beginning: a history of women in management. In E.A. Fagenson (ed.) *Women in Management: Trends, Issues and Challenges in Managerial Diversity*. Newbury Park, Calif.: Sage.

Alvesson, M. & Willmott, H. (1996). *Making Sense of Management: A Critical Introduction*. London: Sage.

Ashkanasy, N.M., Falkus, S. & Callan, V.J. (2000). Predictors of ethical code use and ethical tolerance in the public sector. *Journal of Business Ethics*, **25**, 237–253.

Bird, F. & Waters, J.A. (1989). The moral muteness of managers. *California Management Review*, Fall, 73–88.

Bowie, N.E. (1979). Business codes of ethics: window dressing or legitimate alternative to government regulation? In T.L. Beauchamp & N.E. Bowie (eds), *Ethical Theory and Business*. Englewood Cliffs, NJ: Prentice Hall.

Campbell, D. (1984). *Women at War with America: Private Lives in a Patriotic Era*. Cambridge, Mass.: Harvard University Press.

Cassell, C.M. (1996). Business ethics and discriminatory behaviour in organizations. In K. Smith & P. Johnson (eds) *Business Ethics and Business Behaviour*. London: International Thomson Business Press.

Cassell, C.M. (2001). Managing diversity. In T. Redman & A. Wilkinson (eds) *Contemporary Human Resource Management: Text and Cases*, Harlow: Financial Times/ Prentice-Hall.

Cassell, C.M. & Biswas, R. (2000). Managing diversity in the new millennium. *Personnel Review*, **29**(3), 268–273.

Chafe, W.H. (1977). *Women and Equality*. New York: Oxford University Press.

Cooke, R.A. (1986). Business ethics at the crossroads. *Journal of Business Ethics*, **5**, 259–263.

Davis, M. (1982). Conflict of interest. *Business and Professional Ethics Journal*, **1**(4), 17–29.

De George, R.T. (1987). The status of business ethics: past and future. *Journal of Business Ethics*, **6**, 201–211.

Derry, R. & Green, R.M. (1989). Ethical theory in business ethics: a critical assessment. *Journal of Business Ethics*, **8**, 855–862.

Desphande, S.P. (1996). Ethical climate and the link between success and ethical behaviour: an empirical investigation of a non-profit organization. *Journal of Business Ethics*, **15**, 315–320.

Dickens, L. (1994). The business case for women's equality. Is the carrot better than the stick? *Employee Relations*, **16**(8), 5–18.

Donaldson, J. (1989). *Key Issues in Business Ethics*. London: Academic Press.

Donaldson, T. (1989). *The Ethics of International Business*. Oxford: Oxford University Press.

Drucker, P. (1973). *Management Tasks, Responsibilities, Practices*. London: Harper and Row.

Duska, R.F. (1993). Aristotle: a pre-modern post-modern? Implications for business ethics. *Business Ethics Quarterly*, **3**(3), 227–249.

Ellis, C. & Sonnenfeld, J.A. (1994). Diverse approaches to managing diversity. *Human Resource Management*, **33**(1), 79–109.

Etzioni, A. (1988). *The Moral Dimension*. New York: Free Press.

Farley, J. (1994). Commentary. In E.A. Fagenson, *Women in Management: Trends, Issues and Challenges in Managerial Diversity*. Newbury Park, Calif.: Sage.

French, P.A. (1995). *Corporate Ethics*. London: Harcourt Brace.

Goodpaster, K.E. (1985). Toward an integrated approach to business ethics thought. *Thought*, **60**(2), 161–180.

Hall, W.D. (1993). *Making the Right Decision: Ethics for Managers*. New York: John Wiley & Sons.

Handy, C.B. (1994). *The Empty Raincoat: Making Sense of the Future*. London: Hutchison.

Hicks-Clarke, D. & Iles, P. (2000). Climate for diversity and its effects on career and organisational attitudes and perceptions. *Personnel Review*, **29**(3), 402–416.

Hoffman, W.M. & Moore, J.M. (1990). *Business Ethics: Readings and Cases in Corporate Morality*, 2nd edn. New York: McGraw-Hill.

Hyman, M., Skipper, R. & Tansey, R. (1990). Ethical codes are not enough. *Business Horizons*, March–April, 15–22.

Jackall, R. (1988). *Moral Mazes: The World of Corporate Managers*. Oxford: Oxford University Press.

Jick, T.D. (2000). Values-based management: a tool for managing change. In R.J. Burke & C.L. Cooper (eds) *The Organization in Crisis: Downsizing, Re-structuring and Privatisation*. Oxford: Blackwell Publishers Ltd.

Jones, D., Pringle, J. & Shepherd, D. (2000). 'Managing Diversity' meets Aotearoa/New Zealand. *Personnel Review*, **29**(3), 364–380.

Jones, T.M. (1991). Ethical decision making by individuals in organisations: an issue-contingent model. *Academy of Management Review*, **16**(2), 366–395.

Kaler, J. (2000). Reasons to be ethical: self-interest and ethical business. *Journal of Business Ethics*, **27**, 161–173.

Kandola, R. & Fullerton, J. (1994). *Managing the Mosaic: Diversity in Action*. London: Institute of Personnel and Development.

Kant, I. (1964). *Groundwork of the Metaphysics of Morals*. London: Harper and Row.

Lewis, S., Kagan, C. & Heaton, P. (2000). Managing work–family diversity for parents of disabled children: beyond policy to practice and partnership. *Personnel Review*, **29**(3), 417–430.

MacDonald, J.E. & Beck-Dudley, C.L. (1994). Are deontology and teleology mutually exclusive? *Journal of Business Ethics*, **13**(8), 615–623.

McEnrue, M.P. (1993). Managing diversity: Los Angeles before and after the riots. *Organizational Dynamics*, **21**, 3.

MacIntyre, A. (1989). *A Short History of Ethics*. London: Macmillan.

MacKenzie, C. (1998). Ethical auditing and ethical knowledge. *Journal of Business Ethics*, **17**(13), 1395–1402.

Maitland, I. (1988). The limits of business self-regulation. In T.L. Beauchamp & N.E. Bowie (eds) *Ethical Theory and Business*. London: Prentice-Hall.

Manley, W.W. (1992). *The Handbook of Good Business Practice: Corporate Codes of Ethics*. London: Routledge.

Michalos, A.C. (2001). Ethics counselors as a new priesthood. *Journal of Business Ethics*, **29**, 3–17.

Milton-Smith, J. (1995). Ethics as excellence: a strategic management perspective. *Journal of Business Ethics*, **14**, 683–693.

Molander, E.A. (1987). A paradigm for the design, promulgation and enforcement of ethical codes. *Journal of Business Ethics*, **6**, 619–631.

Murphy, P.E. (1995). Corporate ethics statements: current status and future prospects. *Journal of Business Ethics*, **14**, 727–740.

Ozar, D.T. (1979). The moral responsibility of corporations. In T. Donaldson & P. Werhane (eds) *Ethical Issues in Business*. Englewood Cliffs, NJ: Prentice-Hall.

Pastin, M. (1988). *The Hard Problems of Management: Gaining the Ethics Edge*. San Francisco, Calif.: Jossey Bass.

Prasad, P. & Mills, A.J. (1997). From showcase to shadow: understanding the dilemmas in managing workplace diversity. In P. Prasad, A.J. Mills, M. Elmes & A. Prasad (eds) *Managing the Organizational Melting Pot: Dilemmas of Workplace Diversity*. Thousand Oaks, Calif.: Sage.

Primeaux, P. (1992). Experiential ethics: a blueprint for personal and corporate ethics. *Journal of Business Ethics*, **11**, 779–788.

Rehg, W. (1994). *Insight and Solidarity: A Study in the Discourse Ethics of Jürgen Habermas*. Berkeley: University of California Press.

Rosenblatt, Z. & Schaeffer, Z. (2000). Ethical problems in downsizing. In R.J. Burke & C.L. Cooper (eds) *The Organization in Crisis: Downsizing, Restructuring and Privatization*. Oxford: Blackwell Business.

Schein, E.H. (1985). *Organizational Culture and Leadership*. San Francisco, Calif.: Jossey Bass.

Sims, R.R. (1991). Institutionalization of organizational ethics. *Journal of Business Ethics*, **10**, 493–506.

Sinclair, A. (1993). Approaches to organizational culture and ethics. *Journal of Business Ethics*, **12**, 63–73.

Smith, K. & Johnson, P. (1996). *Business Ethics and Business Behaviour*. London: International Thomson Business Press.

Sorrell, T. (1998). Beyond the fringe? The strange state of business ethics. In M. Parker (ed.) *Ethics and Organization*. London: Sage.

Sorrell, T. & Hendry, J. (1994). *Business Ethics*. Oxford: Butterworth-Heinemann.

Stark, A. (1993). What's the matter with business ethics? *Harvard Business Review*, May–June, 38–48.

Stevens, B. (1994). An analysis of corporate ethical code studies: where do we go from here? *Journal of Business Ethics*, **13**, 63–69.

Sumner, W.G. (1988). A defence of cultural relativism. In T. Donaldson & P.H. Werhane (eds) *Ethical Issues in Business: A Philosophical Approach*. Englewood Cliffs, NJ: Prentice Hall.

Thomas, R.R. Jnr (1990). From affirmative action to affirming diversity. *Harvard Business Review*, **68**(2), 107–117.

Thornberg, L. (1994). Journey towards a more inclusive culture. *HR Magazine*, February.

Trevino, L.K. (1986). Ethical decision making in organizations: a person–situation interactionist model. *Academy of Management Review*, **11**(3), 601–617.

Trevino, L.K. & Nelson, K.A. (1995). *Managing Business Ethics: Straight Talk about How to Do It*, New York: Wiley.

Velasquez, V.E. (1988). *Business Ethics: Concepts and Cases* (2nd edn). New York: Prentice Hall.

Velasquez, V.E. (1992). *Business Ethics: Concepts and Cases* (3rd edn). London: Prentice-Hall.

Victor B. & Cullen, J.B. (1988). The organisational bases of ethical work climates. *Administrative Science Quarterly*, **33**, 101–125.

Walker, B.A. & Hanson, W.C. (1992). Valuing differences at Digital Equipment Corporation. In S.E. Jackson & Associates (eds) *Diversity in the Workplace: Human Resource Initiatives*, New York: Guilford Press.

Webley, S. (1992). *Business Ethics and Company Codes: Current Best Practice in the United Kingdom*. London: Institute of Business Ethics.

Weller, S. (1988). The effectiveness of corporate codes of ethics. *Journal of Business Ethics*, **7**, 389–395.

Woodhams, C. & Danieli, A. (2000). Disability and diversity: a difference too far? *Personnel Review*, **29**(3), 417–430.

CHAPTER 4

Managing Diversity: Developing a Strategy for Measuring Organizational Effectiveness

Michael L. Wheeler

OEStrategies, Inc., New York, USA

SUMMARY

This chapter explores a framework for understanding diversity as a critical factor influencing organizational effectiveness. Practical as well as conceptual, the strategic diversity model as presented herein provides the reader with applicable tactical metrics relative to creating, managing, valuing and leveraging diversity that culminate in an action plan and overall strategic measurement process that allow for flexibility and specificity.

INTRODUCTION

Measuring organizational effectiveness in the context of diversity management is about creating a framework—a strategy—for ensuring a holistic approach to understanding the people factors and forces affecting organizational capability and performance. While

Individual Diversity and Psychology in Organizations. Edited by Marilyn J. Davidson and Sandra L. Fielden.
© 2003 John Wiley & Sons, Ltd.

Strategic Diversity Measurement Model

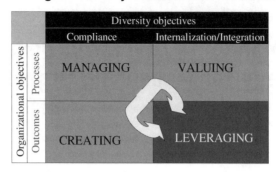

FIGURE 4.1 Strategic diversity measurement model.
Source: Wheeler, M.L. (1996). *Corporate Practices in Diversity Measurement*, The Conference Board

there are many approaches to diversity measurement, and to organizational and human performance, this chapter builds and focuses upon a solid framework and foundation that encompass four essential areas required for developing a strategy for successfully measuring diversity for organizational effectiveness:

- Creating diversity
- Managing diversity
- Valuing diversity
- Leveraging diversity

As can be seen by the strategic diversity measurement model (see Figure 4.1), these four components are *all* part of—and necessary to—the effective measurement strategy (Wheeler, 1996).

This chapter will examine closely the tactical metrics that might be applied to each quadrant of the model and demonstrates how each quadrant is related to (1) compliance, (2) internalization, (3) processes, (4) outcomes and (5) drivers. How these metrics are determined and influenced by business and diversity strategy will also be explained. The sum of these components composes the strategic diversity model wherein lies the flexibility, and critical and practical components necessary for successfully measuring organizational effectiveness within the distinct goals, objectives and context of each unique organization.

ORGANIZATIONAL EFFECTIVENESS DEFINED

'Organizational effectiveness', like the word 'diversity', is a popular term that does not always have a clearly defined meaning—or at least not one that is universally understood by those who use the term. To best understand organizational effectiveness as it will be used in this chapter, is to understand the basis of systems theory (e.g. Katz & Kahn, 1978; Beer, 1980; Nadler & Tushman, 1980; Hall, 1983) and more specifically Harrison's discussion on 'Organizations as open systems' (see Figure 4.2) (Harrison, 1987). Harrison's discussion provides an excellent example of systems theory to help one understand the various factors that can affect organizational performance. With this

Environment (task and general):

- *Task environment* includes all the external organizations and conditions that are directly related to an organization's main operations and its technologies. They include suppliers, unions, customers, clients, regulators, competitors, markets for products and resources, and the state of the knowledge concerning the organization's technologies.

- *General environment* includes intuitions and conditions that may have infrequent or long-term impacts on the organization and its task environment, including the economy, the legal system, the state of scientific and technical knowledge, social institutions such as the family, population distribution and competitions, the political system and the national culture within which the organization operates.

Purposes:

- Includes the strategies, goals, objectives, plans and interests of the organization's dominant decision-makers.

Behaviour and processes:

- The prevailing patterns of behaviour, interactions, and relationships between groups and individuals....

Culture:

- Shared norms, beliefs, values, symbols and rituals relating to key aspects of organizational life.

Structure:

- Includes enduring relationship between individuals, groups and larger units, grouping of positions in divisions, departments and other units; standard operating procedures; established mechanisms for handling key processes such as coordination... human resources mechanisms, actual patterns... that may differ from officially mandated ones.

Figure 4.2 Organizations as open systems.
Source: Excerpted from: Harrison, M.I. (1987). *Diagnosing Organizations: Methods, Models, and Processes*. Applied Social Research Methods Series, Vol. 8, Newbury Park: Sage Publications

framework in mind, 'organizational effectiveness' is defined for the purpose of this chapter as follows:

> Organizational Effectiveness is the purposes, environment, behaviours and processes, culture and structure and the interactive and interrelated factors that inhibit, enable or enhance individual, group and organizational capability and performance.

Three keywords are critical in the context of diversity and organizational effectiveness—inhibit, enable or enhance. By understanding how systemic components—individuals, groups, organizations, and even societal and external influences—affect the ability of individuals, groups and organizations to achieve full potential, one can build a broad or focused, but essentially *comprehensive* foundation for understanding those things that influence performance. At first all these factors may seem overwhelming and even

contradictory to an efficient strategy. But one must be aware of all the resources and contextual issues one has available to build the essential components of the measurement
strategy.

DIVERSITY DEFINED

Like organizational effectiveness, diversity has become a popular word that can mean
many things to many people. It is often a word loaded with assumptions and received or
identified with strong emotions.

DEFINITIONAL APPROACHES AND BIASES

Definitions are often determined or influenced much by the predisposition of individuals,
organizations (including culture and leadership) and the law. For example, it may be
based upon an equal opportunity, affirmative action, legal or punitive model. Or it might
be based upon an oppression model or on a cross-cultural one. It may be fuelled by
personal passion and motives by someone who has a particular bias, or need to address
his or her own personal issue or mission. Definitions might be approached from a "Right
thing to do" or ethical perspective. Each view or approach is valid, but all are not
equally effective in an organizational context. Legal considerations are often required,
and although the business rationale or ethical approach is more subjective, these too
are important considerations for defining and measuring diversity. Therefore, a useful,
inclusive definition that is operational within an organizational context is particularly
important.

DIVERSITY IN THE ORGANIZATIONAL CONTEXT

For the purpose of this chapter and understanding diversity in the context of organizational effectiveness, diversity is defined as follows:

> Diversity is all the ways in which we differ and how those differences enable, enhance
> or inhibit the ability of individuals, groups and organizations to achieve individual,
> collective and/or organizational goals and objectives.

Establishing a clear definition of diversity and organizational effectiveness will assist an organization—and all involved—in more effective development of the diversity
measurement strategy. When it comes to metrics, the definition matters greatly as it will
determine perceptions, strategy, what is valued in metrics and where emphasis will be
placed.

COMPONENTS OF THE STRATEGIC DIVERSITY MEASUREMENT MODEL DEFINED

Working with a model that allows for a broad range of approaches and flexibility, yet at
the same time helps one establish a strategic focus with practical application is critical.
The guidelines identified in Figure 4.3 were used in the development of this model and
should be heeded to help ensure success.

The strategic diversity measurement model presented in this chapter, via the four key quadrants of the model, allow for flexibility *and* focus. A brief discussion of each quadrant begins to make clear how the four pieces comprise a holistic approach to effective measurement.

1. *Creating diversity* is about creating a 'balanced workforce' (Wheeler, 2001). This means understanding inclusion and exclusion and what people—individuals, groups or segment(s) of the workforce—might be excluded from contribution, opportunity, and fair and equal treatment. It is about how their presence—or lack of presence—enhances or inhibits organizational effectiveness. It is about how an internal workforce reflects or does not reflect the local or national population. The metrics most often associated with the creating quadrant of the model are typically those based upon representation by race and gender. Although visible differences are a key element to creating diversity, visible diversity is a minimal objective. Parity, balance and inclusion based upon a wide array of factors are important.

2. *Managing diversity* relates to all those factors that come into play in how people are managed, developed, evaluated and included or excluded from teams, or individual contributions to the business. The most common metrics utilized for the managing diversity quadrant include promotions (based upon race and gender), equity in performance reviews and compensation analysis. What will be highlighted in this chapter is a focus upon leadership commitment and accountability and behavioural metrics.

3. *Valuing diversity* is a more nebulous term, and relates to the 'internalization' (see definition of 'internalization' below) of a value inherent in the organizational culture. The work environment is a critical metric in this quadrant and can provide a barometer for the value of inclusion and diversity. Valuing diversity is sometimes driven and benchmarked by a formal organizational values statement, but will also likely manifest itself in a visibly diverse top management team as well as throughout the organization. Valuing diversity can be 'seen' in a variety of indicators, as will be discussed further in the 'organizational readiness matrix' (see p. 68).

4. *Leveraging diversity* is associated with the 'synergy' of differences and the positive results or benefits of creating systems and processes that draw upon the belief and power that diverse teams, views and opinions can result in better problem-solving, greater innovation, better customer service and ultimately in improved bottom-line results and profitability. It relates to those things that build upon diverse people, perspectives and

- Timeliness, usability and understandability
- Accuracy and dependability
- Differentiation between outcomes and processes
- Links to business (practical)
- Links to external measures (e.g. benchmarks)
- Inclusive of breadth of issues
- Sequential in deployment
- Flexible
  —For future evolution
  —For customizing in each business area

FIGURE 4.3   Guidelines for measurement strategies

teams to create more innovation and creativity and that the presence of diverse individuals improves decision-making and the customer–company link. On the other side of leveraging diversity is the failure to do so, resulting in lost opportunity. Although difficult to measure, 'lost opportunity' can be a powerful perspective when considering metrics.

Each of the four segments—creating, managing, valuing and leveraging—are interrelated and inextricably intertwined. Although there may be programme-specific—or 'tactical'—metrics that may seem totally independent of other metrics, it should become clear how sets of tactical measures all come together to create a comprehensive strategy. Although the focus or emphasis may vary from quadrant to quadrant at different points of time, it is again critical to ensure that tactical metrics indeed exist for each of the four categories to ensure the completion of the strategy. Moreover, there are multiple types of metrics that apply to each of the quadrants to complete the strategic model.

OBJECTIVES, OUTCOMES, PROCESSES, COMPLIANCE, INTERNALIZATION AND DRIVERS DEFINED

For each of the four quadrants of the strategic diversity measurement model, there are subcomponents related to specific objectives, outcomes, process and driver metrics. And, as will be discussed, creating and managing are related to compliance-oriented metrics whereas valuing and leveraging are more internalized measures.

ORGANIZATIONAL OBJECTIVES

Organizational objectives can be identified in a variety of ways—from the formal strategic plan, to mission statements, to annual reports. These may be macro or micro—in other words, may relate to overall organizational objectives or to those of a particular division or function. An understanding of *both* formal and informal objectives is critical. In sum, the best way to identify organizational objectives is to ask: What are the formally stated goals and objectives of the organization, division or function? A variety of metrics can be utilized to determine how effectively these objectives are being met or not being met.

DIVERSITY OBJECTIVES

Diversity objectives are diversity-specific goals and objectives such as:

• Increasing representation by race and gender in senior management ranks
• Reducing turnover among women and minorities
• Improving recruitment of people of colour
• Implementing and rolling out company-wide diversity training

These goals and objectives too may be formal or informal, but should always be aligned with organizational objectives. For example, Table 4.1 demonstrates how business strategy links to a diversity objective and what a metric might look like. Clearly, not all metrics will have a direct link to business strategy, but this should be a critical starting point for an overall strategy.

There is often a gap between the jargon of business leaders and human resources professionals typically responsible for diversity initiatives. Consequently, there is also

TABLE 4.1 Linking business strategy to diversity objectives and metrics

Business strategy	Diversity link	Metric
Globalize	Cultures working together effectively	360 degree feedback Employee attitude surveys
Improve customer focus	Does internal workforce represent the marketplace? Who are the untapped market segments?	Focus groups with customers Feedback on websites
Grow the business	Need more talent Recruitment and retention efforts increased	Where are recruiting? Have expanded recruiting to traditionally minority colleges? Are women and minorities being developed for the fast track?
Innovation	Diverse perspectives generate greater innovation and problem-solving	Are diverse teams in place? Are they effectively managed?

often a lack of clear connection between diversity objectives and how they are aligned with or support business objectives (the author is biased that diversity objectives are indeed business objectives). There is an important caveat to organizationally driven objectives: identifying and linking organizational strategy and objectives to diversity is only the starting point. Eventually diversity-oriented metrics will provide data and information that may indeed influence the direction of business strategy.

Outcomes

Outcomes are and should be very specific. The clearer the outcomes, the better and easier to identify the right metrics. Instead of a general statement or goal that says, 'Reduce turnover', it should say, 'Reduce turnover by 1 per cent.' Of course, the more sophisticated the strategy and metrics become, the easier it is to get more detailed. Yet, in some cases, simple measures are the best.

Processes

Processes are in essence the heart of business practices such as evaluation processes, interviewing etiquette, developmental practices or leadership development programmes. Processes can be modified, or new ones may be created. Process measures are among the most important and are foundational to a change process. They determine those things that will ensure long-term commitment, change and ultimately improved or enhanced organizational effectiveness. Integrating or building diversity metrics into accepted business processes helps create sustainability in the efforts and promotes familiarity and credibility.

DRIVERS

Drivers are those metrics that in fact drive or create incentive for the achievement of goals and objectives. For example, companies might create financial incentives and tie management behaviours or objectives to compensation relative to the recruitment, retention and development of people. These are often called accountability metrics. Accountability metrics can be a driver, compliance and process measure.

COMPLIANCE

Compliance measures or objectives are those things that are required by law, organizational objectives, or accountability metrics. In the United States, affirmative action plans are compliance-driven metrics for Federal contractors. Employment laws and non-discrimination laws are the same. Compliance can be formal (as in legal requirements or formal accountability requirements) or informal (as in a verbal command from a CEO) and are often relied on or adhered to because they typically fall within the realm of the law. Although not fully objective, they typically provide the most concrete measures that companies have at hand.

INTERNALIZATION

Internalization is closely associated with the valuing and leveraging quadrants of the strategic diversity measurement model. Internalization is a state where diversity becomes just another part of business considerations or way of doing business. Indicators of internalization will be discussed further below, but can be reflected in behaviours and environmental metrics.

The specific formulas that may be utilized for the various types of metrics are not as important to this chapter as are the specific objectives, identification of metrics and the process utilized to create a complete plan. The individual(s) responsible for developing strategy should understand all the tools, formulas and models utilized by his or her business. Moreover, he or she should be aware and familiar with the theories, models and current practices that may be brought into the organization's existing scheme of metrics to enhance or improve current processes.

TACTICS FOR MEASURING THE CREATION OF A DIVERSE WORKFORCE

Creation of a diverse or 'balanced' (Wheeler, 2001) workforce encompasses several elements that allow the utilization of a variety of tactics (see Figure 4.4). Again, this is most often driven by demographics—the labour pool or labour force. Creation of a diverse workforce, again, is more often than not directly related to the visible diversity throughout the organization. The efforts of any company should be manifested in the real tangible measurable efforts of increased diversity and inclusion.

When considering performance and organizational effectiveness, the idea of a 'balanced workforce' is an important one. It might be helpful to ask oneself, 'What are those

Representation/composition of the workforce—top down
   EEO1 data/government requirements
   Affirmative action guidelines
Tracking career paths and key assignments
   Hirings
   Promotions
   Participation in mentoring initiatives
Recruitment—job offers /refusals
Length of stay/tenure
Voluntary terminations
National/local demographics—national or industry benchmark comparisons
Strategic staffing initiative
Skills and languages

FIGURE 4.4   Measures for creating a diverse workforce

things that include or exclude individuals or groups from the full participation and con-tribution?' in the workforce and then to focus on those things relevant to the organization and make those the priority issues to focus on for metrics. Sometimes the *lack* of visible diversity is an important indicator. Invisible factors such as sexual orientation may be an important issue and should not be overlooked just because it is not a formal or visible measure. Whatever it is that is the basis for exclusion may indeed be a deterrent to the full utilization of talent and consequently a barrier to full productivity and organizational effectiveness.

The compliance element of this quadrant is at the same time straightforward and complex. Where laws are involved, such as those in the United States with regard to affirmative action, there are relatively clear expectations about what is required to remain compliant and remain within the law. EEO1 requirements (a system of metrics and figures required by the United States Equal Employment Opportunity Commission for all Federal contractors) provided by the government provide some detailed specifications to measure the composition of the workforce. Because of this, companies sometimes consider compliance a sufficient objective. From a diversity perspective, compliance is a minimal requirement.

TACTICS FOR MEASURING THE MANAGEMENT OF A DIVERSE WORKFORCE

Managing a diverse workforce also falls under the realm of 'compliance' for several rea-sons. First, companies are liable for the behaviours of their managers' and employees' management practices and treatment of employees under the law. Beyond representation, there are laws that protect against bias, discrimination and harassment. Second, from a di-versity performance perspective leadership commitment and accountability become im-portant to increasing the commitment to diversity as a business imperative and to ensure the effective management and development of a diverse workforce for maximum organi-zation performance, capability and competitiveness. Consequently, many required train-ing programmes and initiatives are compliance driven—formally and informally—to ensure that leadership carry out the values, mission and duties of the organization as well as ensuring their actions remain within the law and often formally stated organizational values.

Leadership commitment and accountability metrics are often tied to:

• Profile representation or the creation of visible diversity in the organization
• An environment of inclusion where management behaviours demonstrate the values and practices associated with inclusion
• Diversity leadership or the active and proactive commitment to improving organizational effectiveness through people

One of the critical metrics under managing diversity is accountability. Consequently this metric becomes a driver for ensuring the attainment of organizational goals for creating, managing, valuing and leveraging diversity.

'Creating' behaviours

• Achieves numerical goals for women and minorities
• Initiates/participates in outreach activities
• Makes diversity objectives part of staffing decisions
• Ensures diverse interviewing team and candidates
• Invests time and resources to support staffing priorities

'Managing' behaviours

• Communicates, positions diversity as company priority
• Attends EBP meetings
• Participates in diversity training programmes
• Flexibly manages employees as individuals and encourages contributions from all
• Holds self and direct reports accountable for diversity objectives/behaviours

'Valuing' behaviours

• Walks the talk
• Listens and *values* different points of view
• Provides work environment in which individual and cultural differences are valued
• Incorporates diversity/inclusiveness into mainstream dialogue
• Challenges norms/biases
• Broadens perspective and self-understanding
• Champions people development

'Leveraging' behaviours

• People are rewarded for results vs just activity
• Utilizes affinity/networking groups for market/cultural insight and connections
• Diverse viewpoints required to be competitive
• Knows skills, abilities and talents of employees
• Addresses systemic solutions for sustainable results

FIGURE 4.5   Measuring management behaviours

ACCOUNTABILITY

There is an adage that states, 'What gets measured gets done.' Employees are held accountable for financial profits and losses, and often their compensation is directly tied to their performance. This should be no different when it comes to people issues. This is gaining acceptance and credibility as organizations recognize the value of accountability for driving real change in behaviours and in the outcomes of business and diversity objectives. Managers need to understand the link between diversity and business performance.

MANAGEMENT BEHAVIOURS

Management behaviours—defining them, driving them (see Figure 4.5)—have become a priority for many companies and an important piece of the accountability process. Recognizing the complexity of the psyche and personal beliefs, companies are focusing less on trying to change attitudes than they are on trying to change behaviours. Of course, the hope is that in the long run, a change in behaviour will result in change of attitude. Clearly defining expected behaviours also helps provide a basis for both outcomes and processes for better goal attainment. A simple checklist can determine whether or not individuals are exhibiting the expected behaviours within the organization.

As can be seen by Figure 4.6, metrics for managing diversity cover a broad spectrum and should be representative of the business systems and practices—or should be created to improve business systems and practices.

TACTICS FOR MEASURING THE VALUING OF A DIVERSE WORKFORCE

'Valuing diversity', although a little more difficult to measure and define, is possible to see in its manifestation within an organization. This is where the idea of 'internalization'

Promotions
Movement of career paths
Cutbacks/hiring freezes/downsizing—avoiding disproportionate cuts
Succession planning
Performance reviews/practices
Reasonable accommodation
Litigation
Complaints/grievances
Mentoring
Attendance at training for employees and management
Returns from leave, e.g. maternity leave
Behaviours
Visible/active participation in, and commitment to, diversity
Manager effectiveness and commitment to diversity via 360 degree feedback
Achievement of personal diversity actions plans/objectives

FIGURE 4.6 Measures for managing a diverse workforce

comes into play and a move away from compliance. The work environment, or organizational culture and formal and informal practices will tell a lot about an organization and how diversity is valued or not.

WORK ENVIRONMENT

The work environment is a central component for measuring value. The organizational readiness matrix (see Table 4.2), created by the Conference Board's Executive Councils on Workforce Diversity and inspired and influenced by the work of Miller and Katz et al. (Miller & Katz, 1995; Jackson et al., 1981) provides a very useful tool for a

TABLE 4.2   Stages of diversity and organizational readiness

⇐⇐⇐⇐⇐⇐ Transition ⇒⇒⇒⇒⇒⇒

Characteristics	Exclusion (intolerance)	Symbolic pioneers (tolerance)	Critical mass (acceptance)	Inclusion (fully integrated)
Emotion	Disdain/ignorance	Indifference	Acceptance	Respect/value
Business performance	Suboptimal (clueless)	Suboptimal (awareness)	Increasing optimization (pockets of excellence)	Optimal
Executive commitment	The least we can get away with	Reactive/legal compliance	'Right thing to do' Ownership	Business imperative
Leadership positions	Majority white male 'Old boys' network'	Tokenism 'Pioneers'	Strong middle management representation Limited at top	Board/executive committee representation
Diversity focus	Minimal compliance	Compliance focus on numbers	Positive actions Begin business integration	Optimizing global potential
Market focus	None	None	Emerging employee ownership of business solutions/results	Integrated into all aspects of business/ teams
Customer focus	None	None	Conscious diversification of teams	Broad cultural global involvement
Employee involvement	None	Informal networks	Formal councils/ affinity groups	Passionate involvement in business by all

Source: Wheeler, M.L. (2001) *The Diversity Executive: Tasks, Competencies, and Strategies for Effective Leadership*, The Conference Board. Developed by The Conference Board's Councils on Work Force Diversity, inspired and influenced by concepts from the work of F.A. Miller and J.H. Katz (1995) *Cultural Diversity as a Developmental Process: The Path from Monocultural Club to Inclusive Organization*. The Kaleel Jamison Consulting Group, Inc., copyright © 1995 Pfeiffer & Company International Publishers. Published in the 1995 Annual, No. 2. The basis for this model was presented by Jackson, B., Hardiman, R. & Chesler, M. (1981) in 'Racial awareness and development in organizations'. (Working paper: New Perspectives, Inc.)

> Culture and environment
> Language of workplace
> Type of workers—part-time, full-time, job shares
> Utilization of work—life benefits/initiatives
> Parity
> Compensation analysis
> Leadership behaviours/practices
> Networking groups
> Attitudes and perceptions
> Resource and referral usage
> Degree of integration of diversity initiatives into company
> Employee minority events
> Top management accessibility
> Inclusive language
> Barriers to contributions

Figure 4.7   Measures for valuing a diverse workforce.
Source: Wheeler, M.L. (1996). *Corporate Practices in Diversity Measurement*, The Conference Board

quick assessment and understanding of the valuing component of where an organization might exist, and how it might look with regard to valuing diversity—or inclusion. For example, a relatively easy and typical metric is to look at the representation based upon race, gender and ethnicity of a top management team. What is the composition of the executive suite? Although not the sole determinant of an environment of inclusion, it is clearly an important indicator that would demonstrate on some level how committed and developed a company is with regard to the full inclusion of a diverse workforce.

Other indicators, as identified in the model and that relate directly to organizational effectiveness, are the diversity links to the marketplace, customers and business performance. Awareness of these subtle indicators provided by the matrix can be a powerful tool for observational analysis of an organization. Figure 4.7 also provides numerous examples of how the valuing component is actually measured.

TACTICS FOR MEASURING LEVERAGING A DIVERSE WORKFORCE

This important, but least understood and practised component of a measurement strategy provides the greatest challenges *and* opportunities for understanding diversity in the context of organizational effectiveness and performance. Although some believe there are just too many factors that make up revenue per employee to make any strong connections to diversity, there is a growing belief and commitment to the fact that global marketing strategies, productivity and innovation that recognizes customer differences and new and emerging markets are optimized when the workforce reflects the marketplace. According to Hayles,

> When the 5-year, 11-year and 20-year financial performance of companies engaged in diversity and related progressive human resource work is compared to the performance of those that are not doing such work or doing it poorly, the former companies significantly outperform the latter in terms of sales growth, profit growth, and performance in a down turning economy. (Hayles, 1995)

Customer satisfaction and loyalty
Market segments—sales and marketing data
Increased market share
Tapping into new markets
Community/corporate image
Participation in vendor fairs
Relationship with local communities
Successes/failures in foreign cultures and markets
Missed opportunities in markets/product development innovation/customization
Dollars spent with minority and women-owned business enterprises (MWBE)
Advertising dollars spent in diverse marketing initiatives

FIGURE 4.8   Measures for leveraging a diverse workforce.
Source: Wheeler, M.L. (1996). *Corporate Practices in Diversity Measurement*, The Conference Board

There is still much work to be done in this area. Moreover, there is great opportunity for stronger alliances within companies to draw upon cross-functional experiences and expertise to build clearer linkages to diversity and the bottom line. But, the bottom-line component cannot be the sole factor for determining value of diversity initiatives. An overemphasized focus on return on investment (ROI) for each diversity initiative would be futile and send the wrong message to all constituents involved. Although few to date link diversity to organizational effectiveness and performance via the balanced scorecard concept (Kaplan & Norton, 1996), there is growing acceptance of the scorecard concept in recognizing that there are many factors critical to ensuring the optimal performance of an organization and its people. Hence, one should carefully consider a balanced approach to diversity metrics—as the strategic diversity measurement model does—and remember those metrics are part of a greater whole for the organization. Figure 4.8 provides specific examples of the metrics being used to better understand how diversity is leveraged for organizational success.

AN ACTION PLAN: TURNING TACTICS INTO STRATEGY

Table 4.3 provides an example of an action plan that clearly lays out tactical metrics for each piece of the overall strategy. Once the organizational goals and objectives have been identified, then the action plan provides a useful tool for identifying the diversity-specific tactical measures that will help the organization achieve those goals. As noted earlier, under each of the four components of the action plan—from creating to leveraging—there are three types of measures just as critical to short- and long-term success.

- Outcomes
- Processes
- Drivers

The completion of at least 12 total metrics (per the matrix) requires a rather simple, yet thoughtful process for ensuring all the pieces are in place for developing an effective short- or long-term measurement strategy. Subsequently, the action plan can be utilized for establishing immediate objectives or changes, as well as establishing long-term goals. In fact, there are several useful purposes for the action plan matrix:

TABLE 4.3 Creating a strategic action plan: sample metrics

	Creating	Managing	Valuing	Leveraging
Outcomes	Increased workforce representation	Increased retention rates Reduced complaints/ conflicts	Improved climate survey ratings	Increased ethnic/racial or niche market share
Drivers	Hiring and promotion objectives	Utilization of 'benefits' work/life, tuition, employee assistance plans (EAPs) Performance reviews	Compensation tied to diversity	Targeted market financial objectives
Processes	Fairness of selection processes	Management training	Participation in and contribution to diversity initiatives	Utilization of internal networking groups and task forces

Source: Wheeler, M.L. (1996). *Corporate Practices in Diversity Measurement*, The Conference Board.

- A first step
- An assessment tool
- As a quarterly or annual planner
- A benchmark for progress
- To revise plans
- To identify gaps in current measurement strategy

A team effort in the action plan process is most valuable as it begins to model a process of inclusion, and can improve the quality of the product. The plan should be revisited periodically for progress, effectiveness and for periodic revisions. Flexibility is important in often dynamic workplace environments. When considering long-term goals and objectives, particular attention should be given to the processes piece of the model. These are the beginning of metrics that institutionalize or integrate certain factors, goals and objectives into the fabric of the business and become the long-term drivers of what the organization envisions for the future.

CHALLENGES OF MEASURING DIVERSITY

When it comes to human resources related metrics they are often referred to as the 'soft stuff' of business and not given the credibility or importance they deserve as a part of overall business performance, objectives and profitability. Consequently, this is one of the reasons for understanding a systemic and comprehensive approach to diversity measurement as identified in the strategic diversity measurement model.

No matter how well developed diversity metrics are, there will always be some measurement challenges (see Figure 4.9): some are specific to diversity, others are general

- Measures may not be right for the objective
- Benchmarking has limitations
- Measures can backfire—must be prepared to take bad with the good
- Competing hypotheses may surface
- Liability may be an issue
- Measure can limit how people view diversity
- Measures may not apply globally
- Measures can be taken out of context
- Measures/data may be flawed
- Measure may not be as bad as thought or may not provide expected findings
- Diversity measures are too often anecdotal
- Measures do not fit with current business models
- Might get what you asked for
- May get too much data
- Data may get out publicly, can improve or deteriorate public image—media may not understand or may misinterpret
- Comparisons may be 'apples to oranges'
- Homogeneous group efforts are sometimes quicker in results—but not necessarily better

FIGURE 4.9   Challenges and potential drawbacks to diversity measures

problems with metrics. The following are important considerations typically associated with diversity metrics:

- *Denial, disbelief*—sometimes it is possible to have every imaginable piece of data and information yet the receivers of that information are unable to validate it. This is particularly true when it comes to the work of diversity. A historic body of research, and growing body of new research, can effectively be utilized to support internal data.
- *Manipulation of data*—organizations and individuals are always looking for ways to make the data look favourable. Be careful how you use data and be sure it is utilized and presented with integrity.
- *Failure to use available data*—one of the most common problems observed with data collection is the failure to use it. This is most common with employee attitude surveys. For employees to take these seriously, some action and communication must occur.
- *Lack of commitment to action*—too often organizations have data for data's sake, but fail to utilize it as an opportunity for change, improvement or action.
- *Slicing and dicing data*—there is a dichotomy accruing in corporations across the globe. On the one hand we are seeking information on a variety of levels that provide a realistic look at who our workforce is. On the other hand, many people see this as invasive of privacy and in some cases seeking out such information may violate law.
- *What does not get measured*—we know that traditional accounting methods do not take into consideration all the real factors that truly make a difference on the bottom line. The focus tends to be upon tangibles. Even so, when it comes to the human or environmental aspects of the bottom line, even the tangible factors are often not taken into consideration or remain on some ledger separate from the ones that senior management utilize for critical strategic decision-making. Consequently, what does not

get measured may indeed be a significant factor for organizational effectiveness and performance. On many levels, diversity metrics bring to light things that have traditionally not been measured and demonstrates the link to organizational effectiveness.

Still, there are things that do not get measured at all. This may be due to laws, culture, or the sheer inability to measure something. But these things can be very important. For example, while categorizing groups for an employee attitude survey, a company may not include gays and lesbians as a demographic group. Yet that does not mean that the issues, concerns and attitudes of gays and lesbians in the workplace are not important. Or, as is often the case with gays and lesbians, companies may derive attitudinal information from focus groups or employee affinity groups. In the United States, employee attitude surveys traditionally segment data by race and gender. In some countries, this is illegal or unacceptable. Yet, knowing how attitudes and perceptions differ can make a big difference in the decisions companies make.

- *Psychological and sociological implications of performance, creativity, productivity and dedication*—organizational measures rarely capture the psychological implications for business performance. It is critical to understand the individual and group implications of attitudes, behaviours, inter- and intra-group conflict. There are also historical implications to understand this. Black rage is one example that can have an effect on organizations and people—yet is often ignored or misunderstood particularly with relevance to organizational performance.
- *Cultural nuances*—often metrics are not culturally sensitive or inclusive and therefore may not capture accurate assessment. For example, an individual oriented assessment in a group-oriented society/culture will not be the appropriate or more accurate assessment technique.
- *Measuring the wrong thing*—sometimes the wrong metrics are implemented with expectation of certain outcomes. Know and carefully think about what you are measuring and what you are looking for in results to be sure the two are aligned.
- *Missing data*—sometimes the data that are not there are the most important. Know the limitations of data.
- *Assumptions* and *understanding of the creators and audience/receiver of the data*—diversity metrics are often loaded with political agendas and individual's agendas. The use of the strategic diversity measurement model and action plan helps establish a well-rounded, more objective and thought-out process that takes into consideration all involved.
- *Too much data*—organizations rarely lack metrics and the expertise to implement and utilize them. In fact, more often than not, they are overloaded with measures of profits, losses and performance. Consequently, in the organizational context, especially with regard to organizational effectiveness, top business leaders want to know at a glance what they need to know. The individual responsible for diversity must have at hand the comprehensive set of metrics, yet must be able to provide that in a concise, easily communicable way. There are a number of ways to do this:

1. Integrate diversity metrics into current measures.
2. Suggest an enhanced metric reporting system utilizing something like the balanced scorecard.

3. Choose the critical measure or two that would be most influential on top management.
4. Utilize creative visuals and charts to simplify complex numbers.

One business executive equates the presentation of data to top management as using the dashboard of an automobile. What are those key things you need to know about how well your 'car' is running. Perhaps there are lights on the dashboard that only light up when there is potential trouble. Think about how diversity fits into the overall 'dashboard' of the organization and what indicators need to be there.

The competent business leader or diversity executive will utilize a full range of abilities to successfully assess an organization's diversity relative to organizational effectiveness. There is an additional quality that one can gain, or that comes naturally to those involved in the work of diversity—and that is intuition. Just as with the organizational readiness matrix, one can learn to spot and identify leading indicators that have an effect on the ability of an organization to maximize the capability of its people and the organization itself. Intuition is important in the development and assessment of the data that will comprise the overall strategy. Diversity as a performance factor for organizational effectiveness is more than the numbers.

CONCLUSIONS

The old adage, 'Be careful what you ask for' holds true with regard to measuring diversity for organizational effectiveness. Despite many challenges, diversity measurement can:

- Redefine measures of success
- Create accountability
- Identify areas to achieve value added
- Drive change
- Bring clarity and common understanding
- Create common efforts towards common goals
- Shape corporate image internally and externally
- Define what diversity is
- Influence decision-making
- Dispel myths

Clearly, measuring diversity in the context of organizational effectiveness is fraught with complexities. But, by keeping metrics in line with organizational goals and objectives, one can help minimize problems and create the focus necessary in the context of a particular organization.

An organization's leadership must be reminded that diversity is fact—a reality that exists no matter the state of the economy, the business or leadership values, or personal beliefs of any individual. Consequently, developing a strategy for measuring organizational effectiveness becomes a very important and fundamental tool for not only assessing and driving organizational change and impact, but it becomes a tool, a vehicle, that ensures the creation, management, valuing and leveraging of a diverse workforce for organizational effectiveness and *sustained and enhanced competitiveness.*

SPECIAL ACKNOWLEDGEMENT

The author would like to acknowledge the Conference Board's two Executive Councils on Workforce Diversity for their support, contributions and foundations to his research reports and to the special focus group—including members of the councils—that created the strategic diversity measurement model and the tactical diversity measurement model (the 'action plan') while exploring the development of models for furthering the work of diversity.

REFERENCES

Beer, M. (1980). *Organizational Change and Development—a Systems View*. Santa Monica, Calif.: Goodyear.

Hall, R. (1983). *A Diagnostic Approach to Organizational Behavior*. Boston: Allyn and Bacon.

Harrison, M.I. (1987). *Diagnosing Organizations: Methods, Models, and Processes*. Applied Social Research Methods Series, Vol. 8. Newbury Park: Sage Publications.

Hayles, R.V. (1995). Why bother with diversity? In *Diversity in Corporate America, 1994–1995*. Minneapolis, Minn.: Institute for Corporate Diversity.

Kaplan, R.S. & Norton, D.P. (1996). *The Balanced Scorecard: Translating Strategy into Action*. Boston, Mass.: Harvard Business School Press.

Katz, D. & Kahn, R. (1978). Organization as social systems. In E. Lawler et al., *Organizational Assessment* (pp. 162–184). New York: Wiley.

Miller, F.A. & Katz, J.H. (1995). *Cultural Diversity as a Developmental Process: The Path from Monocultural Club to Inclusive Organization*. The Kaleel Jamison Consulting Group, Inc., copyright © Pfeiffer & Company International Publishers. Published in the 1995 Annual No. 2. The basis for this model was presented by Jackson, B., Hardiman, R. & Chesler, M. (1981) in 'Racial awareness development in organizations'. Working paper: New Perspectives, Inc. The original concept was adapted by J.H. Katz & F.A. Miller in 1986 (*Developing Diversity*, The Kaleel Jamison Consulting Group, Inc.) and continues to evolve.

Nadler, D. & Tushman, M. (1980). A congruence model for diagnosing organizational behavior. In E. Lawler et al. (eds) *Organizational Assessment* (pp. 261–278). New York: Wiley.

Wheeler, M.L. (1996). *Corporate Practices in Diversity Measurement*. The Conference Board, Report Number 1164-96-RR. New York.

Wheeler, M.L. (2001). *The Diversity Executive: Tasks, Competencies, and Strategies for Effective Leadership*. The Conference Board, Council Report R-1300-01-CR. New York.

PART II

Legal and Cultural Issues

CHAPTER 5

Management of Diversity in the UK—the Legal and Psychological Implications

Jill Earnshaw

University of Manchester Institute of Science and Technology, Manchester, UK

SUMMARY

This chapter explores the extent to which legislative provisions and their associated case law can assist in organizational moves towards greater diversity. It demonstrates the way in which discrimination legislation can protect individuals from being un-favourably treated for reasons which relate to personal attributes such as their sex, race or disability. Discussion also focuses on the way in which employment protection legislation has broadened its remit to cover non-standard workers, in particular those who work part-time. Recognizing that women and ethnic minority workers who are appointed to traditional white male jobs are potentially open to bullying and harass-ment, the chapter describes the various avenues for redress against such treatment and questions the appropriateness of legal remedies. It concludes that the law can play only a limited role in ensuring that individuals are treated on their merits and their rights respected.

Individual Diversity and Psychology in Organizations. Edited by Marilyn J. Davidson and Sandra L. Fielden.
© 2003 John Wiley & Sons, Ltd.

INTRODUCTION

As we have seen from earlier chapters, the fundamental principle of managing diversity in the workplace is that employees should be treated as individuals rather than as a group and that individual differences should be respected and fostered rather than expecting conformity with stereotypical perceptions. In seeking to ensure that this principle is put into effect, the law can play only a secondary role because, for example, it cannot force organizations to employ individuals whom it does not wish to recruit, nor can it insist that those who are taken on are judged on their merits. The contribution which the law can make is to provide a framework within which organizations will know that their actions are deemed by the society of the time to be appropriate and to provide equally to all those employed, a fallback of legal remedies should the rights created by the framework be infringed.

The principal contribution which the law has made in this area has been to outlaw increasingly certain types of decision-making by organizations which are not based on the ability of individuals to do their job. In addition, there have been moves away from standard models of full-time, permanent employment when legislating in the field of employment protection rights towards a recognition of more varied and atypical patterns of employment. This chapter will demonstrate how the discrimination legislation and other relevant legislative provisions are applicable to moves towards a more diverse workforce and its subsequent management. It will also highlight the psychological effects on individuals of unlawful discrimination and investigate the extent to which the law can provide adequate and appropriate remedies.

SELECTING INDIVIDUALS ON THEIR MERIT

DISCRIMINATION LEGISLATION SURROUNDING RECRUITMENT AND PROMOTION

Moving to a more diverse workforce inevitably involves changes to the composition of staff and may mean that jobs which have, for example, traditionally been done by white men are opened up to women and members of ethnic minority groups. In such circumstances, it is clearly important that individuals should be judged on their ability to do the job rather than on preconceived ideas about the suitability and attributes of a particular sex or racial group.

Until recently, employers in the UK were relatively unrestrained by the law in their ability to recruit the workforce of their choice and to maintain its traditional composition. Only decisions based on sex or race were open to legal challenge.[1] However, in 1995, after persistent lobbying by various pressure groups, disability discrimination was given legal protection by the Disability Discrimination Act, modelled in some respects on the US Americans with Disabilities Act 1991 (Doyle, 1993). More recently, the Gender-Reassignment Regulations 1999 were passed to give effect to a ruling of the European Court of Justice (ECJ) that discrimination against transsexuals who had undergone gender reassignment or who were intending to do so was contrary to the 1976 EU Equal Treatment Directive. In contrast, there is currently no legislation to outlaw discrimination on grounds of sexual orientation and the UK Employment Appeal Tribunal has confirmed that such treatment does not lie within the ambit of the sex discrimination legislation.[2]

Each of the pieces of legislation work to avoid the fact of sex, race, disability and the like from playing an improper part in recruitment (and other) decisions by use of the concept of 'direct' discrimination. For example, Section 1(1)(a) of the Sex Discrimination Act 1975 provides that: 'a person discriminates against a woman if *on the grounds of her sex* he treats her less favourably than he treats or would treat a man'.

Direct discrimination thus embodies the notion of a comparison between the treatment of a woman and a similarly placed man where the basis for the differential treatment is her sex. In deciding whether the treatment was, or was not, 'on grounds of sex', case law (*James v. Eastleigh Borough Council* [1990] IRLR 288) has established that the question to be asked is, '*But for* her sex, would she have been treated in this way?' So, for example, if a woman is asked at an interview questions about her plans for a family or how she intends to cope with childcare, and such questions would not have been (or were not) asked of male candidates, such questioning would constitute sex discrimination. The Act applies equally to men, and the Race Relations Act 1976 incorporates a similar notion of discrimination where 'on racial grounds'[3] a person is treated less favourably than other persons.

Although in many respects the Disability Discrimination Act is similar to the legislation on sex and race, there are certain important differences.[4] First, 'direct' discrimination is defined more widely, as less favourable treatment 'for a reason relating to' the person's disability rather than 'on grounds of' disability. This means that, for example, an employer who has no problem with employing blind persons but objects to the presence of dogs on the premises would still discriminate under the Act by refusing employment to a blind person with a guide dog. Secondly, unlike the sex and race discrimination legislation, the employer is provided with a 'justification' defence—no doubt because while in general a person's sex or race should not impact on their ability to do the job in question, a person's disability may very well do so.

Because one of the aims of the 1995 Act was to remove some of the structural barriers to the entry of disabled persons into employment, there is an additional definition of discrimination, namely, that the employer has failed in the duty of 'reasonable adjustment', such duty arising where any arrangements made by or on behalf of an employer or any physical feature of premises occupied by the employer place the disabled person concerned at a substantial disadvantage in comparison with non-disabled people (Section 6(1)). At its most simplistic level, this would cover the issue of wheelchair access to the employer's premises, but it could also extend, for example, to the lighting in an interview room (see *Ridout v. TC Group* [1998] IRLR 628) or insistence that a job be done on a full-time basis. The legal provisions on reasonable adjustments and their relationship to justification defences are complex, but it is nevertheless clear from the developing case law that, depending on the extent of the employer's knowledge of a person's disability, there is an expectation that thought should be given to adapting premises, equipment or the way in which a job has traditionally been carried out, in order to level the playing field for disabled persons.

While the Sex Discrimination Act and the Race Relations Act do not contain provisions on 'reasonable adjustments', they do seek to challenge job requirements which may have a greater impact on one sex rather than the other or on certain racial groups. Thus, what is termed 'indirect' discrimination is the application of a 'requirement or condition' or a 'provision, criterion or practice' which would be to the detriment of a considerably larger proportion of women than men (or vice versa) and which cannot be justified by the employer (Section 1(1) (b) of the Sex Discrimination Act).[5] In consequence, employers have increasingly faced legal claims in respect of, for example, mobility requirements, rigid shift patterns or insistence on full-time working where these act to the detriment of working mothers.

STEREOTYPING

In the early days of the sex and race discrimination legislation, it was not unusual to find instances of overt sexist and racist attitudes on the part of employers. Scrutiny of more recent employment tribunal decisions would reveal that this is now relatively rare, but while on the one hand this may be considered encouraging, it is also the case that the more subtle and often subconscious forms of bias which continue to prevail are less easy both to identify and to change. Racial and sexual stereotyping is something which to a greater or lesser extent a large proportion of the population will face from time to time, but it is no less significant for its pervasiveness because without being checked it can deny employment opportunities to minority groups just as effectively as outright bigotry.

Employment tribunals in the UK have been aware for some time of the difficulties faced by individuals in proving that issues of sex or race have been at the root of decisions not to appoint them or to deny them opportunities for promotion. Led by guidance from the Court of Appeal (e.g. in the case of *Noone v. NW Thames Regional Health Authority* [1988] IRLR 195), they now approach such cases by looking to the employer for an explanation of less favourable treatment, once that (plus a difference in e.g. race or sex) has been established by the applicant. If such explanation is not forthcoming or is found by the tribunal to be unsatisfactory, then an *inference* of unlawful discrimination may be drawn, regardless of the absence of concrete proof.[6]

There is a view that subconscious bias and stereotyping can be identified by analysing the language used by those involved in, for example, the recruitment process and although the use of expert witnesses to testify as to such matters is relatively rare in employment tribunals in the UK, it is not entirely unknown. In the case brought by Alison Halford against the Northamptonshire Police Authority in 1990 (Case No. 13660/90) evidence was given by an occupational psychologist about how sex stereotyping can arise and the conditions which promote it in the work setting. In particular, it was pointed out that the 'rarity' of the individual increases the likelihood of sex stereotyping and that imprecise evaluation criteria or lack of prior agreement on the criteria to be used allow stereotypes more scope to influence the evaluation process. While employment tribunals are not expected to have detailed knowledge of stereotyping and subconscious bias, they will generally be extremely suspicious of recruitment or promotion procedures which are not based on objective criteria related to the requirements of the job and would certainly have concerns where an employer's evidence is to the effect that the individual in question would not have 'fitted in'.

ENCOURAGING MINORITIES TO APPLY

Organizations which seek to introduce diversity into their workforce may be tempted to recruit preferentially members of a particular ethnic minority group or the under-represented sex. However, they may face some difficulty in doing so because, as alluded to earlier, preferential treatment of women will constitute discrimination against men and selective appointment of ethnic minority groups will discriminate against for example the white majority. Only in the case of disability is such 'reverse' discrimination lawful because the Disability Discrimination Act operates asymmetrically—in other words, a claim can be made under this piece of legislation only by a person who is disabled. An employer who seeks to increase the proportion of disabled workers in the organization cannot therefore be challenged legally by equally well-qualified able-bodied workers.

There are, however, certain limited provisions in the Sex Discrimination Act and the Race Relations Act for what might be termed 'positive' discrimination in relation to training and recruitment. Section 47 of the Sex Discrimination Act allows for single-sex training if there is an under-representation of workers of a given sex doing a particular kind of work so that, for example, an organization which has relatively few women managers would be permitted to introduce a 'Women in Management' training programme. In a similar way, where there is an under-representation of a particular minority ethnic group within the workforce in comparison with the geographical area from which recruits are drawn, Section 38 of the Race Relations Act provides that employers may encourage applications from members of the under-represented group. Advertisements urging members of the black community in London to apply for employment in the Metropolitan Police Force would be a good example of the use of this provision.

Other forms of positive action which may assist employees to combine the demands of home and work, such as flexible work schedules or the provision of workplace crèches, are unlikely to transgress statutory requirements even if they benefit more women than men. However, while the use of targets (as opposed to quotas) to increase, for example, minority ethnic representation, is not in itself unlawful, there may be a tendency, as with the encouragement of applications, to discriminate at the point of selection.

EMPLOYMENT PROTECTION RIGHTS FOR A MORE DIVERSE WORKFORCE

By the mid 1970s the contract of employment had ceased to be the sole regulator of the employment relationship and the terms and conditions under which individuals worked for their employer. Employment protection legislation was appearing on the statute books which provided, for example, job security in the form of unfair dismissal protection, and statutory minimum rights in respect of matters such as maternity leave, notice periods, guarantee payments, itemized pay statements and redundancy pay. However, the majority of these new rights were limited to 'employees' as opposed to the self-employed and depended upon completion of a qualifying period of employment which itself was determined by the number of hours worked per week. In essence, the legislation was focused on those full-time, permanent members of the workforce who would nowadays be described as 'core' rather than 'peripheral' or 'atypical'.

During the 1980s and 1990s the workforce began to diversify in ways which meant that the model of employment upon which the statutory employment protection rights were based became increasingly unrealistic as a representation of the way in which people worked (Felstead & Jewson, 1999). Full-time, permanent working gave way to more varied patterns of part-time and temporary work and there was a substantial rise in the numbers of individuals who, while being classified legally as self-employed, were often economically dependent on a single employer or a small number of employers (O'Reilly & Fagan, 1998; Rodgers & Rodgers, 1988; Rubery et al., 1993). By the mid 1980s, it was estimated that one-third of the workforce fell outside the remit of employment protection legislation (Leighton & Painter, 1987).

In 1991 the hours requirement for unfair dismissal rights was challenged legally as being indirectly sex discriminatory and hence contrary to the EU Equal Treatment Directive (76/207) and Article 119 (now 141) of the Treaty of Rome (*R v. Secretary of State for Employment, ex parte* EOC [1994] IRLR 493) on the basis that women's hours of work were in general lower than men's and hence fewer women could meet the statutory thresholds. The case was brought by the UK Equal Opportunities Commission (EOC) and was regarded as a landmark victory because it led to abolition of the hours requirement throughout the various employment protection rights. Pressure from the adoption of the 1992 EU Pregnant Workers' Directive also led (in the Trade Union Reform and Employment Rights Act 1993) to the abolition of the qualifying period for rights to basic maternity leave.[7]

Equally significantly, when the Labour government took office in 1997 it became concerned about confining its programme of proposed new employment legislation to 'employees', in part because of the numbers of people such as homeworkers and agency workers who were generally classed as self-employed and in part because the boundary between employment and self-employment was becoming increasingly blurred. It therefore commissioned research to ascertain the likely effect on the coverage of legislation if rights were to be extended to 'workers'—who would not necessarily be regarded as employees (Burchell et al., 1998). The consequence was that not only were new rights under the National Minimum Wage Act 1998 and the Working Time Regulations 1998 accorded to 'workers', but in addition, the Secretary of State reserved the right in the Employment Relations Act 1999 to extend the coverage of *existing* employment protection rights should the government choose to do so. Furthermore, homeworkers and agency workers, who were felt to be particularly vulnerable groups, were specifically included in the legislation. This combination of government initiative and pressure from the EU may not have brought each and every member of the diverse workforce under the umbrella of the law's protection but it has undoubtedly widened the remit very substantially.

MOVES TO MORE FLEXIBLE, INDIVIDUALIZED WORKING PATTERNS

USE OF INDIRECT DISCRIMINATION PROVISIONS

Given the rapid and extensive growth of part-time working, particularly by women with young children, it was clearly a significant step forward to extend employment protection rights to those who did not work full-time. Historically, however, while part-time working may have held attractions not only to the individuals concerned but also to employers seeking to achieve more flexibility in the organization of working time, it also had significant disadvantages. Although the EOC's victory and subsequent amendment of the legislation meant that henceforth employers could not, for example, deny maternity leave to their part-timers, other areas of working life were untouched by the changes and in many cases, part-time work remained low paid and low status (Grimshaw & Rubery, 1997).

Some of these disadvantages have now been overcome as a result of legal claims based on the indirect sex discrimination provisions discussed earlier in the chapter. Arguably the most significant have been those which have challenged employers' rules on the exclusion of part-timers from occupational pensions, in which EU case law has played a crucial role. As far back as 1986, the ECJ ruled that exclusion of part-time workers from the pension scheme where this had a disparate impact on women would constitute indirect sex discrimination contrary to Article 119 of the Treaty of Rome unless it could be objectively justified.[8] More recently, in the case of *Preston and ors v. Wolverhampton Healthcare Trust* (c-78/98 [2000] IRLR 506, ECJ) it held that the rule under the UK Equal Pay Act 1970 which prevented applicants from backdating pension membership to a time prior to two years before the date they brought proceedings also breached European law.

The indirect sex discrimination provisions have been used in a similar way to challenge inflexible working time arrangements. For example, in the case of *Edwards v. London Underground No. 2* ([1998] IRLR 364), the applicant was a single parent who had a young child and worked from around 8 a.m. to 4 p.m. as a train operator. In 1991 London Underground announced a new shift system which would have meant a much earlier start to Ms Edwards's shift as well as work on Sundays. Ms Edwards was not prepared to work the new system and the Court of Appeal upheld her claim of indirect sex discrimination even though she was the only female train operator out of 21 (95.2 per cent) who could not comply with the new system compared with 100 per cent of the 2023 male train operators. It sanctioned the approach of the employment tribunal to look at the issue of compliance more generally and take into account national figures which showed that 10 times as many women as men were single parents with responsibility for a child.

Even an employer's insistence that a job be carried out on a full-time basis has formed the basis of sex discrimination claims. As early as 1984, Ms Holmes, who was also a single parent, brought an application under the Sex Discrimination Act when the Civil Service refused her request to return to work part-time after the birth of her second child (*Home Office v. Holmes* [1984] IRLR 299). Although at the time there was considerable opposition to the view that refusing a request for part-time work could amount to the application of a 'requirement or condition' such cases have now become more commonplace.[9]

The use of indirect sex discrimination claims as a means of obtaining part-time working or combating disadvantageous treatment of part-timers has not been unproblematic, however. First, it is not always easy (especially e.g. for an unrepresented applicant at an employment tribunal) to show that the 'requirement' in question was one which impacted adversely upon women—as the case involving Ms Edwards illustrates. Second, an employer can always refuse a request for part-time work, or defend successfully treatment which impacts adversely on women (or indeed on a particular racial group), if there is 'justification' for so doing. However, where there is detrimental treatment of part-timers, the requirement to show an adverse impact on women is no longer necessary following the introduction of legislation to outlaw discrimination against part-time workers.

THE PART-TIME WORKER (PREVENTION OF LESS FAVOURABLE TREATMENT) REGULATIONS 2000

These EU-inspired regulations aim to protect part-time *workers* (i.e. not simply employees) against less favourable treatment than a comparable full-timer, but only where such treatment is 'on grounds' that the individual is a part-time worker. It is as yet early days to assess their success or otherwise, but from the time of their implementation they have been the subject of some criticism. First, less favourable treatment of part-timers is not unlawful if it can be objectively justified and it is uncertain how stringently this will be construed, for example, in terms of arguments about additional costs of part-timers. Second, there are significant restrictions on who can be selected as a full-time comparator, in that a part-time worker is normally permitted to choose only someone who is employed under the same type of contract, doing the same kind of work, at the same establishment (see Section 2 of the Regulations for specific wording). Given that an 'employee' contract is not defined as being the same type of contract as a 'worker' contract, it is not hard to see that individuals may struggle to find the appropriate comparator on whom to base their claim. For example, in the hotels and catering industry it is common for bar work only to be done on a part-time basis so that no permitted full-time comparator would exist. Part-time fixed-term staff who feel that they are unfairly treated may gain additional rights now that the EU Fixed Term Work Directive has been implemented in the UK, but this legislation would be likely to permit them only to compare themselves with permanent part-time, as opposed to full-time, workers.

ENSURING PROTECTION FROM HARASSMENT AND BULLYING

Ensuring that legal rights are available to all workers and that 'minority' workers are not discriminated against at the point of recruitment is, of course, only half the battle in providing legal protection to a diverse workforce. It is an obvious point that employers who seek to move towards greater diversity, whether in the sense of opening up traditionally male jobs to women, or to increasing their proportion of minority ethnic workers to reflect more accurately their customer base, or to providing job opportunities for disabled workers, will normally be able to do so only incrementally over a period of time. The initial pioneers in such strategies are particularly prone by virtue of their 'lone' status not only to stereotyping, but also to acts of harassment and bullying, and while, as we shall see, the law provides some redress, it does so only through fragmented provisions which are not specifically tailored to harassment and bullying in the workplace.

USE OF DISCRIMINATION LEGISLATION

Although by the early 1980s it was recognized that sexual harassment in particular was a huge problem for millions of working women, employment tribunals in the UK (and courts in the US) struggled to accommodate harassment within the confines of discrimination legislation, largely because of the need to identify 'less favourable treatment on grounds of sex'. Courts in the US initially regarded such behaviour as a personal matter in which they were reluctant to intrude (Rubenstein, 1983) and only after the Supreme

Court case of *Meritor Savings Bank v. Vinson* (477 US 57, 40 FEP Cases 1822 (1986)) was it accepted that sexual harassment was actionable under Title VII of the Civil Rights Act 1964 which outlaws discrimination 'because of' sex (or race). In the same year the UK Employment Appeal Tribunal (EAT) considered the issue in the case of *Porcelli v. Strathclyde Regional Council* ([1986] IRLR 135) in which a female laboratory technician's male colleagues indulged in unpleasant and humiliating behaviour towards her because they disliked her and wanted to persuade her to leave. They argued in their defence that they would have treated a male colleague whom they disliked equally unpleasantly and that therefore there would have been no differential treatment between the sexes. However the EAT rejected this argument on the basis that some aspects of their behaviour which had a sexual element to it (e.g. handing her a nail screw and asking her if she wanted a 'screw', and showing her a penis-shaped rod-holder and asking her if she had a use for it) could have no counterpart in the way in which they would have treated a man. The effect of the judgment has been that the Sex Discrimination Act has been relied upon not only where a woman has been subjected to unwanted sexual attention, but also where she has been the victim of abusive or bullying behaviour where such behaviour had sexual overtones. In a similar way, racial abuse and harassment have fallen within the ambit of the Race Relations Act.

Although it became increasingly common for victims of sexual or racial harassment to bring employment tribunal claims, the European Commission was concerned at the lack of progress towards stamping out workplace sexual harassment and commissioned a report in order to determine whether specific legislation at EU level was necessary to combat the problem (Rubenstein, 1987). Although the Commission ultimately concluded that it was not, because the existing Equal Treatment Directive (76/207) would be applicable in cases of sexual harassment, it did produce a Code of Practice and a Recommendation (Com(89) 568 final, 22.11.89) about how organizations should deal with issues of harassment at a practical level. The Code was particularly useful because it gave a definition of sexual harassment which was lacking at domestic level, and while it had no legal force in itself, it could be taken into account by tribunals in cases where they were uncertain as to whether the behaviour in question constituted harassment.[10] In other less clear-cut cases such as where female employees are subjected to patronizing behaviour which contains no sexual element as such, the issue can usually be resolved by reverting to the fundamental question noted earlier, i.e. 'but for' her sex, would she have been treated in this way?

The Code defined sexual harassment as 'unwanted conduct of a sexual nature, or other conduct based on sex affecting the dignity of women and men at work', and while many tribunal claims in practice have revolved round issues of proof rather than definition, the Code has been important at an organizational level in that it has often been the starting point for 'Dignity at Work' or similar policies where management might otherwise have struggled to delineate clearly the boundaries of unacceptable behaviour in the workplace.

Despite problems of definition and proof, it is now widely accepted that employees who are harassed on account of their sex, race (or disability) can seek redress via the appropriate legislation outlawing discrimination. In contrast, individuals who are targeted because of their sexual orientation or in connection with their undergoing gender reassignment ('sex-change' operations) struggled to find a legal avenue for their complaints. Attempts to bring claims under the Sex Discrimination Act were invariably rejected because so long as homosexuals of both sexes were, or would have been, equally badly treated (or, in the case of transsexuals, those undergoing gender reassignment from male to female being equally discriminated against as those changing from female to male), it was argued that there was no disparity of treatment between men and women.[11] Arguments that 'sex' should be equated with 'sexual orientation' were routinely rejected both in the UK and the US.[12]

At EU level there has been a disparity of approach between the attitude towards discrimination on grounds of sexual orientation and that involving transsexuals. In *Grant v. SW Trains* ([1998] IRLR 188) the ECJ held that the former was not contrary to EU law, whereas in *Chessington World of Adventures v. Reed* ([1997] IRLR 556) it ruled that discrimination on grounds of gender reassignment was contrary to the Equal Treatment Directive. The UK's response was to produce the Gender-Reassignment Regulations 1999, but, perhaps understandably, not to legislate to protect homosexuals.

Following the successful case brought in the Court of Human Rights by four military personnel who were subjected to intrusive questioning and subsequent dismissal from the armed forces because they were gay, the EAT decided[13] that the term 'sex' was ambiguous and should be construed to include 'sexual orientation'. However, its ruling attracted some criticism and was subsequently overturned by the Court of Appeal. For the future this is likely to be academic because in October 2000, political agreement was reached on a new EU Framework Directive prohibiting discrimination on grounds of religion or belief, disability, age and sexual orientation (EOR, 2000a). In addition, the European Commission, contrary to its stance a decade ago, has proposed a revision to the Equal Treatment Directive which would clearly define sexual harassment at work as discrimination based on sex (EOR, 2000b).

OTHER AVENUES FOR REDRESS

As the previous discussion has emphasized, harassment and bullying which can be linked to a worker's sex, race, etc. can now be remedied via discrimination claims. However, where these aspects are absent and the issue is one of 'mere' bullying or victimization, the situation is less straightforward. Despite lobbying from time to time for legal provisions specifically to protect against bullying in the workplace, no such legislation presently exists. One of the only possibilities for legal redress is a somewhat indirect route which relies upon alleging a breach of terms which are implied into all contracts of employment. In particular, it is an implied term that the employer will not without lawful excuse destroy the relationship of 'mutual trust and confidence' which exists between employer and employee.[14] If an employer fundamentally breaches this term by, for example, bullying, harassing, undermining or victimizing an employee, that employee is entitled to resign and claim to have been unfairly ('constructively') dismissed.[15] The fundamental drawback is that constructive dismissal claims can only be brought if the employee in question actually resigns, and although reinstatement is, in theory at least, a remedy for unfair dismissal, the chances of employees getting their job back as opposed to being awarded compensation are pretty remote.

In reality, most victims of harassment want the harassment to stop and the harasser to be punished as opposed to obtaining financial compensation (Earnshaw & Davidson, 1994) and in this respect, the Protection from Harassment Act 1997 would appear to be an attractive option for legal action. The Act makes harassment both a criminal offence and a civil wrong (tort) and although it was passed to deal with the problem of stalking, there appears no reason why it should not be relied upon by victims of workplace harassment and regardless of whether the harassment is linked to sex or race. In one sense the provisions of the Act are more limited than those of the discrimination legislation because they only make unlawful a 'course of conduct', which must involve conduct on at least two occasions. On the other hand, 'harassment' is defined widely as conduct which the person in question 'knows or ought to know amounts to harassment', and in civil proceedings under the Act, an injunction can be obtained to restrain the defendant's behaviour.

Although the present writer is unaware of the use of the Protection from Harassment Act in this way, two men have recently been jailed for 12 and 21 months respectively for workplace sexual harassment because their behaviour constituted an indecent assault (*R v. Wakefield, R v. Lancashire, 21.1.01*). This is a welcome development because there appears to have been little awareness in the past that this criminal offence will have been committed in the majority of incidents in which women are inappropriately touched by men, even if there is no 'assault' in the way in which this word is commonly understood.

PROVIDING REMEDIES WHERE PSYCHOLOGICAL HEALTH SUFFERS

DISCRIMINATION CLAIMS—COMPENSATION FOR INJURY TO FEELINGS AND PERSONAL INJURY

Whenever individuals make successful claims under the discrimination legislation they can be awarded compensation to cover their financial loss. Sometimes, for example if an employee has resigned because of sexual or racial harassment, this may be fairly easy to quantify. On other occasions, such as where there is an allegation that a person's rejection at a job interview was based on sex or race, tribunals may have a more difficult task because they will have to assess what were the chances that the individual would have been appointed had sex or race not played a part in the decision.

Financial loss aside, however, it is now widely documented that employees who are discriminated against experience distress and humiliation, and that bullying and harassment are harmful to health. Victims not uncommonly suffer a variety of symptoms ranging from nausea, headaches and stomach problems to disgust, depression and guilt (Terpstra & Baker, 1991). It is therefore significant that employment tribunals are specifically empowered to award compensation for injury to feelings, and although this may be a somewhat imprecise exercise, such awards have become commonplace as tribunals have increasingly recognized the emotional impact of discrimination. The case of *Lee v. DERA* (Case No. 3101771/98) serves as an example; Dr Lee's male line manager had objected to her being appointed to her post and continually undermined her. When she complained, no proper investigation took place because the manager's side of things was preferred and ultimately a reorganization was contrived which resulted in the termination of her employment because it was decided that Dr Lee 'did not fit in with Civil Service ethos'. In awarding Dr Lee £25 000 for injury to feelings, the tribunal noted that her treatment had caused her stress resulting in 'loss of sleep, nightmares, headaches, extended and difficult periods, hand-shaking and dental problems'. While this case cannot be said to be the 'norm', in that the average award for injury to feelings in 1999 was only £4060, it is notable that in the same year awards for injury to feelings accounted for around half of the total compensation in sex and race cases (EOR, 2000c).

Although the power to award compensation for injury to feelings has been an important factor in the ability of employment tribunals to provide proper redress to victims of un-lawful discrimination and especially sexual and racial harassment, an equally significant development has been the confirmation by the Court of Appeal in the case of *Sheriff v. Klyne Tugs (Lowestoft) Ltd* ([1999] IRLR 481) that in successful discrimination claims, tribunals are also able to award compensation for personal injury. This ruling has meant that if unlawful discrimination causes individuals to suffer a psychological illness, they can use the relatively speedy and inexpensive route of an employment tribunal rather than having to rely on a slow, expensive and complicated personal injury claim in the civil courts (see below). In the case of *Lee v. British Telecommunications plc* (Case No. 1100824/98) a night-shift worker who suffered racial abuse and threats over a three-year period and eventually resigned was awarded £104 674 including £12 000 for injury to feelings and £6000 for psychological damage. The treatment he had endured had resulted in his sleep pattern and concentration being affected, his self-esteem being lowered and he had even contemplated suicide.

CLAIMS UNDER THE DISABILITY DISCRIMINATION ACT 1995

As discussion in the earlier part of this chapter has indicated, individuals who suffer detrimental treatment related to their disability may bring claims under the Disability Discrimination Act. However, a second, related consideration is whether victims of bullying, harassment or victimization who in consequence suffer a psychological illness, thereby become 'disabled' under the Act. There is no doubt that there is the potential for, for example, depressive illnesses to be brought within its scope because mental impairments are included so long as they are 'clinically well recognized'. However, there is also a requirement for the impairment (whether physical or mental) to have a 'substantial and long-term adverse effect on normal day-to-day activities' before it satisfies the definition of a disability.[16]

Quite what the term 'clinically well recognized' means has been a matter of specu-lation, but case law under the Act now seems to indicate that the condition should fall within one of the recognized classifications of mental disorders.[17] Although a detailed discussion of the Act is beyond the scope of this chapter, it would seem that the somewhat loose use of the terms 'stress' and 'depression' in common parlance to cover a variety of conditions ranging from a few mild symptoms to a major mental disorder means that some psychological consequences of harassment and bullying will not amount to a disability because tribunals will not be satisfied (especially in the absence of expert medical evidence) that a clinically diagnosable condition exists. Because the effect of an impairment will be 'long term' only if it has lasted (or is likely to last) for 12 months, even some clinically well-recognized impairments may be excluded although there is provision for conditions which are likely to recur.[18] In addition, an impairment will only be taken to have an adverse effect on normal day-to-day activities if it affects one or more of a number of listed matters and but for the inclusion in that list of 'memory or ability to concentrate, learn or understand', it is likely that all but the most severe mental illness would fall outside the remit of the Act.

Even if an individual does suffer a psychological illness sufficient to amount to a disability, this does not of itself give him or her the right of access to a tribunal. What it does mean is that an employer may breach the Act if such an individual is then discriminated against by being treated less favourably for a reason related to their disability, or if there is a failure of the duty of reasonable adjustment. To take an obvious example, where an employee is on long-term sickness absence on account of a depressive illness and is ultimately dismissed, there may follow not only a claim for unfair dismissal, for which the current maximum compensatory award is £52 600, but also a claim under the Disability Discrimination Act, in respect of which compensation is unlimited.

PERSONAL INJURY ACTIONS BASED ON CLAIMS OF NEGLIGENCE

Personal injury actions arising out of work-related accidents have been a common feature of the business of civil courts in the UK for very many years. However, while they may occur frequently, they also involve the injured employee in complex legal issues such as proving that the employer could reasonably have foreseen the risk of harm which has been suffered and failed to take such steps as were reasonable in the circumstances to avert such risks. In other words, these claims are fault-based, requiring proof of negligence on the part of the employer.

Personal injury claims have traditionally arisen out of incidents causing physical harm, but in 1995 there was a landmark case involving a social worker who successfully sued his employer in respect of a (second) nervous breakdown caused by pressure of work.[19] Although the flood of claims which was predicted at the time has not materialized in the sense of reported legal cases, research shows that a substantial number of employees who are bullied, harassed or otherwise poorly treated by their employer to the point where their health is suffering, are seeking legal advice (Earnshaw & Morrison, 2001). Solicitors who were interviewed during the study indicated that this type of personal injury claim posed particular problems but also admitted that from time to time employers were settling out of court—and some of these cases have made the media headlines (e.g. Johnstone, 1999). Such case law as does exist has made it clear that employers are not under a duty to protect their employees from 'unpleasant emotions' such as anger or resentment as opposed to psychiatric injury (*Fraser v. The State Hospitals Board for Scotland* Court of Session, 11.7.00) so that, as in the case of the Disability Discrimination Act, to suffer 'stress' will not be sufficient for a legal claim. On the other hand, the House of Lords has recently ruled that where an employee complains of being harassed at work, it may be foreseeable that where no action is taken by the employer, the employee will be victimized and that this may lead to psychiatric injury (*Waters (A.P.) v. Commissioner of Police for the Metropolis* [2000] IRLR 720).

CONCLUSIONS

The legal framework surrounding issues of diversity and the management of a diverse workforce which have been discussed here protect individuals only in the sense that if their legal rights are infringed, they may make a legal claim and, if successful, receive compensation. It is self-evident, however, that monetary awards are a poor way to remedy much of the harm which may be caused, and it has already been noted that in cases of sexual harassment, financial incentives hardly figure in the decision to pursue a legal remedy. Neither should it be overlooked that not everyone whose legal rights are infringed will seek a legal remedy: they may well find such a course of action too stressful, too expensive or simply feel that, win or lose, it will be unlikely to enhance their future prospects within the organization. Those who do, may or may not feel that justice has been done, but in any event it is highly likely that working relationships will have been irreparably damaged.

What this means is that organizations which genuinely desire to move to a more diverse workforce which treats people on their merits and allows for individual differences, need to have policies and procedures in place which are tailored specifically to their needs. The law can provide a framework, for example by laying down minimum provisions for maternity leave, but an organization can then build on these, to give its female workers the flexibility and motivation to retain their commitment while raising a family. In fact, the new provisions on parental leave specifically encourage employers to enter into workforce agreements and only in the absence of such an agreement will the 'fallback' provisions of the regulations apply.

It is also clear that it is almost impossible for the law to play the sort of preventive role which assures employees that their rights will be respected and that they will not be subjected to treatment which may come about when they are seen to be 'different'. It is only organizations which, through their senior management, can create a culture which is accepting of difference and enable individuals to fulfil their potential. No amount of legal rules and regulations can be a substitute for management training which develops good interpersonal skills and makes workers feel valued for the contribution they can make. The law may shape people's behaviour at a societal level, but for organizations, it is the day-to-day interactions at an individual level which will determine people's experience of work.

ENDNOTES

1. Although religious discrimination in Northern Ireland was prohibited by the Fair Employment legislation.
2. See *MacDonald v. Ministry of Defence*, IDS Brief 688, p. 3.
3. Meaning, on grounds of colour, race, nationality or ethnic or national origins.
4. Note: the Act does not apply where the employer has fewer than 15 employees.
5. Currently, the Race Relations Act covers only a 'requirement or condition' which a considerably smaller proportion of persons of the racial group concerned can comply with compared with persons not of that racial group, but new legislation will have to be introduced by July 2003.
6. The EU Burden of Proof Directive, which was implemented by the UK government by the Sex Discrimination (Indirect Discrimination and Burden of Proof) Regulations 2001, formalizes this approach.
7. I.e. the then 14-(now 26) week leave: the qualifying period remained for the right to the extended period of leave.
8. *Bilka-Kaufhaus v. Weber von Hartz* [1986] IRLR 317.
9. See e.g. the recent case of *Lockwood v. Crawley Warren Group Ltd* (1176/99) in which the EAT held that an employer applied a 'requirement or condition' when it refused a woman's request either to work from home or take six months' unpaid leave in order to resolve childcare difficulties and suggested she take two weeks' paid leave and then return to full-time working.
10. E.g. the case of *Wadman v. Carpenter Farrer Partnership* [1993] IRLR 374.

11. E.g. in the case of *Pearce v. Governing Body of Mayfield School* [2000] IRLR 548, it was held that oral abuse of a lesbian teacher, by calling her "lezzie", "dyke", etc. would not amount to sex discrimination unless a homosexual male teacher would have been treated differently.
12. See e.g. *Smith v. Gardner Merchant* [1998] IRLR 510, *Gay Law Students Association v. Pacific Telephone Co,* 19 FEP 1914 (1979).
13. See note 2.
14. See e.g. *Malik v. BCCI SA* [1997] IRLR 462 H.L.
15. Employment Rights Act Section 95(1)(c).
16. See Section 1(1) of the Act.
17. American Psychiatric Association, *Diagnostic and Statistical Manual of Mental Disorders,* 4th edn. International Version, Washington, DC, American Psychiatric Association, 1995.
18. See Schedule 1, Sections 1(1) and 1(2).
19. *Walker v. Northumberland County Council* [1995] IRLR 35.

REFERENCES

Burchell, B., Deakin, S. & Honey, S. (1998). *The Employment Status of Individuals in Non-standard Employment.* London: DTI EMAR Research Series No. 6.

Doyle, B. (1993). Employment rights, equal opportunities and disabled persons: the ingredients of reform. *Industrial Law Journal,* **22**(2), 89–103.

Earnshaw, J. & Davidson, M. (1994). Remedying sexual harassment via industrial tribunal claims—an investigation of the legal and psychosocial process. *Personnel Review,* **23**(8), 3–16.

Earnshaw, J. & Morrison, L. (2001). Should employers worry? Workplace stress claims following the John Walker decision. *Personnel Review,* **30**(4), 468–487.

EOR (2000a). EU Anti-discrimination law agreed. *Equal Opportunities Review,* No. 94, 2.

EOR (2000b). Directive would bar sexual harassment. *Equal Opportunities Review,* No. 92, 45.

EOR (2000c). Compensation awards' 99, *Equal Opportunities Review,* No. 93, 11.

Felstead, A. & Jewson, N. (eds) (1999). *Global Trends in Flexible Labour.* Basingstoke: Macmillan.

Grimshaw, D. & Rubery, J. (1997). *The Concentration of Women's Employment and Relative Occupational Pay: A Statistical Framework for Comparative Analysis.* OECD Occasional Paper No. 26. Paris: OECD.

Johnstone, H. (1999). Woman is awarded £67,000 for stress. *The Times,* Tuesday 6 July, 7.

Leighton, P. & Painter, R.W. (1987). Who are vulnerable workers? In P. Leighton and R.W. Painter (eds) Vulnerable workers in the UK labour market: some challenges for labour law. *Employee Relations,* **9**(5), 308.

O'Reilly, J. & Fagan, C. (1998). *Part-time Prospects; Part-time Employment in Europe, North America and the Pacific Rim.* London: Routledge.

Rodgers, G. & Rodgers, J. (eds) (1988). *Precarious Jobs in Labour Market Regulation: The Growth of Atypical Employment in Western Europe.* Geneva: International Institute for Labour Studies.

Rubenstein, M. (1983). The law of sexual harassment at work. *Industrial Law Journal,* **12**(1), 1–16.

Rubenstein, M. (1987). *The Dignity of Women at Work: A Report on the Problem of Sexual Harassment in the Member States of the European Communities.* Office for Official Publications.

Rubery, J., Earnshaw, J. & Burchell, B. (1993). *New Forms and Patterns of Employment: The Role of Self-Employment in Britain.* Bremen: Nomos.

Terpstra, D.E. & Baker, D.D (1991). Sexual harassment at work: the psychosocial issues. In M.J. Davidson & J. Earnshaw (eds) *Vulnerable Workers: Psychosocial and Legal Issues.* Chichester: Wiley.

CHAPTER 6

Affirmative Action as a Means of Increasing Workforce Diversity

Alison M. Konrad
Temple University, Philadelphia, USA
Frank Linnehan
Drexel University, Philadelphia, USA

SUMMARY

This chapter describes the nature of affirmative action (AA) programmes with particular emphasis on the US and summarizes evidence regarding their effects. A distinguishing feature of AA is that it is proactive rather than reactive, influencing organizations to actively recruit and promote members of historically disadvantaged groups rather than seeking to identify and correct past instances of discrimination. The chapter summarizes empirical evidence showing that AA has been generally effective for improving employment and educational opportunities for disadvantaged groups. The chapter also marshals evidence that calls into question the claims that people have negative attitudes towards AA programmes or that AA programmes stigmatize beneficiaries. We draw implications for future research by presenting evidence that anti-AA attitudes may be linked with racist and sexist beliefs, discussing the importance of documenting the existence of discrimination, and noting the possible benefits to non-beneficiaries of supporting AA.

Individual Diversity and Psychology in Organizations. Edited by Marilyn J. Davidson and Sandra L. Fielden.
© 2003 John Wiley & Sons, Ltd.

INTRODUCTION

Affirmative action (AA) programmes in the US consist of organizational goals for increasing the representation of historically excluded groups, timetables for achieving those goals, and organizational practices designed to achieve the goals within the stated time frames. AA is proactive in that it influences organizations to actively recruit and promote members of disadvantaged groups. Other government programmes designed to protect equal opportunity are reactive and focus on redressing findings of past discrimination. As such, AA is the only equal employment programme that does not require the victims of discrimination to recognize their condition and file a complaint (Crosby & Cordova, 1996). This feature is important because most victims of discrimination do not complain (Edelman, 1992).

AA continues to generate controversy, and AA opponents seem to be gaining ground in many countries around the world. In 1995, the European Court struck down a City of Bremen directive that ordered employers to hire a woman when there is an under-representation of women in the position and job candidates are determined to be equally qualified (Hodges-Aeberhard, 1999). In the US, the 1996 passage of Proposition 209 in California ended AA in college admissions, state and local employment, and in the awarding of state contracts (Smith et al., 1998). Australia's Equal Opportunity for Women in the Workplace Act of 1999 explicitly moved away from the language of AA, reduced reporting requirements, and allowed employers more flexibility in programme implementation (Strachan & Burgess, 2000; see Chapter 8 for more details). Not all recent actions have been negative, however. In South Africa, a decision of the Industrial Court upheld AA, ruling that it was acceptable for employers to consider whether a non-white candidate was historically disadvantaged in hiring decisions (Hodges-Aeberhard, 1999).

AA supporters argue that ongoing structural discrimination justifies the need for AA (Rosado, 1997; Hudson, 1999). Opponents label AA reverse discrimination against members of advantaged groups (Steeh & Krysan, 1996). Some opponents justify their anti-AA views by focusing on the dysfunctional behaviour of disadvantaged groups (e.g. teenage motherhood, criminality), leading one author to conclude that AA opponents 'transpose or hopelessly confuse the causes of inequality with the effects of inequality' (Hudson, 1999: 267). Such confusion abounds because the complexity of status attainment processes in post-industrial societies obscures the impact of discrimination and makes it difficult to challenge the belief that the system would be fair without AA.

Our review of the empirical literature indicates that AA has been effective in increasing the representation of historically excluded groups in organizations, thereby enhancing demographic diversity. Like all government and organizational programmes, AA is imperfect, and there is evidence of unintended negative consequences. Organizations with major problems should be encouraged to improve their AA practices, but developing an AA programme that will please all constituencies is likely to be impossible because redistributing power and status among identity groups is a process that is bound to generate opposition.

We organize this chapter into four sections. First, we describe AA in the United States and compare it with its counterparts in Australia because the US programme is often compared with others and there is much confusion about its nature. Second, we describe evidence regarding the impact of AA on the organizational representation of historically excluded groups. Third, we review the literature on attitudes towards AA. Fourth, we discuss research on the unintended social and psychological consequences of AA for beneficiaries. We conclude with implications for future research.

AA IN THE UNITED STATES

A common misperception about the US AA programme is that it consists exclusively of quotas or preferences. In fact, quotas and preferences comprise a relatively small proportion of US AA programmes and are undertaken exclusively by government and other public entities. Public sector employers may use quotas or preferences when a sufficiently compelling government interest has been demonstrated, for example remedying discrimination by the government entity itself. Even in these cases, AA preference programmes are acceptable only if no reasonable demographically neutral alternative exists, and the preferences are flexible, focused, limited in duration, and not overly burdensome to non-beneficiaries (Day, 2001). Federal government regulations explicitly prohibit private employers from utilizing quotas or preferences (see Revised Order 4, published under 41 CFR 60-2).

By far the largest component of AA consists of procedures and practices undertaken by organizations to proactively prevent discrimination and ensure equal opportunities for historically disadvantaged groups (Konrad & Linnehan, 1995a). Certain employers are required to have AA goals, but employers are not penalized for failure to meet those goals as long as they can demonstrate a good faith effort to attain them (Edelman, 1992). Below, we describe the overall structure of AA in the US to indicate which organizations are covered and illustrate the variety of AA practices undertaken. Then we compare the US AA programme with its counterpart in Australia. In doing so, we hope to add some clarity to the AA debate.

STRUCTURE OF THE US AA PROGRAMME

The US AA programme consists of two distinct parts. First, government agencies may use AA quotas or preferences in employment or in the selection of government contractors (Sarokin, 2000). Second, employers who have 50 or more employees and obtain contracts to do business with the federal government at the level of $50K or more annually are required to develop a written AA plan. Institutions of higher education receiving more than $50K of federal support annually through research contracts (which covers most large US colleges and universities) are required to incorporate both employment statistics and student enrolments into their AA plans (Bowen & Bok, 1998). The Office of Federal Contract Compliance Programs (OFCCP) oversees AA requirements for federal contractors (for detailed information, see the OFCCP website at http://www.dol.gov/esa/ofccp). Below, we describe the written AA programmes required of federal contractors.

AA REQUIREMENTS FOR US FEDERAL CONTRACTORS

US federal contractors are required to develop written AA plans which must contain: (1) a utilization analysis, (2) goals and timetables to reduce or overcome identified areas of underutilization, and (3) a set of specific and results-oriented procedures for achieving the goals and ensuring equal opportunities for historically disadvantaged groups. Utilization analysis is rather fine-grained and takes into account the fact that the demographics of the qualified available labour force are different for different types of positions. Underutilization occurs when the organization has fewer minorities or women in a particular position than would be expected by the availability of qualified workers in the geographical area where the organization can reasonably recruit. In such cases, contractors are required to set goals and develop procedures to help them achieve the goals.

Revised Order 4 in the Code of Federal Regulations (41 CFR 60-2) describes a wide variety of procedures for overcoming underutilization, and these regulations specifically state that private employers may not use demographically linked quotas or preferences to achieve their AA goals. The OFCCP website lists the following as best practices for AA:

1. Organizational leaders demonstrate and communicate a commitment to equal opportunity and AA;
2. Successful analysis and self-monitoring of the organizational workforce to identify and address possible areas of discrimination;
3. Good faith efforts to remove barriers and expand equal opportunities such as innovative outreach and recruitment programmes, employee development and training programmes, executive and management development programmes, succession planning, and employee support and mentoring programmes;
4. Accountability and measurable results from the good faith efforts.

Employers are encouraged to develop programmes that are customized to fit their specific needs. As a result, each organization's AA programme is a unique entity.

Oversight of the US AA programme consists of OFCCP compliance reviews, which are conducted on a random basis, in response to statistical disparities between the employer's workforce and other similar employers in the geographical area, and in response to complaints about specific employers. Approximately 4000 compliance reviews are conducted annually, and roughly 1700 of these result in conciliation agreements where the OFCCP finds what it considers to be evidence of discrimination and the employer agrees to put new procedures and monitoring systems in place and possibly pay a financial settlement to affected employees (see the OFCCP website).

Both private employers contracting with the federal government and public agencies as employers adopt various AA-related practices. Research by Konrad and Linnehan (1995a), which is described in more detail below, identified over 100 separate AA-related practices adopted by organizations. Organizations adopt some AA-related practices voluntarily. They adopt others in response to an OFCCP compliance review. Finally, organizations may be required to adopt specific AA-related practices in order to resolve a discrimination lawsuit.

COMPARISON WITH AA IN AUSTRALIA

Australia's AA programme resulted from the Affirmative Action (Equal Opportunity for Women) Act 1986. Unlike legislation in the US, Australia's Affirmative Action Act covered only women. The 1986 Act outlined eight requirements for organizational AA programmes, specifically:

1. Development and communication to all employees of an AA policy statement;
2. Appointment of a senior manager responsible for AA;
3. Consultation with trade unions;
4. Consultation with employees, particularly women;
5. Analysis of the organization's employment profile by job classification and gender;
6. Review of human resource practices;
7. Setting of goals against which to measure progress;
8. Monitoring and evaluation (Sheridan, 1998).

Organizations with over 100 employees were required to complete a standardized annual report detailing their employment statistics and human resource practices. These reports were graded on a five-point quality scale by the Australian Affirmative Action Agency.

With the election of a conservative coalition federal government in 1996, the legislation was reviewed. The Equal Opportunity for Women in the Workplace Act 1999 initiated changes in Australia's AA programme starting in January 2000 (information on the Act can be found at http://www.eeo.gov.au). Reporting is still required, but employers are no longer required to use the standardized reporting form. Additionally, since 1999, the Affirmative Action Agency has abandoned quality grading of reports and assesses only whether the reports meet minimum requirements (Strachan & Burgess, 2000).

Table 6.1 shows a comparison between AA programmes for private employers in Australia and the US. In Australia and the US, AA is a government programme with a basis in legislation and Presidential Executive Orders, respectively (see Konrad & Linnehan, 1999, for a detailed legislative history of the US AA programme). In the US, AA covers women and people of colour while the Australian specific programme covers only women. The US and Australian programmes include the setting of goals against which progress can be measured. In both Australia and the US, AA is overseen by a federal agency which reviews reports submitted by employers, but (as discussed in Chapter 7) the Australian programme has weaker penalties for non-compliance (being named in Parliament) compared to the millions of dollars in financial settlements reported by the OFCCP. In neither of these countries does AA require private employers to use quotas or preference programmes.

TABLE 6.1 Comparing AA in Australia and the US

	Australia	US
Programme basis	Legislation in 1986 and 1999	Presidential Executive Orders (e.g. EO 11246 in 1965)
Groups covered	Women	Women, people of colour
Organizations covered	Over 100 employees	50+ employees and $50K in annual federal contracts
Includes goal-setting	Yes	Yes
Includes preferences or quotas	No	No
Assessment	Report reviewed by AA Agency	OFCCP compliance reviews (~4 000 annually)
Penalties for non-compliance	Named in Parliament	Financial settlements, possible debarment

Finally, it is important to note that there is no AA in Britain. However, in 1991, a government-led initiative, Business in the Community, launched 'Opportunity 2000' (recently renamed 'Opportunity Now'), a campaign encouraging employers to enhance employment opportunities for women, which was totally voluntary. By 1998, 325 organizations had joined this programme, covering approximately 25 per cent of the British workforce (Halford & Leopard, 2001). The programme encourages its members to adopt a five-point strategy to assist women's career development known as the 'Star of Change':

1. Demonstrate senior managers' commitment to women's development;
2. Invest in resources for staff training and facilities;
3. Change behaviour that fosters inequality;
4. Communicate ownership through workshops and publications;
5. Share ownership by obtaining feedback and monitoring women's career progression (Strachan & Burgess, 2001).

More recently, 'Opportunity Now' has launched a Racial Equality Initiative.

THE EFFECTS OF AA ON WORKFORCE DIVERSITY

Considerable evidence exists to support the effectiveness of AA for increasing the organizational representation of historically excluded groups in the US. In early studies, Leonard (1984, 1986) found that from 1974 to 1980, the employment of African-Americans and white women rose more quickly in US federal contractors (who are required to use AA) than in non-contracting establishments. Similarly, Rodgers and Spriggs (1996) reported that between 1982 and 1992, the employment share held by African-Americans was about 1 per cent higher in contracting than in non-contracting establishments. In addition to increasing workforce diversity among federal contractors, there is research evidence that AA also increased the numbers of women and African-Americans hired by police departments (Sass & Troyer, 1999; Lott, 2000) and the practice of using race as a criterion in admission decisions was recently upheld by the US Supreme Court in Grutter V. Bollinger et al.

AA in US colleges and universities has increased the presence of African-Americans in selective baccalaureate institutions, law schools and medical schools (Simpson, 1996; Bowen & Bok, 1998). Bowen and Bok (1998) argue that these gains have come at very little expense to white students. They calculated that dismantling AA in selective baccalaureate institutions would increase the percentage of white applicants admitted from 25 per cent to only 26.5 per cent while cutting African-American admissions in half. Indeed, where AA has been dismantled in US higher education, the numbers of African-American students have been decimated (Bunzel, 1997; Suhler, 1997). The loss of African-American medical students is particularly distressing since African-American physicians are far more likely than their white counterparts to provide health care for underserved US populations (Komaromy et al., 1996).

Other authors have taken AA research a step further by linking employment statistics to the presence of specific AA-related human resource practices. Konrad and Linnehan (1995a) identified over 100 formalized practices resulting from employers' attempts to enhance equal employment opportunity and fulfil AA directives. They categorized these practices as either identity-conscious (taking gender or ethnicity into account) or

TABLE 6.2 Examples of identity-blind and identity-conscious AA practices

Identity-blind practices	Identity-conscious practices
• Validating all testing and selection procedures and criteria • Posting or otherwise announcing all promotional opportunities • Initiating remedial, job training and work-study programmes • Developing and implementing formal employee evaluation programmes • Developing employee support and mentoring programmes • Developing a management succession plan	• Accessing recruitment sources likely to generate high numbers of female and minority position candidates • Monitoring the gender and race composition of applicant flows • Monitoring the skills and experience levels of all female and minority employees • Ensuring that women and minorities are included in training programmes • Ensuring that some women and minorities are considered for management vacancies • Encouraging women and minorities to participate fully in all company-sponsored recreational and social activities • Training supervisors on their equal employment responsibilities and holding them accountable

identity-blind (those that do not consider gender or ethnicity). Examples of identity-conscious and identity-blind practices are shown in Table 6.2.

The firms in Konrad and Linnehan's (1995a) sample of 138 reported a greater presence of identity-blind than identity-conscious practices, however, federal contractors reported more identity-conscious structures than non-contractors. Contractors who had undergone an OFCCP compliance review had more identity-conscious practices in place than those who had not been reviewed. Experiencing an equal employment lawsuit also increased the presence of identity-conscious practices. These findings suggest that government intervention is important for getting firms to adopt identity-conscious practices.

Importantly, Konrad and Linnehan (1995a) found that identity-conscious practices were associated with a greater presence of people of colour in management and an increase in the rank of the highest-level woman in the organization. Identity-blind practices were unrelated to the presence of women and minorities in the workforce. As further evidence of the positive effects of identity-conscious practices, Highhouse et al. (1999) found that African-Americans were more likely to apply for a job when an employment advertisement specified the use of identity-conscious policies compared to an ad that promoted identity-blind policies.

More recently, the work of Holzer and Neumark (1999, 2000a, b) has shed light on the effects of AA practices on hiring. This work was based on extensive data collected from 3200 companies in four US metropolitan areas: Atlanta, Boston, Detroit and Los Angeles. In their analyses, Holzer and Neumark tried to ascertain whether companies that use AA select women and members of protected groups who are less qualified than white males, thus investigating the allegation of AA's reverse discrimination effect. Their findings showed that firms using AA attracted a more diverse pool of applicants (Holzer & Neumark, 1999), and hired more women and minorities (Holzer & Neumark, 2000a). Companies that used AA in recruitment also used a greater variety of recruitment sources and scrutinized their applicants more intensely than employers who did not use AA (Holzer & Neumark, 2000a).

Significantly, these studies also showed that firms using AA in hiring were more likely to hire women and minorities who failed to meet the educational requirements of the position, and that these employees had lower educational attainment than white males in the same positions. While this finding may appear to support opponents' claims of reverse discrimination, i.e. AA practices force employers to hire women and minorities who are less qualified than white males, Holzer and Neumark's (1999, 2000a, b) analyses refocused this question on what is a more important issue for employers, that of the employee's job performance, rather than educational qualifications. They reported that women and minorities who may be considered 'underqualified' on the basis of educational requirements were just as likely to receive promotions and were paid relatively more than their counterparts in firms that did not use AA (Holzer & Neumark, 1999). More importantly, with the exception of Hispanic men, these employees were rated as least as highly as other employees. One explanation the authors offered for these results was that firms using AA in hiring provided more formal training programmes than firms that did not use AA, an indication that AA-sensitive firms made greater efforts to improve the job-specific skills of their new hires (Holzer & Neumark, 2000a).

Lott's (2000) findings are less supportive of AA. He found that AA increased the hiring of women and minority police officers, however, his research also linked an increase in the presence of women, African-Americans and Latinos on a city's police force with increases in violent crime. Lott argued that the form of AA adopted by police departments (changing the content of tests) may be to blame for these negative outcomes and that, although made illegal in the US by the Civil Rights Act of 1991, norming (developing different cut-off scores for different demographic groups) would be more effective for increasing the officer diversity without reducing quality.

More research is needed on the effects of AA programmes outside the United States. Some significant results have emerged, however. In Japan, Cannings and Lazonick (1994) found that the enactment of the 1985 Equal Employment Law had a significant positive effect on employment opportunities for university-educated women. In Canada, Leck and Saunders (1992, 1996) found that the Employment Equity Act had a positive effect on the number of organizations employing a representative number of women and visible minorities. Additionally, Leck et al. (1995) found that the Act contributed to lowering the wage gap between men and women. In Great Britain, Zabalza and Tzannatos (1994) attributed the 1975–81 rise in the relative earnings and employment of women to the implementation of the Equal Pay Act and the Sex Discrimination Act. In Australia, French (in press) found that organizations utilizing identity-conscious practices employed women at higher management levels than organizations that did not have identity-conscious structures in place.

DO PEOPLE HAVE NEGATIVE ATTITUDES TOWARDS AA?

Studies of attitudinal reactions to AA are important because of their implications for the perceived fairness of organizational decision-making processes. The organizational justice literature has demonstrated that employees who consider decision-making processes to be unfair develop negative attitudes towards the organization and reduce the effort they expend to conduct both required and voluntary organizational tasks (Brockner & Wiesenfeld, 1996). As discussed below, evidence shows that non-beneficiaries often express negative attitudes towards AA in general. Other research demonstrates that the public's knowledge of AA is faulty, however, and attitudes towards AA as actually practised are generally neutral to positive.

Many members of non-beneficiary groups express negative attitudes towards AA programmes (Kravitz & Platania, 1993; Steeh & Krysan, 1996), but members of historically disadvantaged groups are more supportive (Harrison et al., 2001). Members of advantaged groups tend to believe that AA programmes violate organizational justice norms (Bobocel et al., 1998). Leck et al. (1996) found that the extent to which AA was seen as a justice violation predicted workers' intentions to exclude and reject members of beneficiary groups in a large Canadian organization.

One of the difficulties of studying attitudes towards a complex programme like AA is the fact that people have little understanding of the way AA actually affects organizations. Members of advantaged groups tend to believe that AA simply constitutes strong preference programmes that undermine attention to candidate qualifications (Kravitz & Platania, 1993; Bell et al., 1997, 2000), and this belief is associated with negative attitudes towards AA (Kravitz & Klineberg, 2000; Kravitz et al., in press). *When presented with actual AA practices, such as aggressive recruiting and special training programmes, people generally provide positive ratings* (Kravitz & Platania, 1993; Konrad & Linnehan, 1995b).

Other research shows positive attitudinal effects among employees who experience actual AA programmes. Using data from the nationally representative US General Social Survey, Taylor (1995) found that white employees of AA firms had more positive attitudes towards AA than their counterparts in non-AA firms. In a study of over 7000 employees at a large US federal government agency, Parker et al. (1997) found positive attitudinal reactions to perceptions that the organization supported AA for all demographic groups, including white men. Specifically, the perception that the organization supported AA was positively associated with the perceived fairness of decision-making and perceived support for the employee career development.

These findings imply that sharing information about the actual human resource practices involved in AA programmes might enhance public support. Attitudes towards AA may not be easily affected by information, however. Bell et al. (2000) found that negative messages about AA caused white respondents to show more negative attitudes while positive information had no effect. Although they did not test the impact of providing information about the actual characteristics of AA programmes, their findings imply that education may not always be effective for engendering AA support. On the other hand, research by Donovan and Leivers (1993) in a small Australian town showed that negative beliefs about a stigmatized ethnic group were significantly reduced by a two-week paid advertising campaign. Their finding implies that educational interventions can be effective in improving attitudes towards disadvantaged groups and, possibly, programmes aimed at helping them.

ARE AA BENEFICIARIES STIGMATIZED?

Studying the social and psychological outcomes of AA is important due to the implications for AA beneficiaries' organizational experiences. Exclusion and harassment in organizations are associated with strain and negative health consequences (James et al., 1994; Klonoff et al., 2000; Schneider et al., 2000) as well as negative attitudes and intentions to quit (Laband & Lentz, 1998). As detailed below, laboratory research fairly consistently demonstrates the stigmatizing effect of AA on beneficiaries. These same studies show that AA's stigmatizing effects can be mitigated by emphasizing the selected candidate's qualifications. Additionally, laboratory conditions are often unrealistic, and the negative effects documented in these studies have seldom been replicated in the field.

In laboratory studies, members of advantaged groups stigmatize AA beneficiaries as being incompetent (Heilman, 1997; Heilman et al., 1997; Maio & Esses, 1998). Undergraduate women who receive preferential treatment in laboratory settings reduce their estimations of their own competencies (e.g. Heilman et al., 1998). The unintended negative consequences of AA are partly or wholly alleviated when the policy makes clear that merit considerations are central to the decision-making process (Heilman et al., 1998) or when beneficiaries are clearly high performers (Heilman et al., 1997).

The findings are fairly clear but must be interpreted with caution. *An important limitation of the research on self-denigration by AA beneficiaries is that the laboratory conditions generating such results are unlikely to be replicated in field settings.* For example, Heilman et al. (1998) told women that,

> because there have not been enough female participants signing up for this study so far, we now have adopted a policy of giving the leadership role to women if there is only a negligible difference between participants' scores on the SCSI (preferential equivalent [condition]), giving the leadership role to women if they achieve at least a minimum score on the SCSI (preferential minimum standard [condition]), giving women the leadership role (preferential absolute [condition]), and taking gender into account when we select leaders (preferential ambiguous [condition]). (p. 193)

It would be extremely unprofessional for university admissions counsellors or human resource managers to say such things to female candidates (e.g. 'because we have not had many female students before, we have adopted a policy of admitting women who meet minimum acceptable qualifications' or 'because we have not had many women in the job of marketing manager before, we now hire women if they meet minimum hiring standards'). AA as practised in the field is far more subtle and multidimensional. For these reasons, the generalizability of the laboratory findings of beneficiary self-denigration is questionable.

Additionally, the findings of field research have seldom replicated negative social and psychological effects of AA outside the laboratory. Undergraduate students who were AA beneficiaries showed support for AA and believed that AA helped them more than it stigmatized them (Truax et al., 1998). Graduates of an MBA programme had more positive job attitudes when their own gender was given preferential treatment than when decisions were gender-neutral (Graves & Powell, 1994). White women in the US General Social Survey database who were employed by AA or non-AA firms showed no differences in job satisfaction, intrinsic interest in work, and ambition, and African-Americans in AA firms had higher levels of ambition than their counterparts employed in non-AA firms (Taylor, 1994). Finally, white men in the General Social Survey who were employed by AA firms evaluated the work habits of African-Americans more favourably than those from non-AA firms (Herring & Collins, 1995). Women in AA firms, however, had less favourable perceptions of the work habits of African-Americans than those in firms without AA programmes, a finding that is consistent with the stigmatization effect.

IMPLICATIONS AND FUTURE RESEARCH AGENDA

Despite the limitations of research documenting unintended negative consequences of AA and the mitigating factors authors have identified which alleviate those effects, some authors have used this body of findings to justify their opposition to AA (Steele, 1991) or to suggest that AA be radically redesigned to reduce unintended consequences (Heilman, 1997). We meet such suggestions with scepticism because they imply that a non-controversial way exists for organizations to redistribute power, status and economic resources among identity groups. Research has shown that self-interest and the interests of one's identity group as a whole affect attitudes towards AA (Bobo, 1998; Harrison et al., 2001; Konrad & Hartmann, 2001). As such, it is likely that some members of advantaged groups will object to a policy that seeks to distribute more resources to disadvantaged groups regardless of the way the programme is designed. Below, we discuss the effects of prejudice and belief in the existence of discrimination on AA attitudes in order to raise questions for future AA research.

PREJUDICE AND AA ATTITUDES

Negative attitudes towards AA are linked to racism and sexism such that members of advantaged groups with more egalitarian attitudes often support AA (Bobocel et al., 1998; Little et al., 1998; Harrison et al., 2001; Konrad & Hartmann, 2001; Konrad & Spitz, in press). The link between prejudice and negative attitudes towards AA is another reason that it is probably not possible to redesign AA programmes in a way that will end the controversy surrounding them. The foundations of prejudice are complex and deep-rooted in society, and eradicating prejudice has proven to be difficult (Dovidio & Gaertner, 1998).

One suggestion for modifying AA in the US has been to change to a disadvantage-based approach rather than a gender- or ethnicity-based programme. This idea would decouple AA from prejudicial images of women or historically disadvantaged ethnic groups, perhaps reducing the impact of racism and sexism on attitudes towards AA. Sigelman (1997) found, however, that public support for disadvantage-based AA programmes is no stronger in the US than support for current AA policies. Additionally, political scientists have argued that social welfare, another disadvantage-based programme, has been rhetorically bound up with racist stereotypes, the result of which has been a dramatic decline in support among the US public (Carmines & Stimson, 1989). Should disadvantage-based AA programmes be instituted, they could meet the same attitudinal fate.

Also, as stated above, one reason some members of advantaged groups hold negative attitudes towards AA is that they believe AA constitutes strong preferences for members of disadvantaged groups that disregard qualifications (Kravitz & Klineberg, 2000; Kravitz et al., in press). Here, we argue that it is possible that racism and sexism are associated with the belief that AA constitutes strong preferences that violate merit criteria. The racist/sexist notion that disadvantaged groups are inferior in ability and competencies implies that AA beneficiaries are unlikely to be qualified. Hence, the idea the AA disregards merit is a logical outcome of prejudice. Future research should examine whether racism or sexism are associated with the belief that AA constitutes strong preferences with little regard for merit. Research could also examine whether racism and sexism affect people's reactions to educational initiatives about AA such that egalitarians respond more strongly to positive messages about AA.

PREJUDICE, DIVERSITY MANAGEMENT AND THE STIGMATIZATION OF AA BENEFICIARIES

It is also possible that only those individuals holding racist or sexist attitudes stigmatize AA beneficiaries. Criticizing AA programmes may be a socially acceptable way for prejudiced people to express their racist or sexist attitudes (Little et al., 1998), and denigrating the qualifications of an AA beneficiary may simply reflect symbolic racism or subtle sexism. To our knowledge, no studies have examined whether there is a link between AA stigmatization and racist or sexist attitudes. If the stigmatization of AA beneficiaries is limited to those holding racist or sexist beliefs, policies that hold people accountable for their behaviour seem to be a more appropriate response to this unintended negative consequence of AA than dismantlement or 'going back to the drawing board'.

On a more positive note, Gilbert and Stead (1999) demonstrated that raters did not stigmatize women and minorities hired by a company that 'seeks to actively recruit diverse individuals at all levels of the organization' even though candidates hired through AA were stigmatized in their studies. Gilbert and Stead's (1999) findings suggest that the diversity management label may be useful for reducing negative reactions to organizational programmes intended to increase the representation of disadvantaged groups. As Linnehan and Konrad (1999) point out, there is a great deal of overlap between the practices involved in AA programmes and those constituting diversity management.

BELIEF IN THE EXISTENCE OF DISCRIMINATION

Belief in the existence of discrimination is a relatively strong predictor of pro-AA attitudes (Swim & Miller, 1999; Harrison et al., 2001), and advantaged groups are less likely than disadvantaged groups to believe that discrimination against the disadvantaged exists (Bobo & Kluegel, 1993; Tougas & Beaton, 1993; Kravitz & Klineberg, 2000). Matheson et al. (2000) found that even when participants were told that a testing method discriminated against women, many men did not label the women's negative outcomes as discriminatory, whereas most women did. The belief that disadvantaged groups do not experience discrimination partly explains why advantaged groups show less support for AA (Konrad & Hartmann, 2001; Konrad & Spitz, in press).

One reason members of advantaged groups are less likely to believe that discrimination exists is because discrimination is difficult to detect on a case-by-case basis. Only when aggregate data are presented can people readily detect a systematic pattern of discrimination (Cordova, 1992).

Additionally, because the passage of equal opportunity legislation has made overt discriminatory barriers illegal, much contemporary discrimination is constituted of privileges received by the advantaged group. New research shows that advantaged groups are unlikely to recognize their privileges. Specifically, members of advantaged groups identify many sources of informal special assistance as critical to their own success but fail to recognize that the reason disadvantaged groups do not attain the same status is because they do not receive this special assistance (DiTomaso, 2001).

Finally, another difficulty for identifying discrimination against disadvantaged groups is that group members may be reluctant to label poor treatment that they experience as discrimination. Ruggiero and her colleagues (Ruggiero & Taylor, 1997; Ruggiero & Major, 1998) have demonstrated that disadvantaged groups resist labelling experiences as discriminatory because it requires admitting that one has been excluded by others due to prejudice. This admission is painful because it implies social rejection and lack of control over one's own fate. Advantaged groups use the discrimination label more readily because they face relatively little prejudice. Hence, for advantaged groups, admitting that one has been discriminated against in a single situation does not have the same implications of social rejection and lack of control in one's life overall.

Researchers may be able to increase support for AA by documenting the existence of current discrimination against disadvantaged groups as well as the lingering effects of past discrimination. Such documentation seems to require continuous updating to counter claims that discrimination and its effects no longer influence people's outcomes in contemporary society.

POTENTIAL BENEFITS OF ALTRUISM TOWARDS DISADVANTAGED GROUPS

In their insightful conceptual paper, Pratkanis and Turner (1999) identify several costs of resistance to improving the status of historically disadvantaged groups, including failure to identify the true causes of personal and social problems, limited development of personality and coping skills, feelings of hostility and aggressiveness, and susceptibility to propaganda. Alternatively, they identify several potential benefits of altruism towards disadvantaged groups, including improved productivity and decision-making, ability to learn from others, the development of a more complex social self, a sense of belonging, and a purpose larger than oneself. Research documenting the benefits of altruism for the advantaged group could help to garner greater support for programmes and policies that attempt to end disadvantage, such as AA.

CONCLUSIONS

AA programmes are complex and are primarily constituted of formalized human resource practices designed to prevent discrimination against historically disadvantaged groups through aggressive recruiting, targeted training programmes, etc. The use of demographically linked preferences or quotas is generally limited to the public sector, and private employers in Australia and the US do not include preferences or quotas in their AA programmes. Employers are encouraged to customize their AA programmes to meet their particular needs, and the resulting organizational programmes constitute fairly unique entities.

AA-related practices can be either identity-conscious or identity-blind, and evidence links AA-related practices to improved opportunities for beneficiary groups in Australia, Canada and the US. More research linking AA programmes to employment statistics is needed, however, especially in countries outside the US.

Two controversies surrounding AA include the possibility of negative reactions among non-beneficiaries and stigmatization of historically disadvantaged groups. Indeed, evidence shows that non-beneficiaries often express negative attitudes towards AA, but many people erroneously equate AA with preferences or quotas, and attitudes towards AA as actually practised are generally neutral to positive. Evidence suggests that the diversity management label may engender fewer negative attitudinal reactions, despite the fact that diversity management programmes are often quite similar to common AA practices. Also, laboratory research does fairly consistently demonstrate that AA has a stigmatizing effect on beneficiaries; however, laboratory conditions are often unrealistic, and findings from field studies show few negative effects.

Belief in the existence of discrimination enhances support for AA, but it can be difficult to convince advantaged groups that discrimination exists. Contemporary discrimination against historically disadvantaged groups is largely informal and subtle. By comparison, AA is a formal policy and a highly visible target for the disaffected. Also, disadvantaged groups hesitate to attribute negative experiences to discrimination because they do not wish to be socially rejected or lose a sense of control over their own lives. For these reasons, resistance to AA by advantaged groups is likely to be more forceful than resistance to discrimination by the disadvantaged. One thing researchers can do to increase support for AA is to convincingly document the existence of discrimination against disadvantaged groups in order to counter claims that discrimination is a thing of the past. Another thing that researchers can do is to document the costs to the advantaged group of the current state of affairs and the benefits of altruism towards the disadvantaged.

Hence, setting up a voluntary AA programme is likely to be controversial. As such, programme implementation needs to be carefully managed. Communicating the need for AA, perhaps by sharing employment statistics showing deficiencies, can be a useful first step. Sharing information about the actual identity-blind and identity-conscious practices being utilized can counter inflammatory rhetoric and enhance a sense of procedural justice. Publicizing the qualifications of members of AA beneficiary groups can maintain a sense that outcomes are fair and rewards are being distributed according to merit. Many activities associated with AA involve making human resource decisions more transparent, which also should make them appear less arbitrary. The result of a well-managed AA programme can be the increased presence of historically excluded groups combined with an enhanced sense of organizational fairness.

REFERENCES

Bell, M.P., Harrison, D.A. & McLaughlin, M.E. (1997). Asian American attitudes toward affirmative action in employment: implications for the model minority myth. *Journal of Applied Behavioral Sciences*, **33**, 356–377.

Bell, M.P., Harrison, D.A. & McLaughlin, M.E. (2000). Forming, changing, and acting on attitude toward affirmative action programmes in employment: a theory-driven approach. *Journal of Applied Psychology*, **85**, 784–798.

Bobo, L. (1998). Race, interests, and beliefs about affirmative action. *American Behavioral Scientist*, **41**, 985–1003.

Bobo, L. & Kluegel, J.R. (1993). Opposition to race-targeting: self-interest, stratification ideology, or racial attitudes? *American Sociological Review*, **58**, 443–464.

Bobocel, D.R., Son Hing, L.S., Davey, L.M., Stanley, D.J. & Zanna, M. P. (1998). Justice-based opposition to social policies: is it genuine? *Journal of Personality and Social Psychology*, **75**, 653–669.

Bowen, W.G. & Bok, D. (1998). *The Shape of the River: Long-term Consequences of Considering Race in College and University Admissions*. Princeton, NJ: Princeton University Press.

Brockner, J. & Wiesenfeld, B.M. (1996). An integrative framework for explaining reactions to decisions: interactive effects of outcomes and procedures. *Psychological Bulletin*, **120**, 189–208.

Bunzel, J.H. (1997). Hard facts about falling minority admissions. *The Washington Post*, October 12, C3.

Cannings, K. & Lazonick, W. (1994). Equal employment opportunity and the 'managerial woman' in Japan. *Industrial Relations*, **33**, 44–69.

Carmines, E.G. & Stimson, J. (1989). *Issue Evolution: Race and the Transformation of American Politics*. Princeton, NJ: Princeton University Press.

Cordova, D.I. (1992). Cognitive limitations and affirmative action: the effects of aggregate versus sequential data in the perception of discrimination. *Social Justice Research*, **5**, 319–333.

Crosby, F.J. & Cordova, D.I. (1996). Words worth of wisdom: toward an understanding of affirmative action. *Journal of Social Issues*, **52**(4), 33–49.

Day, J.C. (2001). Retelling the story of affirmative action: reflections on a decade of federal jurisprudence in the public workplace. January, 2001, 89 *California Law Review*, 59.

DiTomaso, N. (2001). The American non-dilemma: white views on race and politics. Paper presented at the American Sociological Association, August, Anaheim, Calif.

Donovan, R.J. & Leivers, S. (1993). Using paid advertising to modify racial stereotype beliefs. *Public Opinion Quarterly*, **57**, 205–218.

Dovidio, J.F. & Gaertner, S.L. (1998). On the nature of contemporary prejudice: the causes, consequences, and challenges of aversive racism. In J.L. Eberhardt & S.T. Fiske (eds) *Confronting Racism: The Problem and the Response* (pp. 3–32). Thousand Oaks, Calif.: Sage.

Edelman, L.B. (1992). Legal ambiguity and symbolic structures: organizational mediation of civil rights law. *American Journal of Sociology*, **95**, 1401–1441.

French, E. (in press). Approaches to equity management and their relation to women in management. *British Journal of Management*.

Gilbert, J.A. & Stead, B.A. (1999). Stigmatization revisited: does diversity management make a difference in applicant success? *Group and Organization Management*, **24**, 239–256.

Graves, L.M. & Powell, G.N. (1994). Effects of sex-based preferential selection and discrimination on job attitudes. *Human Relations*, **47**, 133–156.

Halford, S. & Leopard, P. (2001). *Gender, Power, and Organizations*. New York: Palgrave.

Harrison, D.A., Kravitz, D.A. & Lev-Arev, D. (2001). Attitudes toward affirmative action programs: a meta-analysis of 25 years of research on government-mandated approaches to reducing employment discrimination. Paper presented at the meeting of the Academy of Management, August, Washington, DC.

Heilman, M.E. (1997). Sex discrimination and the affirmative action remedy: the role of sex stereotypes. *Journal of Business Ethics*, **16**, 877–889.

Heilman, M.E., Block, C.J. & Stathatos, P. (1997). The affirmative action stigma of incompetence: effects of performance information ambiguity. *Academy of Management Journal*, **40**, 603–625.

Heilman, M.E., Battle, W.S., Keller, C.E. & Lee, R.A. (1998). Type of affirmative action policy: a determinant of reactions to sex-based preferential selection? *Journal of Applied Psychology*, **83**, 190–205.

Herring, C. & Collins, S.M. (1995). Retreat from equal opportunity? The case of affirmative action. In M.P. Smith & J.R. Feagin (eds) *The Bubbling Cauldron: Race, Ethnicity and the Urban Crisis* (pp. 163–181). Minneapolis: University of Minnesota Press.

Highhouse, S., Stierwalt, S.L., Bachiochi, P., Elder, A.E. & Fisher, G. (1999). Effects of advertised human resource management practices on attraction of African American applicants. *Personnel Psychology*, **52**, 425–442.

Hodges-Aeberhard, J. (1999). Affirmative action in employment: recent court approaches to a difficult concept. *International Labor Review*, **138**, 247–272.

Holzer, H. & Neumark, D. (1999). Are affirmative action hires less qualified? Evidence from employer–employee data on new hires. *Journal of Labor Economics*, **17**, 534–569.

Holzer, H. & Neumark, D. (2000a). What does affirmative action do? *Industrial and Labor Relations Review*, **53**, 240–271.

Holzer, H. & Neumark, D. (2000b). Assessing affirmative action. *Journal of Economic Literature*, **38**, 483–568.

Hudson, J.B. (1999). Affirmative action and American racism in historical perspective. *The Journal of Negro History*, **84**, 260–275.

James, K., Lovato, C. & Khoo, G. (1994). Social identity correlates of minority workers' health. *Academy of Management Journal*, **37**, 383–396.

Klonoff, E.A., Landrine, H. & Campbell, R. (2000). Sexist discrimination may account for well-known gender differences in psychiatric symptoms. *Psychology of Women Quarterly*, **24**, 93–99.

Komaromy, M., Grumbach, K., Drake, M., Vranizan, K., Lurie, N., Keane, D. & Bindman, A.B. (1996). The role of Black and Hispanic physicians in providing health care for underserved populations. *New England Journal of Medicine*, **334**, 1305–1310.

Konrad, A.M. & Hartmann, L. (2001). Gender differences in attitudes toward affirmative action programs in Australia: effects of beliefs, interests, and attitudes toward women. *Sex Roles*, **45**, 415–432.

Konrad, A.M. & Linnehan, F. (1995a). Formalized HRM structures: coordinating equal employment opportunity or concealing organizational practices? *Academy of Management Journal*, **38**, 787–820.

Konrad, A.M. & Linnehan, F. (1995b). Race and sex differences in line managers' reactions to equal employment opportunity and affirmative action interventions. *Group and Organization Management*, **20**, 409–439.

Konrad, A.M. & Linnehan, F. (1999). Affirmative action: history, effects, and attitudes. In G. N. Powell (ed.) *Handbook of Gender and Work* (pp. 429–452). Thousand Oaks, Calif.: Sage.

Konrad, A.M. & Spitz, J. (in press). Explaining demographic group differences in affirmative action attitudes. *Journal of Applied Social Psychology*.

Kravitz, D.A. & Klineberg, S.L. (2000). Reactions to two versions of affirmative action among Whites, Blacks, and Hispanics. *Journal of Applied Psychology*, **85**, 597–611.

Kravitz, D.A. & Platania, J. (1993). Attitudes and beliefs about affirmative action: effects of target and of respondent sex and ethnicity. *Journal of Applied Psychology*, **78**, 928–938.

Kravitz, D.A., Klineberg, S.L., Avery, D. R., Kim Nguyen, A., Lund, C. & Fu, E. J. (in press). Attitudes toward affirmative action: correlations with demographic variables and beliefs about targets, actions, and economic effects. *Journal of Applied Social Psychology*.

Laband, D.N. & Lentz, B.F. (1998). The effects of sexual harassment on job satisfaction, earnings, and turnover among female lawyers. *Industrial and Labor Relations Review*, **51**, 594–607.

Leck, J.D. & Saunders, D.M. (1992). Hiring women: the effects of Canada's Employment Equity Act. *Canadian Public Policy*, **18**, 203–220.

Leck, J.D. & Saunders, D.M. (1996). Achieving diversity in the workplace: Canada's Employment Equity Act and members of visible minorities. *International Journal of Public Administration*, **19**, 299–321.

Leck, J.D., St. Onge, S. & LaLancette, I. (1995). Wage gap changes among organizations subject to the Employment Equity Act. *Canadian Public Policy*, **21**, 387–400.

Leck, J.D., Saunders, D.M. & Charbonneau, M. (1996). Affirmative action programs: an organizational justice perspective. *Journal of Organizational Behavior*, **17**, 79–89.

Leonard, J. (1984). The impact of affirmative action on employment. *Journal of Labor Economics*, **3**, 363–384.

Leonard, J. (1986). The effectiveness of equal employment law and affirmative action regulation. In R.A. Ehrenberg (ed.) *Research in Labor Economics* (Vol. 8, pp. 319–350). Greenwich, Conn.: JAI Press.

Linnehan, F. & Konrad, A. M. (1999). Diluting diversity: implications for intergroup inequality in organizations. *Journal of Management Inquiry*, **8**, 399–414.

Little, B.L., Murry, W.D. & Wimbush, J.C. (1998). Perceptions of workplace affirmative action plans: a psychological perspective. *Group and Organization Management*, **23**, 27–47.

Lott, J.R. (2000). Does a helping hand put others at risk? Affirmative action, police departments, and crime. *Economic Inquiry*, **38**, 239–277.

Maio, G.R. & Esses, V.M. (1998). The social consequences of affirmative action: deleterious effects on perceptions of groups. *Personality and Social Psychology Bulletin*, **24**, 65–74.

Matheson, K.J., Warren, K.L., Foster, M.D. & Painter, C. (2000). Reactions to affirmative action: seeking the bases for resistance. *Journal of Applied Social Psychology*, **30**, 1013–1038.

Parker, C.P., Baltes, B.B. & Christiansen, N.D. (1997). Support for affirmative action, justice perceptions, and work attitudes: a study of gender and racial-ethnic group differences. *Journal of Applied Psychology*, **82**, 376–389.

Pratkanis, A.R. & Turner, M.E. (1999). The significance of affirmative action for the souls of White folk: further implications of a helping model. *Journal of Social Issues*, **55**, 787–815.

Rodgers, W.M., III & Spriggs, W.E. (1996). The effect of federal contractor status on racial differences in establishment-level employment shares: 1979–1992. *American Economic Review*, **86**, 290–295.

Rosado, C. (1997). Affirmative action: a time for change? *Latino Studies Journal*, **8**, 36–53.

Ruggiero, K.M. & Major, B.N. (1998). Group status and attributions to discrimination: are low- or high-status group members more likely to blame their failure on discrimination? *Personality and Social Psychology Bulletin*, **24**, 821–837.

Ruggiero, K.M. & Taylor, D.M. (1997). Why minority group members perceive or do not perceive the discrimination that confronts them: the role of self-esteem and perceived control. *Journal of Personality and Social Psychology*, **72**, 373–389.

Sarokin, H.L., Babin, J.K. & Goddard, A.H. (2000). Has affirmative action been negated? A closer look at public employment. *San Diego Law Review*, **37**(3), 575–636.

Sass, T.R. & Troyer, J.L. (1999). Affirmative action, political representation, unions, and female police employment. *Journal of Labor Research*, **20**, 571–587.

Schneider, K.T., Hitlan, R.T. & Radhakrishnan, P. (2000). An examination of the nature and correlates of ethnic harassment experiences in multiple contexts. *Journal of Applied Psychology*, **85**, 3–12.

Sheridan, A. (1998). Patterns in the policies: affirmative action in Australia. *Women in Management Review*, **13**, 243–252.

Sigelman, L. (1997). The public and disadvantage-based affirmative action: an early assessment. *Social Science Quarterly*, **78**, 1011–1022.

Simpson, G. (1996). The plexiglass ceiling: the careers of black women lawyers. *Career Development Quarterly*, **45**, 173–188.

Smith, E.L., Wilkinson, D.M. & Whigham-Desir, M. (1998). A disturbing proposition. *Black Enterprise*, January, 54.

Steeh, C. & Krysan, M. (1996). Affirmative action and the public, 1970–1995. *Public Opinion Quarterly*, **60**, 128–158.

Steele, S. (1991). *The Content of Our Character*. New York: St Martin's Press.

Strachan, G. & Burgess, J. (2000). W(h)ither affirmative action legislation in Australia? *Journal of Interdisciplinary Gender Studies*, **5**(2), 46–63.

Strachan, G. & Burgess, J. (2001). Affirmative action legislation in Australia: the legislative model. Paper presented at the Rethinking Gender, Work and Organization Conference, June, Keele University, UK.

Suhler, J.N. (1997). Affirmative action case has ripple effect; UT Southwestern, SMU say black enrollment down. *The Dallas Morning News*, October 21, 19A.

Swim, J.K. & Miller, D.L. (1999). White guilt: its antecedents and consequences for attitudes toward affirmative action. *Personality and Social Psychology Bulletin*, **25**, 500–514.

Taylor, M.C. (1994). Impact of affirmative action on beneficiary groups: evidence from the 1990 General Social Survey. *Basic and Applied Social Psychology*, **15**, 143–178.

Taylor, M.C. (1995). White backlash to workplace affirmative action: myth or peril? *Social Forces*, **73**, 1385–1414.

Tougas, F. & Beaton, A.M. (1993). Affirmative action in the work place: for better or for worse. *Applied Psychology: An International Review*, **42**, 253–264.

Truax, K., Cordova, D.I., Wood, A., Wright, E. & Crosby, F. (1998). Undermined? Affirmative action from the targets' point of view. In J. Swim & C. Stangor (eds) *Prejudice: The Target's Perspective* (pp. 171–188). San Diego, Calif.: Academic Press.

Zabalza, A. & Tzannatos, Z. (1994). The effect of Britain's anti-discrimination legislation on relative pay and employment. In P. Burstein (ed.) *Equal Employment Opportunity, Labor Market Discrimination and Public Policy* (pp. 329–342). New York: Walter de Gruyter.

CHAPTER 7

Principles and Practice of Gender Diversity Management in Australia

Mary Barrett
Griffith University, Queensland, Brisbane, Australia
Andrew Hede
University of the Sunshine Coast, Maroochydore, Queensland, Australia

SUMMARY

In this chapter we present a number of examples of Australian organizations which are acknowledged as implementing programmes at the forefront of gender-based diversity management. Ironically, perhaps, such apparent success stories in the area of gender advancement in the workplace are becoming problematic at the same time as—and perhaps even because of—the growing prominence of terms such as 'diversity management' and 'productive diversity' in academic, corporate and public policy discussions of how to improve organizational performance and achieve competitive advantage. Accordingly, the examples illustrating some of the most advanced current thinking and practice in Australia in gender-based diversity may also illustrate some of the dilemmas that arise from changing paradigms in diversity management generally.

INTRODUCTION

Diversity is a key characteristic of the Australian workforce. Yet this diversity is so far not reflected in the ranks of management, especially in senior management levels

Individual Diversity and Psychology in Organizations. Edited by Marilyn J. Davidson and Sandra L. Fielden.
© 2003 John Wiley & Sons, Ltd.

(Karpin, 1995: 232). This is apparent from an examination of the workplace situation of Australian women, indigenous people, people from non-English-speaking backgrounds, people with disabilities and older workers.

In this chapter, we begin by briefly outlining the situation of women in the Australian workforce, and contextualize these data by comparing them with similar information for other groups which have traditionally been the object of government policy to remove discrimination hindering workplace advancement. We also review Australian legislation relating to gender and other forms of discrimination and its efficacy, and then consider recent debates in Australia and elsewhere concerning the theoretical bases for dealing with gender and other forms of workplace diversity. Specifically, we consider the shift from equal employment opportunity (EEO)-based arguments to the various 'productive diversity' arguments. Finally, examples of organizational practice are presented and reviewed both for their achievements and for the ways they reflect the dilemmas and paradoxes arising from newer forms of diversity thinking.

WOMEN

Broad societal changes such as access to education, the increased availability of suitable jobs, contraception and increases in the number and acceptability of childcare facilities have all had a major impact on Australian women's participation in the formalized labour market. Towards the end of last century, more than 65 per cent of Australian women aged between 20 and 55 years of age were in paid work (Smith & Hutchinson, 1995), up from 24 per cent in 1947. Smith and Hutchinson predict that this figure will grow by one-third by 2011.

Despite this, Australia is still regularly described as having the most segregated and segmented workforce in the world, with gender being a prime determinant of the type of work people do and how it is organized. The range of industries women work in is narrow and within these they are concentrated in lower-paid jobs at the bottom of the employment hierarchy (Ronalds, 1987; Smith & Hutchinson, 1995). It is often pointed out how inadequately Australian women are represented in senior management. Figure 7.1,

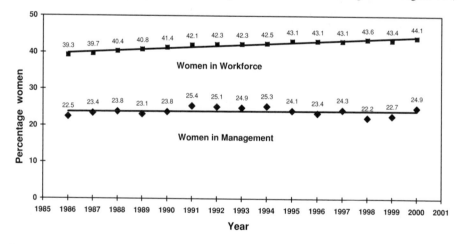

FIGURE 7.1 Women's managerial representation in Australia.
Data source: ABS (1986–2000)

TABLE 7.1 Australian average weekly earnings: full-time adults ($)

	Ordinary Earnings			Total earnings		
	Women	Men	Women's earnings as percentage of men's	Women	Men	Women's earnings as percentage of men's
1989–90	458	552	83.0	471	599	78.7
1999–2000	687	816	84.0	702	867	81.0

Data source: ABS (1989–2000).

which compares women's workforce participation with their representation in the ranks of managers and administrators, makes this clear. While women's workforce participation has grown from 39.3 per cent in 1986 to 44.1 per cent in 2000, there has been scarcely any upward movement in women's representation in management—the figure has hovered around 22–25 per cent for the entire period.

Further, the failure of women's average weekly earnings rates to make more than minimal gains on those of men is evidence of women's continuing secondary status in the workforce. As Table 7.1 points out, movement of women's earnings as a percentage of men's was scarcely more than one percentage point in the period 1989–90 to 1999–2000, irrespective of whether ordinary time earnings or total earnings are considered.

INDIGENOUS PEOPLE

Australia has a sorry history in relation to its treatment of indigenous people and this is clearly reflected in their current economic disadvantage (Norris, 2001). The overall employment participation rate of indigenous people is considerably lower and their un-employment levels much higher than for non-indigenous Australians. On both measures, indigenous women fare worse than men. Those indigenous people who are in work are much more likely to be in low-paid labouring jobs (24.3 per cent of indigenous workers versus 8.7 per cent of all Australian workers) and are much less likely to be in managerial or professional positions (13.9 per cent of indigenous workers versus 26.4 per cent of all Australian workers) (Norris, 2001). Again, on such measures, indigenous women have more employment disadvantage than indigenous men.

NESB GROUPS

Three successive waves of immigration of people from non-English-speaking back-grounds (NESB) have contributed to Australia's present multicultural heritage. The first, in the nineteenth century, brought Chinese, German and Jewish people to Australia. Soon after the Second World War, immigration was primarily from Europe and in-cluded Italian, Greek, Maltese, Yugoslavian, Dutch, Hungarian and Polish people. Since the 1960s immigration has been more diversified, with people from Turkey, India, Sri Lanka, Vietnam and Cambodia in addition to the groups already mentioned. At a for-mal level, government endorsement for the white Australia policy has given way to multiculturalism, which supports the right of all Australians to enjoy their cultural heritage and to equal opportunity regardless of their ethnic background. Nevertheless, the skills and qualifications of migrant workers have often been undervalued or not recognized at all, with many starting small businesses in their own communities as a way of avoiding unemployment or assembly-line work (Shaw, 1995).

PEOPLE WITH DISABILITIES

The 'charity' inherent in the model of employment, which encouraged people with disabilities to participate in a segregated setting, limited the recognition and valuing of the work of people with disabilities as well as their ability to control their pay and conditions. Quinn et al. (1993) emphasized, however, that only 20.4 per cent of people with disabilities are participating in the workforce. Earlier work, such as Cooper and Jongeling (1983), emphasized the limited acceptance of these groups on the part of employers, as well as their restricted access to educational and training opportunities.

OLDER WORKERS

The age of the Australian workforce is increasing, a result of the ageing of the 'baby-boomer' group (i.e. the population 'bulge' created by the larger numbers of people born in the decade following the end of the Second World War), a declining birth rate for the generations following the Second World War, and improvements in health and medical care which have kept people in productive work for longer. Compulsory retirement has been phased out in most state jurisdictions. However, a number of studies show the persistence of negative and unsubstantiated workplace stereotyping based on age, such as the view that older people are more likely to be absent from work, suffer from memory loss or diminished intelligence (Bennington & Tharenou, 1986; McGrath, 1990; CCH, 1995).

LEGISLATIVE FRAMEWORKS

The legal obligations of Australia with respect to workforce diversity arise from its treaties with the United Nations and its special agency for this issue, the International Labour Organization. Australian legislation to make sex discrimination illegal has existed in some state jurisdictions since the late 1970s. Federal legislation includes the Sex Discrimination Act 1984 and the Racial Discrimination Act 1975. There is also a federal Disability Discrimination Act 1992 and various state and territory anti-discrimination statutes which prohibit discrimination on a range of grounds, such as gender, pregnancy, marital status, sexual orientation and so on (Race Discrimination Commissioner, 1998: 7). As well as proscribing discrimination, much legislation has also aimed to encourage change in relation to access, status, power and rewards for people in the workplace. For women, programmes to promote equal employment opportunity have been mandated by legislation for larger employers (i.e. organizations with 100+ employees) for more than a decade under the Affirmative Action (Equal Opportunity for Women) Act 1986 (Ronalds, 1987). Following a regulatory review in 1998 aimed at reducing the compliance burden on business, this Act was amended as the Equal Employment Opportunity for Women in the Workplace Act 1999 (Hede, 2000).

LEGISLATIVE OUTCOMES

From the official data about the situation of women and other groups at whom this legislation has been aimed, it is clear that the efficacy of this legislation has been limited. In the case of women, one indicator of employment equity is their managerial representation. In the federal public service, for example, women comprised 26.1 per cent of the Senior Executive Service (SES) in 2000 as compared with 10.9 per cent in 1990 (PSMPC, 2000). This compares very favourably with the United States where the SES in 1999 comprised 21.8 per cent women, up from 9.5 per cent in 1990 (United States General Accounting Office, 2001). In the overall Australian workforce, a longitudinal study showed that women's representation in the management occupational category decreased during the period 1966–74, increased in the period 1974–84 after the initial sex discrimination was enacted, but remained essentially static in the period 1986–94 (Hede, 1995). However, a subsequent study which focused specifically on larger organizations covered by affirmative action legislation, found that between 1990 and 1995 women's managerial representation improved significantly from 17.2 to 21.7 per cent (Hede & O'Brien, 1996). The difference in findings between the two studies indicates that affirmative action legislation was effective—it improved women's managerial representation in the sector where it had coverage (organizations with 100+ employees) while during the same period women's situation failed to improve in the total workforce. It remains to be seen whether the recent changes in federal equal opportunity legislation which have resulted in less onerous compliance for organizations reduce the demonstrated effectiveness of the former affirmative action legislation.

The main changes to affirmative action in Australia with the implementation from January 2000 of the Equal Employment Opportunity for Women in the Workplace Act 1999 were:

1. The Affirmative Action Agency was renamed the Equal Opportunity for Women in the Workplace Agency (EOWA);
2. Reporting requirements were simplified and made less prescriptive;
3. Changes were made in the recommended content of programmes promoting equal opportunity for women in the workplace;
4. Organizations became eligible to be waived from annual reporting if the Agency is satisfied that they have taken all 'reasonably practical' measures to address equal opportunity issues and have complied with the Act for no less than three consecutive years (AAA, 1999).

DIFFERENCES IN VIEWS OF DIVERSITY

But a full consideration of the effectiveness or otherwise of diversity legislation depends at least partly on what view one adopts of diversity as well as the purpose of adopting diversity strategies. Both of these vary considerably. Textbooks for management students such as Loden (1995), and Davidson and Griffin (2000), divide diversity into two dimensions. First-level dimensions of diversity include differences which are visible to others and either impossible or difficult for individuals to change, such as gender and age. Secondary dimensions of diversity refer to characteristics over which individuals have a degree of control about how they are acquired, modified or removed. Such secondary characteristics include religion, work experience, geographic location, education, organizational role and level, family status, political beliefs, communication style and work style.

But this view does not capture the range of views inherent in different organizational approaches to diversity strategy or management. Bertone et al. (1998), in their review of the American and Australian diversity literature, discern at least five approaches to the issue of managing diversity, as opposed to diversity itself, although the two impinge on each other. They are, to cite these authors (pp. 22–23):

1. The traditional EEO definition, which deals with differences in gender, racioethnicity and age (cf., Overell, 1996). EEO definitions are generally concerned with raising the profile and improving outcomes of designated groups (such as women and the disabled) which have been shown to suffer direct or indirect discrimination in the workforce.
2. Broader definitions which recognize a range of human differences, such as physical ability, personal qualities (both innate and learnt) and sexual orientation (cf., Woods & Sciarini, 1995; Wallace, Ermer, & Motshabi, 1996).
3. Definitions based on the broadest possible concept of diversity, incorporating hierarchical levels, function and backgrounds (Cox, 1993).
4. The notion that a culture of valuing diversity has the capacity to create a pluralistic social order, resulting in organizational cohesion and international harmony (Cope & Kalantzis, 1997) and
5. Business oriented definitions, which view managing diversity as driven by business needs (Overell, 1996; Hay, 1996; Dawkins, Kemp, & Cabalu, 1995).

Business-oriented definitions of diversity management are both multifaceted and, at the moment at least, prominent in the Australian business environment. Because of this prominence, it is worth summarizing some of the most frequently cited business case arguments for a more diverse workforce.

REDUCED COSTS

The reduced cost argument for increased diversity proposes that, properly managed, greater organizational diversity will lead to higher employee satisfaction. This, in turn, will result in higher productivity and lower turnover and absenteeism. Conversely, organizations that do not manage diversity well will have lower productivity and high turnover and absenteeism. All these factors have a direct impact on costs, and hence affect the organization's competitive position.

MARKETING ADVANTAGE

The marketing advantage argument suggests that organizations whose workforces are diverse are better able to appreciate the needs of different market segments. As with the cost argument, this enhances the organization's competitive position. A major Australian bank has taken this argument a step further by developing a 'Women in Business' programme focused on women customers. At a recent conference on women, management and employment relations, the organization argued that the resulting customer pressure had led to changes in the ways women were deployed inside the organization. For example, women borrowers and investors demanded the opportunity to discuss their needs with women bank executives.

RESOURCE ACQUISITION

The resource acquisition argument underlies the goal of many organizations to be the 'employer of choice' in their industry, particularly from a diversity perspective. It suggests that organizations which promote themselves as managing diversity effectively will become known among women and members of other target groups as a good place to work. This in turn enhances the organization's ability to recruit good people from a wider societal base.

CREATIVITY

The creativity argument proposes that more diverse organizations tend to be more creative and innovative than those that are less diverse.

PROBLEM-SOLVING

Closely related to the creativity and resource acquisition arguments, the problem-solving argument suggests that a more diverse organization has access to a larger pool of information which can be drawn upon to solve problems.

ENHANCED SYSTEMS FLEXIBILITY

Finally, the enhanced systems flexibility argument, in the context of valuing diversity, proposes that dealing effectively with diversity forces organizations to become more flexible across a broad spectrum of systems issues. The result is that these internal changes enhance the organization's ability to meet the needs of its customer base and adapt to other aspects of its environment.

PARADIGM DEBATES IN DIVERSITY MANAGEMENT

Bertone et al. (1998) highlight the American origins of much of the literature and company evidence supporting the business case arguments for diversity. Moreover, they highlight the need to distinguish between 'managing diversity' and 'productive diversity' within the range of business case arguments (Bertone et al., 1998: 26). Managing diversity, which is the focus of much of the American literature, tends to refer to avoiding the problems that arise from cultural clash, whereas productive diversity has primarily an economic motivation, and focuses on the benefits to be gained from a culturally diverse workforce. The arguments as summarized above lean towards a 'productive diversity' focus. Yet, as we will see, this in itself is a potential source of difficulty if the economic motivation is less prominent at some point.

The Australian legislation summarized earlier was based on EEO rather than business case approaches, that is, approaches which aim to recognize and further the legitimate aspirations of society's minority groups. According to Overell (1996), EEO is a policy for dealing with social justice issues related to specific targeted groups, whereas 'productive diversity' seeks to derive economic benefits from using previously unrecognized skills and talents and using them in better ways. The other four views in the list by Bertone et al. are idealistic to varying degrees. The most idealistic approach is the view of Cope and Kalantzis (1997), who see moves in organizations to value diversity as having positive ramifications in the broader society and even in international relations.

In the literature as well as in business practice, both the pragmatic and the idealistic arguments appear to be gaining ground—albeit from opposing directions—on EEO-based arguments, which are increasingly seen as flawed. As mentioned earlier, Overell's (1996) critique is that EEO is focused on social justice rather than business goals. Others such as Burton (1992, in Hall, 1995) have argued that EEO approaches are ineffective even in their original aims of reducing disadvantage; that is, that without extending EEO programmes to include broader notions of diversity, the only beneficiaries of such programmes are likely to be professional women and migrants from non-'alien', English-speaking backgrounds. Hall (1995) argues further that 'perpetuating inequality may be productive sometimes' and that differences between employees have been used as the basis of differing pay and conditions (Hall, 1995: 20).

The attack on EEO from more idealistic, even visionary, perspectives is evident in the views of Cope and Kalantzis (1997), for example, who criticize EEO approaches as, firstly, 'accusation based', and secondly, as tending unwittingly to encourage sameness rather than valuing difference. According to Cope and Kalantzis (1997), legislative provisions which point out the ways organizations are failing to advance the outcomes of particular groups tends to create, at best, reluctant compliance rather than a genuine interest in the value of diversity. Moreover, the proposed improved organizational outcomes themselves, which simply aim to 'get more people from different groups into higher positions in organizations', have led to a criterion-based view of merit. This in turn leads to a rigid rather than a genuinely creative approach to diversity since everyone needs to meet the same merit criteria. The 'unwitting sameness' critique is echoed in the view of Greenslade (1991) who, along with some indigenous Australian critics (e.g. Bowd, 1999) label EEO initiatives as having an assimilationist agenda. That is, simply attempting to increase the representation of diverse groups without changing organizational culture does little to further the valuing of difference.

EEO approaches have come under other, more practical pressures. It is often pointed out that EEO programmes have suffered from backlash from white male groups. This has sometimes led to diversity management programmes being instigated in organizations to protect EEO practices aimed at removing disadvantage. Moreover, some women are reluctant to use special programmes such as job sharing, mentoring or networking group participation, or to seek promotion in an organization with an affirmation action scheme for fear of being seen as less committed, or as requiring special treatment to get ahead (Heilman et al., 1993).

The literature suggests that broader definitions of diversity management, when they are separated from EEO or rights-based arguments, as is increasingly the case, have the advantage that they are more likely to acknowledge and value people's multiple identities and group memberships and avoid assuming uniform interests for women, indigenous people or other groups. Yet this broader view, whether it is taken from an idealistic perspective or a business-focused one, may deflect the attention of management from general social justice issues or specific issues of concern to a particular type of diversity.

CURRENT CASE EXAMPLES OF BEST PRACTICE

This section presents some current examples of gender management diversity practice in Australian organizations which are taken as examples of best practice. The first two cases are from organizations which have been studied as instances of good diversity management, including gender diversity management. The remaining seven, non-identified organizations are case examples of organizations the EOWA considers meet their legislative obligations and whose reporting requirements have therefore been waived. After considering the diversity and gender management models these practices reflect, we will return to the dilemmas they present.

The first example involves Telstra, Australia's leading telecommunications provider, which is a company 51 per cent owned by the federal government. A programme was implemented to train managers to value difference, both cross-cultural and gender-based (Rogers, 2000). The programme, which was aimed at 250 senior and middle managers, involved a series of two- and five-day awareness workshops, follow-up skills training workshops and specific issue consultancies. Surveys conducted before and after the workshops indicated that 81 per cent of managers felt they had a deeper understanding of diversity management as a result (Rogers, 2000). Managers' ratings of their ability to communicate the importance of diversity increased from 40 to 58 per cent, and their ability to give gender-sensitive feedback increased from 51 to 62 per cent and culturally sensitive feedback from 36 to 50 per cent. After the workshops, 25 per cent of managers rated themselves as 'proactive' on diversity, with 35 per cent rating themselves 'disinterested' (staff surveys rated 20 per cent of the managers as 'proactive' and 55 per cent as 'disinterested' in diversity). Generally, the Telstra case shows that training programmes can be effective in improving diversity awareness, but as Rogers (2000) points out, it is critical to have follow-up skill development and to ensure long-term commitment.

The second example of diversity management practice is that of a large legal firm, Blake Dawson Waldron, and their approach to the issue of parenting (EOWA, 2001a). The firm piloted an initiative involving a range of support systems for women with parental and other non-work obligations (e.g. remote technology to assist working from home, improved arrangements for teaming). These systems have since been expanded throughout the firm. Staff are also offered options in relation to job sharing, working from home, part-time work, flexible working hours and work while on parental and maternity leave. A key feature of the firm's approach is that those working part-time are accorded full accountability for their projects and workload even when they are not at work. They are required to be contactable via mobile (cell) phone for work emergencies and are given support with children if they have to visit the office on their off days.

The other examples of diversity management to be considered come from confidential reports by the EOWA to determine whether organizations would be waived of their annual reporting obligations. These reports which cover seven organizations assessed in early 2001 (EOWA, 2001b) were made available to the authors with permission of the organizations concerned. The authors also interviewed representatives of the organizations to explore issues in the reports.

Organization A is a major car manufacturer. One of the elements of its diversity management programme is focused on recruitment of women. At present the company is recruiting women into 14 per cent of their engineering positions which is double the market availability of women engineers. To improve recruitment prospects for the firm, the company offers scholarships for women in engineering and currently sponsors more than 30 women in university engineering courses. At present women comprise only 14 per cent of the company's workforce which means there is only a limited pool of female applicants for promotion. A list of women perceived as having high potential for advancement is used in strategic planning for the organization. Women in positions below management level are developed through an executive shadowing programme which involves accompanying an executive throughout their day for two days per month over four months. The company's promotion rates for women are increasing and are above the industry average. Exit interviews are conducted with any women who leave the organization to determine whether there are any systemic issues involved in their leaving.

Organization B is a major company with interests in real estate and construction, both of which are male-dominated industries. The company has extensive overseas operations particularly in the US and Asia. One feature of the company's approach to diversity management is to encourage women to have a career development plan as part of the performance management programme. Women are encouraged to identify a development plan that fits their own aspirations for balancing work and family life. Few women, however, are able to take up overseas appointments. The company has a stated commitment to being responsive and flexible in relation to the needs of women throughout the organization. Managers are charged with being accountable to champion the development of high-performing women. The organization also allocates annual targets for managers to increase the representation of women in professional positions.

Organization C is a major non-bank finance organization recently created by the merging of two credit unions. The organization places emphasis on training, with all managers being trained in merit and equity processes for recruitment, selection and promotion. Currently, more women are being recruited than men at every level. The training for managers also covers issues relating to pregnancy, maternity leave, flexible arrangements for women returning from maternity leave and a new policy on breastfeeding. Induction training for all staff covers sex-based harassment and discrimination. The organization also offers leadership development courses which have been attended by 25 per cent of staff, including almost all those in managerial positions. More than 60 per cent of attendees have been women. The two organizations involved in the merger had different managerial structures and somewhat different cultures. However, their approaches to gender diversity and equity are similar.

Organization D is a medium-sized manufacturer involved in food processing. The organization is distinctive in that women are already well represented in management, whereas the industry is male dominated. The CEO is a woman and women comprise 50 per cent of executive positions, 33 per cent of senior management, 38 per cent of line management and 69 of team leader positions. As there is little turnover in managerial positions there are relatively few opportunities for promotion in this organization. Positions are advertised internally first and staff are encouraged to consider lateral moves to improve their career prospects. In addition to performance appraisal, annual career development discussions are held with all staff to identify their training needs. Flexible working arrangements are negotiated individually with women needing to balance family commitments. The organization faces seasonal fluctuations in demand and manages this with casual employees. Overall, Organization D has no major proactive programmes aimed specifically at women and seems to be one of those rare organizations that have effectively integrated gender diversity management into their general management procedures.

Organization E is a large private high school for girls. Not surprisingly, women comprise the majority of staff (85 per cent) including most managerial positions (75 per cent) as well as the CEO and deputy positions. Recruitment policy is to actively seek women and promotion is usually from within the organization. Gender diversity management in this organization is characterized by the fact that women's issues are very much part of the culture. Such issues are specifically fostered by monthly meetings of a working group devoted to equal opportunity for women. All new staff undergo mentoring which is used to identify any matters relating to equal opportunity. Many of the gender issues that arise in other organizations simply do not arise in this case because of the predominance of women. In such an organization, however, one must ask whether there are any issues relating to employment opportunities for men.

Organization F is one of Australia's largest providers of accounting and consultancy services. This organization, like others in the sector, has an under-representation of women but is endeavouring to redress the situation. Twice as many women graduates are being recruited as men and women are being promoted at the same rate as men. This means that if these two statistics are maintained the representation of women will improve in time. A new major programme based on a US model is being implemented to develop and retain women in the organization. It is specifically designed to help women move from manager to partner, where they are poorly represented, by allocating a one-on-one mentor to those deemed to have high potential. The organization found that women were being offered fewer opportunities for overseas transfers and has addressed this with a new policy based on improved access and transparency.

Organization G is a medium-sized manufacturer of automotive components. Women occupy only 15 per cent of management positions which is typical of the sector. Only 13 per cent of the engineers are women as this organization has to compete for female graduates with car manufacturers such as Organization A. This organization has engineering students on industry-based learning programmes and their recruitment agencies target female candidates for engineering positions. Organization G has a very low staff turnover (less than 1 per cent) which results in few promotional opportunities and limited prospects for improving gender diversity. This has led the organization to offer internal transfers and overseas assignments as career development opportunities. Women staff are encouraged to undertake training in order to improve their prospects of moving into production management and engineering roles.

IMPLICATIONS

The above cases are not claimed to be representative but are seen as illustrative of a range of good gender management practices currently being implemented by Australian organizations. They serve to highlight a number of issues in gender diversity management.

One of the most important questions about diversity management in Australia is that of 'mainstreaming', that is, integrating the provision of EEO into general management rather than having separate proactive programmes. Of the seven cases reviewed above, one could conclude that generally even those organizations which are widely regarded as being at the forefront of good diversity management practice are not doing much that is very proactive or distinctive. This probably reflects the fact that Australian legislation has moved from the more proactive 'affirmative action' to the more steady-state 'equal opportunity'. In an ideal world where equity in employment is fully implemented and systemic discriminatory practices have been eradicated, maintenance via equal opportunity practice would be sufficient. Unfortunately, few organizations could claim to have achieved such a state. All seven organizations were assessed by the EOWA as having taken all 'reasonably practical' measures. In most cases this involves not specific proactive programmes but rather sound practice in implementing merit and equity as the basis for staff management across the range of relevant areas: recruitment and selection; promotion, transfer and termination; training and development; work organization; conditions of service; sex-based harassment; pregnancy and maternity. Such approaches can only produce incremental change at a slow rate—it seems that Australia is resigned to it taking many decades to achieve gender equity in its employment system.

We saw in the first example from Telstra that providing training to managers can improve their awareness of cultural and gender diversity issues. Also, Organization C uses training of managers as a key component of its diversity management strategy. However, as with any programme intended to change organizational culture, it takes time and sustained effort at all levels to move from improved awareness of diversity issues to adoption of pro-diversity values to widespread implementation of behaviours that are fully equitable. One concern is that awareness programmes might merely change some people's language so that they become adept at mouthing the 'politically correct rhetoric' to disguise their prejudiced values and their discriminatory behaviours. This is a key mechanism in the entrenchment of systemic discrimination—the effects can be seen in statistics on women's representation but no instances of discrimination can be identified because the discriminatory behaviours are covert. How easy it is, for example, for a male manager to give preference in promotion to a man over a more capable woman by simply overrating him and underrating her on the supposedly objective selection criteria without betraying his prejudices (which may even be unconscious) by any telltale discriminatory language. Valid measures of diversity management effectiveness are generally not provided by surveys (especially not by self-reported attitudes, values and behaviours) but rather are based on how well an organizational workforce reflects the diversity of the relevant community.

The issues of parenting and work/family balance are being increasingly recognized in Australia. Like most Western countries, Australian society still sees women taking primary responsibility for families either by choice or default. Many organizations are taking active steps to provide support particularly in the form of flexible working arrangements. However, few go so far as to provide childminding facilities—Organization B above reports that they run a programme of activities for children during school vacations. For women in management roles there is a slow breaking down of some of the prejudice against those who give priority to family (e.g. questioning the 'commitment' of any manager who leaves work on time). Interestingly, Organization A reports that by including in their job advertisements that they support a work/life balance, they expanded their applicant pool fivefold.

A number of organizations above have adopted mentoring as part of gender diversity management. This is especially relevant at higher levels of management where the competencies are more subtle and where ongoing constructive feedback on behaviour is essential to development. Mentoring also provides women with access to the complex networks at the top of organizations which serve to entrench the power of those already there and to exclude newcomers who do not fit the mould (typically, white, Anglo-Saxon and male).

The challenge of improving women's representation is particularly difficult in organizations where there is little growth coupled with low staff turnover. In the case of Organization G with less than 1 per cent turnover, it is very unlikely that women's managerial representation will improve from its current 15 per cent level with the sort of steady-state approach encouraged by the low-key approach required by current EEO legislation. By contrast, Organization D which also has low turnover has relatively high representation for women. It seems that this organization established 30 years ago has always had a relative absence of gender discrimination. The founding CEO was a woman who reportedly had a good understanding of, and active interest in, human resource issues. She implemented merit and equity systems at the outset and evidently has enabled women to progress.

CONCLUSIONS

As well as these specific problems, the cases exemplify a number of broader dilemmas and questions for the future of diversity management in Australia.

WHAT NEXT—BUSINESS CASE ARGUMENTS, EEO OR BOTH?

The statistics and organizations we have cited suggest that neither business case arguments nor EEO approaches are likely to be sufficient on their own to produce substantial movement in the situation of women in Australian organizations. The cases make it clear that, like many other change management initiatives, simply pointing out the organizational benefits of a more diverse workforce does not lead to immediate, profound and lasting organizational change. When particular groups within organizations see themselves as likely losers and when the existing organizational culture does not favour diversity initiatives, change is likely to be slow indeed. Specific losses on the part of particular groups as well as less definable issues of organizational culture combine to hinder diversity initiatives. EEO practitioners and managers in the organizations we spoke to argued that more substantial results will need to wait for changes in organizational culture to reinforce the initiatives they have made.

Many EEO practitioners and line managers in our organizations and others argue that EEO approaches smack of 'accusing' particular individuals or groups of a failure to make good progress on the diversity agenda. According to this viewpoint accusations— or what sound like accusations—are more likely to lead to suspicion about diversity and even active backlash against long-standing EEO initiatives. Many argue that backlash is already established in many organizations. Some believe that 'showing' rather than 'accusing' is a better approach, by making videos of interactions in meetings to make visible what behaviours are leading to or symptomatic of disadvantage.

We are less confident that approaches which deliberately downplay EEO or other right-based approaches would work. Bringing about change in organizational culture is a notoriously slow process. Being content to wait for organizational culture change may invite complacency. In any case, other arguments for change based on a business case rarely have to wait decades, nor do they have to accept the most minimal progress as evidence of success. As Krautil (2001) points out, would businesses accept minimal sales targets? Moreover, accepting business case arguments alone—particularly those based on 'productive diversity' rather than merely 'managing diversity'—has its hazards. The productive diversity argument, if used apart from other, right-based arguments, suggests that if at some point the economic motivation for increasing workforce diversity fades, the organization would be justified in abandoning diversity initiatives. This is a real risk, since views of what constitutes managerial best practice are notoriously subject to organizational 'short-termism' and simple fashion in management thinking. Organizations need to continue to work towards including women and minority groups fully in decision-making regardless of the perceived business 'dividend'. Initiatives based on furthering the legitimate aspirations of particular groups cannot be discarded.

MAINSTREAMING OR NOT?

Business case arguments for diversity have considerable value in that they have brought diversity issues into focus as an explicit aim of management and not merely an ancillary or afterthought. Much has been achieved by recognizing that lack of attention to equity issues will cost the organization in the long term since it will lead to cynicism, reduced creativity, labour market and other 'system' rigidities, higher staff turnover, and potential loss of market share. Mainstreaming has placed diversity at the heart of many organizations, made it an important performance criterion in managers' regular performance appraisals, and reminded organizations that diversity management is everyone's job, not just that of a few individuals. Adopting a mainstreaming approach to equity may even, in the longer term, lead to the view that problems of juggling work and life balance are not merely 'women's issues' but that work itself may need reform.

Yet mainstreaming also has its problems. Equal treatment of all organizational groups is not always appropriate and does not result in true equity. Defining diversity too broadly—where differences in organizational hierarchy, function and background come to be as important as fundamental, 'first level' forms of diversity—makes it likely that diversity programmes based on such thinking will not cover specific issues in gender or racial/ethnic issues. Organizations need to target major systemic issues affecting broad minority groups such as race, gender, ethnicity, age, disability (i.e. the sources of first-level diversity) rather than treating all human differences as if they had equal impact and meaning within society and employment.

MONITORING PROGRESS

Our cases strongly suggest that it will continue to be important to collect statistical data at the organizational level on demographic characteristics of staff, to enable analysis of the issues. This is especially important for people affected by more than one of type of potential disadvantage. Good measurement has long been valued in management and this is perhaps the least paradoxical aspect of what our cases suggest needs to be done. Even then there are dangers. It is easy for organizations to derive an overly optimistic view of their progress—say in the appointment of women executives—by comparing the extremely low numbers of women executives 5 or 10 years ago with a larger number now, but one which still falls short of women's general representation in the workforce. Similarly, pointing to absolute increases in the numbers of women on corporate boards is less useful than pointing out changes in the percentage of women to men on such boards. While small, internally focused steps towards enhancing gender and other forms of workforce diversity are useful—particularly as a basis for measuring managerial performance—they should not replace an external view of how well the organization reflects its world. Perhaps analyses like those in this book will help further this goal.

REFERENCES

AAA (Affirmative Action Agency) (1999). Entering a new era in the Year 2000. *Action News: Newsletter of the Affirmative Action Agency*, **40**, December.

ABS (Australian Bureau of Statistics) (1986–2000). *Labour Force Australia, Monthly Reports for August Each Year. Catalogue 6203.0*. Canberra.

ABS (1989–2000). *ABS Economic Indicators, Catalogue No. 1350.0*. Canberra.

Bennington, L. & Tharenou, P. (1986). Older workers: myths, evidence and implications for Australian managers. *Asia Pacific Journal of Human Resources*, **34**(3), 63–76.

Bertone, S., Esposto, A. & Turner, R. (1998). *Diversity and Dollars: Productive Diversity in Australian Business and Industry*. CEDA Information Paper No. 58, Workplace Studies Centre, Victoria University of Technology.

Bowd, D. (1999). Caring for all regardful of race, colour and creed—valuing diversity for better mental health services for all. Paper presented at the 1999 NSW Aboriginal Mental Health Conference, Penrith, NSW, September 1–3. Paper obtainable through the Aboriginal Services Division of the Department of Human Services, South Australia.

Burton, C. (1992). *Managing Difference and Diversity—the Changing Role of Human Resource Management in the 90s*. International Women's Day Seminar Series. Canberra: Public Services Commission.

CCH (1995). *Workplace Age Discrimination: A Guide for Managers and Supervisors*. North Ryde, NSW: CCH Australia Limited.

Cooper, G.D. & Jongeling, S. (1983). Factors affecting employment opportunities for and employer attitudes towards persons with a disability—results of a survey. *Australian Rehabilitation Review*, **7**(1), 23–30.

Cope, B. & Kalantzis, M. (1997). *Productive Diversity: A New, Australian Model for Work and Management*. Sydney: Pluto Press.

Cox, T. Jr (1993). *Cultural Diversity in Organisation*. San Francisco: Barrett-Koehler Publishers Inc.

Davidson, P. & Griffin, R.W. (2000). *Management: Australia in a Global Context*. Brisbane: Wiley.

Dawkins, P., Kemp, S. & Cabalu, H. (1995). *Trade and Investment with East Asia in Selected Service Industries*. Canberra: Institute of Research into International Competitiveness, Australian Government Publishing Service.

EOWA (Equal Opportunity for Women Agency) (2001a). Legal eagles balance work and life. *Action News: Newsletter of the Equal Opportunity for Women in the Workplace Agency*, **45**, Autumn.

EOWA (2001b). Waiving assessment reports. *Confidential Reports*, Equal Opportunity for Women in the Workplace Agency, Sydney, Feb–May.

Greenslade, M. (1991). Managing diversity: lessons from the United States. *Personnel Management*, December, 28–33.

Hall, P. (1995). *Affirmative Action and Managing Diversity: Affirmative Action Agency Monograph, 8*. Canberra: Australian Government Publishing Service.

Hay, C. (1996). *Managing Cultural Diversity: Opportunities for Enhancing the Competitive Advantage of Australian Business*. Canberra: Australian Government Publishing Service.

Hede, A. (1995). Managerial inequity in the Australian workforce: a longitudinal analysis. *International Review of Women and Leadership*, **1**(1), 11–21.

Hede, A. (2000). Affirmative action in Australia: employment equity at the crossroads. In M.J. Davidson & R.J. Burke (eds) *Women in Management: Current Research Issues*, Vol. II. London: Sage Publications.

Hede, A. & O'Brien, E. (1996). Affirmative action in the Australian private sector: a longitudinal analysis. *International Review of Women and Leadership*, **2**(2), 15–29.

Heilman, M.E., Kaplow, S.R., Amato, M.A. & Strathatos, P. (1993). When similarity is a liability: effects of sex-based preferential selection on reaction to like-sex and different-sex others. *Journal of Applied Psychology*, **78**(6), 917–927.

Karpin, D. (1995). *Enterprising Nation: Renewing Australia's Managers to Meet the Challenges of the Asia-Pacific Century* (Report of the Industry Task Force on Leadership and Management Skills). Canberra: Commonwealth of Australia.

Krautil, F. (2001). The emperor's EEO clothes: calling business's bluff. Presentation to the 13th Women, Management and Employment Relations Conference, Sydney, 12 July.

Loden, M. (1995). *Implementing Diversity*. Sydney: McGraw-Hill.

McGrath, J. (1990). Skill shortage provokes rethink on retirement. *Personnel Today*, **6**, April.

Norris, R. (2001). From bad to worse? The development of Australian Indigenous employment disadvantage. *Journal of Economic and Social Policy*, No. 1, 242–249.

Overell, S. (1996). IPD says diversity is next step for equality. *People Management*, December, 12–13.

PSMPC (Public Service and Merit Protection Commission) (2000). *Australian Public Service Statistical Bulletin 1990–2000*. Canberra: Public Service and Merit Protection Commission.

Quinn, G., McDonagh, M. & Kimber, C. (1993). *Disability Discrimination Law in the United States, Australia and Canada*. Dublin: Oak Tree Press.

Race Discrimination Commissioner (1998). *Diversity Makes Good Business Sense: Training Package for Managing Cultural Diversity in the Workplace*. Sydney: Human Rights and Equal Opportunity Commission.

Rogers, M. (2000). Valuing difference and training staff: the Telstra case. Paper presented at 21st Century Business: Delivering the Diversity Dividend, Melbourne, November.

Ronalds, C. (1987). *Affirmative Action and Sex Discrimination: A Handbook on Legal Rights for Women*. Sydney: Pluto Press.

Shaw, J. (1995). *Cultural Diversity at Work: Utilising a Unique Australian Resource*. Chatswood, Sydney: Business and Professional Publishing.

Smith, C.R. & Hutchinson, J. (1995). *Gender: A Strategic Management Issue*. Chatswood, Sydney: Business and Professional Publishing.

United States General Accounting Office (2001). Senior executive service: diversity increased in the past decade. *Report to Congressional Requesters*, USGAO, Washington, DC, March.

Wallace, P., Ermer, C. & Motshabi, D. (1996). Managing diversity: a senior management perspective. *Hospital and Health Services Administration*, **41**(1), 91–104.

Woods, R. & Sciarini, M. (1995). Diversity programs in chain restaurants. *Cornell Hotel and Restaurant Administration Quarterly*, **36**(3), June, 18–23.

CHAPTER 8

Organizational Efforts to Manage Diversity: Do They Really Work?

Penny Dick

Sheffield University Management School, Sheffield, UK

SUMMARY

This chapter examines the claims that the management of diversity can produce positive effects for both individuals and organizations. Empirical studies that have attempted to ascertain relationships between diversity management and outcomes at the level of the individual and of the organization are reviewed. In the chapter, it is argued that the evidence linking the management of diversity to different levels of achievement and affective outcomes is limited and, furthermore, that the majority of studies have focused on diversity per se, not its management. It is argued that the theoretical and methodological assumptions that underpin much of the diversity research may be inappropriate. Specifically, it is argued that approaches that seek to understand diversity management issues by focusing on the psychology of individuals neglect the role of social processes, particularly power, in producing and reproducing inequality. The chapter concludes by arguing that the diversity literature needs to adopt a more theoretical and critical focus to advance understanding in this field.

INTRODUCTION

The purpose of this chapter is to examine the extent to which the strategies and techniques that organizations use to manage diversity actually make a difference. In addressing this question, it is necessary to qualify what is meant by 'efforts to manage diversity' and what sorts of difference such efforts are supposed to produce. To begin with, therefore, the chapter will briefly review some of the more common approaches to diversity

Individual Diversity and Psychology in Organizations. Edited by Marilyn J. Davidson and Sandra L. Fielden.
© 2003 John Wiley & Sons, Ltd.

management alongside some of the claims that are made for their effectiveness. The chapter will focus on conducting a critique of these approaches and claims, by examining the available empirical evidence and the underlying theoretical bases on which these approaches and claims are built.

WHAT SORTS OF EFFORTS DO ORGANIZATIONS MAKE TO MANAGE DIVERSITY?

The management of diversity has much less of a history in the UK compared to the USA, due to differences in the demographic composition of organizations in each country. The USA, for example, not only has far greater racial diversity than the UK, but has also more of a history of civil rights lobbying and attendant legislation including affirmative action programmes (illegal in the UK). Nonetheless, demographic changes in the UK population appear to be having an impact. More women and ethnic minorities entering the labour market, coupled with an increase in the average age of workers (Cassell, 2001), means that organizations in the UK are beginning to pay more attention to diversity management.

As discussed in previous chapters, the management of diversity as a discourse and a set of practices, is concerned with embracing and enhancing all the differences between employees, not just differences in gender and race. Nevertheless, it is probably true to say that many of the initiatives organizations undertake in the name of diversity management do have the interests of women and non-white workers as their target. Historically, efforts targeted at these groups have been largely reactive, in terms of either increasing their numbers in the workplace in response to criticism (e.g. the police service), or in avoiding discrimination claims. Increasingly, to move organizations away from a reactive position with regards to diversity, academics and practitioners are emphasizing the importance of the business case in diversity management (Herriot & Pemberton, 1995; Robinson & Dechant, 1997; Kandola & Fullerton, 1998; Cassell, 2001). From this perspective, the management of diversity is not simply a moral imperative, nor a way to avoid expensive discrimination lawsuits, but a means of enhancing individual and organizational performance (Cox, 1993).

There are a great many techniques and initiatives that fall under the rubric of diversity management, but among the most common are:

• Multicultural workshops designed to increase and improve understanding between culturally diverse groups
• Support groups, such as women's and cultural minorities' networks
• Reward systems that are designed to encourage individual managers to effectively manage diversity
• Human resource systems to monitor the recruitment and advancement of minorities
• Flexible working practices, such as job share and part-time or flexi-hours that enable minorities to combine non-work responsibilities with their jobs
• New organizational forms, particularly team-based working, deliberately designed to be heterogeneous

Barry and Bateman (1996) suggest that diversity initiatives can be grouped into four major themes in human resource management: training and development (e.g.

multicultural workshops); work design (e.g. flexible working practices and team-based working); staffing (e.g. targeting minority groups for recruitment and promotion); and compensations (e.g. reward systems).

Dass and Parker (1999) in a review of the diversity initiatives of organizations, further argue that they can be broadly categorized into three types of approach: episodic, free-standing and systemic. Episodic approaches are highly reactive: the organization responds on an ad hoc basis to problems related to organizational diversity. Thus, for example, a case for racial discrimination might be dismissed as a one-off event requiring no further action, or may result in some form of diversity training. Free-standing approaches involve a more systematic attempt to deal with diversity issues, including the implementation of equal opportunities polices, training in appropriate (and fair) selection and recruitment techniques, and perhaps consciousness-raising activities designed to encourage employees to think more carefully about race, gender or disability, for example. The systemic approach tends to be adopted by those organizations that embrace diversity as a philosophy and that wish to actively promote the benefits of a diverse workforce. In this approach, diversity issues are clearly linked to the organization's strategic goals. Such approaches have been discussed in detail elsewhere in this book.

Apart from the differences in emphasis between the three types of approach, each also has clear implications for what are seen to be important outcomes of a diversity strategy, as well as how such outcomes might be measured and evaluated. Episodic and free-standing approaches with their implicit emphasis on the avoidance of conflict are not likely to have any clearly defined outcomes or evaluation measures associated with them. And even if some outcomes are specified, it is unlikely that they would be evaluated rigorously. For example, in UK police forces, there are very many initiatives designed to increase and manage workforce diversity, particularly in terms of increasing the recruitment and promotion of female, ethnic and black officers. However, although the diversity of police forces is monitored annually by Her Majesty's Inspectorate (HMI), there is very little systematic evaluation of the efforts police forces use to increase workforce diversity, nor of the effects that such initiatives have on current employees. Such scrutiny tends to be left to academics (e.g. Brown, 1998). Following the Stephen Lawrence Inquiry, MacPherson report (1999) (as detailed in Chapter 12), for instance, the police service in England and Wales has been given government-set targets for increasing the numbers of ethnic minority officers recruited to forces. Forces have implemented a number of initiatives in response, including advertising in media known to be frequently accessed by ethnic minorities; hosting open days; and working with local community groups to promote a positive image of the police. Yet the evaluation of these various initiatives appears to be very primitive (monitoring the numbers of applications from minorities) and is not carried out by all forces, despite the considerable resources put into them (Bland et al., 1999).

This rather lacklustre approach to the evaluation of diversity initiatives is not confined to the police service in the UK. Comer and Soliman (1996) in their review of 20 nationwide organizations in the US argue that despite the claims that are made for the effectiveness of diversity initiatives, very few organizations have evaluated the outcomes of such initiatives. They found that even where organizations did report some form of evaluation, this was usually in terms of a headcount of the numbers of employees recruited and/or promoted from different minority groups. As they argue, such counts provide little information about the extent to which diversity initiatives are having an impact at the level of the individual or the organization. Moreover, Wise and Tschirhart (2000) state:

> ...empirical evidence about the consequences of diversity in work organizations is limited, and many of the existing studies present conflicting and inconclusive findings.... Our assessment of the diversity literature suggests that managers are using largely untested assumptions as a basis for diversity policies, strategies and actions. (p. 386)

Overall then, it appears that while many organizations are making efforts to manage diversity, there is very little evidence that the outcomes expected of such initiatives are measured or even articulated in any more than very basic terms. As Comer and Soliman (1996) remark, this is striking, given the considerable resources that are invested in diversity initiatives, and given that there are models of diversity management that specify the sorts of outcomes for which organizations should be aiming (Cox, 1993; Kandola & Fullerton, 1998).

OUTCOMES THAT ARE SPECIFIED FOR DIVERSITY MANAGEMENT PROGRAMMES: DOES EVIDENCE SUPPORT THE CLAIMS?

Academics have been spelling out the sorts of outcomes that organizations can expect from diversity management initiatives for at least the last 10 years. These outcomes can be broadly categorized as individual level outcomes and organizational level outcomes (Cox, 1993).

INDIVIDUAL LEVEL OUTCOMES

Cox (1993) suggests that individual level outcomes from diversity initiatives can be divided into affective and achievement outcomes. Affective outcomes include improved job and career satisfaction, organizational identification and job involvement. Achievement outcomes include improved performance and pay and increase in promotion mobility rates. The basic idea underpinning these predictions is that an organization that sets out to show its employees that it values their contribution regardless of their social category, will not only reap the rewards of having happier and more contented staff, but also will be able to show the tangible effects of such values through the improved performance and upward mobility of their staff.

There is surprisingly, and alarmingly, very little empirical evidence to support the view that diversity *initiatives* result in these sorts of individual level outcomes, though there is considerable research that has examined the effects of different *types* of workforce diversity on such outcomes. For instance, Wise and Tschirhart (2000) in their review of research into the effects of workforce diversity, identified 113 articles that had measured individual level outcomes. The majority of these articles (just under one-third) focused on the performance evaluations of employees on the basis of their sex and race. Promotion mobility, job satisfaction and job involvement were the next most frequently studied outcomes (each accounting for about a fifth of the studies reviewed). Comer and Soliman (1996), however, found very little evidence that practitioners were concerned with measuring the individual level outcomes specified by Cox (1993).

In one of the few studies that has attempted to more directly address the effects of diversity management rather than simply diversity, Hicks-Clarke and Iles (2000) conducted a study into the relationship between a climate for diversity and affective outcomes (refer to Chapter 10 for more details). They conducted surveys in four public sector organizations (NHS trusts) and five private sector organizations (retail companies) in the UK. Climate for diversity was defined as the presence of policy support for diversity and the recognition of equity. Outcome measures included job satisfaction, career commitment and organizational commitment. Their results indicated that a positive climate for diversity was strongly associated with the presence of positive affective outcomes. However, due to the cross-sectional nature of the research methodology, the positive association between (perceived) positive climate for diversity and job satisfaction cannot be taken as meaning that the direction is from a positive climate for diversity to more satisfied employees. It is just as feasible that satisfied employees are more likely than dissatisfied employees to perceive that their organization is behaving morally/fairly. Similar arguments have been used to criticize the overinflated claims of stress/strain research (Kasl, 1986).

Some of the work that has been done on the effects of different types of workforce diversity on individual level outcomes has, nevertheless, made explicit the implications for diversity management initiatives, enabling at least, the development of a research agenda. For example, Jehn et al. (1999) examined the effects of different types of diversity on workgroup performance (achievement outcomes) and on organizational commitment and morale (affective outcomes). Workgroup performance was measured by self-reported evaluations of the group's performance and by efficiency indicators obtained from organizational records. Affective outcomes were measured by self-report. They report that informational diversity (defined as differences in knowledge bases and perspectives) was most likely to increase achievement outcomes. They found that value diversity (defined as differences in beliefs about the nature of the workgroups' goals, targets or mission) was more likely than social category diversity (defined as explicit differences among group members such as race, gender and ethnicity) to result in negative affective outcomes. They conclude: 'Diversity itself is not enough to ensure innovation. . . . For group members to be willing to engage in the difficult and conflictual processes that may lead to innovative performance, it seems that group members must have similar values' (Jehn et al., 1999: 759).

One of the key arguments articulated in this study, is that social category diversity is not necessarily associated with value diversity. Put simply, two women in a group with seven men will not necessarily be that different from the men, especially if they are all from the same functional group or organizational subunit. The implication of this argument is that managers need to pay attention to ensuring that a group of workers share the same values, if they wish to improve affective and achievement outcomes. This suggests that social category diversity need not necessarily be a key focus in designing and implementing diversity management initiatives.

However, a major limitation in Jehn et al.'s study was that their social category diversity results were based on the measurement of only two factors, age and gender. Furthermore, although this is not stated in the study, it would probably be the case that the organization studied (a household goods removal company) was male dominated. This is a critical shortcoming, however, since research suggests the existence of non-symmetrical gender and race effects for social category diversity. For example, a number of studies have found that increasing group heterogeneity (on the basis of sex or race) has more negative effects on the affective outcomes of organizational dominants (white men) and more positive effects on these outcomes for women and racial minorities (Tsui et al., 1992).

Other studies of the effects of diversity on achievement outcomes have examined the position of minorities with regards to promotion rates and performance evaluations. Cannings (1988) in a study of nearly 700 Canadian managers found that gender had a significant effect on chances for promotion, even when factors such as education were controlled for: women were less likely than men to be promoted. A recent study by Lewis (1997) examined whether the performance of women and racial minority staff in federal organizations in the US was rated differently from that of white men. Holding position in the organization, educational background and age as constants, Lewis found that women were more likely than their male counterparts to be rated 'outstandingly good', but, and in support of earlier studies, he found that racial minorities were less likely to be rated 'outstandingly good' compared to their white counterparts. In the main, the available research suggests that minorities are promoted at slower rates than the majority in a wide variety of occupations and professions (Baldwin, 1996).

Overall, these studies suggest that the relationship between diversity and affective and achievement outcomes is complicated. It seems that, at the level of the workgroup, homogeneity in values, but differences in skills and knowledge have the greatest impact on improving achievement and affective outcomes. The effects of social category diversity appear to be contingent on the demographic composition of the organization as a whole and to exert differential effects at the level of the individual. Where minorities are very under-represented, this appears to have negative affective outcomes for members of minority groups and positive affective outcomes for members of the majority. However, as the numbers of minorities increase this trend reverses. Furthermore, being a member of a social category minority appears to have deleterious effects on certain achievement outcomes such as chances for promotion.

One implication of these findings is that diversity initiatives designed to change the demographic composition of the organization may affect minority and majority employees in different ways. This must be a key area for future research, because as Prasad et al. (1997) argue:

> The literature on managing diversity pays little attention to the growing hostility toward policies such as affirmative action and employment equity that actually promote workforce diversity... white rage becomes manifested in a series of actions that oppose diversity... acknowledging the presence of this anger and learning to deal with it needs to be made an important item in the agenda of managing diversity. (pp. 14–15)

Barry and Bateman (1996), taking a somewhat different perspective, suggest that diversity initiatives may become 'social traps': situations that may have short-term positive effects for an individual or group but, over time, have negative consequences. For example, firms who try to accommodate parents with family obligations by providing 'special treatment' (e.g. opportunities to expand personal networks through family-based activities), may, in the longer term, alienate and create dissatisfaction among members of majority groups who are put at a disadvantage through not having opportunities to expand their own personal networks.

On the whole, therefore, evidence to support the idea that the effective management of diversity has a positive effect on affective and achievement outcomes is very limited. The bulk of the research, with the exception of Hicks-Clarke and Iles (2000), simply looks at whether different types of diversity are associated with specific individual level outcomes. This tells us very little about whether diversity initiatives actually 'work'. It is also apparent that the effects of workforce diversity are complex and possibly tied to specific organizational contexts. Further, while there is some evidence to support the view that a diverse workforce is associated with positive individual outcomes, there is clearly considerable variation in these outcomes among both minority and majority employees. Additionally, there are methodological and theoretical limitations that many studies have yet to address. Before addressing these limitations, however, the chapter now turns to the question of whether diversity initiatives affect organizational level outcomes.

ORGANIZATIONAL LEVEL OUTCOMES

Until very recently, there was very little research that had examined the extent to which diversity initiatives had an effect on organizational level outcomes. In Cox's (1993) model, he asserts that the improvements in individual level outcomes, such as job satisfaction and promotion mobility, will have a positive affect on employee motivation which will then filter through to the organizational level to produce improvements in first- and second-level outcomes (see Figure 8.1).

The lack of research in this area is staggering, given that managers themselves who champion managing diversity as a set of practices and a philosophy use the rhetoric of the 'bottom line business case' to support their views (Comer & Soliman, 1996). The majority of studies have examined the relationship between diversity and first-level outcomes. Again, what is lacking in the literature is any clear or systematic account of how specific diversity initiatives affect or influence these outcomes over time.

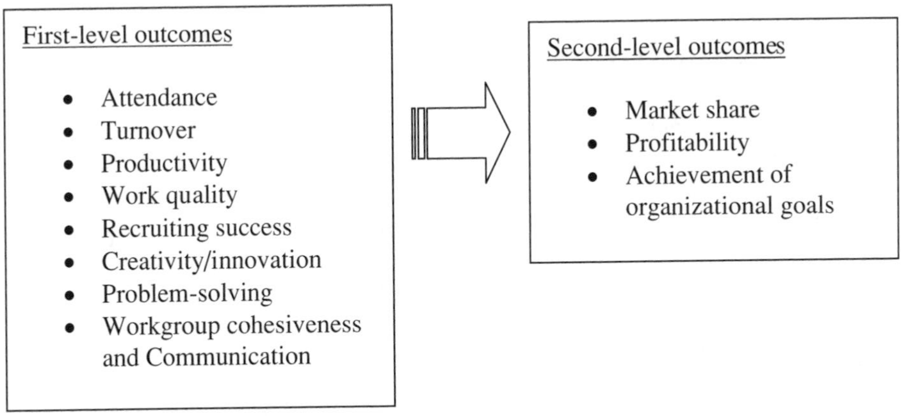

FIGURE 8.1 First- and second-level outcomes resulting from improvements in job satisfaction, promotion mobility and motivation.
Source: Cox, T., (1993) *Cultural Diversity in Organizations: Theory, Research and Practice.* San Francisco, CA: Berrett-Koehler Publishers Inc. Reprinted with permission of the publisher. All rights reserved. www.bkconnection.com

Like many of the studies reviewed in the previous section, much of the research has focused on the relationship between different dimensions of workforce diversity and first-level organizational outcomes, rather than the relationship between these outcomes and diversity initiatives. Research has produced mixed results, suggesting that workgroup diversity can have positive *and* negative effects on first-level outcomes. Cordero et al. (1996) examined the effects of racial and gender group composition on creative productivity among a sample of research and development engineers and scientists. Creative productivity was measured by patents and by managers' ratings of the groups' innovativeness. They found that men were more innovative when they were in the majority in their workgroups, but whites were more likely to benefit from patents and patents pending when in racially diverse workgroups. Other studies suggest that increased conflict and lowered morale associated with membership of heterogeneous workgroups (Tsui et al., 1992) may have adverse effects on first-level outcomes.

Attempts to resolve these contradictory findings have focused on identifying possible mediating variables. For instance, some research suggests that heterogeneity in workgroup diversity is more likely to yield positive first-level outcomes when the task is complex and requires interdependence among workgroup members (Watson et al., 1993); when social category diversity is not commensurate with value diversity (Jehn et al., 1999); and when the workgroup is predominantly composed of organizational dominants (Wharton & Baron, 1987). What is clear, however, is that the relationship between workgroup diversity and first-level outcomes is complex, and attempts to model the large number of variables that may be involved in this relationship are based largely on cross-sectional data. Having already alluded to the problems with this type of methodology, these issues will be dealt with in more depth later in the chapter.

A further problem is that even though some studies have found positive associations between workforce diversity and first-level organizational outcomes, it cannot be assumed that these outcomes would eventually lead to the second-level outcomes proposed by Cox (1993). This is a widespread problem in the work psychology literature, where assumptions about first-level outcomes, including phenomena such as psychological stress and organizational commitment, are assumed to be related to second-level outcomes such as absenteeism and turnover, despite the fact that there is very limited empirical evidence supporting the existence of such links (Arnold et al., 1998).

Recently, a small number of papers have taken the effects of diversity initiatives on both first- and second-level organizational outcomes as their focus. For instance, Perotin and Robinson (2000) found that organizations that had implemented diversity initiatives, such as minority monitoring, reviewing selection procedures and pay rates and having a disability-friendly workplace, were more productive than workplaces that had no such policies. In their study, they found that the greatest increases in productivity were obtained where the organization had implemented diversity initiatives and an employee participation scheme. While participation schemes and diversity initiatives did yield independent effects on productivity, these were not as great as the joint effect. Furthermore, they found the joint effect was further strengthened, the larger the proportion of minorities employed. However, this study, like many in this area, was cross-sectional, making it problematic to assume that it is diversity initiatives (or participation schemes) that result in increased productivity.

Richard (2000) examined the relationship between workforce racial diversity and firm performance. Firm performance was measured in three different ways: by calculating the net income of the firm per employee; by return on equity for the year end in which the study was carried out; and by perceptual measures of market performance. He found that racial diversity was positively associated with firm performance when the firm was pursuing a growth strategy, and negatively associated with firm performance when the firm was following a downsizing strategy. Richard (2000: 174) concludes:

> The results of this study suggest that neither interest group [academics and business executives] is likely to see a direct positive relationship between cultural diversity and firm performance. Instead the effects are likely to be determined by the strategies a firm pursues and by how organization leaders and participants respond to and manage diversity.

An earlier study conducted by Chatman et al. (1998) lends some support to this view. Based on a simulation exercise with 258 MBA (Master in Business Administration) students, which included tasks such as weighting the importance of various attributes that should be used on organizational performance appraisals, and developing suggestions for improving procedures or products, they argue that organizations that develop collectivist rather than individualistic cultures are better placed to increase the effectiveness of a diverse workforce.

Taking a different perspective, Wright et al. (1995) argue that firms that develop high-quality affirmative action programmes are attractive to investors, who respond to such developments by bidding up stock prices. However, the authors acknowledge: 'Investors may have simply reacted to the positive nature of announcements of awards for quality affirmative action programs rather than viewed such programs as providing competitive advantage' (p. 290).

Though few in number, these studies suggest that diversity initiatives can have an impact on 'bottom-line' business outcomes. However, there are studies that suggest that this 'value-in-diversity' perspective is flawed. For instance, Palich and Gomez-Mejia (1999) argue that cultural diversity among international divisions of global firms impedes firm performance due to 'disproportionate levels of misunderstanding and conflict' (p. 598), and they cast doubt on the 'value-in-diversity' perspective by arguing that empirical research has not established links between diversity and various performance outcomes: 'Despite vast conceptual support for this popular view [value-in-diversity], its empirical foundation is weak ... one of the few linkages empirical research has identified is a strong and consistent positive relationship between diversity and turnover' (Palich & Gomez-Mejia, 1999: 600).

Furthermore, a recent study by Lott (2000) suggests that affirmative action programmes in the US aimed at increasing the number of police recruits from minority groupings are associated with increased crime rates, due to overall lowering of recruitment and selection standards.

In summary, therefore, it is fair to say that as Cassell (2001) argues, 'the jury is still out' as to whether managing diversity initiatives 'work'. Part of the problem, as previously discussed, is that there are very few studies that have actually examined the effect of diversity initiatives. Moreover, those that have are limited due to the nature of the methodologies used, which are generally cross-sectional. A larger number of studies have examined the effects of workforce diversity per se on a variety of individual and organizational outcomes. On the whole, such studies suggest that workforce diversity does affect outcomes at different levels, but not only are findings mixed with regard to whether these effects are positive or negative, they also indicate the relationship between workforce diversity and different outcomes is neither direct nor easily explicable. A further issue, particularly for those advocating a 'value-in-diversity' approach, is that the assumed relationship between individual level attitudinal outcomes, such as job satisfaction and morale, and organizational level outcomes such as lowered absenteeism, turnover and increased productivity has yet to be adequately empirically verified.

SOME CRITICAL ISSUES FOR THE EVALUATION OF DIVERSITY INITIATIVES

Having spent some time discussing the available 'evidence' as to whether organizational efforts to manage diversity actually work, the following section aims to examine some critical methodological and theoretical issues that need to be addressed if we are to obtain a more informed and rigorous picture of the effects of diversity initiatives.

There is an increasing call for the diversity management literature to utilize more rigorous theoretical and conceptual approaches (Prasad et al., 1997; Cassell & Biswas, 2000; Dick & Cassell, 2002). Prasad et al. present this issue as follows: 'It is our contention that the elaborate showcasing of the diversity movement has severely limited our understanding of the more problematic aspects of multiculturalism in the workplace. A host of gender conflicts, race tensions and cultural frictions lie hidden in the shadows of the showcase' (p. 12).

Prasad et al. (1997) argue that the unproblematic promotion of diversity management as a desirable practice for organizations to engage in has had the effect of neglecting both theory and a critical examination of the assumptions underpinning diversity 'prescriptions'. However, the development of theory is critical to the future of diversity initiatives. Unless we can begin to frame initiatives in ways that render their actual or probable effects understandable, there is a danger that, like many other so-called 'management fads', diversity initiatives will eventually lose their currency as 'the thing to do', and the lot of minorities will fail to excite the attention of future researchers or practitioners. More fundamentally, we need to develop appropriate theory to enable sensible and sustainable initiatives to be developed in the first instance.

THEORETICAL ISSUES

Organizational culture

It can be a confusing and frustrating task to attempt to identify the theoretical bases of the diversity management literature. However, it is probably reasonable to assert that the majority of the literature that addresses the issue of diversity management is underpinned by the concept of corporate or organizational culture, though this is rarely dealt with at any more than a superficial level. So, for example, many approaches advocate the idea of cultural audits (Walker & Hanson, 1992; Thornburg, 1994; Kandola & Fullerton, 1998; Hicks-Clarke & Iles, 2000), in which the values and attitudes towards diversity that exist in the organization are assessed, so that 'problem areas' can be identified and dealt with. However, this cultural perspective plays down a number of key problems. First, is the problem of treating organizational culture as if it is a relatively homogeneous domain, i.e. that values and attitudes are widely shared within the organization. Smircich (1983), in a comprehensive account of the concept of culture argues: 'Much of the literature refers to an organization culture, appearing to lose sight of the great likelihood that there are multiple organization subcultures, or even countercultures, competing to define the nature of situations within organizational boundaries' (p. 346).

Despite the fact that this warning was issued nearly 20 years ago, it is disturbing to note that many studies appear not to consider these issues, even though they are likely to have a fundamental impact on the way organizational members respond to diversity initiatives. For instance, assuming that a 'culture change' is necessary in order to promote diversity management initiatives leads some organizations to develop and implement 'diversity training' designed to change attitudes and challenge stereotypes. However, Ellis and Sonnenfield (1994) in a review of three US-based diversity initiatives, found that such training undermined its own goals, largely because it alienated white males, who believed themselves to be 'vilified' by the training.

A second and related problem is that some studies argue that the organizational culture in any given company is likely to reflect the values and attitudes of the organizational dominants (e.g. Robinson & McIlwee, 1991 in a study of engineering companies; Fielding, 1994 in a discussion of police culture). This suggests that the values and attitudes of minorities are likely to be different. However, not only does research suggest that social category diversity is not necessarily related to value diversity (Jehn et al., 1999), but also that members of minority groups sustain and emphasize values that apparently compromise their interests (Holdaway & Parker, 1998; Dick & Jankowicz, 2001).

Again, these issues have considerable implications for managing diversity initiatives. If some members of minority groups do not perceive nor experience the organizational culture in their workplace as problematic, to what extent are initiatives designed to change values and attitudes likely to be welcomed or have any long-term effects (Dick & Cassell, 2002)?

Furthermore, approaches that unproblematically prescribe 'culture change' as being necessary for the success of diversity initiatives are positioned within an explanatory framework in which culture is conceptualized as an internal organizational variable that can be manipulated by managers to achieve corporate goals (Smircich, 1983). This position is problematic from a host of theoretical (Hearn & Parkin, 1983; Smircich, 1983), and critical perspectives (Willmott, 1993) but, more fundamentally, it limits our understanding of the subjective effects of organizational culture, most specifically how it frames and organizes individuals' experiences in specific organizational and occupational contexts. For example, Waddington (1999) takes exception to the vilification of police culture and the way it is portrayed as the cause of many ills in the police organization, including the discrimination of women and other minorities. He argues that the 'cult of masculinity' that is a prominent feature of the police culture enables officers to make sense of an inherently problematic organizational experience—their occupation of a 'marginal position in any society that has pretensions to liberal democracy' (p. 302).

Understanding culture as something that serves a purpose, rather than something that has a free-standing existence, may shed more light on the reasons why minorities sustain apparently hostile cultures (Dick & Jankowicz, 2001). It can also move us away from a situation in which we are unproblematically treating some 'values' as 'wrong', and in the process alienating significant sectors of the workplace (Ellis & Sonnenfield, 1994).

Social identity theory

The vast majority of the work that has examined the effects of workforce diversity per se, rather than the effects of diversity initiatives, is underpinned by social identity theory (Tajfel, 1982; Turner, 1987). According to social identity theory, individuals possess both a personal and a collective or social identity, the latter varying according to the groups to which we belong, e.g. women, worker, professional and so on. Social identity theory states that we will be attracted to groups that can enhance our self-esteem and will be less attracted to groups that we perceive to be potentially esteem-damaging. Once we have achieved group membership of any specific group, there is a tendency for our perceptions to be influenced by out-group homogeneity bias: the tendency to perceive groups that are different from our own as sharing similar (largely undesirable) characteristics. It is these processes that are postulated to be at the root of stereotypes which can then lead to unfavourable judgements being made about members of out-groups. This framework has been used to account for the fact that increased group heterogeneity can lead to conflict (Pelled et al., 1999); while increased homogeneity in values (particularly agreement over group goals and processes) leads to improved achievement outcomes (Jehn et al., 1999). It has also been used to account for the asymmetrical effects of workgroup diversity on the affective outcomes of organizational dominants and minorities (Tsui et al., 1992), on the grounds that organizational dominants experience a loss in status (and hence self-esteem) as workforce heterogeneity increases, whereas minorities experience an increase in status.

In terms of diversity initiatives, social identity theorists have postulated that two strategies are likely to be helpful in reducing conflict and promoting effective individual and workgroup outcomes: recategorization and cross-categorization.

Recategorization strategies (Gaertner et al., 1990) involve interventions that cause the salience of one's collective identity (e.g. gender) to be reduced by enhancing a different superordinate identity (e.g. the organization). This type of process is thought to be at the root of findings that suggest that increased task interdependence increases achievement outcomes in diverse workgroups (Watson et al., 1993). Cross-categorization strategies (Marcus-Newhall et al., 1993) involve rendering personal identity salient by crossing one collective identity (e.g. gender) with another (e.g. marketing function). The idea here is that the cognitive system becomes confused by two conflicting collective identities and hence the two cancel each other out, resulting in individuals interacting on the basis of their personal identity (see Jehn et al., 1999 for a study demonstrating these sorts of effects). However, recategorization and cross-categorization strategies can be problematic for a number of reasons (Brickson, 2000), including the fact that they rely heavily on context (for example, how possible is it for organizations to assign workgroups strong unifying goals?), and the fact that real world categorizations such as gender and functional unit acquire salience in a variety of uncontrollable and unpredictable situations (for instance, gender may become highly salient for a woman who has been turned down for a promotion when she was the only woman on the shortlist).

Apart from these issues, there are far more fundamental concerns pertaining to the neglect of power and social processes in social identity theory (Henriques, 1998). By focusing on cognitions as central to the processes of 'stereotyping', 'unfavourable judgements' and 'group attractiveness', the social and historical conditions that have led to women and other minorities being subordinated within organizational hierarchies in terms of access to career opportunities and rewards are ignored. In the same way, the 'status' of white dominants is treated as an unproblematic fact, rather than being critically examined so that the processes that continually reproduce their status can be identified and challenged. The conditions in both organizations and the sociocultural context that produce social differences are, therefore, not accounted for in social identity theory.

Recently, organizational scholars have used the work of Michel Foucault to explain how the status quo is maintained in organizations, often to the apparent detriment of some groups. In these studies, the individual is 'de-centred' in favour of an examination of discourse, defined as 'cultural regimes of knowledge' that are used to make sense of ourselves and others. Discourse, from a Foucauldian perspective, is never neutral nor does it encompass a 'once and for all' body of knowledge. Discourse is derived from specific, historical relations of power and is constantly resisted or reinforced as it is used to make sense of ourselves or others. Thus, a very simple example, is the emergence of 'feminist discourse' as a response to discourses in which women were subordinated and rendered economically dependent on men (Weedon, 1987). Women can draw on feminist discourse to argue for equal pay or equality of treatment at work. However, feminist discourse has been 'resisted' by some groups and individuals and has produced alternative sets of, sometimes, derogatory ideas about what a 'feminist' is, including being 'butch', 'pushy' or 'extreme' (Faludi, 1991). Thus some women, understandably, do not wish to be seen as 'feminists'.

Within the context of organizations, these ideas have been used to examine how power relations in organizations are reproduced, leading to the subordination of some groups and the dominance of others. For example, Collinson (1994) shows how organizational power relations between management and shop-floor staff in a manufacturing organization are reproduced by acts of 'resistance' on the part of shop-floor staff. Such acts included the control of output and inverting the class-based hierarchy in the organization (rubbishing management and celebrating shop-floor skills and knowledge). Collinson argues that these acts 'incorporate an explicit discourse of consent, not only to labour commodification but also to the elite control of the enterprise' (Collinson, 1994: 38). Kondo (1990) studied the relations of power in a sweet factory in Tokyo, focusing specifically on the part-time female workers whose working conditions were far inferior to those of their full-time male colleagues. Kondo argues that the Japanese female identity is dominated by notions of *uchi*, roughly translated as 'home life'. This means that work is never treated as a serious part of the Japanese woman's life, despite the fact that many of them and their families are absolutely dependent on this part-time work for survival. However, *uchi* not only operates to secure these women's consent to appalling working conditions, but also is used by them to resist workplace practices, such as demonstrating absolute loyalty to the firm—these women would often take a few days' unauthorized leave and justify this through *uchi*.

These studies demonstrate that the conditions that give rise to the subordination or unfair treatment of some groups is more complex than cognitive or perceptual error, and further demonstrates that the status quo is unlikely to be changed by simply increasing contact between groups of unequal status in organizations. Indeed, these studies suggest that organizations themselves need to be problematized if we are to adequately understand the processes that lead to subordination (Ferguson, 1984).

METHODOLOGICAL ISSUES

Inevitably, methodology, if it is to be useful, must be informed by appropriate theory. As has been argued previously, much of what is written in the diversity literature is not underpinned by sound theory, and it is therefore unsurprising that the methodologies employed are problematic for two principal reasons.

First is the tendency to use cross-sectional methodologies to identify 'associations' between various dimensions of workforce diversity or (less frequently) between diversity initiatives and various individual level outcomes. Despite the confidence and assurances offered by authors utilizing such methodologies, the fact remains that no assertion about the direction of causality can be made. Thus, we are still in the dark as to whether diversity initiatives and some dimensions of workforce diversity actually have tangible effects at the level of the individual. Longitudinal studies are needed that more adequately track the processes and outcomes of both workforce diversity and of diversity initiatives.

Second, is the tendency to use positivist methodologies. In many studies, individuals are unproblematically placed into categories on the basis of race or gender and 'outcome' measures are taken (often using self-report measures). Associations between the independent variables (race or gender) and the dependent variables (various individual or organizational outcomes) are then sought. These studies neglect the broader historical and specifically organizational context within which these individuals are located. As a consequence, the complexity of the processes that are at play is oversimplified. For example, police forces throughout the UK are frequently admonished by Her Majesty's Inspectorate (HMIC, 1992; 1995) for their poor record on recruiting and retaining women officers. Studies have suggested that the reasons for this are located in the police culture (Brown, 1992); in male police officers' attitudes to women (Flynn, 1982; Balkin, 1986; Young, 1991); and in the nature of police work itself (Martin, 1989; Wilson, 1982). However, there are as many studies that contradict these views as support them (Dick & Cassell, in press). What is clear is that there is enormous variation in the experiences and beliefs of police women and methodologies that attempt to treat the women and their experiences as 'variables' are unable to capture this variability, let alone explain it. In a recent study by Dick and Cassell (forthcoming), they argue that the problem for many police forces is not located in the attitudes of individual men and women, but in the way the job of the police officer is constructed through discourses that emphasize its demanding nature. These discourses operate not just at the rhetorical level, but at the level of material organizational practices, such as the shift system, not handing jobs (arrests) over to colleagues at the end of a shift, and long working hours. These practices continually reproduce dominant discourses about the nature of policing, which in turn render it impracticable for many women to remain in their jobs once they have children.

While not suggesting that positivist methodologies should never be employed, one could argue that positivist methodologies provide a two-dimensional snapshot of the nature and effects of social processes and practices. Diversity management initiatives are complex both in their nature and outcomes and we therefore need to supplement positivist methodologies (preferably longitudinal) with more phenomenological methodologies if we are to advance our understanding and practice in this area.

CONCLUSIONS

Do organizational efforts to manage diversity work? The answer to this question would be 'We don't know.' The evidence is certainly limited and what evidence there is, can be critiqued from a variety of theoretical and methodological perspectives. Based on the evidence discussed throughout this chapter, it appears that there are a number of key issues that future research needs to address in order to adequately answer the question posed in the title of this chapter.

First, research needs to address actual diversity initiatives implemented by organizations, not workforce diversity per se. It is clear that workforce diversity does affect individual and organizational outcomes, albeit in a variety of different ways. What is not clear is what specific practices produce good vs bad outcomes. We also need to explore the reasons for the success or otherwise of different initiatives from a more critical theoretical perspective, perhaps utilizing some of the methodologies and approaches that have been discussed. We need to move away from cross-sectional surveys and self-report data which fail to capture the complexity of the processes involved.

Second, we need to be aware of our own stake as researchers in the diversity management field. As Prasad et al. (1997) comment: 'For the most part, management academics have adopted what might be described as an attitude of *distant cheerleading*. That is, although they continue to endorse the importance of managing diversity, they have rarely engaged the process itself as a serious research act' (p. 5: original emphasis).

However, there are problems in attempting to better the lot of groups in organizations that academics construct as subordinated. Burr (1998) sums up this problem as follows: 'If we argue that a position is justifiable if it leads to the improvement of conditions for certain people, what do we mean by improvement, and can we be satisfied that our understanding would be the same as theirs?' (p. 16).

The tendency in the diversity management literature to treat these issues as unproblematic is possibly part of the reason why many diversity initiatives are treated with disdain by minorities and majorities alike (Ellis & Sonnenfield, 1994). The literature needs to engage with these issues if it is to command any serious voice. As previously argued, this might involve moving away from traditional psychological theories and using approaches underpinned by social constructionism. While these approaches by no means escape criticism (see Burr, 1998 for a summary), they at least move us away from treating phenomena such as 'discrimination' and 'prejudice' as if they are verifiable objective realties and hence towards developing initiatives that engage people rather than alienate them.

Finally, we need to move away from what Prasad et al. (1997) have called the 'commodification of diversity': 'the transformation of any reform movement into a popular entertainment item and fashionable piece of memorabilia' (p. 17). Not only does this tendency result in diversity initiatives being immediately greeted with the scepticism that accompanies all management fads, but also leads to overinflated claims about what such initiatives can achieve with little or no evidence to back these claims up. To move away from this position, we need to develop a far more critical approach. We need to examine the conditions of possibility for the emergence and take-up of the management diversity discourse, and in so doing engage with the more uncomfortable aspects of it, including the 'resistance' to diversity initiatives demonstrated by members of organizational minorities and majorities and a more circumspect analysis of what diversity initiatives can actually achieve in practice.

REFERENCES

Arnold, J., Cooper, C.L. & Robertson, I.T. (1998). *Work Psychology: Understanding Human Behaviour in the Workplace.* London: Pitman.

Baldwin, N.J. (1996). The promotion record of the United States Army: glass ceilings in the officer corps. *Public Administration Review,* **56**(2), 199–208.

Balkin, J. (1986). Why policemen don't like policewomen. *Journal of Police Science and Administration,* **16**(1), 29–38.

Barry, B. & Bateman, T.S. (1996). A social trap analysis of the management of diversity. *Academy of Management Review,* **21**(3), 757–791.

Bland, N., Mundy, G., Russell, J. & Tuffin, R. (1999). Career progression of ethnic minority police officers. *Police Research Series, Paper 107.* London: Home Office.

Brickson, S. (2000). The impact of identity orientation on individual and organizational outcomes in demographically diverse settings. *Academy of Management Review,* **25**(1), 82–106.

Brown, J.M. (1992). Changing the police culture. *Policing,* **8**, 307–322.

Brown, J.M. (1998). Aspects of discriminatory treatment of women police officers serving in forces in England and Wales. *British Journal of Criminology,* **38**(2), 265–282.

Burr, V. (1998). Overview: realism, relativism, social constructionism. In I. Parker (ed.) *Social Constructionism, Discourse and Realism.* London: Sage.

Cannings, K. (1988). Managerial promotion: the effect of socialization, specialization and gender. *Industrial and Labour Relations Review,* **42**, 77–88.

Cassell, C. (2001). Managing diversity. In T. Redman & A. Wilkinson (eds) *Human Resource Management: Issues and Strategies.* London: Addison-Wesley.

Cassell, C.M. & Biswas, R. (2000). Managing diversity in the new millenium. *Personnel Review,* **29**(3), 268–273.

Chatman, J.A., Polzer, J.T., Barsade, S.G. & Neale, M.A. (1998). Being different yet feeling similar: the influence of demographic composition and organizational culture on work processes and outcomes. *Administrative Science Quarterly,* **43**(4), 749–772.

Collinson, D. (1994). Strategies of resistance: power, knowledge and subjectivity in the workplace. In J.M., Jermier, D. Knights & W.R. Nord (eds) *Resistance and Power in Organizations.* London: Routledge.

Comer, D.R. & Soliman, C.E. (1996). Organizational efforts to manage diversity: do they really work? *Journal of Managerial Issues,* **8**(4), 470–484.

Cordero, R., DiTomaso, N. & Farris, G.F. (1996). Gender and race/ethnic composition of technical work groups: relationship to creative productivity and morale. *Journal of Engineering and Technology Management,* **13**, 205–221.

Cox, T. (1993). *Cultural Diversity in Organizations: Theory, Research and Practice.* San-Francisco, Calif.: Berrett-Koehler.

Dass, P. & Parker, B. (1999). Strategies for managing human resource diversity: from resistance to learning. *The Academy of Management Executive,* **13**(2), 68–82.

Dick, P. & Cassell, C. (2002). Barriers to managing diversity in a UK constabulary: the role of discourse. *Journal of Management Studies,* **39**(7), 953–976.

Dick, P. & Cassell, C. (in press). The position of police women: a discourse analytic study. *Work, Employment and Society.*

Dick, P. & Jancowicz, A.D. (2001). A social constructionist account of police culture and its influence on the representation and progression of female officers: a rep. grid analysis in a UK police force. *Policing: An International Journal of Police Strategy and Management,* **24**(2), 181–189.

Ellis, C. & Sonnenfield, J.A. (1994). Diverse approaches to managing diversity. *Human Resource Management*, **33**(1), 79–109.

Faludi, S. (1991). *Backlash: The Undeclared War against Women*. London: Chatto and Windus.

Ferguson, K. E. (1984). *The Feminist Case against Bureaucracy*. Philadelphia: Temple University Press.

Fielding, N. (1994). Cop canteen culture. In E. Stanko & T. Newburn (eds) *Just the Boys Doing Business: Men, Masculinity and Crime*. London: Routledge.

Flynn, E.E. (1982). Women as criminal justice professionals: a challenge to change tradition. In N.H. Rafter & E.A.Stanko (eds) *Judge, Lawyer, Victim, Thief: Women, Gender Roles and Criminal Justice*. Boston: Northeastern University Press.

Gaertner, S.L., Mann, J.A., Dovidio, J.F., Murrell, A.J. & Pomare, M. (1990). How does co-operation reduce inter-group bias? *Journal of Personality and Social Psychology*, **59**, 692–704.

Hearn, J. & Parkin, P.W. (1983). Gender and organizations: a selective review and critique of a neglected area. *Organization Studies*, **4**(3), 219–242.

Henriques, J. (1998). Social psychology and the politics of racism. In J. Henriques, W. Hollway, C. Urwin, C. Venn & V. Walkerdine, *Changing the Subject: Psychology, Social Regulation and Subjectivity*. London: Routledge.

Herriot, P. & Pemberton, C. (1995). *Competitive Advantage through Diversity*. London: Sage.

Hicks-Clarke, D. & Iles, P. (2000). Climate for diversity and its effects on career and organisational attitudes and perceptions. *Personnel Review*, **29**(3), 324–345.

HMIC (Her Majesty's Chief Inspector of Constabulary) (1992). *Equal Opportunities in the Police Service*. London: Home Office.

HMIC (1995). *Developing Diversity in the Police Service. Thematic Inspection Report*. London: Home Office.

Holdaway, S. & Parker, S.K. (1998). Policing women police: uniform patrol, promotion and representation in the CID. *British Journal of Criminology*, **88**(1), 40–64.

Jehn, K.A., Northcraft, G.B. & Neale, M.A. (1999). Why differences make a difference: a field study of diversity, conflict and performance in workgroups. *Administrative Science Quarterley*, **44**(4), 741–763.

Kandola, R. & Fullerton, J. (1998). *Managing the Mosaic: Diversity in Action*. London: IPD.

Kasl, S.V. (1986). Stress and disease in the workplace: a methodological commentary on the accumulated evidence. In M.F. Cataldo & T.J. Coates (eds) *Health and Industry: A Behavioral Medicine Perspective*. New York: Wiley.

Kondo, D.K. (1990). *Crafting Selves: Power, Gender and Discourses of Identity in a Japanese Workplace*. Chicago: University of Chicago Press.

Lewis, G.B. (1997). Race, sex and performance ratings in the Federal Service. *Public Administration Review*, **57**(6), 479–490.

Lott, J.R. (2000). Does a helping hand put others at risk? Affirmative action, police departments and crime. *Economic Inquiry*, **38**(2), 239–277.

Marcus-Newhall, A., Miller, N., Holtz, R. & Brewer, M.B. (1993). Cross-cutting category membership with role assignment: a means of reducing intergroup bias. *British Journal of Social Psychology*, **32**, 125–146.

Martin, S.E. (1989). *On the Move: The Status of Women in Policing*. Washington, DC: Police Foundation.

Palich, L.E. & Gomez-Mejia, L.R. (1999). A theory of global strategy and firm efficiencies: considering the effects of cultural diversity. *Journal of Management*, **25**(4), 587–606.

Pelled, L.H., Eisenhardt, K.M. & Xin, K.R. (1999). Exploring the black box: an analysis of work group diversity, conflict and performance. *Administrative Science Quarterly*, **44**(1), 1–25.

Perotin, V. & Robinson, A. (2000). Employee participation and equal opportunities practices: productivity effect and potential complementarities. *British Journal of Industrial Relations*, **38**(4), 557–583.

Prasad, P., Mills, A.J., Elmes, M. & Prasad, A. (1997). *Managing the Organizational Melting Pot: Dilemmas of Workforce Diversity*. Thousand Oaks: Sage.

Richard, O.C. (2000). Racial diversity, business strategy and firm performance: a resource-based view. *Academy of Management Journal*, **43**(2), 164–172.

Robinson, G. & Dechant, K. (1997). Building a business case for diversity. *Academy of Management Executive*, **11**(3), 21–31.

Robinson, J.G. & McIlwee, J.S. (1991). Men, women, and the culture of engineering. *The Sociological Quarterly*, **32**(3), 403–421.

Smircich, L. (1983). Concepts of culture and organizational analysis. *Administrative Science Quarterly*, **28**, 339–358.

Tajfel, H. (ed.) (1982). *Social Identity and Intergroup Relations*. London: Cambridge University Press.

The Stephen Lawrence Inquiry: Report of an Inquiry by Sir William MacPherson of Cluny (1999). Cmd 4262-1. London: HMSO.

Thornburg, L. (1994). Journey toward a more inclusive culture? *HRMagazine*, **39**(2), 79–84.

Tsui, A.S., Egan, T.D. & O'Reilly, C.A. (1992). Being different: relational demography and organizational attachment. *Administrative Science Quarterly*, **37**(4), 549–580.

Turner, J.C. (1987). *Rediscovering the Social Group: A Self-Categorization Theory*. Oxford: Blackwell.

Waddington, P.A.J. (1999). Police (canteen) sub-culture: an appreciation. *British Journal of Criminology*, **39**(2), 287–309.

Walker, B.A. & Hanson, W.C. (1992). Valuing differences at Digital Equipment Corporation. In S.E. Jackson & Associates (eds) *Diversity in the Workplace: Human Resource Initiatives*. New York: Guilford Press.

Watson, W.E., Kumar, K. & Michaelson, L.K. (1993). Cultural diversity's impact on interaction process and performance: comparing homogeneous and diverse task groups. *Academy of Management Journal*, **36**, 590–602.

Weedon, C. (1987). *Feminist Practice and Poststructuralist Theory*. Oxford: Basil Blackwell.

Wharton, A.S. & Baron, J.N. (1987). So happy together: the impact of gender segregation on men at work. *American Sociological Review*, **52**(5), 574–587.

Willmott, H. (1993). Strength is ignorance; slavery is freedom: managing culture in modern organizations. *Journal of Management Studies*, **30**(4), 515–552.

Wilson, N.K. (1982). Women in the criminal justice professions. In N.H. Rafter & E.A. Stanko (eds) *Judge, Lawyer, Victim, Thief: Women, Gender Roles and Criminal Justice*. Boston: Northeastern University Press.

Wise, L.R. & Tschirhart, M. (2000). Examining empirical evidence on diversity effects: how useful is diversity research for public-sector managers? *Public Administration Review*, **60**(5), 386–394.

Wright, P., Ferris, S.P., Hiller, J.S. & Kroll, M. (1995). Competitiveness through management of diversity: effects on stock price valuation. *Academy of Management Journal*, **38**(1), 272–287.

Young, M. (1991). *An Inside Job: Policing and Police Culture in Britain*. Oxford: Clarendon Press.

CHAPTER 9

Managing Diversity: Caste and Gender Issues in Organizations in India

Elisabeth M. Wilson

Institute for Development Policy and Management,
University of Manchester, UK

SUMMARY

This chapter examines sources of difference within the workforce of India, focusing principally on caste and gender, and sets these within the Indian cultural context. It discusses the use and application of reservation, a form of affirmative action, as a means of enabling disadvantaged groups, principally scheduled castes and scheduled tribes, to gain public sector employment. Reservation has aspects of both positive action and positive discrimination, and its successes and criticisms are discussed. In relation to women, different provisions apply, often based on essentialist assumptions of gender differences. The concept of managing diversity has gained little currency within India, and reasons for this are explored.

INTRODUCTION

India is not merely a country and the largest parliamentary democracy in the world, but also a subcontinent, presenting significant internal diversity. The impacts of both globalization and liberalization have focused increasing attention on Indian entrepreneurialism and expertise, particularly in relation to software development. Joint ventures, foreign direct investment and outsourcing of support services such as call centres by European firms point to India not only as a business partner, but also as a coming source of expert labour. The treatment of diversity within Indian workplaces is therefore a pertinent focus of enquiry.

Individual Diversity and Psychology in Organizations. Edited by Marilyn J. Davidson and Sandra L. Fielden.
© 2003 John Wiley & Sons, Ltd.

This chapter reviews approaches to equal employment opportunities and managing diversity within the Indian context. Sources of diversity in India are discussed, the most salient being caste and gender, followed by an overview of the legislative framework for employment equity, generally known as reservation. The successes of this particular form of affirmative action are discussed, as are criticisms. Reference is made to the application of different approaches to equal employment opportunities in the public and private sectors. There is discussion as to whether the concept of managing diversity can be applied to India, and speculation on the implications for Indian organizations.

SOURCES OF DIVERSITY IN INDIA

Monappa (1997) identifies the principal components of diversity in the Indian context as socio-economic status, ethnic background and linguistic composition. Other writers (e.g. Sivaramayya, 1996) see the main concerns of diversity centring on caste and gender. These major sources of diversity, and others (see Figure 9.1), will be discussed in this section, before considering in the next section how they are dealt with in the Indian context.

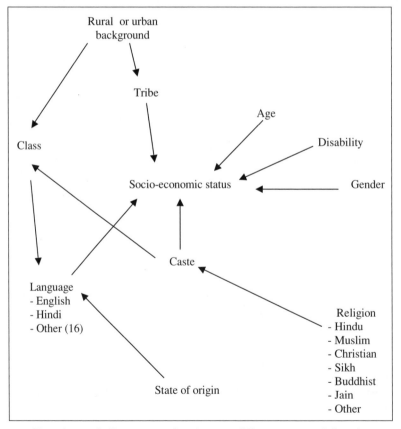

Note: Arrows indicate connections between different aspects of diversity

FIGURE **9.1**   Sources of diversity in India

India has an active workforce of 314 million persons, of which 224 million are male and 90 million female, according to the 1991 census (India at a Glance: Work Participation, 2001). India is a nation spread substantially across and beyond a subcontinent. Within its 32 states there is constitutional recognition of 18 major languages (Bhargava et al., 1995), of which Hindi is the predominant group spoken by 40 per cent of the population, according to government sources (India at a Glance: Languages Spoken, 2001). English and Hindi are the two official languages of the government of India (Budhwar, 2001). This makes for a linguistically and culturally complex nation (Newsom & Carrell, 1994).

The principal social, and hence workforce, difference that distinguishes India from other countries is the caste system, which sprang initially from Hinduism (*Economist*, 1998a). Caste is a hierarchical social system, determined by birth, and distinguished principally by endogamy (marriage within one's own caste or subcaste) and rules about physical and social contact with other castes (Dube, 1996). As Panini (1996: 39) states: 'membership of a caste makes a person part of a person-based social network which controls insiders' information about economic opportunities, transmits skills, and provides varied types of human and material support'.

Visitors to India often despair of understanding caste. This is hardly surprising, as even in-depth studies of villages by Indian sociologists and social anthropologists fail to achieve agreed descriptions of *varna*, the hierarchical relationships between castes (Shah, 1996a). The categorization of groups by themselves and others can, and often does, differ (Unnithan, 1994), and it is said that all one can state with certainty is that Brahmins are at the top of the system and Dalits, formerly known as untouchables, are at the bottom (Shah, 1996a). In fact four main castes are identified (see Figure 9.2): Brahmins (priests), Khatriyas (warriors), Vaisyas (business people), and Sudras (manual labourers). Below these are untouchables, also known as Dalits (oppressed).

Dalits can still be victims of caste-based violence, with allegations that state governments perpetuate violence and collude with dominant castes (*Hindu*, 2000a). Although it is posited that caste is a social construction (Sunstein, 1999), some research indicates genetic differences between men of different castes, thought to be an outcome of social segregation. Despite attempts to change differential outcomes for those of lower caste in educational, social and economic life, its salience persists. As an article in the *Hindu* (2001a: 16) states: 'Inflicted by birth, sanctified by religion, glorified by tradition, caste has had brutal repercussions for a fifth of India's population.'

In the past, and more persistently in rural areas, caste determined occupation. Increasing urbanization has weakened this link considerably (Shah, 1996a), as have government

FIGURE 9.2   Main caste divisions

policies. A recent report in *World Development* (Chari, 2000) paradoxically illustrates both the persistence of caste-based networks, and also the loosening of links with specific occupations. It reports that members of the agrarian Gounder caste are the predominant owners of small companies manufacturing cotton knitwear in Tirupper, and through their networking activities have enabled class mobility (Chari, 2000).

As well as castes, India has a number of tribes recognized as ethnically distinct from other Indians, the greater majority suffering significant disadvantages (Unnithan, 1994), as well as a minority enjoying considerable economic advantages, such as the Coorgs. The 1991 census (India at a Glance: Scheduled Castes and Scheduled Tribes, 2001) indicates that scheduled castes are 16.48 per cent of the population, and scheduled tribes 8.08 per cent, making a total of 24.56 per cent. There is considerable variation between states; for instance, 28.3 per cent of the population are scheduled castes in the Punjab, but only 0.1 per cent in Mizoram (India at a Glance: Scheduled Castes and Scheduled Tribes, 2001).

Class used to be an outcome of caste, but has become increasingly differentiated from it as a response to education, industrialization and urbanization. However, there remains legal and linguistic confusion between the concepts of caste and class (Sivaramayya, 1996; Shah, 1996a). Socio-economic disadvantage is the hallmark of large groups, some of whom are legally recognized as Other Backward Classes (Shah, 1996a) (further discussed later). Fifty-two per cent of the population are literate, although male literacy rates exceed female: 64 to 39 per cent (India at a Glance: Number of Literates and Literacy Rates, 2001). Those who suffer from educational disadvantages are likely also to suffer from economic and social disadvantages. For instance, bonded labour persists despite legal procedures for their identification and rehabilitation; in 1996 surveys identified 48 916 bonded labourers, of whom 11 913 had been rehabilitated by the end of March 1999 (Director-General of Labour Welfare, 2001a). There is a growing middle class, increasingly urbanized, and estimated at between 100 million (*Electronic Design*, 1999) and 300 million (Ghosh & Roy, 1997). About 100 000 graduate from universities annually (*Electronic Design*, 1999), but there is still a significant difference in economic and educational attainment between urban and rural dwellers. Indeed India's President, Mr Narayanan, expressed his concern at divisions between the privileged 'nouveau riche' and a resentful underclass (Kazmin, 2000).

A further source of diversity in the workforce is the split between organized and unorganized labour. The 1991 census indicated that 91 per cent (286 million) of the workforce was in the unorganized sector with only 9 per cent (28 million) in the organized sector (Director-General Labour Welfare, 2001b). Among those occupations specifically mentioned within the informal sector as 'specially distressed categories' are scavengers (rubbish collectors/sorters), an occupation traditionally linked to the untouchable caste. However, other categories cover a wide range of self-employed people, and small businesspeople, as well as casual labourers, partisans and domestic workers (Director-General of Labour Welfare, 2001b). It is likely that the 2001 census (once published) will reveal a larger formal sector.

The caste system is buttressed by the major religion, Hinduism, which is followed by 83 per cent of the population (Ghosh & Roy, 1997). It is a syncretic religion that has incorporated local gods and customs, leading to a wide range of sects and beliefs (*Economist*, 1998a). Other religions represented include 11 per cent Muslims (Ghosh &

Roy, 1997), with the remaining 6 per cent composed of Christians, Sikhs, Buddhists, Jains, and small groups like the Zoroastrians. Although Patel (1996) reports increasing homogenization of culture as a result of liberalization, globalization and urbanization, there are sporadic flare-ups of what is known as 'communalism', communal hostility between different castes, classes and faiths.

Disability is widespread in a country where preventive and rehabilitative services are not available to the vast majority of the population. Estimates are that 5–6 per cent of the population are physically handicapped, a total of 60–65 million (*Times of India*, 1998a). The 2001 census will collect information, categorizing disabilities into sight, speech, hearing, movement and mental (*Hindu* 2001b).

Age is a naturally occurring difference in any workforce. Within India its salience is tied to the acceptance of hierarchy discussed below. Thus seniority may still play a prominent role in promotion decisions (Budhwar, 2001).

However, the most obvious source of diversity in the workforce is gender, with women considerably disadvantaged. Women have a persistently low status and lack equality in many aspects of life (Patel, 1996). This is evident in sex determination of the foetus, dowry demands and bride burning (MacFarquhar, 1994). In India as a whole, there are 927 females for every 1000 males (India at a Glance: Female Sex Ratio, 2001). This varies between 1036 in Kerala where women are more emancipated than elsewhere, to 859 in Annachal Pradesh (India at a Glance: Female Sex Ratio, 2001). Despite progress, a gender gap remains in relation to female education, employment and per capita income (*Hindu*, 2000b). Women represented 24.9 per cent of the workforce in 1992, with a higher percentage of illiteracy than is the case overall (Ghosh & Roy, 1997). This can be explained by the gender gap in education. In terms of human capital theory there are better economic returns from investing in boys' education (Kingdon, 1998). In addition girls may also be offered lower-quality education (Kingdon, 1998).

The growth of opportunities for women seeking work is smaller than the rate of growth of the female labour force (Ghosh & Roy, 1997). While women's participation in the workforce may be underestimated because of multiple roles and the greater likelihood of their being in the informal sector, men are still the primary breadwinners (Ghosh & Roy, 1997). Nevertheless as Monappa (1997) states, the Indian woman cannot be stereotyped. There is an established tradition of women in the professions and government service, alongside middle-class women who conform to the traditional role of homemaker, and poor women who have no choice but to work as urban or agricultural labourers (Monappa, 1997). Writers indicate a distinct difference between educated middle-class urban women, and their rural sisters (e.g. Manchanda, 1995). Where they are employed in the formal sector, women tend to cluster in service sectors such as banking, travel and teaching (Monappa, 1997). Social change has led to changes in attitude towards educated women, and the prejudice against working outside the home is disappearing in urban centres (Ghosh & Roy, 1997), although India has the largest number of educated, economically inactive, women in the world (Mittal, 1994). The Ministry of Labour (Ministry of Labour at a Glance, 2001) of the government of India identifies a number of significant problems still faced by women workers. These include: a declining trend in work participation rate, lack of organization, the adverse effect of mechanization, the non-payment of wages or of equal wages, and economic and sexual exploitation (Ministry of Labour at a Glance, 2001). Gender discrimination is ubiquitous, and there is rising awareness of harassment at work and in public (Aravamudan, 1998).

EQUAL EMPLOYMENT OPPORTUNITIES IN INDIA

RESERVATION

The constitution of India guarantees equality of opportunity to all citizens (Ghosh & Roy, 1997) and officially abolished untouchability and casteism (Raman, 1999). Nevertheless the government of India acknowledges that some groups require special consideration, using a form of affirmative action known as reservation. These groups can be seen in Figure 9.3. Scheduled castes and scheduled tribes are defined by the constitution of India and subsequent legislative acts as disadvantaged groups, and are deemed to constitute 22.5 per cent of the population of India (Monappa, 1997). Because of concern that this left out a large proportion of the population who suffered from similar disadvantages, a further reserved category of Other Backward Classes was created, increasing the proportion of reserved places from 22.5 per cent to 49.5 per cent (Upadhyaya, 1998). Individual states can also set their own quotas, and in some states the percentage of reservations has reached questionable levels, such as 69 per cent of government jobs in Tamil Nadu (Raman, 1999). It has been described as 'a highly programmatic method for redressing past social discrimination' (Sunstein, 1999).

Reservation applies to local council and parliamentary seats, as well as posts in most government services and enterprises (not the armed forces, government scientific posts and the higher judiciary, for example), in addition to giving preferential access to higher educational institutions. For instance, someone from a scheduled caste or scheduled tribe can enter an undergraduate degree with lower marks than other candidates; what is harder to understand is why this special concession, a form of social engineering (Sunstein, 1999), also applies for entry into master's programmes. These benefits are summarized in Figure 9.4. There is persistent criticism that the promulgation of affirmative action policies threatens the concept of merit; for instance, only half of the places in medical and engineering colleges are accessible to young people from higher castes, regardless of their entry qualifications (Raman, 1999).

- Scheduled castes

- Scheduled tribes

- Other Backward Classes

- National sportsmen/women

- People with visual, aural and mobility disabilities

- Ex-military personnel

- 'Sons of the Soil'

FIGURE 9.3   Reserved categories

• Quotas for Government of India and state jobs
• More flexible rules for promotion
• Quotas for council and parliamentary seats
• Entry to higher education institutions with lower marks, for undergraduate and postgraduate degrees

FIGURE 9.4 Main benefits of reservation

As a consequence of reservation substantial advances have been made by some formerly disadvantaged groups (Shah, 1996b; Raman, 1999). For instance in Tamil Nadu it is asserted that several disadvantaged sections of society have moved up the social ladder as a result of reservation in educational opportunities and government jobs (*Hindu*, 2001c). However, much remains to be done. Although caste is no longer the sole determinant of occupation, class and power (Panini, 1996), nevertheless there is persisting social discrimination (*Times of India*, 1998b; Raman, 1999) and inequalities in terms of access to education and employment (Dhesi, 1998). Systemic social disadvantage (Sunstein, 1999) gives rise to inequality in terms of access to both the acquisition of human capital and labour market (Dhesi, 1998).

It is impossible to disentangle politics from other aspects of Indian life. Caste as well as religion continues to be a salient determinant of elections (*Economist*, 1998b), and concern has been expressed at the expansion in the number of caste-based political parties (*Hindu*, 2000b). Although there has been progression in terms of the political representation of disadvantaged groups, with the current President K.R. Narayanan a member of a scheduled caste, this comes at a heavy price in terms of focusing attention on caste as a political issue (Raman, 1999). It is alleged that the rise of the BJP, the Hindu nationalist political party with a religious fundamentalist platform, was built up as a consequence of the extension of the reservation system (Raman, 1999). In addition, while the lower castes may be well represented as politicians, the vast majority of the Indian population, predominantly the lower castes, are impoverished and illiterate (Raman, 1999). The reservation system leads to what has been described in the UK as a hierarchy of oppression, and competition for disadvantaged status (Sunstein, 1999).

As well as fault finding with the outcomes of reservation, its categorization techniques have also come under scrutiny. There have been serious criticisms of the methods used to identify castes by the government-appointed Mandal Commission (Radhakrishnan, 1996; Shah, 1996a). For example, the concept of 'backward class' is ambiguous and excludes Muslims and Christians (Sivaramayya, 1996). Reservation has therefore been persistently criticized, with calls for the abolition of caste and tribe as markers, and their replacement with economic criteria (*Hindu*, 1999a). A major problem has been the lack of clarity as to whether primary considerations are social, educational or economic (Radhakrishnan, 1996). For instance, many upper-caste Hindus such as Brahmins, the highest caste, are not necessarily economically well off (Raman, 1999). There are claims that the more economically advanced segments of scheduled categories have hijacked the system (*Hindu*, 1999b), leading to concern about the 'creamy layers', families and groups who have benefited substantially already as a prior outcome of reservation policy

Has done too much

- 'Creamy layers' benefit at expense of truly disadvantaged

- Stimulates backlash from higher castes

Has not done enough

- Has not sufficiently redressed socio-economic differences

- Categorization is questionable

- Does not usually include women

- Has not changed attitudes sufficiently

FIGURE 9.5   Criticisms of reservation

(Sivaramayya, 1996). An immediate concern is the fact that 'socially advanced', economically privileged lower-caste families avail themselves of quota opportunities, thus taking up places that might otherwise be available to the truly underprivileged lower castes. Figure 9.5 summarizes criticisms. Another serious consequence is the mindset that the reservation system has encouraged that problems of social and economic disadvantage need not be resolved by changing minds or behaviour but by the rigid application of quotas.

However, perhaps one of the worst outcomes of the system is that it satisfies no one. Disadvantaged groups continue to be dissatisfied (*Times of India*, 1998c), as the state has not delivered equality (Radhakrishnan, 1996). The same article quoted above that pointed to the success of reservation for some groups in Tamil Nadu, conceded that there are still underprivileged sections of society, specifically the Dalits (*Hindu*, 2001c). Even in Kerala, the southern state which has been largely under communist control since independence, achieving higher literacy rates and significant redistribution, there continues to be inter-caste economic disparity in respect of the scheduled castes and scheduled tribes population (Deshpande, 2000). Meanwhile, the Hindu majority is resentful of the perceived privileged status of minority groups (Parekh, 1996). Reservation is also said to be manipulated by politicians for their own ends (Jayaram, 1996), and no Minister or political party wishes to be the one who removes a specified category from the reserved list because of the potential political fallout.

The Indian government remains very sensitive to allegations of caste-based discrimination, rejecting suggestions of solutions from outside at a recent UN Human Rights Commission meeting (*AsiaPulse News*, 2000). Government representatives also rejected suggestions that the caste system is racist (*AsiaPulse News*, 2000), and refused to allow the inclusion of caste in the 2001 World Conference against Racism (*Times of India*, 2001). However the government of India has been roundly criticized by groups representing academia, NGOs and civil society in general, contending the caste system is worse than racism (*Hindu*, 2001a).

Reservation has inevitably been the chosen tool to enable equal employment opportunity in India for other groups. Those with visual, aural and mobility disabilities can benefit from a 1 per cent category reservation for government posts (Government of India Annual Report, 1989–90, cited in Monappa, 1997), which must be significantly out of proportion to their representation in the population. The physically handicapped may also be allocated a quota for admission to university (*Times of India*, 1998d). A Disability Act was passed in 1996 but by 1998 there was no government body or official machinery to implement the Act, and promised incentives for employers had not materialized (*Times of India*, 1998a). Although some specialized vocational training courses were offered (*Times of India*, 1998e), action in this field had largely been left to the voluntary sector (*Star of Mysore*, 1998a). However, the promised disability rehabilitation service was inaugurated in 2001, by the Secretary for Social Justice and Empowerment (*Business Line*, 2001). It was intended to encourage collaboration between NGOs, private sector organizations, state, local and central government, to focus both on prevention and on rehabilitation (*Business Line*, 2001). As part of this scheme, the private sector was urged to help by providing employment, quality vocational training, and refocusing purchasing policy (*Business Line*, 2001).

Two further categories entitled to reservation are the military and state residents. First the government of India reserves certain posts for ex-military personnel (Monappa, 1997). Second is the demand by some states that private sector enterprises employ locals in preference to outsiders, particularly where they are in receipt of tax and other incentives. This is known as the 'Sons of the Soil' concept (Monappa, 1997).

As can be seen, most provision for employment equity is in terms of the Government of India, or the state governments respectively, setting aside set percentages of posts in government service and state corporations for the identified categories. Therefore the extension of reservation becomes the goal of any aggrieved group. For instance, there have been calls for separate reservation for the Muslims in relation to education and employment (*Hindu*, 1999b). This, however, would break the 50 per cent reservation barrier imposed by the Supreme Court of India (Shah, 1996a), which took the common-sense view that such a move would be counterproductive.

PROVISION FOR WOMEN

Although equal opportunity for women, as with all citizens, is guaranteed by the constitution of India (Ghosh & Roy, 1997), there is no consistent enforcement. A number of legislative measures have been taken to ensure women's rights at work. These include the Equal Remuneration Act 1976, which applies to both men and women in respect of pay, recruitment, training, transfers and promotion. There are also a number of protective measures preventing work underground and hazardous factory processes (Ministry of Labour at a Glance, 2001). Recognizing the special position of women, there are laws to protect women workers in factories, and plantations, as well as the provision of maternity leave for women employed in the organized sector (Ghosh & Roy, 1997).

Although reservation is the chosen tool for other groups, reservation for women within government and state employment is uncommon, and it has principally been applied in the political sphere. There have been a number of changes recently, initially reserving 40 per cent of places within village and municipal councils for women, although arguments continue about extending to 33 per cent of places in Parliament itself (Raman, 1999).

The Women's Reservation Bill led to accusations of unfairness, for instance an argument that this would give unfair advantages to upper-class women (Ghose, 1998). There is a National Commission for Women, set up in 1992, which among other concerns can intervene in specific instances of sexual harassment in the workplace (Initiative towards Women Empowerment, 2001). Guidelines as to how to deal with sexual harassment were laid down by the Supreme Court judgment in 1992 (Ministry of Labour at a Glance, 2001), and all workplaces in the organized sector were required to set up complaints committees. India has also signed its agreement to the Convention on the Elimination of All Forms of Discrimination against Women (CEDAW) (Initiative towards Women Empowerment, 2001). However, action in relation to women remains piecemeal and lacks the political clout of other groups, despite an active women's movement and some outstanding women politicians and activists.

CULTURAL INFLUENCES

The particular approach to employment equity in India is underpinned by various cultural influences, which are shown in Figure 9.6. First of these is a strong belief in essentialism, that people are born to their estate in life. Both caste and gender may be perceived in this way. Sahay and Walsham (1997) suggest that the stratification of society by caste has been exacerbated by reservation. A consequence is that most Indians accept the need for hierarchy, and are said to feel more comfortable with superior–subordinate relationships rather than contractual arrangements with peers (Sinha, 1988, cited by Sahay & Walsham, 1997). They tend to develop strong affiliations and/or dependence on superiors and colleagues (Budhwar, 2001). This also seems to lead to an acceptance of bureaucracy as a suitable organizational form. They are less responsive to work and productivity goals that are not enmeshed within a relationship (Kakar, 1978, cited by Sahay & Walsham, 1997). Favouritism by superiors is rife (Sinha, 1988, cited by Sahay & Walsham, 1997), friendliness is used as a preferred tactic in influencing subordinates (Bhatnagar, 1993), and conflict dealt with by accommodation (Sahay & Walsham, 1997).

Sahay and Walsham (1997) also suggest that the religious system, more specifically the Hindu religion, gives rise to a number of orientations: the subordination of intellect to intuition, experience to dogma, and outer experience to inward enlightenment. There are also elements of mysticism and pessimism, and a rejection of time and chronology. Time is not perceived in a linear fashion, and there is a significant orientation towards the past. Thus Singh (1990, cited by Sahay & Walsham, 1997) suggests that Indian managers can live with uncertainty, do not value time, and deal with every day as it comes. Contextual sensitivity is important for moral considerations (Miller, 1994). This also leads to attitudes of fatalism and determinism with the locus of control perceived as located outside the individual (Frazee, 1998).

Domestic systems are also influential. Traditionally the joint or extended family has defined its members' roles, and is run by paternal authority, which has been criticized as inducing infantile behaviour in other adults (Sahay & Walsham, 1997). Thus merit, as a system for promotion within organizations, is still deeply suspect in some quarters, with a preference for seniority rather than competence (*Star of Mysore*, 1998b). Work is often conceived as a duty to the family (Sinha & Sinha, 1990, cited by Sahay &

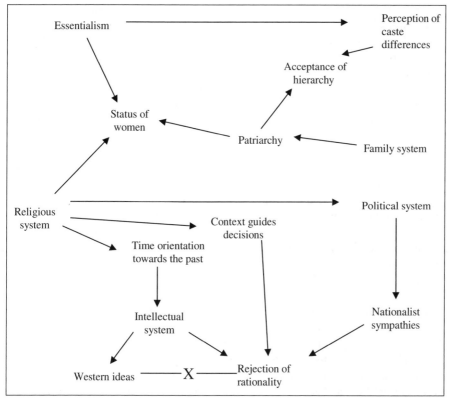

Note: X indicates conflict; Arrows indicate influence

FIGURE 9.6   Cultural influences in the workplace (based on Nabar, 1995; Sahay & Walsham, 1997)

Walsham, 1997), with duty based on an interpersonal moral code (Miller, 1994). The collectivism of Indian culture, and hence social networks, as previously discussed, tend to be defined by family, caste, kinship, linguistic and religious group (Sinha, 1988, cited by Sahay & Walsham, 1997), which are all intertwined, and interpersonal obligations are socially enforceable (Miller, 1994). However, as a response to the growing urbanization of India, there has been pressure on the joint family system (Ghosh & Roy, 1997), and an article in the *Hindu* (2001d) laments the apparent demise of the joint family with the cross-generational support this provided.

Status is generally ascriptive (Trompenaars & Hampden-Turner, 1997) within Indian society, with importance placed on social relationships and high status in society (Frazee, 1998). Thus there has been a tendency to value education and good jobs for their ascriptive and instrumental value, not merely for their intrinsic interest or worth. Budhwar (2001) points out the vicious circle of social networking as an important way of securing work and advancement, which in turn reinforces ascribed status.

As already indicated, politics assumes an importance in India out of proportion to that apparent in other countries. The national/political system adopted socialism and self-reliance after independence, implicitly encouraging nationalism and antipathy towards foreign investment (Sahay & Walsham, 1997). This is being questioned under the on-slaught of liberalization and globalization.

A further major influence is the intellectual system (Sahay & Walsham, 1997). There is a rejection of rationality and logic in the thinking of most Indians. Despite excellent mathematical development, for example, there have been ambivalent feelings towards technology. In addition qualified Indians dislike physical work (Tripathi, 1990, cited by Sahay & Walsham, 1997), with engineers preferring desk to shop-floor roles. Indian managers may have two value systems. Their traditional one inculcated from their family emphasizes relationships, dependency and security, whereas the Western-based manage-ment theory learned at home or abroad stresses individual development, efficiency and teamwork. This tension can create confusion in the execution of both roles and tasks (Sahay & Walsham, 1997).

As evidenced above, Indian culture has a deeply gendered nature, and generally con-servative attitudes towards sexuality. Women are both idealized as devoted and self-effacing, while sometimes being viewed as rebels (Forbes, 1996). Essentialist thinking links current norms and roles for women to legendary figures in Indian scriptures and literature to an extent that cannot be understood in the West (Nabar, 1995). This can be seen as an outcome of both the religious and domestic joint family systems (Sahay & Walsham, 1997). The unconscious emphasis of male superiority can be seen in the use of the term 'manpower planning' in a chapter by Budhwar (2001) describing current human resource management practice. Nabar (1995) explains that the superordinate expectation of all Indian girls is marriage, and ideas about personal choice hardly arise. There are huge contradictions in Indian culture about sexuality: on the one hand there are cele-brations of sexuality within literature and traditional art, and on the other requirements for females to dress and act modestly, with Western dress seen as loose (Nabar, 1995). Sexuality is little discussed within India, and sexual orientation is barely a social, let alone a workplace, topic of interest (Seabrook, 1994).

The influence of culture on individual behaviour should not, however, be overdeter-mined. Singh (1990) using Hofstede's (1991) dimensions of culture found that scores of individuals tended to vary according to their age, education, nature of job and eco-nomic sector. Scores on power distance, the perceived proper gap between manager and employee, were linked to the perceived style of the superior (Singh, 1990). Work stress and stability of employment influenced uncertainty avoidance (Singh, 1990). Coopera-tive colleagues and having a desirable area for living were linked with individualism, as opposed to the collectivism it is assumed pertains in India, and cooperative colleagues and opportunities for earning and advancement influenced masculinity (Singh, 1990). Shukla (1996) found that entrepreneurial behaviour as well as creativity was significantly higher in managers aged 35–39 than those aged 50+, which appears to underscore cul-tural changes. As elsewhere, it is likely that the influence of societal culture is mediated by different organizational cultures (Wilson, 2000).

THE PUBLIC SECTOR

It is within the public sector that major advances have been made as a result of poli-cies of reservation, specifically in relation to the scheduled castes and scheduled tribes. However this has been at a price of persistent criticism as discussed above. In addition to reproaches of the disregard of merit, there are also perceptions of incompetence, for example, that employees have been appointed on the basis of their group membership rather than ability (Shah, 1996b). Concern has also been expressed as to the effect on the efficiency of the public sector as a whole (Panini, 1996; Upadhyaya, 1998). More seriously, there are allegations of the perpetuation of corruption and mediocrity (Raman, 1999).

Within the public service, women have nominally enjoyed equality of opportunity, and this has led to the growth in their numbers and status (Ghosh & Roy, 1997). The constitution of India actually empowers the state to undertake positive discrimination in favour of women (Perumal, 1997–98). However, although it is recognized that within their own social class or caste women are more disadvantaged than men, reservation for women within government and state services has not been widely enacted (Perumal, 1997–98). For instance, Gujarat and Tamil Nadu reserve 30 per cent of posts in state services (Perumal, 1997–98). However, even where reservation is proposed, it may not be fulfilled. Although the government of Andra Pradesh agreed to reserve 33 per cent of suitable posts for women, seven women lawyers who had qualified in 1997 by both written examination and interview as district judges had still not been appointed by the year 2000 (Hindu, 2000c).

For a number of civil service posts there is selection through competitive examinations; women reportedly passed the examinations in greater percentages at lower than at higher levels (Perumal, 1997–98). Women represent 7.5 per cent of total central government employees; however 98 per cent of these are concentrated in lower grades (Government of India, 1997). When considering the possibility of reserving jobs for women, proposals appear tied to gender stereotyping, based on an essentialist approach (ibid, p. 4): 'A better method to ensure greater participation would be to identify certain professions which could be better manned [sic] by women such as education, health, nursing care, secretarial duties, computer etc.'

Merchant (1993) suggests that women officials are pushed into sex-stereotyped services, and even within these specialisms, they rarely reach the top. He suggests that those who do have to change into a sociological male (Merchant, 1993). For instance, sex stereotyping is prevalent within the police service, where the small number of women police officers tend to be used mainly for work with women and children (Sharma, 1998).

There have been serious instances of sexual harassment within the public service. The case of Rupan Bajaj became a cause célèbre (Manushi, 1990). Mrs Bajaj, a senior Government of India official, was sexually harassed at a mixed party by Mr Gill, director-general of police, Punjab. Despite official complaints to the police and the government of India, and the mobilization of a number of influential women within the public sector, there was no satisfactory resolution. Mr Gill remained in post and there was no inquiry. Male reactions were that working women should expect such behaviour (Manushi, 1990). Kishwar (undated) suggests that sexual harassment and slander are used as weapons of subjugation. Issar (1997–98) makes links between post-colonial theories of subjugation and the relationship between men and women in India. She suggests that the hierarchical rigidity demands unquestioning obedience and stifles innovation, affecting the esteem and work output of the lower middle levels. Women officers therefore have a choice of conforming to the prevailing style of management or being marginalized (Issar, 1997–98).

CASE STUDY: THE GOVERNMENT OF INDIA

Thakur and Nadkarni (1996) undertook a survey of the elite Indian Administrative Service (IAS), reporting that the percentage of women officers has remained at 10 per cent since independence. A profile of their respondents, both male and female, indicated that reservation had had no significant effect in terms of attracting women from less advantaged or rural backgrounds, whereas the backgrounds of male respondents were more varied. Women were less likely to be married than men, and more likely to be married to a colleague within the service. A number of rules appeared predicated on the assumption that family and domestic commitments are the prerogative of the wife, and there was gender stereotyping in the type of posts offered to women. In addition women were thought to have restricted access to informal networks. Most of the women, but none of the male respondents, thought that sexual harassment was a problem (Thakur & Nadkarni, 1996).

A United Nations-sponsored development project was undertaken with the aim of increasing the efficiency, effectiveness and accountability of the civil service (Government of India, 1997). *Inter alia* this included: 'a specific objective . . . to review the career development, placement and utilisation of women in higher public service and the establishment of an institutional mechanism to examine women's issues in civil service regulation' (Gaiha et al., 1998).

This expressed concern about the role of women within the public services, and its reflection of gender relations within the bureaucracy of the Government of India, led to a series of three-day gender sensitization workshops for both men and women officers, inaugurated in 1998 (Lal Bahadur Shastri National Academy of Administration, 1998). There was an overall aim of creating an enabling environment so that more women joined the civil services, and women's career prospects were enhanced. These were presented at various locations throughout India. The workshops involved background reading that distinguished sex and gender, and explained gender relations within a gender and development (GAD) framework, as well as factual information and case studies. There were also a series of syndicate activities aimed at identifying problems and offering solutions, including touching on sensitive issues, such as sexual harassment (Lal Bahadur Shastri National Academy of Administration, 1998).

PRIVATE SECTOR

In the formal sector the majority of entrepreneurs are drawn from the trading castes (Sahay & Walsham, 1997). Within the private sector as a whole, caste has been influential, and the formal private sector prefers to recruit via personal contact (Panini, 1996). It is said for instance that the Birlas, the family owning one of the large Indian conglomerates, recruit only trusted members of their relations and caste to sensitive managerial positions (Panini, 1996). Ironically, restrictive socialist policies strengthened caste within the private sector (Panini, 1996). Economic planning was the responsibility of the state, leading to a huge rigidified bureaucracy, which businessmen approached using kinship links and bribes (Sahay & Walsham, 1997). Panini (1996) identified three advantages of caste-based links, in what was known as the 'quota Raj'. First, violations of regulations could be kept quiet, second, caste links were helpful for government contacts, and third, quasi-independent small businesses were set up in the name of kinsmen (Panini, 1996).

It is noted, however, that caste is not always predominant in the workplace; region, language, religion and friendship may work against it (Panini, 1996). Within the private sector affiliations and cliques can emerge based on linguistic differences, which are in many cases tied to different states of origin (Monappa, 1997). Singh (1988) found that managers formed informal groups based on caste, political and provincial considerations. However, with the recent influence of liberalization, it is said that caste and class divisions are rapidly diminishing in India's business sector, particularly with the emergence of knowledge-based and service industries (*Asiamoney*, 2000). There is also more effort at lower and middle levels of organization to select new recruits according to ability and potential (Budhwar, 2001). Increasing competition from foreign firms means pressure to increase performance and productivity, and change work cultures (Budhwar, 2001).

Women's roles within the private sector were strictly circumscribed and in some cases tied to essentialist notions of their skills, with only unmarried females employed in some sectors (Budhwar, 2001). This is now changing with increased pressure for high-calibre employees. A case study undertaken by the All India Management Association and the University of Ohio (AIMA, 1998) looked at the experience of women managers within the private sector. The study reported that less than 5 per cent of middle and senior managers were women. While the majority of men and women believed that both recruitment and promotion were based on merit, a minority identified significant barriers to women's advancement, and the majority believed that pregnancy made women less desirable as employees. Stereotyping was evident in women being seen as insufficiently committed, competitive, ambitious and assertive. A minority considered that even at the senior level, the male managers perceived their female colleagues as women first, with the majority of women considering that they had to sacrifice some of their femininity, and work harder to succeed. Few male managers felt comfortable working for women. There seemed to be some support for the contention (Rosener, 1990) that women's management style is interactive, whereas men preferred a command and control style (AIMA, 1998). Other studies have alleged male prejudice and discrimination against women, citing a 'collective male mindset' (*Hindu*, 2001d). It remains to be seen as to whether the rapid changes in some parts of the formal private sector will open up opportunities for women. For instance, although women form a minority in the IT industry, they are said to be employed on similar terms and conditions to their male colleagues (*Business Line*, 2001).

CASE STUDY: THE ENGINEERING COMPANY

The author investigated an Indian engineering company, here called Indeng. Gender appeared the most salient difference, followed by caste, religion, region/state and language. Other differences also emerging as significant were graduates versus non-graduates, age, and to a lesser extent, disability.

The principal findings were that some aspects of workforce diversity, such as caste, and region of origin, were easily integrated within the company, whereas others, such as gender, were regarded as problematical. Indeng had only recently started to recruit women for other than secretarial positions, and had done this following the lead of other similar companies. There were a number of stereotyped beliefs guiding this; for instance that women were more stable. On the other hand the number of women employed was deliberately kept low in certain locations to avoid extra provisions demanded by law. Despite this background, Indeng had offered advancement to two women with limited qualifications, one at her own request, and one identified through the performance management system. Women felt constrained by the unwritten dress code and what was described as 'the mindset of the workers'. However, there was no overt sexual harassment within the company.

Whereas caste retained its importance in private life, it appeared to be a difference that was easily managed within the workplace. The CEO of Indeng was not high caste, and the incumbent group president was an untouchable, an indication of change. Indeng had systematic recruitment and selection procedures, and saw itself as a modern meritocracy. Caste was therefore seen as irrelevant to this. Class differences were, however, evident between male office staff and operatives, the former conforming to a dress code, and the latter in uniforms. There were four classes of toilet: for directors, managers, workmen and ladies.

State of origin was something of which respondents were aware in relation to colleagues, with more people in lower grades from the local state. However, the managerial cadre could be from anywhere in India, and expected to move around during their career. It was assumed that a wife would follow her husband. Analysis of managers' names discussed with interviewees indicated overwhelming representation by those of the Hindu religion. Occasionally a Christian or Parsee (Zoroastrian) was mentioned, but no Sikhs or Muslims.

Within offices all staff could speak English, which was the managerial lingua franca. Good command of the English language was said to be important, because of written and verbal interaction with others. Qualifications were an important dividing factor. Although operatives on the shop floor were relatively skilled, the abundance of Indian graduates made it easy to deny entry to supervisory and managerial ranks to non-graduates. There was some ambivalence about age. It was strongly stated by some that competence should be the principal criterion for promotion, but there were expressed doubts about appointing managers to senior positions in their thirties. There seemed to be no proactive policy about the employment of people with disabilities, although an operative who was injured had been found an office job.

Despite a sophisticated human resource system, however, the company had no equal opportunity policy as such, and the notion of managing diversity as a business issue was new to them. Differences were therefore managed in a piecemeal way, without any overall strategy.

CONCLUSIONS

India has a diverse population and workforce, but understanding of 'managing diversity' as a positive choice is not common. Legislative provision for equal employment opportunity in India is largely focused on distributive justice, or to be more precise, redistributive justice. Paradoxically this has given rise to cumbersome forms of procedural justice in the guise of reservation, which is open to a number of criticisms.

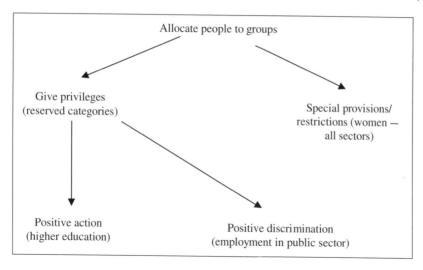

FIGURE **9.7** Legislative approaches to managing diversity

Apart from the threats contained in the 'Sons of the Soil' policies, most provision applies solely to the public sector. The focus of initiatives has been group based, perhaps reflecting the traditionally collective nature of Indian society. The methods used have been to allocate people to groups, and then give them privileges (e.g. scheduled castes and scheduled tribes) or restrictions/special provisions (e.g. women) on the basis of their group membership (Srinivas, 1996). Reservation has aspects of both positive action, in relation to educational advantages it endows, and positive discrimination with respect to public sector employment. This is illustrated in Figure 9.7. However, as Raman (1999) states, the concept of reservation is anathema to many Indians, particularly within the organized private sector, where the absence of an equal opportunities policy is unremarkable. Provision for women is piecemeal, with evident ambivalence about employment equity. Although there are indications of using a 'business case' argument (Wilson & Iles, 1999) for the employment of women, in terms of the special attributes they may bring to the workplace in both the public and private sectors, this is based on assumptions of essentialism. This engenders and embeds stereotyping and job segregation in the workplace, and may compound the disadvantages from which women suffer. Private sector approaches are illustrated in Figure 9.8.

- Rejection of reservation

- Lack of concern, individually or organizationally, for equal opportunities

- Stereotyping of women and gendered job segregation

FIGURE **9.8** Private sector approaches to managing diversity

- Denial of significance of caste differences

The approach to equal employment opportunities in India has been government rather than industry led, and therefore tends to be seen as a legal necessity for government departments and state-sponsored enterprises, rather than a business or moral issue (Wilson & Iles, 1999) that might concern the private sector. Indian approaches to equal employment opportunities can thus be seen as an equal employment opportunity rather than a managing diversity approach (Wilson & Iles, 1999). Attitudinally, as discussed above, the reservation system encourages many Indian managers to feel that equal employment opportunities or managing diversity is not their concern. The implications for Indian organizations are that a wealth of talent may be unused or underused.

This chapter has looked at diversity outside of the Anglo-Saxon assumptions of valuing diversity, and European frameworks for social cohesion. In focusing on India, Western-based views are challenged by the history, politics and socio-economic composition of a country diverse in itself. The successes and failures of reservation, employing similar methods to affirmative action, can give pause for thought to those countries contemplating similar measures, as is happening extensively in Southern Africa.

REFERENCES

AIMA (1998). Gender management: requiring a total revamp. *Indian Management*, March, All India Management Association.

Aravamudan, G. (1998). Killers on the roads. Gender jottings. *Times of India*, 8 August, 14.

Asiamoney (2000). India—a nation in transition. May.

AsiaPulse News (2000). India committed to elimination of caste-based discrimination. 11 August, 45.

Bhargava, M., Aurora, S. & Qureshi, A.N. (1995). Effectiveness of Indian languages on national development. *Psycho-Lingua*, **25**(1–2), 137–149.

Bhatnagar, D. (1993). Evaluation of managerial influence tactics: a study of Indian bank managers. *Journal of Managerial Psychology*, **8**(1), 3–9.

Budhwar, P. (2001). Human resource management in India. In P. Budhwar & Y.A. Debrah (eds) *Human Resource Management in Developing Countries*. London and New York: Routledge.

Business Line (2000). India: Gender neutral. 23 December.

Business Line (2001). India: 107 districts chosen for disability scheme. 9 March.

Chari, S. (2000). The agrarian origins of the knitwear industrial cluster Tiruppur, India. *World Development*, March.

Deshpande, A. (2000). Does caste still define disparity? A look at inequality in Kerala, India. *American Economic Review*, May.

Director-General Labour Welfare (2001a). Bonded labour latest survey and rehabilitation. http://labour.nic.in/dglw/welcome.htm (17/06/2001).

Director-General Labour Welfare (2001b). Other unorganised workers. http.//labour.nic.in/dglw/welcome.htm (17/06/2001).

Dhesi, A.S. (1998). Caste, class synergies and discrimination in India. *International Journal of Social Economics*, **25**(6–8), 1030–1048.

Dube, L. (1996). Caste and women. In M.N. Srinivas (ed.) *Caste: Its Twentieth Century Avatar* (pp. 1–27). New Delhi: Penguin Books India.

Economist (1998a). The diversity of Hinduism. **346**(806), 47.

Economist (1998b). Caste and votes: the Indian elections. **346**(8057), 47.

Electronic Design (1999). India's middle class raises hope. **47**(8), 16.

Forbes, G. (1996). *Women in Modern India*. Cambridge: University of Cambridge Press.

Frazee, V. (1998). Working with Indians (cross-cultural communication). *Workforce*, **77**, 7 S10 (2) July.

Gaiha G., Kashyup, G. & Thakur, S.G. (1998). Action report for engendering the Civil Service based on the US Federal experience. In booklet on *Reading Material for Gender Sensitivisation Workshops*. Mussoorie: Lal Bahadur Shastri National Academy of Administration.

Ghose, S. (1998). Reservations about the Bill. *Outlook*, **IV** (28), 20 July, 68–9.

Ghosh R.N. & Roy, K.C. (1997). The changing status of women in India. Impact of urbanization and development. *International Journal of Social Economics*, **24**(7–9), July–Sept., 902–917.

Government of India Annual Report (1989-90). Ministry of Personnel Public Grievances and Pensions, cited in A. Monappa (1997). *Managing Human Resources*. New Delhi: McMillan India Ltd.

Government of India (1997). *Report of the Fifth Central Pay Commission*, Vol. III. New Delhi.

Hindu (1999a). India. Abolish caste-based quota. 25 May.

Hindu (1999b). India: reservation for Muslims: Supreme Court verdict awaited. 8 May.

Hindu (2000a). Treat caste on a par with racism: panel. 20 April.

Hindu (2000b). EC concern over rise of caste-based parties. 27 December.

Hindu (2000c). India: S.C. notice to Andhra Pradesh Govt. on 'gender bias'. 9 September.

Hindu (2001a). Caste discrimination is racism and more. 15 May.

Hindu (2001b). India: census to collect information on disability. 5 February.

Hindu (2001c). Where caste-based groups turn stake-holders. 11 April.

Hindu (2001d). India: lack of gender-sensitivity regretted. 3 April.

Hofstede, G. (1991). *Cultures and Organisations: Software of the Mind*. London: McGraw-Hill.

India at a Glance. Female Sex Ratio (2001). Government of India http://www.censusindia.net/fsex.html (17/06/2001).

India at a Glance. Languages Spoken (2001). Government of India http://www.censusindia.net/language.html (17/06/2001).

India at a Glance. Number of Literates and Literacy Rates (2001). Government of India http://www.censusindia.net/literates1.html (17/06/2001).

India at a Glance. Scheduled Castes and Scheduled Tribes (2001). Government of India http://www.censusindia.net/scst.html (17/06/2001).

India at a Glance. Work Participation (2001). Government of India http://www.censusindia.net/workpart.html (17/06/2001).

Initiative towards Women Empowerment. Know the Minister (2001). Achievements and Role of Department of Women and Child Development http://wcd.nic.in/mos/achieve.htm (17/06/2001).

Issar, P. (1997–98). The patriarchy of government. *23rd Advanced Professional Programme in Public Administration*. Mussoorie: IIPA.

Jayaram, N. (1996). Caste and Hinduism. Changing protean relationship. In M.N. Srinivas (ed.) *Caste; Its Twentieth Century Avatar* (pp. 69–86). New Delhi: Penguin Books India.

Kakar, S. (1978). *A Psychoanalytic Study of Childhood and Society in India.* New Delhi: Oxford University Press, cited in S. Sahay & G. Walsham (1997). Social structure and managerial agency in India. *Organization Studies*, **18**(3), 415–444.

Kazmin, A.L. (2000). Asia-Pacific: President laments 'national shame' of India's class divide. *Financial Times*, 26 January, 10.

Kingdon G. (1998). Does the labour market explain lower female schooling in India? *Journal of Development Studies*, Oct. 35.1. 39 (2), 39–65.

Kishwar, M. (undated). Sex harassment and slander as weapons of subjugation.

Lal Bahadur Shastri National Academy of Administration (1998). *Gender Sensitisation Workshop (Focus on Women's issues in Civil Service) Curriculum*, Lal Bahadur Shastri National Academy of Administration, Mussoorie, No. 68–70. In booklet on *Reading Material for Gender Sensitivisation Workshops*. Mussoorie: Lal Bahadur Shastri National Academy of Administration.

MacFarquhar, E. (1994). The echoes of Sita. *U.S. News and World Report*, **116** (12), 28 Mar., 54–5.

Manchanda, R. (1995). Hype and heroine: is the new Indian woman a media creation? *Far Eastern Economic Review*, **158** (36), 7 Sept, 48–9.

Manushi (1990). How elite is elite?—women in the civil services. No. 56, Jan–Feb.

Merchant, A. (1993). A Policy Intervention in Training Programme in Public Administration of Government Officials—a Gender Perspective. In Booklet on *Reading Material for Gender Sensitiviation Workshops*, Administrative Training Institute, Mysore.

Miller, J.G. (1994). Cultural diversity in the morality of caring: individually orientated versus duty-based interpersonal moral codes. *Cross-cultural Research. The Journal of Comparative Social Science*, **28**(1), 3–39.

Ministry of Labour at a Glance in the new Millennium (2001). http://labour.nic.in./glance/molglance.html (17/06/2001).

Mittal, M. (1994). *Educated Unemployed Women in India*. New Delhi: Anmol Publications Pvt. Ltd.

Monappa, A. (1997). *Managing Human Resources*. New Delhi: McMillan India Ltd.

Nabar, V. (1995). *Caste as Women*. New Delhi: Penguin India.

Newsom, D. & Carrell, B (1994). Professional public relations in India: need outstrips supply. *Public Relations Review*, **20**(2), summer, 183–188.

Panini, B. (1996). The political economy of caste. In M.N. Srinivas (ed.) *Caste: Its Twentieth Century Avatar* (pp. 28–68). New Delhi: Penguin Books India.

Parekh, B. (1996). India's diversity. *Dissent*, **43** (3), 145–148.

Patel, T. (1996). A suitable survey. *New Scientist*, **152** (2053), 26 Oct., 38–52.

Perumal, N.M. (1997–98). Reservation for women in central support posts. *23rd Advanced Professional Programme in Public Administration*, IIPA.

Radhakrishnan, P. (1996). Mandal Commission Report: A Sociological Critique. in Srinivas M.N. *Caste: Its Twentieth Century Avatar* (pp. 203–220). New Delhi: Penguin Books India.

Raman, S.M. (1999). Caste in stone. *Harvard International Review*, Fall.

Rosener, J.B. (1990). Ways women lead. *Harvard Business Review*, Nov–Dec, 119–125.

Sahay, S. & Walsham, G. (1997). Social structure and managerial agency in India. *Organization Studies*, **18** (3), 415–444.

Seabrook, J. (1994). Out in India (coming out of Indian gay men). *New Statesman and Society*, **7** (320), 16 September, 12 (2).

Shah, A.N. (1996a). The judicial and sociological view of other backward classes. In M.N. Srinivas (ed.) *Caste: Its Twentieth Century Avatar* (pp. 174–194). New Delhi: Penguin Books India.

Shah, A.N. (1996b). Job reservation and efficiency. In M.N. Srinivas (ed.) *Caste: Its Twentieth Century Avatar* (pp. 221–243). New Delhi: Penguin Books India.

Sharma, O.C. (1998). Women police—need and relevance (Bureau of Police Research and Development). In booklet on *Reading Material for Gender Sensitivisation Workshops*. Mussoorie: Lal Bahadur Shastri National Academy of Administration.

Shukla, P. (1996). Effect of age on entrepreneurial behaviour and creativity. *Psycho-Lingua*, **26**(1), 21–24.

Singh, C.B. (1988). Behavioural strategies for influencing immediate superiors. *Psychologia: An International Journal of Psychology in the Orient*, **31**(1), 34–41.

Singh, J.P. (1990). Managerial culture and work-related values in India: reply and comment. *Organization Studies*, **11**, 75–106.

Sinha, D. (1988). Basic Indian values and behaviour dispositions in the context of national development. In D. Sinha & H.S.R. Kao, *Social Values and Development. Asian Perspectives* (pp. 31–55). New Delhi: Sage, cited in S. Sahay & G. Walsham (1997). Social structure and managerial agency in India. *Organization Studies*, **18** (3), 415–444.

Sinha J.B.P. & Sinha, D. (1990). Role of social values in Indian organizations. *International Journal of Psychology*, **25**, 705–714, cited in S. Sahay & G. Walsham (1997). Social structure and managerial agency in India. *Organization Studies*, **18** (3), 415–444.

Sivaramayya, B. (1996). The Mandal judgement. A brief description and critique. In M.N. Srinivas (ed.) *Caste: Its Twentieth Century Avatar* (pp. 221–243). New Delhi: Penguin Books India.

Srinivas, M.N. (ed.) (1996). *Caste: Its Twentieth Century Avatar*. New Delhi: Penguin Books India.

Star of Mysore (1998a). Free computer training. 23 August, 3.

Star of Mysore (1998b). Older colleagues. 31 July, 2.

Sunstein, C.R. (1999). Affirmative action, caste, and cultural comparisons. *Michigan Law Review*, Ann Arbor, March.

Thakur S.J. & Nadkarni A. (1996). How equal is equal?—A study of gender issues in the IAS. *The Administrator*, **XLI**, 2 LBSNAA, Mussoorie, April–June.

Times of India (1998a). Forum decries government's attitude towards the physically handicapped. 20 July, 4.

Times of India (1998b). Dalit judge's successor cleans chamber with Ganga water. 22 July, 1.

Times of India (1998c). SC/ST govt staff protest for promotions. 17 August, 6.

Times of India (1998d). CET counselling from tomorrow. 24 July, 1.

Times of India (1998e). Training course for the adult deaf. Advertisement, 9 August, 10.

Times of India (2001). UN meeting can't discuss casteism, says India. 3 September, 1.

Tripathi, R.C. (1990). Interplay of values in the functioning of Indian organizations. *Indian Journal of Psychology*, **25**, 715–734 cited in S. Sahay & G. Walsham (1997). Social structure and managerial agency in India. *Organization Studies*, **18**(3), 415–444.

Trompenaars, F. & Hampden-Turner, C. (1997). *Riding the Waves of Culture: Understanding Cultural Diversity in Business*, 2nd edn. London and Napierville, Ill.: Nicholas Brealey Publishing.

Unnithan, M. (1994). Girasias and the politics of difference in Rajasthan: caste, kinship and gender in a marginalised society. *The Sociological Review*, **42**, 92–121.

Upadhyaya, K.K. (1998). The political economy of reservations in public jobs in India. *International Journal of Social Economics*, **25**(6–8), 1049–1061.

Wilson, E. (2000). Inclusion, exclusion and ambiguity: the role of organisational culture. *Personnel Review*, **29**(3), 274–303.

Wilson, E. & Iles, P. (1999). Managing diversity: an employment and service delivery challenge. *International Journal of Public Sector Management*, **12** (1), 27–48.

PART III

Specific Forms of Diversity

CHAPTER 10

Gender Diversity and Organizational Performance

Deborah Hicks-Clarke
Manchester Metropolitan University, Manchester, UK
Paul Iles
University of Teesside Business School, Middlesbrough, UK

SUMMARY

This chapter addresses the question of the relationships between gender diversity and organizational performance. It explores the relationship between gender and culture through a discussion of gender attributes, and discusses the managing diversity paradigm and its links to questions of gender diversity. It then explores gender cultures through the concept of the 'gender differential' in relation to the links between gender and performance before analysing studies of managing diversity, gender and climate. The managing diversity paradigm is then explored through an analysis of the business case for managing diversity, the costs and benefits of managing diversity, and research on diversity climates. The relationship between diversity climate, gender and performance is then explored through the work of the authors on the impact of diversity climates on work and organizational attitudes. The chapter concludes with a discussion of the importance of people to organizational performance and its relationship to gender diversity.

INTRODUCTION

This chapter sets out to discuss the connection between gender diversity and organizational performance. As the area of diversity as a whole and gender diversity in particular

Individual Diversity and Psychology in Organizations. Edited by Marilyn J. Davidson and Sandra L. Fielden.
© 2003 John Wiley & Sons, Ltd.

becomes more central to issues surrounding the work environment, it is important to understand its place in organizations. This chapter firstly discusses women in the modern work environment, including discussion of statistical data relating to the number of women in work today. Secondly, it goes on to look at gender and organizational culture and climate, and how these influence the attitudes and perceptions of individuals, and ultimately their own performance. Managing diversity is also considered in this chapter, as well as effective ways of managing difference in organizations. Finally, the link between gender and performance is discussed and conclusions drawn for research and practice.

The issue of gender and performance is an important and complex one. It is often contended, as we will see from the chapter, that there is a direct link between diversity in terms of gender in an organization and the 'financial success' of an organization. However, one of the most crucial elements seems to be the effective management of that diversity, in order to get the full creativity and therefore profitability from diversity. To succeed at this, organizations may need to completely readdress the way that they approach diversity, equal opportunities and their wider HR practices, such as recruitment and selection. Changing this old set of beliefs and behaviours may be difficult, but if companies want this success, then they must do it.

GENDER AND CULTURE

GENDER ATTRIBUTES

The differences between men and women have been widely researched in recent years. There are many different viewpoints concerning what characteristics or attributes each of the sexes can claim as their own. Many now increasingly take Bem's (1974) view that all individuals who are good managers can be placed along a continuum of 'total or complete' femininity to 'total or complete' masculinity (see Figure 10.1).

Indeed, the leadership qualities of each gender (see Kanter, 1989) can be seen as having positive characteristics in different situations. How one understands success can be related to gender to some degree. Rosenthal (1995) argues that men and women believe personal success to be attributable to different factors. Women have a tendency to 'explain away' their success, and believe it is due to hard work, not ability. Men, on the other hand, believe it to be linked to 'natural ability' (Rosenthal, 1995: 26).

This leads us to a discussion of what men think of women's performance. This is an important consideration, as men tend to be in the senior positions in an organization, and their views will influence the individual success of women, as well as the wider culture of expectations and achievement. If men assume that women will not achieve as much as a male in the same position, this could have two different influences on the

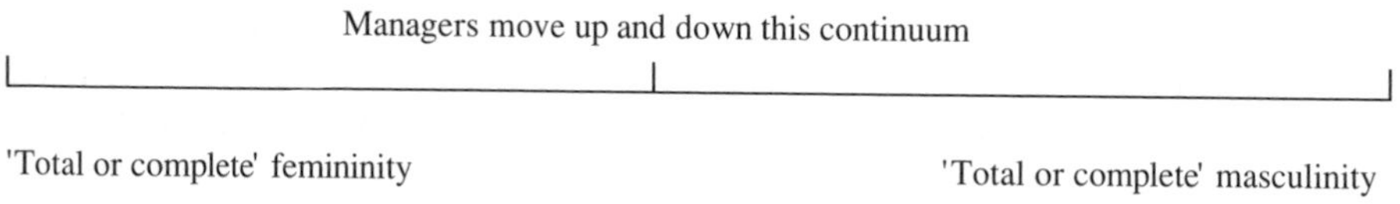

Managers move up and down this continuum

'Total or complete' femininity   'Total or complete' masculinity

FIGURE 10.1   Continuum of gender

women. Firstly, it may mean that men themselves explain away women's achievements, giving male colleagues the credit for achievement. Secondly, it may mean that women become locked in a loop of 'self-fulfilling' prophecies, where they assume that they cannot achieve a particular aim or goal, and therefore do not. Both of these situations are obviously disadvantageous to organizations. If individuals are being credited with achievements they have not made themselves, then this can create dissatisfaction and perhaps lead to the wrong person being promoted. Second, the issue of self-fulfilling prophecy is important in that talented individuals are not using their skills to the full, and in the long run disadvantaging organizations.

The issues discussed above also impact on the wider culture of the organization. If the organization's culture is not inclusive and rewarding those who achieve the goals set them, staff may leave, and the pool of talent wishing to join the organization will diminish. Such cultures do themselves no favours in the longer term. However, in the short term changing the culture from one that is exclusive to one which is inclusive of women can be difficult, and takes time. The process of culture change through the stages originally suggested by Lewin in 1948 (Lewin, 1999) and adapted by many authors since (freezing/unfreezing/moving/refreezing) takes time and effort by the organization. If the culture is one of exclusivity, then it is unlikely to be willing to change without a struggle. The change literature suggests that in order for diversity and its benefits to be recognized in an organization, then its top management must be committed to it. The problem in many organizations is getting that commitment in the first place, as many in that layer of management may be 'old guard' males who support the original culture. Business arguments and ethical reasons have been put forward to support such cultural change. These arguments are discussed below.

MANAGING DIVERSITY

The managing diversity paradigm has been seen as a supporter of the business argument for equality. Differing from the equal opportunities paradigm in both its origins and tenets, it offers reasons why diversity should be managed in a particular way and suggestions as to how to manage that diversity (see Wilson & Iles, 1996 for a detailed comparison of the two models).

The issue of gender diversity grows more important each year for organizations. As more and more women return to the workplace and continue to work throughout their working lives, the inequality that women endure is seen by some as 'par for the course', and by others as intolerable in the twenty-first century.

Laws supporting equality, at least on the work front, have been on the statute book in Britain for almost 30 years. However, some would argue that little really has changed in that time by the presence of such laws, and that it is the continued numbers of women in the workplace that is slowly influencing organizational culture. It could be suggested that as women bear children, and men by their very nature do not, then gender inequality in the workplace will always exist. Women, it has also been held by popular opinion, do not really want high-flying jobs, but would rather be at home with their families. This argument has been supported in recent years by tabloid newspapers reporting on the number of women who have given up such jobs in order to 'spend more time with their families', a term once used almost exclusively to describe the activities of failed politicians. However, in this case the term is taken as a positive and not a negative one. That is the newspapers painting similar activity (i.e. retiring from the fast-paced work arena) as a positive and 'correct' move for women and a rather more negative move for men.

This gender biasing has become part of the norm in our society. Within organizations, the top positions are still filled by men, as are most senior management posts. This is despite 69 per cent of women now being part of the British workforce. However, women are still much more likely to work part-time than men, and when they do, it tends to be by choice, whereas for men it is more likely to be because there are no other employment opportunities. Part-time positions tend to be lower paid and of lower status (Source: Equal Opportunities Commission report 'Facts about Women and Men in Great Britain 2001', www.eoc.org.uk). The EOC quote statistics from the *Labour Force Survey*, Spring 2000 and state that 'Overall, 69% of working age women and 79% of working age men are in employment' (p. 1). Further analysis shows that 43 per cent of women work part-time, whereas 8 per cent of men work part-time. In terms of pay differential, women who work full-time earn '82% of the average hourly earnings of male full-time employees' (p. 1) (Original source *Labour Force Survey*, Spring 2000). The 'double shift' that has been discussed with reference to women's dual role as both worker and homemaker/carer has been cited as influencing women's decisions not to take on more challenging work roles and therefore, not being 'fully committed to work'. This, it can be argued, is both stereotypical and part of the problem women experience. It is also possible to assume that men in our society will experience some problems concerning the work–life balance issue, and this issue cannot truly be seen as a 'women-only' one. However, it is fair to say that women do have unique concerns in our society, especially with respect to gendered work and organizational cultures.

GENDER CULTURES

In terms of organizational culture, it is possible to identify a number of different environments that influence the work-related actions and perceptions of individuals in work. Indeed, Maddock and Parkin (1993) identified several different work cultures which they claim engender different organizational environments. These have a particularly negative influence on women working within them. Maddock and Parkin's gender cultures are a useful way of examining organizational culture from the viewpoint of gender relations. These gender cultures show us that women are working in a number of different environments; therefore, it is not possible to assume that each woman's work and organizational experience will be the same.

In terms of performance excellence, organizations are expecting more and more from their employees. The issue of long-hours culture and organizational demands are increasingly important for both women and men. Women with a double shift (i.e. both career and domestic responsibilities) may experience a particularly hard time, as many gender-blind organizations are not acknowledging the issues at all. This is not to suggest that women cannot perform to an excellent standard, but that to ignore outside influences in an individuals' life would be foolish in the extreme. As new legislation is brought into the UK to allow parents time off when dependants are ill, the UK government as well as its EU counterparts seem more aware than ever of these issues.

Hicks-Clarke and Iles (2000) have shown that the environment one works in does have an influence on individuals' attitudes and perceptions, and therefore also on work performance, making this issue important for organizational performance.

THE GENDER DIFFERENTIAL

The pressures for visibility and the long-hours culture may well be entrenched in our culture; however, equating this with better performance is at best tenuous and at worst foolish. To assume that if one is working very long hours and present in the organization at all times, then one is performing better, appears to be mistaken. Indeed, authors such as Cooper (2000) suggest that the opposite is often the case, with long-hours cultures leading to burnout and much lower performance from staff. Countries other than the UK, such as Sweden, have a culture whereby if one is seen working very late, then the assumption is that the person is not able to complete all their job during the time they should, which indicates a lack of ability rather than more commitment!

So, what is the difference in terms of gender performance for women and men? Perhaps the best way to look at this is in terms of the measurement of that performance. What measurements are used: e.g. financial, team cooperation? The measure used will have an enormous bearing on what is seen as high performance. 'Cloning' is one issue, as many of the individuals setting performance criteria are male senior managers and chairmen, so that it is often the 'male' view of performance that is accepted. Therefore, as has been argued by a number of different authors such as Alimo-Metcalfe (1993), the use of male criteria may mean that women are often judged on an 'alien' measurement. The success of an organization can be measured in many different ways, via financial measures such as how much profit an organization makes, through to their contribution to the natural environment. Profit-making and non-profit-making organizations may well have different agendas, but use the same performance criteria for staff. In non-profit-making

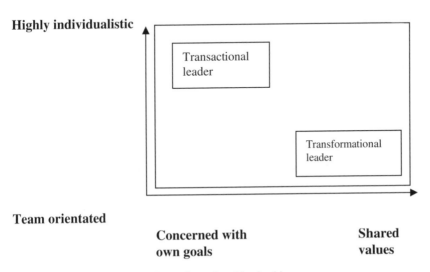

FIGURE 10.2 Transactional and transformational leadership

organizations, despite not being concerned with the making of profit, these criteria are often money-related. When one looks at other areas that are arguably equally important, such as getting the best out of employees, then women (Kanter, 1989) are seen as being better transformational leaders, ones who work well with their staff and encourage commitment to jointly owned goals, as compared with more traditional male 'transactional' leaders (see Figure 10.2). Transactional leadership is more about taking control of subordinates and not involving them in the decision-making process. Organizations are increasingly seeing the importance of teamwork skills for managers, as these will influence the effective performance of the organization.

MANAGING DIVERSITY, GENDER AND CLIMATE

Managing diversity is seen as a way of achieving the most from a workforce by regarding employees not just as members of a particular group (and therefore perhaps deficient in some way, as compared to a white male norm) but as individuals with particular needs (Thomas, 1990, 1991; Cox, 1993; Kandola & Fullerton, 1994). Managing diversity has come into particular prominence because it is often argued that adopting it will confer 'business benefits', as compared to the common perception that equal opportunities costs money. One aim of this chapter is to analyse the business benefits claimed for diversity, especially the impact of diversity climates on performance.

In some ways the importation of managing diversity into the UK parallels the importation of human resource management (HRM) as a new vocabulary from the USA in the late 1980s (e.g. Storey, 1995). Just as HRM, in contrast to personnel management, was seen as a strategic, proactive, long-term, corporate-wide approach to managing people involving questions of culture and values, so managing diversity was seen as signifying a more strategic, proactive, long-term and corporate-wide approach to difference than EO (equal opportunities), typically perceived as involving tactical reactions in a piecemeal way to external triggers such as legislation, and focusing on numbers rather than culture or values (e.g. Wilson & Iles, 1996). However, just as HRM may make less cultural sense in countries that do not see people as 'resources' as compared to the USA, managing diversity may also not be culturally appropriate in all societies. Jones et al. (2000) argue that managing diversity is based on the demographic and dominant cultural assumptions of the USA, and may fail to address, or even obscure, key local 'diversity' issues. They argue that in New Zealand, the dominant discourse of managing diversity has embedded in it cultural assumptions specific to US management, and call for a genuinely multi-voiced discourse that focuses on local demographics, culture and political differences. The US model of diversity or difference tends to take itself as a model of universal best practice, intended to facilitate the cross-cultural management effectiveness of US multinationals as a competitive asset (e.g. Fernandez, 1991; Humphries & Grice, 1995; Labich, 1996). Jones et al. (2000) draw particular attention to the specific indigenous status of Maori, biculturalism, the Treaty of Waitangi, and partnership as key concepts in rethinking ethnic difference, warning against the imposition of culturally specific leadership and management models and formulations.

Similarly, Prasad et al. (1997), arguing from a Canadian perspective, have made similar points, as well as pointing out the positivist, managerialist and unitarist assumptions and neglect of power differences underlying the managing diversity position. Managing diversity may focus our attention away from racism, oppression and the specificity of discrimination and disadvantage in its focus on individual differences and multicultural aspirations and values so that 'everyone will benefit' (Thomas, 1991: 168). Such a view of EO, put forward by many managing diversity proponents, also fails to acknowledge the various approaches within EO developed in the UK (e.g. liberal versus radical approaches, Jewson & Mason, 1986, or long versus short agendas, e.g. Cockburn, 1991) as well as the use of the business case by some EO proponents in the 1990s in Britain and the EU, especially the focus on 'mainstreaming' EO within organizational culture and policies (e.g. Lawrence, 2000). This suggests that the business case for both managing diversity and EO needs to be further explored.

Others have argued (e.g. Mavin & Girling, 2000) that there is a danger that the social justice and ethical arguments in favour of equity may be ignored by managing diversity, and that managing diversity may be driven by senior white men as a way of 'de-grouping' people and individualize initiatives in a way that 'dilutes' the aims, philosophy and objectives of EO. They also suggest that 'those who see managing diversity as the business case for managing equal opportunities ... may be disappointed in the outcomes ...' (Mavin & Girling, 2000: 246).

THE BUSINESS CASE FOR MANAGING DIVERSITY

The ethical or political arguments often used by organizations to implement EO can also be applied to managing diversity; 'fairness' and 'equity' might be regarded as reason enough for organizations to implement policies reflecting such concerns. However, such arguments alone often do not appear to be enough to endear such a concept to organizations and managers concerned with financial performance. Wilson and Iles (1996) argue that managing diversity's apparent strength comes from its 'business case'. For example, many employees of organizations will soon be from currently under-represented groups, especially at managerial levels, e.g. ethnic minorities, people with disabilities and women. As greater economic independence has been gained by women and more financial security gained by ethnic groups, they have also become more important customers and clients. Such employees often wish to have the same opportunities as white men, but may wish to be able to do things in their own way, and not necessarily to have to conform to organizational rules created by white men.

THE COSTS AND BENEFITS OF MANAGING DIVERSITY

Harisis and Kleiner (1993) argue that if diversity is not managed effectively, then the costs can be high in terms of lost productivity, higher turnover, higher absenteeism, strikes and industrial conflict (see Figure 10.3). Managing diversity initiatives may help generate a positive climate for diversity. For example, Youngblood and Chambers-Cook (1984) were reported by Cox and Blake (1991) as showing that when child day-care is introduced into an organization, absenteeism is reduced. Kandola and Fullerton (1994) surveyed UK organizations in order to discover why companies were changing to managing diversity. They found that most organizations who adopted managing diversity did so because they believed it to make good business sense.

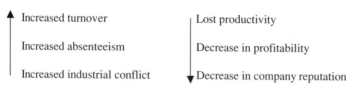

FIGURE 10.3   Problems faced when not managing diversity effectively

Cox and Blake (1991) contend that if diversity is managed effectively, then labour turnover and absenteeism can be reduced, and therefore the costs associated with such outcomes can also be reduced. They outline five other reasons why well-managed diversity is an asset to any organization. Firstly, it becomes easier to recruit people with qualities which the organization requires. Secondly, as ethnic and minority markets grow, minorities will be keener to buy from organizations seen as diverse and supporting diversity. Thirdly, diversity will lead to the organization becoming more creative and innovative. Fourthly, this may in turn improve organizational problem-solving. Finally, the effective management of diversity will enhance organizational flexibility.

Archival studies in the US financial sector have shown positive relationships between top team heterogeneity and strategic change, especially the adoption of innovative strategies (e.g. Wiersema & Bantel, 1992). However, heterogeneity has typically been defined in terms of age, education and functional experience, rather than in terms of race, gender or nationality (given the predominance of white males in financial services' top teams). More suggestive evidence of the positive effects of diversity on performance comes from the work of Cox who shows that multicultural MBA (Master in Business Administration) teams may at the beginning of a project be less productive than monocultural teams, but outperform them subsequently, especially in terms of innovation. This suggests that task phase may be a key moderator of the positive effects of diversity, as well as the nature of the task. Diversity may have positive impacts on innovative tasks, but negative impacts on routine tasks (e.g. Iles & Hayers, 1997).

In addition to the arguments from social psychology of the ways in which team diversity may inhibit group think and promote innovation, there are other theoretical approaches that suggest that diversity may have positive impacts on performance. Women employees in management may bring skills such as listening, empowerment, coaching, team building and development, in line with changing business requirements for example. There are theoretical arguments to support the contention that diversity can confer business benefits to organizations, including gender diversity, if diversity is effectively managed.

The resource-based view of the firm suggests that effectively utilizing critical but previously poorly tapped human resources in non-traditional skill pools may confer competitive advantage (e.g. Grant, 1991). Requisite variety perspectives derived from systems theory suggest that as organizational environments grow more diverse and complex, then internal environments need also to become more diverse. Stakeholder theory (e.g. Freeman, 1984) suggests that as stakeholders become more diverse, then organizations able to manage such stakeholders by allocating resources in a manner consistent with stakeholder concerns may be more effective; internally diverse organizations may better serve diverse stakeholder groups. However, despite these theoretical arguments,

Employee surveys

Employment data

Performance reviews

360 degree feedback

Focus groups

Benchmarking

Diversity-specific surveys

Customer feedback.

Informal employee feedback

Attitude surveys

FIGURE 10.4 Measures used to evaluate diversity initiatives

there is little empirical evidence for the proposition that managerial diversity and/or its effective management impacts positively on job or organizational performance. Shroder et al. (1997) in a study of the relationship between gender diversity and firm performance in US firms show that percentages of women in management were associated with such measures of financial performance as return on investment, return on equity, return on assets and profitability. More longitudinal research is needed, using other diversity dimensions and in other social contexts, to assess whether the supposed business benefits of diversity are realizable.

Wentling (2000) has examined how diversity initiatives in eight multinational corporations headquartered in the USA have been evaluated. All the companies were attempting to evaluate their initiatives, using different methods, while recognizing the difficulties of measurement, Figure 10.4 shows some of the methods used.

Employee surveys and employment data were most commonly used, followed by performance reviews, 360 degree feedback, focus groups, benchmarking, diversity-specific surveys and customer feedback. Less frequent measures employed included informal employee feedback, attitude surveys and peer reviews. Success of diversity initiatives was mostly measured through leadership commitment, diversity representation at all levels, measurement against stated goals and strategic plans, and promotion, hiring, turnover, retention and absenteeism rates. Performance ratings, attitude and behavioural change, employee satisfaction, complaints, workgroup performance and external recognition and awards were less frequently used success measures. Most considered that their diversity initiatives had been very effective and had had a positive impact on the organization. However, most also felt that some components of such initiatives were hard to evaluate, such as their impact on the bottom line, on profitability, on productivity, on return on investment, on behaviour, on attitudes and on internal readiness to launch such initiatives as part of the organizational culture. This suggests that one promising concept for studying the potential benefits of diversity is the concept of organizational climate, and in particular whether a 'positive climate for diversity' is associated with individual and organizational benefits.

MANAGING DIVERSITY AND DIVERSITY CLIMATES

The organizational climate of a work environment can influence employee attitudes and perceptions, as well as other performance outcomes. Climate and culture are often used as interchangeable terms; however, they do differ. Schneider et al. (1994: 18) argue that climate is one aspect of culture; climate is the 'atmosphere that employees perceive is created in their organizations by practices, procedures, and rewards'. Employees cluster their organizational experiences and events into meanings, and these form the basis of organizational climate. Climate is therefore heavily dependent on organizational policies and procedures. Culture they describe as 'referring to . . . the broader pattern of an organization's morals, values and beliefs' (p. 18). They contend that executives' behaviour also affects the organization's culture. Individuals within the organization can then try to understand and assess organizational priorities, which leads to the creation of different climates.

Culture researchers tend to view culture as an all-embracing concept, while climate researchers such as Burke et al. (1992) often view climate as part of culture and discuss it in terms of climate for something, such as climate for diversity. Indeed, Schneider et al. (1994) point out that since organizations define many different priorities, they will manifest many different climates. The priorities set by management are held to lead to organizational climates, as understood and interpreted by employees.

Therefore, culture is seen here, following Schneider and Reichers (1990, 1993), as a set of shared meanings or understandings about the group/organization and its problems, goals and practices. Climate in contrast is taken to be a strand of culture, defined as the perception of particular aspects of the organization based largely on organizational rules and regulations and individuals' interpretation of those rules and regulations.

Kossek and Zonia (1993) use this formulation to contend that diversity climates are affected by EO policies, by access to resources and opportunities in the organization, and by how individuals and groups view those policies. They argue that women are often more aware of restrictions on their advancement and opportunities than are men.

Kossek and Zonia (1993: 63) give examples of attitudes and behaviours that comprise diversity climate, such as whether individuals agree with measures to increase the number of diverse individuals at different levels of the organization. Kossek and Zonia (1993) argue that their results show that hierarchical levels in the organization and gender both affect employee perceptions of diversity climates. In summary, women were more likely to support the organization's attempts to bring in diversity policies than men, and were more likely to show positive attitudes to diversity in general.

Kossek and Zonia (1993) did not examine individual and organizational outcomes as important aspects of diversity climate. In addition, they conducted research in one organization, a US university with a highly qualified and specific set of respondents.

Cox (1993) has also developed a model of diversity climate that considers both individual and organizational outcomes. This interactional model is seen as applicable to many different types of diversity; for example, it can be as equally well applied to job function as to gender. However, more research has been conducted on gender, ethnicity and

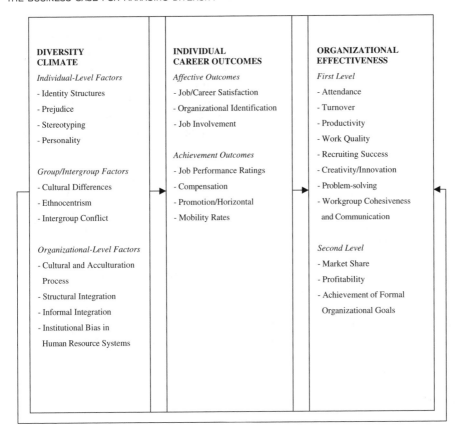

FIGURE 10.5 An interactional model of the impact of diversity on individual career outcomes and organizational effectiveness
Source: Cox, T. (1993). *Cultural Diversity in Organizations: Theory, Research and Practice*. San Francisco: Berrett-Koehler

nationality than on other types of diversity. Gender is seen as visible and unchangeable, unlike job function and other diversity dimensions, and therefore Cox (1993) focuses mostly on such diversity.

Cox (1993) views diversity climate as involving three different sets of factors: individual level factors, group/intergroup factors and organizational level factors. These in turn relate to individual career outcomes, and organizational effectiveness (see Figure 10.5).

Individual career outcomes include both affective and achievement outcomes, such as job/career satisfaction. Individual career outcomes are in turn related to organizational effectiveness, which also comprises a number of factors, split into first-level (such as labour turnover) and second-level types (such as profitability).

Cox (1993) argues that the possible outcomes of diversity climate include how individuals feel about their work and their employer, i.e. effectiveness outcomes, and how well the individual performs in the organization, i.e. achievement outcomes, measurable in the form of HR measures such as job performance ratings.

Cox (1993) contends that if individuals do not feel valued because of their race or gender, this will then affect their organizational identity and job/career satisfaction, as well as job involvement and ultimately job performance and organizational performance.

Majority group members are considered to have different perceptions from minority group members. Minority group members are more likely to be aware of the effects of group membership than majority group members. Cox (1993), for example, quotes surveys of managerial/professional work in the USA which found that women, but not men, saw gender as influencing promotion decisions.

In summary, Cox (1993) argues that organizations which develop a climate which encourages and supports all employees and in which all employees have equal opportunities will be better positioned than competitors. Employees will be more motivated and creative, and therefore diversity in HR is a potential positive asset to organizations. However, minority and under-represented employees (such as women in management) may find that they are able to progress only so far up the career ladder in an organization before coming up against a glass ceiling, and can progress no further. Mandell and Kohler-Grey (1990) argue that organizations are inhibited from valuing diversity because of the pervading image of a manager as male, middle class and white. As a result, the potential benefits offered by diversity will not be realized.

Some research has attempted to explore the effects of diversity or EO policies on employees. For example, Day and Schoenrade (2000) in a study of homosexual employees in the USA found that employees' affective organizational commitment was related to reported disclosure of sexual orientation, anti-discrimination policies and top management support for equal rights. In addition, anti-discrimination policies and top management support were also positively related to job satisfaction, but none of the independent variables was related to job stress or continuance organizational commitment (i.e. commitment due to perceived benefits or costs of leaving, rather than emotional identification and involvement). This finding does suggest that aspects of diversity climate (e.g. perceptions of policies and management support) do influence organizational attitudes such as commitment and job satisfaction.

DIVERSITY CLIMATE, GENDER AND PERFORMANCE

Hicks-Clarke and Iles (2000) studied diversity climates within the retail industry and the UK national health service (NHS) and what factors of diversity climate impact on managerial career and organizational attitudes and perceptions, showing the impact of climate perceptions on individual career and organizational attitudes and perceptions, such as commitment, job satisfaction, satisfaction with supervisor, career commitment, career satisfaction and career future satisfaction. All of these relate to individual and therefore, it is suggested, organizational performance, and the results of this study are discussed in the following section. Figure 10.6 shows the model created for PCFD.

'Climate for diversity' was assessed by scales measuring diversity support (policies and procedures supporting diversity, such as EO policy existence and the availability of mentoring, childcare, flexible working hours and career breaks) and equity recognition (perceived organizational justice, recognition of the need for diversity, and perceived organizational support for diversity). One question of interest was the relationship between perceived climate for diversity and demographic variables such as gender and management level. Statistical analysis showed that senior managers were significantly more likely to perceive the presence of organizational justice and organizational support for diversity, and more likely to recognize the need for diversity in their organizations.

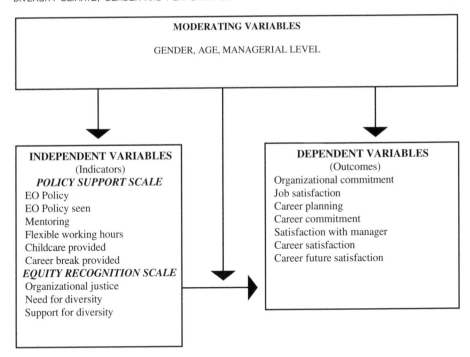

FIGURE 10.6 Positive climate for diversity (PCFD)

Men were more likely to perceive organizational support for diversity than women, but less likely to recognize the need for it. Men were also more likely to perceive the availability of mentors in their organization, but less likely to perceive the availability of childcare. Regression analysis confirmed these findings, and also showed that the higher the management level, the more likely managers were to perceive that flexible working hours and career breaks were available.

Another question of interest was the impact of climate for diversity on a range of career and organizational attitudes, especially those centred on employee commitment and satisfaction. In general, regression analysis showed that climate for diversity (as assessed by support for diversity and perceived equity) significantly influenced employees' organizational commitment, job satisfaction, career commitment, career satisfaction and career future satisfaction, as well as satisfaction with supervisor; the more positive the perceived diversity climate, the more positive were employee attitudes and perceptions. Policy support specifically influenced organizational commitment, satisfaction with supervisor, career satisfaction and career future satisfaction; equity recognition significantly influenced these variables as well as job satisfaction, career planning and career commitment. Of the policy support variables, the availability of flexible working hours appeared to significantly influence the widest range of outcomes, including job satisfaction, satisfaction with manager, career satisfaction, career future satisfaction, and organizational commitment. Of the equity recognition variables, perceived organizational justice emerged as the strongest predictor, significantly influencing job satisfaction, satisfaction with manager, career satisfaction, career future satisfaction, career commitment, organizational commitment and career planning. Perceived organizational support for diversity significantly influenced satisfaction with manager and career future satisfaction. In general, the diversity climate variable of equity recognition, especially the two dimensions of perceived organizational justice and perceived organizational support for diversity, seemed more significant in influencing employee career and organizational attitudes and perceptions than the existence of an EO policy or other policy initiatives.

Of particular interest is the finding that further factor analysis of the support for diversity scale, identified two factors, accounting for 69 per cent of the variance. Factor 1 was labelled 'management support for women'; factor 2 was termed 'management support for minorities'. This suggests that respondents differentiate between support for women and support for minorities, rather than subscribing to a general 'support for diversity' position, and that interviews with managers could usefully reveal the different meanings 'supporting diversity' had for respondents.

Further support for the proposition that respondents differentiate 'support for women' from 'support for minorities' is the finding that analysis of variance shows that 'support for women' influences both career future satisfaction and job satisfaction, while 'support for minorities' influences satisfaction with manager and organizational commitment. Support for women was significantly influenced by gender, with men believing that there was more support for women than women did, but gender was not related to support for minorities.

Factor analysis of recognition of the need for diversity revealed only one factor, accounting for 62 per cent of the variance. In addition, separate analyses of the retail sample only as distinct from that of the whole group of NHS and retail managers reported earlier, showed no significant differences between genders and management levels in terms of either the outcome (satisfaction/commitment) or climate for diversity (equity recognition) variables, suggesting that the sample was too small for adequate statistical analysis and/or that survey analysis was not the most appropriate way of exploring diversity climates in the retail company. Hicks-Clarke and Iles (2000) did, however, show that retail managers were less likely to enjoy childcare provision and less likely to be able to undertake career breaks than the NHS managers, but more likely to express satisfaction over their career futures and with their present careers.

Interview data suggested that mobility seemed a problem for women within the retail organization. Lack of an apparent support for and recognition of the need for diversity may also limit their opportunities. In the retail organization the chairman's 'sexist' attitude seemed to lead women to feel unsupported, although this was tempered by the belief that his attitude was not common among the other board members. Some women saw the female board member as a positive statement and role model, showing that women with children could make it in the organization. Others believed that her life was so different from their own that she was merely used as a token with little effect, as she was showing what they thought of as a 'male' attitude to work, had a nanny and spent no time with her children. Many felt that she had almost cut off her femininity to gain her position, so that she was sacrificing more than they, 'normal' women, ever would. She was also thought to have to work much harder than the men on the board to achieve her position, so that most women could not identify with her. A few women saw her as a positive role model, but did not want themselves to be in that position.

Hicks-Clarke and Iles (2000) argued that organizations will need to reassess their policies and procedure to ensure equity and support diversity if they are to develop a positive climate for diversity, with the apparently positive effects on employee job, career and organizational attitudes that this seems to engender. Knowledge, communication and acceptance of these policies and procedures also seem important. In the interview data, it was shown that an organization may have a policy which individuals may find beneficial, for example career breaks or paternity leave. However, some individuals either had no knowledge of it, or had to discover it for themselves. Policies and procedures put in place may need to be paid more than lip-service. During the reported interviews, it came to light that although certain policies were in place (for example part-time work and career breaks for managers) individuals felt that the organization did not fully support managers taking these routes. As a result interviewees felt that their careers would suffer if they took these options.

Another interesting finding was that both men and women seemed to support initiatives that benefited men, e.g. paternity leave. It seemed that men may be taking their lead from rights given to women, such as maternity leave, were expecting similar rights for themselves, and were gaining the support of women also for these rights.

The demographic mix of the organization also appeared to be an important factor in affecting diversity climates. Often interviewees mentioned that a mix of genders at management level was important. It was felt that organizations needed to address the question of gender balance at management level. It appeared that the more mixed an organization at management level, the more aware managers were of each others' needs. This, in turn, appeared to have a positive effect on perceived equity and organizational justice.

Another important factor identified clearly in the retail company interviews was the importance of top management commitment to a positive climate for diversity. The chairman in one organization was constantly quoted by interviewees as being 'sexist'. This image seemed to influence women's satisfaction with the organization in particular. It also appeared to have made them aware that they may be limited in their aspirations within the organization. This was countered to some extent by there being a woman on the board. However, interviewees often saw her as a 'token female'.

Other factors which have an influence on climate for diversity may include the demographic mix of the department. From the interview data gathered here, demographic mix appears to be an important factor in the climate of the organization, both at department level and indeed board level.

Another important factor appears to be the issue of mobility. One organization insisted on full mobility for their managers for at least the first five years. If a manager was to be successful in reaching senior management, it was accepted by staff that they would have to move around the whole UK. Another issue relating to mobility was the written rule which stated that trainee managers were not able to buy houses for the first five years of their employment; again, this was to enable full mobility of staff. This rule, to which staff had to sign up in their contracts, appeared to have a great effect on women who wished to have families in particular. Moreover, the issue of dual-career couples was also highlighted by this practice. Generally speaking, women tended to put their career second to their partners. Therefore, their mobility was again limited, even if they did not have family responsibilities in the form of children or relatives to take care of Finally, Hicks-Clarke and Iles (2000) concluded from their research that there is increasing evidence that HRM practices, especially those which engender organizational commitment, do seem to have a positive impact on organizational performance and success. Women respondents, and male respondents' partners, had often put their careers more on hold, and would generally move if their male partners 'needed to' in order for their careers to progress. Women were the ones usually sacrificing their career chances with this choice. Mobility is therefore another area that could well be addressed by future research, as could the influence on women and men of dual-career partners and domestic responsibilities.

THE IMPORTANCE OF PEOPLE TO ORGANIZATIONAL PERFORMANCE

Employee commitment may have a number of different foci (e.g. to work itself, to a job, to a career, to a profession, as well as to an organization) and may be instrumentally based (e.g. calculative or continuance commitment) dependent on a perception that the organizational rewards and benefits outweigh the stresses or sacrifices of leaving. It may also be normatively based (e.g. a feeling that personal values and organizational values are congruent) or affectively based (feelings of attachment, loyalty and identification to the organization). The latter seems more likely to generate high performance in employees (e.g. Suliman & Iles, 2000a, b).

The resource-based view (RBV) of the firm, with its focus not only on tangible but also intangible resources and its focus on competence-based competition, has led to the appreciation of the contribution of people practices to organizational success. 'People are our greatest asset' is now not simply an empty rhetorical phrase, repeated ritualistically, usually before downsizing.

In part, this recognition of the growing importance of HRM to firm performance is due to the increasingly widespread influence of the RBV of the firm (e.g. Storey, 2000) with its emphasis on the importance of the firm's internal resources, especially its human assets and its HR practices, for sustainable competitive advantage. There are disputes over 'soft' and 'hard' HRM (e.g. emphasis on business-focused calculation and planning versus communication, training and motivation) and about whether HRM refers to any approach to managing people, or to a specific perspective. For Storey (1995: 5), HRM is a 'distinctive approach to employment management which seeks to achieve competitive advantage through the strategic development of a highly committed and capable workforce using an array of cultural, structural and personnel techniques'— what others (e.g. Walton, 1985) have referred to as 'high commitment management'. Believing that it is the human resource that gives firms competitive edge, HRM aims for flexible committed employees through careful selection and development: since HR decisions are of strategic importance, top management involvement is necessary, and HR polices need to be integrated into the business strategy. Line managers therefore need to be closely involved as deliverers and drivers of HRM, in appraisal, training, team briefing, communication and leadership, and managing organizational culture is seen as more important than managing procedures or systems.

In particular, the HRM model stresses integrated action on selection, training, reward and career development, with restructuring and job redesign to allow flexibility, devolved responsibility and empowerment. There are disputes about how much of this is rhetoric and how much is actually practised, in the UK and USA in particular, and also about what impact HRM policies and practice have on organizational outcomes, especially financial and bottom-line results.

In the UK, for example, Patterson et al. (1997) and Guest (1997) have shown that, compared with investment in research and development, a focus on HRM practices had by far the most impact on company performance and was a major difference between high- and low-performing firms. Michie and Sheehan (2000) have shown that what they term 'high road' HR practices (intensive recruitment and selection, extensive appraisal, training and development, extensive consultation, involvement and communication) are associated with higher financial performance and productivity (especially over the long term) than 'low road' practices such as short-term hiring and firing, little training and low pay/low discretion jobs. Similar 'bundles of HR practices' are associated with firm performance in research in the United States (e.g. Huselid, 1995; Huselid et al., 1997). There is still controversy over whether there is 'one best way' of universalistic HR practices that work for any firm in any situation or whether firms should adopt a contingency perspective of 'best fit', adopting their particular HR bundle of practices to their particular corporate strategy. However, overall, there is now much more evidence that investment in HR 'pays off' in its positive impacts on firm performance. This suggests that diversity practices, as one aspect of HRM, may impact positively on firm performance.

CONCLUSIONS

As we have seen, there have been few studies explicitly examining the connection between gender and performance. The research reviewed shows a link between environment or climate and attitudes and perceptions, and a link between such attitudes and individual (and by implication organizational) performance. Cox has hypothesized the link between organizational climate, individual attitudes, individual performance and firm or organizational performance, and Hicks-Clarke and Iles (2000) also propose this relationship, although more detailed work still needs to be conducted. Authors including Shroder et al. (1997) have gone further than hypothezising the relationship between gender and firm financial performance and have drawn direct connections between those organizations which employ women at managerial levels and the success of a company. They state the 'business case' for women in organizations in that the more diverse the workforce is, the more talent and skills will be present. Managing this diverse workforce is an important issue, as if it is not managed effectively then this talent and potential competitive advantage could be lost. Shroder et al. (1997) found a relationship between the number of women in management in companies and the financial performance of the organization. In simple terms, the more women an organization had at middle management level, the more financially successful the company was. Rosener (1995) also agrees with these results in her own work on women in management and firm financial performance.

It seems that there are several steps necessary to setting up an organization to be able to effectively make full use of its female managers. Firstly, to create the right climate for diversity to flourish. Secondly, to ensure that there are high percentages of women middle managers in an organization. This links with Hicks-Clarke and Iles (2000) which showed that women at middle and junior management level were much more heterogeneous compared with women at senior management level, who tended to 'state the party line' with regard to diversity issues, and often acted in a way which has been described as showing very 'male' personality traits. Therefore, one could hypothesize from this research that the very differences that women bring to a management position are the very qualities that lead to organizational financial success. Once a woman is at a higher level, the climate may not allow her to show this difference, and then the advantages may be lost. Therefore, it is important to create a positive climate for diversity at the top management levels of organizations in order to gain the benefits of gender diversity.

Huselid (1995) considered the importance of what was termed 'high performance work practices' on firm performance, showing a strong link between the work practices an organization has in place and the successful financial performance of an organization. The importance of HR practices is highlighted as having 'a direct and economically significant contribution to firm performance' (p. 636). Huselid suggests that earlier research such as Wright and McMahan (1992) considers the importance of individuals in the workplace and their full utilization.

A number of areas have been considered by researchers as benefiting from positive organizational climates (Hicks-Clarke & Iles, 2000) or cultures (Sheridan & Slocum, 1975). These areas include turnover (Sheridan, 1992), productivity (Cutcher-Gershenfeld, 1991) and firm financial performance (Gerhart & Milkovich, 1992). The importance of good HRM practices and the linkage between such practices and firm financial performance is also supported by Huselid et al. (1997). They surveyed 293 firms for HR practices and financial performance. Strategic HRM, which they describe as involving the design and implementation 'of a set of internally consistent policies and practices that ensure a firm's human capital contributes to the achievement of its business objectives' (p. 172) was seen as important, and they also found a link between HRM practices and firm financial performance.

Given the increasing evidence for the impact of HRM policies and practices on firm performance, then it is likely that managing diversity policies and practices will also be linked to organizational performance. Such policies and practices may well have their impacts through their effects on organizational climate, as this has been shown to affect a range of career and organizational attitudes that have been shown to be related to both individual behaviour and organizational performance.

These studies confirming the importance of people and HRM to organizational performance lend further weight to arguments that managing diversity, including gender diversity, can enhance organizational performance. If people, and how they are managed, are so important to organizational performance, then their commitment and motivation are likely to be critical. This appears to be affected by diversity climates experienced by men and women. Since men and women often seem to experience different diversity climates, with generally less support for women and less recognition of the need to manage gender diversity, then women's commitment in particular, and by implication their performance, is likely to suffer if they experience the diversity climate as negative. This is likely to have deleterious effects on organizational performance, reinforcing the message that gender diversity can contribute to enhanced organizational performance, but only if managed effectively.

REFERENCES

Alimo-Metcalfe, B. (1993). Gender, leadership and assessment. In D. Lane (ed.) *Applying the Assessment Centre Method to the European Experience*. London: Chapman and Hall.
Bem, S.L. (1974). The measurement of psychological androgyny. *Journal of Consulting and Clinical Psychology*, **42**(2), 155–162.

Burke, M.J., Borucki, C.C. & Hurley, A.E. (1992). Reconceptualising psychological climate in a retail service environment: a multiple-stakeholder perspective. *Journal of Applied Psychology*, **77**(5), 717–729.

Cockburn, C. (1991). *In the Way of Women: Men's Resistance to Equality in Organisations*. Basingstoke: Macmillan.

Cooper, C.L. (2000). The psychological implications of the Americanisation of work in the UK. *Stress News*, April, **12**(2), www.isma.org.uk/stressnews.htm

Cox, T. (1993). *Cultural Diversity in Organisations: Theory, Research and Practice*. San Francisco: Berrett-Koehler.

Cox, T. & Blake, S. (1991). Managing cultural diversity: implications for organisational competitiveness. *The Executive*, **5**, 45–46.

Cutcher-Gershenfeld, J. (1991). Japanese team-based work systems in North America: explaining the diversity. *California Management Review*, **37**(1), 42–64.

Day, N.E. & Schoenrade, P. (2000). The relationship among reported disclosure of sexual orientation, anti-discrimination policies, top management support, and work attitudes of gay and lesbian employees. *Personnel Review*, **29**(3), 346–363.

Fernandez, J.P. (1991). *Managing a Diverse Workforce: Regaining the Competitive Edge*. Lexington, Mass.: Lexington Books.

Freeman, R.E. (1984). *Strategic Management: A Stakeholder Approach*. London: Pitman.

Gerhart, B. & Milkovich, G.T. (1992). Employee compensation: research and theory. In M.D. Dunnette & L.M. Hough (eds) *Handbook of Industrial and Organizational Psychology*, 2nd edn (vol. 3, pp. 481–569). Bombay: Jaico Publishing House.

Grant, R.M.C. (1991). The resource-based theory of competitive advantage: implications for strategy formulation. *California Management Review*, **33**, 114–135.

Guest, D. (1997). *Human Resource Management and Performance: A Review of Research*. London: CIPD.

Harisis, D.S. & Kleiner, B.H. (1993). Managing and valuing diversity in the workplace. *Equal Opportunities International*, **12**(4), 6–9.

Hicks-Clarke, D. & Iles, P. (2000). Climate for diversity and its effects on career and organisational attitudes and perceptions. *Personnel Review*, **29**(3), 324–345(22).

Humphries, M. & Grice, S. (1995). Equal employment opportunity and the management of diversity: a global discourse of assimilation? *Journal of Organizational Change Management*, **8**(5), 17–32(16).

Huselid, M. (1995). The impact of human resource management practices on turnover, productivity, and corporate financial performance. *Academy of Management Journal*, **38**, 3.

Huselid, M.A., Jackson, S.E. & Schuler, R.S. (1997). Technical and strategic human resource management effectiveness as determinants of firm performance. *Academy of Management Journal*, **40**(1), February.

Iles, P.A. & Hayers, P.K. (1997). Managing diversity in transnational project teams: a tentative model and case study. *Journal of Managerial Psychology*, **12**(2), 98–118.

Jewson, N. & Mason, D. (1986). Theory and practice of equal opportunities: liberal and radical approaches. *Sociological Review*, **34**(2), 307–334.

Jones, D., Pringle, J. & Shepherd, D. (2000). Managing diversity meets Aotearoa. *New Zealand Personnel Review*, **29**(3), 364–380.

Kandola, R. & Fullerton, J. (1994). *Managing the Mosaic*. London: Institute of Personnel Management.

Kanter, R.M. (1977). *Men and Women of the Corporation*. New York: Basic Books.

Kanter, R.M. (1989). *When Giants Learn to Dance, Mastering the Challenges of Strategy Management and Careers in the 1990's*. London: Simon and Schuster.

Kossek, E.E. & Zonia, S. (1993). Assessing diversity climate: a field study of reactions to employer efforts to promote diversity. *Journal of Organisational Behaviour*, **14**, 61–81.

Labich, K. (1996). Making diversity pay. *Fortune*, **134**, 5.

Lawrence, E. (2000). Equal opportunities offices and managing equality changes. *Personnel Review*, **29**(3), 381–401.

Lewin, K. (1999). Group decision and social change. In M. Gold (Ed.) *The Complete Social Scientist: A Kurt Lewin Reader*. Washington: American Psychological Association.

Liff, S. (1997). Two routes to managing diversity: individual differences or social group characteristics. *Employee Relations*, **19**(1), 11–26.

Littlefield, D. (1995). Managing diversity seen as core economic value. *People Management*, **1**, 12. London: IPD.

Maclachlan, R. (1995). *Large Companies and Racial Equality*. London: Commission for Racial Equality.

Maddock, S. & Parkin, D. (1993). Gender culture: women's choices and strategies at work. *Women in Management Review*, **8**(2), 3–9.

Mandell, B.W. & Kohler-Grey, S. (1990). Management development that values diversity. *Personnel*, March, 41–47.

Mavin, S. & Girling, G. (2000). What is managing diversity and why does it matter? *Human Resource Development International*, **3**(4), 419–434.

Michie, J. & Sheehan, M. (2000). Labour market flexibility, human resource management and corporate performance. Paper presented to British Academy of Management Conference, September, Edinburgh University.

Patterson, M.G., West, M.A., Lawthorn, R. & Nickell, L. (1997). The impact of people management practices on business performance. *Issues in People Management*, No. 22. London: CIPD.

Prasad, A., Mills, A. & Prasad, M. (1997). *Beyond the Organisational Melting Pot*. London: Sage.

Rosener, J. (1995). *America's Competitive Secret: Women Managers*. Oxford: Oxford University Press.

Rosenthal, P. (1995). Gender differences in managers' attributions for successful work performance. *Women in Management Review*, **10**(6), 26–31(6).

Schneider, B. & Reichers, A.E. (1990). Climate and culture: an evolution of constructs. In B. Schneider (ed.) *Organisational Climate and Culture*. San Francisco: Jossey-Bass Publishers.

Schneider, B. & Reichers, A.E. (1993). On the etiology of climates, *Personnel Psychology*, **36**(1), 19–39.

Schneider, B., Gunnarson, S.K. & Niles-Jolly, K. (1994). Creating the climate and culture of success. *Organisational Dynamics*, **23**(1), 17–29.

Sheridan, J.E. & Slocum, J.W. (1975). The direction of the causal relationship between job satisfaction and work performance. *Organizational Behavior and Human Performance*, **14**, 159–172.

Shroder, B., Blackburn, V. & Iles, P.A. (1997). Women in management and firm: financial performance: an exploratory study. *Journal of Managerial Issues*, **IX**(3), Fall, 359–372.

Storey, J. (1995). *Human Resource Management: A Critical Text*. London: Routledge.

Storey, J. (2000). *HRM: A Critical Text*, 2nd edn. Oxford: Blackwells.

Suliman, A. & Iles, P.A. (2000a). The multi-dimensional nature of organisational commitment in a non-western context. *Journal of Management Development*, **19**(1), 71–82.

Suliman, A. & Iles, P.A. (2000b). Is continuance commitment beneficial to organisations? Commitment–performance relationships—a new look. *Journal of Managerial Psychology*, **15**(5), 407–426.

Thomas, R.R. Jr (1990). From affirmative action to affirming diversity. *Harvard Business Review*, **68**(2), March/April, 107–117.

Thomas, R.R. Jr (1991). *Beyond Race and Gender: Unleashing the Power of Your Total Work Time by Managing Diversity*. New York: AMACOM.

Walton, R.E. (1985). From control to commitment in the workplace. *Harvard Business Review*, **63**, 2.

Wentling, R.M. (2000). Evaluation of diversity initiatives in multi-national corporations. *Human Resource Development International*, **3**(4), 435–450.

Wiersema, M.F. & Bantel, K.A. (1992). Top management team demography and corporate strategic change. *Academy of Management Journal*, **35**, 91–121.

Wilson, E. & Iles, P.A. (1996). Managing diversity: evaluation of an emerging paradigm. Paper presented to the British Academy of Management Conference, Sheffield University.

Wright, P. & McMahan, G.C. (1992). Theoretical perspectives for human resource management. *Journal of Management*, **18**(3).

Youngblood, S.A. & Chambers-Cook, K. (1984). Child care assistance can improve employee attitudes and behaviour. *Personnel Administrator*, **29**(2), 45–46 and 93–95.

CHAPTER 11

Analysing the Operation of Diversity on the Basis of Disability

Carol Woodhams
Manchester Metropolitan University, Manchester, UK
Ardha Danieli
University of Warwick, Coventry, UK

SUMMARY

This chapter examines the limitations of diversity theory as it applies to disabled employees. By employing a 'dissolving difference' model of diversity that contrasts with models of equality management, the chapter initially argues the usefulness of a diversity management approach to disability-based inequality. It presents the results of an empirical study that demonstrates a perceived lack of 'groupness' about disabled employees that, on the face of it, is consistent with the underlying principles of the model. Nevertheless, the chapter goes on to argue that in its translation from rhetoric to reality and particularly in its dependence on business-driven arguments, the 'dissolving difference' perspective and the workplace view of disability are incompatible.

INTRODUCTION

There are many areas of debate and tension that remain concerning the theory and practice of managing equal opportunities and managing diversity (Cassell, 2001). As is evidenced throughout the chapters in this book, there is little standardization of the meaning of diversity and little agreement over its key principles. One of the primary debates focuses on the extent to which diversity is new or different from traditional forms of managing equal opportunities (Kandola, 1995). Some authors suggest that managing

Individual Diversity and Psychology in Organizations. Edited by Marilyn J. Davidson and Sandra L. Fielden.
© 2003 John Wiley & Sons, Ltd.

diversity is a distinct alternative (Kandola & Fullerton, 1998; Ross and Schneider, 1992), while others treat it as an all-singing all-dancing approach (IPD, 1996). One of the dimensions of diversity where the distinctiveness is most clearly emphasized is the business rationale that underpins it. However, while this underpinning is important in relation to the ability of diversity approaches to deliver equality for disabled people (see Woodhams & Danieli, 2000), of more relevance to this chapter is an aspect of the distinctiveness/sameness debate that is less clearly delineated, namely the management of diversity's theoretical treatment of minority groups and of individuals as representatives of such groups (women, ethnic minorities, etc.).

A comprehensive analysis of the theoretical approaches to managing diversity carried out by Liff (1996), concluded that there are four possible approaches to the treatment of difference based on group labels. The less original version of managing diversity, i.e. the interpretation that extends rather than rewrites the management of equal opportunities, would encompass three of Liff's four managing diversity approaches (valuing, accommodating and utilizing differences). These approaches perpetuate the use of group labels, treating them as important and defining, emphasizing the need for wider inclusion of more groups. Within this chapter little differentiation is made between these versions of diversity, and managing equal opportunities, as they share a perspective on the use and usefulness of group labels. More original and distinct versions of managing diversity rely less on notions of group membership. The approach of 'dissolving difference' (Liff, 1996) that rejects the usefulness of group categories, is the stance that is most distinct from managing equal opportunities in its treatment of group-based characteristics, and therefore is most useful as a comparative tool within this chapter.

This chapter will initially argue that in the case of managing diversity aimed at disabled employees, the more distinct and individual the model of diversity employed, the more promise it holds for disabled employees. We will present qualitative data drawn from a study of managers' perceptions of disability, which suggests that managers' perceptions are almost entirely individualistic and that the intra-category variability is so extreme that it renders the use of this particular group label almost useless. The conclusion is drawn that at a *theoretical* level, an approach that *dissolves* difference would appear to be the most appropriate for the inclusion of more disabled people into paid work. However, at the level of *practice*, it becomes evident that there are tensions with it as it applies to disability at two levels. Firstly, it states that the practice of diversity management for disabled employees is not as positive as the theory suggests; and secondly, it argues that even the *theoretical* applicability of diversity theory is upset by an internal contradiction between the dissolution of difference and the need for business justification.

DIVERSITY, EQUALITY AND THE TREATMENT OF GROUPS

In their most distinct forms, traditional approaches to managing equal opportunities and managing diversity offer very different perspectives on the use and usefulness of group-based classifications. On the one hand, in managing equal opportunities there is an emphasis on the role of groups in the reduction of opportunity. One of the founding principles of traditionally framed liberal equality is that an individual's membership of a minority group will unfairly reduce their chances to succeed (Jewson & Mason, 1986). While in theory the aim is to become 'blind' to social differences for the purposes of making employment decisions on, for example, recruitment or promotion, nevertheless, equal opportunity *practices* go on to treat the workforce as a collection of individuals who can be categorized into groups according to a range of social differences. In other words, the operation of organizational policies and practices is designed to benefit primarily one group of individuals that share at least one characteristic. So for example, maternity leave, part-time working and career breaks will benefit the employment of women on the grounds that they are generally the primary nurturers and carers of the family (Holterman, 1995). Such policies are of course attempts to remove unfair barriers and so create a level playing field. Although many of the measures that are put in place to promote the abilities of women to manage their caring activities alongside their work will not benefit all women, they will apply (or could potentially apply) to a large proportion of women. Additionally, the monitoring of equal opportunities relies on group-based characteristics to evaluate the extent to which policies are being successfully implemented (Taylor, 1994). Hence we have employment statistics reported in terms of the number of men and women in full-time and part-time employment.

Most versions of managing diversity (e.g. Ross & Schneider, 1992; Ford, 1996; Liff & Wajcman, 1996; Kandola & Fullerton, 1998), on the other hand, place less emphasis on social groups. As stated in the introduction, in its most distinct form, managing diversity attempts to dissolve assumptions of collective difference based on group labels, while emphasizing the unique experiences that life and social experiences create within every individual. It contests the usefulness and validity of group-based policies and practices as a means of securing equality for all individuals within organizations. Instead, managing diversity should 'not exclude anyone—even white middle-class males' (Kandola & Fullerton, 1998: 6). It changes the objectives for equality policies and practices to focus not on equality in groups, but instead to set the goal as 'the opportunity to be acknowledged for the person one is and to be helped in making the most of one's talents and reach one's own goals' (Liff, 1996: 13). Practices emphasize the need to move to a culture and climate that celebrate differences and thus differences are to be viewed positively rather than negatively. In practice this means focusing on a much broader base of profile characteristics to include: 'Not only different genders and races, but also different cultures, lifestyles and ways of thinking' (Platt, CEO and Chairman, Hewlett Packard, quoted in Brimm & Arora, 2001).

Similarly, Caudron (1994: 56) suggests differences should go beyond 'Obvious physical differences to include differences in communication styles, problem solving, professional experience, functional expertise, management level, training and education and work ethics.'

For the purposes of this chapter the theoretical model of diversity that is under evaluation will be one that is idealistic, inclusive and distinct, one that emphasizes individuality and rejects the use of group-based assumptions of shared experience as opposed to managing diversity approaches that extend traditional forms of managing equality. The data presented in this chapter will emphasize the advantages suggested by this model, particularly in response to the challenges posed by managing disability-based diversity.

DISABLED PEOPLE AS THE NEW 'GROUP'

Disabled people represent a group of individuals that have recently had their identity as a minority group strengthened by legislation. The Disability Discrimination Act (1995) confirmed the status of disabled workers as the UK's latest minority group deserving of equal opportunities within a work context. It has provided a statutory foundation and a rationale for the good practice of examining organizational policies and practices towards disabled employees and potential employees to protect them against discriminatory activities. It is the most recent piece of equality legislation that draws on a traditional framework, identifying the relevant 'victims' at the level of a group (by using a generic definition) while implementing rights to fair treatment at the level of the individual. As such it recognizes the sameness and difference aspects of managing equal opportunities. Under Part 1 of the Act a disabled person is someone who has a 'physical or mental impairment which has a substantial and long-term adverse effect on his [*sic!*][1] ability to carry out normal day-to-day activities' (Disability Discrimination Act, 1995, 1 (2)).

This definition categorizes someone as part of the group of disabled people by providing parameters with regard to three key aspects of the definition: i.e. what is a physical or mental *impairment*, what is meant by a person's ability to carry out *day-to-day* activities, and when that impairment might have a *substantial* and *long-term* adverse effect upon the ability to carry out normal day-to-day activities (Cooper & Vernon, 1996; Doyle, 1996). The distinction between *impairment* and *disability* is important because, as we will show, an impairment need not necessarily lead to a disability if it can be accommodated or if adaptations to the individual's environment can be made which offset the potential effect of the impairment (see Barnes, 1999 for further discussions on this link).

Even a very superficial inspection of the Disability Discrimination Act's definition however, reveals some of the complexity of trying to identify disabled people as a group (see also Chapter 1). If we view disability as derived from impairment and view impairment as located at points on a three-dimensional scale of medical condition, time and severity, at the lowest end of the three scales would be mild, temporary illnesses that few people would label as disabling conditions, such as minor mood swings or a headache. At the point that is temporally constant, but still non-severe, would be conditions such as mild depression or *recurrent* headaches. Increasing the severity of these conditions at some point would bring them into the company of those commonly considered disabling; so, for example, if occasional headaches become repetitive migraines which result in an inability to carry out day-to-day activities, the impaired individual would qualify as disabled. At the same time individuals may not have static impairments, they may get 'better' and in doing so they no longer qualify as part of the group. Of course, while some individuals may leave this particular group, they may be replaced by others who have become disabled through accidents or ill health. The term 'disabled', then, reveals little about the nature of the person's impairment, the workplace consequences of that impairment or the types of support they may require (Cunningham & James, 2001).

However, given that historically organizations have based their equal opportunities policies on group-based differences, they have been able to rapidly extend this approach to the latest group of those suffering from discrimination who are now protected by the Disability Discrimination Act (1995) (Woodhams, 1998). The evidence in this chapter argues the ineffectiveness of this approach. It will suggest that there are anomalies around 'disability' that render a group-based approach even less effective than might be the case with other minority groups and that, theoretically, a more satisfactory alternative may be found within a distinct individual managing diversity approach.

RESEARCH METHODS

The data discussed in this chapter are based on two sources: responses from human resource/personnel managers to a questionnaire survey and responses to a series of in-depth interviews. Both aimed at investigating how 'disability' was perceived in organizational terms. The questionnaire survey ($n = 526$) included both private and public sector UK organizations. Responses to the questionnaire indicated that managers had had great difficulty in explaining their understandings of disability and in providing information on the number of disabled people they employed. As a result, it was decided to conduct some interviews to explore this in more depth. Twenty-one interviews were conducted with similar respondents drawn from a mix of UK organizational sectors. The sample included 6 public sector organizations (two local authorities, a hospital, a regional police headquarters, a further education college and a civil service department) and 15 private sector employers (including a supermarket chain, two high street retailers, two banking organizations, one large hotel, one media organization, one mixed service organization, and six manufacturing organizations (including two concerned with energy production, one engineering organization, one food production company and two in chemicals)). Interviews lasted between 45 minutes and 2 hours, were tape recorded and transcribed. Both the survey and the interviews were conducted after the Disability Discrimination Act had been passed but before there was a requirement for employers to implement it. Hence while all respondents were aware of the Act, most respondents were still operating policies according to pre-Disability Discrimination Act practices.

The findings reported in this chapter are of course limited to the views and perceptions of a particular group of managers—human resource (HR)/personnel managers. We chose these respondents because they were more likely to be aware of and have considered issues surrounding disability given that managing equal opportunities is likely to fall within their remit in the organization. However, with the devolution of human resource management (HRM) to line managers, it would be interesting to find out the views of other organizational members further down the hierarchy and in different functional specialisms, together with the views of trade unionists. We have not explicitly examined the views of those of whom we have written, i.e. those who are classified as, or who self-classify as, 'disabled'. This is clearly a limitation and we run the risk of accusations of objectifying disabled people. We may have had responses from managers who had some form of impairment themselves, but if we did, they chose not to share that with us and we must respect their right not to do so.

MANAGERIAL PERCEPTIONS OF DISABILITY

The most prominent finding that emerged from the qualitative data collection around the understanding of 'disability' was that there was very little sense of a homogeneous, cohesive 'disabled' group. Most managers were unable or unwilling to talk about disability in general terms and would only discuss issues of impairment individually. Although political correctness may have played a part in their reluctance to generalize, most interviewees were unable even to provide 'disability' statistics for their organizations, hence managers often reported, 'I don't know how many disabled workers we have' (HR Manager, Chemical Manufacturing).

It could be argued that most interviewees were unable to provide statistics on the number of disabled people they employed in their organization because they had not conducted monitoring exercises, or had yet to incorporate this 'new' group into their monitoring practices. This may be the case; however, we would suggest that this is also a result of managers grappling with the notion of who, in their perception, can and cannot be classified as disabled. Unlike other disadvantaged groups who are more easily identified by observable characteristics, when discussing disability, respondents would use a concrete point of reference to anchor their speculations, utilizing a range of individuals. They deliberated on a case-by-case basis over which of their personal contacts might best 'fit' into the category of disabled without claiming that such individuals might be in any way representative of a group because as one respondent highlighted, 'No two people will necessarily have the same type or degree of disability or impairment' (HR Manager, Bank).

In exploring this dilemma, it became apparent that there were a number of other factors that affected managers' perceptions of disability.

IMPAIRMENT, JOB TYPE AND WORKING ENVIRONMENT

In assessing whether or not an individual was seen as disabled, interviewees and survey respondents often referred to the relationship between type of impairment, type of job and working environment. In other words, individuals were only seen as disabled if their impairment was of consequence within their particular environment, and perhaps had given rise to some need for adaptation within their particular job role, as the following quote illustrates: 'Many people with a disability can appear and behave in the same way as an able-bodied person subject to the environment they are in. In some respects my answers depend on the disability, and each case would have to be dealt with on an individual basis' (Senior HR Manager, Local Government Authority).

In an attempt to quantify the number of disabled people in the organization another manager stated: 'I suppose it depends if it (their impairment) affects their job or not, sometimes we have to make changes' (HR Manager, Chemical Manufacturing).

It would appear from these responses, that it is only if an impairment affects an individual's work that the label 'disabled' is appropriate. If there is an adverse effect, this can be offset by 'making changes' either to the way the work is performed, or to any environmental factors that may be impacting on an individual's ability to perform at a level which managers find acceptable. The difficulty of applying the label 'disabled' to individuals is therefore contingent on factors that are external to the individual person.

The extent to which managers feel able, or are willing, to alter the environment in order to offset the potential effect of an impairment can also depend on the extent to which an individual has particular skills which the employer needs or which are in short supply in the labour market. This can on occasions override concerns managers may have about employing some individuals. But having made the necessary environmental adjustments, managers are then at a loss as to whether such individuals can then be included under the group category 'disabled', as a manager commented: 'He came to us at a time when we really needed skilled people. I was very unsure at first whether or not it would work out but he does his job just the same as everyone else and, particularly since the move, it's not necessary to walk very far. Is he disabled? Is that the sort of thing you mean?' (Human Resources Manager, Bank).

Responses to different types of impairments have to be tailored not only to the specific needs of the individual but also to the particular job. In explaining how this was achieved one respondent reported: 'We've put in a special screen for the woman with the sight disturbances and worked out some special leave for another. It's our new approach to disability management' (Equality Manager, Bank).

One manager went further, placing a specific emphasis on the disabling role of society within his definition. His explanation of disabled status was probably influenced by his organizational definition and was given as: 'Someone who experiences discrimination on the basis of physical or sensory impairment, learning difficulty or emotional or mental distress. Disability is not caused by individual disabled person's particular impairments, but the way in which society fails to meet their needs' (Personnel Manager, Local Government Authority).

In this definition the individual impaired body is not the *cause* of disability, rather it is society's reactions to the impairment which can result in an individual falling within the category of 'disabled'. Taken to its logical conclusion, such a definition would result in the category of disability being understood as a social construction and would support a social model of disability (Barnes, 1993). A central theme that runs through many of the above quotes is the extent to which impairments are seen to affect the productivity of individuals.

IMPAIRMENT AND PRODUCTIVITY

The link between impairment and productivity was mentioned by a number of respondents as important in whether they labelled someone as disabled or not. Some respondents placed greater emphasis on how the severity of the impairment affected the performance of individuals relative to other impaired individuals as the following quote illustrates:

> The extent of the disability can make a big difference. We have some disabled people whose disability in no way affects their productivity, whilst others, for example (those) on the Sheltered Placement Scheme [a Government Scheme subsidizing salaries of disabled workers] may have their productivity severely affected. (Middle Manager, Food Manufacturing)

Others placed more emphasis on the extent to which the environment had been adapted to offset any potential lack of productivity as the following comment highlights: 'When he first started I'll admit I was pretty sceptical. He is so severely disabled I just couldn't see how it would work. But now, after a few years and a lot of changes, he does it so well that we don't see him as disabled any more' (Personnel Manager, Energy Production).

Of course the use of the phrase 'we don't see him as disabled any more' is probably not meant literally, and used rather glibly, but this should not detract from the point that is made over the relative and temporary nature of the concept.

In many instances, the association between impairment and productivity was strengthened to the extent that, *dis*ability was equated to *in*ability. This is not to say that the two were considered to be entirely synonymous, only that some managers considered employees only to be *disabled* in circumstances where they are considered *unable*. One manager came up with a distinctly original definition that illustrates this point:

'[A disabled person is] someone incapable of doing the full range of duties of the principal job for which they are employed' (Personnel Manager, Engineering Firm).

Managers' concerns with the level of productivity of people with impairments were therefore generally cast in negative terms. It would thus be difficult to make a case that the adaptations that were made could be seen as a celebration of difference. Indeed, there is no acceptance within any of the diversity models that diversity management should be supportive of differences in employees' productivity. On the contrary, the aim of adapting the environment appeared to be a need to eliminate differences that might affect performance so that disabled employees could be seen as equivalent to those with no impairments. As such it can be seen as a similar strategy to that implicit within more traditional approaches to managing equal opportunities, i.e. an attempt to remove barriers in order to create a 'level playing field' where thereafter successes are achieved on individual merit.

While the above workplace factors were influential on managers' perceptions and categorizations of individuals as disabled or not, another important factor that respondents drew on related to their exposure to impairment outside the workplace and their familiarity with individuals.

PERSONAL FAMILIARITY WITH DISABILITY

While employment-based issues tended to be considered in relatively negative terms, familiarity with disability outside the workplace tended to be referred to in a more positive light. So for example, one respondent commented, 'It's funny, but I guess only having one leg does make him disabled, but he's my dad and I hardly notice it because he has an artificial one' Personnel Advisor, Further Education College.

And another stated, 'My cousin is deaf, but I was always told not to call her disabled, just deaf. She's not disabled. She's fine' (Personnel Officer, Media).

When familiarity was combined with an above-average work performance it also had a mitigating effect against the ascription of disability status as the following manager reported:

> He has worked here for nearly four years. He really enjoys coming in and hardly misses a day. At one time I spoke to his mum because we wanted to increase his hours but it was going to cause problems with his allowance. He was really disappointed, but he settled down again. Nowadays we hardly notice him. He's just like everyone else. (HR Manager, Retail Organization)

Apart from the somewhat patronizing tone of the above quote and the limitations imposed by the benefits system on individuals' ability to work the hours they might wish and so achieve some level of independence, the political significance of the comment that 'Nowadays we hardly notice him' should not be ignored. Familiarity can be positive but it can also render some people so much part of the norm that they become invisible and their needs ignored.

IMPAIRMENT AND 'OTHER' DIFFERENCES

So far we have discussed how managers' perceptions of disability were influenced by a variety of interacting factors within and outside the workplace. However, managers' perceptions of disability were also influenced by another set of characteristics, unrelated to the impairment itself, but which themselves have been identified as leading to forms of discrimination in the workplace, namely age and gender. So, for example, one respondent commented, 'It's been hard for him since his sight has started to get really bad. He's learning to cope but I don't know how much longer he'll be able to work. Of course it would be even more *tragic* if he were younger' (emphasis added) (Disability Equality Advisor, Civil Service).

The notion of disability as a *tragedy* has been adamantly rejected by disability rights activists both because of the negative perceptions of disability that it suggests and because it places individuals as 'victims', shifting the focus of attention of causes of disability from the social to the individual (Oliver, 1990). While the 'tragedy' of disability may still be part of the public perception of disability, of particular concern here is that this is referred to by a *disability equality advisor* whom one might expect to be more sensitive to such matters! While the above respondent interjected age as a significant factor into perceptions of disability, the person he was referring to was also of course a gendered subject and this was an important consideration for another of our respondents who stated: 'It must be much more difficult if you're a man to lose your job through disability' (Personnel Officer, Media).

Clearly disability is not considered in isolation from other forms of group-based characteristics. These cross-cut disability and lead to perceptions of double (Stuart, 1992) or multiple forms of disadvantage. However, it is not just a question of different forms of inequality cross-cutting each other, but rather that managers perceive a hierarchy of disadvantage within the category of 'disability'. The consequences of this perceived hierarchy suggests that some individuals will be seen as more eligible for adaptations within the workplace, thereby contradicting the notion that all differences should be equally valued or that all individuals should be given the opportunity to reach their full potential (Kandola & Fullerton, 1998). A similar issue is raised by Kirton and Greene (2000: 113) who argue that differences cannot all be viewed equally as Kandola and Fullerton's (1998) analysis suggests. The data presented in this chapter suggest that this is far from the case in relation to disability.

Finally, many of the managers stressed that the use of the disability 'label' is not one that should be bestowed by others, but should be within the control of the individual as the following quote illustrates: 'It might be that they think that it's none of our business what sort of a state they're in as long as they're doing their jobs well, and on one level I can see their point' (Personnel Officer, Media).

Self-identification and classification are therefore an important dimension of disability that may or may not be made public by the individual and as such is similar to other invisible forms of inequality such as sexual orientation. As with sexual orientation, the above respondent qualifies the right of individuals not to declare whether they have an impairment or not, *as long as they are doing their job well*. However, unlike other forms of invisible differences, the transitory nature of the category of disability and the interaction of the level of severity with the nature of the work and environment, differentiates disability from these other group-based differences. It is difficult to see how for example age, gender or ethnicity, or the nature of the job, might render someone as more (or less) homosexual or lesbian.

In summary, the number of factors that seemed to impinge on the stability of the status of disability was many and varied. See Figure 11.1 for a diagrammatic summary.

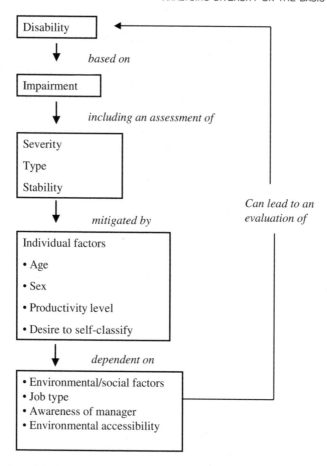

FIGURE 11.1 A model of managerial perception of disability in employment

Managers mentioned the severity of impairment, stability of condition, the effects of the job type and accessibility of the environment, the skill with which they performed their work, their familiarity with the impairment and the individual, and the age and sex of the disabled individual. Every disabled individual was regarded as different from the next and their status as 'disabled' was dependent on the number and type of factors that affected them.

DISCUSSION

The data we have presented suggest that managers were genuinely unable to discuss the issues of 'disabled' people as a meaningful category in a work context. The concept 'disabled' emerged as a term that had little application or relevance to an intuitively comprehensible grouping of people. Managers only talked about 'disabled' employees in very precise and very individual terms. Their understanding of 'disability' was affected by characteristics that were additional and (sometimes) completely unrelated to the nature or severity of the impairment. They specified the practical implications, work abilities, and personal characteristics of each disabled employee, and did not generalize from one disabled individual to another. 'Disability' was regarded as a concept that could change with time and circumstances, not only in the sense that the individual is possibly going to 'get better' or 'worse', but also in the sense that at the point when the effects on employment are no longer problematic, the status was removed. 'Disability' emerged from the findings as an interactive term, altered and shaped by a host of additional factors that are themselves subject to the particular workplace context.

It is argued on the basis of these results that the role of additional characteristics in the perception and definition of 'disability' articulated by these respondents cannot be underestimated, and is intrinsically bound up in the status that the label 'disabled' confers. The step between perceiving an individual as having an impairment and viewing them as disabled brings into play this large number of additional variables. Other distinctions that could have been investigated included whether particular impairments were familiar or unfamiliar, past or present, whether or not impairment interferes with communication, whether or not it is infectious, whether it is potentially fatal/curable, whether the effects are continuous or intermittent. It is difficult to estimate the number of factors that may provide for the distinction of sets of impairments from each other.

Disability emerged from the findings as a set of impressions, an 'index of consequences' created on the basis of a series of assessments, only some of which are directly related to the form of impairment, and many of which are equally dependent on context. It is therefore argued that the cohesion of the disabled group is severely disturbed by the findings.

The results also affect the 'groupness' of people with impairments. As stated within social identity theory (see Tajfel, 1981), the establishment of membership in a group requires establishing not only common intra-group characteristics of these categories, but also inter-group differences, i.e. from 'others'. So in relation to gender, ethnicity and sexuality, women are defined as not 'men', ethnic minorities are defined in relation to other ethnic groups and homosexuals are defined as 'not heterosexuals'. With disability it was clear that the establishment of group membership was problematic on both counts.

Establishing inter-group differences in relation to disability would require comparisons with non-disabled people. This was problematic because managers' points of reference were, in the first instance, whether an individual's impairment could be offset by changes made to the job and/or environment so that the impairment did not adversely affect their performance. It would appear that only if their *subsequent* level of performance fell short of the performance of non-disabled people that the category of 'disabled' became appropriate. The temporal instability of impairment together with the environment in which the individual employee is located is of more significance for managers' perceptions of disability, than any perceived contrasts with other groups. Similarly, establishing common intra-group characteristics for disabled people was equally problematic. Managers' inability and unwillingness to generalize about disabled people, i.e. treat them as a homogeneous group, resulted from their recognition of the salience of factors such as nature of the impairment, the degree of severity, their familiarity with the individual, along with, in our examples, characteristics such as age and gender. Where intra-group comparisons were made with other impaired individuals, this served only to differentiate the degree to which some impaired people were more disabled than others and to some degree how their productivity compared with that of others.

At a managerial level, the 'groupness' and cohesion of disability all but disappeared. Managers saw almost nothing other than a number of individuals with individual requirements, individual needs and often individual solutions. Their contextual and social interpretation of disability is akin to the way we employ concepts of 'ethnicity' and 'femininity' as representatives of a set of social characteristics whose existence lies in the interpretation of the observer. It is concluded that 'disability', as a concrete concept, does not exist. The popularist notion enshrined in equality legislation and social practice that there is a shared understanding of 'disability', is no more than a social myth. In reality it has a multitude of identities that are themselves unstable, shifting and subject to redefinition. Generally this supports a socially weighted explanation of disability, i.e. it refutes the direct and singular connection between impairment and disability that is often assumed, although as discussed there is still a trace of a perception of impairment as a tragedy for the individual and a ranking of individuals according to other forms of discrimination.

DISABILITY AND DIVERSITY—THE SOLUTION?

Given the above discussion, how useful is the concept of managing diversity for managing disability in the workplace? The first point to be made is that this managerial understanding of disabled people clearly contradicts the perspective enshrined within liberal equality theories and versions of managing diversity that *extend* equality, that disadvantaged individuals can and should be identified as representatives of groups. There is a massive discrepancy between the way that liberal equality theory requires the identification and use of group labels, and the managers' interpretation of disabled people, that has very serious implications for the typical standardized and bureaucratic operational approach to equality procedures. In practice, if a group cannot be easily identified, it cannot be monitored; if it has no homogeneous requirements, its needs cannot easily be met. When this finding is cited against the overriding emphasis on the *how* (as opposed to the *why*) of equality procedures within the liberal framework, the implications clearly undermine much of the framework's already weak potential (Woodhams & Danieli, 2000).

Theoretical approaches to managing diversity parallel the managers' understanding of disabled people as individuals and, therefore, on the face of it hold more promise. It emerged, in line with Liff's (1996) understanding of the 'dissolving differences' diversity perspective, that differences were seen not as systematically distributed on the basis of membership of this group, but as unique and individual. In fact, from this perspective, group-based differences are not really 'seen' at all. The emphasis moves away from a perspective of non-discrimination on the basis of group appearance. It is much less on the (somewhat ironic) need, within group-based models, to consciously notice group difference so as to promote its disappearance. There is instead, with individually designed solutions, the ability to redress individually felt oppression often based on the cross-cutting of multiple forms of discrimination which were so prevalent within the understandings of the managers (Kirton & Greene, 2000). In theory then, managers would find this approach intuitively compatible with their own internalization.

In addition, prescriptions for practice initiatives reportedly stress individualism in a manner that could work positively. Disabled employees might find more freedom, flexibility and greater developmental potential within an individualization of job profiles and selection assessment methods, an individualization of supportive options (working hours, leave options, work locations), a flexible approach to appraisals and development, alternative methods of mentoring, coaching and providing feedback and a more individualized method of assessing strengths and weaknesses. They might benefit from policies that attempt to seek information on training needs and ambitions at an individual level and respond through tailored career management or through a wide choice of benefits offered 'cafeteria' style (see Jamieson & O'Mara, 1991, for a good example of this type of model of diversity). They would also benefit from an evaluation of diversity initiatives as opposed to the monitoring of groups. Under managing diversity, the need for group membership dissolves, with the consequence that disabled people would not continually have to justify their minority group status. They would not have to have their status (which is often changeable, sometimes invisible and frequently personal) evaluated and described. The individualization of initiatives and the lack of emphasis on homogeneous group status could be very beneficial. Nevertheless, the applicability of diversity is not without problems.

DISABILITY AND DIVERSITY—THE PROBLEMS?

As critiques of the principles of managing diversity generally appear elsewhere in this book, this section will be limited to those points that may disproportionately impact on employees with disabilities. Our critique will focus on two main issues: firstly, on the difficulties of translating theory into practice, and secondly, on uncovering internal contradictions within a model that on the one hand requires a positive regard for difference, and on the other needs a business justification.

One of the problems with the application of diversity lies not within the theoretical rhetoric, but in the practical reality. As previously argued (Woodhams & Danieli, 2000), the satisfying of individual need is problematic for organizations driven by profit maximization and limited resources. The typical organizational interpretation of diversity in the end retains its focus on groups and group-based solutions. As an example, despite the wide basis for inclusion in the Hewlett Packard programme given in the quote on p. 195, the initiatives that have flowed from this policy include a focus on age discrimination at their sites in Grenoble, language discrimination in Belgium, sex discrimination in Hewlett Packard Austria, sexuality discrimination in Hewlett Packard California, disability discrimination in Germany, etc. (Brimm & Arora, 2001). In other words, the implementation of diversity policy still seems to require a degree of homogeneity of need, treatment and measurement. For economic reasons and particularly in the face of the variety of workplace requirements that are bound to arise in response to a very heterogeneous group, the need for a business justification of policy is problematic. The diversity rhetoric may cope well with and celebrate differences within individuals, but the reality of the business case is that implementation remains based on collective and group-based characteristics (Woodhams & Danieli, 2000). In other words it is difficult to make a profitable business case on the basis of individual needs.

Even more problematically, the understanding of disability that emerged during the interviews highlights a theoretical contradiction inherent in managing diversity approaches. On the one hand, the business rationale for the incorporation of difference within managing diversity approaches proposes that employee uniqueness can only be of positive consequence to performance and productivity. On the other hand, the concept that was most closely linked to managers' understandings of disability, was that of *in*ability at work. The negative consequences of impairment on job performance were found to be the most decisive factor in the defining of an impaired individual as disabled or not. This chapter is not arguing that people with impairments are not able to work as productively as non-disabled comparators. There is evidence to suggest that the productivity of disabled workers is equal to or even exceeds that of non-disabled workers (Zadek & Scott-Parker, 2000). What we are arguing is that under the diversity model, there is a direct incompatibility between the managerial understandings of disability and managers' needs to be convinced by cost-driven business arguments. Previous research by Cunningham and James (2001) found that disabled employees were associated with increased costs rather than cost benefits. Furthermore, positive stereotypes of features of difference are often used to 'sell' the abilities of previously under-represented groups. In this case, intra-group diversity is so extreme and social group membership so loosely identifiable, it could be argued that there are few all-pervasive stereotypes, either positive or negative. The point is echoed by Roberts (1996) who suggests that the approach of 'selling' minority groups for their culturally imparted skills may not apply to a culturally diverse group. How can a theory that so strongly highlights the positive in its approach to employee difference be equally emphatic about the need for a business justification?

CONCLUSIONS

In this chapter we have sought to present a case for a more careful examination of the applicability of managing diversity to a 'new' category of people who have only relatively recently achieved recognition as a group worthy of legislative protection against discrimination. In examining managers' perceptions of disability, we have suggested that their perceptions are most closely aligned with an individualistic approach to managing diversity that attempts to 'dissolve difference' (Liff, 1996). Nevertheless, we have also argued that their ability or willingness to alter the working environment in order to accommodate disability-based 'difference' is driven less by positive terms of celebrating difference for its individual and organizational benefits, and more by its usefulness as a mechanism for ensuring that the performance of an impaired individual is no worse than that of anyone else. Therefore, as a tool to effect organizational progress, the managing diversity approach of 'dissolving difference' has weaknesses for both organization and disabled employees. Furthermore, its perspective on groups and their group status generates further problems.

With the incorporation of a critical political perspective, it could be argued that the dissolution of the disabled group status and the appreciation of all of our unique differences as people might, in the end, not be beneficial to an increased representation in the workforce. The raised profile of disabled people within society generally has substantially benefited from the presentation of disabled people as a coherent political group (Oliver, 1990). Attempts to subdivide the group into impairment-driven categories are seen as destabilizing and unhelpful in the promotion of collective power. The same point can be made within employment, and is particularly relevant for a group that has only recently emerged as a political force with the influence to enact social change. Vince (1996), for example, argues that the diversity movement could be viewed as an attempt to take the politics out of intervention, to individualize social relations and to create a compliant workforce that would be indifferent to the radicalizing impact of collective experiences. Ouseley (1996) echoes this point: 'Diversity approaches that encourage managers to ignore the realities of inequality and discrimination that create such (difficult) conditions for people from certain groups will mean that the status quo is maintained' (p. 7).

Finally, we wish to make a plea for more work on examining how diversity is *actually* being implemented in the workplace especially in relation to disability. This would require consulting those who are at the receiving end of organizational perceptions, policies and practices on managing diversity. The instability of the concept of disability, i.e. that any one of us might experience an impairment, makes this form of discrimination a concern for everyone, not just those who are already experiencing it.

ENDNOTE

1. It would appear that despite sex discrimination legislation, the importance of language has not been taken on board by those responsible for writing the legislation!

REFERENCES

Barnes, C. (1993). *Disabled People in Britain and Discrimination*. London: Hurst and Co.
Barnes, C. (1999). Disability studies: new or not so new directions? *Disability and Society*, **14**, 577–580.
Brimm, L. & Arora, M. (2001). Diversity management at Hewlett Packard Europe. In M. Albrecht (ed.) *Managing Diversity in the Workplace* (pp. 108–124). Malden, Mass.: Blackwell Business.
Cassell, C. (2001). Managing diversity. In T. Redman & A. Wilkinson (eds) *Contemporary Human Resource Management* (pp. 404–431). Harlow: Pearson.
Caudron, S. (1994). Diversity ignites effective work teams. *Personnel Journal,* September, 54–63.
Cooper, J. & Vernon, S. (1996). *Disability and the Law*. London: Jessica Kingsley.
Cunningham, I. & James, P. (2001). Managing diversity and disability legislation: catalysts for eradicating discrimination in the workplace? In M. Noon & E. Ogbonna (eds) *Equality, Diversity and Disadvantage in Employment* (pp. 103–117). London: Palgrave.
Doyle, B. (1996). *Disability Discrimination—The New Law*. Bristol: Jordans Publishing.
Ford, V. (1996). Partnership is the secret of progress: equal opportunity policy and diversity programmes. *People Management*, **2**(3), 8 February, 34–36.
Holterman, S. (1995). The costs and benefits to British employers of measures to promote equality of opportunity. In J. Humphries & J. Rubery (eds) *The Economics of Equal Opportunities* (pp. 137–154). Manchester: Equal Opportunities Commission.
IPD (1996). *Managing Diversity*. An IPD Position Paper. London: The Institute of Personnel and Development.
Jamieson, D. & O'Mara, J. (1991). *Managing Workforce 2000: Gaining the Diversity Advantage*. San Francisco: Jossey-Bass.
Jewson, N. & Mason, D. (1986). Theory and practice of equal opportunities policies: liberal and radical approaches. *Sociological Review*, **34**, 307–334.
Kandola, R. (1995). Managing diversity: new broom or old hat? In C.L. Cooper & I.T. Robertson (eds) *International Review of Industrial and Organisational Psychology* (pp. 131–167). Chichester: John Wiley & Sons.
Kandola, R. & Fullerton, J. (1998). *Managing the Mosaic: Diversity in Action*. London: Institute of Personnel and Development.
Kirton, G. & Greene, A.M. (2000). *The Dynamics of Managing Diversity: A Critical Approach*. Oxford: Butterworth Heinemann.

Liff, S. (1996). Two routes to managing diversity: individual differences or social group characteristics. *Employee Relations*, **19**, 11–26.

Liff, S. & Wajcman, J. (1996). 'Sameness' and 'difference' revisited: which way forward for equal opportunity initiatives? *Journal of Management Studies*, **33**, 79–95.

Oliver, M. (1990). *The Politics of Disablement*. Basingstoke: Macmillan.

Ouseley, H. (1996). Quoted in S. Overell, Ouseley in assault on diversity. *People Management*, **2** May, 7–8.

Roberts, K. (1996). Managing disability-based diversity. In E.E. Kossek & S.A. Lobel (eds) *Managing Diversity* (pp. 310–331). Cambridge, Mass.: Blackwell.

Ross, R. & Schneider, R. (1992). *From Equality to Diversity: A Business Case for Equal Opportunities*. London: Pitman.

Stuart, O. (1992). Race and disability: just a double oppression? *Disability Handicap and Society*, **8**, 249–268.

Tajfel, H. (1981). *Human Groups and Social Categories*. Cambridge: Cambridge University Press.

Taylor, G. (1994). *Equal Opportunities: A Practical Handbook*. London: The Industrial Society.

Vince, R. (1996). Employing critical thinking to develop theories of managing diversity. *Proceedings of the British Academy of Management Conference*, Aston, 16–18 September.

Woodhams, C. (1998). The changing face of equal opportunities; disabled employees and equality. Paper presented at British Academy of Management Conference 'Corporate Transformation', University of Nottingham, September.

Woodhams, C. & Danieli, A. (2000). Disability and diversity—a difference too far? *Personnel Review*, **29**, 402–416.

Zadek, S. & Scott-Parker, S. (2000). *Unlocking Potential: The New Disability Business Case*. London: Employer's Forum on Disability.

CHAPTER 12

Managing Racial Equality and Diversity in the UK Construction Industry

Andrew W. Gale and Marilyn J. Davidson
University of Manchester Institute of Science and Technology, UK
Peter Somerville
University of Lincolnshire and Humberside, UK
Dianne Sodhi and Andy Steele
University of Salford, UK
Sandi Rhys Jones
Rhys Jones Consultants, UK

SUMMARY

This practice chapter presents a review of the limited literature highlighting numerous multifaceted factors responsible for the under-representation of black and minority ethnic (BME) groups in the UK construction industry (the UK's biggest sector). In addition, good practice examples for improving the situation in the construction industry with respect to racial equality are presented, adapted from the good practice guidelines for race and gender equality recently published by the authors.[1]

INTRODUCTION

The construction industry is Britain's biggest industrial sector and yet has the worst record for the employment of women and black and minority ethnic workers. Consequently, it seems appropriate to focus on this particular industry in relation to the management of racial equality and diversity. In 1998, only 1.9 per cent of chartered civil engineers and 0.9 per cent of chartered builders were women and only 3.4 per cent of construction

Individual Diversity and Psychology in Organizations. Edited by Marilyn J. Davidson and Sandra L. Fielden.
© 2003 John Wiley & Sons, Ltd.

professionals were female (Fielden et al., 2000, 2001; Dainty et al., 2001). While there have been numerous studies investigating gender inequality in the construction sector, there has been limited research focusing on racial inequality. That which does exist paints a rather gloomy picture. A report commissioned by the Construction Industry Training Board (CITB) on the under-representation of ethnic minorities in the industry found that less than 2 per cent were black or Asian (Holloway, 1999). This compares with a national average of 6.4 per cent (of working age) (Modood et al., 1997). The report further details the extent of racial abuse within this sector: 39 per cent of ethnic minority construction employees had experienced racial remarks and although the majority of firms (97 per cent) had an equal opportunities policy, only 50 per cent actively monitored it (Holloway, 1999).

The aim of this practice chapter is to present a review of the limited, recent literature highlighting a large number of factors responsible for the under-representation of BME groups in the UK construction industry in the private and public sector (particularly the social housing sector). In addition, good practice examples for improving the situation in the construction industry with respect to racial equality will be presented, adapted from the recent new guidelines (Somerville et al., 2002b) recently published by the authors.

RACIAL INEQUALITY IN THE UK CONSTRUCTION INDUSTRY

Evidence of racial and particularly institutional discrimination within the public sector was highlighted by the Macpherson Report in 1999 on the inquiry into the death of the black teenager, Stephen Lawrence. Institutional racism was defined in the Macpherson Report as:

> The collective failure of an organization to provide an appropriate and professional service to people because of their colour, culture, or ethnic origin. It can be seen or detected in processes, attitudes, behaviour which amount to discrimination through unwilling prejudice, ignorance, thoughtlessness and racist stereotyping which disadvantage minority ethnic people. (The Stephen Lawrence Inquiry, 1999: 28)

The report was critical of the police as well as social housing providers. More recently, the National Health Service and the Fire Service have also come under criticism in relation to institutional discrimination. However, at the same time, it is widely recognized that the private sector is also not beyond criticism with respect to its approach to equality of opportunity and racial discrimination.

One of the most detailed investigations into the issue of racial inequality in the UK construction industry was carried out by Holloway (1999) and focused on five main geographical areas: the South East, Midlands, North West, Scotland and Wales. Over 700 postal questionnaires were sent to organizations working in the construction industry or concerned with construction training: the top 100 construction companies, all the training and enterprise councils and local enterprise councils in Britain (i.e. government-funded vocational training organizations), a selection of relevant national trade and professional industry bodies, and a list of training providers including colleges and privately funded vocational training agencies. A selection of employers and training providers were followed up for interviews and focus groups were carried out with black and Asian people working or training in the industry. Black and Asian clients at jobcentres and community advice centres in each of the five areas were also interviewed and focus groups were held with school students in each of the five areas. In all, 205 organizations returned completed postal questionnaires, 371 training, employed or self-employed black and Asian people in the industry were interviewed or participated in focus group discussions, and 254 potential entrants to the industry (black and Asian school students and unemployed people) participated in the study.

The main findings of Holloway (1999) can be summarized as follows. Potential Asian entrants had a particularly negative image of the industry, as being 'for white people only', as demonstrated by a lack of Asian site workers and by posters, leaflets and the media that portray the industry as 'a white man's trade'. Moreover, there was a common view among potential entrants that the work was of low status and with low prospects for promotion. A high proportion of those already in the industry (predominantly white) had relied on family and friends as a source of information for entering the industry. In this respect, BME groups were at a disadvantage, because they were far less likely than white people to have family or friends in the industry.

There was broad agreement among potential entrants and those already working or training in the industry concerning the barriers to BME entry into the industry. These related to: a perceived difficulty in getting contracts, a fear of racism, and a perceived difficulty in getting a job. These factors actually boil down to one, namely an expectation and/or experience of racial discrimination. Most black and Asian people in the industry felt that there were differences between the opportunities available to white people in the industry and those available to black and Asian people. Examples given included: the dominance of white people in the industry resulting in preference being given to other white people; direct exclusion on grounds of 'race' such as 'on the phone you are classed as white, until you are invited in and the reality hits'; and indirect exclusion, reflecting the customs and practices of the industry which tend to exclude black and Asian people, for example word of mouth recruitment.

Two-fifths of potential entrants cited family pressure to work in other industries as a barrier to entry into the industry. This pressure occurred mainly in relation to black African, Indian, Bangladeshi and Chinese respondents, and not so much for black Caribbean and mixed race respondents. Some Asian communities were more likely to see the construction industry as not conferring positions of the desired status, although this view was contested by other Asian communities such as the Sikh community.

Some respondents referred to the lack of role models within the industry for black and Asian people, while others mentioned the difficulties in obtaining loans from financial institutions to develop their businesses. This caused their businesses to remain small, resulting in exclusion from tendering for larger contracts and the impression that the black contractor is seen as more of a risk (Holloway, 1999).

While a number of young BME people had completed the CITB entry test successfully, this had not led to their gaining sponsorship or work placements with employers, due to employer discrimination and the reported feelings that the employer saw them as being potentially problematic. Experiences of racist name-calling and racist jokes were common. A quarter of respondents in the industry had experienced harassment, bullying and intimidation. In particular, pressures to meet unrealistic targets and pressures to conform socially were frequently mentioned (Holloway, 1999). In addition, over a third of respondents in the industry thought that their training experience or working life was different from that of white people, for example: being given less desirable types of work (e.g. refurbishment of toilets), being treated more harshly, having to prove their worth, being paid less money, and being treated less favourably in access to training courses.

Finally, Holloway's (1999) study found that hardly any organizations showed awareness of any discrimination in relation to BME people. Most organizations gave little or no
support to BME workers who were being bullied or victimized or facing racist behaviour
from their colleagues. Those who complained about such behaviour sometimes experienced further victimization as a result. Although nearly all responding organizations
stated that they had an equal opportunities policy, only one-third of construction companies had action plans in place to implement this policy. Moreover, few construction
companies took any form of positive action towards achieving racial equality in their
organization, e.g. presentations to schools with a high BME population, presentations
to parents in BME communities, provision of information in community languages, inclusion of BME staff in their presentations and of BME role models in their marketing
materials, specific encouragement to potential BME applicants in advertising and recruiting, providing positive action training programmes (no construction companies provided
these), and setting targets for BME people to be employed within the organization (no
construction companies had done this) (Holloway, 1999).

Given the scale of public monies (i.e. government investment) in the UK directed at
the social housing sector and its relationship with the construction industry, it is also
important to consider issues of racial discrimination within this particular public sector. Recent research on the employment and career opportunities of ethnic minorities
within the registered social landlord (RSL) sector (Somerville et al., 2000) for example,
highlighted the discriminatory practices within these organizations, despite evidence of
equal opportunities policies. RSLs are providers of housing to economically underprivileged sectors of the community. The report found that only 1.6 per cent of the senior
management teams were from the BME community and that generally, they tended to be
located in the lower-level jobs within the non-technical disciplines. It has been argued
that this suggests a lack of commitment to the principle of equality of opportunity and has
been linked to the failure of RSLs to set in motion the cultural change required to make
equal opportunities a core value of the organization (Sodhi & Steele, 2000). Moreover,
researchers consistently emphasize that a starting point for organizations addressing the
issue of racial discrimination is to develop comprehensive and effective equal opportunities policies which adopt a diverse, inclusive and mainstream approach (Somerville &
Steele, 1998; Sodhi & Steele, 2000; Bhavnani, 2001; Somerville et al., 2002a).

When Somerville et al. (2000) examined equal opportunities policies of RSLs, they
discovered that these were overwhelmingly concerned only with ensuring equality of
treatment in a formal abstract sense, without also acknowledging real differences or
valuing diversity. In many mainstream RSLs, equality of treatment on paper appeared
to coexist with inequality of treatment in some aspects of practice. For example, this included the procedures by which staff were promoted, and with widespread indifference
to real equality (as evidenced by a lack of review mechanisms), lack of named individuals responsible for promoting, monitoring and implementing the policy, and lack of
ownership of the policy by the staff of the organization and the communities it served.
These authors concluded that most mainstream RSLs appeared to make no special effort to attract job applications from BME communities and less than one in 15 (6.7
per cent) of mainstream RSLs consulted BME communities about their recruitment and
staff selection practices. Importantly, mainstream RSLs which did make special efforts
to advertise within BME communities, were likely to employ far more BME staff at all
levels within their organization.

Not surprisingly, these researchers also found that a higher proportion of BME staff compared to white staff in mainstream RSLs felt that their organization's approach to recruitment and selection, promotion and regrading was unfair, and the major reasons for this unfairness related to:

- Overt discrimination for or against particular individuals or types of staff
- Lack of awareness or understanding of other cultures
- Lack of understanding or commitment to achieving equality of opportunity
- Specific direct and indirect discriminatory practices
- Lack of clarity or transparency in promotions procedures
- Poor or non-existent feedback on unsuccessful job applications (Somerville et al., 2000)

BME staff were reportedly more likely to experience racism from colleagues than from tenants or members of the public; for example, the presence of one or two racist staff against whom their employer took no action. Racism from colleagues was regarded as more serious possibly because it was more difficult to handle within the organization.

In general, less than half of those interviewed by Somerville et al. (2000) felt that their organization was encouraging and supportive of BME staff, compared with over a third who suggested that it was indifferent or discouraging; those working for BME-led RSLs were more likely than those working for mainstream RSLs to regard their organization as encouraging and supportive. Moreover, nearly half of those interviewed were unable to give any examples of good practice on career progression for BME staff, or of organizations with successful positive approaches; those working for BME-led RSLs were more likely than those working for mainstream RSLs to be able to provide such examples. Over two-thirds of RSLs apparently offered no form of positive action, and three-fifths did not encourage the development of BME staff support groups.

No mainstream RSL was clearly operating above the government's Commission for Racial Equality's minimum standard (CRE, 1995a, b, c) in any of the six specified areas of organizational activity, and a large proportion of such RSLs did not appear to be operating even at this level in at least some areas of activity. For example, in the area of policy and practice, some RSLs did not have a policy on racial equality, and most of them did not appear to have a race equality strategy. Furthermore, it should be noted that the majority of mainstream RSLs had no BME members on their boards (Somerville et al., 2000, 2002a).

In addition to specific barriers against getting entry to approved lists, according to Sodhi and Steele (2000) BME contractors commonly experience barriers to winning contracts arising from a number of factors. Firstly, there is a lack of personal contacts with RSL officers responsible for letting contracts—since they are not known to the officers, the officers do not invite them to apply to go on the list or to tender for contracts. As a consequence, they are not members of the 'old boys' networks'.

Since BME firms are generally small and often recently formed, they lack an established reputation which carries weight with RSLs. The culture of many RSLs is also detrimental for BME contractors in terms of stereotyping and ignorance of BME cultures, and in terms of cultivation of 'favoured' contractors who are more likely to be white. Furthermore, most RSLs take no positive action of any kind to correct the under-representation of BME contractors who appear to be more likely to be asked to do work 'at risk' without being awarded the contract when the job is done.

In addition, Sodhi and Steele (2000) proposed that the increased emphasis on 'part-nering' encouraged by Egan (1998) tends to place smaller companies such as BME contractors at a disadvantage. This is because such partnerships tend to exclude small companies and also the focus of partnerships is on large projects. Small companies are therefore increasingly squeezed out, resulting in a 'closed shop culture'. Furthermore, the increasing importance of 'Constructionline' as a form of national approved list of building contractors (as envisaged and recommended by Latham, 1994) is problematic for BME contractors because it requires three references for every category of work, and this imposes a heavier burden on small, less experienced firms (Sodhi and Steele, 2000).

Finally, it is also important to emphasize that the accelerating growth of managerialism indicated by Latham (1994) and Egan (1998), may in certain respects be counterproduc-tive for racial equality. The uncompromisingly 'top-down' market-oriented approach of Egan (1998) is difficult to square with the realities of life on a building site as revealed by detailed painstaking research. If this managerialist approach is promoted therefore, it is likely to lead to harsher treatment of BME contractors and BME-led RSLs (who are likely to be seen, however unfairly, as less efficient). In addition, it may also result in further reductions in the opportunities available to BME people potentially and actually working in the construction and RSL sectors, due to the 'streamlining' of organizational structures and operations and the growth of partnering with favoured organizations who are more likely to be white.

With regard to RSLs, it is likely that there is also here a link between managerialism and institutional racism, but this is complicated by the role of the Housing Corporation (an independent body set up by the government responsible for the regulation of the RSL sector). The dominance of a managerial approach is clear from the emphasis placed on the 'core business' of RSLs which does not include the promotion of equality of opportunity, and from the marginalization within the sector of more 'socially oriented' RSLs such as BME-led RSLs. The Housing Corporation's BME strategy (Housing Corporation, 1998), however, aims to counter this racist bias.

GOOD PRACTICE EXAMPLES FOR CONSTRUCTION COMPANIES

Any activity which promotes equality of opportunity for BME groups can be viewed as good practice. In this section, we provide some examples of good practice for con-struction companies in promoting racial equality. These examples have been abridged from the authors' new publication entitled 'Building Equality in Construction, Vol. II, Good Practice Guidelines for Race and Gender Equality—for Building Contractors and Housing Associations (Somerville et al., 2002b).

These guidelines represent some of the outcomes from a research project funded by the Department of Environment Transport and the Regions. The project forms part of the work of the Centre for Diversity, Inclusion and Equality in Construction Centre at the University of Manchester Institute of Science and Technology (UMIST), and was carried out in partnership with UMIST, Rhys Jones Consultants and the University of Salford.

This new document provides guidance on the development of an equal opportuni-ties policy and issues relating to the implementation of equal opportunities and the management of diversity in the UK construction industry. It also highlights examples of good practice to promote race equality in the construction industry. It complements and builds on an earlier report *Building Equality in Construction: Good Practice Guidelines for Building Contractors and Housing Associations* (Davey et al., 1998), produced to promote sex equality in the construction industry which should be read in conjunction with these guidelines.

The development of these guidelines has been an incremental process, incorporating feedback from those working in the UK construction industry and the social housing sector at various stages throughout the project. This has been achieved primarily through an action learning approach, i.e. analysis, action and evaluation, with groups across the UK representing contractors and social housing sector employees. The following recommendations are divided into five categories:

1. Attracting young BME people into the industry;
2. Widening the recruitment net;
3. Innovative approaches to training;
4. Retaining employees;
5. Starting the process.

ATTRACTING YOUNG BME PEOPLE INTO THE INDUSTRY

The building industry needs to attract more good people. The current skills shortage in many areas has emphasized the difficulties of recruiting people with the basic skills, knowledge and motivation to build a competent workforce. In particular, there is concern that very few BME people are attracted to building as a career, at a time when the number of such people entering other non-traditional careers is growing.

There is therefore a need to raise awareness of the opportunities offered by the construction industry, to improve conditions and to present an image and a reputation that will attract and keep high-quality recruits—black and white, as illustrated in the quotations in Figure 12.1.

Royal Holloway University of London (Holloway, 1999) found low levels of awareness about construction particularly among Pakistani and Indian potential entrants as the following comment illustrates:

All you do is stick bricks on top of bricks. You only need cement and bricks, put the doors on and screw the things in. (Black school student, 13 years old)

Members of community groups commented on the need for information:

Knowledge of the promotion prospects was virtually non-existent with some groups left with the opinion that the work is of low status and you do not need to have qualifications to get into the industry. (Local Asian Councillor, Manager of Indian Community Centre)

FIGURE 12.1 Quotations related to low levels of awareness of opportunities offered by the construction industry

School visits and career events

Visits to primary schools in the local area are an effective method of encouraging interest in construction and improving the construction industry's image and understanding of the industry, not only among children and young people but also among the people who influence them, their parents and teachers. It is important to remember that while there is a need to warn of the dangers inherent on a construction site, this should be balanced by creating a sense of excitement and interest in the process itself. Schools in areas with high concentrations of members of the BME communities should be targeted. Moreover, it is important to define the objectives of visits and to ensure that all children have an equal opportunity to participate. Career events are often organized by schools and colleges and are an opportunity for contractors to encourage new recruits. Such events are also opportunities to meet potential clients—schools and universities frequently commission building work.

Curriculum centres

The CITB curriculum centres enable schools, colleges, local enterprise councils and education business partnerships to work together to develop construction as a context for learning. The CITB (a government-funded agency responsible for training in the construction industry) is involved in organizing site visits, in-service training for teachers, school–college partnerships, curriculum developments, visits to primary and secondary schools, the provision of mentors, the delivery of National Vocational Qualifications (NVQs) for 14–19-year-olds and university liaison. We recommend the industry:

- Become involved with CITB curriculum centres to demonstrate commitment to the long term success of the industry
- Encourage more BME and white employees to get involved in the centres; do not just leave it to senior managers

For example, the CITB in the North West organized a two-day residential conference for sixth-form girls in October 2000 which provided opportunities to visit sites, talk to people in the industry and obtain information on courses and sponsorship. Feedback from the girls who took part was very positive. Of the 40 girls that attended, 100 per cent said that it had been a valuable experience and that if it was repeated they would recommend it to a friend. Over 50 per cent expressed an interest in joining the industry. Furthermore, the CITB welcomes involvement in curriculum centres by contractors and, in return, offers participants courses in presentation skills—an excellent way to promote the industry.

University sponsorship, placement and liaison

Contractors interested in forging links should contact their local universities and colleges and provide sponsorships for BME students at university and ensure that they work with the company during their course and probably afterwards. In addition, they should consider giving guest lectures, getting involved in research projects and advertising jobs at the firm to students and university staff.

Site visits

Visits to construction sites should not only stimulate children's interest in construction, but also provide opportunities for parents and teachers to learn about construction and thus offer more informed guidance. Site visits can be made to new buildings, rehabilitation or specialist construction projects. Contractors can also arrange visits to manufacturers and suppliers.

Shadowing and work placements

Work placements are an opportunity for the contractor to learn more about potential new recruits as well as to encourage BME and white people to enter the industry, therefore the industry should:

• Provide BME young people with the opportunity to shadow staff for two or three days. This is an effective way of highlighting the range of occupations on site, the challenging nature of the industry and its suitability for BME groups
• Offer work experience for BME young people before they choose their A levels, preferably in the summer after their GCSEs
• Consider paid holiday work for A level students
• Provide short placements for teachers, careers advisors and youth leaders so that they can find out about the industry and advise children appropriately

The CITB run employers' seminars to provide information on how work experience programmes are organized, to explain what employers can do to maximize the experience of students on placements and to offer advice on key issues, e.g. health and safety. Furthermore, research undertaken by the CITB suggests that there is limited availability of information on construction in schools:

> I don't think the school has any literature about the construction industry, I have not come across any . . . it isn't a job I would be recommending to my students, we hope that most of our students will follow a planned career path and construction is a job not a career. (Female Head of Year, Blackpool)

WIDENING THE RECRUITMENT NET

There are specific steps that employers can take to widen their recruitment base and encourage diversity in the workforce. Advertising and selection criteria are key to this and, when recruiting, we suggest that particular attention is paid to criteria regarding age, construction experience, professional qualifications and technical skills (see Table 12.1).

Encouraging minority groups into the manual trades

Innovative ideas are needed to reach under-represented groups and encourage them to consider employment and training in building, particularly in the manual trades. One effective method is to develop 'dynamic duos', black and white people working in pairs, who appreciate the need to attract under-represented groups, can visit target areas and who are able to answer questions about the training and the company. These people should be in a position to offer practical and financial help to anyone interested

TABLE 12.1   Recruitment guidelines for advertising and selection

---

Advertising
- Advertise all vacancies externally using sources which allow the widest possible range of applicants to see the advert
- Consider using BME press and BME community organizations for advertising
- Use the website set up for BME staff in the social housing movement—Career Opportunities for Ethnic Minorities (COFEM)
- Think about attracting a wide range of people when designing advertisements, through the use of pictures, profiles of BME and other minority groups
- Include statements on the organization's commitment to equal opportunities, such as '... working towards equal opportunities' and 'we welcome applications from under-represented groups' in advertisements, brochures and so on
- Highlight the need for experience in management, project management, consultancy gained working for other industries, housing associations or local authorities rather than focusing solely on construction
- Highlight possibilities for job share, flexible hours, part-time work and training
- If mentoring and support networks are in place, talk about them
- Consider floodlighting a site for evening visits, as happens in France

Selection criteria
- Use a structured procedure
- Ensure that selection criteria do not discriminate unfairly; criteria should be clear, relevant and objective
- Confine questions to the requirements of the job and ensure consistency
- Accept equivalent experience and qualifications, where possible
- Include BME staff on recruitment panels wherever possible
- Ensure that more than one person carries out interviews, ideally there should be three people on the panel
- Keep a record at each stage and the reasons for the decision
- Use the formal recruitment methods described by the CIB's Working Group 8

---

in attending any meetings and/or arrange a home visit. They should also be present at subsequent meetings so that potential new recruits are reassured that a friendly face will be present.

Databases of minority-led firms

As well as recruiting individuals to the industry, building contractors can help improve equal opportunities by giving minority-led firms the opportunity to obtain subcontract work. For example, there is evidence to suggest that many more BME people are setting up their own businesses, partly as a result of being unable to progress in traditional employment in the construction industry. To help in identifying minority-led firms, a number of databases have been developed. For example, in the North West, Building Positive Action (this is currently held by North British Housing Association); in London, London Equal Opportunities Federation (LEOF); and in Bristol, Elm Housing Association. Organizations should:

- Consider subcontracting work to firms from the databases, especially when providing housing or services for BME and other under-represented groups
- Consider providing financial support for the databases of minority-led firms

Undoubtedly, supporting the databases of minority-led firms demonstrates commitment to equality, gains publicity for the company and potentially can put them in contact with housing associations.

Taster courses

Short or taster courses designed to provide basic skills can provide an effective method of attracting BME people on to courses and give them some experience of construction. A short course also gives trainees a good start in a trade of their choice and enables established BME tradespersons to become multi-skilled.

INNOVATIVE APPROACHES TO TRAINING

Providing attractive packages

The construction industry needs to increase the quantity and quality of training, especially for BME groups, and detailed suggestions for innovative training strategies are listed in Figure 12.2. These recommendations will help the industry provide qualified professional employees and tradespeople. Improving opportunities for local people reduces vandalism on site, reduces property mistreatment, increases tenant involvement and improves building design. It will also enable contractors and housing associations to work together in partnership and gain a competitive edge for future contracts.

- Lift age restrictions and open up courses to a whole range of BME groups
- Offer supplementary courses in maths, English and communications/negotiation skills for work in the construction industry; English as a second language; and computing and multimedia studies
- Highlight the provision of training opportunities and good links with local training providers in promotional material or discussions with BME applicants
- Draw attention to possibilities for BME tradespersons to attend college, take courses offered by the CITB and/or supervise apprentices
- Ensure that BME workers are not isolated by recruiting other people belonging to the same ethnic group, offering them a BME mentor and/or encouraging networking with other BME staff in the organization, i.e. through a BME support group. Bramall Construction (a company based in the north-west of England) have a policy of pairing BME trainees to avoid isolation on site
- Provide opportunities for apprentices to gain qualifications which will make them employable and competent. Ideally these should be City and Guilds or NVQs in the manual trades at level III—not just I and II
- Monitor the training programme of the contractor, client and/or CITB by regular, personal contact in addition to forms and questionnaires
- Monitor the cost and quality of training by setting aside houses specifically for training purposes and nominating a training supervisor
- Display the work produced by trainees to senior managers in the company, the client, partners and visitors such as potential new recruits, local residents and schoolchildren
- Consider flexible hours and taster/short courses
- Consider culturally specific activities, e.g. prayer time

FIGURE 12.2   Suggestions for innovative training strategies

DIY and maintenance for tenants

DIY courses run with housing associations enable contractors to work in partnership with housing associations, develop a pool of BME people potentially interested in working in construction and gain contact with people listed in the directory of minority-led firms. Funding could initially be provided through 'Housing Plus' or 'New Deal' or innovation and good practice grants, but the savings in maintenance costs arising from fewer unnecessary call-outs and less property mistreatment would make the courses self-financing in the longer term.

RETAINING EMPLOYEES

Building contractors should aim not only to build a good workforce by recruiting BME staff, but also encourage them to stay by helping them to develop their careers—good people are a valuable resource.

Preparing for apprentices

An apprentice may find it daunting to arrive on site for the first time and have little idea about what to expect. When BME workers arrive on a site, supervisors, foremen and co-workers may react with varying degrees of curiosity, friendliness, resentment, surprise, indifference or hostility. Consequently, construction companies should:

- Involve and inform the workforce by outlining the organization's commitment to hiring BME staff, the practical steps which have been taken to ensure equality and the company's belief in the ability of BME and other minority groups to do the job
- Provide opportunities for new apprentices to meet other apprentices and to learn about the company, the type of work and the working conditions before starting on site
- Produce a trainee's handbook with introductory information, an outline of training and health and safety structures
- Ask the supervisor to ensure follow-up of any complaints of harassment
- Start training on site during the spring or summer, rather than the winter

For example, a contractor in the Manchester area worked with the CITB to provide training for young local bricklayers and joiners which encouraged team spirit, reduced vandalism (e.g. fewer windows broken) and increased the respect shown by local people. Other contractors worked closely with housing associations and local authorities to provide apprenticeship schemes.

Retaining apprentices

Building contractors often experience a high drop-out rate among apprentices, both BME and white, for various reasons. While some apprentices recognize that the manual trades provide good employment opportunities and wages in the longer term, building contractors have to attempt to satisfy the short-term expectations, needs and aspirations of apprentices. To reduce wasted time and effort in recruitment, it is important to find out why apprentices leave and try to resolve problems where appropriate. Nevertheless, it should be noted that an apprentice leaving does not necessarily represent a failure, especially where a contractor introduced professional recruitment methods and/or the individual has benefited from the training. For example, one contractor based near Stockport (north-west England) suspected that apprentices had been poached by construction companies prepared to pay higher wages. He introduced exit monitoring to find out if this was the case or if there were problems with training and/or recruitment.

Improving working conditions

The world of work is changing dramatically. More people are rejecting poor conditions and long hours, and technology is offering different ways of carrying out traditional tasks. We need to learn from the manufacturing process, using system building or the off-site production of components where appropriate, so that work is conducted indoors and flexible hours can be provided more easily. Also, it is important to compare what other industries and professions are providing in terms of working hours and support mechanisms.

STARTING THE PROCESS

Running a pilot project

Achieving results and bringing about change demand that actions are measured against targets. Activities proposed in the full version of these guidelines that are feasible and appropriate to undertake include:

- Develop a pilot project, likely to attract media attention, and a series of supporting actions
- Meet with other managers to discuss possible pilot projects in more detail and identify further action
- Extend meetings to potential clients and/or partners
- Encourage open discussion, welcoming ideas and minimizing criticism, to encourage innovation and change
- Sustain momentum by arranging follow-up actions and meetings
- Once a pilot project and supporting practical steps have been agreed, define objectives, specific activities, timetable for completion, outcomes and benefits

Developing and using measurement tools, and promoting the results

It is also important to develop appropriate measurement tools through discussions with participants.[2] As detailed in Table 12.2, this involves defining parameters, identifying practical steps, developing specific measures, testing and incorporating the results into overall performance measures, as well as promoting the results.

Getting involved in equal opportunities initiatives and activities enables contractors to gain insight into current thinking and behaviour within housing associations, contributing to informed decisions about future business and marketing activities. Taking practical

TABLE 12.2 Pilot projects—strategies for developing and using measurement tools, and promoting the results

---

Measurement tools
- Establish a baseline, against which progress can be measured
- Identify ways of measuring outcomes, for example numbers of applications from BME groups; number of apprenticeships; and number of careers events, etc.
- Keep a qualitative record of innovations, successes and problems. The records are useful for illustrating accounts during discussions and presentations to clients, the media and work colleagues
- Use the measurement tools to gain feedback about the successes and costs of action to promote equality
- Identify and build upon successes
- Establish learning points and take remedial action
- Encourage people to admit to problems and to learn from difficulties
- Increase motivation by recognizing progress, giving recognition, giving praise where due and avoiding criticism
- Encourage a sense of shared responsibility, especially when problems are encountered. Avoid allocating blame
- Communicate successes to employees, clients and potential new recruits
- Keep material to publicize interest and action such as photographs, articles in the building press and letters of recommendation

Promoting the results
- Contact housing associations, the Housing Corporation, the National Housing Federation and those involved in Housing Plus, New Deal and Local Labour schemes to ask about working in partnership
- Inform potential partners about action taken to promote equality
- Show measurement tools and supporting evidence to demonstrate commitment
- Improve the industry's image by highlighting opportunities for BME people
- Try to obtain media coverage to promote the company and the industry, especially when involved in specific projects

---

steps to promote equality enables building contractors to demonstrate commitment and initiative to housing associations, other clients and the public.

CONCLUSIONS

Certainly, it is clear that both immediate short-term and more strategic long-term action is required in the UK construction industry, in order for racial equality to be achieved.

We endorse Bhavnani's (2001) assertion that racism is complex and multifaceted in both its operation and specificity. As repeatedly emphasized throughout this book, the successful implementation and management of diversity (in this case, in the construction industry) require the adoption of an inclusive and mainstream approach. In the words of Bhavnani (2001: 121):

> Any intervention to combat racism has to be inclusive. The strategy to combat racism has to question, be critical and say the unsayable. The relevance of racism to people's lives and work has to be made clear to all. Racism must not be sidelined from other initiatives to make changes in the organizational culture. It is imperative that all groups are involved in these processes, not just black minorities or white middle managers.

ENDNOTES

1. These guidelines were part funded by the DETR and delivered in partnership with UMIST, Rhys Jones Consultants and the University of Salford. The guidelines do not necessarily represent the views of the DETR.
2. To find out more about developing an equal opportunities policy in the construction industry, see:

   - CRE (1995a) *Racial Equality Means Business: A Standard for Racial Equality for Employers*

     This can be used to develop racial equality strategies and measure their impact. It covers six areas where organizations can apply and use a race equality programme: policy and planning; selection; developing and retaining staff; communication and corporate image; corporate citizenship; and auditing for racial equality. It also sets five levels in implementing a programme, which can also be used to assess progress.

   - CRE (1995b) *Racial Equality Means Quality*, and
   - CRE (1995c) *Racial Equality and Council Contractors*
   - Employment Department (1992) *Equal Opportunities: Ten Point Plan for Employers*

     Provides guidance on setting up an equal opportunities policy and a basic toolkit, which gives practical advice on how you can offer equality of opportunity to people from ethnic minorities, women and people with disabilities.

   - CITB and CIB (1996) *Constructive Guidelines in Equal Opportunities, a Simple Checklist for Construction Companies*, the Construction Industry Board Working Group 8

     Provides guidelines on what construction companies can do to set up an equal opportunities policy from scratch and to help those with equal opportunities policies in place to review them.

   Finally, the Change the Face of Constructions Toolkits provides complementary examples of good practice (see Somerville et al., 2002b).

REFERENCES

Bhavnani, R. (2001). *Rethinking Interventions in Racism*. London: Trentham Books.

Commission for Racial Equality (1995a). *Racial Equality Means Business: A Standard for Racial Equality for Employers*. London: CRE.

Commission for Racial Equality (1995b). *Racial Equality Means Quality*. London: CRE.

Commission for Racial Equality (1995c). *Racial Equality and Council Contractors*. London: CRE.

Construction Industry Board/Construction Industry Training Board (1996). *Constructive Guidelines on Equal Opportunities. A Simple Checklist for Construction Companies*. London: The Construction Industry Board Working Group 8. Construction Industry Board Ltd.

Dainty, A.R.J., Bagilhole, B.M. & Neale, R.H. (2001). Male and female perspectives on equality measures for the UK construction sector. *Women in Management Review*, **16**(6), 297–304.

Davey, C., Davidson, M., Gale, A., Hopley, A. & Rhys Jones, S. (1998). *Building Equality in Construction: Good Practice Guidelines for Building Contractors and Housing Associations*. Manchester: UMIST/Building Positive Action/Rhys Jones Consultants.

Egan, J. (1998). *Rethinking Construction*. Report of the Construction Task Force. London: DETR.

Employment Department (1992). *Equal Opportunities: Ten Point Plan for Employers*. Employment Department, PL 922 (Rev. 2).

Fielden, S., Davidson, M.J., Gale, A.W. & Davey, C.L. (2000). Women in construction: the untapped resource. *Construction Management and Economics*, **18**, 113–121.

Fielden, S.L., Davidson, M.J., Gale, A. & Davey, C.L. (2001). Women, equality and construction. *Journal of Management Development*, **20**(4), 293–304.

Holloway (Equal Opportunities Consultancy Group) (1999). *The Under-representation of Black and Asian People in Construction*. Report for the Construction Industry Training Board. London: Royal Holloway University of London/CITB.

The Housing Corporation (1998). *Black and Minority Ethnic Housing Policy*. London: The Housing Corporation.

Latham, M. (1994). *Constructing the Team: Joint Review of Procurement and Contractual Arrangements in the UK Construction Industry*. Final Report. London: The Stationery Office.

MacPherson et al. (1999). *The Stephen Lawrence Inquiry: Report of an Inquiry by Sir William MacPherson of Cluny*. London: Stationery Office.

Modood, T., Berthoud, R., Lakey, J., Smith, P., Virdee, S. & Beishon, S. (1997). *Ethnic Minorities in Britain: Diversity and Disadvantage*. London: Policy Studies Institute.

Sodhi, D. & Steele, A. (2000). *Contracts of Exclusion: Promoting Equality and Social Inclusion in the Commissioning Activities of Registered Social Landlords*. London: LEOF.

Somerville, P. & Steele, A. (1998). *Career Opportunities for Ethnic Minorities*. Salford: University of Salford/The Housing Corporation/National Housing Federation.

Somerville, P., Steele, A. & Sodhi, D. (2000). *A Question of Diversity: Black and Minority Ethnic Staff in the RSL Sector*. London: The Housing Corporation.

Somerville, P. Steele, A. & Sodhi, D. (2002a). Black and minority ethnic employment in housing organisations. In P. Somerville & A. Steele (eds) *'Race', Housing and Social Exclusion*. London: Jessica Kingsley.

Somerville, P., Sodhi, D., Steele, A., Gale, A., Davidson, M.J. & Rhys Jones, S. (2002b). *Building Equality in Construction*. Vol. II *Good Practice Guidelines for Race and Gender Equality—for Building Contractors and Housing Associations*. Manchester: UMIST.

Stephen Lawrence Inquiry (1999). *Appendices*. London: Stationery Office.

CHAPTER 13

Is Diversity Inevitable? Age and Ageism in the Future of Employment

Chris Brotherton

Heriot-Watt University, Edinburgh, UK

SUMMARY

This chapter reviews some of the evidence that indicates that age discrimination is a problem right across the spectrum. The chapter presents some of the policy responses at organizational, national and international levels to age discrimination. The chapter reviews the psychological evidence on age and ability—which demonstrates that there is no empirical basis for detrimental treatment being given to people on the basis of age. The chapter ends by calling for a positive celebration of difference and diversity.

INTRODUCTION

This chapter will argue that age is not categorical—it has a very wide range of social definitions. Yet age can invoke adverse social dialogue, particularly in employment settings. Since we, each of us, have age, we ought to begin by querying these dialogues and the premises on which they are founded. Questions are important in diversity—we need to question the basis on which we relate within and between groups; we need to question the assumptions on which decisions are made that lead to the exclusion of groups from the processes of organizations; we need to question the basis on which social judgements are made when they lead us to negative views of ourselves and others. Viewed positively diversity is about us—the age, the gender, the ethnicity, each of us has. Viewed positively diversity is about difference that is properly managed. As we shall see, so much about age is poorly managed at individual and organizational levels. This chapter explores some of the evidence and the processes underlying this claim.

Individual Diversity and Psychology in Organizations. Edited by Marilyn J. Davidson and Sandra L. Fielden.
© 2003 John Wiley & Sons, Ltd.

Gender, ethnicity and nationality are the categories that claim immediate attention in discussions of diversity. Age has received somewhat less attention. Yet, age is a central concern in employment opportunities. Our organization's capacity to select, recruit and develop people of all ages is becoming increasingly important as the distribution of age across the workforce profile shifts towards the upper parameters. Age provides society with a litmus paper test of its ability to treat people well and fairly at work. Age provides further tests of society's ability to celebrate social identity and positive personal worth. We all have age—yet it goes uncelebrated in most cultures. In the theories of psychology that inform diversity age has a status that distinguishes itself from gender and ethnicity. Age comes to us through a developmental process that is usually considered in that area of psychology concerned with individual differences. Gender and ethnicity are usually considered in those areas of social psychology concerned with social identity and social categorization.

SOME INTERNATIONAL TRENDS AND THEIR POLICY IMPLICATIONS

Wherever we live in the world, we are not members of youthful societies. The world demographic shift is dramatic. In 1950, people aged 60 years or over represented around 8 per cent of world population, but by 2025 they will be 14 per cent (International Labour Organization, 1995). This is a consequence of both fertility rates falling—between 1950 and 1990 the birth rate for the total world population fell from 38 to 27 births per thousand people—and people are living longer. Over the same period life expectancy at birth rose from 46 to 63 years. The effect on the dependency ratio—the number of active working people available to support each non-working person—is striking. In Western Europe the dependency ratio is expected to fall to around 1.5 by 2025, while in East Asia the old-age dependency ratio is expected to fall to 2.4 by 2025. The ILO (1995:1) tells us that

> the increasing burden of old-age dependency is not just the result of population ageing, it is also profoundly affected by changes in the 'labour force participation rate': the proportion of people in a particular age group who are working, or wish to work. In recent years there has been a marked decrease in the participation rates of older workers; a trend that has been amplified by recession.

In the 1980 census of population for the United States the number of persons 65 and older climbed by 28 per cent over figures for 1970. In the United States today there are more than 25 million people in the 65 years and older age group. Between 1961 and 1981 census figures show that the number of people of pensionable age in Britain (65 for men and 60 women at that time) rose by 2.1 million to 9.7 million. Meanwhile, there are fewer people of pensionable age in some kind of pensionable employment. Japan has the largest growth in its over 65 population, with 14 per cent in 1996 and a predicted 22.2 per cent in 2043.

Within industrialized societies improvements in medicine, nutrition, exercise and life-style have increased our life expectancy by an average of 22 additional years since 1900. These are population figures. The numbers of people within the population as a whole reaching 65 and going beyond it have increased, but individual life span has not. The upper boundary of life, the maximum number of years an individual can live, is around

115–120 years of age. Apparently, one Charlie Smith (c.1842–1979) lived to be 137 years old. In 1956, the US Social Security Administration began to collect information about American centenarians who were receiving benefits. Charlie Smith was visited in 1961. He gave his birth date as 4 July 1842, and his birthplace as Liberia. By the end of the nineteenth century, Charlie had settled in Florida. He worked in turpentine camps, and at one point owned a turpentine farm in Homeland, Florida. Charlie Smith's records at the Social Security Administration do not provide evidence of his birth date, but they do mention that he began to earn benefits based on Social Security credits by picking oranges at the age of 113 (Freeman, 1982). Social Security Administration interviews with 1127 people who lived to be over 100 years old yield bizarre reasons as to why some of these people felt that they lived so long. 'Because I sleep with my head facing the north'; 'Because of eating a lot of fatty pork and salt'; and 'Because I don't believe in germs' were among the reasons given for their own longevity. More rational reasons given by the other individuals who lived to be 100 were their organized, purposeful behaviour, discipline and hard work, freedom and independence, balanced diet, positive independence, positive family relations, and the support of friends (Segerberg, 1982).

Conventional economic wisdom has led to a philosophy whereby older workers make way for the young when jobs are scarce. The underlying assumptions of the philosophy are questionable. The ILO (1995: 1) points out that

> it has conventionally been thought that early retirement makes economic sense be-
> cause older workers are less cost effective than younger ones—assuming that as
> they grow older their skills are outdated and their productivity falls, whilst seniority
> requires that they receive steadily higher pay. This may not be true: even if older
> workers do indeed earn more, their earnings do not necessarily continue to rise until
> the end of their working lives. Nor is the productivity question as clear cut as once
> thought. . . . even when older workers cost more than their younger colleagues, this
> can be more than compensated by the accumulated know-how.

It can be argued that the withdrawal of older workers does not necessarily benefit younger workers. Referring to early retirement schemes in Belgium, France, Spain and the UK, the ILO concludes that 'the total impact of such measures on the problem of youth unemployment was negligible. New entrants to the labour market often lacked the experience and know-how necessary for the jobs vacated by older workers. More often, the jobs just disappeared' (ILO, 1995: 2).

Governments across the world are beginning to call into question the notion that chronological age should be seen as the indicator of when a worker should retire. Functional age or working capacity can be considered more appropriate as an indicator of an older worker's ability to cope with the demands of a job. A physically fit older individual can outperform more sedentary younger people. A combination of health promotion, job redesign, training and improved working conditions, adapted to the needs of older workers, should make it possible for organizations to make better use of the capacities of these workers. There is then a range of policy options to be considered. Not least that unless older workers are employed to their full capacity industrial economies will find that their potential for growth is severely limited by a shortage of skills.

Many countries are adjusting their retirement policies so as to make it less attractive for people to discontinue work before the statutory chronological age. Labour forces are likely to become significantly older in the next several decades, although the effect varies markedly across a range of countries. There is an ageing effect on the population figure, for even in the most conservative data, that provided by the Organization for Economic Cooperation and Development (OECD), there will be an increase in the cohort for age 45–59 as well as an increase in the number of people aged 60 and over. The cohort of workers aged 45–64 years in 2015 will be better educated than their counterparts today. The share not having completed upper secondary schooling is likely to fall by over one-third. This trend is likely for all OECD member countries, although large international differences in the distribution of education levels will persist. Rising educational attainment should ease the absorption of older workers. Recent decades have seen a strong increase in the demand for more educated workers and an associated deterioration in the opportunities for less educated workers (OECD, 1997). Poorly educated youths, particularly men, appear to have been most disadvantaged. However, older workers have also been negatively affected. Older workers displaced from production jobs, a group with low educational attainment on average, are at high risk of remaining jobless for an extended period of time and typically experience large earnings losses if they do become re-employed (Podgursky & Swain, 1987; Fallick, 1996).

Any downturn in the labour market creates a higher rate of redundancy among older workers who suffer from unemployment relatively more and for longer than other categories. In 1991, for example, 48 per cent of the older unemployed in Australia had been out of work for longer than 12 months, and 25 per cent for longer than 3 years. For unemployed workers of all ages these figures were 23 and 6 per cent respectively (*Employment Gazette*, 1995).

In Japan, older workers are allegedly 'forced' to quit and become unemployed or see their conditions of employment worsen as they reach the mandatory retirement age. The jobless rate is particularly high among older people (*White Paper on Labour*, Part III 1995).

In developing countries with relatively advanced systems of social security and protection such as India, for example, the situation is the same. Within the statutory retirement age, able-bodied and able-minded older people are forced out of the job market. In Vietnam about one-fifth of retired workers cite retirement rules as making them stop work (*Asian Population Studies*, 1994). The situation is worse in developing countries where literacy levels are low: illiterate workers have little chance of any employment. Older women are more likely to be out of the labour force in developing countries. In Mexico, 68.6 per cent of men between 60 and 64 are economically active while only 9.3 per cent of women are working (Ham-Chande, 1995).

RECRUITMENT OF OLDER WORKERS

Older workers account for a smaller share of new recruits than of total employment in most OECD countries. Among workers aged 45–64 years, their recruitment share ranges from a low of 28 per cent of their employment share in Belgium to a high of 56 per cent in Australia. By comparison, the share of young workers (aged 15–24 years) in recent recruitment is more than twice their share of employment, while they are almost equal for prime-age workers (European Union Labour Force Survey, 1997). The disproportionately low share of older workers among recent recruits illustrates that many firms who employ a significant number of older workers, nevertheless tend not to recruit them (Hutchens, 1988).

There is an apparent tendency for many employers to prefer younger job applicants and so older job seekers may be disadvantaged in recruitment.

DISCRIMINATION AND OLDER WORKERS

'Discrimination against older workers is a long-standing problem. In fact, older workers were targets of discrimination already in the "golden age" of full employment in Europe in the post-war years.' Alexander Samorodov (1999), writing for the International Labour Office, continues: 'Older workers are disadvantaged with respect to employment, job and income security in a labour market.' Discrimination against older workers has only intensified with the lapse of time. Recently, older workers in Germany have been in the first line for working time reductions nationwide while workers in other age groups have not initially been selected. An obvious manifestation of discrimination occurs in vacancy announcements which impose an age limit of 40 or 45 years. However, age discrimination makes itself felt some 10–15 years before the official retirement age, sometimes earlier, if wage increments depend on length of service. Relatively older people who are still in their prime might find themselves targeted for dismissal. Among Canadian workers who were permanently laid off between 1981 and 1984, about 41 per cent of those aged 55–64 had left the labour force by January 1986, compared with 14 per cent of those aged 24–54. One reason is that older job seekers may be obliged to accept lower earnings if they return to work. Less evident, indirect discrimination, which is sometimes difficult to substantiate, might comprise 'offers' made specifically to older workers, such as early retirement options which are presented as voluntary, but where some pressure might be brought to bear. Other forms of indirect discrimination include tacitly withdrawing, or not offering, services which older workers might need more than others, thus making such workers more likely to retire. Usually employers justify such discrimination by involving 'the needs of the business', the need 'to keep production costs down, and be competitive.' Between 1991 and 1996, for example 67 per cent of respondent organizations in a survey on managers' attitudes to age and employment in the United Kingdom had made an effort to reduce the size of the workforce. Nearly six out of ten respondents reported that 'efforts had focussed on older employees.' (Samorodov, 1999: 14–15).

RESPONDING TO AGE DISCRIMINATION

Legislation against age discrimination has proved difficult to implement and hard to enforce (*Financial Times*, 1996a). A survey in the UK (*Financial Times*, 1996b) indicated that 85 per cent of the respondent managers believed that they should treat age as an equal opportunities issue, at least as important as race, sex and disability in the workplace— each of which is addressed by anti-discrimination laws. This did not prevent 55 per cent of the same managers using age criteria in appointing subordinates, and 25 per cent from taking age into consideration in decision in promotion.

For many countries a model for legislation in this area has been taken as that enacted in the United States as long ago as 1967. This aims to promote employment based on ability rather than age; prohibit age discrimination in employment; help employers and workers overcome problems arising from the impact of age on employment. Initially the Age Discrimination in Employment legislation covered workers of between 40 and 65 years, mainly in the private sector. Now the legislation covers workers from 40 years of age with no upper limit. The legislation has probably been reasonably effective in at least preventing 'blatant' discrimination. However, the legislation is incomplete and the proportion of older people among the long-term unemployed remains high. An employer is still allowed to use age as a selection criterion providing it can be shown to be a valid qualification. There is then a potentially large inadequacy in the legislation. In France, age limits in recruitment advertising are banned. Several Australian states have comprehensive age discrimination legislation. Some legislation is in place in Austria, Canada, Greece, New Zealand and Spain. Ireland is reviewing its anti-discrimination legislation with an eye to future age-related protection.

The International Labour Organization has developed the Older Workers Recommendation, 1980 (no. 162) which is a comprehensive international standard for legislation covering equality of opportunity and treatment. The recommendation indicates that the employment problems of older workers should be dealt with in the context of a comprehensive and balanced strategy for full employment.

At the level of the enterprise, due attention should be given to all population groups, so ensuring that 'employment problems are not shifted from one age group to another'. According to Recommendation 162, older workers are to enjoy without discrimination equal opportunity and treatment with other workers in the public and private sectors with regard to vocational guidance and placement services, training facilities, paid educational leave, promotion, employment security, equal remuneration, social security and welfare benefits, conditions of work. In principle, workers should, according to the recommendation, make their own decision on how and when to retire from employment. The recommendation outlines several mechanisms whereby pension and other arrangements are made flexible so as to smooth the transition from work to retirement. In the UK, the government has begun to take some tentative steps towards implementing some aspects of the ILO Recommendation but there is a long way to go before it is fully realized. The Employers' Forum on Age has been set up as a network to 'confront the changes needed to achieve the business benefits of a mixed-aged workforce'. The main purposes of the forum are to support member organizations in managing the skills and age mix of their workforces; to remove barriers to achieving an age-balanced workforce by influencing key decision-makers in government, education, training, recruitment and the trade union movement (Employers' Forum on Age, 2000). The forum subscribes to what it describes as a hard-hitting age diversity strategy which asks firms to measure their commitment against age prejudice and to take the message to employees, customers, suppliers and the wider community. The strategy asks member organizations to commit at the top level so as to build age awareness into all aspects of the business; have a Code of Practice for age diversity in employment, develop policies for a better balanced workforce, increase stakeholder involvement, and to report and measure success. The Employers' Forum on Age sees existing legislation on discrimination as being sufficient and wishes simply to reinforce this position with the adoption of a Code of Practice. The forum says that many employers have yet to grasp that there has been a demographic shift in population with a dramatic drop in the numbers of young people coming on to the labour market. They also report from their own surveys which show that ageism is widespread. Some organizations, they report, define an older woman as being over 35 and an older man as being over 42. The

Employers' Forum on Age provides a rich source of case studies of good practice in terms of the aims it espouses. Yet its membership remains small, with just 165 members representing under 3 million employees (or a little over 10 per cent of the total UK workforce).

McVittie and McKinlay (2000) state that it remains to be seen to what extent the voluntarist approach will succeed in enhancing employment prospects of older workers. They cite a 1998 study carried out before the publication of a voluntary Code of Practice, in which just 40 per cent of organizations surveyed stated that they had in place written equal opportunities policies which made specific mention of age. McVittie and McKinlay also provide evidence that even where age discrimination is specifically included within an organization's equal opportunities policy the outlook for older workers remains bleak. They cite a study of the British Broadcasting Corporation which found that notwithstanding the Corporation's very public commitment to equal opportunities workers aged 50+ were over a 15-year period increasingly excluded from its workforce. The systematic targeting of older workers for redundancies together with the predominant recruitment of under-50s for vacancies left the Corporation with an age profile far younger than that found in other public sector employers. The study, McVittie and McKinlay say, concludes that in spite of the Corporation's commitment to equal opportunities, measures carried out to improve its efficiency had left older workers 'unprotected in the workplace and a low priority in equal opportunities terms'.

In his own research McVittie reports that he had interviewed human resource (HR) managers or recruitment managers of 12 medium to large enterprises in Scotland. Participants for the study were recruited following job advertisements by their organizations in a national newspaper which explicitly claimed that the organizations were 'committed to equal opportunities'. He found an apparent inconsistency between the claims made in their job advertisements to be employers committed to equal opportunities and the age balance of the workforces. On being asked to account for the imbalance the respondents gave three types of account:

1. *The balance results from the actions of older workers and job seekers* which says something like 'it's just the way it works out' and so avoids attributing the age balance to any particular or planned factors in the recruitment process.
2. *A description of the job and worker* such as 'our jobs do hold you to certain targets, there's expectations and objectives set'. The respondent does not say that the jobs are unsuitable for older workers because of the job-related factors. Instead the respondent offers a heavily qualified view of why older workers themselves might find the job inappropriate.
3. *A description of the selection procedures required for recruitment and how they relate to groups of jobseekers.* Here the HR manager says something like 'the age-balance doesn't have anything to do with the recruitment process'. 'Something is stopping people applying to us.'

What is clear is that at no point in the interviews do the participants state that they are opposed to employing older workers. Nor do they state that some jobs are only suitable for younger workers. McVittie tells us that 'the accounts they offer for age balance of the workforce however justify the existing marginalization of older workers within the organization and have the ideological effect of maintaining the existing inequality' (McVittie & McKinlay, 2000: 7–8.)

McVittie's findings begin to offer an indication of some of the processes that maintain age discrimination. Lest his qualitative study appears not to be properly representative, a quantifiable study shows similar patterns. A recent survey conducted by the Chartered Institute of Personnel and Development (the HR managers' professional body for the UK) reported that one person in 10 said that they had not bothered to apply for a job because the advert contained an age criterion that made it clear that they would not be considered. One in eight people surveyed felt that their age had served to prevent them getting a job but had no hard evidence to prove it. Nearly 7 per cent of 16–24-year-olds had been told that their age was a factor in being rejected. On the positive side, many employers are taking steps to tackle age discrimination (Worman, 2001).

WHY CONSIDER AGE?

In a major text, Furnham (1997: 627) writes:

> Normally, young people are more inclined to initiate and accept change than are older ones. They tend to be less risk-aversive and are more willing to try out new things. More importantly, new and low-ranking in the organisation, young people have little to lose from change. For their part, older members of organisations tend to be more set in their ways, have much stake in the status quo, and therefore tend to be more wary about change. Along with chronological age is deference to age, which may inhibit change. To the extent that older more conservative people occupy leadership roles in organisations, and to the extent that organisational members acquiesce to or despise them, organisational change may be slow in coming.

True, organizations are faced with change but it is hard to believe that organizations use reactions to change as a selection criterion although it is feasible that retention policies could be formulated with such a view in focus. In another text McKenna (2000) tells us that a report produced by the pressure group Eurolink Age blames restricted opportunities for people over the age of 50 on discriminatory attitudes:

> It is said that too many employers believe that old people are not up to the job or possess the right skills, and there is widespread belief that older people's jobs are more expendable than young people's. . . . However, at the turn of the millennium there are implications that more companies are prepared to hire older staff. According to the Membership Manager of The Employers' Forum on Age, the important message is that in the 1980s and early 1990s many financial institutions downsized too rapidly. By weeding out a whole stratum of staff of a particular age, they lost a vast amount of knowledge, and damaged the future of their business. Many are now looking to bring in new people with experience to try to regenerate and improve creativity and motivation among existing staff. (McKenna, 2000: 256)

The loss of older workers through downsizing could lose the vital core of the business organization. In all of this it is difficult to avoid the conclusion that there is a lack of analysis on the part of the management in organizations. The skills and knowledge requirements of the organization appear to be little considered when early retirement policies are utilized in downsizing exercises. Nor are the training implications of replacing older with younger organization members. As Samorodov (1999) points out, as older people progress there is an increasing gap between the skills and knowledge gained at school and that acquired in the job, but the importance of job-based knowledge ought not to be underestimated. Lifelong learning is being seen as an increasing priority by many companies as well as by individuals.

In a recent large-scale study, using a range of inventories of personality, Warr et al. (2001) report finding that almost half of the personality attributes examined were not significantly linked to age. Those attributes that are consistently related to age are social confidence, assertiveness, independence, vigour, responsiveness to other people, supportiveness, intellectual efficiency, psychological mindedness, and the extent to which individuals are optimistic, worried or relaxed. Warr et al. further report consistently greater scores at older ages for personality attributes such as being conscientious, modest, conventional, careful in interaction, sympathetic and helpful; and consistent negative age patterns were found for sociability, outgoingness, desired social context, abstract thinking, career achievement motivation and a preference for variety. In terms of the arguments being developed in this chapter, Warr et al.'s findings are important. Those characteristics of personality that are related to increased age ought to make older workers more valued employees. However, those that are related to younger workers seem likely to be those that will appear strong at selection—particularly if the selection procedure is heavily based on interviews or group discussion techniques.

Warr et al.'s findings ought to come as no surprise. It is half a century since Viteles (1954) wrote of the higher morale and positive attitudes of older workers towards the company expressed in the work of Hull (1939). Warr's earlier work is also supportive of older workers' employment:

> The overall finding from more than 100 research investigations is that there is no significant association between age and work performance. The average correlation co-efficient is about +0.06, but separate correlations in the literature range from −0.44 to +0.66.... It is clear from this wide range that the importance of age varies between different jobs and between different aspects of performance. However, the general pattern is clear: in overall terms, there is no difference between the performance observed for older and younger staff in the same job. Incidentally, in almost every case variation within an age-group far exceeds the average difference between age groups. (Warr, 1996)

There are hints in Warr's research on personality that age may affect an individual's ability to process complex information. However, these hints do not find substantiation in the literature on intelligence. Salthouse's (1991: 82–83) major review concludes that:

a) little or no negative effects associated with increased age seem to be evident in most measures of accumulated knowledge or previously acquired information....

b) age-related declines account for 10% to 20% of the total variance, and corresponding to differences between 20 year olds and 65-year olds of between .5 to 1.5 young adult standard deviations, are often found with measures of efficiency of current processing....

c) age relations vary across different measures of cognitive functioning, with some of the variation perhaps attributable to the differences in the type of cognition being assessed, and some of it possibly due to the differences in either the amount of processing required or in the importance of speed factors and

d)   although quite plausible arguments can be constructed attributing some or all of the age differences to artefacts related to differential representativeness such as, health, education, and perceptual motor speed, impact on only a limited segment of the population the bulk of the available evidence seems to suggest that these factors are not sufficient to account for all the observed age trends.

These are important issues, particularly when we consider the fact that jobs of all kinds are increasingly based on cognitive processes rather than making physical demands. Older people are, on the basis of research evidence, no less well placed to do work of this kind than younger people. Secondly, any personnel process which progresses on the basis of older people being less capable than younger seems to be based on ill-founded assumptions.

THE EXPERIENCE OF ORGANIZATIONS

There are a considerable number of companies across the world that do not encourage older workers to retire and have been profitable and efficient. Sonnenfield (1978) provided the example of Thomas Greenwood, president of Globe dyeworks in Philadelphia, who had retained workers hired by his grandfather commenting that 'As long as a man can produce, he can keep his job.' Greenwood also cites 'The 87-year-old president of Ferle Inc, a small company owned by General Foods, which employs workers whose average age is 71', commenting that 'Older people are steadier, accustomed to work discipline' (Sonnenfield, 1978: 190).

Sonnenfield also quoted other American companies with similar policies, i.e. 'U.S. Steel has permitted 153,000 non-office employees to continue working as long as they can maintain satisfactory levels of performance and can pass medical examinations. Polaroid has found that those employees who chose to remain on the job after the age of 65 tend to be better performers' (Sonnenfield, 1978: 190).

In Britain the Employers' Forum on Age (EFA, 2000) website provides case studies of Oxfordshire County Council promoting an equal opportunities policy that provides an action plan for a more balanced workforce age profile. This council supports modern apprenticeships, information technology and computing facilities and PR campaigns aimed at attracting young people when it found its age profile was dramatically skewed towards the middle-aged. The forum also report, by way of example, Peckham and Rye, licensed delicatessen operators based in Glasgow, which suffered very high staff turnover in its low skilled and low-paid work, who targeted new recruitment at the long-term unemployed aged 25 and over. They introduced basic skills training with modest qualifications levels and with further training progressions. Turnover and retention became much more manageable within about six months of the change being introduced and the company continues to be an EFA example of good practice.

IS DIVERSITY INEVITABLE?

Elsewhere I have presented the view that the deterministic forces of demographic change are interpreted as implying that diversity is inevitable. The arguments that are presented by those authors who see diversity as inevitable mistake the interplay between demographic differences with differing rates of economic growth as leading to major redefinitions of labour markets (Brotherton, 1999). However, government's efforts to harmonize workplace standards has been extraordinarily slow in areas such as gender and race. Harmonization in terms of age is, as we have seen in this chapter, virtually non-existent. It might be thought that managing diversity in terms of age is in advance of that observed in terms of race and gender. However, here too progress is slow. It is possible to find examples where companies have made positive gains in terms of their labour market position by targeting different age groups and intervening in some way to improve their position. But the evidence is that the innovations are partial and to that extent weak given the needs of both organizations and people. Diversity ought to empower people and organizations so that the full potential of effort and ability can be realized without being spoiled by discrimination, bias and prejudice. In the knowledge economy and the global marketplace diversity could be celebrated, since thinking rather than physical skills are to the forefront of demand. Yet diversity has to be fought for at each stage. It seems that in every group that is not absolutely and firmly embedded in the power structure that engages workers some individuals readily become marginalized, sidelined and discharged. If the sheer scale of marginalization is doubted, reflect on the point that this chapter has quite deliberately and self-consciously not offered a definition of 'age' or 'old'. Rather, the illustrative evidence has spanned almost 100 years of active life span, except where the discussion has been about policy matters. In this respect age does not provide a category for a social psychology of diversity in the way that race and gender do. A category is the process of understanding what something is by knowing what other things it is equivalent to and what things it is different from. With age all of the scientific evidence that is available on ability and on personality indicates that age itself does not provide a basis for assuming difference. Yet differences are assumed in the implementation of policy.

CONCLUSIONS

It seems that we live in cultures that see early life as 'development' and later life as 'decline' (Gergan, 1994). These viewpoints give little sense of hope or optimism. Cultures, and as Gergan points out, the social scientists within them, need to articulate for some positive and enabling possibilities. This needs to occur both for people as cultural beings and for those managers operating policies in organizations that draw on processes in ways that are informed by cultural views. I have argued elsewhere that social science—particularly social psychology—provides a rhetoric and a dialogue for management (Brotherton, 1999). If that dialogue is restricted in its vision the outcome is an impoverished agenda for the powerful actors in organizations who are set problems by the process of change—and which they fail to understand.

Diversity offers the prospect of people being valued for their own sakes as well as for the contributions that they may make. Diversity thereby offers the prospect of improving not just the social images of particular groups or categories but the level of narration we have with ourselves about our own lives and our own self-images and esteem. Gergan shows us how older people are able to enhance their own sense of well-being through reporting on positive aspects of their life histories (Gergan, 1994: 200). Positive dialogue is then directly beneficial to individuals. It is also likely to be good for the way individuals contribute to organizations and to society. But such conclusions are rested on a range of conditional possibilities—only some of which are in our own hands, none of which are socially determined, none of which are inevitable.

REFERENCES

Asian Population Studies (1994). United Nations, ESCAP. New York. Series No. 131-B, 11–52.

Brotherton, C.J. (1999). *Social Psychology and Management: Issues for a Changing Society*. Milton Keynes: Open University Press.

Employers' Forum on Age. (2000). Website.

Employment Gazette (1995). London: April, 146.

European Union Labour Force Survey (1997). Brussels: Eurostat.

Fallick, B.C. (1996). A review of recent empirical literature on displaced workers. *Industrial and Labour Relations Review*, March, 5–16.

Financial Times (London) (1996a). 15 April.

Financial Times (London) (1996b). 12 August.

Freeman, J. (1982). The old, old, very old Charlie Smith. *The Gerontologist*, **22**, 532.

Furnham, A. (1997). *The Psychology of Behaviour at Work*. London: Psychology Press.

Gergan, K. (1994). *Social Relationships*. Cambridge, Mass.: Harvard University Press.

Ham-Chande, R. (1995). *The Elderly in Mexico: Another Challenge for a Middle-income Country*. Malta: UNIA/CICRED.

Hull, R.L. (1939). Measuring employee attitudes—a proving ground for personnel policy and practices. *Conference Board Management Record*, November, 165–172.

Hutchens, R. (1988). Do job opportunities decline with age?. *Industrial and Labor Relations Review*, October, 89–99.

International Labour Organization (1995). *World Labour Report*. Geneva: ILO.

McKenna, E. (2000). *Business Psychology and Organisational Behaviour*, 3rd edn. London: Taylor & Francis.

McVittie, C. & McKinlay, A. (2000). When equal opportunities are unequal: justifying the marginalisation of older workers. Paper delivered to the British Psychological Society Social Psychology Section Conference, Nottingham, September.

OECD (1997). *Employment Outlook*. Paris, July.

Podgursky, M. & Swain, P. (1987). Job displacement earnings loss: evidence from the displaced worker survey. *Industrial and Labour Relations Review*, October, 17–29.

Salthouse, T.A. (1991). *Theoretical Perspectives on Cognitive Aging*. Hillsdale, NJ: Lawrence Erlbaum Associates.

Samorodov, A. (1999). *Ageing and Labour Markets for Older Workers*. Geneva: International Labour Organization Employment and Training Papers 33.

Segerberg, O. (1982). *Living to be 100: 1200 who did and how they did it*. New York: Charles Scribner's Sons.

Sonnenfield, J. (1978). Dealing with the aging work force. In M.C. Gentile (1996) *Differences that Work*. Harvard Business Review: Harvard, Mass.

Viteles, M.S. (1954). *Motivation and Morale in Industry*. London: Stapes Press.

Warr, P. B. (ed.) (1996). *Psychology at Work*, 4th edn. Harmondsworth: Penguin.

Warr, P., Miles, A. & Platts, C. (2001). Age and personality in the British population between 16 and 64 years. *Journal of Occupational and Organizational Psychology*, **74**, 165–199.

White Paper on Labour, Part III. (1995). Tokyo: Ministry of Labour.

Worman, D. (2001). Making ageism a thing of the past. *People Management*, 8 March, 63.

PART IV

Diversity Training and Its Effectiveness

CHAPTER 14

Designing a Diversity Training Programme that Suits Your Organization

Roberta Youtan Kay
Private Practice, Nipomo, California, USA

Donna M. Stringer
Executive Diversity Services, Inc., Seattle, Washington, USA

SUMMARY

This chapter explores how organizations can most effectively provide diversity training programmes for managers and employees. It begins by examining why an organization would decide to provide such training and the questions to ask in establishing the goals for such an initiative. Guidelines are offered for how to design effective training programmes, including content, process and selection of a training team. The latter part of the chapter offers a number of case studies to demonstrate the types of issues that might arise in such training and some of the approaches trainers might use in handling those issues.

INTRODUCTION

When diversity training seminars became popular in the United States about 20 years ago, many were emotionally charged, confrontational and counterproductive. Consequently, the view of early diversity seminars was that they often did more damage than good because they left people feeling defensive and polarized. However, the lessons of the past have cleared the way for the thousands of professionals in the field today who bring great value to current diversity training. These trainers are able to provide tailored training

Individual Diversity and Psychology in Organizations. Edited by Marilyn J. Davidson and Sandra L. Fielden.
© 2003 John Wiley & Sons, Ltd.

that raises the awareness of the participants so that they can gain greater understanding and skills to communicate with each other and effectively work together. These sessions include awareness about oneself, information about others who are culturally different, and tools to be more effective in cross-cultural communication and working relationships.

Many executives may still be unclear about what is involved in managing diversity and may not be fully aware of how cultural competency, inclusiveness and affirmative action or other legal issues may affect a particular organization. They may not recognize a need to provide training in these areas or what the ramifications would be of doing so. If it has been decided to provide training, then the question may revolve around whether it should be conducted by in-house staff or outsourced to other professionals. This chapter is intended to answer the most frequently asked questions about cultural diversity training and provide guidance for finding the appropriate programmes and/or providers for different types of organizations.

WHY PROVIDE TRAINING?

As organizations employ more diverse employees and serve more diverse customers, both the opportunities for success and the risk of failure increases.

The opportunities for greater success with employees and customers are well documented. As highlighted throughout this book, many studies now show that diverse work teams view situations from a broader range of perspectives, producing more creative solutions to problems and greater product innovation (Executive Diversity Services, 2000). Diversity in an organization's employees can enhance productivity if employees feel valued by the way the organization treats them—allowing them to perform at their fullest potential. Information regarding customers indicates that when an organization's employees, managers and board members are visibly diverse, it increases the diversity of its customers. People like doing business with companies where they see themselves reflected in the organization. And finally, companies that utilize diverse vendors or suppliers are also more successful in gaining access to multicultural markets.

Diversity is not without its risks, however. While diverse teams produce both greater quality and quantity of creative solutions and innovations, they also take longer to form than homogeneous teams—understanding and trusting each other takes time (Executive Diversity Services, 2000). Most importantly, one cannot assume that because diversity is present that it will perform effectively. Misperceptions and conflicts are common and almost predictable if people are not able to acknowledge, understand and work effectively with diverse co-workers or clients.

Several of the 'best practices' for effective organizational diversity initiatives provide the primary reasons for diversity training (Executive Diversity Services, Inc., 2000; DiversityInc, 2001). As demonstrated by Figure 14.1, effective diversity initiatives begin by linking diversity to the organization's mission, goals and organizational culture—integrating it into the organization's values so it is part of the entire context, not something set aside. Like many other organizational efforts, effective diversity is promoted and supported by knowledgeable, committed leaders, so identifying who these people will be is important in the early stages of planning. Initiatives will include goals and activities that meet the needs of employees, clients and vendors. This will virtually always include training and development programmes to provide awareness, information and skills

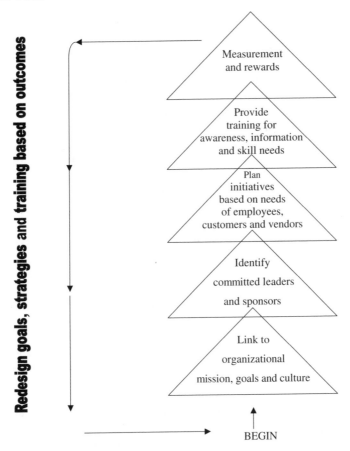

FIGURE 14.1 Best practices for diversity initiatives

for management and employees. Measuring results and rewarding effective diversity management in evaluation, pay and promotion systems provides the motivation for both managers and employees to take the initiative seriously even when it might not be a personal value.

Having done these things, the organization is now in a position to reassess its initiative and redesign the new goals, strategies and training based on the outcomes achieved. It is an ongoing process of identifying goals, taking action and measuring results. It is not a one-time behaviour but an ongoing process to achieve organizational change.

These, then, are the reasons organizations would want to provide diversity training: because diversity can be a primary factor in achieving organizational goals in a competitive global environment and because people cannot be expected to achieve success if they are not provided with the information and skills for doing so.

ESTABLISHING GOALS

The approach your company or organization takes to training depends upon the answers to the following questions:

- Is your need for diversity training proactive (i.e. preventative; recognizing that the workforce is continuously changing and that the global community is a realistic client base) or reactive (arising as a result of an incident of conflict among employees or, perhaps, a lawsuit)?
- What is the organizational context for this training? That is, how will you define the training programme's ability to help the organization achieve its goals? What is the current demographic make-up of your employees, of your clients, of your vendors or suppliers, of the community in which you conduct business?
- How committed and prepared is your leadership team to actively sponsor a diversity change process and participate in their own development of cultural competency? Does management understand and support the idea of diversity training?
- How ready is your workforce for this diversity training? Who supports the idea of training and why? Is there harmony among your existing employees or is there tension in the organization about diversity issues?
- What, specifically, would you like to have happen as a result of this training? Do you want participants to be aware of how cultural differences affect perceptions and behaviours? Do you want them to have greater awareness of their own cultural responses in the organizational environment? Do you want them to better understand co-workers or clients? Do you want them to have specific tools for effectiveness across differences? Do you want them to be able to assess the effectiveness of organizational policies, procedures and practices? Do you want all of the above?
- How much time and budget can you commit to this effort? It is important that training be designed for success. If you have limited time and budget you will need to develop limited goals . . . or plan a longer-term process with incremental goals.

Most organizations are interested in awareness raising for an initial training session. This approach helps participants understand their own biases and values and get a better understanding of other people's perspectives, helping to build empathy and increase communication between those who are different. Skill building usually begins with supervisors and managers but should ultimately be extended to employees as well. While the types of skills required for managing diversity are different from those needed by employees, it is important that employees also receive some specific tools that can be applied in their daily work. Culture-specific training, primarily geared to learning more about the major cultures represented in the workforce and client base, is most effective following an initial awareness-training programme. If culture-specific training is conducted too early, it can serve to create or reinforce stereotypes rather than expand understanding.

Good diversity training should provide all three elements: awareness, new information and skill-building tools, although the balance will depend on the organization's goals and participant experience. Training usually begins with a greater portion of awareness, some new information and a few tools; more advanced training sessions reverse that mix. This combination can facilitate prejudice reduction, growth of cultural competency and an understanding of the meaning and impact of various behaviours, values and communication styles of several groups. It is important, however, that the goals of training be consistent with the organizational context and be limited to the time and budget available. Table 14.1 can be used to consider the basic mix of these items, including

TABLE 14.1 Suggested balance for training content based on developmental stage of participants (%)

Content	1st Stage: basic awareness	2nd Stage: information and tools	3rd Stage: skill building	4th Stage: cultural competence
Awareness of self and others: Values, Behaviours, Styles; Awareness of how similarities and differences impact perceptions, behaviours, and potential conflicts	55	15	10	15
General information about culture	15	25	05	05
Tools for greater effectiveness across differences	13	30	15	10
Application of tools to workplace situations	10	20	60	30
Cultural-specific information	1 (examples only)	10 (examples only)	10 (included in case studies)	40

content about specific cultural groups divided into four potential stages towards cultural competency.

DESIGNING A TRAINING PROGRAMME

There are many issues to be considered in designing training programmes regarding diversity. Among those are establishing realistic expectations—including appropriate time frames for creating the personal and organizational changes required, assuring that the training is theoretically grounded and information provided is accurate, designing the training to fit the organizational and participant needs, fitting the training to the organization's business and political environment, and labelling the training effectively to avoid misperceptions about its purpose and content (Gudykunst et al., 1996).

The first step in designing a training programme is identifying, as specifically as possible, the goals or purpose for the training and the outcomes expected. This is done through a needs assessment that can be as simple as interviewing the organizational person(s) responsible for the diversity initiative and as complex as conducting multiple interviews and/or focus groups with both management and employees. If you are embarking on an organization-wide initiative, of which training is only one component, a full-scale organizational assessment will ultimately serve the initiative and the training design well.

Determination of goals and outcomes will affect the level of commitment your organization must make. Contracts vary from a two-hour, introductory experience for all employees, to a one-, two- or three-day training. We have worked on a major governmental contract that provided three-day training for all managers and a one-day training for staff. One should consider the motivation for, and the message that may be associated with, such an arrangement: is the arrangement appropriate for the situation and does the organization value all of their employees equally? (Of course, allotting more time for training allows for a more in-depth approach, combining awareness raising with skill development and some culture-specific information, which is important to include when training managers and supervisors.)

In designing your programme, it is important to differentiate between training about valuing diversity and one on affirmative action or legal mandates. Essentially, the goal of affirmative action in the United States has been to achieve equality of opportunity in the work environment by changing organizational demographics and targeting groups such as women and minorities, who were previously excluded. In valuing diversity, we are emphasizing the appreciation of differences, creating an environment in which everyone feels valued and accepted; in other words, we are looking at how people are treated once they are in the workforce, regardless of how they got there.

The content of your training will be determined by the organizational goals and an assessment of the participants' existing understanding or skills. The process will be determined to some degree by the organizational culture and participant learning styles. For example, if an organization is technology-prone, the use of PowerPoint presentations and computer-based elements may be effective. If the organization is one that values personal growth and relationships, more small group exercises can be utilized.

Regardless of the content or processes selected, however, attention must be given to a balance of content and process (Bennett, 1994). If one is teaching content that is relatively low intensity (e.g. greeting protocols in different countries), matching it with high-intensity process such as role-playing or demonstrations by the students themselves can lead to increased skills. When teaching high-intensity content (e.g. value differences across cultural groups), it is important to use a lower-risk process such as lectures, stories, videos so that you obtain increased understanding. If you match low-risk content with low-risk process the learner is likely to 'check out' or quit paying attention, and if you match high-risk content with high-risk process you are likely to lose the learner altogether. They may literally leave the room or, at best, stay there but disengage from the class because it is too threatening.

Sequencing training is also an important issue in training design. Moving participants through a learning sequence that attends to the development of learning is critical to success. In other words, you sequence information from easiest to hardest, from awareness to information to skills, from lower-risk content and process to higher risk. We would not expect a child to play soccer before s/he had learned to walk. We should not expect diversity training participants to leave their prejudices behind before they understand where they come from in the first place.

And, of course, too much content in too short a time is a guarantee for failure. Expecting people to develop self-awareness, learn new information and apply tools for skill building in a two-and-a-half-hour session is unlikely to be successful. One of the greatest errors that organizations make is to assume that, because their budget or time is limited, they need to achieve every one of their diversity goals in one short session. One approach we find successful is to identify everything the organization wants their employees to learn, identify the budget and time they have available, and then explore how to provide the desired information/skills over a longer period of time. For example, we worked with a military organization that wanted the equivalent of three days of training for each employee but only had budget for four (4) hours. We designed a long-term process to provide four hours of training for each employee each year for a six-year period. Each year we revisited their original goals for any changes that might have occurred and re-examined that year's training content/process to be sure it was still a good fit. The advantage of this approach is that it allows the organization to get everything it wants, spreads the training over time so it is a consistent theme in the organization, and— perhaps most importantly—allows employees a year to apply what they have learned and return to learn the 'next level'. It is developmental for both the employee and the organization.

An approach that seems to work quite well—and is especially cost-effective for organizations that have 1000 employees or more—is that of selecting internal trainers and providing them skills through a 'train the trainer' process. The external consultants train a core group of employees in diversity issues generally and in the curriculum for the organization specifically. This cadre of trainers is then available to roll out the programme to all employees. One internal trainer is typically paired with one external consultant for each workshop. The ideal pairing would be one that models visible diversity (i.e. both gender as well as ethnic mix), if possible, for each team. Employees respond well to this type of arrangement, as the internal person has an intimate knowledge of the company's culture and the outside consultant is viewed as having greater expertise in the field, bringing in a very different (professional) perspective.

While using internal trainers is an effective way to reduce the expense of a large training initiative, it is also a superb way of weaving diversity expertise into the fabric of the organizational culture. When the initial training is completed, the organization is left with a cadre of experienced individuals who can continue to provide training for new employees, serve as consultants in the organization's ongoing work, and be general resources to the organization on a number of diversity issues. At the same time, internal trainers are often not the most effective choice for training executives and managers, because they may not be seen as having the same level of expertise or experience with management issues that external consultants may have. It is usually most effective to have the external consultants provide the training for executives and managers while the internal trainers conduct training for non-managerial employees. Again, of course, this depends on the organizational culture and the level of the organization from which internal trainers are selected.

FINDING THE RIGHT TRAINER OR TEAM

There are hundreds of private management consultants who provide diversity training. In selecting a consultant there are three primary areas to be concerned about—beyond the practical issues of availability and cost (Wederspahn, 2000). The first is programme content. In choosing your provider, consider how much the consultant or organization can tailor their curricula to meet the specific needs and concerns of your organization. While there are some organizations that have packaged training programmes available, which can be less expensive, you will want to ensure that the package effectively meets your organization's needs.

The second area of concern is the consultant's experiences or competencies in the area of providing diversity training. Paige (1993) has provided an extremely useful list of trainer competencies. He offers competencies in three areas: cognitive, behavioural and personal. Cognitively, it is important that your consultant be thoroughly grounded in both theory and information in the areas of diversity and adult training. Ask about their education, how they stay current on the information, what professional organizations they belong to, what contributions they have made to the professional field. Can they discuss with you the current research, the current direction of the field, the current ethical issues? Behaviourally, the consultant should be able to engage a training audience, facilitate difficult discussions, and act in ways that are perceived as respectful by a wide range of diverse participants. And, look for personal attributes as well. Diversity consultants should be aware of their own cultural biases, exhibit enthusiasm and commitment to diversity (beyond selling you a programme), value different points of view, and have the ability to empathize and demonstrate interpersonal sensitivity.

The third area of concern should be whether the consultant has an understanding and ability to deal with the unique nature of diversity training. It is very important to realize the uniqueness of diversity training as it compares to other types of training done in workplace settings. Often, the HR staff conduct training in related areas such as conflict management, teambuilding or communication skills, for example. However, there are some inherent differences in diversity training that involve risk factors and the potential for on-the-spot conflict and discomfort for participants that other types of training do not create. Consequently, the facilitator of diversity training needs to possess some additional skills to deal with the types of issues that might arise. Therefore, the in-house HR staff are often well advised to seek outside consultants to do this type of training.

The competent and highly experienced diversity trainer should be prepared to deal with participant resistance and defensiveness and should have ways to cope with such resistance. Some strategies that could be put into play during a training session might be to often refer to conceptual or theoretical frameworks to help the participant understand their own responses. Another important skill is to acknowledge the normality of their responses but at the same time, be able to challenge the learner not to rationalize or deny their behaviour, especially when such rationalizations are being used to intellectualize difficulties they might be experiencing regarding multicultural interactions.

Paige (1988) has provided an invaluable list of risks that trainers must be prepared to recognize and manage in training sessions, including the risk of increased self-awareness, self-disclosure, identity loss, failure, alienation, embarrassment and humiliation, personal change or growth, emotional stress and ambiguity. This can provide some guidance in consultant selection. Ask consultants what risks they see for participants in this training and what techniques they use for managing these risks in the classroom.

CASE STUDIES IN DIVERSITY TRAINING

The following cases help illustrate the scope of issues that can be addressed in the workplace.

NEO-NAZI

A city about 50 miles away from Los Angeles, California, contracted with us to do a series of one-day, awareness-raising trainings for their employees. This city is known as a place that has attracted many residents who were fleeing some of the violence and unrest of Los Angeles. Over the past several years, however, the demographic changes of this smaller city have begun to mirror those of Los Angeles. Consequently, problems of cultural conflict, incidents involving skinheads, and general concerns of increased incidents of violence in the city prompted the training administrator and senior HR analyst to contact us. They were taking a proactive approach to deal with general concerns expressed by the community.

After meeting with these two HR administrators, we determined that the best approach for a prejudice awareness and anti-discrimination training would be to do a 'train the trainer' with selected city employees. Thirteen people were recruited, representing diverse departments, ethnicities and perspectives. There were five women and eight men. After providing these people with a five-day, train-the-trainer intensive experience, we shared the facilitation responsibilities by having one of us partner with two of these city employees for each of the one-day workshops that were to follow. There were 19 in all.

One particular subgroup that one of the authors facilitated with two of the in-house employees was for the street maintenance workers—very blue collar and not too well educated. One man in the group made it clear that he was a neo-Nazi. He was trying very hard to derail the training by blatantly not participating and doodling swastikas on his agenda directly in front of the author. Through the morning sessions and at breaks, she engaged him in a couple of side conversations. She talked to him about her being Jewish and how he, theoretically, would wish her dead based on that one fact alone. As she persisted in interacting with him, he became less and less defensive and eventually began to participate and connect with her as a human being. At the end of the day, he made a point of thanking her for the workshop. The following week, when she returned for another training, he stopped to say hello and to apologize for his previous behaviour, jokingly saying that he probably should repeat the morning portion of the training since he was really not mentally present for it the first time he attended.

SEXUAL ORIENTATION

One of the authors was selected to be part of a team of diversity trainers, specifically with backgrounds in psychology, to work on a contract for a large federal agency covering the western region of the United States. This agency was interested in psychologists because of some previous diversity trainings that had created many problems a few years previously. Due to a climate of blatant intolerance towards difference, especially that of sexual orientation, this organization needed a carefully designed and skilfully implemented programme. The agency administrators felt that facilitators with a psychological orientation could more readily handle what had been some volatile and explosive issues in the past.

Their goals were to learn about the cultural norms of different groups, to overcome communication problems due to limited or heavily accented English, and to create an atmosphere where it would be all right to disagree with members of other groups without

248 DESIGNING DIVERSITY TRAINING THAT SUITS YOUR ORGANIZATION

worrying about being called prejudiced. These concerns were disclosed through an in-depth cultural audit that was conducted among agency employees.

The first author facilitated one of these sessions for the agency in a small town in Arizona. At the start of the session, an irate man who was a long-time employee of this agency immediately challenged her. As mentioned above, one of the major diversity issues of concern to this agency was that of sexual orientation. Some very visible acts of discrimination had been directed at gay men and lesbians in this particular workforce, which was primarily white, straight and male. A philosophical debate ensued in this training over the issue of listing sexual orientation as a category of diversity. Because some participants perceived this categorization as an attack on their religious beliefs, a difficult atmosphere resulted for a period of time. It took a lot of delicate work, employing some of the facilitator's psychotherapy skills to dissipate the anger and establish a learning atmosphere once again. People left, not necessarily transformed, but definitely thinking about issues generated in the session that they probably had not thought much about before.

QUICK FIX

A pharmaceutical company had requested a training programme to address racial conflicts that had developed among some employees. People were not communicating with each other—there were old hurts that had been festering for years among some very visible and influential people at the company. The HR director worked with us to create a very basic, introductory workshop that would act as a catalyst for further communication.

After a series of very short (two and a half hours each) awareness-raising workshops, a major shift occurred in the company. The workshops did provide an opportunity for lifting some serious communication barriers. People were beginning to talk more openly to each other, employing a new vocabulary and some simple techniques that had been covered in the training sessions. Our suggestion was to provide follow-up sessions by creating some ongoing, voluntary dialogue groups. This is currently being assessed, based on employee feedback and self-evaluations.

FEMALES ARE DIVERSE

An old-established Fortune 500 company requested a five-day train-the-trainer programme. The authors were shocked to find out that many of the participants did not know the first thing about diversity. The people in attendance were assigned to go to this train-the-trainer programme, as opposed to volunteering, and several of them were chosen only because they were female, which made them 'different' or 'diverse' from the majority of the company's workforce. When consultants do train-the-trainer workshops, it is imperative that they give complete and honest feedback to the participants at its conclusion, assessing their capability and skill level to do this very challenging work. People who do this work need to understand what is involved, be prepared to deal with the many potentially volatile subjects that can arise in trainings, and, most importantly, they must have a real commitment to the work. After going through the train-the-trainer process, several of these participants recognized that they were not emotionally prepared to facilitate diversity trainings and chose not to.

GLOBAL COMPETENCIES

We worked with a major United States airline in providing diversity training for its 18 000 flight attendants in sites located in the United States, London and Hong Kong. Each of those locations included participants from a minimum of seven national groups, multiple ethnic populations and both genders. The training was one day in length and provided by one of our professional diversity trainers partnered with an airline manager who had completed a five-day train-the-trainer class. The goals were to provide individuals with greater awareness of their own cultural patterns, information about cultural behaviour patterns their passengers might exhibit, and tools for reducing conflicts and improving effectiveness across many global behaviours/practices. The content included exploration of perception differences; cultural values, communication styles and non-verbal behaviours that can lend richness to a work environment but can also result in misperceptions and conflict.

Global/national issues showed up persistently. In London, we experienced tension between the British and Scandinavian participants and people from France and southern European countries around the communication style used in classroom discussions. The former typically exhibited a more formal, reserved manner with the latter exhibiting much more effusiveness and confrontational styles. Our trainers were able to point out the difference, help participants understand the difference, identify where those same issues can arise with co-workers or passengers, and apply several communication tools to achieve greater effectiveness. This allowed participants self-awareness, cross-cultural information and tools—all three in the resolution of a single classroom issue.

In Hong Kong, we saw differences in classroom behaviours as well. While US citizens working in Asian countries would readily ask questions or challenge the instructors, most Asian participants would not do so. While all participants spoke English, some were more limited in their abilities than others. As a result, we designed a process that allowed people to have small group 'summary' discussions at the end of each training module. This allowed people to ask questions of their peers if they did not feel comfortable asking questions of the instructors, and it allowed those who were less fluent to get 'translations' from those who had greater language capacity. Again—participants were experiencing greater self-awareness, specific information about other national/cultural groups, and the ability to apply some tools immediately at the end of each module.

GENERATIONAL DIFFERENCES

The second author was asked to intervene in conflicts within a work team following the team's attendance at a two-day diversity awareness training. The team was a research group in a Fortune 100 manufacturing company. There were 17 members on the team: 3 women, 14 men; 15 European-Americans, 2 Indian foreign nationals. The manager of this team contacted the author, indicating that the team had found the diversity training helpful but that they were still struggling with conflicts that he believed were based on gender and educational degrees.

Every member of the team was interviewed face to face, asking them to identify the team's strengths and challenges and to discuss any conflicts they were experiencing, with whom and what they thought the conflict was based on. Virtually every member of the team identified the national, gender and educational diversity (engineering, chemistry and marketing) as strong assets to their effectiveness. The real issues, identified in these interviews, were age and tenure.

The team was almost evenly split between 9 people who had been with the team between 20 and 35 years and 8 who had been with the team fewer than 3 years. Historically, it had taken a minimum of 10 years to become a 'senior researcher' and the longer-term employees were insisting that it could be no other way. They had been expected to 'serve their time' and the younger group should too. Furthermore, they believed the work to be so complex that it cannot be learned in fewer than 10 years. The newer individuals were anxious to move up in the company and had no intentions of staying with an organization for 10 years before having their expertise and skills recognized in the form of a 'senior researcher' title.

A series of three day-long sessions were conducted with this team. The first session assigned some hands-on activities, one conducted with an older team and younger team; the other conducted with two teams mixed by tenure. The results were not surprising: the age-segregated teams performed equally; the age-mixed teams outperformed the age-segregated teams. This led to a discussion regarding the values that different levels of tenure, company experience and newer educational experience could bring to problem-solving. The second session focused on discussing the specific tasks required to become a senior researcher, the time required to learn each task, and alternative ways/time frames for learning these tasks. Results of these talks resulted in greater understanding of the complexity of tasks on the part of the younger team members. The older team members were also able to identify places where the learning process could be speeded up as well as a greater appreciation for a commitment of the younger members to gain in-depth understanding. The final session explored—successfully— compromises between the two groups, resulting in older/younger partnerships for the purposes of mentoring and speeding up the time frames for promotion to senior researcher status.

There are several interesting observations about this case study. First, the team was open to intervention because they had attended a diversity awareness training session that led them to believe they could resolve their differences. Second, the problem initially identified by the manager was not the problem identified by the team when they were included in assessment interviews. And finally, because the team had gained tools during diversity training, they were able to appreciate each other across age/tenure differences, and to identify solutions that left every team member feeling valued and more able to contribute to the organization.

CONCLUSIONS

The cases described in this chapter help to illustrate the many elements involved in approaching diversity training. An expanding global marketplace and the demographic changes occurring in workforces all over the world, suggest how important it is for organizations to learn more about diversity issues, determine the need for diversity training programmes, and select the programme and a provider that are suitable for achieving organizational goals.

REFERENCES

Bennett, J. (1994). *Balancing Content and Process*. Portland, Oregon: Intercultural Communication Institute.

DiversityInc. Best Practices for Diversity (2001). See website: www.DiversityInc.com

Executive Diversity Services, Inc. (2000). The business case and best practices for implementing diversity initiatives. Unpublished paper, available from www.executivediversity.com (Seattle, Wash.).

Gudykunst, W.B., Guzley, R.M. & Hammer, M.R. (1996). Designing intercultural training. Chapter 4 in Dan Landis & Rabi S. Bhagat (eds), *Handbook of Intercultural Training*, 2nd edn. Thousand Oaks, Calif.: Sage Publication.

Paige, R.M. (1988). *Risk Factors in Cross Cultural Training*. Minneapolis: University of Minnesota.

Paige, R.M. (ed.) (1993). *Education of the Intercultural Experience*, Yarmouth, Me: Intercultural Press.

Wederspahn, G. (2000). Finding suitable providers. In *Intercultural Services: A Worldwide Buyers' Guide and Sourcebook*. Houston: Gulf Publishing Company.

CHAPTER 15

Diversity Issues in the Mentoring Relationship

David Clutterbuck

European Mentoring Centre and Sheffield Hallam University, Sheffield, UK

SUMMARY

Mentoring is increasingly used to help achieve organizations' diversity management objectives. At one extreme *all* mentoring relationships involve diversity, because learning occurs across the gaps in experience, perspective, influence and ability. However, the more different mentor and mentee are in their backgrounds, the greater the skill required by both parties to make the most of the relationship, especially where the mentee is a member of a relatively disenfranchised group. This chapter explores some of the issues surrounding mentoring across this spectrum of diversity. A more detailed exploration of this topic can be found in the book *Mentoring for Diversity* (Clutterbuck & Ragins, 2001).

INTRODUCTION

A PROBLEM OF DEFINITION

One of the big problems with the vast majority of literature on both mentoring and diversity is that it fails to define precisely what is being studied. Many of the mentoring studies, particularly from North America, do not distinguish between relationships which are in the line (i.e. between supervisor and direct report) and those which are off-line, although the dynamics of these two types of relationship are very different. Others lump together formal and informal relationships, and even those that attempt to distinguish between

Individual Diversity and Psychology in Organizations. Edited by Marilyn J. Davidson and Sandra L. Fielden.
© 2003 John Wiley & Sons, Ltd.

these relationship types usually use very simplistic distinctions that fail to recognize the wide spectrum between formality and informality, into which most mentoring falls. Relationship purpose is also a significant but largely ignored variable.

Studies in diversity often show similar confusion. Is the purpose of an intervention equal opportunities—the enfranchisement of minorities or disadvantaged groups—or is it more about better use of talent?

THE MEANING OF MENTORING

Mentoring is often confused with coaching, counselling, tutoring and other forms of development. In practice, while mentoring shares many behaviours with these roles, it occupies a distinct place in the spectrum of one-on-one development. Coaching largely concerns tasks and skills. Feedback from the coach is an important element in the process, which is largely driven by the coach. Mentoring concerns the development of capability and personal wisdom. It is the mentee who drives the process and provides his or her own feedback, in general. Wisdom, in this sense, is defined as the ability to extrapolate from and apply in new ways the learning one has acquired in the form of information (an output of teaching), knowledge (an output of tutoring) and skills (an output of coaching). The difference between an old man and a sage is that, while both have years of experience, the latter is able to use his or her insights from that experience to help others develop their own insights.

Coaching and mentoring meet at the point where the learner begins to take charge of their own developmental agenda. Counselling is a process for assisting people to understand themselves and their environment, and to cope with the difficulties this poses. At the therapeutic end, it has no crossover with mentoring, but effective *developmental* mentors (for the distinction, see below) will typically involve themselves in helping the learner establish viable coping strategies and career/self-development plans. There is, of course, a cycle of roles here, for the outcome of these mentoring/counselling activities is often a need for coaching in specific skills.

Even within the core of mentoring itself, there are two fundamentally opposing concepts. One, which can be referred to as the *US traditional* or *godfathering* model, starts from an assumption that the focus of the relationship is the mentor's extensive experience and willingness to exercise power and influence on behalf of the mentee (typically called a protégé). It is often characterized by long-term relationships that may involve a degree of mutual dependence. It is also often confused with line management roles and is a hands-on role, where the mentor assumes personal responsibility for the protégé. The very word 'protégé', which derives from the same root as to protect, emphasizes this sense of patronage.

The following is a typical definition of this approach: A mentor is … 'A person who oversees the career and development of another person, usually a junior, through teaching, counselling, providing psychological support, protecting and at times promoting or sponsoring' (Zey, 1984).

In essence, schemes based on this approach to mentoring seek to emulate the 'old boy' networks of privilege. The evidence from a variety of mainly US studies is that it does not translate easily into an environment where the scheme's purpose is to undermine privilege and enfranchise groups previously excluded (e.g. Chao et al., 1992; Fagenson-Eland et al., 1997; Ragins & Cotton, 1999; Viator, 2001).

The second, competing, philosophy of mentoring derives primarily from European experience, but is also evolving in the United States, Canada and Australia. *Developmental mentoring* emphasizes the mentee's role in managing the relationship, and focuses on the achievement of personal insight, intellectual challenge and increasing self-reliance. In formal schemes, the relationship is supported by the organization for a relatively short time—typically two years—after which the mentee moves on, or the relationship becomes less intense and more informal. Developmental mentoring is always an off-line activity, in which the difference in perspective and experience between the two partners is valued as a source of mutual learning. The hierarchical status or power of the mentor is far less important than the learning potential from the relationship—on both sides. There is also scope for peer mentoring and upward mentoring. (Jack Welch, CEO of General Electric, reportedly had an upward mentor, for example.)

The received definition of developmental mentoring is 'Off-line help by one person to another in making significant transitions in knowledge, work or thinking' (Megginson & Clutterbuck, 1995).

In between these two competing philosophies lies a whole mix of approaches, which accommodate mentoring to diverse environments. Some national cultures, such as the UK and Scandinavia, are comfortable with a relatively unstructured, hierarchy-free approach. Other cultures, with high power distance, such as Indonesia or France, prefer for the mentor to be more masterful. The difficulties arise when mentoring occurs across cultural divides. Although corporate culture often has an evening-out effect, there is enormous room for conflict and misunderstanding of role. In an experiment with English and Dutch expatriate mentors and local young engineers (all Western educated) in Brunei (Clutterbuck, 1995), we found that the expectations of how the relationship should be managed were completely opposite. The mentees expected a relationship in which they received a great deal of instruction and personal support; the mentors one where the learner would be self-driven and regard the mentor as a source of intellectual challenge. The solution, in this case, was to encourage mentors and mentees to seek a compromise with which they could both feel comfortable.

Another useful way of looking at developmental mentoring is as a source of personal reflective space (PRS). PRS is a way of describing the inner dialogue (talking to oneself) that happens when people slip into deep thought about one topic, which has been disturbing them for some time. They ask themselves questions from different perspectives, trying better to understand the issue, and very often reach new insights that open up further options to deal with it. In mentoring, the mentee invites a trusted outsider to join in this dialogue. The mentor asks more penetrating questions, challenges assumptions more forcefully, suggests new ways of looking at things, and generally raises the pace and quality of the thinking process.

THE MEANING OF DIVERSITY

In the same way, as discussed throughout this book, diversity has taken on a diversity of meanings. Does it, at one extreme, refer to inadequate access to power for specific groups, based on gender, race or disability? Does it refer more broadly to the management task of integrating and using—to the maximum benefit of the organization and its members— the talents of all employees? Or is it about valuing and exploiting differences in culture, background and personality, perceiving diversity as a source of competitive advantage?

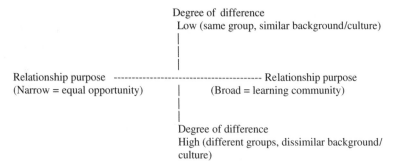

Figure 15.1   Two defining dimensions of diversity programmes

How the organization views diversity will significantly influence the ways in which it applies mentoring and the outcomes it expects.

Figure 15.1 illustrates some of the choices an organization may have to make. The issue of degree of difference is discussed later, but there clearly is a significant variation in the nature and impact of the relationship where the two people have much in common and where they have relatively little in common. The opportunity to create strong rapport is much greater in the former, but the learning potential is smaller, so the relationship is likely to concentrate on psychosocial support (Ragins & Cotton, 1991; Dreher & Cox, 1996). At the other extreme, while high difference in background, experience and culture creates great opportunities for learning, it also makes it difficult to achieve the necessary levels of rapport.

Relationship purpose, as defined by the overall scheme objectives, tends to position the mentoring initiative and people's instinctive reaction to it. On the negative side, both the mentee target group for an equal opportunities mentoring scheme and the intended mentors may resent this overt focus; and a more general scheme may be seen by managers as too 'soft' to be worthy of significant commitment. On the positive side, either focus can be a powerful signal to the organization that change is both desired and required.

MENTORING AS A STRUCTURED APPROACH TO DIVERSIFIED MANAGEMENT

Formal mentoring programmes to support equal opportunities objectives have become an established element of the corporate development portfolio. In particular, many companies have experimented with 'glass ceiling' programmes to support women in overcoming institutional and attitudinal barriers to advancement into middle and senior management. In recent years, however, a range of new diversity applications have emerged. Some enable ethnic groups in multicultural organizations to redefine the balance between corporate culture and the cultural identities people bring with them into the organization. Some attempt to capitalize on the inherent diversity of all employees, encouraging them to respect, value and learn from other people's different perspectives. And some have found new ways to address the inequalities of power in organizational structures, for example by reversing the hierarchy.

As the majority of service organizations become increasingly driven by virtual teams, networks and complex alliances, capitalizing on diversity will become more and more important as a source of competitive advantage. The more diverse an organization is in its cultures, its technologies and its disciplines, the wider the range of responses it can muster to deal with competitive threats and opportunities—as long as the habits of dialogue, knowledge sharing and constructive challenge are well embedded into the systems, practices and the common culture. Mentoring is emerging as one of the most practical and powerful methods of building that organizational competence.

The following examples illustrate some of the wide variety of types of scheme originated recently:

- At An Post, the Irish Post Office, women managers are taking part in an intriguing experiment where mentors are drawn from more senior levels not just within the postal service, but from large companies at either end of the supply chain—both customers and suppliers. The aim is to provide as many as possible different perspectives on the roles to which the women aspire.
- At SAS, the Scandinavian air carrier, structured mentoring began with a programme for women leaders and rapidly diversified to meet the needs of a variety of other groups. People are encouraged to seek a mentor from a different nationality or culture, a different gender or someone younger than themselves. The vast majority (95 per cent) of these relationships have found that the inbuilt diversity gives the relationship an extra dynamism and helps to sustain the interest of both parties.
- At the World Bank, some 2000 mentoring pairs have been set up, almost all at the instigation of groups of people from the same geographical regions. In each case, they have recognized the value in both networking together and creating close developmental relationships with people outside their natural groups.
- At Procter and Gamble (P&G), a planned traditional glass ceiling approach—in which powerful male executives would adopt more junior female managers, to 'groom' them for promotion—was abandoned in favour of relationships where the executives became the mentees and the more junior women became the mentors. The programme had as one of its objectives overcoming a much higher labour turnover among women managers than among men—a goal which has now been achieved. The executive mentees have gained significant insights into diversity issues in general, and a greater empathy with the issues female employees face. Given that most of P&G's customers are women, this empathy is inevitably reflected in marketing policy.
- At the Cabinet Office in the UK, an innovative programme of leadership development provides mentors for civil servants with disabilities ranging from blindness, and loss of limbs to schizophrenia.

SOME KEY ISSUES IN DIVERSIFIED MENTORING

STRUCTURING THE MENTORING SCHEME

As the volume of diversity mentoring schemes grows, it becomes easier to identify good practice from those that succeed and fail. Some of the critical lessons we have observed include the following.

The importance of clear purpose

One multinational service organization recently required its European operations to provide mentors for all women staff above a certain level. Matches were made by diktat, lunch appointments made—and mentor and mentee sat there wondering what they were supposed to do. Most of these intended relationships never got off the ground because there was no clarity about roles, nor about expected outcomes. Successful programmes always ensure that everyone involved is clear about what is expected in terms of behaviour and outcome, for mentee, mentor and the organization.

Understanding the perspective of the intended audience

Many programmes founder because they fail to take into account the wishes of the potential mentees. A public sector organization found that a much-publicized programme aimed at racial minorities attracted a good supply of mentors but very few mentees. Feedback from the intended audience revealed that they were unhappy about being targeted in this way, because it suggested that there was something wrong with them. A similar story emerges from a large engineering company, where an intended mentoring programme for women was radically changed after consultation with them. The women argued that this would devalue the process, because it would be seen as a remedial programme. Instead, they wanted (and got) a programme for any employee, but one which women were encouraged to join.

Being realistic about numbers

A common issue for mentoring programmes in general is how to balance quality against quantity. While on the one hand, it is unrealistic to expect most line managers to have the developmental competence of a professional mentor, a poor mentor can have a devastating effect on the mentee and on other people, too. Very few companies have successfully implemented an 'allcomers' programme and even in those that have succeeded, finding enough effective mentors is a continuing headache.

This has an immediate impact on the numbers that can be helped at any one time. The programme designers therefore need to think through clearly who are the priority audiences, who might be the most appropriate mentors for them and how supply is likely to affect demand. In general, people with real jobs in the organization can rarely cope with more than three formal mentoring relationships.

Scarcity becomes even more of an issue when mentees seek mentors from the same gender or racial group. By definition, these are likely to be fewer in number at the higher levels in the organization. The management of expectations therefore becomes a significant influence on the reputation and success of the programme.

The need for choice

Even more than for mentoring in general, diversity mentoring relationships demand that both parties *want* to be there. Where the mentor perceives there to be strong reciprocal benefits from exploring and understanding other perspectives, the relationship tends to be much more successful than when the mentor is either reluctant, or simply trying to be altruistic. There is also some evidence that mentees tend to be more proactive when they have exercised some choice in the selection of their mentor. Good practice appears to be that mentees are guided in their selection, but left to make up their own minds.

The need for training

Again, even more than for mentoring in general, diversity mentoring demands that mentors and mentees clearly understand their roles, responsibilities and the context in which the relationship operates. Successful diversity training programmes typically spend time on both developing mentoring competence and raising awareness of the relevant diversity issues. Key topics for the latter include the nature of group disempowerment, how stereotyping occurs, and basic differences between how different cultures or genders may approach the same issues.

POWER AND EMPOWERMENT

Because people may have different expectations about tapping into the mentor's power and influence, it is critical to ensure that both parties come to a shared understanding about what is and is not appropriate. Really effective developmental mentors manage to 'park' the power issues and work with the mentee to develop his or her own ability to influence their environment. By helping the learner grow in self-resourcefulness—for example, through building their networking capability—the mentor gives them a lasting advantage. Mentors, who actively use their influence on behalf of the learner, are in essence *disempowering* them in terms of being able to achieve under their own steam.

In a developmental context, an acceptable definition of power is *the ability to make desirable outcomes happen*. Power is thus a mixture of personal competence and the quality of one's connection with the working environment. The mentor in a diversity programme, therefore, enfranchises the mentee by helping them develop a greater mastery of their environment—which usually begins with an understanding of the barriers, both internal and external, to their achievement.

BALANCING DIFFERENCE AND SIMILARITY

A recurring issue is whether it is better for the mentee and mentor to come from the same diversity group. Table 15.1 puts some of the arguments into context. In summary, it seems that each case needs to be examined on its individual merits and that en masse solutions will generally be inappropriate.

A practical case is Tricia, who wanted to become an HR director. She needed to learn how to think and behave like a director, but without compromising the feminine qualities that underlay her effectiveness as an HR professional. Because she had no female role model to work with inside the organization, she found one outside—a former CEO. Once she achieved her promotion, she dissolved that relationship and established a new one, this time with a highly experienced, male HR director, who had 'seen and done it all'. In this case, gender was irrelevant to her choice.

TABLE 15.1 Same group mentoring: the pros and cons

Issue	For	Against
Perspective	Greater empathy with mentee's issues and experiences Research suggests higher levels of psychosocial support in same race mentoring than cross-race More role modelling occurs between same gender pairs than cross-gender	More difficult to help mentee take different or broader perspective Research suggests career outcomes for mentees are less satisfactory than in cross-race mentoring
Networking	Same race/gender networks can be more close-knit and sociable	Mentee's and mentor's networks may be too similar to add value to the relationship
Power (where same group mentors are not well represented in the higher levels of the hierarchy)	Easier to establish rapport when the authority/hierarchy gap is relatively small	Mentors are likely to have less insight into politics and prospects
Relationship purpose	Favours relatively new developmental objectives	Favours relatively broad development objectives

Source: From Clutterbuck, D. (1995). *Mentoring and Diversity.* Reprinted by permission of Butterworth Heinemann.

MANAGING STEREOTYPES

Stereotyping is a common issue (although not always recognized as such) in both same group and cross-group mentoring relationships. In same group relationships, mentor and mentee may share stereotypes, and therefore not question them. In cross-group mentoring, either or both party may be making assumptions that unconsciously limit the potential of the mentee.

A critical issue here is the extent to which the perceived disadvantage acts as the focus of the relationship. At one extreme, we have the example of the mentor who pointedly never referred to the problems encountered by a wheelchair-bound mentee, with the (unintended) result that the mentee felt increasingly patronized. At the other extreme, relationships that place a disadvantage at the core of discussions have a poor record of helping people set and achieve ambitious goals. Again, a balance is needed to allow people to put their disadvantage into perspective and concentrate on what they can achieve and how. One of the most helpful things a mentor can do is help the mentee construct a realistic 'bank balance' of advantages and disadvantages they have in the workplace. When multiple factors are taken into account, including education, experience, personality, class and so on, the mentee can work on a much more rounded picture and balance building on strengths against coping with weaknesses.

Among the insights that effective diversity mentoring pairs tend to share are that:

• They do (both) have stereotypes
• Even benevolent stereotypes (such as 'Women are better at "soft" management tasks') can limit people's ability to achieve

• Recognizing and being open about stereotypes is the most effective way of dealing with them

The mentee's own stereotypes may be a prime barrier to achievement. Various experiments in recent years have demonstrated that people relapse easily into unconscious stereotypes. It appears, for example, that defining a scheme as aimed at helping black people may actually stimulate stereotypical behaviour in the black mentee, when s/he is faced with a white mentor. The issues the mentor addresses are then shaped by the observed behaviour, distorting and devaluing the mentoring process.

The key, of course, is the development of deep trust and genuine, open dialogue. Where the relationship works, these two aspects seem to grow together. In cross-group mentoring, the more the mentor can demonstrate a personal interest in understanding and learning from and about the mentee's world, the easier it is to develop trust and dialogue.

MEASURING OUTCOMES

Practical experience in designing mentoring programmes of all kinds indicates that, far from constraining relationships, clear expectations about outcomes provide both focus and energy. Establishing the measurement processes alongside these expectations provides an additional boost ('what gets measured gets done'). This is not about setting up bureaucratic procedures—paradoxically, we find that having a strong shared perception of objectives and priorities encourages mentor and mentee to adopt a high level of informality, because they do not have to worry about why they are there or whether they are doing the right thing. Mentees report they are much less concerned about taking their mentors' time in these circumstances, whereas when there is less clarity about role and purpose, they may be reluctant to do so.

Measurement is usually needed for three reasons:

• To provide immediate help and guidance to relationships that are not working
• To gather information on the operation of the programme, with a view to continuous improvement
• To demonstrate that the programme is working and worthwhile

Many mentors and mentees are reluctant to confront the issue of whether their relationship is working. Each fears rejection, and understandably so. In training before relationships begin, it should always be impressed upon participants that they have a responsibility towards each other to discuss openly the quality of the relationship, at some point within the first three meetings. The initial, rapport-building stages of the relationship therefore become a form of probation (sometimes called a trial marriage), the outcome of which may be that the mentee needs a different kind of mentor, or none at all. The mentor also has an opportunity to withdraw, if s/he feels uncomfortable in the role. If a split is agreed, the mentor may help in the search for a replacement. It is quite common for relationships which have been terminated in this way to reassert themselves some time later, when the mentee has matured.

The scheme coordinator's role includes making sure that each pair has had this dialogue and, where necessary, helping them prepare for it, or rehearse it, or even sitting in as a facilitator in extreme cases. (Obviously, the latter involves issues of confidentiality.)

After about six months, it is useful to review how relationships are progressing, typically with telephone or questionnaire responses from all participants. In particular, bringing mentors back together again to discuss the results reinforces the programme and provides an opportunity for further training.

Both of these types of measurement are aimed at the *process*. Evaluation at the end of the first year—or at a suitable date when significant progress might reasonably be expected to have occurred—is typically aimed at *outcomes*. This is where measurement takes on a harder edge. Outcomes measured might include:

- Retention of people in the target group(s) v. retention of employees overall
- Promotions of people in the target groups
- Changes in competency scores as measured in annual appraisals
- Proportion of people with a personal development plan
- Participants' perception of their own improvements in confidence, stress management or work/life balance . . . and so on

It is also helpful for the mentoring pair to conduct their own review about the same time (even better if it can be used to feed into the overall programme review). Many relationships have by this time achieved some or all of their initial objectives and a decision must be made as to whether to focus on new objectives or to celebrate success and move on. Failure to have this discussion often leads to a gradual drift away on the part of the mentee, leaving the mentor unsure whether they have done a good or a poor job—an uncertainty that may affect their willingness to take on the role again.

Good practice in measurement and review recognizes that the programme will be strengthened by identifying the positive (and negative) outcomes of the relationship to *all* the parties involved—the mentee, the mentor, the organization and significant third parties, such as the mentee's line manager, who also has a stake in the process.

SUSTAINING THE DIVERSIFIED MENTORING PROGRAMME

A high proportion of all mentoring programmes fade away. Surprisingly, there has been very little research into the reasons why some flourish and others do not. The observations that follow, therefore, are based on field experience, with no attempt at quantitative analysis.

A key factor in sustainability appears to be the nature of the top-level support. Some of the most successful programmes have been those where the chief executive plays an active role and is prepared to talk to participants about his or her experiences as a mentee. However, chief executives move on and, if they are the sole champion, the programme loses momentum. Involving as many as possible of the top 50 in the programme, both as participants and as contributors to the design and management process, provides a cushion against such change. Keeping these people in the loop about the benefits the programme is producing for the organization helps as well.

A strong caucus of support from mentors can be built up through *developers' clubs*. These are a means of rewarding managers who contribute significantly to developing others, by inviting them to discuss development issues with top management once or twice a year. Mentors report that this provides the role with a sense of status, that encourages them to continue.

A strong coordinator, with sufficient time allocated to help new mentors and mentees get started, is also important. Participants need a central source for advice and reminders. The coordinator can at the same time gain greater influence by gradually letting go of direct control over key processes, such as matching. Instead of finding mentors for mentees, the coordinator can provide an on-line process that guides their choices and brings in help from the centre only on request.

An expectation that mentees will become mentors in turn also helps sustain the process. So does using previous mentors and mentees as ambassadors for the programme.

Finally, the coordinator and the top management champions must be prepared to evolve and adapt the programme to changing needs. Some initially productive glass ceiling programmes have died, because they failed to adapt to changing perceptions about whether they should focus solely on women, for example, or should expand to include men. Being in tune with the current needs of the organization is essential.

Some companies have solved this problem by acknowledging that the resource for formal mentoring is limited, and selecting every two years or so which specific target audiences they will focus on. They work hard to ensure that audiences which will lose their priority status have the concept of mentoring sufficiently ingrained that people will continue or seek out informal relationships.

It can be argued that the presence of a thriving informal mentoring network within an organization is the best guarantee of continuation for formal mentoring. Formal, organizationally supported mentoring provides the training ground for subsequent informal relationships, and people who have enjoyed one role often embrace the other with enthusiasm.

CONCLUSIONS

ISSUES FOR FURTHER RESEARCH

In current research, we are trying to develop an expectation-based model of mentoring relationships, which begins with how the context and environment of the relationship affect the behaviours and outcomes participants expect. The model goes on to examine how expectations affect behaviour and how behaviour affects outcomes—a complex process which can only be understood (if then) through a longitudinal study. In developing this research project, we have uncovered an array of issues where knowledge is at best scanty. Many of these have particular relevance to diversified mentoring. For example:

- How do successful mentoring pairs park the power issues?
- How can we measure the *quality* of mentoring relationships?
- When is it best to have a same group mentor or a mentor from a different background?
- How do the mentee's stereotypes affect their expectations and ambitions; and what can the mentor do to help the mentee deal with these issues?
- How can mentors be helped to recognize and deal with their own stereotypes?

What we do know, from both fieldwork and the limited amount of specific research in these areas, is that the attitude of the participants is a critical factor. The willingness to accept the other person as having a legitimate point of view and set of experiences; the perception that the mentoring relationship is a valuable opportunity to learn, for both mentor and mentee; and the courage to be genuinely open, enquiring and, when necessary, confronting—these are all essential elements of the fully effective diversified mentoring relationship. Whether we expect *all* diversified mentoring relationships to meet these attitudinal criteria is a matter for debate; for many organizations, *any* sharing of perspective and understanding is a step forward. One of the key areas of research data that we lack is any kind of comparative evaluation of the impact of diversified mentoring at the programmes—what do highly successful programmes do and what do they expect of participants, compared to less successful ones?

Like every mentoring pair, we have so much to learn!!

REFERENCES

Chao, G.T., Walz, P. M. & Gardner, P.D. (1992). Formal and informal mentorships: a comparison on mentoring functions and contrast with nonmentored counterparts. *Personnel Psychology*, **45**, 619–636.

Clutterbuck, D. (1995). Mentoring in a multicultural environment, *Proceedings of the 2nd European Mentoring Centre Conference*, Sheffield Business School.

Clutterbuck, D. & Ragins, B.R. (2001). *Mentoring for Diversity: An International Perspective*, Oxford: Butterworth Heinemann.

Dreher, G.F. & Cox, T.H. (1996). Race, gender and opportunity: a study of compensation attainment and the establishment of mentoring relationships. *Journal of Applied Psychology*, **81**(3), 297–308.

Fagenson-Eland, E.A., Marks, M.A. & Amendola, K.L. (1997). Perceptions of mentoring relationships. *Journal of Vocational Behavior*, **51**, 29–42.

Megginson, D. & Clutterbuck, D. (1995). *Mentoring in Action*. London: Kogan Page.

Ragins, B.R. & Cotton, J.L. (1991) Easier said than done: gender differences in perceived barriers to gaining a mentor. *Academy of Management Journal*, **34**(4), 939–951.

Ragins, B.R. & Cotton, J.L. (1999). Mentor functions and outcomes: a comparison of men and women in formal and informal mentoring relationships. *Journal of Applied Psychology*, **84**(4), 529–550.

Viator, R. (2001). An examination of African-Americans access to public accounting mentors: perceived barriers and intentions to leave. Manuscript submitted for publication.

Zey, M.G. (1984). *The Mentor Connection*. Homewood, Ill.: Irwin.

CHAPTER 16

Networking and the Modernization of Local Public Services: Implications for Diversity

Jean Hartley and Lyndsay Rashman

Warwick Business School, University of Warwick, UK

SUMMARY

This chapter argues that public service organizations are an important location in which to examine issues of diversity (here focusing on gender and ethnicity), in part because public sector organizations employ large numbers of women (and to a lesser extent minorities), and in part because they have explicit values about equalities which are not simply pragmatic but are also based on democratic concerns. The chapter then turns to examine local government specifically and argues that diversity has been undertheorized in the major period of organizational and cultural change which is currently taking place, which includes networking within and between organizations as a crucial element of change. Diversity concerns three sets of issues: equalities of representation, equalities of employment and equalities of service delivery. The modernization agenda (i.e. major public sector reforms) appears to be having differential impacts in particular arenas of activity, and there are some tensions between different elements. The final section of the chapter examines networking as a key part of inter-agency working, which is a significant development in local government organizations. There are several reasons for caution in the view that networking is a force for improvement in diversity opportunities. Some of the social and organizational psychology literature suggests that networking can lead to the concentration of power. However, in spite of this caution, some means whereby networking can be used to help enhance equalities in representation, employment and access to services are explored.

Individual Diversity and Psychology in Organizations. Edited by Marilyn J. Davidson and Sandra L. Fielden.
© 2003 John Wiley & Sons, Ltd.

INTRODUCTION

Contrary to the stereotype, public service organizations are fascinating locations in which to examine issues of gender and diversity, especially during periods of organizational and cultural change.

The stereotype is based on the argument that publicly owned organizations are automatically more bureaucratic, less efficient, less innovative and less creative than private sector organizations. What can be learnt from public service organizations? Surely it would be more valuable to search out those private sector companies which are leading edge in terms of their human resource management (HRM) policies and practices if we want to understand the changing demands on and roles of women and minorities in the workplace?

Well, no. The stereotype is a legacy of a period of neo-liberal or even monetarist economics, which has often failed to take account of some wider issues of organizational functioning, sustainability, organizational purpose and efficiencies as seen by a wide range of stakeholders. There are a number of very important reasons why examining the developments occurring in the public service sector is of wider relevance in discussions of gender and diversity. We therefore begin by setting the scene in terms of employment and the functions of public services. We will concentrate particularly on the public services of local government (called state and local government in the USA), as this is the context from which our empirical data are drawn.

The first point to note is that public services are big business in both employment and capital assets. Taking employment as an indicator, there are over 5 million employees in the public sector in the UK (MacGregor, 2001). In a workforce of over 29 million, this is 17.6 per cent, or over one in six of the workforce. Even in the USA, with its 'market' approach to democracy and employment, the figures are still substantial at 15 per cent of the workforce. Thus on straightforward numbers and proportions terms the public sector is worth taking seriously (Flynn, 1997).

The numbers employed in the public sector are also growing, albeit modestly. While employment had declined in the public sector in the UK in the previous 20-year period, there has more recently been a slight increase. In 1999 and 2000 this was of 93 000 jobs, or 1.9 per cent per year (MacGregor, 2001). The private sector increase over the same period was 0.3 per cent per year. Education and the National Health Service, where about a third of public sector jobs are located, have shown the most increase—nearly as high as in the private service sector (12.3 per cent for education, 11.4 per cent for health compared with 15.5 per cent for private sector service jobs over the decade, MacGregor, 2001). Nearly half of all public sector jobs are in local government. Table 16.1 illustrates these trends over time.

TABLE 16.1   Public sector and local government employment in the UK (employment by thousands)

	1981	1991	1998	2000
Total workforce	26 000	28 920	28 498	29 011
Public sector	7 185	5 848	4 944	5 093
Local government	2 899	2 947	2 579	2 690

Source: Derived from MacGregor (2001, p. 36).

TABLE 16.2   Employment in local government by gender in 2001

	Male		Female	
	No. (thousands)	Percentage	No. (thousands)	Percentage
Full-time	490	44	618	56
Part-time	130	12	928	88
Total	620	29	1546	71

Source: Figures derived from the Local Government Employers' Organization Survey (2001).

These figures show that public services employment is a substantial and growing part of the economy. The public service sector has traditionally employed large numbers of women and minorities, for a range of reasons including more flexible and part-time employment terms and conditions (Geddes, 2001). Employment in the public sector can also contribute significantly to economic regeneration (Geddes, 2001), especially where other employment opportunities are weak.

The public sector also employs a high proportion of women and minorities[1] compared with the private sector. For example, as shown in Table 16.2, women constitute 71 per cent of the workforce in local government compared with 45 per cent in the economy as a whole (Equal Opportunities Commission, 2000; Local Government Employers' Organization, 2001). Women outnumber men in both full-time and part-time work. The effect is most pronounced among employees working part-time. Comparable figures on ethnicity are harder to obtain and interpret. Eighty-two per cent of local authorities report that they have established mechanisms for collecting data about ethnicity on more than three-quarters of their staff and applicants and 64 per cent report these statistics annually. The government, as a response to the Stephen Lawrence inquiry (Macpherson, 1999) (see Chapter 12 for more detail) has proposed to strengthen workforce monitoring by requiring local government councils to compare their workforce profile with the ethnic profile of the local population. There is still some way to go to obtain reliable ethnicity data in local government (Owens, 2001).

The trends for employment also suggest that the future is female. The growth of jobs in the service sector (whether public or private) has created more opportunities for women, especially for those prepared to work part-time (Institute for Employment Research, 2001). Female employment is predicted to grow by 1.5 million across all sectors in the period to 2010 (with health and education growing by 4 per cent). This employment trend is found across the industrialized world. In the USA, it is reported that US businesses were 'startled' in 1987 by the Workforce 2000 report that in the new millennium the majority of US workers (across all sectors) would be women and non-white males (cited in Lorbiecki & Jack, 2000).

There are further reasons for an interest in the public sector in terms of gender and diversity. The public sector has explicit values about equalities. Originally, this was couched in terms of equal opportunities, but more recently has been described as equalities or as diversity. This is more than the competitive advantage sometimes described as the driving force behind the equalities elements of HRM in the private sector (see for example, Cassell, 2001). For many public service organizations in the UK, the espoused values (Argyris, 1999) of equalities have been articulated in policy statements, policies, practices and for some an Equal Opportunities Unit (or similar) for many years (e.g. Rashman, 1991; Holder, 1995; Thobani, 1995). Here, diversity is pursued not solely as a pragmatic concern but also as a set of values about democracy, equality of access to services and equality of employment.

There has been a succession of models in use in local government, from equal opportunities, based on a principle of 'sameness', diversity management, which emphasizes 'difference' (Lorbiecki & Jack, 2000) to more recent emphasis on social inclusion, but their success in effecting organizational change has been questioned (Lorbiecki & Jack, 2000; Newman, 2001a). In addition, as mentioned earlier in Chapter 12, a high profile case of racial discrimination by police in London led to a wide-ranging inquiry about 'institutional racism' in that police force. The resulting Macpherson Report (1999) has been used by a range of public service organizations to examine how far representation, employment and service delivery are based on equal treatment. The Race Relations (Amendment) Act places a new statutory duty on public bodies to promote racial equality and to eliminate discrimination in public services. These issues provide a different lens with which to view diversity in the context of organizational change, compared with the private sector.

The public sector is also relatively well unionized (both in the UK and USA) compared with the private sector, and although trade unions may struggle with the practicalities of equalities as much as any other organization (Cockburn, 1989), their values of collective and individual representation support equalities and diversity, to a certain extent. For both trade union and organizational reasons, public sector organizations have been prepared to make explicit their values about diversity. Elsewhere, we have argued that research into public sector organizations can be valuable in making explicit processes which may be more occluded in the private sector, such as political processes or the roles and interests of different stakeholders in organizational performance (Hartley, 2000; see also Brunsson, 1985; Scott, 2001).

Finally, a reason for being interested in public service organizations is that they are currently undergoing major change, including in some cases restructuring, reform and 'modernization'. Public service managers in the UK describe more change occurring than do their private sector counterparts (Worrall & Cooper, 1998). We turn to analyse the kinds of changes which are occurring and the demands that these are making on public sector leaders, managers and staff.

ORGANIZATIONAL CHANGE IN THE PUBLIC SECTOR

The local government modernization agenda is typical of many of the changes taking place across the public service sector. It is part of the current British government's ambitious programme of reform in the structures and processes of governance and of service delivery. The intention is to shift the centre of gravity beyond the state and towards civil society, including active participation and engagement of users, citizens and communities (Benington, 2000). In addition, the aim is to develop 'joined-up' working between different tiers and spheres of governance (local, regional, national and European). The third key element in the modernization agenda is the emergence of networked governance (in addition to hierarchies and markets), with the aim that there should be new patterns of leadership and the management of influence through interorganizational networks and partnerships. Networks are expected to operate between different public agencies and also between the public, private and voluntary sectors (Benington & Harvey, 1999; Pettigrew & Fenton, 2001).

Much of the literature about equal opportunities which emerged in the latter part of the twentieth century was based on an analysis of hierarchical organizations. The emphasis on networking as a form of governance and service delivery raises new opportunities and constraints on gender and ethnicity which deserve to be analysed and understood. The shift in emphasis from hierarchical modes of decision-making towards

TABLE 16.3 A framework for the local government modernization agenda (LGMA)

Perceived problems	Central government's solutions	Desired outcomes
Leadership and legitimacy		
Localities lack a clear sense of direction	Cabinets and directly elected mayors Separation of executive and representative roles Community planning	A vision for the whole community Recognized leaders Strong leadership Clear accountability Better quality of life
Need for a new democratic legitimacy	Make it easier to vote Consultation, engagement and participation	Increased voter turnout Revitalized local democracy More stability in council funding Improved local financial accountability
Need for a new ethical framework	New framework of standards of conduct	Respect from citizens Support from partners
Quality and integration of services, and accountability		
Lack of coherence and of vertical and horizontal integration to deliver local services to meet the cross-cutting needs of users, citizens and communities	More 'joined-up' government Partnership working New community leadership powers for councils	Shared vision Harnessing the energies of local people and organizations Integrated delivery through information and communication technologies (e.g. e-government) Ability to deal with cross-cutting issues
Quality of services too variable	Put the needs of service users ahead of service providers Universal inspection Beacon Councils	Quality services for all Clear service standards Spread of good practice
Some councils failing to deliver acceptable standards of service	Best Value Universal inspection New powers for central government to act on service failures Local Public Service Agreements	Continuous improvement of services More say for service users Increased flexibilities for well-performing local councils

Source: Hartley et al. (2000).

consultative policy-making with diverse stakeholders suggests complex dynamics of leadership through influence, persuasion and coordination. Diversity management, formerly confined to single institution policy, practice and culture will present challenges to partnerships that cross traditional organizational boundaries.

The issues which central and local government are attempting to address with the Local Government Modernization Agenda (LGMA) have been summarized (Hartley et al., 2000) and are shown in Table 16.3. Some of the perceived problems (for example, legitimacy, accountability, improving the quality and integration of services) are shared with other public services such as health and criminal justice services (e.g. Benington, 2000; Newman, 2001b). The proposed solutions are here primarily concerned with local government.

The focus here is to explore the impact of the very dramatic, widespread and intended transformational changes on gender and diversity (see also Davies & Thomas, 2000; Newman, 2001a).

Newman (2001b) suggests that the UK government since 1997 has been somewhat gender-blind, and that this applies also to minority awareness. Paradoxically, the emphasis within the government on being 'in touch with the people' (the title of the 1998 White Paper on local government) appears to be based on a relatively undifferentiated concept of 'the people'. In part, this has been explained through the source of policy-making: 'In Downing Street's inner sanctum, the occupants are predominantly young, male, white graduates: a generation who grew up feeling that the gender issue was sorted (perhaps by their own mothers) and are inclined to think feminism is yesterday's politics' (Coote, cited in Newman, 2001b: 9).

The key dimensions of the LGMA—networks and partnerships, stakeholder consultation and the invigoration of local democracy—aim to widen participation and inclusion but have tended to use broad concepts of community, rather than emphasizing diversity and difference. There is a risk that, rather than create a radical alternative, the modernization of public services may reproduce gendered and racialized notions of organization.

As we examine the impacts of organizational and cultural change in local government, in part as a result of the LGMA, we assess the diversity impacts in a number of areas.

DIVERSITY IN THE PUBLIC SECTOR

Much of the debate about diversity, particularly from an HRM or an organizational behaviour perspective, has tended to focus on employment as a key indicator of equalities. While this is significant (and has been touched on in the previous section), diversity in the public sector means much more than this. There are at least three sets of issues. First are the issues about *equalities of representation*. These concern the role of elected representatives in the democratic process. How well are women and minority groups represented in the democratic chambers, whether at national, regional or local level? The second set of issues concerns *equalities of employment*. This is the area familiar to HR researchers and practitioners. What are the proportions of employees, both managerial and non-managerial, who are employed by the organization, and what are the barriers and opportunities for employing a diverse workforce? The arguments for equalities in this area have been well rehearsed in the private sector and are applicable also in the public and voluntary sectors.

The third set of concerns is with *equalities of service delivery*. In other words, what are the diversity concerns about how services are distributed and delivered? This is a crucial issue for many public service organizations, and has prompted, in several organizations, the employment of a monitoring officer or unit concerned to examine the distribution of services according particularly to gender and to ethnicity. This is because public service organizations, as a matter of policy and of faith, are committed to service provision according to need rather than according to ability to pay (the market mechanism for access to services in the private sector).

EQUALITIES OF REPRESENTATION

In examining equalities of representation, we explore both formal and informal political institutions and processes. There is an argument that elected representatives need to be as diverse as the populations they represent (e.g. Local Government Employers' Organization, 2001; Newman, 2001b) if democracy is to thrive. This is not to suggest that elected representatives can only speak for those who share a similar background, identity or experience. Part of the skill and role of an elected representative is to be able to understand, articulate and act as an advocate for a variety of groups and identities. However, across the political chamber (Parliament, regional assembly or local council), a failure to reflect diversity is likely to reduce the quality and variety of debate and to reduce legitimacy in the eyes of constituents. For example, research with young people has indicated that democratic engagement appears to be declining and that part of the reason is attributable to conventional party politicians in both national and local government being seen as irrelevant—'men in suits' (Geddes & Rust, 2000). Improving the image of government is crucial if more people are to be encouraged to participate in local democracy, including standing for election. Under the current British government, with its emphasis on public participation, i.e. direct as well as representative democracy, we also need to consider how traditionally marginalized, diverse voices can be heard in the political debates and other political processes (Newman, 2001a, b).

The evidence on formal politics is initially not very encouraging, though there are some promising developments. At the local level, in a survey undertaken in 1997 in England and Wales, diversity was limited (Canavon & Smith, 2001). Of 21 276 councillors (i.e. elected officials) who replied to the survey (just under half the councillor population), 97.5 per cent described themselves as white and only 2.5 per cent as non-white (compared with 6 per cent of the UK population). Under 5 per cent of councillors from minorities were women.

In addition, 73 per cent of councillors were male and only 27 per cent were female (i.e. only half as many women councillors as one might expect from the population). The proportion of women councillors varied substantially from council to council, with the lowest percentage being 5 per cent and the highest being 55 per cent. The numbers of women entering politics has been rising over a number of years, but the turnover rates for women councillors are high. The Chair of the Local Government Association Equalities Committee has commented that an alarmingly high number of councillors are standing down within or at the end of their first term of office (*Municipal Journal*, 2001).

Two-thirds of councillors (66 per cent) had no caring responsibilities (either children or elderly parents). The numbers in employment (53 per cent) were slightly higher than the percentage in the UK population in employment (about 43 per cent). The average age of councillors was calculated to be 55.6 years—with a small proportion of councillors under the age of 30 (Canavon & Smith, 2001).

What might be the impact of modernization on the diversity of councillors? Those initiatives with most impact on councillors include new political arrangements, community leadership and e-governance. New political arrangements, required by legislation, mean that the vast majority of councils (except those serving small populations) have to separate their executive and scrutiny functions (DETR, 1998; Davis & Geddes, 2000). On the one hand, such arrangements are intended to clarify the roles and decision-making of local councillors, and this could help in terms of the diversity of councillors, making it easier for new councillors to learn and contribute. On the other hand, the empirical evidence so far suggests that the new arrangements are leading to a concentration of power in the hands of the executive (compared with the controlling group or full council). The most recent survey, undertaken in 2001 when local government councils were in transition (some having brought in new arrangements, with others still considering what structures to create or how to introduce change) showed that male councillors dominated the executive roles, with 88 per cent of leaders and 82 per cent of deputy leaders being male (Canavon & Smith, 2001). Only 23 per cent of executive or chair posts were held by women. Less than 2 per cent of ethnic minority councillors were in executive positions. While the directly elected mayor option for new political arrangements has turned out to be less popular than the government originally anticipated, few of the names being canvassed for the position are either women or from minority backgrounds. Some councils with diverse populations have argued that the elected mayor option is likely to be seen as highly divisive. Overall, the new political arrangements appear to have narrowed rather than widened diversity.

On the other hand, the interest in e-government may provide new opportunities for women and minorities. For those outside traditional power networks, electronic communication provides avenues to share experiences and to lobby for change (Tsagarousianou et al., 1998; Hartley & Benington, 1999). The fastest growing user group of information and communication technologies is older women. Electronic networking between women and ethnic minorities, and the wider electronic distribution and scrutiny of cabinet documents, could enhance diversity.

In addition, there have been some advances in terms of the selection (by political parties) and election of women and minorities in some of the new forms of regional governance resulting from devolution. The Welsh Assembly, the Scottish Parliament and the Greater London Authority all have a higher proportion of women and minorities than either national or municipal/local government. In the Welsh Assembly 41 per cent of Assembly Members are women.

This is attributed to a number of equalities-related processes including the selection process, being offered a 'winnable' seat, and the voting system (proportional representation). In the case of the Welsh Assembly, this also included a system of 'twinning' of constituencies. For the Labour Party selection process, there were two panels of prospective candidates, one of men and one of women. Each party member involved in selection had two votes (for one man and one woman) and the candidate with the highest vote was entitled to choose which of the two constituencies they would stand for, and the other constituency then had the person of opposite gender for their candidate. In addition, for the Assembly selection process, all panels were given training in interviewing and selection to reduce selection bias.

Brown et al. (1999) suggest a number of mechanisms to enhance diversity of representation (not only gender but also ethnicity, age and other characteristics). These include the voting system, promoting the role of the councillor, party selection procedures, induction and training for new councillors, mentoring and support networks, improving the allowances (remuneration) for councillors, providing better and greater administrative support, reviewing the hours and times of meetings, and also challenging and shifting the political culture of many councils and political chambers, which some (whatever their characteristics) have found intimidating and confusing.

Issues of representation are not only about the identification, recruitment and support of elected representatives. There are barriers to remaining a councillor. A recent survey (Canavon & Smith, 2001) reported that councillors found time pressures, a sense of marginalization, the centralization of power, the pressures to conform to party policy, the council culture, the lack of appropriate role models and the negative image of local government in the public mind as factors which made them unwilling to stand for re-election. This is particularly an issue for younger councillors and also for women and minorities.

So far, we have considered the issue of equalities of representation in terms of formal politics based on elected representatives. However, there are two further forms of politics which we need to consider here: the role of quangos (i.e. quasi-autonomous non-governmental organizations) and the role of public participation. The last two decades in particular have seen the rise of the 'quango state' (Skelcher, 1998). There are a large number of appointments of 'the great and the good' to public agencies, boards and task forces by the government of the day. These are to some extent, the networks of individuals rather than the networks of organizations to provide public services. There are suggestions, though little empirical data, that the current government has drawn from a wider range of people in its appointments (Newman, 2001a). However, as quangos can be considered to be governance through elites, there is some concern about the unelected and unaccountable nature of such appointments.

Finally, we consider the role of public participation in the policy process. The current government has emphasized 'the third way' (Blair, 1998; Giddens, 1998) which includes an emphasis on citizen responsibility and the need to engage citizens directly in areas which concern them. This is a key emphasis within local government. Initiatives such as Best Value include consultation (with a range of stakeholders including users) as a core component. Inspection assesses how far this has been undertaken.

The duty to consult, along with the duty of community leadership, suggests a wider range of voices may be heard in the policy process. However, which voices finally influence policy is not guaranteed from consultation. There is a danger that consultation will lead to cynicism if it does not lead to action and be seen to lead to action. Furthermore, politics can be characterized as the management of conflict and different interests in society. How politicians conceive of, and address, differences of interest still remain very important.

In addition, some experimental research on communication and decision-making by social psychologists is relevant here. For example, Mulder (1971) investigated the proposition that where there are large differences in the expert power of group members in a system, then participation *increases* those differences. In a small group laboratory discussion and decision-making exercise, he found that those with more information (more expert power in the terms of French & Raven, 1968) tended to dominate the decision-making, and their influence increased with the length of the discussion. Where differences in power were low, there were no such differences in participation and influence rates. Such findings have been found in work settings as well. Kolaja (1965) found that managers and professionals tended to dominate Yugoslavian works councils and put forward the majority of the proposals which were accepted by the councils. This also happened in UK industrial democracy settings (Brannen et al., 1976; Batstone et al., 1983). These findings suggest that no participation could, in some circumstances, be better than bad participation. However, power differences can be reduced or managed with appropriate support and training. This raises important questions about how public participation can be appropriately applied to reflect diversity in communities (with diverse power bases and processes). It also raises questions about how those who run public meetings and other forms of participation (both councillors and managers) can learn to ensure there are equalities of voice in participatory interaction.

Equalities of Employment

Initial research and debate work on employment tended to focus on the numbers, types and remuneration of different subgroups within the workforce (for example, women compared with men managers, job descriptions and job remuneration across comparable skills and experience). Later work has focused on questions about the skills and capabilities of different groups (for example, whether women in general have different management skills or styles, whether women leaders have particular characteristics). A third approach has explored the processes of men and women working together, either in terms of how men and women are perceived, how they work together and what skills can be learnt across gender and ethnicity. For example, a study of black managers in eight London local authorities (Rick et al., 1999) found that black managers were more likely to be disciplined than their white counterparts. This reflected both assumptions and perceptions of capability and also how frequent and how informative was the feedback given to managers to course-correct their performance without recourse to discipline.

We noted earlier that public services employ large numbers of women, and that the proportion of women and minorities is higher than in the private sector, including in comparable large organizations. While the percentage of women managers has increased over the last decade across all sectors, only 9 per cent of chief executives in local government are women (Broussine & Fox, 2002). The number of chief executives from minority groups is substantially smaller. Remuneration remains below that of white men.

Furthermore, the loss of public sector jobs over the last two decades has had an impact on middle management due to delayering, downsizing and restructuring. Yet middle management is the level at which women and minorities are developing their careers. In addition, the contracting out of services under the previous government has also had a detrimental impact on jobs, in terms of pay and conditions and in terms of the numbers employed and career paths available, especially at lower grades in the organization (Geddes, 2001). The period of compulsory competitive tendering (CCT) was seen to have a disproportionately large impact on women's jobs (Escott & Whitfield, 1995).

The current government has continued the pressures for the externalization of services, particularly through Best Value (Martin et al., 2001) and through the development of

Public Service Agreements and public–private partnerships. These are likely to continue to reduce wages and narrow job and career opportunities. This is predicted to occur for all types of staff, with the impact occurring particularly for two groups: managers, some of whom have been breaking through the glass ceiling over the last decade, and for low-paid part-time jobs where the largest proportion of female employees are concentrated in public services. Geddes (2001) reports on the Best Value pilot programme research, which shows that 25–30 per cent of local authority pilots were recommending the competitive tendering of services in at least some services, over 40 per cent were recommending partnership and 15 per cent were recommending sales of services and facilities. The downward pressure on the quantity and quality of jobs is likely to continue. Many of the areas which have been externalized or where there is mixed private–public provision are services which employ large numbers of women, for example in home care services. A survey from the main local government trade union, conducted by an opinion company, found staff morale very low (UNISON, 2000).

The modernization agenda may, on the other hand, provide new opportunities for women and minorities through the skills and practices of networking, though the precise processes whereby change occurs need to be examined very carefully. This is examined in a later section.

Equalities of Service Delivery

Public sector organizations are politically managed and have accountability to a wide range of stakeholders, not just those who receive their services. They cannot choose their markets but are required by legislation as well as by policy to provide services to meet users' needs, regardless of background. Yet budget constraints may often mean that they have to ration services as well as meet users' needs. Public service organizations also have democratic as well as service delivery imperatives. How a service is delivered (the manner of delivery, equality of access to the service, etc.) is important and may in some cases contribute to well-being, self-esteem and a sense of citizenship.

In terms of many public service organizations such as local government, the health service or the criminal justice system, many services are disproportionately used by the poor and socially excluded. Many others are disproportionately used by the young and the very old. Among the poor and the old are to be found a higher proportion of women and minorities. In addition, the responsibilities of women in caring roles for both young children and elderly relatives mean that their quality of life may be substantially shaped by the quality of services for their dependants. The issue of equalities of access to services is therefore not an academic point, but a real and substantial issue for public services. What has been the impact of modernization on the delivery of services?

A key programme in local government intended to improve services is Best Value. This includes the requirement for a 'fundamental review' of each service area over a five-year cycle. Part of the challenge of the review is to ask searching questions about whether the service is needed and whether it is meeting the needs of citizens and users. Consultation with citizens, users and other stakeholders has to be conducted at some stage in the review, whether about current services or about options for future services and style of delivery. Other initiatives, such as the Beacon Council Scheme, have also indirectly encouraged some local authorities to develop a more explicit concern with the needs of users (Hartley et al., 2002). The Better Government for Older People was established specifically to create innovative approaches to services for older people through inter-agency networking and collaboration.

All these initiatives have either directly or indirectly required or encouraged consultation with local people over specific services. A number of commentators have suggested that the modernization agenda represents the opportunity for a shift from producer-led to citizen-centred service delivery (e.g. Benington, 2000). However, the focus has perhaps been more on particular user groups (for example, older people, families with children) rather than on diversity. This has meant that equalities issues have not always been directly addressed. For example, the Best Value initiative has not integrated either equality or social inclusion into its framework, and the Commission for Racial Equality has expressed concern about this gap. In the research on the Best Value pilot programme, among the 41 authorities taking part, most had published a statement on equalities in relation to Best Value and had adopted the 'positive about disability' policy, but few had distributed their statement on equalities to all staff (Martin et al., 2001). Crucially, in an era of performance measurement, very few of these pilots had adopted local equalities performance measures in relation to Best Value and very few had adopted local performance indicators for reducing social exclusion through Best Value. Although consultation with users has increased under Best Value, research with 23 authorities implementing Best Value found that consultation with 'hard to reach' groups was very limited (Allison & Hartley, 2000).

On the other hand, Best Value has empowered some front-line staff. Trade union members in a national survey reported that they are now consulted about service delivery and that they have enhanced contact with service users (UNISON, 2000). But the impact on actual service delivery is mixed: 22 per cent of those surveyed say that working practices have worsened, while 21 per cent say working practices have improved under Best Value. Many staff report increased working pressures with the advent of Best Value.

A variety of mechanisms might be considered as ways to improve equalities of service delivery, within the organization and within the wider community. New forms of service delivery provide opportunities to raise questions about issues of difference, and imbalance of power within decision-making forums, and encourage different voices to be heard. There is some pressure building up to resurrect the notion of contract compliance in the externalization of services. This builds in the requirement for suppliers and providers of services to meet council requirements on recruitment, workforce composition, terms and conditions, and training and qualifications. From January 2001, it has been possible for local authorities to take workforce issues into account when contracting out services under Best Value. The Commission for Racial Equality and the Equal Opportunities Commission have been arguing for equality-based criteria for performance measurement for both individuals and services and generic equality standards to tackle race, gender and disability discrimination in public services. These could provide a basis for monitoring internally provided and contracted-out services. The Equality Standard for Local Government (2001) provides a framework for mainstreaming equalities into all aspects of a local council's work, covering both employment and service delivery and the possibility of extension to include additional discrimination policies, such as age, sexuality and religious beliefs. Further, the Equal Opportunities Commission is calling for a duty of public services to promote sex equality, in line with the recent amendment to the Race Relations Act, which requires public services to actively tackle racial discrimination. It has been argued that such a duty would revolutionize public services by requiring an evaluation of the impact of every spending decision (Mellor, 2001). The Beacon Council Scheme might be used more widely to celebrate not only excellence in service but demonstrable equalities in service access and delivery. It could also be used to share learning on these issues between organizations.

THE DIVERSITY IMPLICATIONS OF NETWORKING

It has been suggested that both councillors and managers need to develop or enhance networking skills in order to engage in inter-agency partnership working and policy learning (Hartley, 1998; Benington & Harvey, 1999). This involves leadership and the management of influence beyond the boundaries of the organization (Hartley & Allison, 2000). The reasons for the shift from bureaucratic organizational functioning to network-based functioning are complex but reflect changes across both the public and private sectors (Pettigrew & Fenton, 2001).

In local government, networking skills are highly relevant in at least three ways. First, there is the increased need for networking across services, departments and agencies in order to deliver 'joined-up' government. This involves networking laterally across agencies and vertically between different tiers and spheres of governance. Second, the new political arrangements (analysed in an earlier section) mean that there is a changing interface between political and managerial leadership, which needs to take into account a more fluid way of working between local government councillors and strategic and service managers. Third, there is an increased role for networking in community leadership, because the role of the local authority organization is not simply to provide services but also to help local communities to articulate their aspirations and needs.

It is sometimes said that women's social skills make them particularly adept at networking as a form of influence and leadership (e.g. Marshall, 1984). In addition, the leadership style of women has been characterized, in some quarters, as more transformational than transactional (e.g. Alimo-Metcalfe, 1995), and thus better adapted to the complex set of interrelationships which exist in networked, intraorganizational and interorganizational working, where listening, interpreting, influence and negotiation are key skills. This style, often deployed by women in roles of mediation, liaison and interpretation, traditionally has been undervalued or even made invisible, but is now crucial to new forms of governance.

However, there may also be grounds for concern about networking as an organizational process, in terms of diversity. First, given the stratified nature of local government organizations, with white men being in the clear majority in the most senior positions, there may be a danger that men are embracing new models of leadership at the strategic level (e.g. local strategic partnerships between different agencies) but leaving the 'real' work of detailed, operational joining-up of services between agencies to those (especially women) who are located in service management or middle management.

Second, even where it can be shown that women and minorities have the skills for networking and interorganizational leadership, it cannot be assumed that promotion is on the basis of competence. The links between competence and promotion are not strong. Perceptions of competence have been shown, repeatedly, to be related to gender and ethnicity (Marshall, 1984; Billings & Alvesson, 2000). The stereotype of the accomplished manager remains closer to the stereotype of the male than the female (Schein, 1975). In a recent survey of eight London boroughs, men rated other men higher in terms of managerial competencies, and white people rated other white people higher in terms of managerial competencies (Rick et al., 1999). In addition, there is some suggestion that women are less likely to be clear that promotion is not automatically related to competence.

Some commentators have argued that women fare better in the new networked organizations because they are better able to cope with the lack of security, the flexible demands and the non-traditional career paths which can develop. However, Hartley and Mackenzie Davey (1997) argue that there may be causes for concern. Research from the USA suggests that networked organizations are more likely to concentrate power and that the concentrations of power are based on groups with similar or shared characteristics. Such people are likely to be highly educated, socially skilled, mobile, available to work long hours and good at networking. They are also likely to be similar to those already in power. Herriot (1989) showed that selection processes in organizations often led to the selection of people with similar characteristics to the selectors. Thomas (1995), in discussing race, argues that the intense anxiety which is generated by working under competitive, insecure conditions makes people more suspicious of outsiders and out-groups. While managers may pay lip-service to the idea of diversity, networked organizations, by definition, operate on the basis of who you know. The 'old boy network' is a powerful force for the status quo, and this may be reinforced during times of uncertainty and change. Hartley and Mackenzie Davey (1997) note that while women have been described as better at forming networks, they appear to be less good at exploiting them for career purposes. Also, their location in vertically segregated occupations (including the lower and middle levels of management) tends to mean that their circles of influence are, in any case, more circumscribed. Perhaps networked organizations reinforce rather than replace the status quo, in terms of employment—though their role in promoting citizen-centred governance and joined-up services may be very valuable and therefore there may be some tensions which require articulation and negotiation.

It is therefore important that research addresses some significant questions about networking. We formulate these questions in terms of women working with men, but the questions are potentially equally pertinent for minority councillors, managers and staff.

First, what mechanisms are women politicians and managers using to negotiate, lead, manage and influence change in public service organizations? How do they operate? Are there different styles or different conditions? What can men and women learn from each other in these circumstances? Second, are women's networking style and approach different from men's and do they 'work' in modernization? (And how do we evaluate success, given the multiple and complex criteria and activities?) Third, do men and women perceive any changes in the gendered construction of organizations, for example in the culture of the organization, in what is made explicit and the extent to which patterns of equality and inequality are challenged or reinforced? Many researchers would say that changing the organizational culture is both the hardest and the most important element of achieving diversity (Cassell & Walsh, 1997). Fourth, what new job opportunities are emerging under modernization—and to what extent are they occupationally segregated by gender? What jobs are declining or disappearing and what new roles are being created that might increase potential for the integration of diversity in cross-functional services?

Fifth and importantly, what theories and frameworks of gender and diversity are most useful in helping to explain the differential impacts of change due to networking and to modernization? This is a critical area which, given the complexity of the organizational and cultural changes taking place in local government (and other public services), may require more than one theory or explanation. Already, there are concerns to contextualize theories of diversity, recognizing for example, that US and UK approaches to diversity and diversity management have pronounced differences (Lorbiecki & Jack, 2000; Cassell, 2001). This may also be true of differences between the public and private sectors. Dealing with three types of equalities in the public sector inevitably raises tensions and contradictions between the different intentions and consequences of policy and practice.

CONCLUSIONS

We conclude this chapter by summarizing some of the challenges of diversity in the LGMA and how these might be addressed. Table 16.4 synthesizes the earlier discussion into features of public services: local government leadership on the one hand and the provision of quality services on the other. The table summarizes the main problems of diversity for local government, within the three sets of issues: representation, employment and services. These issues have been covered in the course of this chapter.

While we have outlined some causes for concern with networking as a panacea for community and organizational ills, there is some ground for optimism through using networking as a means to achieve positive changes for diversity. Table 16.5 sets out the opportunities of the LGMA for diversity and how networking can, and in some cases

TABLE 16.4 Problems of diversity for the LGMA

	Representation	Employment	Services
Leadership and legitimacy	Composition of elected member body not representative of diversity in local community Unequal representation in executive positions	Unequal representation in senior posts within public sector organizations and on partnership boards and networks	Mediating/balancing conflicting views and aspirations in increasingly complex networked and cross-functional partnership arrangements
Quality and integration of services and accountability	Creating equitable consultation that takes differences of power into account and which includes 'hard to reach' groups and is accountable to different, diverse and excluded sections of local community	Risk of erosion of employment rights in new organizational forms of service provision Risk of increased occupational segregation, especially in low-paid, part-time jobs	Prioritizing, resourcing and designing non-traditional forms of service delivery, to meet diverse needs of service users Addressing diversity within service standards

TABLE 16.5 The contribution of networking to solving the problems of diversity for the local government modernization agenda

	Representation	Employment	Services
Leadership and legitimacy	Transparent selection process, induction, role models, mentoring and support networks for under-represented groups Networking to share common vision, goals and good practice	New roles of facilitation, relationship-building and mediation Greater mobility across traditional organizational and career boundaries	Joined-up levels of local, regional and national governance Facilitation of inter-organizational learning
Quality and integration of services and accountability	Encouragement to participate in partnerships and cross-functional boards to redress past power imbalances	Increased flexibility in working arrangements Zones and projects create local jobs for local people	Integration of diversity in service standards Service design recognizes difference and focused on user needs

is, being used to support changes. We have explored these issues in the course of this chapter.

The emphasis on more inclusive, representative and participative approaches to policy development and action, through partnerships and networked governance, renews the challenge to the unequal representation of women, minorities and other socially excluded groups, as councillors, in employment (as managers or staff) and as service users and citizens. The growing importance of policy networks shifts the locus of power from traditional hierarchies and creates new opportunities to tackle inequality and social exclusion. Responses to the reform agenda suggest that public sector organizations are responding in different ways. While there are some cautious grounds for optimism, governance through networks has had limited impact on issues of diversity and difference so far.

The impacts may be different for different features and processes of the organization, both because public sector organizations are complex (in terms of functions, services, professions and contexts) and because the raft of initiatives created by central government has been so varied and so numerous. We might anticipate that different initiatives may have different impacts on different elements of equalities. Local government organizations individually and increasingly through their alignment with local partner agencies, have some scope to interpret central government reforms. Through their local strategic choices and priorities, the responses of networked organizations to diversity issues may reinforce the status quo or seek to change culture, policy and practice.

ENDNOTE

1. For the purposes of this chapter, we use the Commission for Racial Equality definitions of race and ethnicity (where available and/or useful). In the UK, ethnic diversity tends to focus on

black and Asian heritage classifications. European heritage tends largely to be encompassed by the term 'white', though some commentators argue for definitions such as 'Irish'. We take the view that such analysis is only useful for broad indicative purposes and that in many situations multiple identities (not all of which are in the public arena) may be significant.

REFERENCES

Alimo-Metcalfe, B. (1995). An investigation of female and male constructs of leadership and empowerment. *Women in Management Review*, **10**, 3–8.

Allison, M. & Hartley, J. (2000). *Balancing Creative Tensions: Better Practice in Implementing Best Value*. London: Department of Environment, Transport and the Regions.

Argyris, C. (1999). *On Organizational Learning*, 2nd edn. Oxford: Blackwell.

Batstone, E., Ferner, A. & Terry, M. (1983). *Unions on the Board*. Oxford: Blackwell.

Benington, J. (2000). The modernization and improvement of government and public services. *Public Money and Management*, **20**(2), 3–8.

Benington, J. & Harvey, J. (1999). Networking in Europe. In G. Stoker (ed.) *The New Management of Local Governance*. London: Macmillan.

Billings, Y. & Alvesson, M. (2000). Questioning the notion of feminine leadership: a critical perspective on the gender labelling of leadership. *Gender, Work and Organization*, **7**(3), 144–157

Blair, T. (1998). *Leading the Way: A New Vision for Local Government*. London: Institute for Public Policy Research.

Brannen, P., Batstone, E., Fatchett, D. & White, P. (1976). *The Worker Directors: A Sociology of Participation*. London: Hutchinson.

Broussine, M. & Fox, P. (2002). Rethinking leadership in local government—the place of 'feminine' styles in the modernised council. *Local Government Studies*, **28**, 91–106.

Brown, A., Jones, A. & Mackay, F. (1999). *The 'Representativeness' of Councillors*. York: Joseph Rowntree Foundation.

Brunsson, N. (1985). *The Irrational Organization*. Chichester: Wiley.

Canavon, M. & Smith, P. (2001). *Representing the People: Democracy and Diversity*. London: Local Government Association.

Cassell, C. (2001). Managing diversity. In T. Redman & A. Wilkinson (eds) *Contemporary Human Resource Management*. London: Prentice Hall.

Cassell, C. & Walsh, S. (1997). Organization cultures, gender management strategies and women's experience of work. *Feminism and Psychology*, **7**, 224–230.

Cockburn, C. (1989). Equal opportunities: the long and short agenda. *Journal of Industrial Relations*, **20**, 213–225.

Coote, A. (2000). *New Gender Agenda*. London: Institute of Public Policy Research.

Davies, A. & Thomas, R. (2000). Researching public sector change: the argument for a gender-inclusive framework. *Public Management*, **2**, 547–554.

Davis, H. & Geddes, M. (2000). Deepening democracy or elite governance? New political management arrangements in local government. *Public Money and Management*, **20**(2), 15–20.

DETR (1998). *Modern Local Government: In Touch with the People*, London: The Stationery Office.

Employers' Organisation (2001). *The Equality Standard for Local Government*. London: Employers' Organisation for Local Government.

Equal Opportunities Commission (2000). Analysis of Labour Force Survey, Spring.

Escott, K. & Whitfield, D. (1995). *The Gender Impact of CCT in Local Government*. Manchester: Equal Opportunities Commission.

Flynn, N. (1997). *Public Sector Management*. London: Prentice Hall.

French, J. & Raven, B. (1968). The bases of social power. In D. Cartwright & A. Zander (eds) *Group Dynamics*. New York: Harper and Row.

Geddes, M. (2001, in press). What about the workers? Best value, employment and work in local public services. *Policy and Politics*, **29**.

Geddes, M. & Rust, M. (2000). Catching them young? Local initiatives to involve young people in local government. *Youth and Policy*, **69**, 42–61.

Giddens, A. (1998). *The Third Way: The Renewal of Social Democracy*. Cambridge: Polity Press.

Hartley, J. (2000). Leading and managing the uncertainty of strategic change. In Flood, P., Carroll, S., Gorman, Z. & Dromgoole, T. (eds) *Managing Strategic Implementation* (pp. 109–122). Oxford: Blackwell.

Hartley, J. (1998). *Competencies for Community Leadership*. London: Improvement and Development Agency.

Hartley, J. & Allison, M. (2000). The role of leadership in the modernization and improvement of public services. *Public Money and Management*, **20**, April–June, 35–40.

Hartley, J. & Benington, J. (1999). *Community Governance in the Information Society*. London: Foundation for Information Technology in Local Government.

Hartley, J. & Mackenzie Davey, K. (1997). The gender agenda in organizations: a review of research about women and organizational psychology. *Feminism and Psychology*, **7**, 214–223.

Hartley, J., Allison, M. & Moran, D. (in press a). *Networking, Learning and Change Management: the Better Value Development Programme*. London: DTLR.

Hartley, J., Benington, J. & Davis, H. (2000). The long-term evaluation of best value. Working paper, Local Government Centre, University of Warwick.

Hartley, J., Rashman, L., Downe, J. & Storbeck, J. (2002). *Monitoring and Evaluation of the Beacon Council Scheme: The Process Outcomes Evaluation*. London: Improvement and Development Agency and the DTLR.

Herriot, P. (1989). Selection as a social process. In M. Smith & I. Robertson (eds) *Advances in Personnel Selection and Assessment*. Chichester: Wiley.

Holder, J. (1995). Challenging racism: the BBC mentor scheme. In C. Itzin & J. Newman (eds) *Gender, Culture and Organizational Change*. London: Routledge.

Institute for Employment Research (2001). *Projections of Qualifications and Occupations: 2000/2001*. Sheffield: Department for Education and Employment.

Kolaja, J. (1965). *Workers' Councils: The Yugoslav Experience*. London: Tavistock.

Local Government Employers' Organization (2001). *Local Government Employment Survey 2000*. London: Local Government Employers' Organization.

Lorbiecki, A. & Jack, G. (2000). Critical turns in the evolution of diversity management. *British Journal of Management*, **11**, Special Issue, S17–S31.

MacGregor, D. (2001). Jobs in the public and private sectors. *Economic Trends*, **571**, June, 35–40.

Macpherson, W. (1999). *The Stephen Lawrence Inquiry: Implications for Racial Equality*. Report of an inquiry by Sir William Macpherson of Cluny. London: Stationary Office.

Marshall, J. (1984) *Women Managers: Travellers in a Male World*. Chichester: Wiley.

Martin, S., Davis, H., Bovaird, T., Downe, J., Geddes, M., Hartley, J., Lewis, M., Sanderson, I. & Sapwell, P. (2001). *Improving Local Public Services: Evaluation of the Best Value Pilot Programme. Final Report*, London: DETR.

Mellor, J. (2001). EOC welcomes historic bill to increase women's representation. Press release: 20 June 2001. London: EOC.

Mulder, M. (1971). Power equalisation through participation? *Administrative Science Quarterly*, **16**, 31–38.

Municipal Journal (2001). Representing the people. *6 July*, 3.

Newman, J. (2001a). Changing governance, changing equality? New Labour, modernisation and public services in the UK. Conference paper, Gender, Work and Organizations Conference, University of Keele, June.

Newman, J. (2001b). *Modernising Governance: New Labour, Policy and Society*. London: Sage.

Owens, D. (2001). Personal communication. Centre for Research in Ethnic Relations, University of Warwick.

Pettigrew, A. & Fenton, E. (2001). *The innovating organization*. London: Sage.

Rashman, L. (1991). The effect of gender on the organisational influence of women trainers. MA thesis, University of Manchester.

Rick, T., Tamkin, P., Pollard, E. & Tackey, N. (1999). *The Organizational and Managerial Implications of Devolved Personnel Assessment Processes*. Brighton: Institute for Employment Studies.

Schein, V. (1975). The relationship between sex role stereotypes and requisite managerial characteristics among female managers. *Journal of Applied Psychology*, **60**, 340–344.

Scott, W.R. (2001). *Institutions and Organizations*, 2nd edn. Thousand Oaks, Calif.: Sage.

Skelcher, C. (1998). *The Appointed State: Quasi-governmental Organizations and Democracy.* Buckingham: Open University Press.

Thobani, M. (1995). Working for equality in the London Borough of Hounslow. In C. Itzin & J. Newman (eds) *Gender, Culture and Organizational Change*. London: Routledge.

Thomas, D. (1995). People of color in the new career environment. Conference Paper, Academy of Management, Vancouver, August.

Tsagarousianou, R., Tambini, D. & Bryan, C. (1998). *Cyberdemocracy: Technology, Cities and Civic Networks*. London: Routledge.

UNISON (2000). *Against the Odds: Delivering Local Services. Report of an NOP survey of UNISON local government members*. London: UNISON.

Worrall, L. & Cooper, C. (1998). *The Quality of Working Life: The 1998 Survey of Managers' Changing Experience*. London: Institute of Management.

CHAPTER 17

Workable Strategies and Effectiveness of Diversity Training

David L. Tan
University of Oklahoma, Norman, Oklahoma, USA
Lee A. Morris
Research and Training Associates, Oklahoma City, Oklahoma, USA
James Romero
University of Oklahoma Health Sciences Center, Oklahoma City, Oklahoma, USA

SUMMARY

This chapter discusses the changing demographics in the US workforce and the role that diversity training can play in dealing with these important changes. Some of the myths and realties of diversity training are explored. Also presented is a workable diversity training model and the evaluation of its effectiveness. Finally, some practical suggestions are provided for the development and implementation of a successful diversity training programme.

INTRODUCTION

Due to the demanding, competitive, interrelated and ever-changing nature of the world's economy, governments and private industries alike are compelled to develop and implement strategies to handle all internal and external environmental factors facing them. For some sectors of the economy, these responses have to come quickly and effectively—perhaps for some on a daily basis—or else they face the consequences of permanent loss of business opportunities or the inability to regain or re-establish a comparative advantage.

There should be no denying that the external environment is important to all organizations—public, private, governmental, quasi-governmental, non-profit and for-profit alike. The effectiveness in responding to the challenges posed by the external environment,

Individual Diversity and Psychology in Organizations. Edited by Marilyn J. Davidson and Sandra L. Fielden.
© 2003 John Wiley & Sons, Ltd.

however, requires proper leadership and management of internal matters (Bryson, 1995)—which is to say, the proper control and utilization of human, financial and physical resources within an organization are necessary in order to respond to the external environment. Perhaps one of the most important of these elements is the workforce within an organization.

In the United States, the demographic composition of the nation's population and its workforce, as predicted by the now famous Hudson Institute's *Workforce 2000: Work and Workers for the Twenty-First Century* (Johnson, 1987), has changed drastically, making it incumbent on all organizations to seek and implement alternative approaches and paradigms of leadership, management and motivation. In light of the potential that old or existing theories and practices may not work effectively in handling today's new changes and challenges, it may be crucial for leaders to develop a fresh approach to addressing issues related to personal productivity and success, teamwork, group commitment and organizational productivity (Apps, 1994). Indeed, some have taken the position that old strategies and theories do not in fact work and are counterproductive to organizations and definitely to groups who now constitute a larger part of the new workforce—women, ethnic minorities, the aged and the physically challenged (Klenke, 1996; Tan et al., 1996).

Strategies to accommodate a more heterogeneous workforce can be critical for organizational survival and prosperity. In this vein, organizations must learn new and innovative ways of dealing with this important change. The old ways, as Apps (1994) postulates, have not usually permitted organizations to view changes in an innovative way. The new way, states Quinn (1988), is to recognize polarities in the workforce, to see their strengths and weaknesses, and to integrate and differentiate.

To be sure, leaders must recognize the changing workforce, develop a workable individual and organizational mindset to deal with new attitudes and values, and implement a set of coherent strategies to meet all new challenges of the workplace. As a first step, leaders must recognize that 'homogeneous selectivity'—that is, the recruitment or promotion of a certain type of person, usually those similar in race, ethnic background, religious preference or gender—may no longer be appropriate nor even make good business sense, both internally and externally. In order to recruit and retain good workers and to ensure that their commitment and productivity remain high, a different kind of organizational culture may need to be developed—one that has to move beyond a token understanding of issues related to diversity.

The ideal culture would be one that keeps morale and productivity high and one that fosters a greater understanding and harmony among all the diverse working and managerial ranks (Tan et al., 1996; Yukl, 2002). The failure to address issues related to diversity may hinder not only individual productivity but organizational success as well. If workers, regardless of their ethnicity or gender, cannot achieve the level of success of which they are capable, ultimately the whole organization may suffer. Therefore, it may be incumbent on leaders and managers to address important issues related to productivity, particularly those resulting from the lack of understanding of diversity in the workplace. Given the potential that many existing theories of leadership and management do not take into consideration a more heterogeneous workforce, diversity training has been recognized as an acceptable solution to the problem of handling diversity in the workforce in the United States (Apps, 1994; Tan et al., 1996). The need for diversity training has created a cottage industry, and needless to say, there has been a wide variance in effectiveness of these programmes.

IMPORTANCE OF DIVERSITY TRAINING

Based on our many years of experience in dealing with diversity training programmes and in evaluating their successes and failures, we have come to understand several factors that are likely to lead to a more successful diversity training programme in most organizational settings. The first is that a successful programme should educate its intended audience about the myths and realities of diversity in the workplace. Surprisingly, despite the writing on the wall for over a decade in this country, many leaders, managers and workers still do not recognize or perhaps simply reject the reality of the changing demographics of the US population and its labour force. Some of our participants believe that valuing or managing diversity is just another code-name for affirmative action or civil rights programmes aimed at correcting the legal, social and moral health of organizations. Some leaders and workers do in fact believe that programmes dealing with diversity are merely schemes forced upon them and their organizations to replace European-American men with people of colour and women rather than as a needed business strategy to maintain morale and productivity in order to compete in a national or global economy (Tan et al., 1996).

To be sure, diversity training, if it is to be effective, should be designed to address and change some of the myths related to diversity, to introduce to the participants the realities and importance of diversity, and to discover and develop new and innovative ways of valuing, managing and facilitating diversity in the workplace. It is not too uncommon for us to come across people who have fundamental differences of opinions about diversity in the workplace, and we understand that some people can enter a diversity training programme with a high degree of anxiety, fear and suspicion. Consequently, changing the mindset of a usually unreceptive audience is an important and often difficult objective of any diversity programme, but it is one that is likely to contribute to a better outcome if it can be achieved. Strategies to handle this important objective are discussed later.

Before any curricular strategies can be discussed, it is important to note there can never be a universal diversity training programme. A training developer cannot simply pick a programme off a shelf, even one with a proven record in another setting, and implement it in exactly the same way expecting great success from it. In our experiences, a diversity training programme can only be successful if it takes into consideration the uniqueness of each organization. Specifically, it must take into account the characteristics of the targeted audience, their leaders, their issues and the organizational culture in which they work. In some instances, we have even designed a separate programme for each group within the same organization. For example, in one organization, we designed one programme specifically for managers and supervisors and a second one for support staff only, since the nature of the issues and circumstances faced by each group was very different and required different attention and resolutions.

In order to develop a customized diversity training programme, the diversity trainers have to implement a few pre-training procedures, the first of which is the exploration and development of a proper context for diversity training. This is an important procedure since it can set the tone for the entire diversity training programme. The context can then be used as a springboard for developing a programme that best suits the needs of the organization. Over the years, we have developed a systematic mechanism for assessing the current attitudes and needs of people in a given organization. This mechanism, which we call the 'cultural audit', has proven to be an extremely useful tool in understanding the general and specific circumstances dealing with diversity, responsibilities, fairness, morale, culture and general productivity of the workplace. This instrument was developed based partly on the work of Gardenswartz and Rowe (1993) and partly on interview data we collected from our participants. To be sure, this tool helps us in identifying the appropriate curricular components that need to be developed in order to achieve desired training outcomes.

Our cultural audit instrument has essentially three main parts. The first reflects *individual attitudes and beliefs* of employees relative to diversity issues. The second part asks employees to rate their perceptions of the *organization's values and norms* relative to diversity issues; and the third part examines the employees' perceptions of *management's practices and policies* relative to diversity issues. These three parts can vary in length and can accommodate unique issues associated with each organization. The instrument is then administered, producing results that are used as bases for the development of a customized diversity training programme.

We have found that our cultural audit instrument is particularly useful in ferreting out the perceptions on diversity between the various subgroups in an organization. We usually find a high level of disagreement on many issues, such as whether or not racial minorities and women are assisted in their career advancement within the organization; whether managers effectively use problem-solving skills to deal with linguistic and cultural clashes; whether there is an appreciation of diversity reflected in the workplace and its reward system; whether there is a favouritism towards European Americans in the workplace; whether racial, ethnic and gender jokes are tolerated in the formal work environment; and who should be responsible for the problems of solving diversity issues in the organization. Any similarities or dissimilarities in these and other issues are dealt with in our training sessions.

Since there is usually a great deal of disagreement between various subgroups in any organization, it is critical that a climate of comfort and safety be established, before, during and after a diversity training exercise. The proper context and purpose of training (as explained earlier) must be clearly communicated to, and understood by, a majority of the participants. Usually, this process takes some time and effort to develop and does require organizational champions, leaders and opinion makers to facilitate the process. A sense of ownership of the decision-making process in the development of the diversity training programme is helpful. It is also helpful to decrease the belief that there are hidden agendas behind the training exercise. The key is to persuade as many people as possible to buy into the mutual benefits of the exercise. Inevitably, there will always be perpetual resisters in any organization, but there will be opportunities to deal with them in training.

Once a diversity training programme is developed, we usually negotiate on the length of the programme and the frequency of delivery. We are partial to a multiple-day format because it allows opportunities for timely follow-ups and reflection of materials. Pertaining to the training process itself, we can offer a few pieces of advice. The first is that when we allow our participants to establish ground rules for their training, we find this to be an excellent way of fostering their sense of ownership and of taking responsibility for their own behaviour and outcome during the training process. Second, when we encourage our participants to speak for themselves, to refrain from personal attacks, to be open to new or different ideas, and to express themselves freely in all discussions and activities, our effectiveness increases. Third, when we assure our participants that their expressed opinions are held confidential and are not recorded nor repeated to anyone, we are more likely to find more people engaged in meaningful discussions. Fourth, when we make efforts to convince our participants that we, as programme trainers, have no 'hidden agendas' and that our primary responsibility is to facilitate their discussions, we find that we can better achieve our programme objectives and also assist our participants in the resolution of their problems.

A WORKABLE DIVERSITY TRAINING MODEL

Having worked with various organizations of all types (from federal governmental agencies to private corporations), we have developed our own unique style. Even though our programme can vary from one organization to the next, there are some important commonalities worth mentioning. The first is that we feel all diversity training programmes should be experiential in nature. By that we mean it should be a programme built around real organizational incidents using strategies such as meaningful simulations, relevant case scenarios, cutting-edge videos, appropriate instrumentation, and meaningful discussions appropriate to each organization. We have also found consistency in the objectives of our programmes, which usually include, but are not limited to, the following (Morris, 1994):

- The exploration of the primary dimensions of diversity
- The analysis of the impact of assimilation on the ability of others to succeed
- The exploration of personal values, stereotypes and prejudices
- The examination of the impact of destructive 'isms' on others
- The assessment of employee readiness to value diversity
- The identification of current barriers that could impede the cultural change process
- The analysis of ways to prevent sexual harassment in the workplace

These objectives usually form the basis for our training programme. Some specific examples of our curricular components have included a highly interactive cross-cultural simulation session; an exercise designed to increase awareness of the ways in which people have discriminated against, judged or isolated others; a presentation showing confrontations of people from different cultures; an exercise designed to identify barriers that can impede cultural changes; an intercultural learning activity; a set of case scenarios; a gender discrimination exercise; and a sexual harassment training module (Morris, 1994).

EFFECTIVENESS OF DIVERSITY TRAINING

In order to gauge the effectiveness of our efforts, we usually have an evaluation mechanism in which we ask our participants to offer their opinions on the programme's objectives and outcomes, before and after their exposure to our training programme. These items have included their:

- Personal knowledge of diversity issues
- Readiness to value diversity in the workplace
- Knowledge of the impact of assimilation or socialization on people's ability to succeed in the workplace
- Knowledge of barriers which impeded cultural change in the workplace

- Awareness of their own personal stereotypes and prejudices
- Knowledge of the impact of stereotypes and prejudices in the workplace
- Knowledge of identifying and preventing stereotypes and prejudices in the workplace
- Knowledge of the impact of sexual harassment in the workplace
- Knowledge of identifying and preventing sexual harassment in the workplace

The before-and-after scores provide us with immediate feedback about our successes and failures. We also ask them to tell us the ways in which we can improve our training programme.

In order to show some examples of the complexities and successes we have had with our diversity training programme, we have decided to use two cases for illustration. The first was our training programme designed for a federal agency. In this example, over 700 managers and supervisors participated in a series of 40 three-day workshops offered in several cities throughout the south-western region of the United States. Two trainers—one male and one female—facilitated each workshop. At the end of each training seminar, all respondents were asked to evaluate the programme as a whole and its components, including the trainers.

When statistical analysis was used to compare the level of awareness, knowledge, readiness or experience among the participants from all 40 workshops, before and after the workshops, we found appreciable statistically significant ($p < 0.05$) increases in awareness, knowledge, readiness and experience in all of our desired outcomes (see Table 17.1). The largest increases appeared to be in their:

1. Knowledge of diversity issues;
2. Knowledge of barriers which can impede cultural change process in the workplace;
3. Knowledge of impact of stereotypes and prejudices in the workplace;
4. Readiness to value diversity in the workplace;
5. Knowledge of identifying and preventing stereotypes and prejudices in the workplace (Tan, 1994).

In addition, the participants felt that our programme was personally enriching to them and had practical work applications.

We must stress, however, that a good proportion of our success can be attributed to our facilitators, who performed an outstanding job despite the difficulties and complexities associated with introducing a highly charged subject to an often unreceptive audience, which in this case happened to be essentially white males. It clearly took some patience, finesse and persistence on the part of our facilitators to stay focused on the achievement of the programme's objectives. We also attributed a great deal of our success to the careful and deliberate development of our programme based on our initial assessment of the unique circumstances and needs of our intended audience. Subsequent improvements in our programme were made possible by immediate feedback we received from the participants.

The second case was a programme we designed for a state agency in Oklahoma and we again found statistically significant increases in everything we had hoped to accomplish (see Table 17.2). The three largest increases in that programme were their:

1. Knowledge of barriers that impede cultural change process in the workshop;
2. Knowledge of diversity issues;
3. Knowledge of identifying and preventing sexual harassment in the workplace.

TABLE 17.1 Before and after effects of diversity training: a federal agency

Desired outcomes	Before workshop	After workshop	Extent of change	No. of cases	T-value	Significance
1. Knowledge of diversity issues	6.01	7.90	1.89	197	18.89	0.00
2. Your readiness to value diversity in the workplace	6.50	8.14	1.64	196	14.90	0.00
3. Knowledge of the impact of assimilation (socialization) on people's ability to succeed in the workplace	6.13	7.84	1.71	195	15.51	0.00
4. Knowledge of barriers which impede cultural change process in the workplace	6.03	7.86	1.83	195	16.97	0.00
5. Awareness of your own personal stereotypes and prejudices	6.51	8.04	1.53	197	13.29	0.00
6. Knowledge of the impact of stereotypes and prejudices in the workplace	6.66	8.17	1.51	196	14.52	0.00
7. Knowledge of identifying and preventing stereotypes and prejudices in the workplace	6.37	8.01	1.64	197	15.42	0.00
8. Knowledge of the impact of sexual harassment in the workplace	7.24	8.52	1.28	196	12.74	0.00
9. Knowledge of identifying and preventing sexual harassment in the workplace	7.04	8.36	1.32	197	13.53	0.00

TABLE 17.2 Before and after effects of diversity training: a state agency

Desired outcomes	Before workshop	After workshop	Extent of change	No. of cases	T-value	Significance
1. Knowledge of diversity issues	5.81	8.49	2.68	220	−24.21	0.00
2. Your readiness to value diversity in the workplace	6.78	9.13	2.35	220	−6.07	0.00
3. Knowledge of the impact of assimilation (socialization) on people's ability to succeed in the workplace	5.82	8.28	2.46	216	−19.88	0.00
4. Knowledge of barriers which impede cultural change process in the workplace	5.60	8.67	3.07	218	−7.12	0.00
5. Awareness of your own personal stereotypes and prejudices	6.47	8.62	2.15	217	−17.13	0.00
6. Knowledge of the impact of stereotypes and prejudices in the workplace	6.53	8.57	2.04	217	−6.74	0.00
7. Knowledge of identifying and preventing stereotypes and prejudices in the workplace	6.33	8.44	2.11	218	−4.81	0.00
8. Knowledge of the impact of sexual harassment in the workplace	6.23	8.54	2.31	216	−18.10	0.00
9. Knowledge of identifying and preventing sexual harassment in the workplace	5.83	8.44	2.61	216	−19.82	0.00

The overall results showed clearly that the diversity training workshops had brought about significant changes in the participants, which ranged from a change of 31–55 per cent (Tan, 1997). Despite the successes we experienced from this programme, we saw the need for a follow-up study, which should consist of an assessment of whether the changes in the knowledge level and attitudes of our participants have translated into appropriate behaviours, actions and policies that have benefited the workplace, but we have not been given the opportunity to perform this assessment yet.

CONCLUSIONS

Through our experiences with the above organizations and others, we understand fully that diversity training is a very sensitive and often difficult topic to introduce, particularly when the audience is unreceptive or does not fully understand the value of diversity. The difficulty is further compounded by the need on the part of the trainers to walk a very fine line between creating a climate of directness and honesty and injecting a blend of impersonal humour, outrage and scholarship during the training process. For any diversity programme to succeed, we believe strongly that there must be a proper balance between the two. To be sure, some personal characterizations of the messages are needed but not at the expense of dissuading participants from comfortably expressing their viewpoints with feelings of guilt or rejection. Role playing, simulation exercises, innovative videos and relevant discussion have allowed us to accomplish this objective very well. Experienced and flexible trainers are definitely necessary to react to and accommodate the unique and ever-changing circumstances of each training group or session.

Before entering any training programme, we usually detect a strong sense of reservations from the participants about diversity training and many admittedly do not know what to expect. That is where we usually begin our work. By considering and planning ahead the psychological and sociological realties surrounding this difficult subject, we have managed to achieve considerable success. We are most pleased when we hear from our participants that our programme has helped them to understand diversity issues— such as why they viewed other cultures as threatening; why they often described other cultures in negative terms; why they usually resorted to general stereotypes and prejudices in their encounters with people of a different culture or gender; or why they automatically assumed their own language, culture or gender to be superior to others. From our assessment results, we understand that many of our participants appreciated the opportunity to assess their own attitudes and values (many for the first time) and to understand how their attitudes have contributed towards their propensity to discriminate against, judge or isolate others. We do not attempt to force our participants to reveal their feelings unless they feel comfortable in doing so. The opportunity for personal reflection, however, is an important factor related to the success of our training programme. So is the opportunity for our participants to discuss and understand diversity concepts in a non-threatening but highly interactive way. These are all keys to a successful diversity training programme.

Despite our successes with our approaches to diversity training, we have often felt the need to return and assess whether the changes in attitudes have led to something meaningful for the organizations, vis-à-vis actual behaviours and actions that have benefited the organizations. Similar to the interconnectedness of the world's economy, it would be unwise to examine diversity issues in isolation from all the social and organizational contextual factors that can influence organizational behaviour. In conclusion, we believe that the management of diversity in the workplace will ultimately lead to organizational effectiveness, both internally and externally. For most, if not all, organizations, dealing with diversity issues is not a choice but a necessity.

REFERENCES

Apps, J.W. (1994). *Leadership for the Emerging Age*. San Francisco: Jossey-Bass.

Bryson, J.M. (1995). *Strategic Planning for Public and Nonprofit Organizations*. San Francisco: Jossey-Bass.

Gardenswartz, L. & Rowe, A. (1993). *Managing Diversity: A Complete Desk Reference and Planning Guide*. Homewood, Ill.: Business One Irwin.

Johnson, W.B. (1987). *Workforce 2000*. Indianapolis, Ind.: Hudson Institute.

Klenke, K. (1996). *Women and Leadership: A Contextual Perspective*. New York: Springer Publishing.

Morris, L. (1994). *Training Manuals of the FAA and the University of Oklahoma Diversity Training*. Norman, Okla.: College of Continuing Education, University of Oklahoma.

Quinn, R.E. (1988). *Beyond Rational Management: Mastering the Paradoxes and Competing Demands of High Performance*. San Francisco: Jossey-Bass.

Tan, D. (1994). *FAA Southwest Region and the University of Oklahoma Diversity Training Program: Final Summary Report*. Norman, Okla.: College of Continuing Education, University of Oklahoma.

Tan, D. (1997). *The Department of Rehabilitation Services and the University of Oklahoma Diversity Training Programme: Evaluation Report*. Norman, Okla.: College of Continuing Education, University of Oklahoma.

Tan, D., Morris, L. & Romero, J. (1996). Changes in attitude after diversity training. *Training and Development*, September, 54–55.

Yukl, G. (2002). *Leadership in Organizations*, 5th edn. Upper Saddle River, NJ: Prentice Hall.

PART V

Recognizing Stereotypes, Attitudes and Bias

CHAPTER 18

What You See Is What You Get: Popular Culture, Gender and Workplace Diversity

Alison Sheridan and Jane O'Sullivan
University of New England, Armidale, Australia

SUMMARY

In this chapter, the role popular culture can play in limiting the realization of diversity within organizations is explored. Drawing on mainstream Hollywood cinema, we examine representations of gender and work in popular cultural texts that contribute to, and go some way towards explaining, the disparity between the spirit of diversity management and its manifestation. Masculinity continues to be privileged over femininity and shapes organizational practices and behaviours. In this chapter we argue that in order to enter and survive within many organizations, people who are seen to be too different from the privileged and notionally mainstream identity group must somehow camouflage their difference in order to 'pass' as being of the dominant group. As such, diversity is compromised rather than celebrated, and its benefits to organizations severely curtailed.

INTRODUCTION

In 1997, *GI Jane* (1997, Ridley Scott) exploded onto the Hollywood screen depicting Lieutenant Jordan O'Neil (Demi Moore), a highly trained killing machine, hardly recognizable with her face besmirched with mud and blood, head shaved and biceps bulging. As if these were not sufficient markers of her performance of masculinity, later in the film, hands tied behind her back and still able to give her senior officer a broken nose, she raises her battered face from the dirt and struggles to her feet. Through bloodied

Individual Diversity and Psychology in Organizations. Edited by Marilyn J. Davidson and Sandra L. Fielden.
© 2003 John Wiley & Sons, Ltd.

lips she spits out her defiant challenge 'suck my dick'. Seemingly, she had successfully negotiated the minefield of gender inequity in that bastion of homosociability—the military. A woman had made it into this elite team of soldiers—she is a US Navy SEAL! This can be read as an illustration of inclusivity, as it exemplifies gender equity, access and greater diversity within the armed forces.

Clearly this sequence lends itself to more than one interpretation, because while it does reflect the nature of workforce diversity, it is cause for a very qualified level of celebration. Lieutenant Jordan O'Neil (GI Jane) has in effect masked any markers of difference; and in this context that difference is her femininity. In addition, the level of credence you may be willing to give to this example of diversity in a workplace may be qualified in a couple of ways. First, you may be thinking the above incident is only fiction—one presented in a Hollywood film. Second, it is a very extreme transformation from femininity to masculinity and takes place within a workplace culture, the military, that is renowned for its erasure of difference to facilitate uniform behaviours.

In brief, your qualms are justified. We have indeed selected an extreme case to introduce our argument that the actual level of diversity in current workplaces is not as great as it would seem. There may be different faces in the workplace, but they rapidly become camouflaged to pass almost undetected within the normative structures and processes of organizations. We do, however, take issue with the sentiment 'only fiction' in that this would imply that such texts are irrelevant to the 'real world' of work. Mainstream Hollywood cinema forms a significant part of our cultural diet, be it in the form of a trip to the movies or a night in front of the television. In these activities that are coded as leisure and pleasure, one is not conscious of the role popular fictional texts play in both reflecting and constructing stereotypic representations of women and men in the workplace. Nevertheless they do (Marshment, 1997; Hassard & Holliday, 1998) and there is a growing literature on the role the media play in affecting norms and, in turn, influencing attitudes held by the audience. Studies have shown how the media not only affect personal attitudes directly but also indirectly through beliefs about group norms (Morton & Duck, 2000).

We argue that workplace diversity largely remains an ideal that has not yet been realized. Within most organizations there exists a disparity between the spirit of diversity management and its manifestation. Further, we argue that representations of gender and work in popular cultural texts contribute to, and perhaps go some way towards explaining, this disparity between diversity rhetoric and diversity within the workplace. In this chapter cinematic representations of women and men in the workplace are analysed to reveal how gender as an organizing principle within organizations (Acker, 1998) limits the scope for diversity within workplaces. Masculinity continues to be privileged over femininity and shapes organizational practices and behaviours. In essence we argue that in order to enter and survive within many organizations, people who are seen as not belonging to or complying with the privileged and notionally mainstream identity group must somehow erase or camouflage their difference in an attempt to 'pass' as being of the dominant group. In that sense, diversity is compromised rather than celebrated, and its benefits to organizations severely curtailed. To illustrate our argument we will be focusing on *Working Girl* (1986, Mike Nichols) and *In the Company of Men* (1999, Neil LaBute), two films we believe capture the kinds of stereotypic representations of women and men in the workplace that are touched upon in a wide variety of other mainstream fare. As such, we are providing an example of how the reproduction of inequalities is programmed into ongoing social processes (Garnsey & Rees, 1996), such as the seemingly innocuous process of viewing a popular film. We argue that analysing popular culture, in this case popular films, can bring about a fuller appreciation of the role of ideology in constructing cultures that fail to achieve real diversity in the workplace.

DIVERSITY IS ONE THING, MANAGING IT IS ANOTHER

'Managing diversity' is a term that has multiple meanings within organizational studies, depending on the situation and perspective of those employing it. It has been represented in a variety of forms and apparently motivated by a variety of factors (De Cieri & Olekalns, 2001). In the literature, managing diversity has been represented as referring to policies seeking to respond to the changing workforce demographics, with a large number of factors being included under the umbrella of 'diversity'. Robinson and Dechant (1997) trace how the term 'diversity' has evolved over time. From the traditional definition of diversity concerned with attributes (differences in gender, racioethnicity and age) they track a move to a broader usage of the term which includes different physical abilities, qualities and sexual orientations. They also point to a further use of the term 'diversity' where the focus is on the variety of attitudes, perspectives and backgrounds among group members or, as Thomas and Woodruff (1999) note, behaviour diversity. The term has even been used within some companies to capture the differences that people bring to organizations from their 'different hierarchical levels, functions and backgrounds' (Robinson & Dechant, 1997: 22).

As to what prompts firms to embrace a managing diversity policy, the reasons are also varied. As the term 'equal opportunity' with its overtones of social justice is less often invoked in the business literature (Sinclair, 2000), the term 'managing diversity' has gained greater support as it has been presented as providing real gains to businesses. For businesses to benefit from having a diverse workforce it is argued that it is not enough to be able to identify different faces, there is also a need to be able to draw upon the richer mix of experiences and perspectives they bring to the workplace. Rather than it being seen as a legal requirement, it has been framed as an initiative that 'smart' organizations take up (Gilbert & Ivancevich, 2000). Cost savings and the ability to attract and retain talented staff are often cited as strong arguments for pursuing diversity initiatives (Robinson & Dechant, 1997; De Cieri & Olekalns, 2001). A further reason for formal diversity initiatives to be enacted is the claim that companies can drive business growth by appropriating their employees' different perspectives to better target markets and to employ more creative approaches to problem-solving. Maas (1999: 97), for example, argues the objective in managing diversity 'is to fulfil business goals through cultivating and coordinating talents of the organization's members'.

Despite the range of definitions and general debate surrounding managing diversity there remain real barriers to the inclusion of differences within organizations. While there may be formal managing diversity policies operating within organizations, there continue to be impediments to the valuing of difference within organizations (Gilbert & Ivancevich, 2000). For instance in Australia, while women represent 43 per cent of the paid workforce, they continue to dominate the clerical, sales and service occupations and

TABLE 18.1   Women in the Australian labour force

Women as a proportion of the paid workforce[a]	43.4
Women as a proportion of managers[a]	23.2
Women as a proportion of board members of publicly listed companies[b]	3.4

[a] Australian Bureau of Statistics (2001).
[b] Sheridan (2001).

make up the vast majority of part-time workers (Australian Bureau of Statistics, 2001). It seems that women's entry into paid work has been acceptable if they have remained in the domains traditionally dominated by women. As outlined earlier in Chapter 8, entry into traditionally male domains has been more problematic. As can be seen in Table 18.1, while women in Australia now represent 24 per cent of managers, they are clustered in the junior and supervisory levels. At the most senior levels of management, women make up less than 5 per cent of the positions. The demographic profile of top management remains very homogeneous. While some women may be allowed to join the senior ranks, their access is highly conditional on them adopting the assumptions and practices which pervade these ranks (Newman, 1995). We believe that the cinematic representations of the workplace that reinforce notions of appropriate roles for women and men represent a significant barrier to the realization of diversity within organizations.

IDEOLOGY AND MAINSTREAM FILM

In our discussion of popular constructions of workplace culture we have confined ourselves to a selection of cinematic texts that might be considered to have appealed to a large enough audience to make a good deal of money at the box office and later in the video market. In this respect, it is reasonable to expect that this kind of cinema will be designed for widespread, or majority, appeal. It is cinema that is unlikely to take too many risks in terms of its treatment of what are considered by the majority to be believable or acceptable expressions of identity and context. As a consequence of this level of conservatism, issues of sexuality, race, gender and class tend to reflect the ideals, and conventions, of the dominant culture; that is, they will be supportive of mainstream ideologies. As Smith (1987) notes, the concept of ideology brings into focus how forms of thought are consciously produced by the dominant group, and that these influence the expression of the local or particular so that they accord with the dominant group's interests. Ideologies serve to disguise or to defend authority, and in doing so, they operate to promote habits and behaviour patterns conducive to the welfare of the dominant group (Collins, 1998).

In explaining the nature and operations of ideology, Turner (1993: 133) observes that:

> . . . implicit in every culture is a 'theory of reality' which motivates its ordering of that reality into good and bad, right and wrong, them and us, and so on. For this 'theory of reality' to actually work as a structuring principle it needs to be unspoken, invisible, a property of the natural world rather than human interests. Ideology is the term used to describe the system of beliefs and practices that is produced by this theory of reality; and although ideology itself has no material form, we can see its material effects in all social and political individuals. The term is also used to

describe the workings of language and representation within culture which enable such formations to be constructed as 'natural'.

One of the most common features of mainstream cinema is its widespread commitment to narrative conventions that are geared to producing seemingly natural reflections of 'reality'. To achieve these goals the films disguise, or efface, the fact that their representations are constructed, and selected with particular effects in mind. What seems so real serves to disguise that it is all mediated by the ideologies of the film-makers, and the contexts in which they produced the films. Clearly, it is largely impossible for anyone to completely step outside ideology, as we are all so thoroughly enmeshed in it. What we are suggesting here is that, in respect to popular cinematic representations of workplaces, it is possible and productive to subject them to close scrutiny in order to identify the exclusivity of their representations and how these contribute to maintaining the dominant order in organizations. In Table 18.2, we list chronologically a range of films mentioned in this discussion. Those subjected to some analysis are highlighted in bold.

TABLE 18.2 Filmography

Film title	Date	Director	Country	Main protagonists/ antagonists	Actors
Baby Boom	1987	Charles Shyer	USA	J.C. Wiatt	Diane Keaton
Wall Street	1987	Oliver Stone	USA	Bud Fox	Charlie Sheen
				Gordon Gekko	Michael Douglas
Working Girl	1988	Mike Nichols	USA	Tess McGill	Melanie Griffith
				Katherine Parker	Sigourney Weaver
				Jack Trainer	Harrison Ford
The Doctor	1991	Randa Haines	USA	Jack MacKee	William Hurt
Regarding Henry	1991	Mike Nichols	USA	Henry Turner Sarah	Harrison Ford Annette Bening
Falling Down	1993	Joel Schumacher	France/ USA	D-Fens Prendergast	Michael Douglas Robert Duval
Philadelphia	1993	Jonathan Demme	USA	Andrew Beckett Joe Miller	Tom Hanks Denzel Washington
The Temp	1993	Tom Holland	USA	Kris Bolin Peter Derns	Lara Flynn Boyle Timothy Hutton
Disclosure	1994	Barry Levinson	USA	Tom Sanders Meredith Johnson	Michael Douglas Demi Moore
The Associate	1996	Donald Petrie	USA	Laurel Ayers	Whoopi Goldberg
Brilliant Lies	1996	Richard Franklin	Australia	Susy Connor Gary Fitzgerald	Gia Carrides Anthony LaPaglia
Courage Under Fire	1996	Edward Zwick	USA	Captain Karen Walden Lt. Colonel Sterling	Meg Ryan Denzel Washington
GI Jane	1997	Ridley Scott	USA	Lt. Jordan O'Neil Master Chief Jack Urgayle	Demi Moore Viggo Mortensen
In the Company of Men	1997	Neil LaBute	Canada/ USA	Chad Christine Howard	Aaron Eckhart Stacy Edwards Matt Malloy

WORKING GIRLS AND SMIRKING BOYS

If anyone was ever in any doubt about the continuing differences between men's and women's experiences of the workplace in the last 10 years or so, a viewing of the two films *Working Girl* (1988) and *In the Company of Men* (1997) would make this distinction very clear. Each of these two narratives depicts the main protagonists negotiating their career path through the gendered structures of their respective workplaces. In *Working Girl*, the protagonist, Tess McGill (Melanie Griffith), is a young woman aspiring to a career in management within a large company. From her perspective, the barriers to her opportunities for moving into management from her secretarial position seem insurmountable. For the two male protagonists in *In The Company of Men*, their status as white middle-class males makes their movement into senior management seem less an opportunity than a right.

WORKING GIRL

In *Working Girl*, when Tess McGill, a brassy blonde from the mainland, lands in Manhattan, and surreptitiously appropriates the identity, and corporate wardrobe of her absent boss, Katherine (Sigourney Weaver), she is in effect preparing to pass as a legitimate participant in the corporate world. Katherine, whose identity Tess seeks to replicate, is 'an imposing female senior manager . . . [who] presents as tall, lean, shoulder-pads in place—indeed androgynous' (O'Sullivan & Sheridan, 1999: 18). Further, the representation of Katherine echoes other cinematic representations which construct apparently successful career women as being scheming and manipulative (Brewis, 1998). Katherine, as the woman 'who has achieved organizational success is depicted as overly competitive, overly aggressive and as willing to go to any lengths to secure [her] organizational future' (Brewis, 1998: 88). As such, the representation of Katherine in this film acts to confirm the suspicions of working men that their female colleagues are a threat and that working women have no legitimate claim to organizational success.

In a bid to erase any markers of diversity, Tess replicates Katherine's dress. In doing so, she achieves a much modified version of her previously flamboyant femininity, but one that is just sufficiently short of the androgynous appearance of Katherine to win the variously romantic and fatherly affections of her male colleagues. After her little ruse is discovered, and Tess's true identity uncovered, she is out of a job. Tess does, however, have a rather kittenish appeal once reinstalled in her blue jeans and sweater, and armed with a file full of Katherine's indiscretions, she is soon upwardly mobile again. In a lobby, confronted by a group, including Katherine, Katherine's disaffected fiancé and deal broker, Jack, and a disgruntled client, Mr Trask, Tess shoots from the hip. No longer cross-dressed (or as Tasker (1998: 19) suggests, a 'cross-class dresser') but still angry, and hungry for a place in the organization, Tess exposes Katherine as the fraud and subsequently orders her to get her 'bony ass' out of the building. Now all this may sound like a standard Hollywood cat fight, corporate-style, but there is a twist in the tail of this narrative. While in order to gain access to a business career, Tess had to erase her difference and take on the trappings of the corporate closet, once there she does indeed offer a significant, and successful alternative approach to business analysis and problem-solving. For a full appreciation of the benefits offered by her unconventional and diversified approach to business practices and the depiction of women as being unnatural in positions of authority within the workplace, let us take a closer look at the altercation mentioned above and the two female characters in more detail.

Katherine, having returned to the workplace after a lengthy absence following an accident, finds that Tess has been masquerading as her. She discovers that Tess has been negotiating a major deal between her much-valued client, Mr Trask of Trask Industries and the company, Metro Radio. In a bid to retrieve her position as the boss, and legitimate negotiator, Katherine quickly moves to fire Tess, and doing a bit of masquerading herself, tries to pass off the proposed deal as her own brainchild. Just as the elevator doors are closing behind Katherine, Jack and her recently reclaimed client, Tess desperately urges Trask to 'ask ... [Katherine] about the hole in ... [the] deal'. Galvanized by this remark, Trask intercepts the closing door, and, in a state of agitation, Katherine grabs the news clipping Tess is brandishing, announcing in a disparaging tone 'the People page!' Adopting a derisive tone, she proceeds to read aloud about some seemingly inane account of house-hunting by a beauty queen and her radio personality husband who are planning to take a 'bite out of the Big Apple' [move to New York]. What eludes Katherine is the fact that this radio personality is, as Jack points out, 'Metro's major asset' who was syndicated to all their stations and 'No. 1 in his slot. The cornerstone of their programming.'

At this point Trask begins to take Tess seriously, and to suspect Katherine of trying to steal the credit for the deal. He chooses to join Tess and Jack in the lift to the top floor. Now Tess has the opportunity to explain how she developed the idea for Trask Industries to purchase a radio station. While Trask Industries had stated they were interested in moving into media, it was Tess's idea for Trask to invest in radio rather than buying television stations. This seems to be a demonstration of the benefits to business of different backgrounds and perspectives being brought to bear on a major decision. From her reading of an eclectic and unlikely range of magazines and papers including *Forbes* (a well-respected business weekly magazine) and the social pages of *The Post* (a tabloid), Tess identified the business opportunities for Trask Industries. Moving between the stories of the society wedding, the charity ball and Trask's stated desire to expand she can see the potential for Trask taking over a radio syndicate. Or as she puts it: 'I started to think Trask—radio? Trask—radio! And then I hooked up with Jack and he hooked up with Metro and so now here we are!'

Having initially identified the possibilities by this unconventional means, and continuing to be an avid reader of the popular press, Tess is also able to sound the alert because she has read about the planned move of the star disc jockey to 'the Big Apple'. In doing so she identifies the potential risks Trask Industries face in taking on a radio station in which the key personality is looking to leave. Trask, apparently convinced by her logic and impressed by the 'fire in her belly', asks if she would like to work for him and be willing to 'go out on a limb every day for ... [him]—legitimately'. She jumps at the chance.

It seems this film offers a clear illustration of the benefits of diversity to business. The message seems to be that Trask Industries can drive business growth by appropriating a broader range of skills and expertise among employees, in this case through Tess's different perspective. In the final scene of the film, where we see Tess (once again donned in the corporate uniform) installed in her middle-management office with a personal secretary with whom she is willing to take turns making the coffee and with whom she hopes to maintain a two-way channel for input and initiatives, we may glimpse the promise of an ongoing diversity of workplace practices. However, as the triumphant music accompanying the closing credits rises to a crescendo, the camera pulls back to reveal Tess's office window on corporate culture as a rapidly disappearing dot in the Manhattan skyscape. This diminution of her presence suggests that she will not really make a mark on the established workplace culture of Trask Industries. It would seem that difference and any chance of change to the dominant culture are simply overwhelmed by the enormity of the existing system. As Casey (1995: 142) suggests in her analysis of the culture of a large corporation, the disciplinary apparatus embedded in the workplace culture acts to eliminate or control difference—whether it be age, gender or race—to achieve appropriate fit between employees and the corporate culture. This elimination of difference can be seen even more clearly in the machinations of the smirking boys in the next film that we analyse.

In the Company of Men

Kennedy (1996: 87) argues that in response to the changing social environment, including workplace opportunities for women and men, white men are demonstrating an increasing paranoia in which 'white male selfhood . . . [is] a fragile and besieged identity'. While Kennedy's discussion focuses on the film *Falling Down* (1993, Joel Schumacher), this is one of a number of films that trace the relationship between models of masculinity and the changing workplace. See for example *Wall Street* (1987, Oliver Stone), *Regarding Henry* (1991, Mike Nichols), *The Doctor* (1991, Randa Haines), *Philadelphia* (1993, Jonathan Demme), *Disclosure* (1994, Barry Levinson) and *Brilliant Lies* (1996, Richard Franklin).

Faludi (1999) also points to the increasing perception of white men in crisis as the prompt for her study into the stories of American men. In the film, *In the Company of Men*, this fragility of white male identity manifests itself in an unchecked scourge of difference—a complete rejection of diversity in the workplace.

The film is set in the context of a workplace that is relentlessly masculine and where a competitive ethos feeds into both work and play for the two main players, Howard (Matt Malloy) and Chad (Aaron Eckhart). These men are old college buddies who now work together in a company in which a culture of competition is evident. Early in the film it is established that while Howard may have line authority, he does not have true patriarchal authority. It is his subordinate, Chad, who is the bearer of the markers of hegemonic masculinity. Throughout the film, unbeknownst to Howard, Chad is looking to restore himself to what he perceives as his rightful position of authority in the workplace through undermining Howard's performance.

In their 'play' the two men are apparently a team as they seek to sexually exploit and harm a junior female worker. Far be it from Chad or Howard to tangle with the likes of Katherine from *Working Girl*, or any other competitive, aggressive, or indeed confident, professional woman. To make their game more 'therapeutic' in terms of restoring their sense of superiority as men over women, they specifically target a woman who meets their criteria of being in some way weak and defenceless:

Chad [to Howard]: Say we were to find some gal...and this person's a vulnerable...young thing, wall flower—disfigured in some way. Some woman who's beginning to feel that life—I mean a full, healthy sexual life—romance, stuff like that,
is just lost to her forever. And we both hit [on] her...and on we play...and then
one day out goes the rug, and we're pulling hard! And Jill—she just comes tumbling
after. Trust me, she'll be reaching for the sleeping pills within a week! And we will
be laughing about it until we are old men. What do you think? Restore a little dignity
in our lives.

Their 'gal', Christine (Stacy Edwards), is a deaf typist who has recently started work
in the offices where they are posted and, for them, she has the added bonus of being
sexually attractive.

Over the pair's six-week posting to this work site, the film is able to focus on the
men's relationships in isolation from their normal work environment. The depiction of
the offices suggests a state of flux. There are renovations going on—walls are half fin-
ished, spaces are temporarily petitioned and the office furniture and technology seem to
leave much to be desired—all of which reinforce a sense of impermanence and change.
This is perhaps indicative of the uncertainties surrounding career tenure that feed into the
paranoid motivation for the two men's self-affirming game. Citing grievances about affirmative action policies and 'growing job insecurity in an age of post-industrial restructuring', Kennedy (1996) identifies an increasing 'fear of falling' among white middle-class
Americans. This he characterizes as a reaction to 'losing control over self and society; a
fear which has distinctly anxious connotations for white males who must confront their
diminishing ability to assume normative roles of power and authority and transcend the
politics of identity formation' (Kennedy, 1996: 89).

To counteract this kind of fear and restore their 'dignity', Chad and Howard embark
on their game. While the game of leading a woman on, only to dump her, is men against
women, it is also a battle between what are coded as superior and inferior versions of
masculinity. A quick comparison of the two men, Chad and Howard, reveals how they
are at extremes of the spectrum of gender traits in terms of physical and emotional
performance. Chad is the extreme manifestation of hegemonic masculinity. He is tall,
with chiselled good looks—a Calvin Klein model type—but also disturbingly like the
ideal of Aryan manhood. This last point is greatly exacerbated by his evident cruelty
and his assumption of his absolute right to discipline the alien other; where the other
can be in terms of race, sexuality or gender. Such behaviours reaffirm the right of the
white, Anglo-Saxon man to dictate organizational structures and behaviours. Howard,
on the other hand, is shorter, balding, wears glasses and seems to have an air of harried
anxiety and is unlikely to be a winner in the contest of the workplace or the 'wooing' of
Christine. In the final scenes of the film, it becomes clear that Chad, the 'ideal man', wins
out in both the work and play situations. Despite his display of paranoia and arguably
sadistic personality disorder (American Psychiatric Association, 1987), he is rewarded
both in winning the deaf 'gal's' affections (which he ridicules) and in gaining Howard's
job. Chad seems to embody LaBier's (1986) observations that the attitudes of toughness,
aggressiveness and competitiveness and the ability to intimidate and humiliate others
and to 'get' one's enemies are valued attributes in many organizations. As Chad puts it,
'business is all about who's sporting the nastiest sack of venom and who is willing to
use it'. His reading of the workplace is apparently accurate as his abhorrent behaviour
is rewarded in this film's narrative.

A closer analysis of the film highlights the factors that sustain the highly masculine work environment. In the following sections we look at these factors; the temporal and spatial features of the workspace; the nature of the informal and exclusive communications between men; and the assertion of a masculine hegemony.

TEMPORAL AND SPATIAL FEATURES OF THE WORKSPACE

Howard and Chad are introduced to us en route to their new workplace. Their conversations take place in transit lounges, planes, a hire car and finally in the hotel bar. That Howard and Chad are able to simply decamp from 'home' for a lengthy period of time to pursue a work project out of town is an example of the type of gendered organizing practices that limit the realization of diversity within companies. Commitment to work is often taken to be demonstrated by temporal availability (Hochschild, 1997). This is an assumption that indirectly discriminates against women, given the continued unequal division of labour in the home. These men are apparently unencumbered by family responsibilities and able to go where work requires them. That employees are able to accommodate long and unsocial hours is an assumption underpinning many organizational practices. Little has been achieved within organizations to accommodate more diverse work schedules (Acker, 1998), particularly within the executive ranks. It comes as no surprise then that in *In the Company of Men* the workplace seems to be occupied day and night. In this respect it is entirely predictable that Howard's and Chad's work and 'play' take place in the same space. This representation could be said to both reflect and construct the normalizing of long and unsocial hours in the workplace.

The physical features of the workplace within the *mise-en-scène* code it as masculine. The intersection of venetian blinds, door frames, filing cabinets and desks form harsh edges and straight lines of demarcation. These can be said to reinforce a sense of inflexibility and containment. These combine with the large plate glass windows and glass walls to create a sense of surveillance—a kind of cross between a fish bowl and a bird cage. The low-key lighting has a somewhat washed-out effect creating a monochromatic blue/grey impression, only punctuated by the executive uniforms of white shirt and black tie and dark trousers worn by all of the men. There is no space in which femininity can be expressed in this environment and the high angle close shot of a single vase of flowers situated on a filing cabinet is in stark contrast to this. The flowers, however, are presented to Christine as part of the game of building her up only to tear her down.

The executive uniform may be worn by the Afro-American junior executives in an attempt to pass as 'white' and certainly this erasure of difference is consciously sought by them. When Howard asks an Afro-American junior colleague if he would be interested in Christine, the younger man replies in reference to her disability '. . . in a company like this—with these guys around? No fucking way!' This exemplifies this man's attempts to erase, or at least not draw attention to, his own markers of difference that may otherwise be highlighted by associating with another 'other'. Such cautionary tales of the workplace culture proscribe any real acceptance of diversity.

Another Afro-American junior colleague in this same organization is unable to avoid Chad's racist intimidation and humiliation. Installing himself behind Howard's desk, and assuming his official authority, Chad takes the opportunity of giving one of these 'othered' juniors a dressing-down—quite literally. After mock-schooling the junior's pronunciation ('Is it Keif or Keith' and 'It's "ask" not "ax"'), Chad asks this latest victim if he 'has the balls for this job', adding, 'You want a job like mine... you need the big brass ones for the task.' After closing the venetian blinds, precluding scrutiny, Chad demands that the junior show him his 'clankers', with the comment, 'They asked me to recommend someone for the management training program before I go... so you decide.' As the young man stands exposed before him, trousers lowered and face registering total humiliation, Chad swings back and forth in his chair, evaluating. At this point Chad asserts 'I'm not a homo...'. Even though Chad is at pains to assure the young man, and perhaps himself, that his inspection is not motivated by sexual desire, this interrogation can only be characterized as sexual harassment. Nevertheless, if Chad were to acknowledge this as an instance of same sex desire he would be appalled. The heteronormative nature of Chad and all he represents would cite homosexuality as a marker of diversity to be excluded from the workplace.

In case the racism and sexism motivating and enabling this instance of supremacist abuse are not already sufficiently evident, when Chad tells the young man to pull up his pants, he adds, 'And get me a cup of coffee before you take off—black's fine.' This is a classic instance of the abuse of power, and later, when Howard asks Chad why he chose to humiliate Christine, Chad's simple explanation is 'Because I could.' This seems to constitute a display of personal power in the absence of any satisfyingly extensive and publicly recognized influence—the kind of white middle-class male backlash against a perceived marginalization identified by Kennedy (1996) and Faludi (1999).

INFORMAL AND EXCLUSIVE COMMUNICATIONS

'What's the difference between a golf ball and a g-spot? I'd bother spending twenty minutes looking for a golf ball.' In this linguistic 'horseplay' (Hearn, 1985), Chad is sharing a misogynistic joke with Howard in an informal and exclusive conversation between buddies as they move through the workplace.

This scene reinforces the importance of informal networks and conversations as factors limiting the realization of diversity in the workplace. The restricted access to, or exclusion from, informal interaction networks for those not of the dominant order, has been well recognized in the literature (Harriman, 1996; Wajcman, 1999). The value of these networks is found in how closely tied they are to the allocation of instrumental resources that are critical for effective performance in a job and for career development, as well as the expressive benefits of friendship and social support (Ibarra, 1993). Not having access to such networks disadvantages individuals in terms of not being privy to all the information about what is going on within the organization and not having the connections to assist in career development. Cannings and Montmarquette (1991), in considering the impact of networks on men's and women's career progression, demonstrated that the greater success of men relative to women in gaining promotion is men's greater use of informal networks. Informal linkages become even more important at higher levels in the organization, where information sharing and decision-making are greatly entwined with social networks.

The nuances of a company and its culture are revealed more in informal conversation than through more formal channels. The traditional situations in which male colleagues informally fraternize, such as drinks after work, informal lunches and weekend games of golf, are not readily accessible to women because they are seen as 'too different'. This same exclusion also holds for those who differ from the dominant white male group in other ways such as race and sexuality and so limits their access to an important career advantage. The representation of the men's interactions in the workplace in this film reflects the importance of the informal communications that go on within organizations. Not only are their conversations in the workplace quite informal—they occur in corridors, prior to meetings, in the men's room—they are also clearly shaped by their own interests and their antagonism to women. As such, they reflect a culture of exclusion, rather than inclusion, which is reinforced by the absence of women in professional roles in the film. Chad can crack misogynistic jokes, comfortable in the knowledge that his male colleagues are of a similar mind and will appreciate the humour.

Hegemonic Masculinity and Its 'Others'

The expression of masculinity in the film can be analysed with different points of emphasis. The first point relates to the absence of women from professional roles. The men are clearly in the positions of authority and women in support or subservient roles in the workplace, and this is reinforced by the architectures of power as noted above. That Christine has a disability could be read as the company being open to embracing diversity. However, she is employed on a temporary basis, in a support role with no authority. This lack of authority characterizes all the women depicted in the workplace in the film. Secondly, the misogyny expressed by the men, in particular Chad, also articulates an anxious backlash (Kennedy, 1996). Thirdly, there are clearly differences in the embodiment of masculinity, which we have seen to privilege white over black, but which interestingly also sets up a hierarchy between Chad's embodiment of hegemonic masculinity relative to Howard's feminized status.

It is perhaps ironic that one of Chad's jokes which elicits Howard's smirking camaraderie touches on the issue of abjection and marginalization of women. Chad's joke 'I don't trust anything that bleeds for a week and doesn't die', reflects an image of the female body as leaking and 'out of control' (Kristeva, 1982). The anxiety it can evoke is the state of abjection described by Kristeva (1982). While Kristeva uses the term 'abject' in relation to men and women, it is most often applied to a patriarchal notion of women as somehow a threat to stable and self-sufficient notions of self-hood. It is argued that abjection is 'associated with all that the subject perceives as unclean and potentially polluting: food, bodily wastes, and vomit, for example, all of which serve to remind the subject that it cannot escape basic biological drives over which it has no influence' (Gamble, 1999: 185).

This suggests a reading of Howard's embodiment of emotion as a feminizing one and on various occasions Howard's body betrays his unease in the role of the predatory patriarch. He spends a protracted period of time in the toilet, trousers around his ankles, while Chad pontificates on the progress he's made in the ensnaring of Christine. Also, after the full and irreversible effects of their game are realized, Howard's body registers its revulsion, and he is seen weeping, and later vomiting in a stairwell. Indeed, throughout the film Howard is coded as feminine in comparison to the strength and emotional atrophy of Chad, and he is the one seen squirming on the end of the telephone, as he strives to disengage himself from a conversation with his mother. As Connell (1987: 183) notes, 'hegemonic masculinity is always constructed in relation to other subordinated masculinities as well as in relation to women' and must negate other masculinities. Understanding this basic 'rule' renders Chad's success in winning Christine and the management job unsurprising.

IN THE COMPANY OF OTHERS

While we have focused on *Working Girl* and *In the Company of Men* to illustrate our arguments, these are not isolated instances of cinematic stereotyping of women and men in the workplace. Many other films reinforce the stereotypes of who should be in authority. GI Jane is a striking and seemingly extraordinary example of the attempt to disguise her difference within the military, nevertheless she is in fact operating within similar territory to her forerunner, Captain Karen Walden (Meg Ryan) in the film *Courage Under Fire* (1996). While GI Jane is able to erase all markers of femininity by undergoing an extremely painful metamorphosis in order to successfully negotiate the treacherous terrain of the US military, her counterpart, Captain Walden, is not so successful. Captain Walden is a Black Hawk helicopter pilot and the senior officer in an all male crew. The fact that she is in line for the posthumous awarding of the Medal of Honor is poor compensation for the fact that she quite literally 'crashes and burns' as a result of the insubordination and homosocial paranoia of the dominant male, Monfriez (Lou Diamond Phillips) in her crew. After their helicopter crashes, Walden and her crew are in enemy territory. Despite her resolution not to abandon one of her injured men, Walden's handgun proves to be no match for the phallic power symbolized by the M16 wielded by Monfriez. This hegemonic male successfully subverts her authority over the other less mutinous, younger males. As they escape, Captain Walden and her helicopter are obliterated by enemy fire.

This funeral pyre may be excessive, nevertheless there are numerous such cautionary tales which make up mainstream cinema. Membership of the dominant identity group may not guarantee a meteoric career trajectory, but to have any chance of being a high-flyer, the message is clear that markers of difference need to be kept in the closet. This is apparent in the operations of homophobia in the workplace as explored in the treatment of Andrew Beckett (Tom Hanks) in the film *Philadelphia* (1993, Jonathan Demme). Early in the film, in the guise of a heterosexual white middle-class male, Andrew is identified as a natural candidate for a partnership in his corporate law firm. The narrative of the film concerns Andrew's attempt to expose the law firm for having wrongly dismissed him on the basis of claims of incompetence. The film makes it explicit that the maintenance of a heteronormative workplace is the partners' real motivation for his dismissal (Holliday, 1998).

Moving to more light-hearted fare, in the comedy *The Associate* (1996, Donald Petrie), Laurel Ayres (Whoopie Goldberg), as an Afro-American woman, literally masks her identity in order to gain entry to the upper echelons of the world of commerce. In order to be taken seriously in her industry, Laurel cross-dresses as Robert Cutty, an aged and excessively white male. Her own markers of identity resist such a transformation and can only be contained with the help of a white latex mask and wig. This transformation is rewarded immediately in terms of access to power and money. There are a number of films that chart the modification and manipulation of femininity in an attempt to access senior echelons of the workplace. See for example, *Baby Boom* (1987, Charles Shyer), *The Temp* (1993, Tom Holland) and *Disclosure* (1994, Barry Levinson).

Ramsay (1995) has advocated the need to make more explicit the resistant behaviours that women experience daily in the workplace. While discussion of these issues at an abstract level may be interesting, Ramsay (1995: 177) suggests it is only through 'description, recognition and identification that resistant behaviour can be challenged and changed'. Film is a visual medium and as such is ideally suited to the task of description, recognition and identification of human behaviours. While the films may seem to provide stereotypical representations of women and men within the status quo, they can nevertheless be appropriated as exemplary texts in diversity education a bid to resist, challenge and change these outcomes. In this chapter we have been concerned to expose the obstacles to diversity in the performance of a variety of categories of identity, including gender, race and sexuality and to articulate a significantly qualified response to some seemingly positive representations of workplace change.

CONCLUSIONS

In the films we have looked at diversity has not been widely realized. While it sounds good in theory, the practice falls short of the rhetoric. The status quo continues in the form of a broadly accepted notion of the workplace in which any markers of difference that actively challenge or differ from the hegemonic model of masculinity are either eradicated or camouflaged. Difference is disciplined and punished and, as a consequence, diversity is suppressed.

While the cinema audience may explode with cheering when GI Jane reigns supreme or be hushed in reverence for the heroic last stand taken by Captain Karen Walden, these films should not only be seen as celebrations of change but also as cautionary tales that can be appropriated to bring about an awareness of barriers to the realization of workplace diversity. As such they can provide a powerful tool in diversity education. Those involved in diversity education can use these texts to make visible the sorts of obstacles to diversity and forms of resistance in the workplace. It would seem then that the 'picture *is* political' as Marshment (1997) would have it, and if deployed in this way the picture can also be educational. GI Jane, Captain Walden and the diverse crew of workers examined in this chapter can be recruited in the service of diversity awareness: their stories can illustrate the subversion of diversity initiatives and support the awakening of people's consciousness of the power of dominant ideologies.

REFERENCES

Acker, J. (1998). The future of 'gender and organisations': connections and boundaries. *Gender, Work and Organisation*, **5**(4), 195–206.
American Psychiatric Association (1987). *Diagnostic and Statistical Manual of Mental Disorders*, 3rd edn. Washington: American Psychiatric Association.
Australian Bureau of Statistics (2001). *Labour Force Australia (Cat No. 6203.0)*. Canberra: Australian Government Publishing Service.
Brewis, J. (1998). What is wrong with this picture? Sex and gender relations in disclosure. In J. Hassard & R. Holliday (eds), *Organization Representation, Work and Organizations in Popular Culture*. London: Sage Publications.

Cannings, K. & Montmarquette, C. (1991). Managerial momentum: a simultaneous model of the career progress of male and female managers. *Industrial and Labor Relations Review*, **44**(2), 212–228.

Casey, C. (1995). *Work, Self and Society after Industrialism*. London: Routledge.

Collins, D. (1998). *Organizational Change, Sociological Perspectives*. London: Routledge.

Connell, R.W. (1987). *Gender and Power*. Sydney: Allen & Unwin.

De Cieri, H. & Olekalns, M. (2001). Workforce diversity in Australia: challenges and strategies for diversity management. Working paper 9/01, Melbourne: Department of Management, Monash University.

Faludi, S. (1999). *Stiffed, the Betrayal of the American Man*. New York: William Morrow and Company Inc.

Gamble, S. (ed.) (1999). *The Icon Critical Dictionary of Feminism and Postfeminism*. Cambridge: Icon Books.

Garnsey, E. & Rees, B. (1996). Discourse and enactment: gender inequality in text and context. *Human Relations*, **49**(8), 1041–1045.

Gilbert, J. & Ivancevich, J. (2000). Valuing diversity: a tale of two organisations. *Academy of Management Executive*, **14**(1), 93–105.

Harriman, A. (1996). *Women/Men/Management*, 2nd edn. Westport, Conn.: Praeger Publishers.

Hassard, J. & Holliday R. (eds) (1998). *Organization Representation, Work and Organizations in Popular Culture*. London: Sage Publications.

Hearn, J. (1985). Men's sexuality at work. In A. Metcalf & M. Humphries (eds) *The Sexuality of Men*. London: Pluto Press.

Hochschild, A. (1997). *The Time Bind, When Work Becomes Home and Home Becomes Work*. New York: Henry Holt.

Holliday, R. (1998). Philadelphia: AIDS, organization, representation. In J. Hassard & R. Holliday (eds) *Organization Representation, Work and Organizations in Popular Culture*. London: Sage Publications.

Ibarra, H. (1993). Personal networks of women and minorities in management: a conceptual framework. *Academy of Management Review*, **18**(1), 56–87.

Kennedy, L. (1996). Alien nation: white male paranoia and imperial culture in the United States. *Journal of American Studies*, **30**(1), 87–100.

Kristeva, J. (1982). *Powers of Horror: An Essay on Abjection*. New York: Columbia University Press (translated by Leon S. Roudiez).

LaBier, D. (1986). *Modern Madness: The Hidden Link between Work and Emotional Conflict*. New York: Simon and Schuster.

Maas, J. (1999). Making diversity work. *Sloan Management Review*, **40**(4), 97–98.

Marshment, M. (1997). The picture is political: representation of women in contemporary popular culture. In V. Robinson & D. Richardson (eds) *Introducing Women's Studies*, 2nd edn (pp. 125–151). Houndmills: Macmillan.

Morton, T. & Duck, J. (2000). Social identity and media dependency in the gay community: the predictions of safe sex attitudes. *Communication Research*, **27**(4), 438–460.

Newman, J. (1995). Gender and cultural change. In C. Itzen & J. Newman (eds) *Gender, Culture and Organizational Change, Putting Theory into Practice*. London: Routledge.

O'Sullivan, J. & Sheridan, A. (1999). Misrepresentations: women, management and popular culture. *Women in Management Review*, **14**(1–2), 14–20.

Ramsay, E. (1995). The politics of privilege and resistance. In A. Payne & L. Shoemark (eds) *Women, Culture and Universities: A Chilly Climate? Conference Proceedings*, Sydney: University of Technology.

Robinson, G. & Dechant, K. (1997). Building a business case for diversity. *Academy of Management Executive*, **11**(3), 21–31.

Sheridan, A. (2001). A view from the top: women on the boards of public companies. *Corporate Governance, The International Journal for Effective Board Performance*, **1**(1), 8–14.

Sinclair, A. (2000). Women within diversity: risks and possibilities. *Women in Management Review*, **15**(5/6), 237–246.

Smith, D. (1987). *The Everyday World as Problematic, a Feminist Sociology*. Boston: Northeastern University Press.

Tasker, Y. (1998). *Working Girls: Gender and Sexuality in Popular Cinema*. London: Routledge.

Thomas, R. & Woodruff, M. (1999). *Building a House for Diversity; How a Fable about a Giraffe and an Elephant Offers New Strategies for Today's Workforce*. New York: American Management Association.

Turner, G. (1993). *Film as Social Practice*, 2nd edn. London: Routledge.

Wajcman, J. (1999). *Managing like a Man, Women and Men in Corporate Management*. Sydney: Allen & Unwin.

CHAPTER 19

Male Managers' Reactions to Gender Diversity Activities in Organizations

Anna Wahl and Charlotte Holgersson

Stockholm School of Economics, Stockholm, Sweden

SUMMARY

This chapter aims at problematizing men's reactions to equal opportunity and gender diversity activities in organizations. It is based on two different empirical studies conducted in the Swedish private sector, that both include interviews with male top managers. The empirical results are analysed with feminist theory on organization and management. The results indicate that the gender structure of the organization (i.e. numerical gender distribution, degree of segregation in tasks and positions and distribution regarding power and influence) has a decisive impact on men's reactions to gender diversity. In one of the studies male managers expressed gender-absent perceptions on management. As a result they did not see the point in changing the organizations' gender distribution on management levels and therefore a majority displayed negative reactions to gender diversity activities. Similar reactions could be found among some of the managers in the second empirical study. These were all men, in male-dominated organizations with male-gendered cultures. However, male managers in numerically women-dominated organizations displayed less gender-absent perceptions on organizations and management. Consequently, they expressed less negative reactions to gender diversity. Men who work with women in key positions are unable to reproduce the common perceptions of women as non-existent, not competent and not career oriented. We have called this *local feminism* since the interviewees concerned promote equal conditions for women and men in their daily work as organization leaders without necessarily identifying this as efforts particularly directed at women. The emergence of men as *local feminists* in organizations with many women and where women are influential may thus be seen as a direct consequence of the gender structure.

Individual Diversity and Psychology in Organizations. Edited by Marilyn J. Davidson and Sandra L. Fielden.
© 2003 John Wiley & Sons, Ltd.

INTRODUCTION

This chapter aims at problematizing men's reactions to equal opportunity and gender diversity activities when analysing work for change of the gender order in organizations. It is based on two different empirical studies conducted in the Swedish private sector. The first study is the result of a committee of inquiry appointed by the Swedish Government (SOU, 1994; Wahl, 1995). The second is based on interviews with top executives within a large Swedish company (Holgersson & Wahl, 2001). The empirical results are analysed with feminist theory on organization and management in order to contribute to the diversity discourse when it comes to ways of thinking and methods for change.

GENDER AND ORGANIZATION

The gender order in society is reproduced in the gender order of organizations, and vice versa. Every organization has a gender order that reflects the power relation between men and women. In organizations, meanings of gender are expressed through perceptions, structures and processes (Kanter, 1977; Acker, 1992; Baude, 1992; Wahl et al., 1998). Gender structures in organizations can differ when it comes to gender distribution, with respect to numbers in both professions and positions, and to power and influence (Wahl, 1992, 2001). An organization's gender order is related in several ways to that of society and cannot thus be separated from the more general context of gender order in society (see Figure 19.1).

Research on management and gender has grown over the past 25 years. A relatively large amount of attention has been devoted to women in executive positions since the 1970s within the research tradition called 'women in management'. This tradition has, however, primarily focused on the individual and has therefore concentrated on the presence or absence of particular characteristics in female executives. This type of research on women as executives was not related to any broader feminist theory but has been based on the traditional, gender-absent approaches of management theory. Results from studies are often discussed in terms of attitudes, prejudices and sex role patterns, without links being made to more general theories about gender and gender systems. Several researchers have, however, criticized the explanations of the women in management tradition with their focus on the individual, and have instead advocated more contextual explanations for the existing imbalance between the sexes in executive positions (Kanter,

---

GENDER STRUCTURE:
1.   Numerical gender distribution
2.   Degree of segregation in tasks and positions
3.   Distribution regarding power and influence

GENDER ORDER:
1.   Gender structure
2.   Symbolic aspects such as norms, values and notions of gender

FIGURE 19.1   Gender structure and gender order in organizations—key theoretical concepts. Sources: Wahl, A. (1995). *Könsstrukturer iorganisationer*, EFI Stockholm and Wahl, A. et al. (2001). *Det ordnar sig. Teorier om organisation och kön*, Studentlitteratur Stockholm

1977; Marshall, 1984; Cockburn, 1991; Wahl, 1992, 1995). A contextual perspective in research requires a more critical view of structures in organizations, as well as relations in society as a whole, as they are not regarded as self-evident. In this type of approach, the explanation for the low number of women at senior management level lies in the structural obstacles women as a social category encounter. In feminist studies, gender and management are both defined as socially constructed concepts. Treating gender, that is femininity and masculinity, as socially constructed concepts means that they are not regarded as absolute or true in content.

A body of research studying male managers as belonging to the gender category of men has developed, contributing to a further understanding of management and organizations (Collinson & Hearn, 1994, 1996). The critical studies of men have indicated the dialectic relationship between constructions of masculinities and constructions of management. Masculinities and femininities are often constructed as opposites of one another. Women are therefore confronted with specific problems at management level since they belong to the 'other' sex. Masculinities have been made part of management (Collinson & Hearn, 1996; Wahl, 1998). Theories about men's homosocial behaviour (Lipman-Blumen, 1976; Kanter, 1977) and men's homosocial desire (Roper, 1996) describe the importance of men confirming other men in organizations. The dominance of men among managers can thus be understood as a question of men choosing other men, rather than of men actively rejecting women (Lindgren, 1996).

MEN'S PERCEPTIONS OF WOMEN AND MANAGEMENT

In this section some results from a study based on a committee of inquiry will be presented. The study was conducted in 1993–94, and focused on the executive levels of management in the Swedish private sector. The data were collected through a questionnaire distributed to 58 per cent of all companies with more than 200 employees to survey business and industry. In-depth interviews were conducted with a selection of male (11) and female (9) chief executives, and with agents of change (9 women) who worked with projects concerning increasing the number of women at the executive level. The report was published in English in the book *Men's Perceptions of Women and Management* (edited and co-authored by Wahl, 1995). This section in the chapter is based on a summary of the results of the study.

Overall, the main conclusion from this study was that men lack knowledge on the importance of gender in work life. Male executives have ideas about women which seldom accord with women's own descriptions. Men regard it as a matter of course that they define what a manager should be like, and that priority is given to their perception of how organizations should be run. Male executives are, however, unaware of the priority given to their perceptions. They regard their descriptions and assessments as being objective in general and thus gender neutral. They regard it as self-evident that competence governs recruitment to executive positions, but what competence actually consists of is not clarified. The conclusion of this line of reasoning is, nevertheless, that men are competent and women are not. Women regard men's lack of knowledge as a problem. What is even more problematic, however, is that men do not regard this as a problem. Most male executives consider that things work well as they are. They do not perceive change as necessary. They do not regard it as a problem for companies that

there are few women at senior levels, and they do not consider that this has effects on
business activities and profitability.

GENDER DIVERSITY

Sweden is often considered to be more successful when it comes to equality between
women and men, compared to most other countries. This concerns women's participation in politics and in the labour market overall. It is, for example, considered normal
for women in Sweden to have small children and to work and have a career. This has
been made possible through a number of support systems, of which an important one
is municipal day care for children. It is also due to the shift in attitudes, from considering equality a 'women's issue' to a 'society issue' or an 'organization issue'. Creating
equal terms for women and men in the labour market involves changing organizational
structures and is therefore a question of power.

Swedish equal opportunity policy is characterized by its focus on women in the labour
market. During the first half of the twentieth century, equal opportunities were mainly
about women's equal rights to education and to occupations from which they had previously been excluded and the abolition of special women's wages. From the 1960s and
onwards, when married women with children started to enter the paid labour market, the
question of childcare appeared on the agenda. Creating municipal day care and introducing parental allowance solved this question. Research, however, shows that women
still have lower wages than men and that women still carry out the great bulk of unpaid
work in the home (Åström, 1995).

The value of the initiatives carried out in the past years can, however, be seen at the
structural level. There is a platform for equal opportunity issues in practically every
workplace throughout Sweden. There is a base for women's demands. The more radical
gender elements in the contemporary debate, such as a woman's party or quotas and also
policies aimed at increasing representation for women and more female executives, have
at least in part originated from equal opportunity policies (Åström, 1995). Today, men
and women in Sweden are active to the same extent on the labour market. In 1999, the
economic activity rate among women aged 20–64 was 78 per cent compared to 84 per cent
for men. The labour market is, however, segregated. Women work to the same extent in
public and private industry, whereas the majority of men work in private industry. Most
occupations are either dominated by men or women, only two occupations have an equal
gender distribution, i.e. journalists/authors and chefs/cooks (Statistics Sweden, 2000).

TOP MANAGEMENT

The male bias in top management levels in business life can be seen as an expression
of gender order in the labour market. A majority of all companies in private industry in
Sweden have top management consisting entirely of men, and the top management of
99 per cent of companies are dominated by men. Overall, the proportion of women at
top management level in privately owned companies is 6 per cent (Höök, 1995).

In our study, male and female senior managers by and large displayed quite different
ideas as to why there were so few women at senior levels, and whether it was important

to try to change this. Women regarded the problem as a profitability problem, whereas men regarded it more often as a woman's problem. Women viewed themselves and other women as competent, whereas men saw women as having deficiencies in a number of aspects. The male top executives referred to children and the family as a problem of decisive importance—for women. Women, on the other hand, stressed quite different kinds of obstacles, especially the fact that men and women do not pursue careers on equal terms (Asplund, 1988; Wahl, 1995).

The idea was widespread among male top executives that women do not want to become managers, an idea that is not shared by the female executives. Men based their statements on their *perceptions* (as opposed to experiences) about women; only one of the men interviewed had a woman in his top management group. Women based their statements on actual *experiences* of working together with men *and* women, and over half of the women interviewed had women in their senior management groups. The results of the interviews with these executives substantiated previous research and revealed a lack of actual real knowledge about women senior executives, primarily on the part of the men, and an absence of dialogue between men and women (Franzén, 1995).

Clearly, the male executives' perceptions about women in management were not supported by available research in the field. The female top executives had reflected much more on the relationship between the distribution of the sexes and male-dominated organizational structures. As a consequence of men choosing men, it is a common occurrence that senior management groups and boards of directors are all-male worlds. Thus, the norm that managers are men is perpetuated and consolidated. Since it is never problematized or openly discussed, this norm is, however, recreated tacitly and in an implicit way. Senior management groups and boards of directors are presented as gender neutral. The absence of women allows misconceived, stereotypical notions about women to flourish, i.e. women do not want to pursue careers, women do not wish to become managers, women lack confidence and women give their families a higher priority than their careers. Management is in fact developed by men in senior management and is accordingly about relationships between men (Wahl, 1995).

WORK FOR CHANGE

In our survey of privately owned companies, 50 per cent had organized equal opportunities activities. Half of the companies surveyed did not have a plan of action for equality between men and women, even though they are required to do so by law (Höök, 1995). One in three companies said, however, that they had an explicit policy of wishing to increase the number of women managers they employed. There appeared to be a will to change in some organizations who had committed employees working on testing, developing and disseminating ideas about how to increase the number of women in management positions.

The most common methods used according to the interviews carried out with agents of change in this field were:

- Integrating and setting goals
- Working with recruitment and appointments
- Managerial training

FORM	Women only	Women and men	Men only
PERSPECTIVE	Power	Complementary	Absent
INTEGRATION	Independent	Semi-integrated	Integrated

FIGURE 19.2   Combinations of factors in equal opportunity programmes.
Sources: Holgersson, C. and Höök, P. (1997). *Ledarutveckling för kvinnor—uppföljning av en satsning på Volvo*, and Höök, P. (2001) *Stridspiloter i vida kjolar*, at EFI Stockholm

- Networks
- Specific projects
- Managerial training for women
- Mentoring programmes

The change agents who were interviewed fell mainly into two categories: external agents and internal agents. The external agents were often consultants commissioned by organizations to carry out projects. There were also consultants who arranged independent programmes, or managerial training courses, that were open for managers from different organizations. The internal change agents worked on projects in their own organizations.

Most projects and programmes can be described with the assistance of the factors *form* (only women, only men or women and men), *perspective* (gender absent, gender complementary or with a power perspective) and the *degree of integration* in the organization (Wahl, 1995; Holgersson & Höök, 1997; Höök, 2001) (see Figure 19.2).

A number of combinations of these three factors exist today as regards methods listed above. There seems to be a *maturity axis* in time, affecting how work is carried out. For example, in managerial training for women, there is often a programme for women only that is not especially well integrated in the organization in the early stages of development. With a power perspective, it could be labelled as 'personal development'. On the other hand, without a gender perspective, it might be categorized as a self-development course such as 'boosting your self-confidence'. In due time, the specific programme for women is more integrated into the organization. These programmes, that follow years after the first initiatives, often have the form of networks and project groups, focusing on women who want to increase their knowledge and acquire more scope for action, i.e. power (Wahl, 1995; Höök, 2001).

The other kind of result described was the increased visibility of women in the organization or the increased visibility of the issue of gender diversity. This result should be seen in the light of the agents' claims that there was a general perception among managers that there were no suitable, competent women to turn to. If the programme has had a gender-absent perspective, however, sometimes a negative effect of visibility could occur. It depended on attitudes towards women's situation in the organization. For example, if there was no general understanding as to why a training programme should be solely for women, this could be interpreted as an injustice to men, rather than a way of dealing with a gender bias in the organization. As a consequence, this type of programme would often be difficult to defend in the long run. It is obvious that women-only training courses enable women to become more aware of their situation in the organization and acquire new knowledge on these issues. A number of agents also claimed that attending these courses also changed women's perceptions with respect to other women. Women learned to acknowledge other women in the organizations to a greater extent, as well as their skills and competencies. They realized the importance of giving other women support, and of building female networks. Furthermore, women who had previously been sceptical of the value of special development programmes for women, often changed their view once they had been on such a course themselves (Wahl, 1995).

MEN AND GENDER DIVERSITY ACTIVITIES

As equal opportunity activities became more integrated into the organization's activities, through mainstreaming and diversity policies, men have become more involved in the process. It is important for men to realize that they themselves reproduce the biased structures in organizations. Men will continue to reproduce these structures uncritically, unless they learn to think in a different way. Integrating men in the programmes is, therefore, not done without encountering problems. It is important to introduce a power perspective in the programmes, so that the acquisition of knowledge and new ways of thinking can take place.

Having men involved in a mentoring programme, for example, can be advantageous if there is a power perspective. Then men's awareness is increased, and at the same time, a dialogue can be initiated between men and women. However, if there is a gender-absent perspective, there can be a risk that men will dominate and that the norms of male dominance will simply be reproduced.

On a more optimistic note, our research illustrated that mentoring programmes which acknowledged gender issues also helped change male attitudes in a positive direction. Some men became aware of problems such as home/work conflicts, etc. that they have never thought about before in relation to working life. Obviously, a change in perceptions and attitudes towards diversity issues in organizations is an important result of this work. Changes in attitudes can also result in changes in behaviour. The results to a large extent involve linking women's issues to the organization's activities and not treating them as separate issues, but integrating them throughout all the processes and systems within the organization.

The lessons to be learnt about the degree of success of the various programmes and projects described by the agents dealt with the importance of support and backing from senior management. In successful programmes, senior management sent signals down the organization emphasizing the importance of the programme and this was noted, especially by male managers. It was also important to have access to the senior management in the course of the work and not just at the beginning, an issue that was raised by several of the interviewed agents of change. Some argued that it was also necessary that senior management really believed in the importance of increasing the number of women in management positions, and that their actions were based on conviction and not just lip-service.

A large proportion of the lessons drawn from this study were about men. Overall, men lacked knowledge and motivation about the issue relating to gender equality. Men did not feel involved, and they did not understand the problem. Men chose other men for managerial jobs, and most male top managers lacked the experience of working with women on the same level (Wahl, 1995).

THE GROUP—A CASE STUDY OF MEN'S REACTIONS TO GENDER DIVERSITY ACTIVITIES

In this next section, we will discuss our second investigation which involves a case study of men's reactions to gender diversity activities in an organization known as the Group. The Group is a Swedish organization in the media industry with operations in a large number of mainly European countries and with approximately 10 000 employees. The Group comprises over 50 different independent companies, organized in six different business areas and each headed by a chief executive officer. The organization is highly decentralized, which Group management regards as the base for diversity and creativity. According to the official corporate objectives and vision, the Group values talent, entrepreneurship, professionalism and integrity. The Group also claims to be receptive to change, having short decision-making paths and allocating great freedom of responsibility.

In 2000, the Group launched a three-year project called Tora with the objective of increasing the number of women in executive positions within the organization. The project management team stated that half of the Group employees were women and half of the customer base consisted of women, thus, in order to make business profitable, it was necessary to use all talent and potential among employees. During the first year of the project the proportion of women managers was 41 per cent, with the number of women in management groups increasing from 16 to 24 per cent. The aim of Tora was to increase the number of women in management groups to at least 30 per cent, using different change methods, i.e.

- Setting clear goals
- Reviewing key employees with special focus on women
- Making working conditions more flexible
- A mentoring programme with a power perspective
- A study of the recruitment strategies within the Group as a way of raising gender awareness and equality issues

We aim to focus on just one of the methods above, namely the last one: the results from the study of different ways in which managers and key employees were recruited and identified within the organization (Holgersson & Wahl, 2001). This was investigated through 10 interviews with chief executives (9 men and 1 woman) within the Group, since chief executives were responsible for identifying and recruiting key persons in the individual companies.

The objective was to investigate differences in experiences within the Group, rather than the most typical or dominant experiences. The selection of interviewees was therefore steered to ensure interviewee diversity according to numerous criteria for distribution. They were chosen in order to represent companies of varied size; with varied gender distribution in relation to both organization and management team; from different business areas and types of operations; from different levels in Group hierarchy; and with a certain degree of geographical dispersal. The interviewees related to the phenomena studied from different angles and each individual had his or her own definition of a key person, of how identification can be interpreted and of the relevant types of recruitment to be described.

EXECUTIVE VIEWS ON THE LACK OF WOMEN IN TOP POSITIONS

All interviewees considered the lack of women in top posts in the Group to be a problem and half of these regarded the problem to lie primarily with group management. The reasons for seeing it as a Group problem rather than their own company problem did however vary. Some interviewees already employed women in senior posts and thus did not see a problem in their company. One interviewee failed to understand why the Group considered it a problem since he believed that selection should be based on competence, which in turn should lead to the recruitment of women, as well as men. There were, however, also interviewees lacking women in senior posts who did not consider this a problem, but considered the low proportion of women at top level as a problem for the Group.

Some interviewees claimed that women carry the problem within themselves, since they were not as geographically mobile as men, were unsuited to the working hours, lacked self-assertion and were too discreet and quiet. Others, however, considered the problem to be within their own company, not just at group level. They expressed the view that men were also part of the problem, variously describing men as cowardly and fearing conflict. According to two interviewees, men fearing conflict could lead to women being perceived as difficult to work with, since they were seen as being more direct and more ready to solve conflicts. Another interviewee related how men felt threatened by competent women. Yet another claimed the low proportion of women in senior posts to have its source in men, with men choosing to surround themselves with other men. This was primarily due not to men feeling as strangers in relation to women, but rather to a feeling of belonging in relation to men. This resulted in men appointing and surrounding themselves with other men. The interviewee stressed sameness rather than difference as the guiding factor.

A majority of the interviewees considered women at least as competent as men, and were in several cases credited with greater competence. The interviewees also revealed various ways of arguing in favour of change. One chief executive explained the necessity for getting more women into the organization in order to achieve a specific change in product. Conversely, two other interviewees claimed that product change had led to a greater proportion of women in the organization.

Some interviewees were positive towards the Tora project, although half of them claimed that it largely lacked relevance within their own organization since many women already held senior posts. Two interviewees suggested that the Tora programme was irrelevant to their companies, despite men dominating at decision-making level, since everyone was content with the situation as it stood. According to one of these interviewees, the chief issue was finding competent people.

These results may seem contradictory in the way the male managers expressed positive attitudes towards women in general, but more negative attitudes towards the Tora project. This could be a sign of a resistance to change when it comes to actual programmes in their own organization. Despite a positive attitude to gender diversity as a principle, there is often resistance when it comes to actual change of gender order (Wahl, 1995; Höök, 2001).

Executive Views on Management and Culture in Relation to Gender

Some managers pointed out specialist competence as a guiding principle, while others saw all-round competence (e.g. as expressed in the ability to collaborate) as important. Several interviewees stressed the importance of flexibility in viewing the tasks of management, and that overtime was not essential. One interviewee had banned overtime, considering it important that all work was carried out during working hours and that the need to work overtime was a negative warning signal. Examples of the opposite were also present in the findings, as illustrated by one interviewee who stated that management commitment could be seen through working long hours. It was also expressed that the art of selecting a leader meant getting 'the right "man" in the right place'.

What did interviewees have to say about competence and management in relation to gender? Three interviewees expressed what is termed a complementary view of women and management, believing that women could contribute something different in their management. A further three passed over this view and instead emphasized the competence of women as clear in itself, in one case even as superior. These maintained that the organizational conditions were unequal for women and men, which explained the scarcity of women in senior posts. In two interviews, women were described as lacking the aggression and self-confidence required in executive posts. Companies with a relatively high proportion of women managers were perceived as being oriented gender-wise towards women at business sector or product level. In other words, women managers were a result of operational orientation. Chief executives of certain companies stated that the issue of gender distribution for some posts had become part of company culture. This issue was regularly taken up at meetings; for example, as one interviewee put it, 'Talk has to be followed by decisions and actions, that's important if the issue is to acquire credibility in the organization.'

Most interviewees revealed how different business sectors, professions and departments were gendered. These most often corresponded but were not always clear-cut. For example, the position of editor could be gendered for men or for women. Sometimes contradictory gendering was commented on; the evening paper business, for example, could be gendered for men, despite a large proportion of women readers. Gendering was often expressed directly by an interviewee stating that a certain business sector or profession was for men or for women. Sometimes this was more indirect through expressions such as 'fire-fighter', 'cowboy' and 'farmer' when speaking of managers (see Table 19.1).

TABLE **19.1** The statements on gendering in the Group

Female gendered
Profession: editor
Department: circulation department, administration, customer service, subscription department
Business: magazines (both through products and customers), publishers
Content of operations: culture, lifestyle, entertainment

Male gendered
Profession: news reporter, management team, chief executive and 'crown prince',
   Group board of directors
Business: news, financial reporting, business information, evening paper

---

Interviewees used cases to illustrate their own organization culture. These almost only occurred when the issue of women or the situation for women in the Group arose. These illustrative cases dealt mostly with women, emphasizing those having achieved success in the company or the Group. In four interviews women's minority position was illustrated by pointing out the occasional woman visible in the Group. These cases exemplified the exposed position of women compared to men in corresponding circumstances, showing women's difficulty in being acknowledged as 'all-rounders' and—according to an interviewee—women becoming 'too male'. One case was taken up to show that a woman could combine a management job with having children. The post was adapted to suit the woman, not the opposite way round, which was an excellent solution according to the interviewee.

The vast majority of interviewees were men, and the majority of these described how they themselves had recruited a woman or made a woman visible in their company. One interviewee described how he had successively begun to notice women's competence and how he later had passed on his observations to others. He told of the first women he had recruited and his scepticism at that stage. This was followed by a decade of successful recruitment of women during which his attitude to women in his organization changed totally. He previously considered women having children a problem, but in the interview said there was no problem. 'It's not just women having children nowadays', he added jokingly. He described several occasions where women had accompanied him and, for example, been presented to the board. He also described discovering the existence of misogyny, and was surprised about the opposition to women in a certain organization. Some of the cases dealt with men. Two interviewees told of efforts to recruit men to their women-dominated company. This proved difficult in both cases since finding competent women was much easier, according to interviewees. There were also the spontaneous comments of interviewees about changes they have seen concerning women and men at the Group. Several of the interviewees felt that numbers of women in more senior posts was increasing and gave specific examples of this.

HOW GENDER ABSENT ARE PERCEPTIONS WITHIN THE GROUP?

The dominant view among senior managers in Swedish private sector business is that the low proportion of women in management presents no problem. If identified as a problem, then it is a problem for women. It is very rarely described as an organization problem (Wahl, 1995). Compared to Swedish business in general, a large proportion of company heads in the Group seemed, however, to view the low numbers of women managers as a problem. Unusually, a significant number of interviewees described this as an organizational problem. Furthermore, another difference was that several interviewees spoke of men as sources of the problem. Thus, awareness of the problem appeared to be broader and more nuanced in the Group than in Swedish business in general.

Gender distribution in several of the companies (numerically dominated by women) meant that chief executives were able to see the problem from a different angle. Men generally dominated top positions in business. Consequently the majority of these men had no experience of working with women at the same level. As previously discussed, this helps perpetuate the notions of women as inadequate leaders and/or uninterested in a career (Wahl, 1995). In several Group companies women were in fact in the majority, even at higher levels, and men were therefore less likely to reproduce stereotypical concepts of women as managers.

Therefore, the Group did not appear to be an organization with a markedly gender-absent perspective on management. The companies displaying insight into gender and diversity issues also seemed to possess different attitudes towards change. Several of these companies had switched from identifying women as the problem and ceased efforts to adapt women to the organization, and instead focused on the problem of organizational structure and climate. This had resulted in several organizations trying to change organization structure. Changing job descriptions and making the organization of work more flexible makes combining management and children a possibility for both men and women. One interpretation of this is that men are also being recognized as a gender category, not simply as the gender-neutral norm. Several companies also endeavoured to change organizational culture through, for example, discouraging or even counteracting overtime.

Running a project for change such as Tora also plays a part in creating awareness and thus change at Group level. This is shown by the active support of the Group executive for the change process, which has also been noted by earlier research (Cockburn, 1991; Wahl, 1995). The unusual awareness regarding gender within the Group may be interpreted as a result of the different gender structures (see Figure 19.1) among companies within the Group. Several companies in the Group were numerically female dominated and women had a relatively greater influence on operations. This could be an explanation of the lack of gender absence and the greater degree of insight into the problem.

WHO INTERPRETS AND DEFINES MANAGEMENT?

Various constructions of negative gender stereotyping were expressed in the interviews. In the companies dominated by men, women were often portrayed as inadequate, either lacking aggressiveness or being too quiet. Where women were expected to change the product in a specific way, this often resulted in views of women as being different and complementary (see Figure 19.3).

This view of women as different might at first appear equal, but is usually discriminatory and linked to the view of male competence as superior and female competence as complementary and subordinate (Wahl, 1998). The view of women expressed in such descriptions can be recognized from organizations dominated by men (Wahl, 1992, 1995; Holgersson, 2001). Women leaders in companies dominated by men may still be considered as 'too masculine', while in the companies dominated by women they attract no special attention since their competence is self-evident.

> **Unexploited resource**: Women are inadequate but can compensate for this, thus representing an unexploited resource in the organization ('sameness').
>
> **Different resource**: Women are inadequate but have other qualities and experiences compared with men, and can thus represent a different and complementary resource in the organization ('difference').

FIGURE **19.3**   Discourses on women in organizations.
Source: Wahl, A. (1998). Deconstructing Women and Leadership, *International Review of Women and Leadership*, **4**(2), 46–60

Not surprisingly, a more positive view of women was also expressed in the companies dominated by women where they are described as unquestionably competent. This was also confirmed from interviews with both men and women managers in a previous study of organizations dominated by women (Wahl, 1998, 2001). It is interesting to note that a negative or complementary view of women is expressed in only 3 companies of the 10, compared with two-thirds of the companies in the survey of Swedish private sector business presented earlier in the chapter (Wahl, 1995). Statements made by the chief executives reveal a more positive view of women in the Group than in business in general.

In several of the companies women were described as specialists, i.e. people carrying out a special function, often belonging to a certain profession. In the interviews, specialist skills were portrayed as incompatible with managerial positions. Management competence and specialist competence were clearly in contradiction. In this way management competence and all-round competence become one and the same. But all-round competence was not something available through education as with specialist competence. All-round competence is achieved when individuals get the opportunity of gaining the required experience. Kanter (1977) writes on the importance of finding oneself in a positive spiral. Once a person has been identified as leader material, then this person will be offered positions and opportunities to become still more competent. An earlier study of organizations dominated by women, with many women in leading positions, showed that the period of development as a leader was regarded as being of particular importance by the women. They compared their situation with the 'normal' situation in organizations dominated by men and established that they were given greater opportunity to grow and develop as leaders (Wahl, 1998, 2001).

In some of the companies, commitment is linked to management competence, and commitment is measured in terms of hours spent working. Kanter (1977) noted that since finding out the real reasons for success and failure is difficult, management suffers a great deal of insecurity. By making work priority number one, managers show loyalty and willingness to do their utmost for the company, thereby reducing their insecurity. Thus, the requirement of long working hours is not a performance requirement but rather a loyalty requirement, since loyalty is measured in time. Since women often have other commitments besides work, such as home and children, they do not possess the same opportunity of showing loyalty and are therefore regarded as unsafe bets compared to their male colleagues.

Interviews with company heads and chairpersons suggest the requirement of total commitment to work as still dominant in Swedish business (Franzén, 1995; Andersson, 1997; Linghag, 1998; Holgersson, 2001). However, interviewees in the Group companies dominated by women reported that overtime was not encouraged. This indicated that loyalty can be shown in other ways. What these other ways were was not revealed in the analysis of the interviews, but presents an interesting question for further research.

GENDERED CULTURES

Gendering is a term used to show that notions of gender are social and cultural constructions (Acker, 1992; Wahl et al., 2001). These notions then are up for negotiation and ever changeable. The interviews conducted show several examples of such changes. Empirical material revealed that professions, job positions and business sectors were gendered in the Group. These often corresponded to the gendering of business as a whole. There were exceptions, however. Being an editor may be regarded as typical for men in one company and typical for women in another. One company with a woman as chief executive, and with a dominant number of women employees, existed in a sector otherwise dominated by men. Sales personnel in one company had changed from being predominantly gendered by men to being outnumbered by women.

Two typical models of contrasting gendered organizational cultures within the Group are outlined below:

- Traditional, male-dominated culture where 'long hours' were stressed as important. Evening overtime, long days and frequent travel were required. Measured results represented the basis for judgement of leaders. The chief executive was described as 'a lonely cowboy'. A recurrent description of the environment is 'laddish'.
- Culture dominated by women (which were often led by men), where competence is given greater emphasis than long working hours and working methods. Commitment, identification, informal environment and feeling at home were described as important in relation to management. *Not* working late into the evenings was described by some as important. Flexibility and the opportunity of combining work and children were stressed.

Basic elements in both of these organizational cultures were independence, a spirit of enterprise and commitment. Commitment might be measured through long hours (e.g. positive note is made of e-mails being sent at 10 p.m.) in the male-dominated cultures, while culture dominated by women might measure commitment in terms of well-being.

Gendering of operations in certain companies had contributed to the formation of a 'sanctuary', where women were described neither as inadequate or different. It seemed the culture of 'independence and freedom' which existed in the different companies within the Group, could create both opportunities and hindrances for women. This culture resulted in gendering being seen as a local issue for each company. According to our interpretation, gender structure in this way gains a significant influence on the formation of local gender orders. The term 'gender order' embraces somewhat more than the term 'gender structure'. Besides the quite easily observed three measurements of distribution dealt with above as organization gender structure, gender order also includes more symbolic aspects such as organization norms, values and notions of gender (Wahl et al., 2001). Gendered characteristics in organizations can be seen as gender symbols, making it hardly surprising that contradictions, ambiguities, ambivalence and time-related changes exist (Acker, 1992; Gherardi, 1995; Wahl et al., 2001).

The local gender orders influence the actions of the chief executives. Some of the chief executives interviewed can be interpreted as feminists within their organization since they incorporated a positive view of women which also resulted in action. Their actions did not, however, go beyond their organizations, but rather represented a response to an environment with many competent women, and which they themselves led. We have called this 'local feminism', since the interviewees concerned promoted equal conditions for women and men in their daily work as organizational leaders, without necessarily identifying this as efforts particularly directed at women. The emergence of men as *local feminists* in organizations with many women and where women are influential, may therefore be viewed as a direct consequence of the gender structure.

CONCLUSIONS

In the two studies reported in this chapter, different reactions from male managers have appeared. In the government inquiry (Wahl, 1995) male managers expressed gender-absent perceptions on management. As a result, they did not see the point in changing the organizations' gender distribution on management levels and therefore a majority displayed negative reactions to gender diversity activities. Similar reactions could be found among some of the managers in the Group. These were all men, in male-dominated organizations with male-gendered cultures. However, male managers in women-dominated organizations displayed less gender-absent perceptions on organizations and management. Consequently they expressed less negative reactions to gender diversity.

These results are summarized in Figure 19.4 and indicate that the gender structure of the organization (i.e. numerical gender distribution, degree of segregation in tasks and positions and distribution regarding power and influence) has a decisive impact on men's reactions to gender diversity. Men who work with women in key positions are unlikely to reproduce the common perceptions of women as non-existent, not competent and not career oriented. However, it is important to note the influence of power in these processes. Male managers who were identified as local feminists were not in high status organizations within the Group.

Male managers' reactions vary in relation to the context and it is not certain that local feminists act the same in all situations. It would be interesting to study men who in

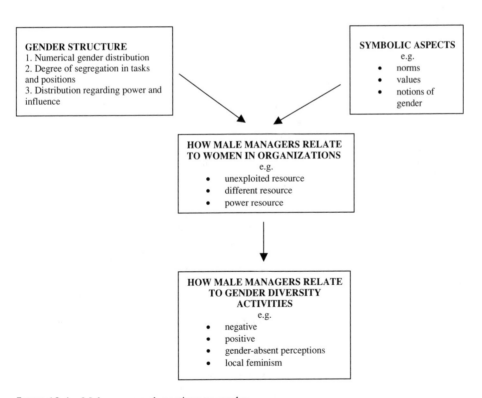

FIGURE 19.4   Male managers' reactions to gender

their normal context act as local feminists in a different kind of setting, for example in a homosocial context with other male managers of higher rank. Most of the men in the very top positions do not share the experience of working with women on the same level. The homosocial rituals here are dominated by the gender-absent discourse. It is probably difficult for one single man to refrain from participating in homosocial rituals and to break these rituals by sharing experiences from the local feminist position.

What then are the contributions from gender research on working for change in organizations in relation to the diversity field? We want to highlight two basic and interrelated ways of thinking: the structural perspective and the power perspective. As reviewed in the two studies presented in this chapter, the structural context is essential when analysing, both in theory and practice, actions for change. It is important not to interpret reactions as individual characteristics, but as results of the situation. Therefore, the problem is not women but the gender structures in organizations. Changing structures means working with those in power positions, i.e. men.

With a power perspective we can move beyond the discourse of 'sameness' and 'difference' towards seeing women, or other subordinated social categories, as interpreters of reality (Wahl, 1998). Instead of being defined by the dominant group as an unexploited and inadequate resource or a different and complementary resource that can be used, women, and other subordinate groups, can be seen as a *power resource* (cf. Wahl, 1998) that exercises power and thus initiates and influences organizations. This implicates that working for change means problematizing dominant ways of thinking and organizing.

REFERENCES

Acker, J. (1992). Gendering organizational theory. In A. Mills & P. Tancred (eds) *Gendering Organizational Analysis*. London: Sage.

Andersson, G. (1997). Karriär, kön och familj. In A. Nyberg & E. Sundin (eds) *Ledare, makt och kön* (SOU 1997: 135). Stockholm: Fritzes.

Asplund, G. (1988). *Women Managers. Changing Organizational Cultures*. Chichester: Wiley.

Åström, G. (1995). Society in a gender perspective. In A. Wahl (ed.) *Men's Perceptions of Women and Management*. Stockholm: Fritzes.

Baude, A. (1992). *Kvinnans plats på jobbet*. Stockholm: SNS.

Cockburn, C. (1991). *In the Way of Women*. London: Macmillan.

Collinson, D. & Hearn, J. (1994). Naming Men as Men: Implication for Work, Organization and Management. *Gender, Work and Organization*, **1**(1).

Collinson, D. & Hearn, J. (1996). *Men as Managers, Managers as Men*. London: Sage.

Franzén, C. (1995). How the perceptions of male and female executives differ. In A. Wahl (ed.) *Men's Perceptions of Women and Management*. Stockholm: Fritzes.

Gherardi, S. (1995). *Gender, Symbolism and Organizational Cultures*. London: Sage.

Holgersson, C. (2001). The social construction of top executives. In S.-E. Sjöstrand, J. Sandberg & M. Tyrstrup (eds) *Invisible Management*. London: Thomson.

Holgersson, C. & Höök, P. (1997). Chefsrekrytering och ledarutveckling som arenor för konstruktion av ledarskap och kön. In A. Nyberg & E. Sundin (eds) *Ledare, makt och kön* (SOU 1997: 135). Stockholm: Fritzes.

Holgersson, C. & Wahl, A. (2001). *Identifiering av nyckelpersoner och rekrytering av chefer inom Valhalla koncernen—en studie ur ett könsperspektiv*. Stockholm: EFI (Research report).

Höök, P. (1995). Women at the top—a survey of Swedish industry. In A. Wahl (ed.) *Men's Perceptions of Women and Management*. Stockholm: Fritzes.

Höök, P. (2001). *Stridspiloter i vida kjolar. Om ledarutveckling och jämställdhet*. Stockholm: EFI.

Kanter, R. M. (1977). *Men and Women of the Corporation*. New York: Basic Books.

Lindgren, G. (1996). Broderskapets Logik. *Kvinnovetenskaplig Tidskrift*, **17**(1), 4–14.

Linghag, S. (1998). Chefskapets paradoxer. In C. Franzén, S. Linghag & S. Zander *Arbetsglädje i livet—om ledarskap på 2000-talet*. Stockholm: Näringslivets Ledarskapsakademi.

Lipman-Blumen, Jean (1976). Toward a homosocial theory of sex roles: an explanation of the sex segregation of social institutions. *Signs*, **1**(3).

Marshall, J. (1984). *Women Managers. Travellers in a Male World*. Chichester: Wiley.

Roper, M. (1996). Seduction and succession: circuits of homosocial desire in management. In D. Collinson & J. Hearn (eds) *Men as Managers, Managers as Men*. London: Sage.

SOU (Statens Offentliga Utredningar) (1994). *Mäns föreställningar om kvinnor och chefskap*. Report 3. Stockholm: Fritzes.

Statistics Sweden (2000). *Women and Men in Sweden. Facts and Figures*. Örebro: SCB.

Wahl, A. (1992). *Könsstrukturer i organisationer*. Stockholm: EFI.

Wahl, A. (ed.) (1995). *Men's Perceptions of Women and Management*. Stockholm: Fritzes.

Wahl, A. (1998). Deconstructing women and management. *International Review of Women and Management*, **4**(2), 46–60.

Wahl, A. (2001). From lack to surplus. In S.-E. Sjöstrand, J. Sandberg & M. Tyrstrup (eds) *Invisible Management*. London: Thomson.

Wahl, A., Holgersson, C. & Höök, P. (1998). *Ironi och sexualitet. Om ledarskap och kön*. Stockholm: Carlssons.

Wahl, A., Holgersson, C., Höök, P. & Linghag, S. (2001). *Det ordnar sig. Teorier om organisation och kön*. Lund: Studentlitteratur.

CHAPTER 20

Bias in Job Selection and Assessment Techniques

Mike Smith

University of Manchester Institute of Science and Technology, Manchester, UK

SUMMARY

This chapter starts by examining the egalitarian fallacy that all groups are equal in all human characteristics. It then distinguishes between the concepts of fairness and bias. Fairness is an essentially subjective concept based upon personal notions of how the world *should* be. Bias is a statistical concept concerned with the accuracy of prediction. The remainder of the chapter examines ways of establishing whether bias exists in selection. *Reports of rejected candidates* usually offer very poor evidence of bias. Similarly, *opinions of experts* are also poor evidence of bias. The *proportions of employees* belonging to different groups are better, but not conclusive evidence since they often depend upon assumptions similar to those involved in the egalitarian fallacy. Nevertheless disproportionate numbers are often a signal that further investigation is required. If the *rank position of certain questions or facets* of a selection system is markedly different for certain groups there is strong evidence that bias exists. However, the strongest evidence of bias is given by the *regression approach* which compares performance at selection with subsequent job performance. The regression approach does not make the unrealistic assumption that selection methods are perfect. Neither does it assume that all groups are equal. It looks at the errors in prediction (residuals). If the residuals for one group are systematically different from those of another group then bias is almost certain to exist. The chapter gives a non-statistical explanation of this approach.

Individual Diversity and Psychology in Organizations. Edited by Marilyn J. Davidson and Sandra L. Fielden.
© 2003 John Wiley & Sons, Ltd.

INTRODUCTION

Concepts of fairness often depend on an ideological stance. For extreme egalitarians it is an axiom that 'all men and women are born equal'. It directly follows that any measure showing differences between individuals must be wrong and must be biased. This crude proposition is untenable. It is patently obvious that people differ in many ways: some are larger, some are smaller, some are more excitable, some have a knowledge of nuclear physics, some are colour blind, some are strong, etc. In fact, there are many, many ways in which people clearly differ. The extreme egalitarian view may be refined in two ways that make it more tenable. First, it may be asserted that when all characteristics are considered, individuals do not differ, i.e. in sum total we are all the same but we may differ on the component characteristics. This too is a difficult position to sustain. Much will depend on the way that characteristics are combined and the proposition is impossible to either prove or disprove in practice because it will be impossible to measure every characteristic a person has. The second refinement of the extreme egalitarian view is to accept that while individuals may differ on certain characteristics, *on average* people in one group will be equal, *on average* to people in all other groups. This too is a difficult argument to sustain. Anthropological studies using objective, measures such as height, eye colour and blood group have shown that differences between groups do exist. Anthropological studies involving psychological characteristics are more difficult to interpret because the measures are less objective, but these studies have also shown that some differences between groups exist. While it is probable that in prehistory all groups were equal, selective migration and different evolutionary pressures will have produced different characteristics in different populations. Group differences are anathema to many people, because they have been used to disadvantage or persecute certain categories of people, and repugnance at such atrocities is thoroughly justified. Nevertheless, emotional repugnance is a very dubious basis for denying group differences. We simply do not know whether different groups of people are equal or are different in some way. This has important implications in employee selection: it is difficult to establish whether the methods used are fair or unfair unless you know for certain whether or not there actually are real differences.

THE DISTINCTION BETWEEN FAIRNESS AND BIAS

Many authors make no distinction between the concepts of fairness and bias. However, the distinction needs to be made. In essence, fairness is a subjective concept. It involves people making value judgements about how situations should be. These judgements have always changed from generation to generation. In the fourteenth century the privileges of a monarch were considered to be totally fair because they were ordained by God and were equitable recompense for the heavy burdens of state. Today many of the trappings of the feudal system are regarded as anathema and unfair. Each generation considers its ideas of fairness to be superior to those of the last generation. Without doubt future generations will look back upon our concepts of fairness with incredulity. A cynic might define fairness as a part of the value system which a powerful or articulate elite unfairly impose upon people who are not members of that elite.

Bias, on the other hand, is an empirical, statistical concept which is concerned with prediction. If a measure accurately predicts, for all groups, a desired outcome then it is not biased. If a measure is inaccurate in predicting a desired outcome for some groups but not for others it is biased. Unfortunately, this distinction is less clear than it appears. As a later section will show, the presence or absence of bias might depend upon the desired outcomes (job criterion) which are used. The choice of the criterion is, in many instances, a subjective decision.

Modern definitions of bias in employee selection acknowledge that group differences might, or might not, exist. The following definition contains the essence of most accepted definitions of bias:

> candidates who are equally likely to succeed in the job are equally likely to receive a job offer irrespective of their ethnic group, sex, age or disability (see Cleary, 1968; Cole, 1973; Jensen, 1980; Schmitt & Chan, 1998).

Such definitions have a number of merits. First, they make no assumption about the levels of suitability in different groups. If one group is naturally more suited than another, so be it. Members of the group will tend to obtain more job offers but the decision will be based on 'ability' rather than group membership. It is likely that *some* members of both groups will receive job offers since overlap, probably a very large overlap, will exist—it is virtually unknown for *all* members of one group to be 'higher' than all members of another group. Second, this definition is realistic and acknowledges practical reality. No method of selection is perfect and mistakes are made. Hence, some qualified people in all groups will be wrongly rejected. Fairness exists when the probability of rejection is proportional to the true differences between the groups (see Thorndike, 1971). In parenthesis, it should be noted that some very bad methods of selection, such as choosing candidates at random, are often fair because the probability of being wrongly rejected is the same for both populations. Third, the definition emphasizes the ability to do a job. It is in the best interests of applicants, the organization and society to have positions filled by competent people. Fourth, the definition takes bias out of the realm of opinion and ideology by reducing it to a factual question 'are people in one group offered fewer jobs than equally capable people in another group?' This factual question can be resolved by looking for empirical evidence. Many types of empirical evidence are available. These types of empirical evidence have different strengths and they need to be discussed in greater detail. However, before the merits and disadvantages of the different types of evidence can be understood it is necessary to list the commonly used methods of selection and their validity.

THE VALIDITY OF SELECTION METHODS

Psychologists have investigated methods of selection for at least 85 years. They have been particularly concerned with their validity because validity gives an index of the accuracy of selection where a correlation of 1 is perfect accuracy and a correlation of 0 is the accuracy of random selection. Unfortunately, there are several practical difficulties in assessing validity. First, there is the criterion problem: what measures can be used to decide whether an employee is good or bad? Many criteria exist but in practice they

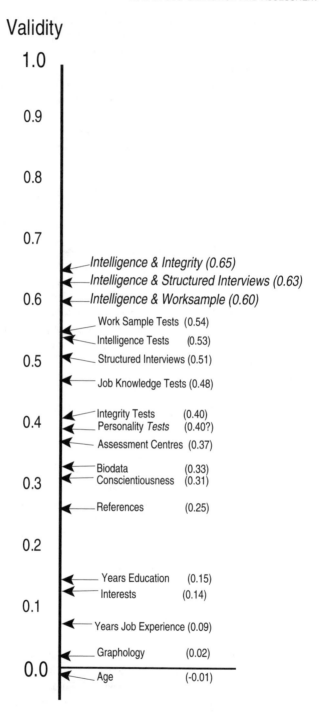

FIGURE 20.1 Accuracy of selection methds: performance and training criteria combined, based on Schmidt & Hunter (1998). *Psychological Bulletin*, **124**(2), 262–274

are usually combined into two types: performance information and training information. Ideally, performance information is based on some objective index of job performance such as the number of components produced or the value of sales. Such objective indices are difficult to obtain in many jobs—especially management jobs and jobs in the welfare sector. In practice, therefore, the performance criteria are usually based upon subjective data such as a rating by a person's superior. This distinction between 'hard' and 'soft' criteria could, as a later section shows, have an important bearing on whether a method can be proved to be fair or unfair. Training criteria are often used because conditions during training are more uniform and the outcome, the grade at the end of training or weeks taken to achieve a set standard, is more objective. The second problem in assessing the accuracy of selection methods concerns sample sizes. Most validity studies use samples which are too small from a scientific viewpoint. The small sample sizes arise from the practical reality that there are often not enough recruits in organizations. However, there is a statistical technique, meta-analysis, which allows the results from small samples to be combined so that conclusions can made on the basis of large samples which do meet stringent scientific criteria.

Using meta-analysis, occupational psychologists are now in a position to estimate the validity of a wide range of selection devices. Figure 20.1, based on Schmitt and Hunter (1998), combines the validities obtained for the two main types of criteria, production and training, into one diagram. The figure is largely self-explanatory. However, subsequent sections of this chapter will show that there is a distinction between unstructured and structured interviews. The diagram only gives the validity for structured interviews. The validity of unstructured interviews is much lower and typically in the region of 0.15. Once the validity of different selection methods has been outlined it is logical to assess the ways in which the fairness of selection methods can be considered, i.e. opinions of candidates, opinions of experts, proportions employed, ranking of questions and comparisons with subsequent performance.

TYPES OF EVIDENCE OF BIAS

OPINIONS OF CANDIDATES

Rejected candidates often claim that a selection system has wrongly rejected them because the system is biased against the group to which they belong. Undoubtedly many of these candidates will have been wrongly rejected due to the simple fact that no selection system is totally accurate and that mistakes will occur. Many candidates will have genuinely received a raw deal at the hands of incompetent and unthinking selectors. However, many accusations made by rejected candidates will be unfounded and will arise from their need to maintain pride. The claims of rejected candidates may be poor evidence of bias for a second reason. Rejected candidates are exquisitely sensitive to faults and errors in, say, their own interviews. They may note that, for example, their interviewer is disorganized and ignorant of basic information given in their application form. These faults are then used to support claims of bias such as, 'you can tell he had already made up his mind because he had not even read my form!' However, the logic of this argument rests upon a false assumption that the interview of the successful candidate was perfect. In fact, the interview of the selected candidate may be equally chaotic and misinformed.

The way applicants perceive selection methods has been a major focus of research. Gilliand (1993) identified two important aspects of perceptions of organizational justice: procedural justice and distributive justice. Procedural justice concerns the consistency with which rules are implemented. In a procedurally just system, for example, all candidates will be treated in a similar (equivalent), courteous way and asked only for information which is clearly relevant to the performance of the job (Smither et al., 1996). Distributive justice concerns the correctness of the final decision—usually in terms of a reasonable balance between what a person puts into a situation and the rewards they receive. In a distributively just system the candidate with the highest ability will be selected. The job relatedness of a selection system has been found to increase an applicant's perceptions of distributive justice (Gilliand, 1994). Procedural justice and distributive justice are conceptually different but, in fact, they are highly correlated (Sheppard & Lerwicki, 1987; Brockner & Wisenfeld, 1996; Leck et al., 1996). The justice implications of tests and other selection methods have been exhaustively considered by authors such as Konovsky and Cropanzano (1993), Hogan and Quigley (1996) and Tenopyr (1996).

Many investigators such as Ployhart and Ryan (1998) have attempted to identify the factors which influence perceptions of fairness. Unsurprisingly, procedural fairness is increased when all candidates are treated in a consistent way, and distributive fairness is increased when candidates receive a job offer themselves. These results lead Chan et al. (1998) to suggest that notions of justice contain a self-serving bias where poor-performing candidates reduce the threat to their egos by claiming that a test is not relevant to their future performance in the job.

Unfortunately, there may be tension between the views of candidates and the accuracy of selection methods set out in Figure 20.1. Latham and Finnegan (1993) compared the perceptions of applicants, interviewers and lawyers to three types of interviews: unstructured interviews, patterned interviews and situational interviews. Patterned and situational interviews have higher validity and legal defenceability. They tend to be preferred by both interviewers and lawyers. However, applicants tend to prefer unstructured interviews—possibly because they feel that they have greater control over the impression they make. In a similar vein Harland et al. (1995) found that, in a printing firm, employees believe that a selection system consisting of an interview and a personality test was less likely to be fair than a system consisting solely of an interview. Furthermore, perceptions of fairness improve only slightly when the use of the personality test was explained. More recently Harris (2000) found that structured and highly 'job focused' selection systems can result in negative perceptions about the fairness of the process, its outcomes and effectiveness. As suggested by Latham and Finnegan, candidate perceptions of fairness stand in stark contrast to the perceptions of human resource professionals. Hayes et al. (1993) surveyed human resource professionals' opinions regarding the fairness of selection practices on disabled versus general applicants. Structured interviews, work samples, personality tests and cognitive ability tests were rated highly for job relatedness and fairness. Unstructured interviews, biodata and clinical personality tests were rated as being less job-related and fair.

Candidate opinions are immensely important because a candidate who has a negative opinion of the way he/she is treated during selection is much more likely to make a legal

Selection method	Observed percentages	Expected percentages	Ratio	% Successfully defended
physical ability tests	14	4	3.5:1	58
cognitive ability tests	18	8	2.3:1	67
unstructured interviews	57	29	2.0:1	59
structured interviews	6	12	0.5:1	100
assessment centres	1	5	0.2:1	59
work samples	4	26	0.15:1	86
biodata	0	7	—	—
honesty tests	0	3	—	—
personality tests	0	7	—	—

FIGURE 20.2 Percentages of contested cases compared with the percentage that would be expected from their frequency of use and the percentage of cases successfully defended

challenge to the organization's methods. Terpstra et al. (1999) analysed Federal Court cases involving nine methods of selection. They noted the frequency with which the methods were challenged and the frequency with which the challenges were defeated. Terpstra et al., related the number of challenges to the frequency with which the various methods were used and obtained the results set out in Figure 20.2. The results suggest that the majority, 64 per cent, of legal challenges were successfully defended. Although physical tests are among the least frequent methods of selection they give rise to a disproportionately high number of challenges. Cognitive ability tests and unstructured interviews are also disproportionately likely to attract legal challenges, but defending cognitive ability tests has a slightly higher than average probability of success. Structured interviews, assessment centres, work samples, biodata, honesty tests and personality tests are unlikely to attract a legal challenge. In the unlikely event that structured interviews and work samples are contested, they are highly likely to be defended successfully.

The research on candidate perceptions, especially the findings that ideas of justice have a self-serving basis, means that the claims of rejected candidates are very poor evidence of bias in a selection system. Generally it will only be safe to conclude that bias has taken place when a rejected candidate is able to cite one or more specific and relevant irregularity that is corroborated by other, independent evidence.

OPINIONS OF EXPERTS

If the perceptions of candidates are not good evidence of biased selection, an alternative may be the opinions of experts. An expert psychologist might, for example, be asked to look at a test and pronounce upon the bias contained in the questions. Past experience has shown that this too is a very unsatisfactory type of evidence. First, experts may disagree with each other and contradictory advice may be purchased by different sides of a dispute. Even the opinions of the authors of a test may be in error. For example, on one television programme Weschler, the author of the Weschler Intelligence Scale for

Children, admitted that two questions might be biased against black children. Yet when the data were analysed, it was found that black children were slightly more likely to give the correct answers to these questions (Miele, 1979; McLoughlin & Koh, 1982). The work of Sandoval and Miille (1980) provide little support for the use of the opinions of experts, even when the experts belong to the minority groups concerned. Furthermore, Jensen (1980) and Cole (1981) suggested that people with PhDs in psychology were inaccurate when asked to identify questions that were biased.

PROPORTIONS EMPLOYED

The proportions of majority and minority groups employed are frequently put forward as evidence of bias. Typical statements will include 'only x per cent of women are managers' or 'only y per cent of police officers are from a minority group'. While such claims may give rise to a suspicion of bias which should be investigated, they do not provide clear evidence of bias. In many cases, the logic of such claims leads to absurd conclusions. For example, women teachers outnumber men teachers by a huge margin but this does not mean that education authorities are systematically biased against men. Other factors, especially the personal choices made by men and women, which have little to do with the fairness of selection systems, are probably responsible for the huge imbalance in favour of women teachers.

A more subtle and justifiable approach is to consider the proportions of applicants who are offered jobs. Suppose, for example, that an organization has 200 male applicants and 100 female applicants for a job. In itself, this imbalance does not imply bias because women might have chosen to apply elsewhere or to abstain from the labour market (however, the organization would do well to check that the imbalance in applicants was not caused by its own actions!). If 100 of the male applicants (50%) received job offers while 35 women applicants (35%) received job offers the evidence of bias is more compelling, since comparing applicants automatically removes contamination by factors such as individual choice. Such reasoning led to the 4/5 rule which was once contained in USA government guidelines on selection. In essence, the 4/5 rule claimed that a selection system is biased if the rate of job offers for minority applicants is less than 4/5 the rate of job offers for majority applicants. Thus in our example the selection system would be biased because the hiring rate for women is 3.5/5. The 4/5 ratio is largely arbitrarily, but it does allow minor deviations from parity which might be caused by random events.

In the last decade or so the 4/5 rule has fallen out of use because of one major weakness. The 4/5 rule makes the assumption that the pool of talent in groups is necessarily equal—the egalitarian fallacy that was discussed at the start of this chapter. There may be circumstances where the pool of talent in the applicants from the majority group is higher than the pool of talent in the minority group and a hiring rate of less than 4/5 is fully justified. This weakness in the 4/5 rule can often be exploited by biased employers who invoke the idea of different levels of talent to justify a whole series of recruitments where the hiring rate for the minority group is less than 4/5 the hiring rate for the majority group. While it is unscientific to assert that all groups are equal, the number of times a majority group has higher talent than a minority group should be roughly equivalent to the number of times that a minority group has higher talent. Hence there should be at least some selection situations where the hiring ratio for the minority group exceeds 6/5 the hiring ratio for the majority group. In 1989, the US Supreme Court ruled that near statistical imbalance in the workforce is not sufficient to establish a prima facie case of disparate impact (*Wards Cove Packing Company v. Antonio*). Another impact of this decision is to place the burden of proof on the plaintiff when fairness of a selection system is at issue. This case and other legal issues are described in greater detail by Schmidt et al. (1992).

RANK ITEM DIFFICULTY

Comparing the difficulties of questions for the majority group and the minority group is a scientifically valid way of detecting bias. At its simplest, this method involves analysing the answers on each question for each group and then ranking the questions in order of the difficulty. If the rank order of certain questions is different, there is evidence that the question is biased against one of the groups. The approach is easy to understand using the following hypothetical example. Supposing 100 people for each of two groups are given a test containing 10 questions which are identified by the letters A–J and the percentage in each group who obtain the correct answers is calculated. The following outcome detailed in Figure 20.3 might result.

It can be seen that the scores of group Y are generally lower than the scores of group X. In itself, this is not good evidence of bias because the two groups might differ in terms of ability. When the rank order of questions for the two groups is inspected, it can be seen that they are generally very similar and show small differences which are in the order of one or two places. These small differences represent little more than random error. However, there are two questions (B and D) where the differences between the ranks are much larger than the ambient statistical noise. In both questions, the rank for group Y is much lower than the rank for group X. This is clear evidence that while the majority of questions have the same meaning for both groups, questions B and D have different meanings which make them disproportionately hard for group Y. The item difficulty approach has a substantial advantage because it does not make any assumption about the level of ability in the two groups.

Question	A	B	C	D	E	F	G	H	I	J
% correct majority group	90	83	71	67	58	49	34	26	17	11
% correct minority group	90	29	69	16	57	51	34	24	19	13
Rank majority group	1	2	3	4	5	6	7	8	9	10
Rank minority group	1	6	2	9	3	4	5	7	8	10
Difference	0	4	1	5	2	2	2	1	1	0

FIGURE 20.3 Hypothetical example demonstrating the rank method of demonstrating bias, from Terpstra, Mohammed and Kethley (1999). *International Journal of Selection and Assessment*, 7(1), 26–33

THE REGRESSION APPROACH

The regression approach is based upon the very widely accepted view that equally suitable candidates should have an equal chance of receiving an offer of employment irrespective of their background (Cleary, 1968; Einhorn & Bass, 1971: see also Steffy & Ledvinka, 1989). The regression approach is sometimes called the equal risk model and it is the approach which has found most favour in the courts. The regression approach makes no assumption whatsoever about the levels of ability of various groups and it does not make unrealistic assumptions that a selection system can be perfectly accurate. Unfortunately the regression approach is statistically complex and the following account describes only the main features. In essence, the regression approach compares scores which people obtain during selection with their subsequent performance at work. It is easiest to explain using test scores because they take the form of numerical data. However, the same principles apply to other methods of selection such as interviews, references and biodata. Ideally a test score is obtained for each individual in a large sample and the scores are locked away so that they cannot influence the rest of the selection procedure. Every individual is then hired (this is an unrealistic assumption but the results obtained in practice can be corrected statistically) and after a short period of time, usually six months, the job performance of everyone in the sample is assessed. With operative and sales jobs the assessment is relatively easy because 'hard performance data' (items produced or sales figures, respectively) can be used. In many management, service and caring jobs the assessment uses 'soft performance data' such as ratings from supervisors. A test score and the work performance for each candidate can then be plotted on a scattergram as shown in Figure 20.4.

Each dot represents one applicant. In this simplified example the scales on the two axes are equivalent: selection scores range from 1 to 10 and performance is judged

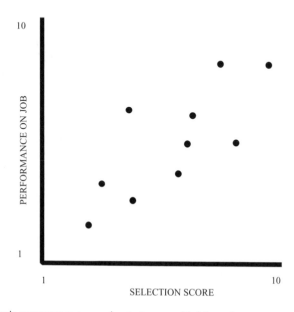

FIGURE 20.4   Basic scattergram comparing test score with job performance

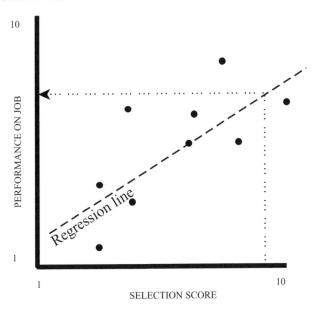

FIGURE 20.5   Fitting a regression line to predict job performance from test score

on a scale 1–10. For clarity, only a small sample of applicants is shown. In practice much larger samples are essential.

Once the scattergram has been produced a trend line (a regression line) is calculated and drawn on the graph. The regression line gives the prediction that can be made from the selection score to subsequent performance. In this example (see Figure 20.5) a candidate who scores 9.5 on the test would be expected to obtain a rating of 7.5 for work performance.

If the prediction is perfect, all points would lie on the regression line. Unfortunately, however, no selection method is perfect. Most of the points will lie close to the regression line but some will be further away. The more the points deviate from the trend line, the less accurate the selection system. The distance of each point from the regression line is called the residual. The residuals are shown in Figure 20.6.

The average of the residuals (to be statistically correct, it is the average of the *square* of the residuals) is an index of the accuracy of the selection method, and fairness can be unambiguously defined in terms of regression lines and residuals. Instead of using a single regression line for the whole sample, a regression line is fitted using data from the majority group and a separate regression line is fitted using data from a minority group. If a test, or any other method of selection, is fair there should be no significant difference between the slope of the two regression lines. Thus, without making any assumptions, examination of regressions gives unequivocal evidence of fairness or bias. For example, the trend lines for two groups shown in Figure 20.7 are very similar and any differences are so small that they are probably due to random error and the method would be deemed fair.

In practice, the regression lines can show many configurations, some of which indicate fairness and some of which indicate bias. A classic paper by Bartlett and O'Leary (1969)

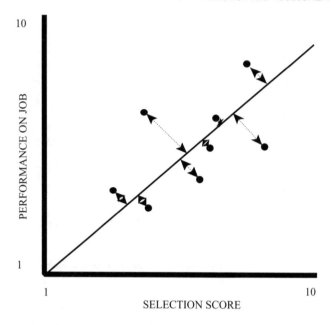

FIGURE 20.6 Residuals from regression

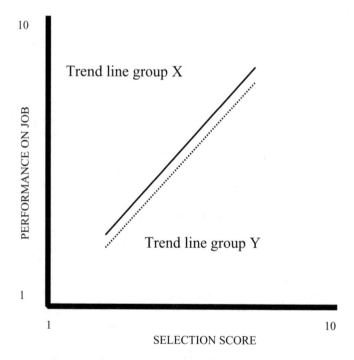

FIGURE 20.7 Separate, but very similar regressions for two groups—unbiased

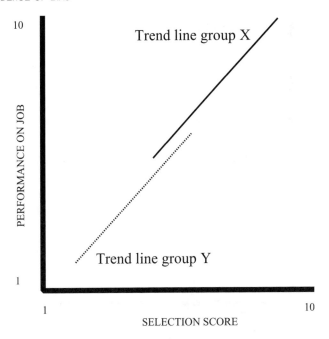

10

PERFORMANCE ON JOB

Trend line group X

Trend line group Y

1

1   10

SELECTION SCORE

FIGURE 20.8   Separated regressions but similar slope—unbiased

has become accepted as the authoritative source; only three of the configurations will be described here. The second configuration shown in Figure 20.8 is only slightly different from that shown in Figure 20.7. For some reason known only to the deity in the sky, only the less able people belonging to group Y apply to an organization. So, when the organization analyses the relation between selection and performance it finds that the 'Y' applicants tend to obtain poor scores on the test and they also tend to produce fewer widgets per hour and they tend to appear out the bottom left of the graph. However, the slopes of the regression lines are similar. There is no unfairness in this configuration because people of the same ability to do the job have the same chance of receiving a job offer.

The third configuration is very different and is shown in Figure 20.9. For both groups, a high score will tend to be associated with higher job performance. But this trend is much more pronounced for group 'X'—the trend is magnified by being an 'X'. Statistically this means there is a significant interaction between the regression line and group membership. There is a clear difference between the trend lines for the two groups and this difference indicates bias. If the performance of people in group X is predicted from the trend line for group Y (i.e. they are selected on the same basis using the test score) their subsequent performance will be seriously underestimated and group X will be disadvantaged. Conversely, if the performance of group Y is predicted from the trend line of group X, the performance will be seriously overestimated and they will receive more favourable job offers.

The process of calculating trend lines and residuals is laborious and tedious. A more elegant method which produces the same result is described by Cohen and Cohen (1983: 313). Statistics enthusiasts might wish to note that Cohen and Cohen use an analysis

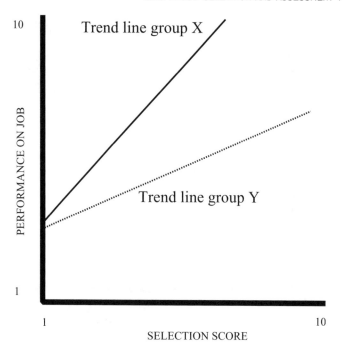

FIGURE 20.9   Separate regressions: differing slopes—biased

of variance where job performance is the dependent variable while the test score and group membership are independent variables. The interaction term between the two independent variables is examined and if the interaction term is significant, the two trend lines will differ (as in Figure 20.9) and the selection method would be biased.

PROBLEMS WITH REGRESSION APPROACH

Although the regression approach is scientifically very strong it has two problems concerning issues noted earlier—criteria and sample size.

Previous sections of this chapter have called attention to the distinction between 'hard' and 'soft' criteria. Hard criteria are objective data such as number of widgets produced, while soft criteria are subjective data such as an appraisal rating by a supervisor. A problem may arise when soft criteria are used in analyses of fairness since subjective judgements used as criteria may, themselves, contain bias. For example, a bigoted supervisor might be prejudiced against a certain group and consciously or unconsciously downgrade the value of the work produced by that group. If the bias of the supervisor is similar to the bias of a selection device the two sources would appear to cancel each other out and would mask the true bias which exists. These issues were raised by both Bray and Moses (1972) and Boem (1972). However, an authoritative study by Schmidt et al., (1973) concluded that when irrelevant artefacts are removed from studies, subjective criteria are no more likely to generate instances of single group validity (unfairness) than objective criterion measures. More recently, Ford et al. (1986) found objective and subjective criteria were related to ethnic group in very similar ways, and Oppler et al.

(1992) noted that differences observed between black and white ratees in performance do not necessarily imply bias; such differences could reflect actual and true differences between such samples. An excellent review of performance evaluation is given by Arvey and Murphy (1998).

Research into the fairness of selection methods is dogged by the sample size problem. The regression approach is very powerful but, in order to work properly, it requires large sample sizes—preferably larger than 172 (see Schmidt et al., 1976). Such sample sizes are difficult to obtain for majority groups because few organizations employ that number of people in a single occupation. Since the number of a minority group in an organization will be much smaller, it is even more difficult to obtain reasonable samples which can be used with the multiple regression approach. For example, supposing that the largest job in an organization employs 10 per cent of the personnel and that 7 per cent of employees belong to a minority group. In order to obtain a sample of 172 minority employees in the largest job an organization would need to employ almost 25 000 people in total. Very few organizations outside the government sector reach this size. Consequently, the statistics concerning fairness are usually based on small samples—sometimes they are as small as 30. It is a fundamental rule of statistics that estimates based on small samples are unreliable and fluctuate widely from sample to sample. While the statistics for a majority group will be relatively stable, they will be compared with unstable estimates for the minority group and, by the laws of chance alone, half of the comparisons will show lower results for the minority group and the unwary might conclude that a true difference exists.

Sample sizes are not a problem when comparing a diversity of sexes since the number of men roughly equals the number of women and decent sample sizes can be obtained for both groups. However, sample sizes can produce acute problems in countries such as the UK where the ethnic minorities comprise about 7 per cent of the population. To make matters even more difficult it is often necessary to subdivide the ethnic minority into Afro-Caribbean, Asian, Chinese and 'other' ethnic groups. The sample size problem is less acute in the USA where about 20 per cent of the population belong to ethnic groups. Consequently much of the research which is quoted in this and other chapters is based upon research from the USA.

PROBLEMS IN GENERALIZING AMERICAN RESULTS

Such generalization of research findings needs to be made with great caution because the context may be different. While the UK and USA share similar languages and an Anglo-Saxon approach to business and law, there are notable differences in addition to the relative proportions of ethnic minorities. The main wave of coloured immigration to the USA was caused by the slave trade from Africa in the eighteenth and nineteenth centuries. These immigrants arrived into an economic system built on slavery, sub-servience and rigid segregation. US slavery was abolished in 1863 but segregation laws were in force until as late as 1954. In contrast, the main wave of immigration to the UK was voluntary and occurred in the 1950s long after the British abolished slavery in 1807 (France repealed slavery in 1848). There have never been segregation laws in Britain. Furthermore, immigration to the UK was more diverse and included a higher proportion of immigrants from the Indian subcontinent. In themselves these differences mean that there are huge psychological contrasts with the relations between ethnic communities.

BIAS OF SPECIFIC METHODS OF SELECTION

Once the methods of selection have been identified and a scientific approach to establishing bias has been developed, it is possible to consider the bias of individual methods. Searching the literature for evidence of bias in selection methods is difficult because many authors do not clarify the concept of fairness and there is a litter of studies that have little scientific value. Many studies focus upon the average scores for two groups. This information is useless unless there is incontrovertible evidence that the two groups are, in fact, equal. Other studies involve experimental simulations of doubtful relevance. Typically a group of students is given some information. Half of the students are given one version relevant to a majority group and the other half are given a version relevant to the minority group. The students are then asked to make a hypothetical decision about, for example, which candidates they would appoint and what salary they should be offered. Some authors even quote research on the marking of student essays and exam answers as evidence of bias in selection situations. Unfortunately these simulations are very artificial and there may be real doubt about whether the findings generalize to actual situations. These effects usually account for only 1 or 2 per cent of the variance. It may be this is an overestimate caused by artificial situations or experimental artefacts. On the other hand, it may also be that the results are an underestimate because pressures in a real situation are more intense and may produce larger effect sizes.

The two most authoritative reviews of the bias of selection methods have been produced by Reilly and Chao (1982) and Baron and Janman (1996). Figure 20.1 suggested that the single most valid selection method is a *work sample* test. Work sample tests come in many forms and two of the most frequently used forms are the in-tray exercise and group discussions. In theory, work sample tests should show no greater group differences than actual job performance since work samples simply mirror a job. However, it is possible that bias might creep into the way that in-trays are scored because factors such as vocabulary and handwriting could influence assessors. Kesselman and Lopez (1979) found no difference in the validity of in trays for black and white applicants. Baron and Janman note that few studies have looked at differences in performance on in trays for different groups. Those studies that have investigated differences in performance, do not provide evidence of group differences or differential validity. Group discussions are also a common type of work sample. Often a candidate's score is based entirely on the judgement of assessors and there is clearly room for bias. Furthermore, the composition of a group could be an important factor since the race or sex of other participants may exert an influence. Considerable research has investigated the effect of the assessor's sex or race. The results have not been entirely consistent. Some investigators suggest that both black and white raters tend to give higher scores to their own group. Other investigators have found that the effect, which is very small and accounts for about 1 per cent of the variance, is limited to black assessors giving slightly higher ratings to black candidates. Baron and Janman (1996) observe, 'there seem to be no published studies of differential validity against external criteria'.

Tests of *mental ability* are one of the most valid methods of selection. The fairness of these tests has received much more attention than any other selection device. The numerous studies and meta-analysis have generally failed to find evidence of bias. When bias has been found it has generally been in favour of the lower scoring group—using a regression equation based on the whole population will tend to overestimate the subsequent performance of the lower scoring group. Overall there is strong evidence in favour of using cognitive ability tests (Baron & Janman, 1996).

Reilly and Chao (1982) reviewed studies of the fairness of *interviews*. Again, there was little scientific evidence available. However, one study of semi-structured interviews (Exxon) did examine the regressions for black and white candidates and found significant validities for whites, but no significant validities for blacks and females. Arvey (1979) located three studies examining the ethnic fairness of interviews but found no evidence to suggest differential validity. In 1989 Harris reviewed employment interviews. Only a few studies examined the regression lines for different groups and, in general, there were no differences for males and females or for different races.

Since many personal history or background experiences are related to gender, age, sex and ethnic group it is possible that biodata may be biased. The majority of studies reviewed by Reilly and Chao were concerned with the average scores of groups. Four studies examined validities and regressions. There were no significant differences between black and white groups. However, some gender differences were found and different scoring keys may be needed for males and females.

Bartlett and Goldstein (1976) reported data on the fairness of references for large samples of black and white applicants. The vast majority of references for blacks and whites were favourable (98.1 and 99.1 per cent, respectively). There was a significant relationship between the reference report and termination (for all reasons) for whites but there was no significant relationship for blacks. When involuntary terminations were considered, references had some validity for both groups. On the data available, it is difficult to judge whether references are fair, but the validity of the method is so low that any unfairness which does exist should be small.

In general, the picture concerning the differential validity of predictors is uncertain. There is too little research on many selection methods to justify any firm conclusion. The main exception to this generalization is the well-researched area of ability tests which are usually fair and when exceptions occur, they generally favour the lower scoring group.

OTHER ASPECTS OF FAIRNESS IN SELECTION

This chapter has concentrated on psychometric aspects of bias because they involve the most intricate and least accessible concepts for the layperson. However, fairness is affected by other stages of selection—especially drawing up personnel specifications and attracting applicants.

JOB ANALYSIS AND PERSONNEL SPECIFICATIONS

Personnel specifications are usually drawn up after a job has been analysed. As their name suggests, they attempt to specify the knowledge skills and abilities which people must have in order to succeed at a job. They entail considerable potential for unfairness because they can be worded in a way that disadvantages people. At the most obvious and repugnant level a personnel specification could include a blatant statement such as 'blacks need not apply'. A slightly more subtle, but still unfair, statement might be 'bright, strong lad needed'. Statements of this kind are illegal and must not be used. Sometimes, unfair requirements are included unintentionally. For example, a police force may specify that applicants need to be 1.7 m tall. Although the requirement does not specify or prohibit any particular group the requirement may have a disproportional effect on certain groups. A height requirement will almost certainly discriminate against ethnic groups of small stature such as pygmies. A height requirement could also discriminate against women. Similarly, age limits, coupled with demands for certain experience, can discriminate against women. For example, a civil service specification setting an age limit of 35 and 6 years' relevant experience would be more difficult for women to meet because, when career breaks for child rearing are taken into account, they are less likely to have accumulated the 6 years' relevant experience. However, such requirements can be included in personnel specifications provided that there is a clear link to job performance. For example, a height limit for police officers of 1.7 m may be deemed unfair but a height limit of, say, 1.5 m may not be unfair since shorter police officers may not be able to perform crucial tasks such as, in the USA, shooting a pistol over the top of the roof of a car. This example demonstrates that requirements bearing disproportionately on one or more groups may be acceptable *provided* that there is a clear link to job performance.

ATTRACTING CANDIDATES

Once a person specification has been produced, the next step in a selection system is to attract candidates by adverts or other methods. The way that a job is advertised can give rise to unfairness in two ways: the design of the advertisement and the place of publication.

Adverts need to be designed so that they do not imply that applications from one group are more acceptable than applications from other groups. A part of the problem is semantic and another part is graphic. The words in adverts should be carefully chosen to avoid stereotypes. For example, adverts should avoid terms such as 'fireman' and 'salesman' and should use neutral words such as 'firefighter' or 'salesperson'. The graphics and illustrations used in adverts should be scrutinized with equal care so that the people pictured in an advertisement depict diverse groups that reflect the composition of the local community.

The placement of adverts may also have a discriminatory effect. For example, placing the adverts in a newspaper which is rarely purchased by members of minority groups is likely to inhibit applications from members of these groups. Indeed, it may be necessary to make a conscious effort to target publications which are likely to be read by a diverse range of applicants. The use of 'word of mouth' to advertise a job can be particularly discriminatory, despite the fact that there is some evidence that candidates attracted by informal contacts tend to be better employees. Unfortunately, 'word of mouth' communication is likely to rely upon an existing workforce who will pass the information to people who are similar to themselves. Consequently, in most situations, 'word of mouth' recruitment is likely to reinforce the status quo and the status quo may not exploit the full range of talent and abilities available in a truly diverse workforce.

AFFIRMATIVE ACTION POLICIES

Finally, the impact of affirmative action policies needs careful consideration. Heilman et al. (1998) note that research on affirmative action has documented many negative consequences of preferential selection procedures in work settings. Research has shown detrimental effects of the way that the beneficiaries perceive themselves and the way that they react to the work situation. Women who believe they have benefited from affirmative action have been shown to report lower job satisfaction and organizational commitment. They also show greater role stress and greater apprehension when they are about to be evaluated. Affirmative action may also have negative consequences for non-beneficiaries. The non-beneficiaries are less likely to engage in 'citizenship' behaviour. Much depends upon the nature of the affirmative policy and the way that it is communicated. In the absence of any explanation workers tend to consider that the selection or promotion is on the basis of group membership alone and are likely to show negative reactions. However, when it is explained that group membership is only a part of the policy and that merit still plays a significant role in selection and promotion decisions many, but not all, negative reactions are alleviated (see Heilman et al., 1998).

ALTERNATIVE SELECTION METHODS

An alternative approach which might avoid the disadvantages of affirmative action policies would be to seek selection methods which maintained validity while reducing the possibilities of unfair impact. Chan and Schmitt (1997) compared traditional pencil and paper situational judgement tests with similar judgement tests which were administered using video recordings. They found that while the face validity of the video and written versions was similar, the adverse impact of the written version was reduced with the video version because the video version required less reading comprehension and was more acceptable to black undergraduate students. Unfortunately, this study only concerns face validity rather than the scientifically more important predictive validity. In addition, the use of undergraduate students as subjects means that generalization of the findings to realistic work settings must be made with extreme caution.

Schmitt et al. (1997) conducted computer simulations to assess whether adding alternative predictors to measures of cognitive ability would reduce adverse impact. The alternative predictors were structured interviews, personality (conscientiousness) and biodata. In brief, they found that by adding additional predictors with at least moderate validity, they could improve the accuracy of the regressions while at the same time maintaining and even increasing the overall validity of the selection system. The best results were obtained when they added three alternative predictors which had individual validities of 0.3 and where there is little intercorrelation between the additional methods. If the results of these simulations can be generalized into practice any adverse impact of ability tests can be reduced by up to 74 per cent by combining the ability test results with the results from three other, independent and moderately valid alternative predictors—without any loss in the accuracy of selection.

CONCLUSIONS

It is clear that there have been major advances in thinking since the initial concern over bias in selection in the 1960s. The crude egalitarian view that all people, or all groups, are equal in everything has been retreating in favour of the view that diversity exists and that diversity might mean that some groups may have an advantage in some jobs but not in others. However, this realization remains at an abstract level. Few researchers have even attempted to specify which groups have advantages or disadvantages for a given list of jobs. Furthermore, it remains difficult or impossible to say with any certainty which group of people are better than another. We are therefore left in the situation that applicants from one group might, in truth, be better, equal or worse than applicants from another group. We simply do not know and each individual must therefore be assessed on his/her individual merits. Despite its woolliness this view has had an enormous influence upon what is regarded to be scientific evidence of bias. Methods which depend upon an assumption of equality, such as average scores of the two groups or the proportions of the two groups employed, have been abandoned. Their place has been taken by the regression approach and the item difficulty approach which make no such assumption. Statistical models of fairness have long since been worked out in some detail. Their major problem is that they require empirical data from large samples. Unfortunately, large samples, especially large samples of ethnic minorities, are not available. Consequently the main research need in the area of selecting from diverse pools of applicants is to obtain more high quality data on ethnic minorities. A larger set of data would allow more rigorous and sophisticated analyses. It would allow us to explore the generalization that differential validity is rare and that the larger proportion of unfairness is produced the way person specifications are produced, the way a job is advertised and the use of traditional selection methods such as unstructured interviews. A larger set of data from Europe is needed to confirm that results obtained with ethnic minorities in the USA can be generalized to other countries such as the UK. Such studies would not only be fascinating but they would help those who need to select among an increasingly diverse array of applicants.

REFERENCES

Arvey, R. D. (1979). *Fairness in Selecting Employees.* Reading, Mass.: Addison-Wesley.

Arvey, R.D. & Murphy, K.R. (1998). Performance evaluation in work settings. *Annual Review of Psychology*, **49**, 141–168.

Baron, H. & Janman, J. (1996). Fairness in the assessment centre. In C.C. Cooper and I.T. Robertson (eds) *International Review of Industrial and Organisational Psychology 1996*. Chichester: Wiley.

Bartlett, C.J. & Goldstein, I.L. (1976). A validity study of the reference check . Unpublished paper, University of Maryland. Quoted by Reilly and Chao (1982), note 28.

Bartlett, C.J. & O'Leary, B.S. (1969). A differential prediction model to moderate the effects of heterogeneous groups in personnel selection and classification. *Personnel Psychology*, **22**, 1–17.

Boem, V. R. (1972). Negro–white differences in validity of employment and training selection procedure. *Journal of Applied Psychology*, **56**, 33–39.

Bray, D.W. & Moses, J.L. (1972). Personnel selection. *Annual Review of Psychology*, **23**, 545–576.

Brockner, J. & Wisenfeld, B.M. (1996). An integrative framework for explaining reactions to decisions: interactive effects of outcomes and procedures. *Psychological Bulletin*, **120**, 189–208.

Chan, D. & Schmitt, N. (1997). Video-based versus paper-and-pencil method of assessment in situational judgement tests: subgroup differences in test performance and face validity perceptions. *Journal of Applied Psychology*, **82**(1), 143–159.

Chan, D., Schmitt, N., Jennings, D., Clause, C.S. & Delbridge, K. (1998). Applicant perceptions of test fairness: integrating justice and self-serving bias perspectives. *International Journal of Selection and Assessment*, **6**(4), 232–239.

Cleary, T.A. (1968). Test bias: prediction of grades of negro and white students in integrated colleges. *Journal of Educational Measurement*, **5**, 115–124.

Cohen, J. & Cohen, P. (1983). *Applied Regression/Correlation Analysis for the Behavioral Sciences*. Hillsdale, NJ: Lawrence Erlbaum.

Cole, N.S. (1973). Bias in selection. *Journal of Educational Measurement*, **I**(10), 237–255.

Cole, N.S. (1981). Bias in testing. *American Psychologist*, **36**(10), 1067–1077.

Einhorn, H.J. & Bass, A.R. (1971). Methodological considerations relevant to discrimination in employment testing. *Psychological Bulletin*, **75**, 261–269.

Ford, J.K., Kraiger, K. & Schechtman, S.L. (1986). Study of race effects in objective indices and subjective evaluation of performance: a meta-analysis of performance criteria. *Psychological Bulletin*, **99**(3), 330–337.

Gilliand, S.W. (1993). The perceived fairness of selection systems: an organisational justice perspective. *Academy of Management Review*, **18**, 694–734.

Gilliand, S.W. (1994). Effects of procedural and distributive justice on reactions to a selection system. *Journal of Applied Psychology*, **79**(5), 691–701.

Harland, L.K., Rauzi, T. & Biasotto, M.M. (1995). Perceived fairness of personality tests on the impact of explanations for their use. *Employee Responsibilities and Rights Journal*, **8**(3), 183–192.

Harris, L. (2000). Procedural justice and perceptions of fairness in selection. *International Journal of Selection and Assessment*, **8**(3), 148–157.

Harris, M.M. (1989). Reconsidering the employment interview: a review of recent literature and suggestions for future research. *Personnel Psychology*, **42**, 691–726.

Hayes, T.L., Wendt, A.C. & Craighead, R.A. (1993). How can you fairness select applicants with disabilities? Here's what HR professionals think. *Applied Human Resource Management Research*, **4**(1), 14–26.

Heilman, M.E., Battle, W.S., Keller, C.E. & Lee, R.A. (1998). Type of affirmative action policy: a determinant of reactions to sex-based preferential selection? *Journal of Applied Psychology*, **83**(2), 190–205.

Hogan, J. & Quigley, A.M. (1996). Physical ability testing for employment. In R.S. Barrett (ed.) *Fair Employment Strategies in Human Resource Management*. Westport, Conn.: Quorum Books.

Jensen, R.A. (1980). *Bias in Mental Testing*. London: Methuen.

Kesselman, G.A. & Lopez, F.E. (1979). The impact of job analysis on employment test validation for minority and non-minority accounting personnel. *Personnel Psychology*, **32**, 91–108.

Konovsky, M.A. & Cropanzano, R. (1993). Justice considerations in employee drug testing. In R. Cropanzano (ed.) *Justice in the Workplace: Approaching Fairness in Human Resource Management*. Hillsdale, NJ: Erlbaum.

Latham, G.P. & Finnegan, B. (1993). Perceived practicality of unstructured, patterned, and situational interviews. In H. Schuler, J.L. Farr & M. Smith (eds), *Personnel Selection and Assessment: Individual and Organisational Perspectives*. Hillsdale, NJ: Erlbaum.

Leck, J.D., Saunders, D.M. & Charbonneau, M. (1996). Affirmative action programmes: an organisational justice perspective. *Journal of Organisational Behaviour*, **17**(1), 79–89.

McLoughlin, C.S. & Koh, T.H. (1982). Testing intelligence: a decision suitable for the psychologist. *Bulletin of the British Psychological Society*, **35**, 308–311.

Miele, F. (1979). Cultural bias in the WISC. *Intelligence*, **3**, 149–164.

Oppler, S.H., Campbell, J.P., Pulakos, E.D. & Borman, W.C. (1992). Three approaches to the investigation of subgroup bias in performance measurement: review, results and conclusions. *Journal of Applied Psychology*, **77**(2), 201–217.

Ployhart, R.E. & Ryan, A.M. (1998). Applicants' reactions to the fairness of selection procedures: the effects of positive rule violations and time of measurement. *Journal of Applied Psychology*, **83**(1), 3–16.

Reilly, R.R. & Chao, G.T. (1982). Validity and fairness of some alternative employee selection procedures. *Personnel Psychology*, **35**, 1–62.

Sandoval, J. & Miille, P.M.W (1980). Accuracy of judgements of WISC-R item difficulty for minority groups. *Journal of Consulting and Clinical Psychology*, **48**(2), 249–253.

Schmidt, F.L. & Hunter, J.E. (1998). The validity and utility of selection methods in personnel psychology: practical and theoretical implications of 85 years of research findings. *Psychological Bulletin*, **124**(2), 262–274.

Schmidt, F.L., Berner, J.G. & Hunter, J.E. (1973). Racial differences in validity of employment tests. *Journal of Applied Psychology*, **58**(1), 5–9.

Schmidt, F.L., Hunter, J.E. & Urry, V.W. (1976). Statistical power in criterion-related validation studies. *Journal of Applied Psychology*, **61**(4), 473–485.

Schmidt, F.L., Ones, D.S. & Hunter, J.E. (1992). Personnel selection. *Annual Review of Psychology*, **43**, 627–670.

Schmitt, N. & Chan, D. (1998). *Personnel Selection: A Theoretical Approach*. Thousand Oaks: Sage.

Schmitt, N., Rogers, W., Chan, D. Sheppard, L. & Jennings, D. (1997). Adverse impact and predictive efficiency of various predictor combinations. *Journal of Applied Psychology*, **82**(5), 719–730.

Sheppard, B.H. & Lerwicki, R.J. (1987). Toward general principles of managerial fairness. *Social Justice Research,* **1**, 161–176.

Smither, J.W., Millsap, R.E., Stoffey, R.W., Reilly, R.R. & Pearlman, K. (1996). An experimental test of the influence of selection procedures on fairness perceptions, attitude about the organisation and job pursuit intentions. *Journal of Business and Psychology*, **10**, 297–318.

Steffy, B. & Ledvinka, J. (1989). The long range impact of definitions of 'fair' employees selection on black employment and employee productivity. *Organisational Behaviour and Human Decision Process*, **42**(2), 297–324.

Tenopyr, M.L. (1996). Gender issues in employment testing. In R.S. Barrett (ed.) *Fair Employment Strategies in Human Resource Management*. Westport, Conn.: Quorum Books.

Terpstra, D.E., Mohammed, A.A. & Kethley, R.B. (1999). An analysis of Federal Court cases involving nine selection devices. *International Journal of Selection and Assessment*, **7**(1), 26–33.

Thorndike, R.L. (1971). Concepts of culture fairness. *Journal of Educational Measurement*, **8**, 63–70.

Wards Cove Packing Company v. *Antonio* (1989). Supreme Court, 3115.

PART VI

The Future—the Management of Diversity beyond the Millennium

Cultural Diversity Programmes to Prepare for the Twenty-first Century: Failures and Lost Opportunities

Norma M. Riccucci

Rutgers University, Newark, USA

SUMMARY

This chapter addresses the failure of American organizations to embrace the opportunities presented by the changing demographics of the nation's population. It summarizes the changing demographics, illustrating changes in the racial, ethnic, age and gender make-up of American society. It looks at some of the efforts organizations have developed to address these changes in an attempt to become more diverse in terms of social composition. It then addresses the pitfalls of the approaches, and the programmes and activities that organizations could pursue to become more diverse and, ultimately, reflective and representative of the American populace.

INTRODUCTION

In the last decade or so, many organizations in the United States have been attempting to prepare for, and manage, diverse workforces as a matter of competitive survival. This is due to the fact that America's workforce looks markedly different than it ever has before. In a way, it can be described as polytypic. Compared with even 20 years ago, more white women, people of colour, disabled persons, new and recent immigrants, gays and lesbians, and intergenerational mixes (i.e. baby boomers, Generation Xers and Generation Nexters) now work in America. In response to these predicted, and in many ways, realized changes, some public and private sector organizations developed and implemented an assortment of diversity programmes with the ultimate goal of remaining viable and competitive.

Individual Diversity and Psychology in Organizations. Edited by Marilyn J. Davidson and Sandra L. Fielden.
© 2003 John Wiley & Sons, Ltd.

Now, after over a decade since the various demographic forecasts were made, researchers are beginning to look at the problems underlying the way in which organizations developed and implemented their diversity initiatives. This chapter begins by briefly reporting the changing demographics which are occurring in workplaces throughout America. It then examines some of the programmes that organizations have introduced to prepare for increased social and cultural diversity in their workforces. Finally, it looks at what went wrong with the manner in which American organizations responded to increased diversity in the workplace.

THE CHANGING DEMOGRAPHY OF US WORKFORCES

Predictions and estimates over the past 20 years or so suggest that because of demographic changes to the US population, the composition of public and private sector workplaces is changing. The workforce changes which have already begun to occur include:

- Increases in the number of women
- Increases in the number of people of colour
- Increases in the average age of workers
- Increases in foreign-born or immigrant workers

A very simple, yet striking way to portray the demographic shifts at least as they pertain to white men, women and people of colour is presented in Figure 21.1. As the data show, women will account for about 48 per cent of the workforce by the year 2008. White men will account for about 37 per cent, and men of colour around 15 per cent.

Table 21.1 provides greater detail on important demographic changes which have implications for employment. It illustrates changes in the workforce based on gender,

TABLE 21.1 Workforce participation rates, 16 years and older, by gender, race and ethnicity, 1978, 1988, 1996, 1998, and projected 2008

Group	Participation rate (%)					Percentage point change 1978–2008
	1978	1988	1996	1998	2008	
White	63.3	66.2	67.2	67.3	67.9	4.6
Men	78.6	76.9	75.8	75.6	74.5	−4.1
Women	49.4	56.4	59.1	59.4	61.5	12.1
African-American	61.5	63.8	64.1	65.6	66.3	4.8
Men	71.7	71.0	68.7	69.0	68.3	−3.4
Women	53.2	58.0	60.4	62.8	64.6	11.4
Asian and other[a]	64.6	65.0	65.8	67.0	66.9	2.3
Men	75.9	74.4	73.4	75.5	74.0	−1.9
Women	54.1	56.5	58.8	59.2	60.5	6.4
Hispanic origin[b]	—	67.4	66.5	67.9	67.7	0.3
Men	—	81.9	79.6	79.8	77.9	−0.4
Women	—	53.2	53.4	55.6	57.9	4.7

[a] The 'Asian and other' group includes (1) Asians and Pacific Islanders and (2) American Indians and Alaska Natives. The historical data are derived by subtracting 'black' from the 'black and other' group; projections are made directly, not by subtraction.
[b] Data by Hispanic origin are not available before 1980. Percentage point change is calculated from 1988 to 2008.
Source: Bureau of Labor Statistics (BLS) website: http://stats.bls.gov (Participation refers to the percentage of a specific group participating in the workforce. So, by 2008, for example, 61.5% of all women will be participating in the workforce.)

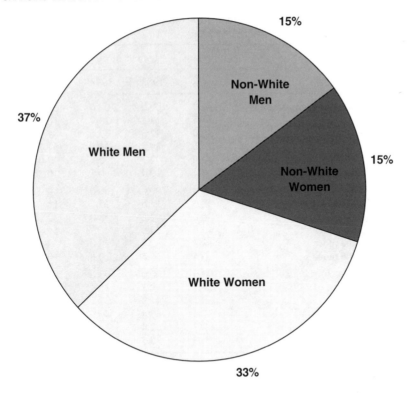

Figure 21.1 The complexion of the United States workforce by 2008.
Source: Based on data obtained from the Bureau of Labor Statistics (BLS) website,
http://stats.bls.gov

race and ethnicity from 1978 to 1998, and projected changes to 2008. The table shows
a decline in the participation of white men in the workforce, with an increase of white
women (12.1 per cent). In addition, the table shows remarkable increases of women of
colour in the workforce, while the projections for men of colour show slight decreases
in their workforce participation.

Table 21.2 illustrates the ageing of the labour force. As we can see, there is a steady
increase in the age group, 40 and older. By 2008, this age cohort is expected to represent
a majority share of the civilian labour force for both women and men. While there are
drops in labour force participation of the younger age cohorts, the changing *values* of
younger generations (e.g. the Generation Xers and Nexters) will create challenges for
public and private sector managers to the extent that younger and ageing persons will be
working alongside one another.

Changes to the labour force and workforce go well beyond race, ethnicity, gender and
age. As noted, there will be greater diversity based on such characteristics or factors
as ability, sexual orientation, foreign-born status and so forth. In addition, as a number
of reports predicted (see, for example, *Workforce 2000*, 1987), jobs in the twenty-first
century would require much more technological skills, due to shifts in the American
economy, from a manufacturing to a service base. Employers were thus urged to train and
educate their workers in order to prepare them for the new technologies needed to perform

TABLE 21.2 Distribution of the labour force by age and gender, 1978, 1988, 1998, and projected 2008 (%)

Group	Labour force			
	1978	1988	1998	2008
Total, 16 years and older	100.0	100.0	100.0	100.0
16 to 24	24.5	18.5	15.9	16.3
25 to 39	36.0	42.3	37.6	31.9
40 and older	39.6	39.2	46.5	51.7
65 and older	3.0	2.7	2.8	3.0
75 and older	0.4	0.4	0.5	0.5
Men, 16 years and older	100.0	100.0	100.0	100.0
16 to 24	22.6	17.6	15.5	16.1
25 to 39	36.6	42.6	38.0	32.2
40 and older	40.8	39.9	46.5	51.8
65 and older	3.2	2.9	3.0	3.4
75 and older	0.5	0.5	0.6	0.6
Women, 16 years and older	100.0	100.0	100.0	100.0
16 to 24	27.1	19.7	16.4	16.6
25 to 39	35.1	41.9	37.1	31.7
40 and older	37.8	38.4	46.6	51.7
65 and older	2.7	2.4	2.5	2.5
75 and older	0.3	0.3	0.4	0.4

Source: Bureau of Labor Statistics (BLS) website: http://stats.bls.gov

the new jobs (for more detail see Chapter 22). Advances in communications, information management, and biotechnologies along with the continuing shift of production from goods to services, and the continued trends towards globalization have indeed led to a *digital* revolution, resulting in dramatic changes to the nature of work in American society.

ORGANIZATIONAL RESPONSES TO CHANGING DEMOGRAPHICS

Based on the predicted demographic shifts, public and private sector organizations began to develop diversity programmes, particularly because failing to do so could jeopardize their viability, profitability and competitiveness. Many organizations developed 'cultural awareness' training programmes and/or policies to address problems and concerns such as sexual harassment and accommodations for disabled workers.

Table 21.3 provides a more detailed account of the various diversity programmes that some public and private sector organizations have offered. The list is derived from a survey conducted in 1993 by the Society for Human Resource Management (SHRM) and Commerce Clearing House (CCH). The survey population comprises 785 human resources specialists from public and private sector organizations. Obviously, the list is not comprehensive, but is intended to provide an idea of the types of programmes which have been developed.

TABLE 21.3 Types of diversity programmes developed by employers

Programme/policy	Per cent in existence (based on survey respondents)
Sexual harassment	92.7
Physical access for disabled workers	75.8
Parental leave	56.7
Literacy training	35.1
Breaking through the glass ceiling	33.1
Redesigning jobs for older workers	27.4
Subsidized day care	25.6
English as a second language	23.0
Mentoring for people of colour	21.8
Fast-tracking for people of colour	17.6
Partner benefits—gay and lesbian workers	14.9

Source: Based on data obtained from '1993 SHRM/CCH Survey' Commerce Clearing House, Inc., May 26, 1–12.

PROBLEMS IN ORGANIZATIONAL RESPONSES TO CHANGING DEMOGRAPHICS

In 1987, the Hudson Institute published a report, *Workforce 2000*, which predicted radical shifts in the demographic make-up of the American labour force (also see, for example, *Civil Service 2000*, 1988 and *New York State Work Force Plan*, 1989). As noted, many organizations began to respond by developing diversity programmes. Ten years later, the Hudson Institute published an updated report entitled *Workforce 2020* (1997), where the messages to employers about the importance of preparing for diversity were virtually the same as in the 1987 report. It would appear that employers in the US, although continuing to espouse the urgency of preparing for diversity in the workforce, may be ignoring the recommendations and prescriptions of demographers, policy analysts, and researchers. It may be the case that diversity receives a good deal of lip-service, but nothing more, from employers. That is to say, what employers claim they are doing today to prepare for increased diversity in the workplace is what they said they were planning to do in the mid 1980s.

Another problem that exists around organizations' efforts to prepare for the twenty-first century is that too much emphasis may be given to diversity initiatives that are driven by federal mandates. For example, as we saw in Table 21.3, sexual harassment policy, 'reasonable accommodation' of disabled workers, and parental leave were the most popular strategies. While these programmes are certainly essential, they address only a fraction of diversity concerns and issues. Moreover, they may be motivated or compelled not by a genuine concern for diversity but rather as measures to avoid liability claims for possible discriminatory practices under the laws which, for example, call for reasonable accommodation (the Americans with Disabilities Act of 1990), parental leave (the Family and Medical Leave Act of 1993), and which proscribe sexual harassment (Title VII of the Civil Rights Act of 1964 as amended).

In effect, other diversity efforts which are not driven by federal law (e.g. professional development programmes aimed at career advancement of people of colour) are not adopted. In fact, the SHRM/CCH survey (1993) shows that such programmes in the form of mentoring and fast-tracking of people of colour have been less popular (see Table 21.3).

The SHRM/CCH survey also found that diversity management is a low priority when compared to other issues and concerns such as profitability and market share. Over 50 per cent of the survey participants reported that diversity initiatives take a back seat to such measures as revising compensation systems, restructuring and downsizing (SHRM/CCH survey, 1993). Yet, as the demographic predictions made clear, relegating the importance of diversity programmes can only, in the long run, negatively affect worker productivity, profitability and market share.

Another problem surfaces from the tendency of some organizations to simply substitute the term 'diversity' for affirmative action and equal employment opportunity (EEO). That is to say, existing affirmative action programmes become the 'new' diversity initiatives. This phenomenon has become particularly popular, given the erosion of affirmative action by court rulings throughout the US. Relabelling affirmative action efforts seems to be the case for many organizations, including the federal government. A recent report by the US Merit Systems Protection Board (1993), *Evolving Workforce Demographics*, stated that federal agencies are developing very few new diversity programmes to address the demographic changes, but rather simply continued with their old affirmative action programmes. Often the programmes are relabelled 'diversity programmes' (see, for example, Cameron et al., 1993; Gard, 1994; Riccucci, 1997).

While EEO and affirmative action programmes are critical to diversity efforts, particularly since they are driven by legal mandates, they are different from diversity measures. In the US, EEO is largely viewed as a means to prevent discrimination in the workplace on the basis of such factors or characteristics as race, colour, religion, gender, national origin, ability and age. Affirmative action, on the other hand, which emerged in response to pervasive employment discrimination, embodies proactive efforts to redress past discriminations as well as to diversify the workplace in terms of race, ethnicity, gender, physical abilities and so forth. Affirmative action has been viewed as a legal tool to ensure EEO and diversity.

Diversity or managing diversity is the next iteration on the continuum. It refers to the ability of top management to develop strategies as well as programmes and policies to manage and accommodate diversity in their workplaces. It includes the ability of organizations to harness the diverse human resources available in order to create a productive and motivated workforce. Key here is management's ability to develop ways to address such challenges as communication breakdowns, misunderstandings and even hostilities which invariably result from working in an environment with persons from highly diverse backgrounds, age cohorts and lifestyles.

Thus, to the degree that organizations confound the concepts of EEO, affirmative action and diversity, each area is potentially diminished. In particular, relabelling affirmative action programmes as diversity initiatives severely curtails the broader efforts needed to manage diversity in the workplace.

Another very critical problem in organizations' efforts to prepare for diversity in the workplace is a failure to prepare for the backlash by white males (and their labour unions).

Indeed, we have not made much progress beyond the backlash that evolved out of the US Supreme Court's 1978 *Regents v. Bakke* decision, which popularized the concept of 'reverse discrimination'. Once again, as we are seeing throughout the country, white males are filled with fear and anger. As a *Business Week* cover story entitled 'White, Male and Worried' succinctly pointed out,

> Often for the first time in their lives, [white males] are worrying about their future opportunities because of widespread layoffs and corporate restructuring. Outside the corporation, white men are feeling threatened because of racial and gender tensions that have been intensifying in recent years (Galen, 1994: 51).

This fear is, in part, a new manifestation of the old backlash against affirmative action. That is, many continue to believe that diversity, just like affirmative action, will lower standards. As the *Business Week* article said, 'At the heart of the issue for many white males is the question of merit—that in the rush for a more diverse workplace, they will lose out to less qualified workers (Galen, 1994: 52). This is an old argument which has little empirical foundation, yet it has been a forcefully convincing one for those opposed to affirmative action and now, diversity efforts.

Government and corporate officials did not develop measures to address the inevitable problem of backlash. Perhaps there was a belief on their part that the driving force behind diversity initiatives is not statutory or common law—as it is with affirmative action—but rather economic (i.e. in terms of 'competitiveness' and 'viability'). As a corollary, businesses and government could claim they have no legal pressures to embrace diversity, but are doing so 'voluntarily'. Officials may have then concluded that diversity programmes and policies would be accepted unconditionally by white males, unions and even white male managers. But, as we are seeing with the nationwide assault against race- and gender-based employment programmes, this has not been the case.

The backlash problem also stems from organizations' failure to address the fears of white men about the *effects* of policies and programmes aimed at promoting diversity. Organizations will need to work with white males so that they understand that models of diversity are based on inclusion, not exclusion. That is, diversity programmes do not seek to displace white males, but rather to prepare workers and managers to work in a heterogeneous environment, one where *everyone* can compete equally for organizational resources. So, diversity efforts will go beyond race, gender, ability and age to cover, for example, career planning for everyone.

Another part of the backlash problem has been failing to educate all workers that diversity initiatives, just like affirmative action, will not lower standards. There appears to be a misguided assumption that people of colour, white women and other protected-class persons are unqualified for their jobs, and are hired only because of their gender, race, etc. White males in particular, will claim, for example, that if a person of colour scores lower on a written or oral exam, but is nevertheless hired, standards have been lowered. Employers need to educate all workers to understand that this is a myth, given the biases which exist in how people's competencies and qualifications are judged. That is to say, oral or written tests for determining a job applicant's qualifications are often plagued with cultural biases or subjective measurement scales (see Chapter 20).

Employers might strive to rectify the exams; if they do not, they should at least educate all workers about these discrepancies in order to eradicate the myth that the use of such tests will actually lead to the hiring or promoting of qualified or best qualified job candidates.

Another serious shortcoming in organizations' preparations for increased diversity relates to a failure to provide workers, in particular women and people of colour, with the skills and tools necessary to fill high-tech jobs. As noted earlier, advances in technology have led to changes in the nature of work in the US. The degree to which employers actually provided on-the-job training for high-tech jobs remains unclear. However, an interesting development points to evidence that employers have done little to prepare workers for the new jobs of the twenty-first century. In October of 2000, the US Congress passed a bill that increased significantly the number of visas available for educated foreign-born persons in order to temporarily fill highly specialized jobs in the US, especially those in the computer and technology industry. The measure was spurred by the great demand for jobs in high-tech industries and low supply of American labour with the requisite skills. This raises questions around why the US has not been preparing Americans for these highly specialized jobs, or why public and private organizations have not been training existing workers, especially women and people of colour, to fill these high-technology jobs.

Perhaps the most critical shortcoming around organizations' efforts to prepare for increased diversity in the workplace is that many employers have not integrated their diversity initiatives into the broader, long-term goals and missions of the organization. Rather, diversity measures have tended to be 'one-shot' deals. For example, the SHRM/CCH survey (1993) of public and private human resources specialists revealed that over 70 per cent of diversity training programmes are one day or less in length. The survey concluded that this strategy results in failure.

If employers are genuinely interested in developing successful programmes, they will need to change the *culture* of their organizations so that diversity is not just supported but valued. Managing diversity means managing cultural change, which is not just a simple, one-shot programme, but an initiative that must exist over time. It requires incorporating diversity efforts into continuous improvement and total quality management (TQM) programmes. A key requirement is *accountability*, where behaviour changes on the job are measured and rewarded when set diversity goals have been achieved. In effect, diversity initiatives become a standard way of doing business.

CONCLUSIONS

Many organizations across the country prepared for workforce 2000 by mounting a variety of diversity programmes. Some employee populations are already so diverse that such programmes are essential. But, as we are finding, there are a host of problems with the way in which diversity programmes have been conceptualized and implemented. And some organizations pontificate on the importance of such programmes, but they do very little to actually develop and execute diversity programmes. If organizations in the US are truly interested in remaining competitive and viable, particularly in a global economy, they will need to develop viable diversity programmes and policies or reconceptualize and overhaul their existing ones.

REFERENCES

Cameron, K., Jorgenson, J. & Kawecki, C. (1993). Civil service 2000 revisited. *Public Personnel Management*, **22**, 669–674.

Civil Service 2000 (1988). Washington, DC: US Office of Personnel Management.

Galen, M. (1994). White, male, and worried. *Business Week*, 31 January.

Gard, K.K. (1994). MSPB reevaluates workforce 2000 for the 1990s. *Public Administration Times*, 1 February, 1/13.

New York State Work Force Plan (1989). Albany, NY: New York State Department of Civil Service.

Regents v. Bakke (1978). 438 US 265.

Riccucci, N.M. (1997). Cultural diversity programs to prepare for workforce 2000. *Public Personnel Management*, **26**, 35–41.

SHRM/CCH (Society for Human Resources Management/Commerce Clearing House) (1993). *1993 SHRM Survey*. Commerce Clearing House, Inc., May 26, 1–12.

US Merit Systems Protection Board (1993). *Evolving Workforce Demographics: Federal Agency Action and Reaction*. Washington, DC: USMSPB.

Workforce 2000 (1987). Indianapolis, Ind.: Hudson Institute.

Workforce 2020 (1997). Indianapolis, Ind.: Hudson Institute.

CHAPTER 22

Cultural Diversity in the IT-Globalizing Workplace: Conundra and Future Research

Nada Korac-Kakabadse
University College, Northampton, UK
Alexander Kouzmin
Graduate College of Management, Southern Cross University, Australia
Andrew Korac-Kakabadse
Cranfield School of Management, Cranfield, UK

SUMMARY

This chapter explores effects of information technology (IT) at the beginning of the third millennium, and its ramifications for labour organization, business and culture. IT is conceptualized as a catalyst for a period of seminal change within the global economy. The lack of IT awareness, social diversity, and the need to tap the creative synergy of sociocultural differences, through the better understanding of IT effects on culture, are highlighted.

A need for self-reflection and a critical examination of adopted management models, especially those within embedded ethnocentric contexts of shared beliefs, values and cognitive structures, are also explored. It is argued that organizations need to learn to manage cultural diversity. The need for the development of organizational ideologies that build on cognitive structures, culturally sensitized to diversity, is central to a generic strategy for managing increasingly culturally diversified organizations that make up the globalized economy in the third millennium.

Individual Diversity and Psychology in Organizations. Edited by Marilyn J. Davidson and Sandra L. Fielden.
© 2003 John Wiley & Sons, Ltd.

INTRODUCTION

As a result of *economic* pressure (permanent unemployment, permanent underemployment, decline of the middle class); *changing business needs* (shift from products to services, shift to human-based services, focus on core business, cost reduction, customer focus); *demographic changes* (female-dominated workforce, ageing workforce, decline in youth population); *organizational dynamics* (globalization, minimalist/line organization, externalized work, demise of traditional organization, demise of traditional management); *social change* (increased affluence, post-materialistic values, emerging leisure society); and *technology advancement* (invisible collaboration, virtual companies/teams, global communications/interaction, personal corporate infrastructure, mobility and opaque work domains), the nature of the social contract is fundamentally changing. The current dynamic in society and in organization, besides some perceived enhancement in efficiency, carries the erosion of social contracts.

Some have argued that IT has had an epochal impact on the development process, as it punctuates the shift from traditional development to an emerging social totality with its own distinct organizing principle (Baudrillard, 1983; Jameson, 1984; Lyotard, 1984; Kellner, 1988). This shift is exemplified by networked organizations, de-differentiation and an increased demand for symbolic goods [ones that may be consumed symbolically— gazed at; dreamt about; talked about; photographed; and handled, such as information goods; education; arts; culture; and leisure pursuits (Leiss, 1978: 19; Douglas & Isherwood, 1980)]. IT has been credited with bringing into being the 'globalization' option (an advanced and complex form of internationalization that implies a degree of functional integration between internationally-dispersed economic activities that has combined and uneven effects across social space and time) in the way that industrialization had brought about the capitalist–industrial state (Dicken, 1992: 2). Like industrialization, it implies a progressive economic and administrative realization and differentiation of the social world (Weber, 1949; Bell, 1976; Simmel, 1978).

There are strong suggestions that the emergence of the global option would have been inconceivable without advancements in IT, particularly telecommunications (Forester, 1985, 1987, 1989; Castelles, 1989; Henderson, 1991), since the root of global restructuring is a 'techno-economic' process, establishing a whole range of new organizational possibilities facilitated by computer-related physical technology and creating a world so different that it can only be understood as constituting a new techno-economic paradigm (Freeman & Perez, 1988; Perez & Soete, 1988). With regards to social change, IT is seen as a source of culture, where culture is perceived as ways of working, belief, attachment and contact (Gransey & Roberts, 1992) and where IT's economic value of manipulating culture to enhance rational control is a pivotal issue for all organizational actors. To the extent that IT succeeds in this mission, corporate IT becomes a medium of nascent totalitarianism (control through the uniform definition of meanings).

Others (Freeman, 1987; Korac-Boisvert, 1992; Korac-Boisvert & Kouzmin, 1994) have argued that IT developments have been a major material condition for the emergence of the global option in as far as they have enabled particular labour processes and sometimes entire production facilities to be dispersed across the globe (internationalization), while allowing managerial control to remain centralized in the 'world cities' of core societies (Weill, 1990, 1992).

The adoption of new IT continually (re)defines work-related and social roles, contributing to a significant shift in the international pattern of specialization and competitiveness

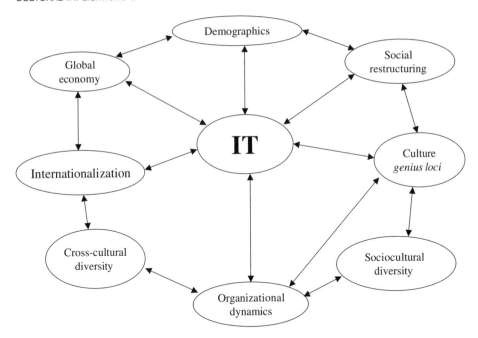

FIGURE 22.1 Symbiotic forces driving the IT-globalizing workplace (Compiled by authors)

at a rate that is often faster than related organizational and socio-economic theories can address (OECD, 1987: 214, 1992a,b; Tushman & Nelson, 1990; Korac-Boisvert & Kouzmin, 1994; Kouzmin & Korac-Boisvert, 1995; Korac-Kakabadse & Kouzmin, 1997a) (see Figure 22.1). Moreover, the social restructuring trend has been further propelled by the increasingly sophisticated demands of prosperous customers (consumerism, changing actor profiles, de-differentiation); the accelerated rate of development of newly industrialized countries with lower labour costs; and the erosion of protectionism which was, itself, fuelled by the greater mobility of actors, capital and information (punctuated by spectacular advances in IT that have eluded the sovereign powers of any one nation) (Korac-Boisvert & Kouzmin, 1994; Kouzmin & Korac-Boisvert, 1995).

CULTURAL IMPLICATIONS OF IT

Organizations provide a *genius loci* or 'spirit of a place' in terms of an 'orientation' and knowing where one is in relation to one's context and in terms of 'identification', involving knowing how one is able to relate to action (Schulz, 1980). The *genius loci* provides individuals with dimensions of the experience of safety and belonging; openness and honesty; love and appreciation; social and culture rules; freedom and responsibility; support, control and power; and membership. Through work practices, organizational culture, rules and procedures, structures, management style and rewards, organizations define the work realm for individuals.

The adoption of new IT also conveys a powerful cultural load, having the capacity to involve all organizational actors in its use—being inserted into organizational life both in material and in discursive ways (Webster & Robins, 1986; Hill, 1988; Muetzelfeldt, 1988; Korac-Boisvert, 1992). Materially, IT provides the potential for a wide range of data collection, storage and processing. IT provides information on demand, builds banks of shared knowledge, and enables real-time, structured learning events to transcend boundaries of time and space, thus becoming a tool for building solutions (McAteer, 1994: 68). IT can also be used as a tool for understanding other cultures and tapping into their creative synergy, rather than merely being a tool for presenting 'other' cultures as something exotic or dismissing them as having *ethnie* 'differences' that dominant cultures often equate with 'inefficiency' (Korac-Boisvert, 1992).

IT's discursive presence is most prominent in a cultural setting concerned with the future of work and organizations (Forester, 1985, 1989; Roszak, 1986; Webster & Robins, 1986). Within a sociological context, IT influences social system continuity, control, identity, and the integration of members. For example, the microelectronic advancements of the 1990s have been particularly influential on labour organizations. The use of job clustering (combining several jobs into one) is often facilitated by the use of IT as opposed to job simplification (a reduced task set) emphasized by the Taylorist influence (Hammer & Champy, 1993: 51–52). Furthermore, when assisted by direct access to centrally formed databanks, by means of computer networks and other forms of interactive IT, employees at the lower levels of organizational structure have the potential to become multi-skilled, equipped with the kind of planning and logistical information hitherto held only at the disposal of middle managers. The distribution of the power within the workforce, however, is not predetermined (Child, 1987). While the 'democratic' thrust of economic rationalism claims that a technology-powered economistic society is viable (Child, 1985, 1987; Dizard, 1985), these optimistic views often overlook the fact that in network or web organizations, the policy trajectory is less visible than in top-down organizations; that centre–periphery power relations are less easily recognized both by participants and by analysts; and, that strategic control is centralized while operational decision-making is concurrently decentralized (Muetzelfeldt, 1992; Korac-Boisvert & Kouzmin, 1994; Kouzmin, et al., 1997).

Ongoing decentralization renders state control more difficult—it does not make it superfluous: the innovative processes of non-Taylorist rationalization cannot only be influenced, but are shaped, by political means (Piore & Sabel, 1984). Thus, a fundamental political problem is whether processes and outcomes of decentralization take place under some sort of political (and, possibly, socio-economic) control by state agencies. State agencies have to decide whether to leave workplace operations to the market, with the implicit or tacit acceptance of unrealistic assumptions of rationality and 'good' defined in terms of efficiency, rather than effectiveness, or to regulate workplace operations further in ways which are likely to be more generally accepted, given the growing pressure of social demands flowing from dysfunctional economic rationalist solutions (Kouzmin et al., 1997).

CROSS-CULTURAL DIVERSITY: A NEGLECTED ORGANIZATIONAL CAPACITY

Societies with Anglo-American work ethics have created value systems which emphasize that individuals can succeed if they have talent and commitment. There are also *ethnie* value differences within these work ethics that are often neglected in increasingly multicultural organizations. These differences are visible even in the cross-cultural setting between 'psychologically close' cultures (Sappinen, 1992), as exemplified by Australian CEOs working in British subsidiaries, where cross-cultural conflict appears to have been the unintended consequence emerging 'not in the start-up period but when cooperation had become routine' (Meyer, 1993: 101).

Notwithstanding the Australian heritage, as well as historically close cultural ties with Britain, manifested by a common language and common political, legal and educational systems (Kanter, 1991); close similarity in terms of the four work-related values (power distance, uncertainty avoidance, masculinity/femininity and individualism/collectivism) (Hofstede, 1980, 1992, 1993); attitude dimensions (Ronen, 1986); and similar economic reform strategies, British and Australian management have not shared the same formative context experience. The similarities posed by close cultural ties (defined in the cultural, social and economic sense) have led Australian foreign direct investment to flow predominantly towards Britain rather than to geographically proximate trading partners. However, these same ties often lead Australian and British managers to 'inter-cultural over-confidence' (Meyer, 1993: 93) and cognitive arrogance that overlook the differences which may stem from the different fields of experience of each society (Kelley, et al., 1987; Huo & McKinley, 1992).

Differences in national formative contexts may often impact on the interrelationship between business strategy, environment and control system attributes, and strategic management (Ouchi, 1979; Douglas & Rhee, 1989; Schneider, 1989; Porter, 1990; Huo & McKinley, 1992; Kouzmin & Korac-Kakabadse, 1997). Similarly, an organization's formative context (whether it has experienced organic and/or acquisition-based growth), history and circumstance determine organizational success (Kakabadse, 1991: 164). French managers, for example, require considerable attention in terms of social skills training, while an in-depth study of senior managers in the UK, France, Germany, Sweden, Ireland, Austria, Spain and Finland suggested that the French, in particular, resent interference in their work or in the management of their functions (Kakabadse, 1993). They also find criticism difficult to take and display a high need for control in terms of implementing their views and intentions. A French view of interference is seen by managers of other European organizations as comments made by one colleague to another which might require some consideration (Kakabadse, 1993). A study by Kakabadse and Myers (1995a) strongly supports this position. Ethnic culture affects the process of strategy formulation, particularly in scanning, selecting, interpreting and validating information as well as establishing priorities (Schneider, 1989). Differences in *ethnie* culture are, therefore, likely to result in different interpretations and responses to the same strategic issue (Schneider & De Meyer, 1991).

In the case of Australia, geographic isolation (Blainey, 1966) may have been instrumental in forming the Australian manager's proclivity for higher independence, egalitarianism (Western, 1983), dominance and assertiveness than is the case with British managers (Barry & Dowling, 1984). Ignored differences in, or perhaps peripheral, cultural values between Australian and British managers have been found to be of particular concern in the management of day-to-day activities, business etiquette and interpersonal interaction (Fenwick & Edwards, 1994). A comparison between Australian and US managers also reveals subtle differences in their values, attitudes and beliefs concerning a range of management-related topics (Dowling & Nagel, 1986; Posner & Low, 1990).

Similarly, Australian managers tend to make independent decisions, often posing difficulties in an increasingly cross-cultural relationship (Korac-Boisvert, 1992) where rhetorical management strategies (giving orders, setting procedures, supervision) are extrinsic and cannot always be assumed to work in the future. Australian managers need to learn to accommodate more collegial decisions, arrived at through negotiation, discussion and compromise, and to be sensitive to cross-cultural issues when designing reward policies. For example, 'self-actualization' needs (Maslow, 1962) appear to generate high preferences for reward items such as participation (power distance dimension) and work challenge (individualism dimension) in Britain and its ex-colonies (Hofstede, 1980). However, participation may not work as a reward for actors from a high power distance society (Hofstede, 1980, 1993). Similarly, work challenge may be ineffective as a reward in a collectivist culture.

Contemporary managers must find psychological rewards and inspiration for actors whose psychological development patterns are unfamiliar to them, i.e. find new ways to tap the intrinsic motives of organizational actors to achieve optimum performance (Hodgson, 1988). Managers should foster an organizational culture that accommodates *ethnie* and individual employee differences by giving employees the power of self-determination. There is a need to harness the diverse talents of actors who willingly perform jobs because their sense of purpose and identity is tightly coupled to the core values of the organization. As Peters and Waterman (1982: 238–239) put it, managers need to *enable* the average employee to become a 'winner'.

In addition to technological development and the emergent globalization of work environments, increased global mobility has transformed many ethnocentric organizations into multicultural and multinational organizations. Although migration flows largely from non-OECD (Organization for Economic Cooperation and Development) countries to the OECD, there is considerable movement of member-country nationals within the area (Garson & Puymoyen, 1995). Also, the consolidation or emergence of regional economic blocks (the European Economic Area, Association of South-East Asian Nations, American Free Trade Agreement and Asian-Pacific Economic Cooperation (APEC)), along with particular political developments (such as events in the former Yugoslavia Algeria and Haiti), have intensified and strengthened the regional aspect of migration (Garson & Puymoyen, 1995). Consequently, labour laws will become more significant and be determined by global trading agreements (GATT) and individual trading block issues. Managing these interactions within intimate relationships and the global mind-set perspective will require new skills from all stakeholders (Roobeek, 1990). Leaders in contemporary globalized organizations will need to synthesize ethnocentrism and cultural relativism, as, in their extreme forms, both pose equal dangers. The former becomes insensitive to cross-cultural differences, whereas the latter becomes blind to cross-cultural similarities (Kouzmin & Korac-Kakabadse, 1997).

Managers of multinationals need to consider, among other things, the European respect for structure and the chain of authority as well as the Asian concern for the broad-based involvement of all participants (Keen, 1991). Furthermore, managers need to accommodate actors from cultures that accept chance (French) and intuition or fate (Arabic) as functions of organizational life, including actors from diverse, sometimes antagonistic, cultures (Foucault, 1965, 1979). A willingness to learn to communicate effectively with actors not familiar with the language system (jargon, context and cultural idioms) of the host society is also a requirement. Thus, motivation by personal success in the form of wealth, recognition and self-actualization may produce increased productivity in organizations with predominantly British (Australian, and other former colonies) and American cultural backgrounds (Hofstede, 1980). These are cultures that value individualism (Hofstede, 1980), as exemplified by the number of Australian law firms and media organizations.

However, the same strategy may have no, or an adverse, effect within an organization which has a predominantly homogenized cultural background, such as a Japanese IT consultancy firm, which harbours consensus decision-making and promotion of cohorts rather than individuals as an expression of Japanese 'groupness'. Similarly, motivation by individual job security may be successful among employees with a cultural proclivity for strong uncertainty avoidance, high power distance and a need for belonging, such as Greek, French, Spanish, Portuguese, Yugoslav and Asian actors (Hofstede, 1980). Motivation by success and belonging, on the other hand, may produce higher productivity in organizations with a workforce which is predominantly of a North European culture (Hofstede, 1980; Keen, 1991).

The impact of cultural factors may be felt most strongly in the need for belongingness, love and esteem of culturally different actors. In organizations with a predominantly Greek culture, such as in labour-intensive factories in Australia, the positions of these needs may interchange and cause a reversal in the hierarchy—Greek culture (Hofstede, 1980), characteristically, considers love to be contingent upon one's status in society (Maslow, 1971: 51–52). Self-actualization needs determine intrinsic reward preferences, whereas needs below the level of self-actualization appear to determine extrinsic reward preferences; different cultures value different reward preferences. Besides culture, an actor's individual growth along the hierarchy of needs is also influenced by gender, personality, age group and organizational position.

However, psychologically insecure actors, irrespective of their ethnic cultural background, hesitate to undertake challenging jobs. The acceptance of challenge is a key element in seeking a competitive edge, and retraining the workforce is a critical issue. Often a reason for failure is the actor's inability to adjust to responsibility (Dowling & Schuler, 1990). Furthermore, psychological insecurity also generates resistance to learning new skills (Dowling & Schuler, 1990). In the process of rationalizing the irrational, to make them more secure and in control, psychologically insecure actors often miss the hidden meaning and significance of the actions that shape the organization (Morgan, 1986). The rationality expressed by Taylor (1911) may have disguised an extreme form of compulsiveness, just as the contemporary manager's excessive concern for clear-cut targets and goals may disguise his/her basic insecurity in life, anxiety, inferiority or insignificance (Kanter, 1977; Morgan, 1986; Manz & Sims, 1990).

In a comparative analysis of European manufacturers in which a total of 957 top managers (chairmen, chief executive officers, managing directors, general directors) participated, *ethnie* differences requiring improvement were revealed in terms of job satisfaction, orientation to discipline, specialist versus general management orientation, team orientation, organizational orientation, other areas of business practices, as well as organizational and management performance (Kakabadse & Myers, 1995b). The study suggests that there are significant differences (positive and negative) in management perceptions of organizational orientation and change, as well as in the quality of management (Kakabadse, 1993; Kakabadse & Myers, 1995a). Similarly, a comparative study of US, Japanese and South Korean managers and US, UK and Irish managers (Alderson & Kakabadse, 1994) revealed significant variations in attitudes towards work ethics.

Social diversity, exemplified by differences among actors and the multiplicity of cultures within organizations, needs further consideration. Underestimation of the impact of even subtle cultural differences on the establishment and maintenance of effective interpersonal relationships may undermine the strategies for an effective information search and, thus, decisions, outcomes and organizational effectiveness. Considering that one of the criteria for the effectiveness of any social organization is its ability to utilize its resources (human and artefacts) to carry on a useful exchange with its environment and that sociocultural differences often cause the underutilization of the potential of an organization's human assets, overcoming cultural ignorance and increasing broader cultural understanding require urgent attention in the global option (Kouzmin & Korac-Kakabadse, 1997). Since differences are often subtle, impediments are often left unaddressed, often leading to a creeping crisis (Korac-Boisvert & Kouzmin, 1994). Until actors are willing to accept other values and behaviours that are dissimilar to their own, they will continue to carry a judgemental perspective that can, in spite of themselves, be prejudicial, discriminatory and oppressive (Carnevale & Stone, 1994: 25).

THE CULTURAL 'LEAP FORWARDS' IN GLOBALIZING IMPERATIVES

By changing current culture, organizations can prevent a significant waste of talent among multi-ethnic actors and gain a competitive advantage. In pragmatic management terms, there is a business case for change driven by the need for increased productivity, if not for purely altruistic reasons. Besides altruism, cultural changes are also influenced by many other factors, such as the organization's founder, its history, changing market, IT advancement, actors' changing profile and leadership (Bennis, 1993; Korac-Boisvert & Kouzmin, 1994; Kouzmin & Korac-Boisvert, 1995; Korac-Kakabadse & Kouzmin, 1997a, b). In a broader context, organizational culture forms an important ideological element within a global restructuring of capital, labour and markets and a shift towards a more fluid organizational philosophy of 'flexible accumulation' (Harvey, 1989). In order to harness these changes consciously, organizations need, in addition to a progressive cultural policy, an infrastructure and 'new-age' leadership vision, or an egalitarian ideology (Korac-Boisvert & Kouzmin, 1994) actually to sustain globalization.

In order to respond effectively with dynamics of cultural change, organizations build an organizational psycho-structure that sustains cultural change through the action-oriented management of diversity. Only through the ideology of social diversity can the organization accommodate sociocultural differences (Pringle, 1994). The implications of this qualitative shift in ideology, from the homogeneous to heterogeneous culture, are profound, requiring an actor to set aside his/her own personal filters or perceptions in order to examine the perception of others and recognizing that these values are as valid as his/her own. Contemporary actors need to be inventive, as it is the actor who constantly reinvents him or herself (Foucault, 1986: 40; Bennis, 1993).

Cross-cultural training and development are critical for effective technology transfer (intra- and interorganizationally), as well as a qualitative leap forward, regardless of the cultural distance between focal and host cultures (Aviel, 1990; Bigelow, 1994; Korac-Boisvert & Kouzmin, 1994). With hub and satellite office arrangements made possible by the 'information superhighway', the nature of the workforce and work styles will become significantly diverse. Economic democratization of the workplace needs to go beyond equality principles towards a de-ethnocentricity that recognizes a wide diversity of cultures and practices through the diversity of organizational content as well as a plurality of interests. In Bakhtin's (1968) terminology, organizations need to provide a 'hybridization' medium which brings together the exotic and the familiar through actors' broader cultural awareness. Organizations need to change in order to accommodate actors from a variety of cultures, providing equal opportunity for the fulfilment of each actor's intellectual, emotional and socio-economic aspirations alike, irrespective of the cultural or ethnic differences (Korac-Boisvert & Kouzmin, 1994). The emerging global option highlights the need to think realistically about how culturally to create an effective worldwide business (Zuboff, 1983; Kakabadse, 1991: 53; Ali & Falcon, 1995).

The focus, therefore, needs to be on the methods by which cultures are built, on hidden assumptions to be examined, and on the questioning of the cultural authority of one society to speak for 'the other'. There is a need to move beyond foundationalism, relativism and single epistemologies towards plural ontologies, to investigate specific social and cultural processes and the dynamics of the production of particular forms of knowledge. There is a need to work towards a sociological account of the information age and to gain a better understanding of potential cultural challenges at the beginning of the third millennium. This entails focusing on the interrelationships between cultural segments within culture, on symbolic goods (with the focus on intellectual fields) (Bourdieu, 1971, 1979), on conditions of supply and demand for symbolic goods (the process of competition and monopolization), and on the struggle between the 'established' and the 'outsiders'.

BEYOND EQUITY: UNITY THROUGH CULTURAL DIVERSITY

The conceptualization of unity through diversity, or unity permeating difference, is becoming more acceptable today as part of some of the changes which have given rise to the information age, undermining the cultural integration of the nation-state. The concurrent incorporation of the state into large units and the transformative effects of global economic and cultural flows require a global unity within which diversity can take place. This is exemplified by the current efforts to create a European identity, sponsored by the EC (European Commission), in such a way as to allow cultural variation and unity through diversity (Schelsinger, 1987). The effort to create an 'imagined community' for Europe, generating unifying symbols which differentiate Europeans from others, also draws sustenance from areas of cultural conflict such as the notion of *ethnie*; the set of symbols, myth, memories, heroes, events, landscape and traditions woven together in popular consciousness (Smith, 1990) and which are grounds for a common culture. Reconstructing all national European cultures and constructing new symbols for an emerging European superstate and transnational culture are problematic, although with the further development of the European Union it is expected that trade between EC member states will rise and that collaborative and joint-venture projects will be increasingly perceived as low risk initiatives (Burns et al., 1995).

Moving from the national state to the transnational or the global one, whereby the world becomes united to the extent that it is regarded as one place and one global culture, poses a number of challenges (Robertson, 1990; Wild, 1994). There are arguments both for and against cultural integration and homogenization at the global level. This is evidenced by multinational capitalism—Americanization, Japanization and media imperialism—which assumes that local differences are being obliterated by universal forces exemplified by increased international flow of people, capital and symbolic goods (Gassner & Schade, 1990). Factors that mediate between national cultures, global financial markets, international law and various international agencies and institutions form the transnational or 'third culture' (Gassner & Schade, 1990).

The globalization process leads to the acceptance of the view that the world is a singular place, acting as a form capable of generating and sustaining various images of what the world is, or should be. Notionally there would be a common culture, although not on the level of content (the possession of an integrated set of beliefs and values) but, rather, more on the level of form; an underlying and formal, generative possibility for a recognizable complexity of variation. From this perspective, the global culture does not point to homogeneity or to a common culture, but, rather, to the increased awareness of all actors that in their daily interaction, through a variety of cultural contacts with others, they can increase the range of conflicting definitions of the world with which they are brought into contact. In this sense, the formation of a global culture entails an intellectual 'leap forward' through the education of all actors, engendering a generative ideology and not a superior, coherent set of values. Synergizing the emerging call for 'ideological leadership' and the sociological and anthropological assumptions that dominate ideology, plays a crucial role in sustaining a social order and integrity.

The 'global-village' (Toffler, 1980) culture can be conceptualized as a 'museum without walls' (Malraux, 1967) in which all styles, traditions and cultural forms of the past can be represented, and where the principle of organization becomes an eclectic montage, with the nearest juxtaposed to the most distant (Bann, 1984; Robertson, 1988) and where a generative formal articulation of meaning occurs in which commonality entails the capacity to recognize differences as legitimate and valid (Pringle, 1994). Cultures and subcultures require an interpretivist framework allowing for the conceptualization of a multicultural and heterogeneous society (Maccoby, 1994).

While models, metaphors and analogies can be helpful if critically examined and limitations understood, they can also be misleading (Simon, 1962). However, they may also revalue different management preoccupations in cross-cultural settings, even with cultural similarity and 'psychic closeness' (Kanter, 1991), let alone 'psychologically distant' cultures. The universal adoption of inappropriate management models can be psychologically painful and developmentally depriving (Korac-Boisvert, 1992). A historical review of the Anglo-Saxon work ethic and value system suggests that it has produced a fertile ground for world-leading breakthroughs in product and process technology, whereas the Japanese work ethic has perfected many of these innovative breakthroughs. Arguably, Anglo-American cultures in increasingly globalized organizations need to explicate an ideology that builds on the philosophy of individualism, celebrates cultural diversity, and is sensitive to the global and local contexts that further nurture creativity and innovation. The required ideology should actively construct a 'communal sense' (Barnard, 1938) and strengthen organizational performance by securing great commitment and flexibility from employees (Selznick, 1957; Ouchi, 1981; Peters & Waterman, 1982; Kanter, 1990).

The strength of an organizational ideology that shapes organizational culture provides the key for securing 'unusual effort on the part of apparently ordinary employees'

(Peters & Waterman, 1982: xvii). In today's multicultural organizations, ideology must celebrate diversity (Morgan, 1983; Van Maanen, 1994) and accommodate driven people whose ideas provoke, enrage and move the great lumbering cart of theory onwards. 'The idiosyncratic, exciting, innovative maverick thinker, the active deconstructionist and marginal people, alike' (Weir, 1993: 17) are all 'social wealth creators'. Ideology needs to synergize diversity with a culture encouraging the questioning and challenging of the status quo, the finding of new solutions, the taking of risks in support of trialing innovative methods, and providing an environment which assists individuals in challenging their own basic belief systems.

In a new global circumstance of polyculturalization, captured by the 'museum without walls' (Malraux, 1967) metaphor, there is an urgency for 'visitors' (all actors) to adopt the role of interpreting the great variety and wealth of diverse cultural traditions, presented to a new audience in a meaningful manner, without venturing into areas of judgement or value hierarchization (Bauman, 1985, 1988, 1990). Reference to the *fin-de-millennium* pathos may indicate a need for a shift from old frames and the development of more flexible modes of classification; a new frame which entails a more flexible generative structure within which a wide range of differences can be recognized and tolerated. In this sense, the formation of a global culture entails the education of the populace into a new set of generative values. There is a need for reflexive, cross-cultural analysis within an appropriate appreciation of the ethnic formative context. The most basic task of corporate leaders is the *individualizing* of corporations, requiring the adoption of a new management philosophy that is based on purpose, process and, above all, people, recognizing and employing the untapped ability that each individual brings to work every day (Bartlett & Ghoshal, 1995).

Although initiating and managing such a process is often laboriously difficult, there are substantial rewards when a new cultural pattern evolves that enhances both individual and organizational development. It is the intellectual skills of the actors which are relevant to, and enhance the quality of, organizational life. Altering organizational scripts and changing organizational culture is more often than not a daunting task, even God-like, for in attempting to change the 'formative context' one is in, one also creates new kinds of action with new values. Progress is often uneven at best, and the resistance to change formidable, as rather than handing down previously constructed patterns of interactions as a context for ongoing ones, actors need first to investigate their validity and subject them to psycho-structural 'audits' in order to accept them and *enact* new ones.

Organizations that choose to resist cultural change will continue to frustrate and burn out actors, perhaps causing a large proportion of talented employees to exit either physically (brain drain) or psychologically (by not reaching their potential or not giving their all), seriously endangering the organization's potential for achieving a competitive advantage. Actors become demotivated 'by the thoughtless, irritating, unconcerned way by which they are treated; by conventional operating practices and by old attitudes, myths and prejudices' (Hoernschemeyer, 1989: 39). Under such adversity, actors retreat to positions and perceptions of familiarity; it is often easier to label uncomfortable and seemingly difficult problems as ones of *ethnie* difference, justifying their so-called insurmountable nature instead of effectively managing these differences by developing cultural interfaces, effective dialogue and promoting organizational learning (Kakabadse & Myers, 1995a).

The very strength of the unity through diversity concept is that it facilitates active learning processes which occur in a multicultural environment, what Revans (1985) called 'comrades in adversity'—actors learn from each other by sharing and comparing their problems and opportunities with one another, learning to distinguish differences between the problems that stem from individual actors and those that stem from business (Kakabadse & Myers, 1995a). Apart from sharing experiences and solutions to problems, there is also the opportunity to challenge each others' firmly held views and beliefs which are often blocking insights into, or acceptance of, new knowledge.

Change induced by learning processes is essential if performance is to increase, enabling the effective achievement of socio-economic democracy in a world characterized by perpetual novelty and challenge. The new globalized frontier requires actors who are able to see through the complexity of underlying structures that generate change (Senge, 1992; Kouzmin & Korac-Boisvert, 1995; Korac-Kakabadse & Kouzmin, 1997a, b). Actors must be able to reflect on the self and be tolerant of other actors, creating the learning processes that make unity through diversity and self-organization possible. The required skill is to stimulate a debate in a manner that is feasible to the managers and to the actors of the organization (Jacques, 1951; Kakabadse & Myers, 1995a). IT may facilitate this process and, as such, may be a mediating factor in 'getting the dialogue right' by reinforcing the establishment of a common language and providing an avenue for participation within the organization via electronic mail, video-conferencing and other electronically-mediated communication tools, including satellite-facilitated worldwide employee development programmes and electronic brokerage (the connection of many different buyers and suppliers instantaneously through a central database—the electronic market) (Korac-Kakabadse & Kouzmin, 1997a). However, IT will provide an avenue for sustained productivity only if its management allows employees to have a direct stake in the future (Beaumont & Sparks, 1990), not by being a vehicle for the better manipulation of organizational actors.

CONCLUSIONS AND FUTURE RESEARCH DIRECTIONS

In a global economy, competitiveness will largely be determined by the use an organization makes of its talent (Lessem, 1990). It is talent and intellectual skill which are relevant to, and enhance, the qualities of interdependency and synergy of complex organization. These scarce resources, effectively managed, provide a competitive advantage for organizations (Sadler, 1994). Organizational models based on images of managers as grey-suited, middle-aged men from a dominant ethnic group occupying impressive hierarchies of substantial size, have considerably less merit in the 1990s and beyond (Hall & Gordon, 1973). The emergence of a myriad of smaller, innovative and flexible organizations, deregulation and global marketplaces are realities imposing the need for organizations to be more proactive with human resources and with sustained adaptation becoming increasingly necessary.

In the global marketplace, organizations can no longer afford to pass over talented people merely because their gender, ethnic backgrounds or economic utility do not fit traditional managerial profiles. The 'option of limiting management to one gender is becoming an archaic luxury that no organization will be able to afford' (Adler, 1994: 36). Stereotyping and/or 'male-as-standard' norms seriously hamper organizations recruiting top talent. While actors who are physically different from the norm and who come from minority groups find themselves discriminated against, it appears that the greatest waste of talent, nationally and internationally, 'remains the discrimination against women when filling jobs' (Sadler, 1994: 15).

With new organizational and managerial imperatives, where traditional, functional management is often a recipe for disaster and small, well-focused actions often produce significant and enduring improvements, new skills for making sense out of chaos are required (Freedman, 1992; Korac-Kakabadse & Kouzmin, 1997a, b). Contemporary organizations, especially in a globalized context, require leaders able to see through the complexity of underlying structures that generate change (Senge, 1990; Korac-Kakabadse & Kouzmin, 1997a). They must be 'researchers' who study their own organizations and 'designers' who create the learning processes that make self-organization possible (Senge, 1990) and make gender and social segregation impossible. Changes induced by learning processes are essential for performance enhancement and the enabling of the effective achievement of socio-economic democracy in a world increasingly characterized by perpetual novelty and change. It could be argued that more important than the perspective of specific theories dealing with women and culture are the generic and important concepts of learning, action and social change.

Organizations that choose to resist such cultural change in the face of mere economic imperatives will continue to frustrate and 'burn out' actors, causing a large proportion of talented employees to *exit*. This failure of organizations to recognize, develop and maintain their pool of highly talented women, ethnic and other managers and its cost to the labour force, was officially acknowledged in the USA in 1988 by the Department of Labor's 'Glass Ceiling Initiative'.

Neither have the behavioural implications of '24/7' connectivity been addressed. We are now in the age of technology and worldwide communication virtual networks. We use information technology so that interactions between service provider and client can be in either 'real-time' or 'virtual'. An increased use of virtual interventions comprising 'canned' or playback interventions, stored and administered by technology, is also rising. Consultants, coaching mentors and some psychologists have already used this technology in learning—such as how to do psychotherapy and to diagnose through software, designed as an expert system, based on decision trees, heuristics and fuzzy logic. In order not to invisibly 'cage' individuals, more research and considerably more thought must be put into the design and implementation of such techno-interventions and services in the globalized workplace.

An increased use of 'technology' is the means by which organizations govern employees, not only by shaping their conduct but also by shaping the identity of individuals (Rose, 1996; du Gay, 1997). There is a pressing need for further research in the area of the coping strategies that actors use when they encounter multicultural and diverse contexts—ones that can be called 'IT-holding environments' (virtual electronic networks). The study of adolescent coping strategies on entering diverse environments suggests that to cope with cultural diversity, one needs to possess a sequential relationship with others and that such relationships are context dependent (Coleman et al., 2001). This suggests that the wider the range of strategies an individual has to cope with cultural diversity, the better he/she will be able to effectively manage a culturally diverse or monocultural environment (Coleman et al., 2001). There is a need for an understanding as to whether similar conditions hold for mature individuals working within IT-holding environments.

Given the support of the context-dependent nature of coping strategies, there is a need for more case studies within a collaborative inquiry framework, to increase actor understandings and to develop shared meanings of actors' contexts. In the field of cultural diversity, ideologies and lifestyles compete for hegemony (Coleman et al., 2001). The dominant class, represented by global enterprises, often imposes culture on others in a globalizing world through an economy of symbols promoting specific interests and exemplified by the shapes of office buildings, shopping malls and factories (Kirchberg, 1998) with little or no consideration of the host cultures.

Most issues are not technological but human and organizational. Thus, those who are in management roles need to look for ways to mitigate the effects of IT change by effectively responding to IT and adopting new ways of working. They are also being required to attend to the needs of staff members and user communities while responding to pressures to continually adopt and develop new technologies. Managers will need to strategically use the 'human moment', through face-to-face communication, in order to add colour to employees' lives, help build confidence and develop trust at work. This skill is currently ignored—at the peril of organizational fragmentation and dysfunctionality. While managers will not be expected to be therapists, they will be expected to identify warning signs of impending employee burnout and to help employees deal with high-stress situations. When correctly designed and implemented, with proper organizational adaptation and change management programmes, IT technology *may* significantly enhance business effectiveness.

The challenging question of what technology can do to one goes, largely, unanswered in its more multidimensional vein. Business models and IT-driven re-engineering exercises, in both public and private sectors, either refuse to acknowledge the legitimacy of the question or, if acknowledged, are embarrassed by the question. This 'silence' on the behavioural sustainability of IT and, increasingly, information and communication technology (ICT) innovation and R & D criticality raises issues of complicity and ignorance—the latter, at least, being amenable to persuasion from lines of argument presented above.

IT innovation/instability is 'big business', to say the least. Whether it is sustainable in human resource management terms, let alone in cultural diversity terms, is *the* emerging organizational policy issue of our time. Since we have spent much of the twentieth century seeking to understand the 'socio-technical' ramifications of machine technology on the shop floor, our calculated disregard of the emerging imperative to understand the 'socio-technics' of a digital/virtual/real-time age, runs a perilous risk—perhaps with 'techno-stress', the onus of proof will, at last, need to rest with proposers of IT innovation, rather than with victims of managerially-induced IT abuse. Perhaps individual litigation, certainly class action, will tell—after all!

REFERENCES

Adler, N.J. (1994). Women managers in a global economy. *Training and Development*, April, 31–36.

Alderson, S. & Kakabadse, A. (1994). Business ethics and Irish management: a cross-cultural study. *European Management Journal*, **12**(4), 432–441.

Ali, A. & Falcon, T. (1995). Work ethic in the USA and Canada. *Journal of Management Development*, **14**(6), 26–34.

Aviel, D. (1990). Cultural barriers to international transactions. *Journal of General Management*, **15**(4), 5–55.

Bakhtin, M.M. (1968). *Rabelais and his World*. Cambridge, Mass.: MIT Press.

Bann, S. (1984). *The Clothing of Clio: A Study of Representations of History in Nineteenth Century Britain and France*. Cambridge: Cambridge University Press.

Barnard, C.I. (1938). *The Functions of the Executive* (30th anniversary edn). Cambridge, Mass.: Harvard University Press.

Barry, B. & Dowling, P. (1984). *An Australian Management Style?* (pp. 1–49). Australian Institute of Management Research Report, Canberra.

Bartlett, C. A. & Ghoshal, S. (1995). Changing the role of top management. *Harvard Business Review*, **73**(3), 132–142.

Baudrillard, J. (1983). *In the Shadow of the Silent Majorities*. New York: Semiotext.

Bauman, Z. (1985). On the origins of civilization. *Theory, Culture and Society*, **2**(3), 77–82.

Bauman, Z. (1988). Is there a postmodern sociology? *Theory, Culture and Society*, **5**(2–3), 114–123.

Bauman, Z. (1990). Modernity and ambivalence. *Theory, Culture and Society*, **7**(2–3), 17–24.

Beaumont, J. R. & Sparks, L. (1990). Information technology as a source of competitive advantage. *International Journal of Information Resource Management*, **1**(1), 28–37.

Bell, D. (1976). *The Cultural Contradictions of Capitalism*. London: Heinemann.

Bennis, W. (1993). *An Invented Life: Reflections on Leadership and Change*. Reading: Addison-Wesley.

Bigelow, J. (1994). International skills for managers: integrating international and managerial skill learning. *Asia Pacific Journal of Human Resources*, **32**(1), 1–12.

Blainey, G. (1966). *The Tyranny of Distance*. Melbourne: Sun Books.

Bourdieu, P. (1971). Intellectual field and creative project. In M. Young (ed.) *Knowledge and Control* (pp. 64–83). London: Collier-Macmillan.

Bourdieu, P. (1979). The production of belief: contribution to an economy of symbolic goods. *Media, Culture and Society*, **2**(1), 48–53.

Burns, P., Myers, A. & Kakabadse, A. (1995). Are national stereotypes discriminating? *European Management Journal*, **13**(2), 212–217.

Carnevale, A.P. & Stone, S.C. (1994). Diversity: beyond the golden rule. *Training and Development*, **48**(10), 22–39.

Castelles, M. (1989). High technology and the new international division of labour. *Labour and Society*, **14**(1), 7–42.

Child, J. (1985). Managerial strategies: new technology and the labour process. In D. Knights & H. Willmott (eds) *Job Redesign: Critical Perspectives on the Labour Process* (pp. 107–141). London: Gower.

Child, J. (1987). Information technology, organization and the response to strategic challenges. *California Management Review*, **30**(1), 33–50.

Coleman, H.L.K., Casali, S.B. & Wampold, B.E. (2001). Adolescent strategies for coping with cultural diversity. *Journal of Counselling and Development*. **79**(3), 356–364.

Dicken, P. (1992). *Global Shift: The Internalization of Economic Activity*. New York: Guilford Press.

Dizard, W. P. Jr (1985). *The Coming Information Age*. New York: Longman.

Douglas, M. & Isherwood, B. (1980). *The World of Goods*. Harmondsworth: Penguin.

Douglas, S.P. & Rhee, D.K. (1989). Examining generic competitive strategy types in US and European markets. *Journal of International Business Studies*, **20**(3), 437–463.

Dowling, P. & Nagel, T. (1986). National work practices: a study of Australian and American business majors. *Journal of Management*, **12**(1), 121–128.

Dowling, P.J. & Schuler, R.S. (1990). *International Dimensions in Human Resource Management*. New York: PWS-Kent Publishing Company.

Du Gay, P. (1997), Organizing identity: making up people at work. In P. du Gay (ed.) *Production of Culture/Cultures of Production* (pp. 33–46). London: Sage.

Fenwick, M. & Edwards, R. (1994). Managing the British subsidiary: is cultural similarity misleading? A study of Australian manufacturers. Paper presented at the Australian and New Zealand Academy of Management's (ANZAM) Annual Conference on 'Vanishing Borders: The Managerial Challenges', Wellington, December, 1–20.

Forester, T. (ed.) (1985). *The Information Technology Revolution*. Oxford: Basil Blackwell.

Forester, T. (1987). *High-tech Society*. Oxford: Basil Blackwell.

Forester, T. (ed.) (1989). *Computers in the Human Context: Information Technology, Productivity and People*. Oxford: Basil Blackwell.

Foucault, M. (1965). *Madness and Reason: A History of Insanity in the Age of Reason*. New York: Random House.

Foucault, M. (1979). *Discipline and Punishment: The Birth of the Prison*. New York: Vintage.

Foucault, M. (1986). What is enlightenment? In P. Rabinow (ed.) *The Foucault Reader* (pp. 78–84). Harmondsworth: Penguin.

Freedman, D.H. (1992). Is management still a science? *Harvard Business Review*, **69**(6), 26–38.

Freeman, C. (1987). The challenge of new technologies. In OECD (ed.), *Interdependence and Co-operation in Tomorrow's World*. Paris: OECD.

Freeman, C. & Perez, C. (1988). Structural crisis of adjustment, business cycles and investment behaviour. In G. Dosi, C. Freeman, R. Nelson, G. Silverberg & L. Soete (eds) *Technical Change and Economic Theory* (pp. 38–66). London: Pinter.

Garson, J.P. & Puymoyen, A. (1995). New patterns of migration. *OECD Observer*, **192**, 8–12.

Gassner, V. & Schade, A. (1990). Conflicts of culture in cross-border legal relations. *Theory, Culture and Society*, **7**(2–3), 64–71.

Gransey, E. & Roberts, J. (1992). The experience of growth in small high technology firms. Paper presented to the 9th European Group of Organizational Studies (EGOS) Colloquium, Berlin, May.

Hall, D. & Gordon, F. (1973). Career choices of married women: effects on conflict, role behaviour and satisfaction. *Journal of Applied Psychology*, **58**(1), 42–48.

Hammer, M. & Champy, J. (1993). *Re-engineering the Corporation: A Manifesto for Business Revolution*. New York: Harper Business.

Harvey, D. (1989). *The Condition of Postmodernity*. Oxford: Basil Blackwell.

Henderson, J. (1991). *The Globalization of High Technology Production: Society, Space and Semi-conductors in the Restructuring of the Modern World*. London: Routledge.

Hill, S. (1988). *Competition and Control at Work: The New Industrial Sociology*. London: Gower.

Hodgson, R. (1988). Purposing: the fundamental dynamics. *Business Quarterly*, **52**(4), 8–11.

Hoernschemeyer, D. (1989). The cornerstones of excellence. *Quality Progress*, **22**(8), 37–40.

Hofstede, G. (1980). *Culture's Consequences: International Differences in Work-related Values*. Beverly Hills, Calif.: Sage.

Hofstede, G. (1992). *Cultures and Organizations: Software of the Mind*. London: McGraw-Hill.

Hofstede, G. (1993). Cultural constraints in management theories. *Academy of Management Executive*, **7**(1), 81–94.

Huo, P.Y. & McKinley, W. (1992). Nation as a context for strategy: the effects of national characteristics on business level strategies. *Management International Review*, **32**(2), 103–113.

Jacques, E. (1951). *The Changing Culture of the Factory*. London: Tavistock.

Jameson, F. (1984). Post-modernism and the consumer society. In H. Foster (ed.) *Postmodern Culture* (pp. 74–83). London: Pluto Press.

Kakabadse, A. (1991). *The Wealth Creators: Top People, Top Teams and Executive Best Practice*. London: Kogan Page.

Kakabadse, A. (1993). Success levers for Europe: the Cranfield executive competencies survey. *Journal of Management Development*, **13**(1), 75–96.

Kakabadse, A. & Myers, A. (1995a). Qualities of top management: comparisons of European manufacturers. *Journal of Management Development*, **14**(1), 5–15.

Kakabadse, A. & Myers, A. (1995b). *Boardroom Skills for Europe* (pp. 1–35). Cranfield: International Management Development Centre, Cranfield School of Management.

Kanter, R.M. (1977). *Men and Women of the Corporation*. New York: Basic Books.

Kanter, R.M. (1990). *When Giants Learn to Dance*. London: Unwin Hyman.

Kanter, R.M. (1991). Transcending business boundaries: 12,000 world managers view change. *Harvard Business Review*, **69**(3), 151–167.

Keen, P. (1991). *Shaping the Future: Business Design Through Information Technology*. Boston, Mass.: Harvard Business School Press.

Kelley, L., Whatley, A. & Worthley, R. (1987). Assessing the effects of culture on managerial attitudes: a three-culture test. *Journal of International Business Studies*, **18**(2), 17–31.

Kellner, D. (1988). Postmodernism as social theory: some challenges and problems. *Theory, Culture and Society*, **5**(2–3), 17–23.

Kirchberg, V. (1998). Stadtkultur in der Urban Political Economy (City culture in urban political economy). In V. Kirchberg and A. Goschel (eds) *Kultur in der Stadt: stadtsoziologische Analysen zur Kultur* (Culture and the city: analyses on culture in urban society) (pp. 41–54). Opladen: Leseke and Budrich.

Korac-Boisvert, N. (1992). Developing economies and information technology: a meta-policy review. Paper presented at the Australian and New Zealand Academy of Management's (ANZAM) Annual Conference on 'Re-discovering Australasian Management Competence in a Global Context', Sydney, December, 1–34.

Korac-Boisvert, N. & Kouzmin, A. (1994). The dark side of info-age social networks in public organizations and creeping crises. *Administrative Theory and Praxis*, **16**(1), 57–82.

Korac-Kakabadse, N. & Kouzmin, A. (1997a). From 'captains of the ship' to 'architects of organizational arks': communication innovations, globalization and the 'withering away' of leadership steering. In J. Garnett & A. Kouzmin (eds) *Handbook of Administrative Communication* (pp. 681–716). New York: Marcel Dekker Inc.

Korac-Kakabadse, N. & Kouzmin, A. (1997b). Maintaining the rage: from 'glass and concrete ceilings' and metaphorical sex changes to psychological audits and re-negotiating organizational scripts—part 2. *Women in Management Review*, **12**(6), 207–221.

Kouzmin, A. & Korac-Boisvert, N. (1995). Soft-core disasters: a multiple realities crisis perspective on IT development failures. In H. Hill & H. Klages (eds) *Trends in Public Sector Renewal: Recent Developments and Concepts of Awarding Excellence* (pp. 89–132). Berlin: Peter Lang.

Kouzmin, A. & Korac-Kakabadse, N. (1997). From phobias and ideological prescription: towards multiple models in transformation management for socialist economies in transition. *Administration and Society*, **29**(2), 139–188.

Kouzmin, A., Leivesley, R. & Korac-Kakabadse, N. (1997). From managerialism and economic rationalism: towards 're-inventing' economic ideology and administrative diversity. *Administrative Theory and Praxis*, **19**(1), 19–42.

Leiss, W. (1978). *The Limits to Satisfaction*. London: Marion Boyars.

Lessem, R. (1990). Introduction. In Y. Masuda (ed.) *Managing in the Information Society: Releasing Synergy Japanese Style* (pp. i–xxv). Oxford: Basil Blackwell.

Lyotard, J .F. (1984). *The Postmodern Condition*. Manchester: Manchester University Press.

Lyotard, J. F. (1986). Rules and paradoxes or svelte appendix. *Cultural Critique*, **5**(1), 40–53.

McAteer, P.F. (1994). Harnessing the power of technology. *Training and Development*, **48**(8), 64–68.

Maccoby, M. (1994). Creating quality cultures in the east and west. *Research Technology Management*, **37**(1), 57–59.

Malraux, A. (1967). *Museum without Walls*. London: Basil Blackwell.

Managing Office Technology (1996). Temporary staffing is still growing but a little slower. **41**(9), 34.

Manz, C.C. & Sims, H.P. Jr (1990). *Superleadership: Leading Others to Lead Themselves*. Berkeley, Calif.: Prentice-Hall.

Maslow, A.H. (1962). *Toward a Psychology of Being*. Princeton, NJ: Van Nostrand.

Maslow, A.H. (1971). *The Further Reaches of Human Nature*. Harmondsworth: Penguin Books.

Meyer, H.D. (1993). The cultural gap in long-term international work groups: a German–American case study. *European Management Journal*, **11**(1), 93–101.

Morgan, G. (1983). *Beyond Method*. Beverly Hills, Calif.: Sage.

Morgan, G. (1986). *Images of Organization*. Beverly Hills, Calif.: Sage.

Muetzelfeldt, M. (1988). The ideology of consumption within the mode of production. Paper presented to the Sociological Association of Australia and New Zealand Annual Conference, Canberra, May.

Muetzelfeldt, M. (1992). Organizational restructuring and devolutionist doctrine: organization as strategic control. In J. Marceau (ed.) *Reworking the World: Organizations, Technologies and Cultures in Comparative Perspective* (pp. 295–316). New York: Walter de Gruyter.

OECD (Organization for Economic Cooperation and Development) (1987). *Evaluation of Research—a Selection of Current Practices*. Paris: OECD.

OECD (1992a). *Technology and the Economy: The Key Relationships*. Paris: OECD.

OECD (1992b). *Structural Change and Industrial Performance*. Paris: OECD.

Ouchi, W.G. (1979). A conceptual framework for the design of organizational control mechanism. *Management Science*, **25**(7), 833–848.

Ouchi, W.G. (1981). *Theory Z: How American Business Can Meet the Japanese Challenge*. New York: Addison-Wesley.

Perez, C. & Soete, L. (1988). Catch up in technology: entry barriers and windows of opportunity. In G. Dosi, C. Freeman, R. Nelson, G. Silverberg & L. Soete (eds) *Technical Changes and Economic Theory* (pp. 458–479). London: Pinter.

Peters, T.J. & Waterman, R.H. (1982). *In Search of Excellence: Lessons from America's Best-run Companies*. New York: Harper and Row.

Piore, M. & Sabel, C.F. (1984). *The Second Industrial Divide: Possibilities for Prosperity*. New York: Basic Books.

Porter, M.E. (1990). *The Competitive Advantage of Nations*. New York: Free Press.

Posner, B. & Low, P. (1990). Australian and American managerial values: subtle differences. *International Journal of Management*, **7**(1), 89–97.

Pringle, J. (1994). Feminism and management: critique and contribution. In A. Kouzmin, L.V. Still & P. Clarke (eds) *New Directions in Management* (pp. 127–142). Sydney: McGraw-Hill.

Revans, R. (1985). *The Origin and Growth of Action Learning*. London: Chartwell-Bratt.

Robertson, R. (1988). The sociological significance of culture: some general considerations. *Theory, Culture and Society*, **5**(1), 38–43.

Robertson, R. (1990). Mapping the global conditions. *Theory, Culture and Society*, **7**(2–3), 63–99.

Ronen, S. (1986). *Comparative and Multinational Management*. New York: Wiley.

Roobeek, A.J.M. (1990). The technological debacles: European technology policy from a future perspective. *Futures*, **22**(6), 904–914.

Rose, N. (1996). Identity, genealogy, history. In S. Hall & P. du Gay (eds) *Questions of Cultural Identity* (pp. 143–163). London: Sage.

Roszak, T. (1986). *The Cult of Information*. Cambridge: Butterworth.

Sadler, P. (1994). Gold collar workers: what makes them play at their best? *Personnel Management*, April, 14–17.

Sappinen, J. (1992). Adjustment to a foreign culture and measuring expatriate failure and success: two case studies of Finns in Estonia. Research Paper Series 2. Helsinki: Helsinki School of Economic and International Business Administration, Centre for International Business Research.

Schelsinger, P. (1987). On national identity: some conceptions and misconceptions criticized. *Social Science Information*, **26**(2), 111–124.

Schneider, S. C. (1989). Strategy formulation: the impact of national culture. *Organization Studies*, **10**(2), 149–168.

Schneider, S. C. & De Meyer, A. (1991). Interpreting and responding to strategic issues: the impact of national culture. *Strategic Management Journal*, **12**(4), 307–320.

Schulz, N. (1980). *Genius Loci*. Academy Edition.

Selznick, P. (1957). *Leadership in Administration*. New York: Harper and Row.

Senge, P. M. (1990). *The Fifth Discipline: The Art and Practices of the Learning Organization*. New York: Doubleday.

Senge, P. (1992). *The Fifth Discipline: The Art and Practice of the Learning Organization*. Sydney: Random House.

Simmel, G. (1978). *The Philosophy of Money* (translated by T. Bottomere & D. Frisby). London: Routledge and Kegan Paul.

Simon, H. (1962). The architecture of complexity. *Proceedings of the American Philosophical Society*, **106**, 467–492.

Smith, A. (1990). Is there a global culture? *Theory, Culture and Society*, **7**(2–3), 92–101.

Taylor, F. (1911). *Principles of Scientific Management*. New York: Harper and Row.

Toffler, A. (1980). *The Third Wave*. New York: William Morrow.

Tushman, M. L. & Nelson, R.R. (1990). Introduction: technology, organizations and innovation. *Administrative Science Quarterly*, **35**(1), 1–8.

Van Maanen, J. (1994). An interview with John Van Maanen. *OMT Newsletter, Academy of Management*, Winter, 14–16.

Weber, M. (1949). 'Objectivity' in social science and social policy. In E. Shils & H.A. Finch (eds) *The Methodology of the Social Sciences* (pp. 49–112). New York: Free Press.

Webster, F. & Robins, K. (1986). *Information Technology: A Luddite Analysis*. Norwood, NJ: Ablex.

Weill, P. (1990). Strategic investment in information technology: an empirical study. *Information Technology*, **12**(3), 141–148.

Weill, P. (1992). The relationship between investment in information technology and firm performance: a study of the value manufacturing sector. *Information System Research*, **3**(4), 307–333.

Weir, D. (1993). Not doing the business: why there is no decent management research. *The Times Higher Education Supplement*, **30**, 17.

Western, J. (1983). *Social Inequalities in Australian Society*. Sydney: Macmillan.

Wild, A. (1994). Vision of 2022: era of the global works council and individualism. *Personal Management*, **26**(13), 39–49.

Zuboff, S. (1983). The work ethic and work organization. In J. Barbash, R. Lampman, S. Levitan & G. Tyller (eds) *The Work Ethic* (pp. 153–181). Madison, Mont.: Industrial Relations Research Association.

CHAPTER 23

The Future of Workplace Diversity in the New Millennium

Tony Montes
Ashridge Management College, Ashridge, UK
Graham Shaw
Centre for Business and Diversity Ltd, UK

SUMMARY

This chapter explores practical issues and challenges that the future of workforce diversity brings in the new millennium. The dramatic and ongoing changes in the world's political, social and economic arrangements in the last year present profound implications for any notion of inclusiveness and equality that have so far guided communities and organizations. The chapter summarizes current thought leadership and the need for new paradigms to manage diversity, and also proposes a method to measure and progress equity in the workplace. The authors propose a standard that is primarily customizable to any organization's need to address its issues around the management of diversity which impacts on organizational effectiveness, credibility, performance, reputation, and development of capabilities. The standard can be used to benchmark the organization externally and the authors illustrate their current and future application in organizations. It is with optimism that the authors feel that beginning with a shared understanding of where we are and where we want to go with working on our differences and similarities enables us to have a better chance of procuring peaceful and progressive communities.

Individual Diversity and Psychology in Organizations. Edited by Marilyn J. Davidson and Sandra L. Fielden.
© 2003 John Wiley & Sons, Ltd.

INTRODUCTION

Many societies today are being rearranged demographically, politically, socially and economically. Recent world events have reignited polarization and intolerance. In this turbulent environment, it is instinctive to seek the comforts of the stable elements of familiar cultures and avoid or exclude those which differ from or challenge deeply held beliefs and practices. Living and working on this instinct alone can be destructive and only leads to prolonged states of conflict. Now more than ever, valuing diversity has become crucial for the survival of all human communities.

In the world of work, the assertion of people's behavioural differences presents a critical challenge for success now and in the future. There is a compelling need for an environment that is not only perceived to be inclusive and equitable, but is also effectively leveraging diversity for the benefit of all.

This chapter describes this transformation journey that will be everyone's responsibility. Effective management of diversity is a development process that will take several years to achieve and will involve mutuality between changes in practices, attitudes and behaviours with that of changes in culture.

Many organizations have begun to realize the need to move attention beyond equality towards looking at the issues and opportunities that diversity brings. Some have taken the first steps to shift conventional focus, from visible manifestations of difference such as ethnicity, gender, age, etc. towards valuing the wider but less obvious influences that make people unique. In both the private and public sectors, they have begun to realize that it is not just about bringing in and bringing on people from diverse backgrounds, but that what really matters is the ability to integrate the skills and talents that different people from different backgrounds bring. It is about moving towards the age of equity with the whole diverse workforce.

Part of the difficulty in getting started rests with two fundamental issues. The first is that perceptions of equity are subjective (whose reality is it or what standard is it based upon?). Secondly, while there are enough measures to monitor equality and representation, there are few standards that can be used to measure equity for various organizational contexts.

At the centre of this is the need to have a working definition of equity over equality. Current and emerging practice suggests how equity can be measured over a continuum, and provides a rigorous framework that can be used to progress diversity aspirations. In this chapter, the authors propose a standard that is primarily customizable to any organization's need in order to address its issues around the management of diversity. This correlates to organizational effectiveness, credibility, performance, reputation, and development of capabilities. As a collateral benefit, the standard can be used to benchmark the organization externally.

ONE SMALL STEP FOR MAN...

The way for the future of diversity is a giant leap that needs to begin with a small but important step in the way we define and understand its full implications. The 1990s have heralded globalization and resulted in the need to examine how organizations and communities develop as demographics change with mobility, and global awareness increases with the internet. The notion and practice of equality, with all the new issues it has raised and old ones which continue to persist, calls for a wider understanding of its consequences that exposes its limitations. While acknowledging some progress in the key divides of gender, race and ethnicity, these gains have been limited, confined to certain societies, and incremental, judging by the continuous clash and backlash between various socio-economic worlds and persuasions we all live in. Events in 2001 and thereafter have revived polarization and intolerance in almost all aspects of our social, religious and economic lives as well as politics and governance.

Practical actions under the equality movement have not been robust enough to escape criticisms of reverse or positive discrimination, despite all the good intentions and legislation that support the removal of inequality. Legislated fairness becomes a candle in the storm as communities grapple with the reality of economic and political migrants. In Europe, the re-emergence of extremism in politics has partly been traceable to mainstream and traditional cultures being marginalized in their own constituencies where integration has either failed, was non-existent, or not wanted at all by one or the other, with guilt resting with both majority and minority groups. Ghettos from both sides have been created physically and attitudinally. Real equality remains as elusive and aspirational at best across the globe.

There is a new kind of consciousness of national identity which is also being raised by new structures of governance. While devolution in the United Kingdom has not resulted in hyphenated societies and clearly defined classifications such as the US (e.g. African-American, Hispanic-American, to name a few), being Welsh, Scottish, Irish or English provides new opportunities on what it means to be British.

The above realities suggest that perhaps there are important opportunities that we ought to look at in terms of seeking alternative ways of appreciating and valuing differences. Such an understanding should be inclusive enough to allow us to move forward from the one size fits all responses that equality tends to limit itself to. As illustrated, in Figure 23.1, Wilson (1997) differentiates between 'equality' (i.e. sameness) and 'equity' (i.e. when we treat people fairly and recognize differences).

The future of diversity in the new millennium will be an evolutionary move towards the age of equity. The drivers for this evolution are all the developments that comprise our current reality. What happens in the future depends on how we understand the challenges and opportunities that diversity brings, and what we do about them today.

Across the globe and in various organizations spanning all kinds of sectors and communities, significant changes are happening in the way homogeneity in the workforce is decreasing. Opportunities for people who do not come from mainstream populations are beginning to open up albeit in a gradual pace. Mobility, migration, education and changing societal values are combining with organizational drivers which result in a workforce that is increasingly more diverse.

The major shifts in attitudes towards women, and people of various races and ethnic origins, in the workplace over several years have widened their options and opportunities. They now are entering the workforce at various income levels, ages and occupations. For instance, economic realities have created the need for dual career families, diverse customer needs and markets, and the effectiveness of social support systems has given them more control over their ability to pursue careers.

The ways of working, cognitive styles, personality profiles and preferences, beliefs and sexual orientation are increasingly being given more freedom of recognition and

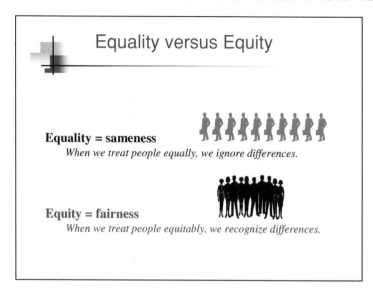

FIGURE 23.1 Equality vs equity
Source: from Wilson, T. (1997). *Diversity at Work*, John Wiley & Sons

expression. Indeed, one leading global corporation has concluded that if the organization is not managing workforce diversity, it is definitely suffering a cost that it does not realize.

THE AGE OF EQUITY

Wilson (1997) gives us a historical basis that traces the movement towards the age of equity:

- *1950–1960: The age of inequality.* This era represented the height of industrialization and the beginnings of the information age. Communities were relatively homogeneous. The tolerance of differences in race, gender, ethnicity, physical ability and culture was defined by measures of 'fitness' to the norm.
- *1960–1990: The age of equality.* The promulgation of equal opportunity legislation marked the years of change. Organizations recognized that management strategy needed to eliminate discrimination and treat employees equally. The term 'legislated fairness' was the underpinning principle by which the fair treatment of the majority of people also tended to ignore differences.
- *2000 +: The age of equity.* The age of equity comes in response to the shortcomings of equality. With equity, we recognize and value differences. The shift to equity occurs when organizations begin to acknowledge and leverage differences and similarities and creates the environment to unleash talent at all levels.

NEW MEANINGS AND PARADIGMS

As experience and research have shown, the way we understand and define diversity has a profound effect on the assumptions we make and the actions we take to develop organizational effectiveness through diversity. (Thomas, 1996, Thomas & Ely, 1996; Wilson, 1997).

The overall meaning that diversity invokes is a picture of diverse races, cultures, ethnicity, beliefs, etc. As such, this invites perception differences born out of stereotypes that are often historically rooted, inherited or acquired.

Inherently, there is nothing wrong with stereotypes at the micro level. At their most basic stage, they become part of our mental models that help us to classify our understanding of what we observe. They form part of our identity and help us to appreciate the identity of others who are like or unlike us. It would be difficult to begin to have any concept of anything outside and inside ourselves without some of our stereotypes kicking in. Through time, we form norms and values that guide the way we live and behave. We become products of our mental models and cultural programming.

The problems begin when stereotypes become so embedded in our attitudes and behaviours that they lead us to take action that is laden with cultural bias. At worst, this potentially leads to discrimination, defined as bias combined with power to impose beliefs to the disadvantage of others (Baytos, 1995). Mental models that are privately held and not publicly tested become self-reinforcing beliefs, whenever they work. They result in culture shock whenever they do not. Culture clashes are nothing more than the result of opposing biases and prejudices facing each other.

DIVERSITY: SIMILARITIES AND DIFFERENCES

A recurrent theme throughout this book has been recognizing that diversity management needs to be integrated into strategic areas. Also, a broader definition beyond the usual demographic characteristics of the workforce such as gender and race has been advocated (Thomas, 1996). Referring to diversity as any mixture of items characterized by differences and similarities, Thomas argues that this definition means that managerial processes need to be focusing on creating enabling environments that consider the diversity of all employees. One problem is that equality has made us used to associate diversity with demographic changes following which we focus on minorities and their notable differences. Diversity in many cases has been used interchangeably with minority. Consequently, strategic workforce plans and actions often address only the differences and not the similarities.

A robust and more inclusive way of dealing with diversity issues that improves the likelihood of support and alignment is about focusing on the collective mixture and not just the distinctive components in a group.

Work on the impact of diverse work teams at the Wharton School (University of Pennsylvania) has developed a useful way of thinking about the key elements of diversity. They refer to three levels:

- *Social category or demographic diversity*—visible demographic characteristics— gender, race, age . . .
- *Informational diversity*—underlying attributes—work experience, educational background, functional background, skills . . .
- *Value diversity*—different views about tasks, targets, goals, mission . . .

We can also add further elements: each of these dimensions has local, national, regional and global dimensions. They also affect not only the workforce of an organization but also its customers and suppliers and other key stakeholders.

This broader view starts to move away from focusing on just the differences that have been at the centre of equality in the traditional sense.

DIVERSITY: THE DYNAMICS OF THE DOMINANT/ SUBORDINATE INTERFACE

Another framework that has helped organizations understand the effects of diversity is the concept of 'dominant and subordinate' subgroups that can be found in organizations (Oshry, 1995). Within any organization, there are dominant groups whose ways of working determine 'the way we do things here'. This often results in the existence of subordinate groups whose talent and capabilities are not maximized—not because they are inferior to that of the dominant group, but because their ideas beliefs and patterns of communication tend to be so different from the dominant group that they become discounted. Over time, because their possible contributions become largely unexpressed, subordinate groups suppress themselves and go for the minimum discretionary behaviour that ensures their survival. The detrimental effect is that some employees adjust behaviour or opt out, due to lack of trust and confidence that the environment will have their own interests taken on board. In leadership development programmes for ethnic minority civil servants in the UK, many potential candidates and stakeholders expressed the view that the biggest barrier for ethnic minority leadership lies in the confidence they have in the system regarding its seriousness in inclusiveness. Competencies and capabilities are not the issue, rather it is a level of trust in the system that needs to be tested. In the end, the talent of each individual is not unleashed which impacts on organizational effectiveness and perpetuates a homogeneous work culture.

Research has shown that well-led diverse teams outperform homogeneous teams (Cox & Beale, 1997). In order to understand systems better and broaden the range of discretionary attitudes and behaviours that organizations need to encourage, there is an increasing need for many group processes that allow people from both groups to confront the dominant/subordinate interface openly and actively. Application of some of these for both private and public sectors in the UK has involved experiencing diversity workshops and interventions in balancing high quality advocacy and inquiry.

The importance of proactively managing diversity has been illustrated, with a key point being that productivity in teams is influenced by how diversity is managed, and is not about the presence or absence of diversity itself.

DIVERSITY AND ORGANIZATIONAL EFFECTIVENESS

In the early 1990s, research was carried out by Thomas and Ely (1996) on the need for a new paradigm for managing diversity. They sought to understand three management challenges that originally focused on three issues:

• How organizations achieve and sustain effective gender and racial diversity in their management and executive levels

- The impact of diversity on an organization's practices, processes, and performance
- The influence of leaders on making diversity an enhancing or detracting element

   Their six-year research with a number of both large and small organizations resulted in the development of a new paradigm for managing diversity. They began with the observation that old and limiting assumptions about the meaning of diversity needed to be modified, before its powerful potential could be unleashed to increase organizational effectiveness. A brief adaptation and summary of their observation are as follows.[1]

   Discrimination and fairness paradigm—organizations often begin with this most common approach which focuses on equal opportunities, fair treatment, and tweaking recruitment processes as part of correcting problems of under-representation that is often backed by legislation. Special career development programmes are crafted for minority groups and the organization's overall cultural understanding is broadened by wide-scale race and equality awareness training. The bid to rid the organization of unfair treatment and remove discriminatory behaviour as a preventative principle is enforced in various ways. Success is gauged by achievement of recruitment and retention targets. Because there is a focus on fair treatment and sameness, the usual consequences are that the staff complement may become diverse but the work and real inclusiveness of the environment does not (Thomas & Ely, 1996). Sameness in behaviour is recognized, individual differences are not and they subsequently become suppressed. Loyalty to the norm is welcome, diverse expressions are deemed counter-cultural.

   The *discrimination and fairness* paradigm promoted assimilation and melting-pot conformism. Looking externally, the emerging changes in demographics attracted many organizations to gain more access to more diverse consumer segments. Realizing that diversity is not just fair but makes business sense to enable them to serve a more diverse public, they adopted the *access and legitimacy* paradigm.

   Under this regime, organizations invest in access to and legitimacy with diverse clients by employing and deploying staff who are similar to or share the same demographic identities and cultural interests of important customer groups. Many consumer product companies or service-oriented organizations have used segmentation to their advantage, and have created service positions that build relationships based on demographic similarities for each segment. A collateral benefit of this is that broader opportunities for women and ethnic minorities, for example, have opened up. The downside has been that access and legitimacy organizations place staff with these specific capabilities into specially identified positions, often forgetting to comprehend the key strengths of those capabilities that could be learnt and built upon as a source for wider competitive ability. In the long run, organizations realize that they know enough to use people's strengths but never seem to learn from them.

   A new and emerging approach to this issue is the *learning and effectiveness* paradigm. This incorporates aspects of the first two paradigms but goes beyond them by concretely connecting diversity to approaches to work. This paradigm recognizes that employees exercise their discretionary behaviour at work as influenced by their cultural make-up. This view enables organizations to leverage differences by creating the processes that value these differences, captures them and synthesizes them into the key functions that matter in delivering results. Such organizations see conflict as a resource and encourages constructive challenge, allows the raising of contrarian positions or countercultural thinking and innovation. These are the organizations that are benefiting from effective management of diversity.

COMPARING THE THREE PARADIGMS

In summary, whereas the discrimination and fairness paradigm focuses on assimilation, (correcting under-representation fairness is seen as same treatment), the access and legitimacy paradigm is more about differentiation, in which the goal is to front-line people into market segments where their demographic influences are the same.

The learning and effectiveness paradigm focuses on synthesizing diverse skills internally in order to build new capabilities that potentially serve wider and even unknown market segments. Assimilation pushes sameness, differentiation tends to invite fragmentation of capabilities.

This new model goes beyond these two paradigms and squarely addresses the persistent issues that result from traditional equality initiatives. It promotes equal opportunity, acknowledges differences, values and leverages those differences. Organizations are able to integrate these differences into new capabilities that tend to make the organization more adaptive to environmental changes in the long run. Employees learn and grow and feel they belong to their organization through their differences, not despite them.

The feature of workplace diversity will no doubt have these three paradigms present in one form or another. Organizations need to decide where they want to be and what will be sustainable for them in their environments.

THE EQUITY CONTINUUM

Wilson (1997) describes the equity continuum as a tool to help organizations progress through their diversity aspirations. In a sense it is a metric that gives an indication of sense of how mature or developed an organization is in terms of creating inclusive and equitable work environments (see Figure 23.2).

The movement towards the age of equity will be everyone's responsibility. It will involve no less than a culture change that will mean valuing and leveraging differences and similarities that impact on the discretionary behaviours of people as 'stakeholders' of organizations. We've said that diversity includes gender, race, age, ethno-cultural background, sexual orientation, disability, religion, education, class, marital status, family status, work style, experience, heritage, cognitive styles, etc. The main objective is to create equitable and inclusive environments that result in superior organizational effectiveness.

Environments such as these operate and have the reputation of having systems and practices which are based on equity and merit, where differences and similarities are recognized and fully utilized. It also allows the organization to create competitive advantage by attracting and retaining the most skilled workforce and benefits from a diverse customer and supplier base.

Movement through Wilson's (1997) equity continuum levels outlined in Figure 23.2 is explained in the following sections.

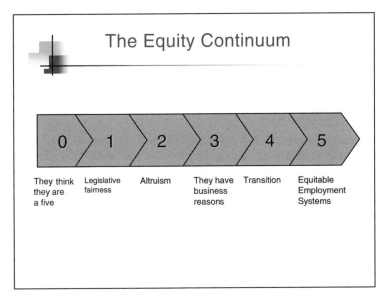

FIGURE 23.2   The equity continuum
Source: from Wilson, T. (1997). *Diversity at Work*, John Wiley & Sons

Level 0: They think they are a five

Level 0 is a situation where the organization is essentially in denial for various reasons. Often this is traceable to complacency or the lack of deeper appreciation of how diverse groups could be disenfranchised without their knowledge ('we don't have any discriminations cases', or 'it ain't broke, why fix it') or they have not fully anticipated current and future changes in demographics and changes in behaviours and motivations in the workforce.

Level 1: Compliance

This is often called legislated fairness. These organizations have primarily a reactive approach to implementing equality initiatives. They are motivated to pursue equity in order to avoid negative consequences that may result from non-compliance with legislated guidelines or other standards (e.g. collective agreements, labour laws, contracts). Initiatives tend to be implemented in reaction to some external pressure (e.g. governmental, union, interest group or stakeholder), as these organizations do not see the benefits of having a diverse workforce.

Level 2: Moving beyond compliance

This level is sometimes called the level where things are done for altruistic reasons. These organizations support initiatives that go beyond securing adequate representation. They want to be recognized as organizations that lend a hand to those who have been historically disadvantaged. Although wanting to do the 'right thing' plays a role in their desire to support traditionally under-represented groups, they also realize that supporting these initiatives can enhance the public perception. These organizations are likely to have one or more diversity initiatives in place, but these are isolated efforts that typically support high visibility programmes or the promotion of designated group members into visible positions. No plan is in place to integrate diversity into all aspects of human resource management nor the larger organizational culture.

Level 3: The business case

These organizations appreciate that managing diversity can yield positive benefits. Their motivation to pursue equity stems from potential business benefits (e.g. becoming the employer of choice, or a model employer).

Whereas those at level 1 are concerned with how failure to attend to diversity will influence costs, organizations at level 3 realize that diversity can yield benefits and positively affect future viability. These organizations recognize the importance of attracting and retaining the best person for the job in order to provide relevant programmes, products and/or services and they are moving in a direction to make that happen. These organizations are in the process of identifying barriers to diversity and developing human resource strategies that encourage and support a diverse workforce. They typically compare themselves to other leading organizations to identify areas requiring improvement and adopt 'best practices'.

Level 4: Integrated diversity

These organizations have internalized diversity as an important value and have embraced diversity as an integral part of the organizational culture. They have ceased to question the value of diversity, as it is the only way they can perceive operating. The fact that diversity is embedded in the organizational culture makes its programmes, products and services more relevant to a wide range of people. As a result, employees take full advantage of its available programmes and there is widespread support and use by its clients and stakeholders.

Level 4 organizations are motivated by the merit principle for all employees and there is a commitment, shared by members at all levels of the organization, which dictates that the best-qualified candidates will always be hired and promoted. These organizations continue to break down barriers that stand in the way of equity and are experiencing the financial and non-financial benefits of a diverse workforce. They are viewed by a wide range of people as an 'employer of choice'.

Level 5: Equitable organization systems

These organizations foster diversity beyond their own boundaries. Their motivation to pursue equity stems from the principle that diversity is an organizational, community, national or even global imperative.

Those at level 5 have internalized diversity as a core value and are commonly acknowledged as industry leaders—an 'employer of choice'. They have fully committed to equity and are merit based, in that the best-qualified candidate always gets hired and promoted. Monitoring and continuous improvement are an ongoing process, aimed at maintaining equitable employment systems through the identification and elimination of emerging barriers.

These organizations have experienced both financial and non-financial benefits as a result of their complete commitment to diversity. They provide relevant programmes, products and/or services to their clients and stakeholders and expect affiliates also to be governed by the merit principle. Motivated by pragmatic action, these organizations often engage in external, long-term, merit-based initiatives and programmes that they believe will have a far-reaching, positive impact on their organization and the global community.

OPERATIONALIZING THE EQUITY CONTINUUM

As we discussed, part of the difficulty in getting started rests with the second fundamental issue that while there are enough measures to monitor equality, there are few standards that can be used to measure equity for various organizational contexts.

From 1998 to 1999, the Trinity Group of Canadian companies initiated the development of a diversity standard that would enable organizations to measure and track their progress in moving through the continuum. The purpose of the initiative was to develop a common standard to guide the implementation and management of diversity programmes in organizations and to operationalize the equity continuum. Soon after the Trinity Group started work they were joined by a group of European-based diversity professionals from major companies working in the Gaining from Diversity Programme of the European Business Network for Social Cohesion (EBNSC—now called CSR Europe). From being a purely 'local initiative' the attempts to develop standards for diversity implementation took on a more global 'feel'.

An initial model was developed by the University of Western Ontario from which prototypes of a practical tool were developed. Subsequent beta testing involved the following organizations: IBM, Ernst and Young, Bell Canada, Nortel, Motorola, Dupont, Scotiabank, Xerox, Canadian Imperial Bank of Commerce, National Grocers, Canadian Public Services Commission, Canadian Bar Association, University of Western Ontario, Shell International, Électricité de France, Lucent Technologies, BP Amoco, Deloitte & Touche, Honeywell, Chase Manhattan Bank, Telecom Italia, Unilever, Microsoft, United Airlines, Mobil Oil.

These organizations were in the midst of either considering their strategies to build global capabilities or examining their need to maximize the diversity of their workforce. The key questions and principles addressed by the continuum are therefore as follows:

- How do we gain recognition that diversity is a strategic business concept?
- How do we gain recognition that diversity requires a vision of strategic implementation?
- Can we develop strategic implementation tools which help build diversity practice across the organization (processes, activities, internal, external) and which indicate levels of improvement?
- How can we benchmark at a level wider than the locality or national level, especially for multinational companies and organizations—the impact of globalization?
- Is it possible to build a common framework of diversity standards across sectors, jurisdictions. . . . ?

THE DIVERSITY ASSESSMENT TOOL

WHAT GETS MEASURED, GETS DONE

A number of organizations that aspire to move forward along the continuum today have chosen to adapt a diversity assessment tool used by the authors (see Figure 23.3). This tool enables them to:

- Benchmark themselves against a clear model of best practice of diversity as it relates to business operations
- Develop standards for the measurement and reporting of diversity initiatives
- Engage in a common framework for discussion between different parts of the same organization, including those operations in different countries
- Create a clear 'leadership framework' for diversity which can operate across the organization
- Identify key areas for the development of strategies and initiatives for best practice

The assessment tool is essentially a survey of perceptions that can be done internally as part of regular internal climate surveys and externally as way to gauge external stakeholder perceptions and reputation with the general public. It measures:

- Five levels of the equity continuum as described above
- Organizational processes
- Organizational activities
- Matrix—activity and validation statements

The distinction between organizational processes and activities is:

- *A Process*: How an organization approaches diversity. The process may also signal 'why' the organization does what it does—the underlying motivation for pursuing diversity.
- *An Activity*: What an organization does. Identifies the actual behaviour of an organization in key business areas.

A more detailed description of what comprises both follows (see Figure 23.3).

ORGANIZATIONAL PROCESSES

The organizational processes that need to be examined are defined as follows:

- *Commitment:* An organization's promise or statement to undertake a course of action.
- *Policy:* A stated course of action that allows an organization to implement tasks more efficiently.
- *Strategy:* A series of steps designed to meet a specific goal.
- *Strategy/planning:* Planning helps translate an organization's policies into action.
- *Implementation:* Carrying out actions according to a plan or procedure; the execution of specific initiatives.
- *Measurement:* Gathering information related to activities that have been implemented. This information can be in the form of feedback/opinions as well as numerical data.

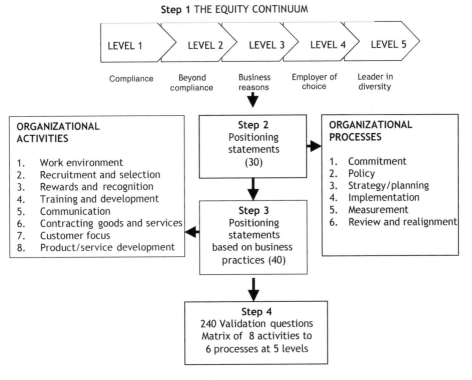

THE STRUCTURE OF THE DIVERSITY ASSESSMENT TOOL

Step 1 THE EQUITY CONTINUUM

LEVEL 1	LEVEL 2	LEVEL 3	LEVEL 4	LEVEL 5
Compliance	Beyond compliance	Business reasons	Employer of choice	Leader in diversity

ORGANIZATIONAL ACTIVITIES

1. Work environment
2. Recruitment and selection
3. Rewards and recognition
4. Training and development
5. Communication
6. Contracting goods and services
7. Customer focus
8. Product/service development

Step 2
Positioning statements
(30)

Step 3
Positioning statements based on business practices (40)

ORGANIZATIONAL PROCESSES

1. Commitment
2. Policy
3. Strategy/planning
4. Implementation
5. Measurement
6. Review and realignment

Step 4
240 Validation questions
Matrix of 8 activities to
6 processes at 5 levels

FIGURE 23.3 The diversity assessment tool process

- *Review/realignment:* Examining data to assess the effectiveness of initiatives. If necessary, adjustments are made to achieve greater benefits or a desired goal.

How it works in principle, is that if an organization wanted to improve the way it conducts a particular activity, it would first make a *commitment* to improve its performance of that activity. Then it would develop a *policy* outlining the overall course of action after which it would create a *strategy and plan* outlining the specific steps it will take. Then it would *implement* its plan, then would take some *measurements* relative to the activity. Finally it would *review* the measurements to determine whether the desired results were achieved, and whether to change its strategy (realign).

After completing these six processes, the organization would make a new commitment and the organizational process would start again.

ORGANIZATIONAL ACTIVITIES

As an important component of how inclusiveness and an equitable environment exist, organizational activities provide a strong indication of the degree to which equity is in place with business ways of operating. They are often about:

- *Work environment:* A combination of all workplace conditions, such as issues of health and safety, employee treatment and behaviour and hours of work.
- *Recruitment/selection:* Finding and hiring employees for the organization.
- *Learning/development:* The process of acquiring new knowledge and/or skills.
- *Accountability/recognition:* Being answerable for meeting certain organizational objectives and being recognized or rewarded for their attainment.
- *Communication:* The sharing of thoughts, opinions or information.
- *Contracting of goods and services:* One party providing another with an article of trade and/or work based on an agreement between them.
- *Programme/product/services development:* Creating a coordinated group of activities, an article of trade, or a plan to provide services.
- *Service delivery:* Providing work (services) to benefit another.

The tool then uses a matrix of validation statements that are constructed to measure the 5 levels against 6 processes and 8 activities which comes to an aggregate of 240 statements which form the survey.

Examples of Recent Applications of the Diversity Assessment Tool

The CSR Europe Diversity Programme

As a whole the *CSR Europe Diversity Programme* seeks to create a greater understanding and a wider acceptance of the concept and practice of *diversity management* within companies; to stimulate the *sharing of business practices*; and to facilitate the *application of tools* for managing diversity through different business processes and operations at a European level. The Benchmarking Programme 2001–2002 was a practical manifestation of this overall goal.

The objective of the Benchmarking Programme

The objective of the Benchmarking Programme was to provide *an opportunity* for CSR Europe member companies to use the diversity assessment tool for the purpose of undertaking *initial benchmarking on diversity issues* in Europe:

- In relation to a model of international best practice
- In relation to other participating companies

The use of the model of best practice developed in the diversity assessment tool (see below) was an important element in providing the framework for benchmarking— *creating a common 'vocabulary'* for a 'conversation' between companies and individuals at different stages of development and with different priorities.

Principal outputs of the Benchmarking Programme

At the start of the programme three principal outputs were foreseen:

- Participating companies would produce *an analysis of their current position* using the framework of the diversity assessment tool, including a *collection of 'evidence'* (practices, programmes, initiatives, policy statements, reports, leadership statements,

etc.) arising from the use of the tool. This would provide a useful *basis for future actions* within the organization.
- CSR Europe would bring together *individual company assessments* and evidence in a single document to enable all participants to understand how others are approaching diversity issues.
- CSR would *publish the results of the benchmarking project* (subject to agreement with participating companies). This will provide a *basis for future actions* within the CSR Europe Diversity Programme. The results to be presented at an *open workshop* towards the end of the project.

Benefits for participating companies

It was anticipated that the project would provide participants with an opportunity to:

- *Raise awareness* of the business implications of diversity issues within their organization
- Stimulate *a more integrated approach* across business units and functional areas
- Identify, publicize and learn from *existing good practices* from across organizations
- Identify priority areas for *future action*
- Establish an *ongoing exchange of experience* with other CSR Europe companies on diversity issues
- *Gain expertise* in the use of the *diversity assessment tool* for future use as an ongoing assessment and planning tool

Principal activities during the Benchmarking Programme

The *main activities* during the project included:

- A *one-day introductory workshop in April 2001* designed to provide further information on the background and development of the project as well as initial training in the *use of the diversity assessment tool.* This enabled company representatives to articulate the specific nature of their internal benchmarking 'project'.
- Having secured internal agreements and involvement from other personnel in the organization, programme participants were given *password protected access* for the company representative to the internet-based diversity assessment tool. The numbers, status and geographical location of the personnel given access in each organization varied between the organizations. How this was accomplished is outlined below in the 'Results' section of this report.
- Personnel from the participating companies then used the diversity assessment tool as *a framework for analysing their own organization.* They collected 'evidence' of policies, procedures, practices, initiatives, programmes, etc. to produce written and verbal reports from this information. They engaged in discussion with personnel in different parts of their organizations.
- During September 2001 the participating companies used the diversity assessment tool to produce an *on-line scoring* of their performance. They also began the *process of collating the 'evidence'* for the reasons for making a particular scoring in the process and activity areas of the diversity assessment tool.

- The second workshop of the programme, held in October 2001, enabled participants to *share their results*. They focused on the overall scoring, why they had made their particular scores and presented some of the 'evidence' for some of the process and activity areas. They also reported on some of the *broader issues* raised in the exercise.
- From November 2001 to November 2002 participants then undertook to *complete their record of 'evidence'* across all the process and activity areas identified in the diversity assessment tool. This process served to *identify a number of key pieces of material* that were illustrative of the work being undertaken and that could be shared between the participants to help in the *process of benchmarking*. Despite the great variation in the perceived level of progress between the participating organizations, four companies produced a wide range of material—*a 'resources bank'*—that they were willing to share with each other and a wider public.
- A *final workshop* was held in March 2002 to enable participants to undertake *a final exchange of ideas, perceptions and materials*, focused on three areas:
  —Developing accountable senior management commitment
  —Integrating diversity into the organization—the 'business case'
   and management accountability
  —Communicating diversity awareness through the organization

There was also discussion about *how to improve the programme* and in what ways CSR Europe/Centre for Business and Diversity could *continue to support* the participating companies.

- The final stage of the project has been to *prepare a report* for circulation to CSR Europe members and a wider audience in the various EU member states and institutions. In addition, the participating companies have launched a Resources Bank to enable the materials identified during the assessment process to be shared among the group.

A Note on Benchmarking

> Benchmarking is perhaps the best means for servicing the human asset by continuously supplying new ideas to sustain superior performance levels.
> Benchmarking is relevant to any organization committed to the ethos of continuous improvement.... Depending on the resources committed, and pace of achievements, benchmarking can lead to:
>
> - incremental improvements to existing performance standards
> - quantum leaps by instigating new practices and ways of working
> - the road to excellence: creating the learning organization.
>
> (*Effective Management of Benchmarking Projects*, Mohamed Zairi, 1998)

Much of the literature on benchmarking identifies three types of benchmarking:

- Strategic
- Process oriented
- Operational

In establishing the benchmarking programme on diversity CSR Europe was attempting to address these sorts of issues.

The diversity assessment tool represents a 'standard', constructed by research and testing, against which participants can test themselves. It represents a structure combining an overall strategic vision of diversity within the organization, within which there is a more detailed breakdown of processes and operational concerns. The 'imposition' of an externally constructed framework (based itself on a model of continuous improvement) was key to gaining a consensus on the scope of diversity issues within organizations. In fact the assessment tool sets a context within which effective benchmarking can take place. By 'giving permission' to the participants to discuss common areas, the programme was able to move from general discussions, able to 'drill down' to identify specific practices and exchange the associated materials.

WHAT DID THE PARTICIPANTS SAY?

Below are a selection of feedback quotations from participants who used the Diversity Assessment Tool.

> The use of the Diversity Assessment Tool as the basis for CSR Europe 'Diversity Benchmarking Programme' has proved very valuable for our members to focus on the business case surrounding the subject. We benefited from a clear and simple measurement system that helped our members not only to identify what they were doing well, but also what should be their next steps. At the same time they could use it as a self assessment tool, as well as a tool for continuous improvement. Above all, the Tool gave us a common business oriented language to involve a wide range of people in the benchmarking process. (Programme Director, CSR Europe, Brussels)

> As a national company we still need to benchmark against international standards. The Diversity Assessment Tool gave us a common language to measure ourselves across the organization. Its focus on the 'business case' enabled us to engage with business units and build on previous audits and surveys. The Tool showed us what we had done well and broadened everyone's understanding of just why diversity is so important today. (Corporate Employee Relations Manager, An Post (The Irish Post Office))

> Environmental and social responsibility are key features of our corporate strategy. The Diversity Assessment Tool provided a valuable new component for our dialogue with different stakeholders about our progress on internal and external issues. (Sustainability Manager, ABB, Italy)

> As a result of recent mergers we have placed social responsibility firmly on the company agenda. The business unit managers in our Corporate Responsibility Task Force were able to use the Diversity Assessment Tool to increase our understanding of the issues and make a first step on our 'diversity journey'. Its language and structure provided a clear framework for thinking about our, increasingly, global business— especially the translation of policy into practice. (Human Resources Manager, Group 4 Falck: Global Solutions, United Kingdom)

> Using the Diversity Assessment Tool across four countries enabled our diversity managers to involve about 200 people in the assessment of our progress. Half our senior team also took part. The Tool promoted a greater awareness of diversity and of our current initiatives, supporting our internal marketing strategy. The Tool also helped us build some new energy around our diversity planning process and pointed to the need to build systematic management commitment as our next big challenge (Corporate Human Resources Manager, Proctor and Gamble, Switzerland)

> Working with our international business units the Diversity Assessment Tool helped us to think more clearly about assessment and measurement. It contributed to identifying current practices and sharing knowledge between business units. Most

importantly it provided a 'reality check' of our values as a business. We have many practices designed to ensure we comply with current legislation and support many local initiatives. The Diversity Assessment Tool helped bring key issues to our attention: the need for a more proactive strategy communicated to all our people. (Community Relations Manager, Manpower Inc., Brussels)

CONCLUSIONS

The future workplace will inevitably become more diverse. The assertion of more dimensions of diversity will be more complex to manage and could pose challenging opportunities and threats for organizational effectiveness. The work environment will have two characteristics:

- Diversity will continue to be about the visible manifestations and the traditionally associated behaviours and stereotypes around race, gender, ethnicity, age and disability.
- In addition, there will be more challenges and opportunities that will emerge in manifestations of individual values, personalities and preferences, that by themselves will keep changing as the environment changes.

The ability to manage diversity effectively will be a big leadership skill. Organizations need to be prepared to create dynamic and flexible environments that will enable them to meet their business needs while ensuring that they constantly have a skilled, motivated and productive workforce. Changing demographics will herald the above realities. Only through being aware and purposeful about managing diversity will organizations ever hope to achieve success and survival.

Knowing where to begin and where to go to will need measures that link perceptions of inclusion and equity with organizational processes and activities. The equity continuum and the diversity assessment tool are robust examples of metrics that can provide direction and purpose to creating truly inclusive environments that maximize organizational effectiveness and individual self-fulfilment and productivity.

NOTE

1. The following summary is reprinted by permission of *Harvard Business Review* from 'Making differences matter: a new paradigm for managing diversity' by D. A. Thomas and R. J. Ely, *Harvard Business Review*, Sept–Oct 1996. Copyright 1996 by Harvard Business School Publishing Corporation, all rights reserved.

REFERENCES

Baytos, L. M. (1995). *Designing and Implementing Successful Diversity Programs*. Englewood Cliffs, NJ: Prentice Hall.
Cox, T. Jnr & Beale, R. (1997). *Developing Competency to Manage Diversity*. San Francisco, Calif: Berrett-Koehler.
Oshry, B. (1995). *Seeing Systems, Unlocking the Mysteries of Organizational Life*. San Francisco, Calif: Berrett-Koehler.
Thomas, D. A. & Ely, R. J. (1996). Making differences matter: a new paradigm for managing diversity. *Harvard Business Review*, September–October.
Thomas, R. Roosevelt, Jnr (1996). *Redefining Diversity*. New York: Amacom.
Wilson, T. (1997). *Diversity at Work*. John Wiley & Sons.

Index